Leonhard Schmitz

A Manual of Ancient History

From the remotest times to the overthrow of the Western Empire, A.D. 476

Leonhard Schmitz

A Manual of Ancient History
From the remotest times to the overthrow of the Western Empire, A.D. 476

ISBN/EAN: 9783337245252

Printed in Europe, USA, Canada, Australia, Japan

Cover: Foto ©ninafisch / pixelio.de

More available books at **www.hansebooks.com**

Λ

MANUAL

OF

ANCIENT HISTORY,

FROM

THE REMOTEST TIMES TO THE OVERTHROW OF
THE WESTERN EMPIRE, A.D. 476.

BY

DR. LEONHARD SCHMITZ, F.R.S.E.,

RECTOR OF THE HIGH SCHOOL OF EDINBURGH.

WITH COPIOUS CHRONOLOGICAL TABLES.

———◆———

PHILADELPHIA:
BLANCHARD AND LEA.
1860.

PHILADELPHIA:
COLLINS, PRINTER, 705 JAYNE STREET.

PREFACE.

THE object of the present work is to furnish a brief but complete summary of the history of antiquity, from the remotest times down to the overthrow of the Roman Empire in the West, in A. D. 476. The history of Greece and Rome is taught in all schools professing to give a liberal education, but this is often done to the entire exclusion of the other nations of antiquity, which, though they did not exercise an equally powerful influence either upon their contemporaries or upon posterity, yet ought not to be passed over by any one desirous to obtain a complete view, and form a correct estimate, of the ancient world. The present manual, therefore, embracing the history of all the nations of antiquity, is designed to present to the student, besides the histories of Greece and Rome, an outline of that of the non-classical nations, and to devote to each of them as much attention as their historical importance may seem to demand.

The history of the Jewish nation does not form part of this manual, because it is felt that the history of that memorable people, in order to be in any way satisfactory, cannot be treated with the same brevity as that of other ancient nations; it must further be assumed, that the history of the Jews is known to every Christian student from his Bible and the religious instruction he has received; the sacred history, moreover, is of that peculiar kind that it ought not to be placed on a level with that of less favoured nations, it being essentially of a religious character, and every one ought to learn it from the Holy Scriptures, rather than from any summary abridgment. In order, however, to assist the biblical student, a brief chronology of Jewish history, from the Creation down to the destruction of Jerusalem, has been added to the Chronological Table at the end of the work.

The whole manual is divided into three books, which may be regarded as three distinct courses of history; the first comprising the Asiatic nations and Egyptians; the second, the Greeks, Macedonians, and the kingdoms that were formed out of the empire of Alexander the Great; and the third, the Romans, Carthaginians, and the nations of south-western Europe.

L. SCHMITZ.

EDINBURGH, APRIL 1855.

CONTENTS

1 * (v)

BOOK II.

HISTORY OF GREECE, MACEDONIA, AND THE GRAECO-MACEDONIAN KINGDOMS.

CHAPTER XII.

CHAPTER XIII.

CHAPTER XIV.

BOOK III.

HISTORY OF ROME, CARTHAGE, AND THE NATIONS OF WESTERN EUROPE.

CHAPTER I.

CHAPTER II.

CHAPTER III.

CHAPTER IV.

CHAPTER V.

CHAPTER VI.

CHAPTER VII.

CHAPTER VIII.

CHAPTER IX.

HISTORY

OF

THE NATIONS OF ANTIQUITY.

INTRODUCTION.

THE name antiquity in its most general acceptation is commonly understood to comprise the whole period from the creation down to the overthrow of the western empire in A.D. 476, and the history of that vast expanse of time is termed the " History of Antiquity," or " Ancient History." But neither the beginning nor the end of this history is the same for all the nations of antiquity. As to the beginning of the human race in general, it is obvious that, unless assisted by revelation, man could have' possessed but very little or no knowledge at all, and after the creation of man many centuries must have passed away before those communities could be formed in the primitive seats of our race, which we term states or nations, and which alone form the subjects of general history. But even the beginnings of these national or political associations, to whatever period they belong, do not yet constitute the beginning of real history, for the accounts of the formation of states and the foundation of cities are generally transmitted to later ages by mere oral tradition, which is ever changing and expanding, until in the end it is impossible to separate its nucleus of truth from what has grown upon and around it. Real history does not commence until the time when contemporary records of some kind or another are drawn up to assist the memory of man in preserving for posterity the memorials of a nation's life. We do not mean to assert that absolutely nothing can be known of those periods about which we have no contemporary records, for tradition also may hand down, and has handed down, a vast amount of information concerning past ages, but such information can never be as perfect and free from error as the accounts drawn up by contemporaries, or by persons living so near the events themselves, as to be able, with a reasonable amount

3

of judgment and discernment, to ascertain the truth. Written records fix for ever that which would otherwise be subject to a perpetual process of change and modification.

The possibility of drawing up records of a nation's history depends upon a variety of circumstances, and, above all, upon the art
of writing. As this art did not become known to all the ancient
nations at once, but was gradually imparted by one to another, it
follows that contemporary records were made in some countries at a
much earlier period than in others, and it must be observed in
general, that the Asiatic nations and the Egyptians practised the
art of writing many centuries before it was introduced into Europe.
Hence we possess authentic and trustworthy accounts of some
Asiatic nations at a period when the history of Europe is still buried
in utter darkness. Asia is the cradle of the human race, in Asia
the first states were formed, and it is from Asia that Europe and
Africa received their inhabitants. Hence the traditions and history
of the Asiatic nations go back to more remote periods than those
of any nation in Europe.

While thus the nations claiming our attention in antiquity widely
differ in regard to the points at which their respective histories and
traditions commence, the point at which antiquity terminates is no
less different with different nations. The epoch generally assumed
as the line of demarcation between antiquity and the middle ages,
is the overthrow of the western empire of Rome, and, so far as the
south-west of Europe is concerned, that event marks, in a sufficiently striking manner, the transition to an entirely new state of
things :—all that was peculiar to the ancient world had then ceased,
and a new order of things had sprung up; the ancient empire was
broken to pieces, new kingdoms were built up on its ruins, and
civilisation, which had before reached a certain culminating point,
now began a new career, struggling through many centuries of
ignorance and barbarism, until in the end it rose to that height
which constitutes the glory of our own age. But upon the eastern
world that event exercised little or no influence, for the Greek empire continued its wretched existence for nearly a thousand years
longer, and the Asiatic nations also preserved their previous forms
and institutions without any material change, until the establishment of Mahommedanism revolutionised nearly the whole of western
Asia and the north of Africa. The nations of central and eastern
Asia, lastly, were not affected at all by the event which so completely changed the aspect of western Europe. But notwithstanding this discrepancy, it is convenient, at least for Europeans, to
regard the fall of the western empire of Rome as the termination
of antiquity, and as the commencement of a new era in history.
Down to this event, therefore, it is our intention in this manual to
carry the history of the ancient nations.

It must not be inferred from the foregoing remarks that the history of the human race is altogether involved in impenetrable darkness during those remote periods, about which neither traditions nor written records have come down to us, for there are other sources from which a certain amount of historical knowledge can be obtained, concerning man as well as concerning the globe he inhabits. The earth, and the mighty revolutions it has undergone since the days of its creation, and before it became the fit abode for man, are not, properly speaking, subjects of a history which is concerned about man alone; but being the scene of his joys and sorrows, its history, as revealed by the science of geology, and its description furnished by that of geography, are interesting, nay, indispensable handmaids to the history of man. Geology, though less necessary to a full understanding of the history of mankind, affords us some insight into the otherwise mysterious revolutions through which the earth has passed before assuming its present form and character. What geology is to the history of the earth, comparative philology has proved to be to the history of man. Ages about which all traditions and all histories are silent, would be like sealed books to us, were it not for comparative philology, a child of the nineteenth century; for the analysis and comparison of languages allow us every now and then to catch a glimpse of the relations subsisting among nations often separated, during the historical times, by thousands of miles; of the state of their civilization, and of their migrations, before they reached the countries in which ultimately they took up their permanent abode. One example may suffice to show the flood of light which comparative philology in our days has thrown upon the history of mankind: it is now established as a fact beyond all doubt, that the nations on the banks of the Ganges and the Indus, as well as the ancient Persians, spoke a language radically identical with those spoken in Europe from the earliest times, including both Latin and Greek, and perhaps even the Etruscan. This great fact has dispelled a mass of false notions formerly entertained in regard to the ancient population of southern Europe. The radical identity of all these languages shows incontrovertibly that there must have existed at one time a close connection among the nations which speak them, and that in fact all these nations must have sprung from one common stock. Of this fact, neither tradition nor history has preserved the slightest trace. The primitive seats of man were in all probability in the north-west of India, or the highlands of Armenia; thence the branches spread in all directions, until the ocean set a limit to their migrations. It has thus been established that most of the races of men, from the Ganges in the east, to the Atlantic in the west, belong to one great family, and it is probable that further investigations will show that all the two thousand languages spoken by man are traceable to one common parent, and will thus confirm the record of Genesis, that all mankind is descended from one common father and one common mother. The study of language will then dispel the idea of several originally distinct races, which physiologists have assumed for the purpose of explaining the physical differences which present themselves among the inhabitants of the several parts of our globe. There can be no doubt that, for practical purposes, it is useful to divide mankind, as it at present exists, into three or even six dif ferent races, each presenting peculiar characteristics, which neither climate nor mode of living apparently ever produces; but thougl this is true of the present age of the world, who will undertake to prove that it was so from the beginning? Is it not possible that for many generations after his first creation man was more plastic and more easily affected by climate and the other influences which at present are nearly inoperative in determining our physical and mental constitution? If a man by living in central Africa does not now become a negro, it does not follow that it was always so; and hence we conceive that the strongly marked differences between existing races afford no ground for assuming, as many have done, that these differences have existed from the day of creation, or that God created not one, but several pairs of human beings.

Another means of furnishing us with some idea of the history of a nation, in the absence of literary memorials, is to be found in its architectural remains; for even if they bear no inscriptions, or such inscriptions as cannot be deciphered and understood, the mere forms and structure of their houses, temples, tombs, and other edifices, often reveal to us at least some parts of a nation's life and history, and that too sometimes in a more vivid manner than written records would have done. Hence the mode of life of the Egyptians, and their ordinary pursuits, were known to the world from their sculptured monuments, long before the clue to the reading of the hieroglyphics had been discovered; and the same may still be asserted of the Etruscans, whose inscribed monuments have not yet been deciphered.

It must not, however, be supposed that ancient history becomes authentic and continuous from the moment the art of writing is discovered and applied to the recording of events, for the earliest records are lost to us in almost every instance; and even if they were extant, they would scarcely furnish more than the skeleton of history. We are therefore dependent upon later writers, who drew up their accounts by the aid of legends and traditions. The value of such accounts depends upon a variety of circumstances, and the historian is obliged to proceed with the utmost caution and wariness in examining, weighing, and discriminating the authenticity of the sources from which he derives his information. As a great many of the historical writings of the ancients have perished, he is often

reduced to the necessity of filling up gaps by combination and con-
jecture, or from analogy. Even at periods about which his sources
of information flow more copiously, he has to contend with difficulties that are unknown to the historian of modern times. Such,
for instance, is the unsettled state of ancient chronology. There
was no chronological era common to all the nations of antiquity;
every people had its own system; and while some reckoned by lunar
years, others computed time by solar ones; with one nation, moreover, the year commenced at one season, while with another its beginning belonged to one quite different. To reduce all these discre-
pancies to one uniform system of chronology is a matter of extreme
difficulty, and we must often be satisfied, after all, with results only
approximating to the truth. We cannot pretend in this work to
enter into a critical examination of this and other knotty points
connected with ancient history, but our object will be to give those
results of modern inquiries which in our judgment appear to be
best entitled to our acceptance.

According to the principle that man, and more especially those
political associations of men which we call states, are the proper
subjects of history, all the nations that ever existed during the vast
period of antiquity come within the compass of ancient history;
but the claim they have upon our attention varies according to the
degree of civilisation they attained, and the influence they exercised
upon their contemporaries or upon posterity. In a work designed
for the instruction of the young, moreover, it would be out of place
to record all that is known of every state and tribe we meet with in
ancient times. A selection therefore has to be made, and a nation
deserves a more or less prominent place in history in the proportion
in which it has either promoted or retarded the progress of man- .
kind in civilisation. In this view ancient history becomes considerably narrowed; it must not, however, be imagined that the less
important nations will be passed over altogether; they will receive
their due share of attention, whenever they emerge from their
obscurity and come in contact with other more influential branches
of the human family. The sacred history of the Jews, however,
or the account of the direct interference of God in the affairs of
the Jewish nation, will be excluded from the present work, partly
because it is, or ought to be, familiar to every one, and partly because it appears to us to be more adapted for religious than for
historical instruction, being altogether distinct from ordinary political history.

There is yet another method by which the domain of ancient
history is sometimes reduced. For there are historians who confine
themselves to the consideration of those nations whose history has
been transmitted to us by the writers of the two classical nations
of antiquity, the Greeks and Romans, and pass over all others
3 *

whose history has become known to us during the middle ages and in modern times, partly from native records, and partly through travellers and missionaries. It will be our endeavour in the present work to set no such limits to our undertaking, but to pass in review all the great nations of antiquity, from whatever sources our information regarding them may be derived, and thus to exhibit before the young student, in broad outlines, as complete a picture of the ancient world as can be produced by the extended knowledge of the present age. Much that it would be interesting to know and to understand more thoroughly, will still remain obscure, being seen only through the mist of the many centuries which separate us from the events presented to our contemplation.

As the development of the human race has, on the whole, followed the daily course of the sun, we shall begin with the nations of eastern Asia, and thence proceed westward till we reach the shores of the Atlantic, beyond which ancient history does not extend.

BOOK I.

ASIATIC NATIONS.

CHAPTER I.

GEOGRAPHICAL SKETCH OF ASIA. — THE EARLIEST SOCIAL AND
POLITICAL FORMS AMONG ASIATIC NATIONS.

1. Asia is traversed by an immense plateau or high table-land,
intercepted by numerous elevations and depressions of the ground,
and occupying nearly one-half of the continent. This extends from
the Black sea in the West, to the sea of Corea in the East of China,
and consists of two main parts, which may be termed the eastern
(the larger) and the western highlands of Asia. The former did
not become known to the classical nations of antiquity until a very
late period, and the ancients call it Scythia, beyond mount Imaus.
This eastern highland bears throughout an almost uniform character, though its chains of mountains have many breaks and interruptions. It is surrounded on all sides by lofty ranges of mountains,
either in such a manner that the enclosed table-land sinks down
towards its centre, from which the mountains gradually rise on all
sides, or the surrounding mountains rise directly from the edge of
the table-land. The former is the case in the north, where mount
Altai forms a kind of circumvallation, while the latter form appears
more in the south, about the Himalayan mountains, the northern
foot of which rises from the very edge of the table-land. These
mountains and highlands were regarded by the earliest inhabitants
of the East as the centre of the earth's surface, as the habitation of
the gods and of the blessed, where peace, and light, and splendour
reigned for ever, and where war and death were unknown. It is
true, all the countries of Asia are grouped around those highlands
as around a mighty citadel; but the notion that they were the abode
of happiness appears to have arisen only from the sublime grandeur
of the mountains, for in reality the life of the tribes inhabiting
them was poor and wretched, when compared with that of the nations
occupying the plains, abounding in the most luxurious vegetation
and in all the richest gifts of nature; for the former were for the
most part nomades, that is, tribes wandering with their flocks and
herds over the extensive steppes, sometimes overrunning as con-

querors the more fertile countries around their high lands.   Their
mode of life, without any towns or fixed habitations, with few wants,
and these easily satisfied, remained the same for ages, and it was
impossible for them to make any considerable progress in civilisation.
Hence they remained far behind the surrounding nations that lived
under more favourable circumstances.

From the central table-land the countries sink down towards the
seas in the most different forms: mighty rivers with numerous
tributaries form extensive water-systems, which are at the same time
the great high roads along which the nations have migrated.   The
northern part of Asia, sloping down from the central highlands, the
modern Siberia, does not come into consideration in ancient history,
but the eastern, southern, and western slopes are the scenes of the
manifold struggles and developments of the Asiatic nations, which
will engage our attention.   In many of these countries, history,
even in the remotest times, meets with regularly organized states,
sometimes even displaying a splendour and magnificence bordering
upon the fabulous.   Wealthy cities with superb temples and palaces
form the centres of civilisation and refinement, and an extensive commerce supplies them with the comforts and luxuries, for which the
East has at all times been proverbial.   But the very bounties of
nature, which almost dispensed with the labour of man, at the same
time rendered him incapable of vigorous exertion, and checked his
progress, or caused him to sink into listless indolence.

2. All the nations we meet with in ancient history—with the exception, perhaps, of the Chinese and a few others — belong to one
of two great races, Indo-Germanic and the Semitic.   The languages
of these two races, notwithstanding their almost endless varieties,
prove incontestably that each of them must have descended from
one common root.   The Semitic race embraces not only those nations
which, according to the Mosaic account, are descended from Shem,
that is, the Hebrews and Arabs, but all the tribes from the Tigris
to the Mediterranean and the Red sea.   It is accordingly encircled
by the far more extensive territories inhabited by branches of the
Indo-Germanic race, which comprises, in Asia, the Indians and
Persians, and in Europe, the Greeks, Romans, Celts, Germans,
Slavonians, and Lithuanians.   It is owing to this greater extension
of the Indo-Germanic race that the languages spoken by its different
branches differ more widely from one another than those of the
Semitic.   For thousands of years these two races have been the
great promoters of civilisation, sometimes the one rising higher in
the scale and sometimes the other.   Their characters diverged at a
very early period, but they have nevertheless exercised a considerable influence upon each other, and at times have contended with
each other for the sovereignty of the world.   The most striking
differences between them may be briefly stated thus: The Semites

are distinguished for their quick and keen perception, for their bold and restless spirit of enterprise, for their obstinate perseverance in the pursuit of their objects, for their spirit of exclusiveness in the possession of what they have gained, for their strong passions and sensual propensities, and, above all, for their strong desire to comprehend the will of the deity, and their lofty aspirations in religion. It is owing to this last circumstance that the religious systems recognising the existence of only one true God, have originated among Semitic nations. The Indo-Germanic race, embracing a multitude of nations of different degrees of civilisation and of different capabilities, is not so easily characterised; but still the more prominent among its branches possess greater clearness and calmness of mind, and greater powers of reflection, than the Semites; they exhibit great genius for organisation, and a wonderful capability for developing the various circumstances in which they are placed, as well as for literature and the arts, in the last of which the Semites have always been far behind them. Their minds being very docile and plastic, they have in later times not only adopted the religious systems of the Semites, but advanced and developed them so much, that at present they far surpass their original instructors. They have, in fact, developed all that is great and noble in man to such a degree, as to outstrip all other races.

3. Many Asiatic nations have, or pretend to have, traditions about their existence as states, which go back many thousands of years before the commencement of the Christian era. It need hardly be remarked that such traditions are of no historical value; the account now universally adopted in Christendom, and at the same time the most plausible in itself, is that contained in the Scriptures, according to which the first pair of human beings was created about four thousand years before the birth of Christ. It is impossible to determine the part of Asia where our first parents were placed by their creator, nor can we trace with any accuracy the gradual increase and extension of our race. All we know is, that in the course of time men spread from Asia over the two other ancient continents of Africa and Europe. The Mosaic account divides all the nations of the earth according to their descent from the three sons of Noah, viz., Shem, Ham, and Japhet—Shem being described as the ancestor of the Semitic race, Ham as the father of the Egyptians and Africans, and Japhet as the progenitor of the inhabitants of Asia Minor and Europe. But we have already observed that language is the only safe criterion in classifying the different branches of the human family, and the study of languages, as it advances, points more and more distinctly to one common stock of human beings — all physiological differences of races being, in all probability, the result of accident and of outward circumstances

4. The character and the institutions, social and political, of the

Asiatic nations have, on the whole, undergone very few changes, and their present condition is not very different from what it was thousands of years ago. All of them reached a certain degree of civilisation, and it cannot be denied that in some instances very great progress was made, but none of them ever advanced beyond a certain point, at which they either remained stationary, or from which they sank back into a state of semi-barbarism. The causes of this phenomenon are found partly in the climate of southern Asia, where the luxurious productiveness of nature supports man without much exertion on his part, and where the easy mode of life allowed him to sink into a state of indolence and apathy, which proved to be the greatest obstacle to a steady and progressive development. Other causes may be found in the social and political relations of the eastern nations, some of which may be traced again to climatic influences.

5. Ever since the beginning of the human race, or at least so far as we can trace its history, the strong has always subdued the weak, the rich has oppressed the poor, and the cunning has cheated the simple. He who had the power, claimed the right to rule over the weaker as his subjects or his slaves; and this state of inequality descended from father to son, and from generation to generation; it was regarded even by great philosophers as the natural and legitimate state of things. Women, being the weaker sex, were treated in Asia only as the means of gratifying the passions, and promoting the comforts of men; the wife, in her relation to her husband, was no more than a servant; and the natural consequence was, that a man took to himself as many such servants as he was able to maintain. Polygamy was the natural offshoot of such a degraded view of the matrimonial relation, in which the husband considered himself to have many rights, but no duties. This evil, which has existed in Asia from time immemorial, and still degrades both sexes in eastern countries, renders a family life similar to that of Europe an impossibility; it destroys the natural relation between parent and child, and causes that between husband and wife to be almost the same as between a master and his slave, which debases both.

6. As a state is only an extended family, it is but natural to expect, in the larger community, vices and virtues analogous to those prevailing in the family. Despotism, therefore, is the form of government which we have to look for in the East; and it may be asserted in general, that the despotism exercised by the head of a state is of a more unmitigated character than that practised by the head of a family; for in the latter the members come into closer and more frequent contact, both with one another and with the head, and the obedience and kind offices of the one party cannot fail to draw forth gratitude and affection from the other. In the state, the despot, living in haughty seclusion from his subjects,

stands to them in no relation that might develop his better feelings. Despotism, which, during the historical periods of Eastern history, is the established form of government, seems nevertheless not to have been the original one, which must rather have contained elements of both liberty and servitude. The earliest form of government in Asia appears to have been the patriarchal, in which the head of a family, or of an aggregate of families, that is, a tribe, exercised the sovereign power. Such a community, proud of its real or imaginary ancestor or founder, of its deeds of valour, and other distinctions, might be either extremely exclusive, or might admit strangers to the same rights and privileges as those enjoyed by the men boasting one common origin. This form of government is generally preserved longest among a nomadic people. Such a people at first scarcely shows any distinction among the parts of which it is composed. A priestly class may, in some instances, begin to separate itself from the rest; but the head and centre of the whole nation is always the chief who has succeeded to those rights and distinctions which, in the belief of all, belonged to their first progenitor by the law of nature. Their wandering mode of life renders it necessary for the nation to be always ready for war, either to repel aggression, or to conquer new pastures for their herds and flocks. The personal contact of the patriarchal ruler with his subjects softens his relation to them in a similar manner as that subsisting in a family between the head and the members. A change takes place, when different tribes join together under one chief, and this change is most striking when a nomadic tribe succeeds in subduing an agricultural people with fixed habitations. In this case the conquered are treated at first in a very different way from the conquerors: the chief treats them as slaves belonging to him by the right of conquest. If the nomadic tribe settle in the conquered country, and amalgamate with the original inhabitants, the chief, in the course of time, assumes the same power and authority over them as over the subject people; both become slaves, and despotism is complete. As the possession of unlimited power, pride, and self-indulgence, are little calculated to improve and ennoble man, despotism generally proceeds from bad to worse. The Asiatic nations have never risen to the idea of political freedom: the man who is a despot in his domestic circle submits with abject servility to the commands and caprices of those whom circumstances have placed above him.

7. Among all the more important nations of the East, we find a more or less complete system of castes, whereby the descendants are bound to follow the same pursuits as their parents. States based upon the system of castes, are probably of later origin than patriarchal states, for it may be assumed that the establishment of castes is always the result of conquest. The classes distinguished for their

knowledge, for their military prowess, or for wealth, subduing others, naturally assume higher powers, and contrive to preserve them for their descendants. Knowledge and valour naturally gain the ascendancy over a nation in its first stage of development, and hence the castes of priests and warriors everywhere appear as the first and most powerful. Wisdom and knowledge are regarded as gifts vouchsafed by the Deity to his ministers alone ; and priests accordingly are the teachers and advisers not only of the people, but also of the rulers, over whom their influence is often so great as to eclipse the power of the military chief—his claims being based on no higher authority than that of the sword. The military caste, from which the ruler is generally taken, forms a kind of nobility, which, like the knights of the middle ages, keeps the rest of the population in subjection by the constant practice and exercise in arms; they secure to their descendants the same rights and privileges by early training and habit. The other castes are always found subordinate to these two, though among them also there is a gradation of rank and dignity. It may appear strange and unnatural to us to compel a son to follow the same trade or profession as his father, as talent and inclination seem indispensable to success ; but we must not overlook the important influence of early training and habit, which, even in our own age and country, generally induce the sons of agriculturists to follow the occupation of their fathers. In the early ages of the world, the institution of castes may even have been very beneficial ; but when it becomes an obstacle to the free development of individual energy, its influence is of a paralysing nature ; and if it remains unreformed, the state itself decays, or continues a monotonous existence, without progress and without improvement. Even while in its highest prosperity, the form of government in such a state is despotic — either the priests exercising an undue influence, or the military chief ruling unchecked, or at least controlled only by priestly authority.

Such are the principal forms of government we meet with in the south and east of Asia, and it is only in the western parts, as we approach nearer to Europe, that we find any modifications forming a kind of transition to the freer institutions of European life.

CHAPTER II.

CHINA.

1. CHINA, which forms a vast empire in the east of Asia, consists of the slopes or terraces from the central highlands of Asia, and of extensive and fertile lowlands traversed by large rivers and inter-

sected by an immense number of canals. Its inhabitants, belonging
to the Mongol race, differ from Europeans more widely than any
other civilised nation. They are the only branch of the Mongols
that has attained any considerable degree of civilisation, but their
progress appears to have been checked thousands of years ago, and
ever since that time the nation has been stationary, so that it can
scarcely be said to have any history at all. Even the repeated conquests of the country by foreign invaders from the highlands of
Asia have produced no changes, for the conquerors being less
civilised than the conquered, generally adopted the manners, laws,
and language of the conquered Chinese. This stationary character
of the nation is regarded in China as the only true basis of happiness and civil order, and is for this reason enforced by its rulers.
What has once been established must for ever remain unaltered,
and all education consists in a mere mechanical training to move
within certain fixed forms; and to do nothing but what somebody
else has done before, is considered as a sign of the most consummate
wisdom. The mariner's compass, gunpowder, and even a kind of
printing, were invented by the Chinese at a remote period; but
while in European countries these things have been the means of
gigantic progress and reforms, the Chinese have never employed
them to any great practical purpose, nor have they carried them
beyond certain rude and clumsy beginnings. The future destiny
of China, therefore, must be a continuance of its stagnation, unless
the nation be shaken by violent convulsions out of its lethargic
condition.

2. The language of the Chinese is as peculiar as the people themselves. Its whole vocabulary consists of about four hundred and
fifty monosyllabic words, which, being pronounced with different
intonations or accents, produce about one thousand two hundred
and three different words. The consequence of this poverty of the
language is, that many words, though pronounced in the same way,
have very different meanings, which, in some instances, are not fewer
than thirty or forty. The inconveniences and misunderstandings
arising from such a language may easily be imagined. The Chinese
language has in reality no grammar at all; for declensions and con-
jugations, and all the variety of other changes, and the numberless
prefixes and suffixes by which in other languages so many relations
are expressed, are entirely unknown, and the relations of words to
one another are indicated by their position alone. The writing of
the Chinese is not alphabetic, but consists of compound and strangely
formed characters or signs representing words, and their vast number forms a singular contrast with the poverty of the spoken language, for the Chinese dictionaries contain between three and four
thousand different signs or symbols of this kind. There can be no
doubt that originally these signs were of a hieroglyphic or pictorial

4

character, and that in the course of time they were so much altered as to become in the end mere conventional symbols. Only very few of these signs represent sounds or syllables.

3. This stiffness and want of elasticity in their language have produced corresponding effects upon the minds of the Chinese, and have also stamped their character upon their philosophy and religion. The ancient religion of the Chinese — we are not speaking here of Buddhism, which was imported at a later period from abroad — was extremely poor and meagre, and it is said that their language does not even contain a word or symbol for a spiritual or divine being. Confucius (properly Kong-fu-tse), their celebrated philosopher, who lived about the year B C. 500, as well as his disciples and followers, never alluded to the existence of a spiritual being as the creator and ruler of the universe, whence Confucianism is little better than Atheism. In his time, it is said, all the relations of social and civil order were in a state of utter dissolution, and he, by inculcating a strict and pure system of ethics, endeavoured to restore the morality and happiness of former ages. To this great object he devoted all the energies of his life; but he did not live to see the fruits of his labours, for it was not till after his death that his countrymen, appreciating his doctrines, really commenced the work of reform, and made his ethical system the soul of their social and political life. This tradition seems to be perfectly correct, and is borne out even by the present condition of the Chinese people. The moral code of Confucius teaches the most absolute submission of children to the will of their parents, of wives to that of their husbands, and of the whole nation to that of its rulers. The idea of freedom or of a self-determining will is not recognised at all.

4. But notwithstanding this total absence of freedom and the paralysing influence of the immutable adherence to established forms and doctrines, there has been, within a limited sphere, a considerable amount of intellectual activity. The literature of the Chinese is rich, and the industry of their learned men and scholars ought not to be undervalued, although the intellectual interests of their country have not been much advanced by them. Poetry in particular, in which the feelings of men have found an outlet even among nations far less favourably circumstanced than the Chinese, has been cultivated to a considerable extent. The novels produced by the Chinese are distinguished by a certain refinement, but are nly pictures of their own life, which strictly moves in certain prescribed forms. Their lyric poetry is freer and more natural. A collection of the best literary productions is ascribed to Confucius; it is related that when he commenced the work of reforming his countrymen, he collected in six books every thing that had been written in earlier ages, and seemed to him suited to assist him in his endeavours. One of these books, which bear the name of Kings,

is lost, but the remaining five are to this day regarded by the Chinese as the canonical and sacred books of their literature. One of them, called Y-king, contains a kind of symbolic philosophy; the Chu-king and Tcheu-tsicou treat of historical and political subjects; the Li-king of customs and ceremonies, and the Chi-king, lastly, forms a collection of three hundred and eleven national songs, which Confucius is said to have selected out of three thousand. In the third century before Christ nearly all the literary treasures of the Chinese were destroyed by fire, whence the authenticity of those books may fairly be questioned, though the Chi-king seems to be genuine, as lyric poems can be most easily retained and propagated by oral tradition. These poems, in the opinion of those conversant with the Chinese language, are full of grace and beauty, and are mostly expressive of grief and sorrow, as if they had been composed at a time when the natural feelings of the nation began to perceive the artificial restraint that was beginning to be imposed upon them.

5. The historical literature of China, so far as antiquity is concerned, is extremely meagre, and cannot be regarded as containing trustworthy records. The Greek and Roman writers furnish us with no information whatever, unless we suppose, as some have done, that the Seres, the silk merchants of the ancient world, are the Chinese. Whatever we know, therefore, about ancient China is derived from native sources, and from the reports of missionaries and travellers—the former of which can scarcely be called authentic, while the latter are often scanty and incomplete; for the Chinese have at all times been extremely vigilant in excluding from their country all foreigners, who might have gathered information, and communicated it to Europeans. The Chinese traditions, tracing the history of the empire back many thousands of years before the Christian era, state that their ancestors came into the country from the mountains in the north-west, and, finding it occupied by barbarous tribes, gradually extirpated or subdued them; and those whose lives were spared adopted the customs and language of the conquerors, and united with them as one nation. But it is admitted on all hands that the earliest periods of Chinése history are quite fabulous; and the most ancient dynasty of Chinese sovereigns that may be looked upon as historical, is that of Hia, which ascended the throne about the year B. C. 2207. As the art of writing is unquestionably very ancient in China, it is not impossible that written records of that remote period may have been preserved; but, in consequence of the general destruction of Chinese literature, which, as already mentioned, took place in the third century before Christ, the historical annals of China which have come down to our time cannot be accepted as trustworthy records. The account of this general catastrophe of Chinese literature runs as follows:—Under the third dynasty, called Cheu, the great chiefs in the various parts

of the empire made themselves almost independent; they recognised the supremacy of the emperor scarcely more than nominally, and threw the empire into a complete state of anarchy by the incessant wars among themselves. One of the chiefs, of the house of Zin, put an end to this state of things by subduing all his rivals, and usurping the imperial throne itself. The most powerful ruler of this (the fourth) dynasty was Shi-hoang-ti, who, in order to crush all attempts of the conquered chiefs to recover their dominions, and to deprive them of all documentary evidence by which they might establish their claims, ordered all literary productions of the preceding dynasties to be burned. After the death of Shi-hoang-ti, however, about B. C. 200, the house of Zin perished as rapidly as it had risen, and was succeeded by the dynasty of Han, which, not deeming a knowledge of the past dangerous to its own existence, ordered the books to be restored. Careful inquiries were made after any remains which might have escaped destruction, and a number of fragments were brought together. But the most important source is said to have been the memory of an old man, who pretended to know by heart all the ancient annals of the empire, and from whose dictation they were restored. Now, even admitting that originally the written records went back as far as the twenty-third century B. C., we can hardly conceive that a nation's history restored in this manner should be authentic and complete. Hence the most competent Chinese historians assert that the commencement of really trustworthy accounts cannot be dated farther back than the eighth century before the Christian era. But, even subsequent to this latter epoch, Chinese history is by no means like what we call history in western Asia or Europe, for we have absolutely nothing but records of external events, consisting of rebellions, usurpations, and changes of dynasties, the people itself being treated as an inert mass, which never comes into consideration. Such a history, which scarcely deserves the name, presents nothing that is either pleasing or instructive; and those who wish to study it must be referred to the works specially devoted to the elucidation of Chinese history.

6. The stationary character of the Chinese nation is mainly owing to three causes:—1. The obstinacy with which the people cling to their ancient habits and customs, and repel every attempt at change or reform; 2. The fact that the empire is separated from the rest of the world by mountains and seas—a separation which the Chinese themselves have strengthened by the construction of the celebrated wall, which runs for about fifteen hundred miles along the northern frontier of China. It extends over mountains, some of which are five thousand feet in height, and runs across rivers and valleys. Its average height is twenty feet, and its breadth at the base twenty-five, and at the top fifteen. The object of this immense rampart, was to protect the empire against the incursions of the Tartars.

This end, however, was not always attained, and even the imperial family at present reigning in China is of Manchoo Tartar origin, and has been on the throne for upwards of two centuries. 3. The absolute power of the emperor, who is regarded as the representative of God upon earth, and is styled "the Son of Heaven." He and his aristocracy of learned men, called Mandarins, treat the great body of the people as imbecile children, and by every means prevent their becoming acquainted with the events that are going on in the world around them. The experiences of foreign nations, therefore, are shut out from the Chinese, and notwithstanding their astonishing skill in some of the mechanical arts and manufactures, they have in general always been far behind the western nations. Their form of government is a kind of patriarchal despotism. Agriculture, the most ancient and most honoured occupation, is under the special patronage of the emperor, who at a stated period in every year performs the ceremony of ploughing a few furrows; and the empress encourages the manufacture of silk, by planting every year with her own hands a few mulberry trees. Events are going on at this moment within the celestial empire, which may possibly break the fetters that have compelled the Chinese for thousands of years to walk like children in leading-strings, and throw down the barriers which have so long isolated their country from the rest of the world, and prevented it from accepting a healthier civilisation.

CHAPTER III.

INDIA.

1. India, the easternmost country of Asia known to the ancients, is bounded on the north by the gigantic chain of the Himalaya mountains, on the south of which it extends in the form of two peninsulas. The western is now called Hindostan, and the eastern Further India, or sometimes India beyond the Ganges. The western peninsula is divided into two almost equal parts by a range of mountains running from east to west. The part on the north of these mountains is the real continental Hindostan, and that on the south was formerly called Deccan. The central part of the northern division contains extensive low lands, which are richly watered by the great rivers Indus and Ganges, and their numerous tributaries. The eastern coast of the peninsula is mostly flat, while the northern and western parts are mountainous, and in some districts form high table-lands. This great variety in the aspects of the country, in its

4 *

elevations and depressions, produces the greatest climatic differences; for while the plains and valleys are in every respect tropical countries, and while the mountainous parts are during the greater portion of the year free from excessive heat, the highest mountains display the phenomena of the polar regions, and the lower parts have all the characteristics of the temperate zones. Hence India within its whole extent, from the Himalaya mountains to its southernmost points, presents a variety of climate and productions, such as no other country in the world can boast of.

2. The variety of the inhabitants of India is almost equally great. We call the people of India Indians or Hindoos — a name which the Greeks derived from the Persians, and which has thence passed into modern languages; but the ancient native appellation was Arya, that is "honourable men," the name assumed by the three higher castes of Indians, to distinguish themselves, as the observers of the sacred laws, from the Mlekha, that is, barbarians, or despisers of the law. Although the complexion of the higher Indian castes is darker than that of their northern neighbours, still they belong to the same Caucasian race, and form the easternmost branch of the great Indo-Germanic family of nations. Their neighbours in the north-west are nearest akin to the Arya in language, and in fact called themselves by the same name. This strong resemblance between the two nations may be either purely geographical, as they inhabit contiguous countries, or it is a proof that their separation from each other is more recent than that of the other branches of the same stock. As all of them must have had one common origin and country, the question presents itself, whether Hindostan itself can have been that country. It seems clear that their common home must have been a country from which they could spread in different directions, for which Hindostan was ill suited; but it is both intimated by tradition, and also highly probable in itself, that the original country of Indo-Germanic race was the mountainous district in the north and north-west of India. From that district the Indians seem to have migrated southward through the Punjaub, and thus to have spread over the peninsula, while other branches moved to the north and west. These immigrants, no doubt, found an earlier race established in India, and remnants of such a race may still be traced in the southern parts. The physiognomy of these latter resembles that of the Caucasian race, but their complexion is darker, and their language is altogether different. Hence it may be assumed that they belong to another stock of nations: they possess some features resembling those of the negroes of Africa.

3. This invading race of the Arya, being possessed of great natural talents and a fine mental organisation, has developed a very remarkable and peculiar civilisation, which, long before Greece reached its intellectual supremacy, displayed a variety, extent, and

refinement, never attained, either before or after, by any other
Asiatic nation. Their intellectual activity was not limited in its
effects and influences to India itself, but even China, otherwise so
impatient and jealous of foreign influence, received the religion of
the majority of its inhabitants from India. The Indians never
appear as conquerors, nor do we hear of any great emigrations, by
which Indian civilisation might have been diffused over other
countries; but there are nevertheless traces of Indian colonies in
the eastern parts of Asia, and Indian settlers are said to have introduced into the island of Java their religion, their laws, manners,
arts, and sciences. Notwithstanding all this, it must be owned that
the influence exercised by India upon the other Asiatic nations
has been comparatively small. In regard to commerce, however,
India occupies the foremost rank among the eastern nations — not
that her merchants travelled much to foreign countries to dispose of
their goods, but, as a general rule, the merchants from western Asia
fetched the products of India, and sold them to their own countrymen
or among Europeans. The commerce of the Indians consisted almost
exclusively in exporting the treasures in which India abounded, or
which their own industry produced. The wealth and productiveness
of the country allowed very little scope for importation from abroad.
What was obtained from India was not so much a supply of the
actual necessaries of life, as of objects of splendour and luxury,
such as pearls, precious stones, ivory, cotton and silk stuffs, spices,
and incense. As regards silk, the general opinion is that it was
only woven in India, the material itself being imported from China;
but there are good reasons for assuming that the breeding of the
silk-worm is very ancient in India, and that it was introduced there
from China at a very remote period. Our accounts of the ancient
commerce of India are very fragmentary and obscure, because the
goods exported from it had to pass through many hands before they
reached the nations of western Asia and Europe; and the most
extravagant notions became current in western countries of the
extraordinary wealth of India. Our present knowledge of the
ancient language of India has somewhat dispelled these notions, and
furnished more correct information about Indian commerce. Goods
exported from a country generally carry their native appellations
with them, and the names of very many articles, originally brought
from India, still retain their Indian names, which have been adopted
into the languages of Europe, for instance, tin, pepper, opal, eme-
rald, and many others. ·

4. Formerly our information about ancient India was derived
solely from the Greeks, who, although the country was not unknown
to them before, and was even connected with some of their mythical
legends, yet did not possess any authentic information about it until
the time of Alexander the Great, who conquered a portion of it, and

made his countrymen and the inquisitive Greeks acquainted with the land, about which, until then, only vague and fabulous reports had been current in the west. But as the occupation of India by the Græco-Macedonians was not of long duration, the information derivable from Greek writers is very scanty and defective, when compared with that which has been gained within the last sixty or seventy years from the study of· the native literature of India, and from a comparison of its language with those of the principal nations of Europe, the radical identity of which was unknown until, towards the end of last century, the English, and especially Sir W. Jones, directed the attention of the learned to it. The language, poetry, and philosophy of the ancient Indians have since that time been subjects of deep and extensive study, and have laid open to us treasures of an intellectual activity in India, of which previously no one had any idea. In addition to these literary remains, temples, sculptures, ruins of cities, inscriptions, coin, and other monuments of very ancient date, enable us to form tolerably correct notions of what ancient India once was. A comparison of what we know of modern India with what has been transmitted to us by the ancient Greeks, seems to show, that in the days of Alexander the Great, it was nearly in the same condition in which it was found in modern times by the first Europeans who visited the country. Hence it is clear that the Indians, though superior in intellect and in the variety and depth of their culture, yet, like other Asiatic nations, were checked in their career at a certain point, beyond which, on the whole, they did not advance.

5. But the historical information derived from the writings of the Indians themselves is likewise very unsatisfactory; for they had scarcely any historical literature at all, and in regard to chronology there are scarcely even two or three points in their ancient history that can be fixed with any precision. Their traditions were embodied in epic poems, which, though we must suppose them to have some historical basis, yet are so full of fanciful and fantastic occurrences, that it is far more difficult to discover the historical kernel than in the epic poetry of any other nation. Those poems, moreover, have not come down to us in their original form, but with numerous alterations and interpolations. The period of epic poetry was not followed in India, as it was in Greece, by one of plain historical narrative, which in fact appears to have had no interest for the imaginative and fanciful Indian. All the historical information transmitted to us by the Indians themselves is limited to a few dry lists of kings, and even these are anything but authentic. They carry us back as far as the fourteenth century before Christ, whence we may assume, that that time forms a kind of beginning of the historical period. The appearance of Alexander in India is interesting, for his historians mention the names of Indian rulers whose

chronology is thereby fixed beyond all doubt. About B.C 56, we hear of a mighty Indian king called Vicramaditya, whose victory over the Sacae forms an era which was adopted by the Indians themselves. But these few events neither throw any great light upon the·internal relations of India, nor serve as a thread for the subsequent history. The introduction of Buddhism fortunately forms another chronological era, about which there is no doubt; but we must defer our account of it until we come to discuss the religion of the Indians. Under these circumstances, our historical knowledge is, on the whole, limited to the social, political, and religious condition of the country, though even here we have no guides to show us the modes of development. All we can say, is that, in the time of Alexander, Indian civilisation had reached a high state of perfection, that this development had commenced about a thousand years before him, and that it continued to bear good fruit for about a thousand years longer, but that then it began to decay.

6. In the time of Alexander the Great, we find India broken up into a number of larger and smaller principalities, which were quite independent of one another; and it appears that, previously to its conquest by foreign invaders, it was never united as one empire. The system of castes has at all times been the foundation of all the political and social institutions of India, and nowhere is it so deeply rooted in the minds of the people, and nowhere, perhaps, has it been so fully developed; for the Indians not only regard the separation into castes as the grand distinction between themselves and the Mlekhas, but trace its origin to the very creation of the human race. The institution itself is founded in India, as everywhere else, upon conquest. Throughout India the three higher castes are distinguished to this day from the lower ones by a lighter complexion and handsomer features, and these higher castes are none other than the Arya, who, as we have already mentioned, at a remote period invaded and conquered India from the north. The four chief castes of the Indians are — 1. The priests or Brahmins; 2. The warriors or Kshatriyas; 3. The tradesmen or Vaisyas; and 4. The servants or Sudras. Mythology describes the Brahmins as proceeding from the mouth of the supreme god Brahma, the warriors as having sprung from his arms, the tradesmen as having arisen out of his loins, and the servants from his feet.

7. The Brahmins have always been the first and most influential caste, and were not only the founders of the intellectual culture and peculiarities of the Indians, but always concentrated in their own body all the intellectual life of the nation. Whatever was opposed to them and their institutions was cast out, or, if successful in maintaining itself, contributed to the decay of the national character. The law always demanded of the Brahmins to lead a pure and holy

life, often to pray and fast, to kill no living being, to take no animal
food except what came from sacrifices, to devote themselves to the
service of the gods, scrupulously to observe a vast number of ceremonies, to study the sacred books, and to expound their contents
to the members of the second and third castes. In compensation
for these numerous and wearisome duties, they enjoyed many and
great privileges, and the other castes were enjoined to show them
the profoundest reverence and submission. The person of a Brah
min was regarded as sacred and inviolable, and even if he were
convicted of a great crime, he could not be put to death, and all
that the king would be entitled to do in such a case would be to
banish him from his dominions. The lands of the Brahmins were
exempt from taxes. Their priestly character alone would have
secured to them a high position in the state; but as they were at
the same time regarded as the sole depositaries of all human wisdom,
they were also the recognised teachers, physicians, and lawyers of
the nation, and the advisers and ministers of the kings.

8. The kings were and still are chosen solely from the military
caste or the Kshatriyas, and although they were regarded as the
chiefs of the nation, yet they ranked below the Brahmins, who
would have thought it degrading to themselves to give a daughter
in marriage to a king, or even to dine with him at the same table.
The Brahmins being the framers of the law, prescribed to the kings
their duties, and the manner in which they had to govern their
dominions, enjoining them to take their highest officers and councillors from among the Brahmins. The king is directed to select
from this caste the wisest man, to entrust to him the most important
state business, and to employ him in carrying into effect all measures of consequence. These regulations show that the fundamental
principle of the Indian state was of a theocratic nature. Rulers
of great energy and power would sometimes break through these
priestly restraints, but they never produced any permanent change,
and Brahminism has for thousands of years been the foundation of
all the political institutions of India. The power of the kings,
however, was nevertheless very great, for they were regarded as the
sole proprietors of the soil, and the cultivators occupied the land
only as tenants, who had to pay a certain proportion of the produce
to the king. But his government interfered very little in local
matters, so that each town or village formed to some extent an independent community.

9. The two castes of priests and soldiers were indeed separated
from the lower ones by a great interval, but the first three are
nevertheless treated as belonging to one another, and as far superior
to the fourth. The first three were styled "the regenerate," and
in consequence of this the Sudras, or fourth caste, were forbidden
to read the sacred books, or to be present when their contents were

expounded. These four castes themselves, however, were subdivided into a great variety of classes, differing in dignity, rights, and privileges, which were transmitted by a father to his children, only by means of his marrying a woman of the same caste to which he himself belonged; and as polygamy is established in India as in other Asiatic countries, the degrading position of woman is somewhat diminished by the fact of her sharing in the rights of her husband. But mixed marriages were nevertheless of frequent occurrence, and as the offspring of such marriages were always regarded as deteriorated in some way or another, a number of mixed castes were gradually formed, which are said to amount to thirty-six, and to each of which a special trade or occupation is assigned. The lowest and most despised of all the castes were the Chandalas, who are best known in our days under the name of Pariahs. They were not allowed to live in towns or villages, or even in their vicinity; whatever they had touched was regarded as unclean, and even to see them was thought to have a polluting effect. When they were seen on the high roads while a Brahmin or merely his suite was passing, they were hunted and killed like wild beasts. The consequence of this was that the Pariahs were a sort of wild and filthy race, living by robbery and plunder. They, like some of the other despised castes of India, seem in fact to be a distinct race, rather than a mere caste, and their condition probably originated in conquest, like that of the Helots in Laconia. The moral effects of this system of castes, which in modern times has lost somewhat of its ancient rigour, are of a most deplorable kind; it has been said that the very idea of humanity does not exist among the Indians, and that they know of no other duties than those of their castes. But still no fetters can be so strong as to prevent the true feeling of humanity from bursting forth occasionally, and Indian poetry in particular often presents to us the noblest feelings of human nature in all their beauty and loveliness. Even the separation of castes was not always observed in practical life with the strictness enjoined by law; for if, for example, a Brahmin was unable to gain the means of living by the discharge of his proper duties, he might serve as a soldier, and carry on agriculture or commerce without losing his dignity as a Brahmin. Cases of this kind still frequently occur.

10. Although it is manifest that such institutions as these must xercise a paralysing influence upon the development of the human mind, still it cannot be denied that there must have been a time in Indian history when those institutions tended to raise and elevate, if not the whole nation, at least certain classes of it. This is most strikingly obvious in the literature, the language, and science of the Hindoos. The Sanscrit, their ancient and sacred language, in which their greatest works are written, is one of the richest, the most euphonious, and the most generally perfect that have ever been

spoken by man. The most ancient works written in this language are the Vedas and the laws of Manu, in which, at the same time, we find the earliest form of the Indian religion. In them we meet with the idea of one uncreated supreme being, existing from all eternity and of himself, comprehending and pervading the universe as its soul. From him, who is himself incomprehensible and invisible, all visible things have emanated; hence the universe is nothing but the unfolding of the divine being, who is reflected in the whole as well as in every individual creature. This original and simple notion of one supreme being was changed in the course of time into polytheism, of which in fact traces appear even in the Vedas themselves. The stars, the elements, and all the powers of nature were conceived as different divine beings that had emanated from the one supreme God. Even in the work of creation a plurality of gods was believed to have been engaged. Brahma', himself created by the first invisible cause, and assisted by the Pradshapatis (the lords of creation), called into being all the various living creatures. Nature after its creation is conceived to be under the special guardianship of eight spirits or gods of secondary rank, among whom Varuna presides over the sea, Pavana over the winds, Yama over justice, Locapalas over the world, Indra over the atmosphere, and Surya over the sun. Numberless spirits of an inferior order are subject to these, and are diffused throughout nature, while the divine substance pervades all living beings from Brahma down to the lowest animals and plants. Within this endless variety of beings the souls of men were believed to migrate, entering after the death of man either into beings of a higher or a lower order, according to the degree in which they had become purified in passing through their previous state of existence. This doctrine of the migration of souls, which we meet with in other countries also, probably originated in India, where it was carried out to its full extent. By way of illustration we may state that, according to the common belief, the soul of a disciple of a Brahmin blaming his master, passed, after his death, into the body of an ass; if he calumniated his master, into that of a dog; if he robbed him, into that of a little worm; and if he envied him, into an insect. This belief led the Indians carefully to avoid killing or injuring any living being; while, on the other hand, they did not scruple to treat a Pariah with inhuman cruelty, because his very condition was regarded as a well-deserved punishment for his transgressions during a previous existence. It must however not be forgotten that this belief acted as a powerful stimulus to strive after moral purity and goodness, inasmuch as it created the notion that by self-denial, self-control, a knowledge of the sacred books, and a conscientious observance of the rules contained therein, the soul of man might return to God, and become worthy of his presence. In all these things, however, the object was to make man conform to certain mechanical rules, rather than to make him strive after real purity of heart.

11. A somewhat different phasis of the Indian religion appears in the national epics, in which the gods are described as having descended to earth, and as taking part in the concerns of men. At this stage the gods appear as real personifications with definite forms; their images are set up in temples and worshipped, and the pure idea of one supreme and invisible god reappears under the name of Brahma (of the neuter-gender), who manifests himself in three divine capacities, bearing the names Brahma (masculine), the creator and lord of the universe; Vishnu, the preserver, and Siva, the destroyer. Vishnu is said to have come into the world in a variety of forms to save it from the influence of evil powers, to punish vice, and to maintain order and justice. These numerous incarnations of the god furnish rich materials for a strange and fantastic mythology. Siva is conceived as destroying all finite things; but as death is only a transition to a new form of life, he was also worshipped as the god of creative power, whence he is the representative of ever decaying and reviving nature. The number of subordinate divinities also increases, and they assume more definite forms. The earth itself is conceived as inhabited by hosts of spirits dwelling in mountains, rivers, brooks, and groves; animals and plants even are worshipped as embodiments of divine powers and properties. This vast mythology, which subsequently became the popular religion of India, may be gathered from the works called Puranas, which occupy a middle character between epic and didactic poetry. They seem to be a compilation from earlier poems, and to have been made at the time when the Indians began to be divided into sects, that is, at the time when the gods of the Trimurti began to be no longer regarded as subordinate to the one great original god, called Para-Brahma, but when one of the three was himself worshipped as the supreme god. For the sectarian divisions consisted in this, that some portion of the people worshipped one of the three gods—the Trimurti—more particularly as the supreme being, while the two others enjoyed less honour; and the priests, with their votaries of one member of the Trimurti, persecuted the worshippers of either of the other two members with obstinacy and relentless fury. At first Brahma seems to have had his separate worshippers, though no temples or images were erected to him, for idolatry was then still unknown. Afterwards there followed the separate worship of Vishnu, and last that of Siva and other gods. In the end, the worshippers of Vishnu and Siva gained the upper hand, and pure Brahminism was suppressed.

12. In the sixth century before Christ[1] a new religion arose in

---

[1] The Cingalese chronology assigns the origin of Buddhism to the year B. C. 525, and others to B. C. 543, while the Chinese place it in B. C. 950.

5

India in the midst of Brahminism. It was and still is called Buddhism, from Buddha its founder, who came forward as the reformer
of Brahminism. The changes which he effected, and the struggles
to which they gave rise, form a most important epoch in the affairs
of India. The history of this remarkable religious reformer is involved in great obscurity, partly because it was written by his
disciples in a legendary form, with additions and embellishments,
and partly because, until recently, it was known only from the works
of non-Indian followers of Buddha, such as the Tibetans, Chinese,
and Mongols, while the most authentic or Sanscrit authorities have
scarcely yet been thoroughly examined. These Sanscrit works are
considerable in number, and are divided into three classes, the first
of which consists of discourses and conversations of Buddha; the
second of rules of discipline; and the third of metaphysical speculations. According to the common legends about the origin of
Buddha, his real name was Sakyamuni or Gautama. He was the
son of a powerful prince, and the most handsome of all men. Even
at his birth he was surrounded by spirits, who continued to watch
over him throughout his life. The fourfold miseries of mankind,
viz., the pains of child-birth, disease, old age, and death, affected
and saddened him so much, that he resolved to renounce all the
pomp and luxury of his high station, and to lead the life of a humble
hermit. After having spent a period of six years in this way, he
returned among men, and began to preach to them the necessity of
despising the pleasures of this world, and of subduing every selfish
feeling. He himself practised these virtues to such a degree, that
he became a superior being — Buddha, that is, an immortal. As
such, he was believed, after his earthly death, to rule over the
world for a period of five thousand years, at the expiration of which
he was to be succeeded by another Buddha, as he himself had been
preceded by four or six other Buddhas. The saints who by their
merits ranked nearest to Buddha himself, and who might become
his successors, were called Bodhisattvas. According to this doctrine,
then, the highest power in the spiritual, as well as the material
world, belongs to deified men, and most of the Buddhists (for this
religion is likewise divided into several sects) do not recognise one
eternal divine creator and ruler of the world, but believe that all
things have come, and are still coming into existence, by some in-
scrutable law of necessity, and by an unceasing process of change.
Only one of these sects worships one supreme god, under the name
of Adi-Buddha. But the non-existence of such a being had been
asserted even before the time of Sakyamuni by certain Indian
philosophers, from whom he appears to have borrowed the idea.
He did not indeed impugn the existence of Brahma and the
numerous other divinities, but he taught that the power of Buddha
was greater than theirs. In other respects he retained the doctrines

of Brahminism, as, for instance, that about the migration of souls.
Rewards and punishments, according to him, were not eternal; but
he taught that the man raised by his virtues to the rank of a god,
as well as the condemned, was subject to an immutable law of
change, and that both must return to this earth to pass through
fresh trials and a fresh succession of changes. The highest happiness, in his opinion, was to escape from this eternal change of
coming into being and dying; whence he held out to the faithful
and the good the hope that in the end they would become a Nirwana,
that is, that they would enter a state of almost entire annihilation.
This state of supreme happiness is conceived differently by the
different sects of Buddhists, but in the main idea all agree.

13. The objects which Sakyamuni himself had in view were far
removed from those metaphysical speculations on which, at a later
time, his followers became divided into sects. His own doctrines,
though intimately connected with his philosophical views, were
essentially practical, for he maintained that there were six cardinal
virtues, by means of which man might attain the condition of
Nirwana, viz., almsgiving, pure morality, knowledge, energy in
action, patience, and goodwill towards his fellow-men. The fundamental principle of Buddhism, therefore, is essentially of an ethical
nature, and the advantages which such a system, notwithstanding
its atheistical character, seemed to afford, were so great, that it
could not but attract great attention at a time when Brahminism,
though still intellectually at its height, had sunk very low in a moral
point of view. Religion, in the hands of the Brahmins, had become
a mere mechanical observance of ill-understood ceremonies, for which
Sakyamuni wished to substitute a truly pious life; at the same time
he endeavoured to put an end to the haughty and domineering spirit
of the priests. He accordingly denied the unconditional authority
of the Vedas, and it was formerly believed that he had even condemned the whole system of castes; but although this latter belief
is erroneous, still it is evident that, a pious and virtuous life being
made the sole condition of eternal happiness, virtually the division
into castes was not recognised, though they continued to exist as
corporations of different occupations and trades, or as political bodies.
The Brahmins alone, as a privileged class, were not only not recognised, but vehemently opposed. This open rupture between the
old and new religion, however, was not produced at once, for Sakyamuni himself did not aim at destroying what he found, but only
wanted to bring about a peaceful reform within the established
religion, and to inculcate the necessity of a really pious life. His
own personal influence, his discourses, and his austerity produced a
great effect, and disciples gathered around him from all classes,
even from the Brahminical caste. Afterwards, however, the Brahmins began to persecute the ascetic Buddhists, at first from envy

and jealousy, and afterwards from a fear lest the new sect should
ultimately overthrow all the religious and political institutions of
the country. But the greater the opposition, the greater was the
success of the new religion; the lower castes in particular, feeling
themselves elevated by the new doctrines, seized with eagerness the
opportunity of getting rid of fetters which had hitherto constrained
them; and the teaching, addressed as it was to all the people without distinction, produced astonishing effects. The Sudras felt called
upon to embrace the new doctrines, and to become members of the
community of saints; and even many of the Kshatriyas, impatient
of the priestly arrogance of the Brahmins, adopted them. In the
end, kings also joined the reformers, and gave a character to the
new religion. About the middle of the third century before Christ,
we meet with a king Açoka, a grandson of Chandragupta, who ruled
over nearly the whole of India, and was devotedly attached to the
doctrines of Buddhism, without, however, persecuting the still
numerous adherents of Brahminism. He not only erected numerous Buddha temples, but strove himself to live entirely in accordance with the ethical precepts of the new religion, practising the
virtues of general benevolence and kindness to all men. He
abolished capital punishment throughout his extensive empire,
erected everywhere hospitals for the sick, and made roads shaded
by trees and provided with wells at certain intervals. He not only
established and extended Buddhism in his own dominions, but even
sent missionaries into foreign countries. The progress of the new
religion was thus immense, but very little is known about the
struggles it had to maintain in India with its great and powerful
rival. All we know is, that the Brahmins continued to exert themselves in maintaining their own religion, and that, after a few centuries, a mighty reaction took place, in which the exasperated
Brahmins succeeded in rousing their followers to a desperate and
bloody contest with their opponents. These struggles, which appear
to have lasted from the third to the seventh century of our era,
terminated in the defeat of Buddhism, which was almost entirely
exterminated in the western peninsula. After the expulsion of the
Buddhists, however, a sect of them called Yainas still maintained
itself, rejecting the authority of the Vedas, and worshipping deified
men. But Buddhism had long before spread beyond the borders
of western India, and had been adopted by numerous other Asiatic
nations. In the third century before Christ, it was introduced into
Ceylon, whence it spread over nearly all the Indian islands, and
over a great part of further India, Tibet, and China, in the last of
which countries it took root as early as the first century after Christ,
under the name of the religion of Fo or Foë, which is the Chinese
name for Buddha. It was especially the lower classes among the
Chinese that eagerly took up the new religion, and to this day

Buddhism is the religion of the majority of the Chinese people. Altogether, this religion is the most widely-spread in the world, extending from the Indus to Japan, and counting about two hundred millions of adherents.

14. The astonishing success of so singular a religious system is certainly one of the most remarkable phenomena in the history of Asiatic civilisation. It has undergone various changes in the countries into which it was introduced, but its most essential points everywhere are traceable to its Indian origin. Buddhism had at first combated the existence of a privileged class of priests, but in its turn it was obliged itself, for the purpose of self-preservation, to institute an order of priesthood. The elements of it lay in the nature of Buddhism itself, which regarded an ascetic life as the holiest that a man could lead. Sakyamuni himself had raised those of his followers who chose an ascetic life, by a kind of consecration, to the rank of Sramanas, which we may interpret by the term " mendicant friars," for they were obliged to vow to spend their lives in celibacy, and to support themselves solely by alms. These Sramanas formed the retinue of Sakyamuni as long as he was alive, and even those who lived in the wilds and solitudes sometimes gathered around him to listen to his discourses. These monks, in the course of time, began to congregate in separate buildings, and thus formed convents, which, by the liberality of their adherents, acquired great wealth, and were placed under strict regulations regarding dress, food, the mode of admission, and the like. These priests differed essentially from the Brahmins by their ascetic mode of life in convents, and by their celibacy. The worship of this new religion was at first very simple. Bloody sacrifices were unknown, because it was unlawful to kill any living being, and because the religion recognised no god to whom sacrifices might be offered. Buddha alone was worshipped, and that in two ways, divine honours being paid to his images and to the remains of his body, the latter of which were preserved in eight metal boxes, deposited in as many sacred buildings or temples. Buildings containing remains of Buddha himself or of distinguished persons who had supported his doctrines, were afterwards greatly multiplied. The Brahmins, in a similar manner, raised vast monuments over the remains of illustrious men, but never paid them any divine honours. Such Buddhist mausoleums are found in great numbers in those countries where this religion is or once was established, especially in Ceylon, where they are called Dagops. In Afghanistan, on the north-west of the Indus, many such monuments of great interest have been discovered in modern times, and are popularly known under the name of Topes. They are all built in the form of cupolas with a few small chambers in the interior. Many of them have been

5 *

opened, and a great number of objects of value, offered by pilgrims, have been found in them.

15. Buddhism, though originating in an opposition to the abuses of Brahminism, degenerated in the course of time into something which is probably far worse than Brahminism. Its dogmas have become wild and fantastic, its form of worship is an empty system of pomps and ceremonies, and its ascetic priests are described as forming a most domineering hierarchy, so that in all Buddhist countries there exists a most marked distinction between the priests and the laity. The priests still live in convents, which are at the same time the schools for the young, and the greatest veneration is paid to them by the people; but they are at the same time bound to strict obedience towards their ecclesiastical superiors. Nowhere is the Buddhist hierarchy so fully and so perfectly organised as in Tibet, where nearly half the population consists of priests, who, together with all the rest of the people, recognise a sort of Pope, styled Dalai Lama, as their head. He is regarded as the living embodiment of a Bodhisattva, whose soul, at the death of the individual in whom it has existed, always migrates into the body of his successor. Many of the institutions and ceremonies of Buddhism have so striking a resemblance with those of the Roman Catholic religion, that it was at one time believed that Christianity had exercised great influence upon Buddhism; but subsequent investigations have shown that the eastern institutions are more ancient than Christianity, and that in all probability Buddhism and Roman Catholicism have arrived at the same results independently of each other. Under such circumstances, the expulsion of Buddhism from India has not been a misfortune, for its purer ethics gave way at an early period to a pompous and wearisome ceremonial, and its influence upon intellectual and literary culture was anything but beneficial. In India, all intellectual pursuits have ever been connected with Brahminism, as is clear from the development of its literature. The Buddhists had indeed a literature, but it was subservient only to the transmission of its doctrines, whereas the national or Brahminical literature embraces all the relations and manifestations of human life, and is deserving of the most careful study.

16. The Vedas, as was remarked above, are the most ancient monuments of the Sanscrit or Brahminical literature, and were, according to tradition, communicated to men by Brahma himself. They were then handed down by oral tradition, until a wise man of the name of Vyasa (the collec or) put them together in their present order, and divided them into four great parts, each of which is subdivided into two sections, of which the first contains prayers, hymns, and invocations, and the second rules about religious duties and theologico-philosophical doctrines. Some few of the pieces

constituting the Vedas are evidently later interpolations, but the
genuine parts cannot belong to a more recent date than the teuth
century before Christ In Sakyamuni's time, they were revered as
ancient works, and there can be little doubt that the most ancient
parts were composed as early as the year B. C. 1400. The book
next in importance consists of the laws of Manu, which was likewise believed to be divinely inspired; for Brahma was said to have
communicated them to his grandson, Manu, the first mortal. The
laws contained in this book are intended as a basis for all the political, religious, and social relations of life. It begins with the
creation of the world, and treats of education, marriage, domestic
and religious duties, of government, the civil and penal law, of
castes, repentance, the migration of souls, and the blessings of the
future life. The age of this work is in all probability much more
recent than that of the Vedas, notwithstanding the tradition, and
much also is traceable to subsequent compilers; but although despotism and priestly rule, as well as a great number of petty and
childish ceremonies, form the main substance of the work, yet the
whole is pervaded by a spirit of profound piety and benevolence
towards man and all living creatures. The great epic poems. the
Ramayana and Mahabharata, are likewise believed to be of divine
origin; they celebrate the heroes who lived and acted at the time
when the gods used to come down upou earth and take a part in
the affairs of men. The Ramayana describes the deeds and exploits
of Rama, the seventh incarnation of Vishnu, and its historical sub-
stratum is, perhaps, the first attempt of the Arya to extend their
dominion in the south. The main subject of the Mahabharata is
the struggle between Pandava and Kaurava, two royal and heroic
families; gods, heroes, and giants here appear in arms against one
another; all the members of the two princely houses perish in a
frightful manner, with the exception of one of the Pandava, who
is miraculously recalled to life. This poem holds a middle place
between real mythology and historical tradition. Both these poems
are of more recent date than the Vedas, but it is generally supposed
that they are more ancient than the institution of Buddhism.
Their authors were Brahmins, and although they were composed
chiefly for the edification of the warrior-caste, yet the lower caste
of the Sudras were not only not excluded from reading them, but
were even encouraged to study them as a means of ennobling and
improving themselves. The cultivation of dramatic poetry belongs
to a much later period, and the most celebrated dramatic poet was
Kalidasa, who is said to have lived at the court of King Vikrama-
ditya, a great patron of men of talent and genius, who appears to
have reigned about the time of the birth of Christ. Kalidasa's
drama, entitled Sakontala, was the first that was made known in
Europe towards the end of last century, when its novelty, beauty,

and singular character created general admiration. What is most striking in this and other poetical productions of India, is the delicacy of feeling and the relations of man to nature, which are of the tenderest and most loving kind; but they nevertheless cannot be measured by the European standard, for the Indians have little taste for the reality of things and for simple beauty, whence their heroes and heroines have no definite forms, but are evanescent and surrounded by a fantastic mistiness. And this is probably the reason why the Indians are little fitted for historical composition.

17. There can scarcely be a doubt that speculative philosophy was cultivated by the Indians before all other nations, and with them, as with some others, it first appears in the garb of poetry. The epic Mahabharata contains a very remarkable episode called Bhagavad Gita, in which the hero Ardshuna and the god Krishna enter into a speculative conversation which may be said to contain the elements of a complete system of philosophy. But in India we meet with the same phenomenon as in other countries, in which speculative philosophy has been pursued with vigour; different systems of philosophy, starting from different premises, were developed, and combated one another. Some of them were regarded as orthodox, because their doctrines agreed with those of the Vedas; others were treated as heretical, because they were irreconcilable with the teaching of the Vedas, or had an atheistic tendency. It was one of these latter systems that was adopted by Sakyamuni, when he rejected the authority of the Vedas, and promulgated his atheistic views. In practical philosophy the Indians did not make the same progress as in their metaphysical speculations; but still they did not entirely neglect it. The invention of the decimal system in numbers, so important in mathematics and in the affairs of ordinary life, which has been generally ascribed to the Arabs, is now well known to have been made by the Indians; the Arabs only imported it into Europe, and thereby have acquired the reputation of being its inventors.

18. The arts, as well as the poetry and philosophy of the Indians, were intimately connected with their religion, and were cultivated chiefly in its service. Architecture, in particular, has produced the greatest and most astonishing works in the form of temples, in which the art of building is seen to proceed from nature, for those temples are grottoes in rocks widened and extended by the hand of man into mighty temples. In some instances the interior only is carefully worked out, but in others the outer parts are finished with equal care, though all is wrought in the living rock. India is very rich in gigantic structures of this kind; European travellers first saw and admired those in the islands of Salsetta and Elephanta, near Bombay; and others were subsequently discovered in the interior of the western peninsula, near the village of Elora. Grottoes,

temples, and human habitations, are there cut in a chain of rocks forming a crescent of about four miles in length; and they present such an abundance of sculptures and ornamental carvings of a most difficult kind, that they cannot have been made otherwise than by many thousand hands employed for an immense number of years. These works of Elora far surpass all others of the same class, both in design and execution. Some of these temples are Brahminical, and others are evidently destined for Buddhist worship; but all must have been constructed at a very remote period of Indian history, and all of them were no doubt originally Brahminical temples. The forms of these architectural works are heavy, overloaded with ornaments, and vague, and they present the greatest variety of straight lines and curves; their chief defect is in regard to simplicity and artistic freedom. The Dagops and Stupas of the Buddhists form the transition to the later temples, which were built of blocks of stone and bricks. Europeans generally call these pagodas, (a corruption of Bhagavati, *i. e.*, a sacred house.) Several of them excite by their vastness no less astonishment than the rock temples of Elora. These pagodas are generally built in the form of pyramids, consisting of several parts with vertical sides, the whole being surmounted by a cupola. They are covered with such a profusion of ornaments that the sight is perfectly bewildering.

19. Sculptures, especially high reliefs in stone, occur in great abundance both in the grotto temples and in the pagodas. Most of the figures are remarkable for great softness, which displays itself particularly in the swelling roundness of the forms, in which bones and muscles are quite concealed. Many of the figures are not only of colossal size, but form most grotesque combinations of human bodies with heads of animals, and often with more than two arms to indicate superhuman strength, while others with several heads are intended to represent superhuman wisdom. These and many other peculiarities show that art in India had not yet come to see that high bodily and mental powers must be expressed by features, forms, proportions, and symmetry, and by a faithful adherence to nature. Indian art thus shows the same peculiarities as Indian poetry; both delight in the expression of softness, combined with what is fantastic and grotesque. The civilisation of India, if viewed by itself and in its seclusion from the rest of the world, is far greater and more important, than if regarded in its connection with that of other nations. India is indeed closely connected with other parts of the world by its language and the literature which mirrors forth the intellectual life of the better part of the nation; but that connection is lost in a period of such remote antiquity, that history, as such, knows nothing of it. Some ideas and inventions no doubt did originate in India, which were afterwards imported into Europe; but their historical recollection has faded away so much, that the

threads can be discovered only by laborious and learned inquiries. It cannot therefore be asserted that India has at any time exercised any considerable influence upon the civilisation of the western world. As to itself, it shares the fate of all eastern countries: it has reached a certain point beyond which it has been unable to advance, and has lost the power of regenerating itself, of renewing its intellectual life, and of opening new paths for itself, by which it might recover and maintain a manly independence.

CHAPTER IV.

IRAN (BACTRIA, MEDIA, AND PERSIA.

1. WE here use the name Iran in its modern acceptation, comprising the Bactrians, Medes, and Persians proper, for these three nations constitute one great branch of the Indo-Germanic race, and are now generally called Iranians, and their country Iran.[1] The people themselves being nearest akin to the Arya of India, called themselves by the same honourable name.[2] Greeks and Romans apply the names Bactrians, Medes, or Persians, to the whole race, according as any of the three branches acquired the supremacy over the others, and thereby threw them into the background. Iran, or the country of the Iranians, is the western highland of Asia, which is much smaller than the eastern highlands; the two are connected by a range of mountains which the historians of Alexander call the Indian Caucasus, and which now bears the name of the Hindoo Kush. The interior of Iran consists of an extensive table-land, the greater part of which has all the characteristics of a desert, especially wanting water and trees, and being of a cold temperature. This table-land, like that on the east of it, is surrounded by mountains which give to the whole country the character of an immense fortress, there being only a few passes by which an entrance can be effected, and these passes run along the most dangerous precipices, or are so narrow that they can be closed by means of gates. Nearly all the more important towns of Iran are built in the vicinity of these passes. The declivities of the mountains on the frontiers form transition countries, some of which are remarkable for their high temperature and their luxurious vegetation; but even these

[1] This name occurs in ancient times only on some coins of the Sassanidæ.
[2] The name is also spelt *Airya*, whence *Iran. Arii*, and *Ariana*, are the names by which the ancients actually designated the greater part of ancient Persia.

have few rivers, and require artificial irrigation to assist agricultural operations.

2. In the history of China and India, no inconsiderable assistance is to be derived from observing the actual state of the countries and of their inhabitants, who have been stationary for many centuries. Such is not the case in Iran, for here great changes and revolutions have thoroughly shaken and altered the ancient condition of both the country and its inhabitants. But, on the other hand, the sources from which information may be obtained regarding its ancient history are more accessible and more generally known ; the classical nations of antiquity having frequently come into contact with the Persians, their writers are far better acquainted with them, and throw much more light upon their history than upon that of India. Besides this information furnished by foreigners, we have the native literature of the Persians, written in the sacred Zend language, which was probably one spoken in the eastern parts of Iran, while the ancient Persic, properly so called, was spoken in the western parts, though both are only dialects of the same branch of the Indo-Germanic stock. The sacred writings in the Zend language, called Zend-Avesta, were unknown in Europe, until, about the middle of last century, a Frenchman of the name of Anquetil du Perron brought them to France, and published a translation of them. These books excited great interest at the time, because they revealed one of the most remarkable of religious systems, which until then had been very imperfectly known. The authenticity of the works, which was at first questioned, has since been established beyond all doubt by oriental scholars. Neither the value, however, nor the antiquity of all the books forming the Zend-Avesta is the same ; the most ancient ones must have been composed before the conquest of Alexander the Great, which opened Iran to the influence of Greek civilisation; for the legends and religious views they contain appear, if not in their original freshness and purity, yet at least free from foreign admixture.

3. The Zend-Avesta contains a very remarkable tradition about the immigration of the Arya into Iran. Once, it is said, the winter in Airyanem-Vaego, the original abode of the people, lasted for ten months, and its severity induced their king Djemshid to emigrate with his people into warmer and more southern countries, which had been blessed by Ormuzd. Djemshid had a golden dagger, a present from Ormuzd, with which he cleft the earth wherever he went ; blessings thus spread everywhere, and the countries became filled with tame and wild beasts, with birds, and men, and red shining fires, which had never before been seen there. This tradition evidently describes the immigration of the Arya from their original homes, in the extreme north-east of Iran, about the sources of the Oxus and Jaxartes; the migration from the north-east to the

south-west was followed by the spread of agriculture, and all the advantages that flow from it as its natural consequences.

4. It is one of the fundamental doctrines with all the Iranians, that originally all things, both moral and physical, were divided into good and evil. Each of these two divisions was presided over by a divine being, the good by Ormuzd, and the evil by Ahriman. Neither of these beings was regarded as eternal, but as produced by Zervane Akerene, that is, uncreated Time, who, after the creation of Ormuzd and Ahriman, entirely disappears, leaving the creation and government of the world, and of all that is contained in it, to those two mighty and divine beings. Ormuzd was from the beginning in a region of light, the symbol of all that is good, while Ahriman dwelt in darkness, the symbol of evil, and the two were perpetually at war with each other. Ormuzd began and completed the creation, which was a creation of light; and Ahriman, though conceived as the destroyer, was nevertheless regarded as a creator; but his creation was the empire of death, and darkness, and evil, which he constituted in such a manner as to oppose to every creature of Ormuzd one created by himself, with similar qualities, but perverted into evil; thus he created the wolf as the counterpart to the useful dog; and in general all beasts of prey, which shun the light, or crawl on the earth; and all troublesome and destructive insects were regarded as creatures of Ahriman. In this manner the whole of the physical world was divided between light and darkness, and all the moral world between good and evil; and the two worlds were conceived as engaged in a perpetual struggle with each other— the evil trying to destroy the good, while the good, in its turn, is bent upon overpowering the evil. It was believed, however, that in the end the principle of good would gain the victory; and, according to some, even Ahriman and his followers were then to be purified and admitted among the blessed. In both these empires, there existed intermediate beings between the supreme rulers and the race of mortals; they consisted of spirits of different grades and ranks. The throne of Ormuzd was surrounded by six arch-spirits, called Amshaspands. Next to them in rank were the Izeds, who stood to the Amshaspands in the same relation as the latter did to Ormuzd. The hosts of other inferior spirits, called Fervers, were innumerable, and pervaded all nature, for every living creature had its Ferver dwelling in it, imparting to it life and motion, and conferring physical and spiritual blessings on those who addressed it in pious and humble prayer. The spirits in the empire of Ahriman were called Devs, six of whom answered to the Amshaspands, and they were the authors of every misfortune, and of all sins. This religious system, notwithstanding its singular dualism, is yet far more spiritual than any of the other polytheistic religions of Asia. It seems to have originated in the worship of the heavenly bodies

which shed their light upon the earth, for this worship prevailed in a
very large part of Asia, where the cloudless sky, with its transparent
blue, clothes all nature with a peculiar brilliancy. Light there
naturally appeared as the vivifying principle, diffusing joy and
happiness over all creation, while darkness seemed to remove and
destroy all that owed its origin and life to light. Hence fire also
was worshipped, as the element containing and diffusing light, and
in special places a perpetual fire was kept up, with certain purifica-
tions and ceremonies. This material worship of light and fire was
raised in the religion of Ormuzd to a spiritual character, for in it
light is no longer a merely physical, but a moral good, and the
symbol of higher spiritual powers. For a long time, worship was
paid simply to the light and fire as they appeared in nature; the
imagination of the Iranians neither conceived the objects of their
worship in definite forms, nor invented any mythological stories
about them. Sacrifices were offered in the open air and on hills,
and Herodotus expressly states that the Persians in his time had
neither statues, nor temples, nor altars. But religion did not
remain in this condition; for, as we shall see hereafter, idolatry
was introduced as early as the time of the Persian empire. At a
still later period, idolatry again disappeared, and its place was supplied by the material worship of fire, and at this stage the religion
of Ormuzd has continued to the present day; for the few surviving
remnants of the ancient Iranians, called Parsi, still cling to the
worship of their ancestors, notwithstanding the furious persecutions
of the Mahommedans. They are found in some of the eastern parts
of Iran, especially in Surate in western India, where Anquetil du
Perron found copies of their ancient sacred books, which were preserved by the priests with great care, and even with danger to
themselves. But the preservation of these books had not been able
to preserve the spiritual element of religion, which has become a
coarse, mechanical, and superstitious fire worship, detested and ab-
horred by the Mahommedan population.

5. According to the ancient and genuine doctrine of the Zend-
Avesta, man became mortal through the sin of his first parents, and
for the same reason he was placed in the middle between the world
of Ormuzd and that of Ahriman. Being free in his choice, but
weak, he would sink under the dominion of Ahriman and his
agents, who watch him night and day, and endeavour to draw him
into the region of darkness, were it not that Ormuzd had revealed
to him the law of light. Under the guidance of this law man is
able to escape from the pursuit of Ahriman and his Devs, and to
arrive at a state of bliss, which was the object of Ormuzd in revealing his law. The sum and substance of this law is, that man must
be pure in his thoughts, words, and actions; and the pure man must
shun the contact of everything proceeding from Ahriman, the source

of all that is impure. If he has been unable to avoid coming into
contact with the impure, he is obliged to undergo a process of purification, consisting of a variety of ceremonies. The worship of the
sacred fire, sacrifices, prayers, and the reading of the sacred books,
constitute the chief religious observances. Contact with dead bodies
of animals or men was regarded as particularly polluting, whence
the people were neither allowed to bury nor to burn their dead; by
the former the earth would have become polluted, and by the latter
the fire. Accordingly, there remained nothing but to expose the
dead bodies in a place where they did not come into contact with
the earth, until the birds of prey or wild beasts had consumed the
flesh, after which the bones were collected and preserved. In all
this, moral and physical purity are blended and confounded. But
one part of the law tells men what to do to induce the earth to yield
them her blessings: they are enjoined to build towns, where priests,
herds and flocks, women and children might congregate in purity;
to cultivate waste lands and improve them by irrigation, and, lastly,
to take care of the cattle and all domestic animals. This part of
the law is evidently intended to promote and preserve civilisation,
and, while Ormuzd thus presides over civilisation, Ahriman rejoices
in wildness and savageness, and everything that is opposed to a
well-organized social system. Hence the Iranians, considering their
own country to be under the special protection of Ormuzd, believed
that the country in the north-east, beyond the river Oxus, was under
the direct influence of Ahriman, because it was inhabited by rude
nomadic tribes which were hostile to them; and they distinguished
that country from their own by giving it the name Turan. Their
aversion to the Turanians, however, arose not from the mere fact
of their being nomades, but because they were hostile to them and
all their social and religious institutions, for some of the Iranian
tribes themselves led a nomadic life.

6. The religion of Ormuzd, by impressing upon its adherents the
necessity of subduing nature, and of combating with all their might
the influence of the empire of Ahriman, could not fail to rouse them
to a life of vigorous activity, and it must have exercised a very considerable influence upon the social and political condition of the
people; but we possess, unfortunately, only very little historical
information about the earliest times. The Zend-Avesta mentions a
division of the people into four classes or castes, viz., priests or
magi, warriors, agriculturists, and tradesmen. The king and the
judges belonged to the first or priestly caste, the warriors seem to
have formed a sort of nobility, and the whole classification must
have been based on differences of descent, but it was never so
strictly enforced and observed as in India, nor does it seem ever to
have embraced the whole nation, as the nomadic tribes, which cannot have been classed with the agriculturists, are not included in
the list of castes.

7. The most ancient, and at the same time the only native records of the history of Iran, are contained in the Zend-Avesta; but they are so entirely mythical that it would be useless to attempt to deduce any history from them. In the middle ages, the Persian poet Firdusi incorporated in a great epic the extant traditions about the ancient exploits of his countrymen; but these traditions are so thoroughly legendary, and so much embellished in the oriental fashion, that they cannot be regarded as a real basis for history. It is only by applying more than ordinary violence that some of them can be made to harmonise with the accounts transmitted to us by the Greeks. We are therefore obliged to take these last as our guides in drawing up our sketch of the history of Persia. But even they do not go very far back, leaving us entirely in ignorance in regard to the most ancient periods. Hence the age of Zerdusht, commonly called Zoroaster, the famous religious lawgiver of the Persians, is buried in utter obscurity.' Some Greek authors state that he flourished about five thousand years before the Trojan war, according to which he would be a purely mythical being. Firdusi relates that he lived in the reign of King Gushtasv, who adopted his doctrines, ordered his subjects to establish the worship of fire, and diffused the Zend-Avesta throughout his dominions. Some critics, identifying this Gushtasv with Darius the son of Hystaspes, believe that Zoroaster must have lived in the sixth century before the Christian era. But there appears to be no good reason for regarding the Gushtasv of Firdusi, and Darius the son of Hystaspes, as the same person; and moreover, if such a man had lived at that time, the Greeks could hardly have left him unnoticed. The probability is, that Zoroaster flourished somewhere about the year 1000 B. C. Shortly after the time of Darius, the Persians began to lose their original character, which it must have .taken centuries to develope under the law of Ormuzd. The Zend-Avesta does not describe Zoroaster as the original author of fire worship, but only as a prophet who developed and completed the whole system. Hence he cannot be regarded either as a purely mythical personage, nor be assigned to so late a date as that of Darius.

8. The most ancient Iranian empire, about which Greek writers furnish any information, is Bactria or Bactriana, with its capital of Bactra or Zariaspa. It formed the north-eastern part of Iran, bordering upon Turan. Most of the accounts we have of Bactria refer to its invasions and conquests by foreign enemies. Thus we are told that Ninus (about B. C. 1230) marched with a vast army into the country and besieged Bactra, which, however, he was unable to take, until Semiramis came to his assistance. Afterwards the Bactrians are said to have submitted to Cyrus, king of Persia, (about B. C. 540,) who appointed one of his sons satrap of Bactria and some adjacent countries. Thenceforth the country continued to form

part of the Persian empire, to which it was tributary, but repeated attempts were made to shake off the yoke. Alexander the Great (B. C. 329) conquered Bactria, like the other parts of the kingdom of Persia, and appointed satraps as its governors; but about the year B. C. 256, the governor Antiochus Theus threw off the yoke of Alexander's successors, and proclaimed himself independent king of Bactria. He was succeeded by several kings whose names are known only from coins, found in modern times at Balkh and Bokhara, and bearing Greek legends. The reign of Eucratidas, who ascended the throne about B.C. 181, appears to have been long and prosperous, for he is said to have ruled over a thousand cities, and to have annexed even a part of India to his dominions. Several of his successors, again, are known only from their coins, which continue to bear Greek legends, until in the end the dominion of the Greek rulers was overthrown by Scythian tribes, which, about B. C. 100, extended their sway as far as the mouths of the river Indus. The coins of the new rulers, who were evidently barbarians, continue to bear Greek inscriptions, but they gradually become so corrupt, that it is clear they were made by people who were not familiar with the Greek language. These Scythian rulers were succeeded by a race commonly called Indo-Scythians, whose chief seat appears to have been on the river Kabul, for their coins are discovered in great numbers between Kabul and Jelalabad. The time when these Indo-Scythians succeeded in gaining the ascendency is unknown; the legends of their coins are still in Greek characters, but we frequently meet with Indian words. When the Sassanidae (A. D. 226) restored the Persian empire, Bactria again became a province of it, and in this condition it remained, until, in the eighth century after Christ, the country was conquered by Mahommedan invaders. A kind of Greek civilisation, the result of Alexander's conquests, had thus maintained itself for several centuries in the distant East, until in the end it was extinguished by barbarians; and were it not for the numerous coins with Greek inscriptions found in those parts, we should hardly know anything of the existence of a Greek empire in the north-east of Iran.

9. The history of Media has been transmitted to us in a more complete and satisfactory form. This country, situated in the west of Iran, was regarded by the ancients as one of the most important parts of Asia, on account of its extent, its favourable situation, the number of its warlike inhabitants, its excellent breed of horses, and its great fertility, especially in the warm plains. At present these advantages no longer exist, for both the population and civilisation have sunk very low, and the artificial irrigation which the country requires has been almost entirely neglected. The history of Media previous to the thirteenth century B. C. is unknown to us; but about that time it was subdued by the Assyrians, whose

yoke the Medes bore for a period of about five hundred years. But they then took courage, and freeing themselves from foreign dominion, restored their country to independence. Under what form of government they lived after their liberation, we have no means of ascertaining, but we are told that the increasing state of lawlessness and anarchy filled the people with fear lest they should be compelled to quit their native country, and that, in consequence, they resolved to appoint a king. They accordingly elected from among themselves Deioces, a man who had already acquired great reputation as a judge in his own district, and was ambitious of gaining the sovereign power among his countrymen. He reigned from B. c. 709 till 656, and from the first surrounded himself with a strong body-guard, and built the capital of Ecbatana, which he fortified with a sevenfold wall. The innermost of these walls enclosed the royal palace and the treasury. At present there are but few remains of Ecbatana, in the neighbourhood of Hamadan. The monarchy which he established was hereditary, and a kind of military despotism. His successor Phraortes, from B. c. 656 to 634, commenced a great war against the Assyrian empire, but lost his life in a decisive battle. In the reign of his son Cyaxares, from B. c. 634 to 594, the kingdom was invaded by Scythian hordes from the countries about mount Caucasus, and was kept in subjection by them for a period of twenty-eight years, at the end of which, Cyaxares and his Medes not only expelled the foreign invaders, but resumed the war against the Assyrians, to avenge the defeat of his father. For this purpose, he allied himself with Nabopolassar, king of Babylon, and succeeded in taking and destroying the Assyrian capital of Nineveh, and subduing the empire. When he died, af·er a reign of forty years, he was succeeded by his son Astyages. The Median empire which was thus restored by Cyaxares, embraced, besides Media, also Assyria, and was further extended by the subjugation of Persia proper and Bactria. It was bounded on the west by the river Halys. Astyages, who reigned from B. c. 594 till 559, was the last king of Media, for in his reign the subject Persians rose against the Medes, and having overthrown their power, subdued the whole of the Median empire. According to Herodotus, the daughter of Astyages married a Persian noble, whose son Cyrus usurped the throne of Media, and thus became the founder of the Persian empire in B. c. 559.

10. The history of Cyrus[1]—setting aside the romance related by Xenophon in his Cyropaedia — has been transmitted to us in a legendary form by Herodotus. According to this, his grandfather Astyages, having been frightened by a dream, gave orders that the son born of his daughter should be killed; but the child was saved

---

[1] Properly Koresh or Kurshid, that is, the Sun.

and reared by a she-dog in the mountains of Persia. He grew up, and became the most distinguished archer and horseman among the warlike Persians. He must have been one of those mighty characters whose mere appearance exercises a peculiar charm upon those coming in contact with them, and who, when successful in great undertakings, are regarded by their contemporaries as direct instruments in the hands of the deity. In regard to his early history, all that can be said with certainty is, that he roused the Persians to an insurrection against the ruling Medes, who were defeated in a pitched battle; all Media then fell into the hands of Cyrus, in consequence of which, the sovereignty passed into the hands of the Persians. The Medes afterwards made several attempts to recover their lost power, but were unsuccessful. The main advantage gained by the Persians was that henceforth they had no longer to pay the heavy land-tax which had hitherto been imposed upon them by the Medes, the latter having now to fulfil the same obligation to them. On the other hand, however, the Persians, who had hitherto enjoyed comparative freedom in their own country, were gradually brought under the same despotism as those nations which had been subdued by their chief. All the countries which had been subject to Media now naturally owned the sway of the new rulers. But that empire did not satisfy Cyrus; in the course of his thirty years' reign (from B. C. 559 to 531) he extended it from the Hellespont, the Ægean, and the frontiers of Egypt, in the West, to the Oxus in the East. Soon after his ascension, he became involved in a war with Croesus, king of Lydia. This king, it is said, had been an ally of Astyages, and now resolved to avenge him on the usurper; but it was probably the fear of being attacked by the successful conqueror that induced Croesus to anticipate the plans of the enemy. He accordingly made war upon Cyrus, but in a battle on the east of the river Halys, the Lydians were defeated, and obliged to make a hasty retreat to their own country. Cyrus, with unexpected rapidity, pursued the enemy through Cappadocia and Phrygia, and appeared before Sardes the capital of Lydia, before Croesus was able to assemble a new army. In a short time the city and its citadel fell into the hands of Cyrus, and Croesus himself was taken prisoner. This important event occurred in the year B. C. 546. Cyrus is said to have ordered the conquered king to be burnt alive, but while standing on the pile, the unfortunate man, remembering a wise saying of Solon, who had once visited him, and refused to own that Croesus, in spite of his immense wealth, deserved to be called happy, exclaimed Solon, Solon! Cyrus, surprised at this, asked what it meant, and upon being informed, ordered Croesus to be brought down from the pile, and to accompany him to the court of Persia. This beautiful story, unfortunately, is irreconcilable with chronology, for Croesus did not ascend the throne of Lydia till B. C.

560, and Solon himself died in that same year or the one following. Certain it is, however, that Croesus for many a year afterwards lived at the court of Persia, enjoying the respect and esteem of both Cyrus and his son Cambyses. The conquest of Lydia was accompanied by that of other nations in Asia Minor; the Mysians, Phrygians, and Paphlagonians, submitted without a blow; but the Greek colonies in Asia, many of which had been subject to Croesus, and the Carians and Lycians, the last of whom had not belonged to the Lydian empire, were resolved to defend their freedom against the new conqueror. But they were unable to maintain themselves, for one Greek city after another, though they defended themselves with true heroism, was obliged to submit, and some of them experienced all the horrors of cities taken by the sword. The inhabitants of Phocaea emigrated, and founded Velia (Elea) in southern Italy. The other Greek cities, after the withdrawal of Cyrus, retained their own republican constitutions, but were obliged to pay tribute to the Persians; they remained wealthy and flourishing, but their free spirit as Greeks gradually disappeared under the Persian rule. Lycia and Caria also were overpowered by Cyrus, and the ruler of Cilicia recognised the supremacy of the conqueror. All Asia Minor was thus reduced. The Lydians afterwards endeavoured to shake off the foreign dominion, but were unsuccessful, and the yoke only became harder and heavier: their arms were taken from them, and they were compelled to live in the enjoyment of the wealth they possessed, in consequence of which they became demoralised and effeminate.

Babylon had not been subject to the Medes, and had therefore to be conquered by force of arms. This conquest was not accomplished by Cyrus without great efforts, but when effected, added vast territories to the Persian empire; for all Syria, together with Phoenicia and Palestine, seem at that period to have been subject to Babylon. The conquest of Babylon, which took place in B. C. 538, is related in different ways. According to the native tradition, Nabonnedus, king of Babylon, met the enemy in the open field, but being defeated in a pitched battle, he retreated to Borsippa, the city of the Chaldaeans, where he was besieged, and afterwards capitulated. His life, however, like that of Croesus, was spared, and he spent the remainder of his days in a small principality in Carmania. According to Herodotus, Cyrus took the city of Babylon by turning the course of the river Euphrates, the city being built on both sides of it, so that he was enabled to march into the very heart of the place as soon as the ordinary bed of the river was dried up. By this conquest, Cyrus at once became the sovereign of all the countries which had been subject to Babylon.

The last undertaking of Cyrus was, according to Herodotus, an expedition against the Mas-agetae, which Ctesias assigns to an earlier period, and accordingly makes Cyrus return victorious; whereas Herodôtus states that he lost his life in a battle against the Massagetae. This nation was probably of the Mongol or Tartar race, living chiefly by the chase and on the produce of their herds and flocks. They occupied the country about the Caspian sea, or the steppes to the north of the river Oxus, and were at this time governed by a queen, Tomyris. Cyrus commenced the war against them, and entrapped them by a stratagem: he left his camp and a great quantity of wine, and when the Massagetae took the camp, they indulged so much in drinking as to become intoxicated, whereupon Cyrus returned and captured a great number of them, and among them the queen's son, who was so mortified at the disaster that, although he had obtained his freedom from the conqueror, he made away with himself. The queen then, filled with grief and revenge, collected a fresh army, and in a terrible battle avenged the loss of her son, and of so many of her people. The body of Cyrus was treated with insult by Tomyris, for she cut off the head, and, throwing it into a bag filled with blood, exclaimed, "Now sate thyself with blood, of which during thy life thou wast so thirsty." This account, preserved in Herodotus, is, like many of his eastern stories, only a popular tradition, though the war against the Massagetae itself cannot be doubted. Certain it is, also, that Cyrus died in the year B. C. 531, that his body was buried at Persepolis, and that he was succeeded by his son Cambyses, in B. C. 530, who was recognised throughout the whole empire without any opposition.

11. Cambyses inherited indeed the warlike disposition of his father, but he was violent and tyrannical, whence his reign, which lasted until B. C. 522, was as unfortunate for those whom he subdued as for his own empire. Its two most remarkable events are the conquest of Egypt, and the murder of his brother, which led to the usurpation of the Magi, so that the government for a time passed into the hands of the Medes; until the Persians, recovering their courage, threw off the yoke. From Herodotus it would seem as if Cambyses had set out on the Egytian expedition immediately after his accession, but this is impossible, for the conquest of Egypt is known to belong to the year B. C. 526. The attack upon Egypt was made without any provocation, and arose simply from his consciousness that he was strong enough to conquer the country he coveted. The story that his anger was roused against the Egyptians by an Egyptian woman, is probably a mere fiction. Egypt was then governed by king Psammenitus. Cambyses, assisted by a treacherous Greek, Phanes of Halicarnassus, invaded Egypt by land and by sea, being supplied with a fleet by the Phoenicians, and the maritime towns of Asia Minor. The land army marched into Egypt through the desert, but the Egyptians met the invaders on the frontier, and a decisive battle was fought in the neighbourhood of Pe-

lusium, in which the Egyptians were completely defeated. After this victory the Persians advanced towards Memphis, then the capital of Egypt, where the people, in consequence of the national antipathy subsisting between the Persians and Egyptians, offered an obstinate and almost fanatical resistance. At length, however, famine compelled them to surrender, and they were treated with fearful cruelty by the conqueror. The Persians being themselves worshippers of light and fire, thoroughly despised the religion of the Egyptians, and Cambyses and his soldiery insulted and maltreated their conquered enemies in every way and on every occasion. According to Herodotus, Cambyses spent the remainder of his life in Egypt, being occupied with designs of fresh conquests, for he wished to carry his arms as far into Africa as his father had carried them into Asia; but nature opposed him. He first sent an army against the Ethiopians, but it perished in the desert under whirlwinds of sand. An expedition to the oasis of Siwah (Ammonium) experienced a similar fate, and these failures only increased the despot's cruelty towards the Egyptians. Another expedition was proposed against Carthage, but Cambyses could not undertake this without the fleet of the Phoenicians, and as they refused to aid their ruler in the subjugation of their own colony, the plan was given up.

Cambyses abandoned himself in Egypt to habits of intoxication, and to the gratification of every whim and passion; which hurt the feelings of his own Persians no less than those of the Egyptians. Being taunted by the son of a noble Persian with being too much given to drinking, he shot the young man with an arrow through his heart; and the father of the youth, who witnessed the deed, when asked by Cambyses whether he now believed him to be drunk, servilely answered, that a god himself could not have aimed more correctly. On another occasion, he ordered twelve Persian nobles to be buried up to their necks in the earth. Among other atrocities, he ordered, in consequence of a dream, his own brother Smerdis to be put to death, and the deed was done by the very man whose son Cambyses had shot.

After this murder a pretender arose, who, with great boldness and address, possessed a remarkable resemblance to the murdered prince, and came forward at Ecbatana under his name to claim the throne. This Smerdis was a Mede, and his brother had been intrusted with the administration of the empire during the absence of Cambyses. Supported by this brother, Smerdis at once took possession of the treasures and the throne of Persia, and the people, tired of the tyranny of ·Cambyses, without hesitation recognised him as their ruler. In order to secure their favour, he adopted a policy opposed to that of the detested tyrant. When Cambyses heard of all this, he set out against the usurper with his army; but his career was cut short, before he had an opportunity of meeting his enemy in battle.　He accidentally wounded himself with his own sword, and died in consequence, mortification having taken place in the wound, B. C. 522.　As he left no children, the army readily recognised the pseudo Smerdis as their king, for as Cambyses had never made the death of his brother publicly known, he was generally believed to be the real Smerdis.

12. This is the view taken by Herodotus, according to whom the empire was governed by a Mede, while every one believed him to be a Persian; but the whole affair seems to have been a revolution, by which the Medes endeavoured to recover their lost power, and for a time were successful.　But, before a year had passed away, seven of the noblest Persians led on their countrymen against the usurper, and overpowed and slew him in his palace.　Upon this there arose a general insurrection against the Medes and their Magi, of whom the Persians slew as many as they could find; and a festival was then instituted to commemorate the event, under the name of the Magophonia.　When the Medes were completely vanquished, the Persians raised one of their own grandees, Darius, the son of Hystaspes, to the throne, B. C. 521.　He reigned until B. C. 486, and this long period was no less important in the history of Persia than the reign of Cyrus himself had been; for Cyrus and Cambyses had enlarged the empire by conquests, but Darius organised and consolidated the unwieldy mass. He divided his vast kingdom into twenty satrapies or provinces, the administration of each of which was intrusted to a satrap or governor, whose duties were not indeed clearly defined; but without some such arrangement the empire could not have been kept together; and under the circumstances, his institutions must have been as good as any that could have been devised, for they lasted till the end of the Persian empire.　In addition to these internal regulations, Darius also, like his predecessors, extended his empire in all directions.　He subdued not only the border countries of India, but the whole valley of the Indus became part of his empire, so that Persian ships sailed up the river as far as it was navigable.　He also made the Arabs tributary, though their country remained free and was not changed into a province. Cyrene in Africa, and Thrace and Macedonia in Europe, together with the Greek islands near the Asiatic coast, had to pay homage and tribute to him.　It appears to have been his ambition also to subdue the countries around the Euxine, and to unite the continent of Greece with his empire.　But in these last undertakings he was not successful. The Scythian nomades on the lower Danube withdrew with their tents and herds, leaving their deserted and barren country to the enemy, who, from want of provisions, were brought to the very brink of destruction, and would on their return have perished on the banks of the Danube, if the Greeks who had been commissioned to guard the bridge on that river had agreed to break it down, as

Miltiades advised. Darius was more successful in quelling the insurrections which broke out in the interior of his empire. Babylon, which made an attempt to shake off the Persian yoke, was re-conquered through the treachery of Zopyrus, a Persian noble, who is said to have mutilated himself in order to win the confidence of the enemy. Miletus and the Greek cities in Asia likewise revolted, and, although at first successful, had in the end to pay dearly for their thoughtless attempt. But we shall afterwards have occasion to recur to these events, and must now turn our attention to the reforms which Darius introduced in his own empire.

13. Darius himself and his successors belonged to the noble family of the Achaemenidae, besides which there were six other great families, from which the generals and great officers of state were chosen by the king. The Persians proper, as the ruling people, were exempt from all taxes; at home they were free and governed themselves, but as soon as they went abroad or to the court, they were slaves like all the other subjects of the king. In all the other parts of the empire a uniform system of administration and taxation was introduced. The administration was facilitated by the division of the empire into satrapies. The military affairs in each province were managed by the satrap, but besides him, there was a royal scribe in every province, who was quite independent of the satrap, and whose business it was to levy the tribute and taxes. Every satrap himself kept a court in his province, and lived in royal splendour, deriving his income from all parts of his province partly in money and partly in produce of the land. As the satraps were generally relations of the king, and were possessed of great power, the provinces were without any redress against their extortions; for if the governors only took care that the tribute to the king was punctually paid, they were allowed to rule according to their own pleasure, and satisfy their avarice in any manner they pleased. Sometimes they even went so far as to defy the commands of their king, and to wage war among one another. On the whole, it may be said that, with the organisation it possessed, the Persian empire was a mere accumulation of heterogeneous masses, kept together only by mechanical means, without any internal bond of union, except fear. No attempts were made to destroy the national character of the provincials, and the Persian government generally left to conquered nations their institutions, laws, and customs, and sometimes even their rulers, if they otherwise obeyed the king's commands and paid their tribute. But notwithstanding this, the provinces generally sank into a state of barbarism, for no laws protected them against the arbitrary and despotic conduct of their governors, the taxation was extremely heavy, and the loss of political independence gradually extinguished that manly spirit without which no nation can rise to greatness.

The Persian army was very numerous, every man capable of bearing arms being obliged to serve, and in time of need they were called to arms to their various rallying places. The soldiers served in their national costumes and armour, which gave to a Persian army a very motley appearance.

The religion of the Persians was the system of the Mede Zoroaster, though it was modified in some points. Fire and the sun were objects of worship, and formed the chief points of the Persian religion. The Magi or priests of the Medes were adopted by the Persians, together with their religion, and were at first a very powerful class of men; but under the military despotism they gradually lost their former power and importance. In science and literature the Persians have left no great name in history; but the noble ruins of Persepolis, consisting of the remains of temples, palaces, porticoes, reliefs, and other sculptures, and walls covered with inscriptions, show that in architecture and sculpture they were by no means behind other Asiatic nations.

The king of Persia, also called the Great King, was a most perfect despot. As in other Asiatic countries, he was regarded as the sole proprietor of the land. In their relation to the king, all his subjects were only slaves, and the king was master over the lives of all his people. Whoever was admitted into his presence had to prostrate himself and kiss the earth. As the throne of Ormuzd was surrounded by spirits of light, so the Persian king, his representative on earth, was surrounded by the noblest Persians and a most brilliant court, which resided in winter at Babylon, in the spring at Susa, and in the summer at Ecbatana. The king's palaces were surrounded with splendid parks, called paradises, and well stocked with fruit-trees and game, and every thing that luxury could devise. The harem of such a Persian sultan was most expensive, being maintained sometimes by the revenues from whole cities or provinces. The influence exercised upon the court and the princes by the intriguing wives of the kings was often of the most pernicious kind, and involved one part of the empire in war with another.

CHAPTER V.

ASSYRIA AND BABYLONIA.

1. ASSYRIA in its narrower sense was situated on the east of the river Tigris, and was consequently a part of Iran; in a wider sense it also includes Babylonia and Mesopotamia, and comprises the

countries about the Euphrates and Tigris, which latter river forms
the boundary between the countries of Iran and those of the Semitic
race. The banks of these rivers were at different times inviting to
princes who appeared there as rulers or conquerors, to build their
capitals on them. The northern part of the country, which is
inclosed between the two rivers, and bears the name of Mesopotamia, is a desert, or rather a steppe, well adapted for nomadic tribes;
but the southern plains of Babylonia, which were intersected by
innumerable canals for purposes of irrigation, were a country of
extraordinary fertility and productiveness, and Herodotus praises it
above all other countries known to him. At present those blessed
districts have become almost a desert under the rude and destructive
government of the Mahommedans; but the ancient ruins of mighty
cities and frontier walls, the canals and other means devised for irri-
gating the country, still attest the high prosperity once enjoyed by
their inhabitants.

2. There was a time when the Assyrian empire was regarded as
the most ancient conquering power in the world; but of its history,
as well as of that of Babylon, only fragments have been preserved
to us by Greek writers and in the Old Testament; and it is sometimes a matter of extreme difficulty to make the profane and sacred
authorities agree with each other. According to the Mosaic account,
Babel or Babylon, the capital of the powerful Nimrod, was the head
of a more ancient empire; and Assur, proceeding from Babylon,
founded Nineveh, the capital of Assyria, which would accordingly
be a colony of Babylon. Greek authorities state the very reverse
of this, for they represent Nineveh as the more ancient city. But
the origin of the Assyrian empire is related by them only in mythical legends, which have acquired great celebrity, though they can
hardly be said to embody the ideas which the Assyrians entertained
respecting their own early history. According to these accounts,
the founder of the Assyrian empire was Ninus, who built Ninus or
Nineveh, and subdued a great part of Asia. His history is connected with that of the fabulous queen Semiramis, who was miraculously saved when only a child, and was possessed of extraordinary
beauty and mental powers. At the time when Ninus marched
against Bactra, she was in the Assyrian army; and when that city
baffled all his efforts, it was conquered by her prudence and valour.
The king was thereupon seized with such admiration of the heroine
that he made her his wife, in consequence of which her previous
husband made away with himself. After the death of Ninus, Semiramis governed the empire, and among other cities built Babylon
with extraordinary splendour and magnificence, and undertook vast
expeditions to extend her dominions by conquest. She subdued
Egypt and a large portion of Ethiopia; but a war undertaken
against India with an army of more than three milllious of men

proved unsuccessful. After this she resigned the government to her son Ninyas, and disappeared from the earth, taking up her abode among the gods. Ninyas, the very opposite of his parents, never quitted the city, and spent his whole life in the midst of women and eunuchs, and in constant amusements.

3. Such is the story of the foundation of the Assyrian empire, as transmitted by the classical writers of antiquity. It is quite clear that we are here in the domain of fable and not of history. Ninus is only the personification of Nineveh, as Romulus in the case of Rome. Semiramis is a Syrian divinity, and perhaps identical with Astarte. There can, moreover, be no doubt that Nineveh was of more recent origin than Babylon; but how and when it was founded, and how it acquired the dominion of a large part of Asia, are questions to which no certain answer can be given. It is equally impossible to say how far the Assyrian empire really extended. The vast conquests mentioned in the story are beyond all question greatly exaggerated; but there can be no doubt that Babylon, Media, and Persia, were subject to it, and that it extended even into Asia Minor.

Diodorus of Sicily, a writer deriving his information from the work of Ctesias, a Greek physician who lived at the court of Persia, gives the subsequent history of Assyria in a form no less fabulous than its beginning. According to him the empire was ruled, for thirty generations after Ninyas, by his descendants, who spent their lives in idleness and voluptuousness like Ninyas, until Sardanapalus, the last of them, even dressed himself as a woman, and acted in a most effeminate and unworthy manner, in consequence of which his subject nations rose in arms against him, headed by the governor of Media. Sardanapalus, at length rousing himself, defeated the rebels in several engagements; but in the end he was overpowered, and being unable to defend Nineveh, he caused a large pile to be erected, on which he burnt himself, with all his treasures, wives, and eunuchs. Nineveh thus fell into the hands of the conquerors, that is the Medes, after the Assyrians from Ninus to Sardanapalus had ruled for a period of 1360 years.

4. This account of the Assyrian empire and its thirty effeminate kings is as fabulous as the story about its foundation, and the only real historical fact in this tradition seems to be, that the end of the empire was as inglorious as its beginning had been glorious. The duration of upwards of thirteen hundred years assigned to the Assyrian empire is likewise more than doubtful, for it is not only opposed to all analogy, but to the express statement of Herodotus, according to whom the Assyrians had been ruling over Asia for a period of five hundred and twenty years at the time when the Medes revolted. This latter statement, probable in itself, is confirmed by the Armenian translation of Eusebius, in which it is stated that

Assyrian kings ruled over Babylon five hundred and twenty-six years, and we know that Babylon shook off the Assyrian yoke at the same time as the Medes, in the eighth century B. C., and both nations had evidently been subject to Assyria during the same period. According to this view the foundation of the Assyrian empire belongs to the thirteenth century B. C., and its final overthrow by the Mede Cyaxares, as we have already observed, to the year B. C. 605, which is about three centuries later than the date assigned to its destruction by Ctesias.

The story about the thirty effeminate kings, and the time in which they are said to have reigned, is moreover opposed to the historical statements of the Old Testament, for here we read of Assyrian kings in the eighth century, who extended their empire, attacked and subdued Babylonia, Syria, Israel, and Phoenicia, and made repeated attempts to conquer Egypt. First we hear of king Phul (about B. C. 770), who extended his empire westward, and approached the kingdom of Israel, which was so terrified that it purchased its freedom for a large sum of money. His successor, Tiglath-pileser (about B. C. 740), conquered the splendid city of Damascus, laid a heavy tribute upon the kingdom of Judah, and transplanted many of the conquered people beyond the Euphrates. He was succeeded by Salmanassar (about B. C. 720), who invaded Israel, and took Samaria after a siege of several years. He led the greater part of the Jewish tribes into the interior, and took all the important towns of Phoenicia, with the exception of Tyre, which baffled his efforts by means of its navy. His successor Sanherib or Sennacherib (about B. C. 712) threatened Judah and attacked Egypt; but sudden misfortunes compelled him to return without having effected his purpose. After his and Assarhaddon's reign (from B. C. 675 to 626), the Assyrian empire sank more and more, in consequence of which Cyaxares, king of Media, allied with Nabopolassar of Babylon, formed the plan to attack and subdue it. With a great force they advanced against Nineveh, and after several reverses against Sardanapalus, the last Assyrian king, they succeeded in taking and destroying Nineveh, B. C. 605, and thus putting an end to the Assyrian empire. As this destruction of Nineveh happened nearly three centuries later than the time assigned to it by Ctesias, some writers have assumed two Assyrian empires, and supposed that after the first destruction a new empire was formed at Nineveh, which lasted until its conquest by Cyaxares. But this supposition is without any foundation : there never was more than one Assyrian empire, and Nineveh was destroyed only once.

5. The destruction of Nineveh by Cyaxares was no doubt complete; and the town of the same name mentioned in later times can have been nothing but a small and insignificant place built upon the ruins of ancient Nineveh. This last city, situated on the east

bank of the Tigris, is spoken of by all writers as a place of such vast extent, that modern London, with all its suburbs, would occupy no more than half its space. This may indeed be exaggerated, or the result of misunderstanding; but Nineveh must, at all events, have been the largest and most important city of western Asia, and its inhabitants' must have possessed immense wealth, in consequence of the extensive commerce carried on by them. Ruins of this gigantic city were unknown until very recently, though travellers had observed the high mounds covering its site, and suggested that excavations might lead to interesting and important discoveries. But in our own days, excavations have been made by Botta, the French consul at Mosul, and still more extensively by Mr. Layard, on the north of the bridge over the Tigris, near the modern Mosul. Walls, palaces, and buildings have been laid open, which, with their numberless sculptures, reveal to us at once the mode of life and warfare of that ancient people. The inscriptions with which these ancient buildings and sculptures are literally covered, may one day help to clear up all that is yet mysterious in the history of Assyria and Babylonia. The sculptures, many of which are now safely lodged in the British Museum, consist of representations of different kinds, as festive processions with the king, his courtiers, eunuchs, priests, and warriors; but especially warlike scenes, representing battles, sieges, war-chariots, and the like. The conquerors and the conquered are generally distinguished by their features and dress, and the latter seem almost in every case to belong to the Semitic race. Both men and animals are drawn in these sculptures, not indeed without faults, but, on the whole, very correctly, and very expressive in their attitudes and movements. They display a state of the arts in Assyria, at a period which cannot be more recent than the eighth or seventh century B. C., such as we could scarcely have expected to find in Asia; for they surpass everything else that is known in the history of Asiatic art. The inscriptions on these monuments are all of the kind called cuneiform, and when one day they shall be deciphered, much new and unexpected light may be thrown upon the traditions that have come down to us about the Assyrians. The people seem to have been akin to the Aryá, but their religion was different, for they worshipped idols similar to those of the Babylonians, of which we shall have occasion to speak presently.

6. The history of Babylon is closely connected with that of Assyria, and the legends of the Greeks, as we have seen, carry this connection to the very origin of the two states. But the splendour and celebrity of Babylon are undoubtedly much more ancient. According to Genesis, it existed even before the dispersion of mankind. This view of the great antiquity of Babylon is supported by the calculations of the Babylonian priests, which were based upon astronomical observations — observations which went back as far as

1903 years before the time of Alexander the Great. Berosus, a Babylonian priest who lived shortly after the time of Alexander, and wrote a history of his country in Greek, also derived his information from native records; but unfortunately we possess only a few extracts from this work. He began with the cosmogony, which in many respects is extremely remarkable, and gave a fabulous account of Babylonian history even during the period before the flood. But his later history appears to be thoroughly authentic, and from it we see that Babylon was conquered and governed by foreigners even before it was subdued by the Assyrians in the thirteenth century. Babylon was no doubt one of the greatest and most ancient cities on earth. It acknowledged, as we have seen, the supremacy of Assyria for a period of upwards of five hundred years, after which, about the middle of the eighth century B. C., it shook off the yoke. At a somewhat later time, it again became subject to Assyria, but only for a short period, for its king Nabopolassar assisted Cyaxares the Mede in conquering and destroying the Assyrian empire for ever, B. C. 605.

Nebuchadnezzar, the son of Nabopolassar, who reigned from B. C. 604 till 561, and is well known from the Old Testament, is distinguished in history as a great conqueror, who raised the Babylonian empire to the summit of its glory. He was engaged in a war against the Egyptian Pharaoh Necho, whom he defeated in a great battle near Circesium (Carchemish), when he received the news of his father's death, which obliged him to return to Babylon. Afterwards, he conquered the kingdom of Judah, and led many of the most illustrious men to Babylon as captives or hostages, among whom was the prophet Daniel. The Jews repeatedly revolted, but were reduced each time with unrelenting cruelty, and their country was almost drained of its inhabitants. In the end, Jerusalem was laid waste, and the bulk of the nation led into captivity. Nebuchadnezzar then directed his arms against Phoenicia, which he completely subdued, and invaded Egypt, where he plundered the lower valley of the Nile. After his death, the kingdom of Babylon began to decay; his successors could no longer think of making conquests, but only how they could defend themselves against the ever-increasing power of the Medes. But it was in vain that Queen Nitocris, the mother of the last king, Nabonedus or Labynetus, endeavoured to render the country and city inaccessible, by making canals, bridges, and lakes; for it was only twenty-three years after the death of Nebuchadnezzar, B. C. 538, that Babylon was taken by Cyrus. Considering this brief duration of the independent existence of the kingdom of Babylon, it could scarcely have attained its celebrity, were it not for its connection with Biblical history, and the splendour of its capital Babylon.

7 *

7. Babylon was situated on both sides of the river Euphrates, which flowed through the centre. Like most other great Asiatic cities, it was built in the form of a large square, and the streets intersected each other at right angles. Herodotus calls it the most magnificent of all cities known to him, and describes its circumference as amounting to about sixty English miles; and indeed, modern investigations of the site show that it cannot have been less; but we must not suppose that the houses were built close together in rows, as in modern cities; on the contrary, there must have been many and large districts inclosed within the walls, which were not covered with buildings, but were used as gardens, groves, and fields. The splendour of the city, the wonder of ancient historians, probably did not exist previous to the last period of independence, but arose in and after the reign of Nabopolassar, when it was the capital of a large empire, and had stepped into the place of Nineveh. The city was surrounded by a wall of burnt bricks, two hundred cubits in height, and fifty in thickness. The royal palace was situated on both sides of the river, and the two parts were connected by a bridge. Near it were artificial terraces, of considerable height and extent, and covered with plants and trees of the most various kinds. These were what are commonly called the hanging gardens of Semiramis, but they were constructed by Nebuchadnezzar, who ordered them to be laid out to please his wife Amuhia, a daughter of Cyaxares, who could not forget the wood-clad hills of her native country. Still more magnificent was the temple of Baal or Belus, built in the form of a square tower of at least three hundred feet in height. It consisted of eight stories, the upper ones being smaller than the lower ones, whereby the whole acquired the appearance of a pyramid. Babylon sank more through the decline of its industry and population, than in consequence of its subjugation by foreign rulers, and in the end all its magnificence became one mass of ruins. Even in the fourth century of our era, its site is described as the haunt of wild beasts, as the prophet had predicted; and such is still the case. The extensive mounds of ruins and rubbish bear no traces of the ancient magnificence of the place. The districts between the several mounds are covered with bricks and fragments of pottery. The walls of the city have disappeared, but the mounds of ruins have for more than two thousand years been used by the neighbouring people as quarries, from which they obtained bricks to build their habitations; nay, whole ship-loads of them have been carried down the river Euphrates. The largest and most important of the ruins of ancient Babylon is situated on the western bank of the river, and is called by the Arabs the tower or palace (Birs) of Nimrod, and by the Jews the prison of Nebuchadnezzar. At its base it is upwards of two thousand feet in circumference, and as there are several indi-

cations of the pyramidal form of the tower of Belus, modern travellers have identified it with that edifice.

8. Babylon continued for centuries to be visited, admired, and described by travellers, while Nineveh was lying in ruins; and this is probably the main reason why so little information has come down to us about the Assyrians, whereas the manners and peculiarities of the Babylonians are often alluded to by the ancients. The language of the Babylonians was the Aramaic, a branch of the Semitic; but it is generally called Chaldaeic, a name by which the Babylonians as a people, also are designated,[1] though it is more commonly limited to that portion of the people inhabiting the district of Chaldaea on the Persian gulf. These Chaldaeans were undoubtedly a foreign tribe, which had immigrated into Babylonia from the north; in their new country they formed a powerful caste, like the Brahmins in India, and most of the Babylonian priests appear to have belonged to it. The mention of such a priestly caste in Babylonia suggests the probability that at one time other castes also may have existed; but during the last generations before the Persian conquest, regarding which we have authentic accounts, the ancient institutions seem to have fallen into decay, and the form of government then was a most complete despotism, as we may see from the descriptions of the prophet Daniel. The Babylonians were then slaves, as Asiatics have generally been during periods of great prosperity; but they forgot their servile condition in their pomp and luxury, in their voluptuousness and sensual enjoyments, of which the profane as well as the sacred writers draw the most revolting pictures. It may safely be asserted that no city ever was more notorious than Babylon for immorality and licentiousness, and the women were in this respect far worse than the men. The causes of this demoralisation, which has made Babylon proverbial, were, on the one hand, the unmitigated despotism of its rulers, and on the other, the great wealth of the people, which was so excessive, that Babylon, as a province of Persia, alone furnished one-third of the entire revenues of the empire. The sources of this wealth consisted in the extraordinary fertility of the soil, and the extensive commerce of the people, for which the situation of the city on the Euphrates was particularly favourable. That river connected the city with the Persian gulf, while roads to the west and north put it in communication with the Mediterranean and the Black sea. Babylon was the main transit-town of the precious merchandise which was brought from India to the west, and was chiefly conveyed by sea to the mouth of the Euphrates. But besides this, Babylon itself was celebrated for the productions of its own industry, consisting of cotton and silk stuffs, costly carpets, and tapestry rich in

---

[1] In the Scriptures, the name is Chasdim, which is etymologically the same as Chaldaeans.

colours and workmanship, which were highly prized even by the Romans in the distant west.

9. The Babylonians, or rather the Chaldaeans, were equally celebrated as diviners; it was especially by means of astrology that they pretended to obtain a knowledge of the future; and as this knowledge was believed to be hereditary in the caste of the Chaldaeans, their predictions were thought to be infallible, and were consequently looked upon with great respect. This art of foretelling the future by observing the stars, was reduced by the Chaldaeans to a regular system, which was called by both Greeks and Romans a Chaldaean science; nay, astrologers in general ultimately came to be called Chaldaeans in the south of Europe. The belief in the possibility of such astrological prophecies arose among the Chaldaeans, from their notion of the divine powers possessed by the stars—a notion of which indications occur even in the religion of Ormuzd. The sun and the moon, being the most prominent among the heavenly bodies, were regarded by the Babylonians as the principal divinities, next to whom came the planets, or the twelve signs of the zodiac. But these divinities were conceived in human forms, and in this anthropomorphism, Baal or Belus, the sun-god, was the supreme divinity, whence western nations identified him with the Greek Zeus, and the Roman Jupiter or Saturn. Belus was further regarded as the founder of the state and city of Babylon, and as the progenitor of the Babylonian kings.

As Belus was the supreme male divinity, so Mylitta, or the moongoddess, was the highest female divinity. Being also the symbol of productive nature, she is often mentioned by Greek and Roman writers under the name of Aphrodite or Venus. Her worship was connected with most revolting obscenity, and seems to have contributed not a little to the demoralisation of the Babylonian people.

10. The five planets were the stars from which, in particular, the Chaldaeans pretended to obtain their knowledge of the future; with them, as with all subsequent astrologers, Jupiter and Venus were beneficent powers, Mars and Saturn hostile, while Mercury was either the one or the other, according to its position. As the priests, by their astrological occupations, were led to observe the stars and their revolutions, which, in the plains of Babylonia, with their bright and transparent atmosphere, was easier than elsewhere, they gradually acquired real astronomical knowledge, which enabled them to calculate with astonishing accuracy the returns of eclipses of the sun and moon. In their chronological calculations they had lunar cycles as their basis, but they devised means for bringing the lunar and solar years into harmony. They knew and employed the division of the day into twelve hours, to determine which they used a sort of water-clock or clepsydra, which was subsequently adopted

by Greek astronomers. This occupation with mathematical calculations also led them to other branches of natural philosophy, such as
mechanics; and in western Asia the Babylonians were the first
people that had a regular system of weights and measures, which
was afterwards adopted by the Syrians and Greeks.

CHAPTER VI.

PHOENICIA.

1. PHOENICIA is the narrow strip of land in the north and west
of Palestine, extending from the town of Dora in the south, to
Marathos in the north. On the west it is bounded by the Mediterranean, and on the east by mount Lebanon, which furnished the
Phoenicians with excellent timber for ship-building. Their coast
country nowhere extended more than a few miles inland, yet their
importance as a commercial people is not surpassed by any other
nation of antiquity.

The question as to who the Phoenicians originally were cannot
be answered with certainty, though it is a well-known fact that their
language was Semitic, and that their whole civilisation bore the
Semitic character. The Canaanites, for this is the name under
which the Phoenicians are spoken of in the Old Testament, were,
according to the Mosaic account, sons of Ham, and not of Shem;
whence they would belong to the same race as the Egyptians and
other southern nations. Greek historians also relate that the Phoenicians were a foreign people, which had originally dwelt on the
Erythraean sea, or the Persian gulf. We cannot here enter into an
examination of this question; but certain it is, that, though they
were foreign immigrants, they became so completely assimilated to
the neighbouring tribes, that they cannot be regarded in any other
light than that of a Semitic people.

2. The very nature and extent of the country they inhabited
obliged them to devote themselves to commerce; and the dominion
which they were unable to found by extending their own country,
they established by their numerous colonies in nearly all parts of
the Mediterranean. Under these circumstances, the Phoenicians,
though numerically a small people, became, by perseverance and
energy, the first commercial nation in the ancient world, and that
too, at a time when Greek civilisation had scarcely commenced its
development. Commerce and navigation were the only means by
which they could secure their existence, and the coast they inhabited

offered the best opportunities, on account of its excellent harbours, most of which are now completely destroyed by the accumulation of sand. Along their coast they built a number of cities, and numerous smaller towns, with which the coast was literally studded. Of all the enormous commercial activity which must once have reigned in those parts, only few traces exist at the present day. Cities and splendid buildings have crumbled away, and vast quantities of ruins and numberless pillars of granite, porphyry, marble, and glass, have in the course of centuries been carried away, or have been used as building materials for other edifices. The most ancient among the Phoenician cities was Sidon, which was built at a time of which history knows nothing. It was the metropolis of most other Phoenician towns, and for a long period remained the most important and powerful among them, until it was eclipsed by Tyre, one of its own colonies. The time of the foundation of Tyre is very doubtful, but it certainly cannot have been later than the twelfth century B. C. The Tyrians themselves afterwards spoke of their own city as more ancient even than Sidon; but though this undoubtedly arose from an excessive partiality for their own native place, yet it cannot be denied that in later times it occupied by far the most prominent position among the Phoenician cities, and threw Sidon into the shade. In this proud position Tyre maintained itself, until in the altered circumstances of the world, it lost its independence, in consequence of which its wealth and glory vanished.

3. The sea opened up to Phoenician enterprise the continents of Africa and Europe, and all the islands of the Mediterranean, while the country was connected by roads and rivers with the great eastern empires, so that the commerce of the Phoenicians was not confined to any one part of the world, but extended over nearly the whole of it. In connection with the Jews, we are told that they sailed down the Red sea to a country called Ophir, whence, among other valuable products, they brought a particularly fine species of gold. It is doubtful what country we are to understand by Ophir, some believing it to be the south of Arabia, and others India, but the latter seems to be the more probable. It cannot be said against this supposition that a voyage to so distant a country was too bold an enterprise for the Phoenicians at so early a period, for a story related by Herodotus proves as clearly as possible that in the reign of the Egyptian King Necho (B. C. 617–601) they circumnavigated Africa, and thus anticipated, by more than two thousand years, the discovery of the Portuguese. King Necho, Herodotus says, was the first to prove that Libya (Africa) is surrounded by the sea, except the part where it is connected with Asia. For he sent out Phoenician sailors and ships, ordering them to return by the pillars of Hercules to the Mediterranean and Egypt. These Phoenicians accordingly sailed down the Red sea into the southern ocean. Each

autumn they landed on the coast of Libya, which happened to be near; they then sowed corn and waited for the harvest; after reaping the corn they again embarked and continued their voyage. In this manner they returned in the third year to Egypt by way of the pillars of Hercules. They related, that while sailing round Libya, they had had the sun on their right hand. All the objections which modern critics have made for the purpose of showing that this narrative is undeserving of credit, are of no weight, and the last sentence of the report contains the most irrefragable evidence of its truth, for as soon as the sailors had passed the equator, the sun must have appeared to them in the north or on their right-hand side. But unfortunately this great discovery was neglected after it had once been made, and no further advantages were derived from it. The ancient nations that were powerful at sea did not consider it degrading to increase by piracy the profits they made by trading, and hence we find the Phoenicians also indulging in this practice, not only at sea, but also on land, for they would sometimes avail themselves of a favourable opportunity, and, making a descent upon a foreign coast, carry off beautiful women and boys, whom they afterwards sold as slaves. This traffic of the Phoenicians in slaves is attested by several passages of ancient writers, and also by the Jewish prophets, who complain of Sidon and Tyre having sold the sons of Judah as slaves to the Greeks.

4. No undertaking appears to have been too arduous for the Phoenicians, for not only did they navigate the seas in the south of Asia, but the pillars of Hercules were no bounds to their enterprise. On the west of Gibraltar they founded in early times the colony of Gadeira or Gades (Cadiz), and from it they sailed in the Atlantic ocean as far as the islands called Cassiterides (the Scilly islands, on the south-west coast of England), whence they brought tin, which was not found in any other part of the ancient world, and was indispensable as an alloy in founding brass. On these same voyages they probably also obtained amber, which was highly valued and used in a variety of ornaments. The country where amber was and still is found in great abundance, is the Prussian coast of the Baltic; but it is doubtful whether the Phoenicians themselves fetched amber from those parts, or whether it was brought to them by other merchants: the latter is the more probable supposition, for we know that amber was conveyed by land to the south of Europe. The Phoenicians were more than ordinarily jealous of competition in their commercial enterprises, and endeavoured by all means to secure to themselves a monopoly in their dealings with distant countries. For this purpose they invented and spread abroad numerous tales about the dangers and terrors to which their seamen were exposed in sailing through the Atlantic ocean. Once, it is said, a Roman merchant-ship followed a Phoenician in the Atlantic,

for the purpose of discovering its secret. But the Phoenicians thwarted the attempt by allowing their own ship to be wrecked in order to draw the Roman into the same disaster. The Phoenician captain saved his life, and, on his return home, he received from the public coffers an indemnification for the loss he had sustained in protecting the trade of his own country against foreign competition.

5. Nations distinguished for commercial enterprise are rarely behind-hand in manufactures and other industrial pursuits, and this rule holds good also with the Phoenicians. Even in the Homeric poems the Sidonians are mentioned as the authors of works of art and skill, and many productions of Phoenician industry, as their textile fabrics and the purple dyes, remained celebrated in antiquity down to the latest times. In the art of weaving, the Phoenicians eclipsed most of their neighbours, and they were believed to be the inventors of purple dyeing, which was afterwards carried on also in other maritime towns of the Mediterranean, as at Tarentum. The purple was not one particular colour, but the name embraced a great variety of shades, from bright scarlet to black. The dye was obtained from a shell-fish, which was found in abundance in several parts of the Mediterranean and also in the Atlantic. The purple of Tyre, however, was regarded as the best, and the cloths dyed in it produced changing colours. Vegetable dyes of great beauty and variety were likewise produced in Phoenicia. The manufacture of glass is said to have been discovered by the Phoenicians through the accidental melting of saltpetre mixed with sand. This manufacture was for a long time kept secret, to secure the monopoly to the Phoenicians. Glass was at first used only as an article of ornament, or made into vessels, pillars, and similar things, which were very much valued, and formed a most lucrative article of commerce. The glass manufactures of Tyre, in particular, were very celebrated, and continued to flourish even beyond the period of antiquity. This commerce and these manufactures account for the immense wealth that was accumulated in the cities of Phoenicia. The Hebrew prophets give the most graphic descriptions of this state of things, but at the same time inveigh against the pride and insolence to which the great wealth gave rise. An invention more important than all these which some of the ancients ascribe to the Phoenicians, is that of the art of alphabetic writing. The question, however, as to whether this honour really belongs to them, has been much discussed, and the result is, that although the Phoenicians cannot be looked upon as the real inventors, they undeniably had the merit of introducing alphabetic writing into Greece, where the most extensive and beneficial use was made of the art, and whereby they conferred an inestimable advantage upon all the nations of Europe. But we shall have occasion to return to this subject hereafter.

6. We possess scarcely any means of forming a correct notion of the civilisation attained by the Phoenicians. Few Greeks and Romans thought it worth their while to study oriental languages, and those who did so, did not enter sufficiently deeply into the study to furnish accurate pictures of the life of nations so entirely foreign to them. The literary productions of the Phoenicians themselves are all lost, nor are there any architectural remains that might throw light upon their state of civilisation. From some descriptions we learn that they were fond of displaying great splendour and magnificence in the construction of their temples, which were chiefly built of wood and metal. Their introduction of the art of writing into Greece, however, shows that they exerted some influence upon the nations with which they came in contact, though they were not able to stamp their whole character upon any one of them. But they themselves did not escape the influence of other nations, and even their religion and mythology show the effects of their commercial intercourse with others; for while they transplanted their own gods and religious ideas to their colonies and other cities and countries with which they were connected, they experienced in return a similar influence of others. It is owing to this system of exchanging gods and ideas regarding them, that so great a confusion has arisen in the accounts of the religions of the ancients; and hence also the facility with which the Greeks and Romans identified their own gods with those of foreign nations.

7. The basis of the Phoenician religion, like that of all the pagan branches of the Semitic race, was the worship of the heavenly bodies; but this worship became coarse and degenerate in consequence of the notion which was gradually formed, that the stars were persons with all the passions of human nature. The great god of the Semitic race, Baal, was called by the Phoenicians Moloch; he was the demon of fire, to whom, for the purpose of appeasing his wrath, men, and especially children, were sacrificed in a most cruel and revolting manner. The statue of the god was made of brass, and when sacrifices were offered, the idol was made red-hot, and the wretched victims were placed in its arms to be slowly roasted to death. Their mothers, who were compelled to be present, did not venture, from fear, to give utterance to their feelings. Such sacrifices of children were offered every year on a certain day, at the commencement of great undertakings, and during any misfortune by which the country was visited. However, the progress of civilisation and the government of Persia, to which Phoenicia ultimately became subject, forbade the perpetration of such horrors. During the siege of Tyre by Alexander the Great, some persons, in despair, proposed to return to the practice which had long been abolished, but the magistrates prohibited it. It is uncertain whether Melkarth also may be regarded as identical with Baal or Moloch. His chief

8

temple was at Tyre, but he was worshipped in the colonies also. The Greeks partially identified him with their own Heracles, from whom, however, they sometimes distinguish him by the attribute of "the Tyrian." Among the female divinities, Astarte occupied the first rank; she was the tutelary goddess of the Sidonians, and was identified by the Greeks and Romans sometimes with Aphrodite or Venus, and sometimes with Hera or Juno.

8. While in their religious views the Phoenicians were complete Asiatics, their political institutions appear to have been more free and elastic than those of other eastern nations, and thus form the transition from Asiatic despotism to European freedom. The country of Phoenicia, small as it was, never formed one connected or united state, but each city was independent, and was governed by hereditary kings, whose authority was probably limited by a council, consisting of the noblest among the citizens. In matters affecting the interests of the whole country, however, the cities seem to have acted as a confederation, and one of them took the lead—an arrangement which sometimes may have led to the permanent supremacy of one city over the rest. But we possess no satisfactory information on these subjects, for not only have we no remains of Phoenician literature, but the works of the Greeks who wrote on Phoenician affairs are lost. Even the relations subsisting between Phoenicia and the empires on the east of it, whose rulers extended their conquests to the Mediterranean and coveted the cities and fleets of the wealthy merchants, are scarcely known to us. About B. C. 730, when King Salmanassar of Assyria invaded and subdued Phoenicia, New Tyre alone, which was then at the height of its power, resisted the aggressor; this city had existed for a long time on an island not far from Old Tyre; it had risen to extraordinary prosperity, and seems at that time to have exercised a hateful supremacy over the other towns, whence these latter even furnished Salmanassar with ships to reduce the only place that was fighting for the independence of Phoenicia. Even Old Tyre joined the enemy. The island city was besieged by Salmanassar for a period of five years, but he was unable to take it. At a later period, Nebuchadnezzar, king of Babylonia, who sent the captive Phoenicians and Jews into his own kingdom, was likewise unable to take New Tyre, although he besieged it for thirteen years after he had reduced all the rest of the country. But this last blow seems to have exhausted the strength and resources of the place, for soon after, when the Persians appeared as conquerors in Western Asia, Tyre, as well as the rest of Phoenicia, was forced to submit, and the country became a Persian satrapy. In this condition, Phoenicia, like other satrapies, had only to perform certain duties, as to pay tribute, and especially to furnish the Persian kings with ships for their maritime undertakings, but otherwise the cities were governed as before by their own kings or judges (suffetes). But their ancient prosperity and splendour were

gone, and never again became what they had been. During this
period the commerce of the Phoenicians was more and more confined
to the eastern parts of the Mediterranean,—the Carthaginians and
Greeks taking their place in the western parts. Once, in the reign
of Ochus, the oppression of the Persian governor goaded the Phoenicians into a rebellion, which was headed by Sidon; but the
attempt failed, and as the king ordered the noblest citizens to be
put to death, the inhabitants of Tyre set their city on fire, and
burnt themselves with all their treasures. Tyre, however, continued
to exist much longer; but when Alexander the Great overthrew
the Persian monarchy, and Tyre, from the proud feeling of its former
greatness, attempted to defy the conqueror, he laid siege to it, and
after seven months took and destroyed the city, B. C. 332. It never
recovered from this blow, and, after the building of Alexandria in
Egypt, its commercial importance was completely gone, though it
continued in a tolerably prosperous condition until a late period of
the middle ages.

9. The colonies which the Phoenicians established in nearly all
parts of the Mediterranean, and by which they not only extended
their commerce but diffused their knowledge, their language, and
their religion, are so numerous that it is impossible to suppose that
all the colonists proceeded from Phoenicia alone; they must have
been joined in these enterprises by large bodies of Canaanites. We
find Phoenician colonies in Cyprus, in Crete, in many of the Greek
islands as far as the coast of Thrace, in Greece itself, in Sicily,
Sardinia, the Balearic islands, and especially on the coasts of Spain
and Africa. The former of these countries attracted them by the
richness and variety of its natural productions. At a time when
the west of Europe was known to the Greeks only from vague
reports, which were worked up by the fancy of their poets, the
Phoenicians had already discovered the valuable metals, especially
silver, in which Spain abounded. Its inhabitants are said to have
been so little acquainted with their value, that they gave to the
Phoenicians quantities of silver for mere toys and baubles. Their
most ancient settlement in Spain was Gades or Gadeira (Cadiz),
founded about the year B. C. 1100, with a famous temple of the
Tyrian Hercules. Gades continued even under the dominion of
the Romans, to be one of the most prosperous and populous cities
in the ancient world. But Gades was not their only colony in
Spain : Turdetania, the western part of modern Andalusia, was
once entirely under their dominion, and this is probably the district
called by the ancients Tartessus, which has been the subject of
so much discussion. Utica in Africa was founded about the same
time as Gades, but all their colonies in Africa were eclipsed by
Carthage, founded about B. C. 814 by emigrant Tyrians. The
history of this important city will engage our attention in a later
part of the work.

CHAPTER VII.

LYDIA.

1. At the time when Cyrus conquered the kingdom of Lydia, it embraced nearly the whole of the peninsula of Asia Minor, for Lycia, and Cilicia appear to have been the only parts of it which maintained their independence. The central portion of Asia Minor consists of an extensive table-land, which affords excellent pasturage for sheep. The southern part is occupied by the chain of mount Taurus, which sinks down towards the Mediterranean, just as the mountains in the west slope down towards the Ægean, and in the north towards the Black sea. The delightful climate, the rich vegetation, and the great fertility of the valleys and coasts, make Asia Minor one of the most beautiful and naturally blessed countries in the world. In addition to this, its coasts abound in excellent harbours, enabling the peninsula to become a most prosperous commercial country. But, notwithstanding all these advantages, Asia Minor has never occupied that position in history to which it might seem entitled. Its civilisation was an exotic plant rather than the product of native growth and development, and after the overthrow of the Lydian empire, it was almost always a part of some other empire, either Asiatic or European. One reason of this may have been the great variety of nations by which it was peopled; for the east was occupied by tribes belonging to the Semitic race, while the western parts, even before their colonisation by the Greeks, were peopled by a race belonging to the Indo-European family; and many of the smaller tribes in the interior, the north and the south, were of unknown origin.

2. The small district in the west of Asia Minor, forming the kingdom of Lydia, appears to have been originally inhabited by Meonians, a branch of the wide-spread Pelasgians, who themselves unquestionably belonged to the Indo-European family of nations. At a later period, about which history furnishes no information, the Meonians were overpowered by the Lydians, after whom the country was thenceforth called Lydia, for in the Homeric poems this name does not occur. These Lydians invaded the country from some other part of Asia Minor, and appear to have belonged to the same race as the Carians and Mysians. Their manners and civilisation were not very different from those of the Greeks, and in the arts of life they were as far advanced as their Greek neighbours. But we know nothing of their language, which must have been superseded by the Greek at an early period.

3. The kingdom of Lydia was governed by two successive dynasties, that of the Heracleids, and that of the Mermnadae—the former commencing with Agron (about B. C. 1200) and ending with Candaules, while that of the Mermnadae begius with Gyges. The earlier dynasty is said to have been genealogically connected with Ninus, the mythical founder of the Assyrian empire, and to have occupied the throne of Lydia for a period of five hundred and five years. Its last king, Candaules, fell in an insurrection of Gyges about B. C. 716. This change of dynasty is related by Herodotus in a very romantic and poetical story, according to which the wife of Candaules compelled Gyges to kill her own husband, and then to marry her. It is possible, however, that this change of dynasty may have been connected with the ascendancy of the Lydians over the Meonians.

Gyges, the first Mermnad king, who is said to have reigned from B. C. 716 to 678, appears, like his successors, as a conqueror, who subdued Colophon and all the Ionian and Æolian colonies of the Greeks along the western coast of Asia Minor. Sardes, with its strong citadel, was the capital of the Lydians. The successors of Gyges were Ardys (B. C. 678–629), Sadyattes (B. C. 629–617), Alyattes (B. C. 617–560), and Croesus (B. C. 560–546), under whom the Lydian empire was conquered by Cyrus. The history of these kings is remarkable, inasmuch as they continued the conquest of the Greek cities, and extended their empire also in the east. But they themselves also were attacked by repeated inroads of the Cimmerians and Treres, nomadic hordes from the north of Asia, who ever since the time of Ardys traversed the country in all directions, and established themselves in various parts, until they were overpowered and expelled in the reign of Alyattes. This king appears to have extended his dominion eastward as far as the river Halys, where he came into conflict with Cyaxares of Media. His successor Croesus ruled over the whole peninsula, with the exception of Lycia and Cilicia, and appears in the traditions as a wise, mild, and beneficent prince; he was beloved even by the Greeks who owned his rule, for they were left undisturbed in the internal affairs of their cities. He was liberal also towards the Greeks in Europe, whose temples he adorned with rich presents, for his wealth was believed to be so immense, that it became proverbial. He was well aware of the danger which threatened him from the east, and did all he could to avert it; but circumstances were unfavourable to him, and his kingdom was overpowered by the Persians in B. C. 546. The whole of it then became a part of the Persian empire, and the greater portion of it remained in that condition until the conquests of Alexander the Great.

8 *

CHAPTER VIII.

EGYPT.

1. WE close our history of the Asiatic nations with a sketch of
the history of Egypt, partly because the ancients regarded that
country as a part of Asia, and partly because its institutions and its
whole civilisation are essentially of an oriental character. Egypt,
in its proper sense, is the valley of the Nile from the islands of
Philae and Elephantine in the south, to the Mediterranean in the
north. The inhabitants themselves called their country Chemi,
and in the scriptures it sometimes bears the name Mizraim. The
Nile, which traverses it from south to north, is the only river the
country possesses, and gives a peculiar character not only to the
country, but also to its inhabitants, who were and are still dependent
upon it for all that the land produces. The long and narrow valley
of the river, which is nowhere broader than about eleven miles, is
bounded on both sides by barren ranges of mountains, and terminates in a deep bay, which, in the course of time, has been filled
up with deposits, and at the head of which the river divides itself
into several branches. The island, thus formed in what was once a
deep bay, was called by the Greeks the Delta, from its resemblance
to the fourth letter of the Greek alphabet. The valley of the river
itself is the only part of the country capable of cultivation and fit
for building towns. The Nile is not only the great high road of
the country, but also its great fertiliser, by its annual inundations
of the whole valley, which commence about the time of the summer
solstice, reach their greatest height about the middle of September,
and then gradually subside. These inundations supply the place of
rain during the hottest season of the year, and from the rich deposit
which the waters leave behind, produce a fertility which in ancient
times entitled Egypt to the appellation of one of the granaries of
the Roman empire. During the period of inundation the whole
valley was under water, and those parts into which the waters had
no natural access, were irrigated by means of canals. The cause
of these periodical risings of the river is the tropical rains in the
mountains of Abyssinia and the interior of Ethiopia. This phenomenon, which has no complete parallel on the whole face of the
earth, could not but exercise a powerful influence upon the Egyptians, and their whole mode of life; for they had to protect their
habitations against the ravages of the waters, as well as against the
constant encroachments of the sand that was blown by the winds

into their country from the west. The activity with which the ancient Egyptians had thus to labour for the preservation of that upon which their lives depended, slackened in the course of time, and modern Egypt is indebted for its fertile soil, to a great extent, to the immense works executed by its ancient inhabitants. The mountains on the east of the valley of the·Nile contained the principal mineral wealth of the country, and furnished the materials for its numerous and gigantic monuments in stone.

2. The peculiarities of Egypt and its inhabitants have at all times had a great charm for foreign travellers, and in ancient times especially for the inquisitive Greeks, whose earliest historian visited Egypt about the middle of the fifth century B. C. The national peculiarities of the Egyptians consisted not only in externals, but also in their whole mode of thinking and acting, which presented features not met with anywhere else, although we find much also that agrees with what is known of other countries. These peculiarities must have arisen partly from the nature of the country and its climate, and partly from the national character of the people. In regard to the last of these points we are very much in the dark; the Egyptians, like most ancient nations, looking upon themselves as autochthones — that is, as sprung from their own soil. Their language, and the innumerable representations of Egyptians in all their social relations and occupations, are our only guides in determining to what race of mankind they belonged. All the essentials of their language are preserved in the Coptic, the language of the Christian population of Egypt, who regard themselves as the living representatives of the ancient Egyptians. The Coptic has indeed long ceased to be a living speech, and is used by the Copts only as their sacred language, just as Latin is employed in the Church of Rome; but the language exists, and has been examined by modern scholars. This much seems certain, that it has no connection with the languages of the Indo-European stock, but some affinity with those of the Semitic. Still, however, the resemblance is so slight, that it would be hazardous to infer from it that the Egyptians were a Semitic race.

But if we take into consideration the descriptions we have of the ancient Egyptians, and the still more authentic information which we derive from their mummies, and the representations on their monuments, we cannot help coming to the conclusion that the ancient Egyptians were a mixed race, consisting of different nations. This view is confirmed by the simple fact that they were divided into castes. The higher castes in Egypt, as in India, were descended from a race endowed with greater intellectual powers, as well as with a handsomer physical conformation; they belonged, in fact, to the Caucasian race, while the lower castes consisted of men forming a kind of transition from the Caucasian race to that of the negroes

The higher castes, which are also distinguished for their less dark complexion, were no doubt immigrants who subdued the native population, though we have no historical traces of such an immigration. The mere fact, however, that the higher castes consisted of members of the Caucasian race, suggests that the invaders came from Asia. There are, moreover, great resemblances between the institutions and the civilisation of Egypt, and those of some eastern countries, which justify the conclusion, that at one time or another the East must have exercised a certain influence upon Egypt — an influence which, according to some, proceeded from Babylon, and according to others, from India.

3. The country in the south of Egypt is often called by the ancients Ethiopia, but is not conceived as a territory with definite frontiers either in the south or west. The same name, however, is sometimes applied to the empire of Meroë, a country above Egypt, enclosed by two arms of the Nile, whence it is called an island. This empire of Meroë was, in the strictest sense, a priestly state, for nowhere was the priesthood ever so powerful, and nowhere was it so perfectly organised as in Meroë. The priests chose the king from among themselves; and, when he incurred their displeasure, he was forced to make away with himself. The state, however, was essentially a commercial one, and the commerce was conducted and protected by the priests, for its principal emporia were in the neighbourhood of temples. Meroë was the country through which the productions of the distant lands of the south were conveyed to the north of Africa, either by caravans, or by boats on the Nile. This commerce was also carried on with Arabia, and through Arabia perhaps with India. There are traces leading to the belief, that in very remote times Arabia was a connecting link between India and the east of Africa, and these have led some historians to consider Meroë as the place to which, in the first instance, Caucasian Asiatics migrated, and whence they proceeded northward into Egypt. The Ethiopians themselves, also, had a tradition, that the inhabitants and civilisation of Egypt were of Ethiopian origin; and according to another tradition, the ancient Ammonium in the Libyan desert, containing the celebrated oracle of Ammon, whom the Greeks identified with their own Zeus, was partially at least a colony of Ethiopians. It may further be observed, that, even at the present day, the country called Ethiopia by the ancients, abounds in monuments strongly resembling those of Egypt, and apparently the prototypes of the latter If, lastly, we bear in mind that the civilisation of Egypt itself gradually proceeded from south to north along the course of the river, it seems natural to suppose that its beginnings must have come from a point beyond the southern boundary of Egypt We must not, however, forget that we are here dealing

with mere probabilities, and that there is no convincing evidence either one way or the other.

4. The life and history of the ancient Egyptians are known to us, not through native historians or poets, but through the works of Greeks, through the Scriptures of the Old Testament, and more especially through the sculptured and architectural works of the people themselves; for those works having withstood the ravages of thousands of years, and the destructive hand of man, still remain, and bear witness to the greatness of the ancient Egyptians, to their skill, their arts, and their mode of life No nation has ever so fully portrayed itself in all its pursuits, religious, social, and military, as the Egyptians. But Egypt, with all its wonders, was comparatively little known until the end of the last century, when a new impulse was given to the study of its history and its antiquities, by the expedition of Napoleon. The most ancient and most remarkable of these monuments are those at Thebes, in the upper valley of the Nile. The city of Thebes, the most ancient capital of Egypt, was situated on both banks of the Nile, and its site is at present occupied by several villages, from which the ruins derive their names. Travellers are inexhaustible in their admiration of the gigantic masses of ruins, of the temples, avenues of columns, obelisks, colossuses and catacombs, in which the district abounds. The temple-palace of Karnak, like some others of these vast structures, probably consisted partially of temples, and partially of residences of the Egyptian kings. This stupendous ruin is connected with another in the village of Luxor by an avenue of colossal sphinxes, no less than six thousand feet in length—the sphinxes standing at intervals of ten feet from one another, but most of them now covered with earth. The portico of the temple of Karnak, to which the avenue of sphinxes forms the approach, is generally regarded as the grandest specimen of Egyptian architecture: one hundred and thirty-four columns support the edifice; the twelve central ones are of gigantic dimensions, measuring thirty-four feet in circumference, and fifty-six in height, with capitals so large, that one hundred men can comfortably stand together upon them. The walls of the apartments and chambers here, as in all the other temples and palaces, are decorated with statues and figures in relief, painted over with brilliant colours. All these monuments are of the greatest interest, not only because they display the state of the arts at a most remote period, but because the sculptures and paintings represent historical occurrences connected with the founders of the monuments. The buildings on the western bank of the river, though not equal to those of Karnak and Luxor, are yet among the finest Egyptian monuments. We there meet with the palace and temple of Medinet-Habu, and a structure in the vicinity called the Memnonium. A plain, not far from it, bears

the name of the 'region of the colossuses,' from the number of colossal statues with which it is covered, partly standing upright, partly overturned, and partly broken to pieces. The two largest of them are fifty-six feet high, one of these being the celebrated statue of Memnon, which was believed in ancient times to give forth a shrill sound every morning at sunrise. Not far from these colossal figures, remnants of a building are seen, which has suffered much from the destructive hand of man, and is generally believed to be the tomb of Osymandias, mentioned by Diodorus. Most of the tombs, however, are under ground, and the necropolis of Thebes, extending from Medinet-Habu for a distance of about five miles in the Libyan hills, is scarcely less remarkable than the temples and palaces of the city itself. The many subterranean chambers and passages form a real labyrinth. The walls of these chambers are likewise covered with figures in relief, and fresco paintings, in many of which the colours are still as fresh as if they were of yesterday. They represent the judgment of the dead, their history and occupations, and are therefore of great interest to the inquirer into the social and domestic customs of the ancient Egyptians. These chambers, moreover, are full of a great variety of utensils and ornaments, and rolls of papyrus, recording things connected with the history of those buried, or rather preserved as mummies in the catacombs. The inhabitants of the village of Gurnua, at the entrance of the necropolis, have for many years carried on a lucrative traffic in the articles found in the necropolis. Among the treasures thence brought to light, we may mention some invaluable MSS. of Greek authors, with whose works we should otherwise be unacquainted.

These catacombs, destined for all classes of the people, are far surpassed in magnitude and splendour by the tombs of the kings, which are situated in a separate and dismal place, well fitted to be conceived as the abode of the dead. Many of them have been opened and ransacked. These, and a hundred other remains, furnish us with the means of forming some idea of the ancient magnificence of that capital of Egypt, and no historian or poet could do this more effectually or strikingly. The execution of these works required an amount of skill and taste which no one would expect at so remote a period; for it is an indubitable fact that the greatest and most important of them must have been built long before the year 1000 B. C.; and as Egyptian art was then at its height, we must date the beginning of its cultivation many centuries earlier.

5. It is a matter of the highest interest to determine the time when those stupendous structures were erected, for it is only when that time is known that we can set the proper value upon its productions. This was formerly a matter of impossibility, but by a

most fortunate and ingenious discovery of the present century, the key has been found for deciphering and reading the hieroglyphics, or sacred symbols, with which many of the Egyptian monuments are literally covered. These symbols consist of figures of the most various kinds, as heavenly bodies, plants, animals, men, members of the human body, utensils, implements, geometrical figures, and fantastic forms. About nine hundred symbols of this kind have been enumerated, the import of which, with very few exceptions, was formerly unknown, although there was no want of ingenious attempts to decipher and explain them. At length the savants of the French expedition found at Rosetta a stone (at present in the British Museum), containing a threefold incription, one in hieroglyphics, the second in the enchorian or popular characters of the Egyptians, and the third in Greek. The stone belongs to the beginning of the second century B. C. The Greek inscription, a translation of the hieroglyphic, and especially the name of Ptolemy in it, led Dr. Young to the discovery as to the nature of hieroglyphic writing, which is partly symbolic and partly phonetic. The discovery was carried out to its full extent by Champollion, a Frenchman. The expectations entertained by scholars in regard to this discovery, however, have been greatly disappointed, for the inscriptions contain no historical records nor philosophical or religious doctrines, but are generally only pompous dedications referring to the royal founders of the monuments. Still these very names of princes, the representations of their exploits, and the chronological information we derive from them, are results which should not be undervalued.

6. All the civil institutions of the ancient Egyptians were based on the system of castes, which was fully developed and strictly adhered to among them. The detail of the arrangement, however, is very uncertain, as our chief authorities, Herodotus, Diodorus, and Strabo, do not agree with one another; but still they are unanimous in stating that the priests and warriors were the two highest and most honoured castes. Strabo regards all the remaining people as one mass, while Herodotus divides them into five castes, herdsmen, swineherds, tradesmen, interpreters, and sailors; and Diodorus mentions only three, shepherds, agriculturists, and artisans. The most important feature, however, in which all agree, is, that the priests and warriors were the ruling castes, and that the rest were subordinate to them. The priests, moreover, ranked above the soldiers, so that the intellectual part of the nation was placed above that representing the power of the sword. It will be remembered that the arrangement in India was of the same character. The kings, bearing the title of Pharaohs, were hereditary, and when a dynasty became extinct, a new king was chosen either from among the priestly or the military caste; and in the latter case, he was at

the same time solemnly raised to the rank of priest by a kind of consecration, whereby he was empowered to perform priestly functions. The king's authority was very great, and he was profoundly reverenced by the people; but he was bound by a series of very minute rules and regulations relating to his official functions, his recreations, and even the food which appeared on his table. These regulations were framed by the priests, who being at the same time the king's councillors and advisers, watched over their observance. Such an arrangement could not fail to lead to collisions, and to excite evil passions both in the breasts of the priests and in those of ambitious kings.

The caste of priests was divided into several ranks; they were either high or low, and were also distinguished according to the divinities with whose service they were connected, as well as according to the temples to which they were attached. Those belonging to the great temples formed different corporations. As the priests were the sole depositaries of all knowledge, human and divine, they might also be distinguished according to their professions as politicians, lawyers, scholars, physicians, architects, &c. They were required to be abstemious in their food and drink, and forbidden to marry more than one wife; but on the other hand they were all-powerful in the state, their lands were exempt from taxes, and they themselves were maintained at the public expense.

The soldiers, amounting, according to Herodotus, to four hundred and ten thousand men, were distributed over the different parts of the country, where they possessed estates that were likewise exempted from taxes. All the soil of ancient Egypt was in reality in the hands of the king and the two highest castes, though the citizens of some of the towns also seem to have possessed lands within their respective territories. Within the caste of artisans or tradesmen, there were, no doubt, various subdivisions according to the different trades and occupations.

8. The art of war was highly developed among the Egyptians, for some of its early kings are described as mighty conquerors, and Egypt itself had often to defend its frontiers against foreign invaders. The armour and mode of fighting of the Egyptians are represented on many of their monuments, where the scenes often remind us of the Homeric descriptions of the war at Troy. The art of besieging also had made much progress, even in the time of the most ancient monuments. The administration of the law was in the hands of the priests, who are said to have conducted all trials in writing. The laws, though some kings had made additions, were on the whole very ancient, and were believed to have been revealed by the gods themselves. Capital punishment was inflicted on murderers (even of slaves), perjurers, false informers, and those who carried on any unlawful traffic. Cowards and deserters were regarded as

dishonoured men. The wealth and intelligence of the Egyptians naturally led them to commercial pursuits, but their trade was carried on by land, by means of caravans, more than by sea, although the mouths of the Nile were then more fit for navigation than they are at present. Their commerce is attested by the fact, that in some of the most ancient tombs at Thebes a number of Chinese vessels with Chinese inscriptions have been found. It is, however, more than probable that the commerce was carried on by foreigners visiting Egypt, rather than by the Egyptians themselves going abroad, for they shunned coming in contact with other nations, for which they entertained generally a thorough contempt. Their own peculiar institutions, laws, and customs, naturally tended to keep them secluded from the rest of the world.

All the occupations of their domestic life are better known to us than those of any other ancient nation, from the numerous paintings and representations in their catacombs; and if, along with these representations, we had a national literature of the Egyptians, we should understand that nation more perfectly than any other. We see them engaged in all the agricultural operations, from ploughing to reaping, in cultivating the vine and fruit-trees, in tending their herds and flocks of sheep and geese, and in pursuing game and wild beasts with bows, arrows, slings, dogs, and even lions, which they were in the habit of taming. Bird-catching and fishing seem to have been among their favourite out-door pursuits. In other representations we see them engaged in the pursuits of town life, some of which are necessary to support existence, while others supply the means of gratifying the love of ease, luxury, or taste. We see them working in wood, cutting and removing stones, weaving, painting, sculpturing, working in gold, jewellery, and the like. Their linens and cottons were excellent, as we still see from the cloth in which their mummies are wrapped. Glass also was manufactured at an early period. A reed, called papyrus, which formerly grew in abundance in the marshy districts of the Nile, was one of the most useful productions of the country, its root being used as fuel, and the leaves wrought into covers, dresses, canvas, and especially paper, (named from *papyrus*), which was celebrated in all antiquity, and remained a common writing material until the time of the middle ages. There can be no doubt that the Egyptians were also acquainted with various chemical processes, and in purple dyeing it would seem that they surpassed even the Phoenicians.

Representations of domestic and social scenes are equally frequent. The kitchen, as well as the drawing-room, and all that is going on in them, are brought vividly before us. From these scenes it is pretty evident that the Egyptians were not quite so gloomy a people as has sometimes been asserted. The halls of the great and wealthy are neither without comforts nor elegance, the furniture appears to be rich and costly, and some articles are beautiful and in exquisite taste. Games, amusements of various kinds, and even bull-fights are figured on their monuments. The feasts and social entertainments seem to be very sumptuous, and the guests are anointed and waited upon by slaves. Women also took part in these social entertainments, which is a proof that in Egypt they enjoyed a higher degree of freedom than in other eastern countries. It is evident that the Egyptians cannot lay any particular claim to temperate habits, for we often see them in situations which are by no means pleasing. The enjoyment of social meetings is often enhanced by dancers and singers. Hence it is not improbable that showing the figure of a dead person at banquets may have been intended as much to encourage enjoyment as to remind the guests of the transient nature of all earthly delights.

9. But notwithstanding their inclination to enjoy life, the Egyptians were a serious and meditative people, and in one way or another religion was connected with all their thoughts and customs. Their religion seems originally to have been a kind of pantheism, or a worship of God in all his manifestations in nature. This view appears to account more satisfactorily for their worship of animals than the explanations of the Greeks, according to whom it arose out of gratitude towards certain animals on account of their usefulness; for it was useful animals alone that they worshipped. The coarse animal-worship of later times was probably only a degenerate and corrupt form of what was in its origin a noble, though erroneous, idea; and the Egyptians, like some other nations, had come to confound the substance with the symbol. In Osiris and Isis, they worshipped the fertilizing powers of nature, under the names of a male and a female divinity. Kneph or Neph was conceived as the spirit of God pervading the universe at the creation, while Phtah was regarded as the real creator, and Ammon or Amun as the king of the gods. The power of evil seems to have been personified in Typhon, who in many respects resembles the Persian Ahriman. Among the animals receiving divine honours in Egypt, we may mention the ox, the dog, the cat, the ibis, the hawk, and some fishes, all of which were worshipped in all parts of Egypt; others enjoyed only a local veneration, while in some places they were regarded as unclean, or were even objects of persecution. Thus the sheep was worshipped only in the district of Thebes and Sais, the goat at Mendes, the wolf at Lycopolis, the lion at Leontopolis, the eagle at Thebes, the shrewmouse at Athribis, and others elsewhere. Whoever killed a sacred animal intentionally was punished with death; if unintentionally, he might escape by paying a fine.. Sometimes even bloody wars are said to have broken out between neighbouring districts, because an animal had been killed in the one, which was worshipped in the other. This strange

superstition and fanaticism maintained themselves among the natives even during the time when the country was governed by Greeks and Romans. The prophets of the Old Testament denounced the absurd worship of animals, the Persians despised it, and to the witty Greeks and Romans it was an object of ridicule. And who can wonder, when we are told that, when a cat died a natural death, all the inmates of the house shaved their eyebrows, and when a dog died, they cut away the hair from all parts of their bodies! These sacred animals, after their death, were embalmed, and deposited as mummies in the sepulchres of men. In some instances, the worship did not extend to whole classes or species of animals, but to one particular animal, distinguished from the rest by certain signs. An animal of this kind was attended to with the greatest care, and the priests charged with it were held in the highest respect. The most celebrated among such animals was the bull Apis, which was kept at Memphis. The animal was always black, with a triangular white spot on the forehead, and the figure of an eagle on its neck. It was believed to confer upon boys attending upon it the power of prophecy. If it reached the age of twenty-five years, it was killed, but otherwise it was allowed to die a natural death. Such an event produced general mourning and lamentation, and its burial was accompanied by all imaginable pomp and ceremony. But the general grief gave way to the most unbounded joy as soon as the priest had discovered (or prepared) a calf with the requisite signs, and produced the new god. The ancients expressly state that Apis was only the symbol of Osiris, whose soul was believed to be in the bull, and to migrate after its death into the body of the successor.

10. This last notion is connected with the belief, which the Egyptians shared with the Indians, that the soul, after the death of the body, migrated into another. The doctrine itself, however, was differently developed by the two nations, for, according to Herodotus, the Egyptians believed that the soul of a man, after his death, had to pass through bodies of all the animals of the land and of the sea, and even through those of the birds of the air; and that then, after the lapse of three thousand years, it returned into the body of a human being. When, notwithstanding this theory of the migration of souls, we hear of the belief of the Egyptians in the existence of a kingdom of the dead, called Amenthes or Amenti, the sojourn of the souls in it cannot have been conceived as permanent, and it was probably regarded only as a transition state in which the mode of migration was determined by Osiris, the judge in the kingdom of the dead. His judgment-seat is often represented in Egyptian paintings, and we there see the actions of the departed regularly weighed in a pair of scales. A similar judgment is said to have taken place in Egypt whenever a person had died. On such an occasion, any one might come forward with accusations against the

deceased, and when the charges were proved, the burial of the body
was forbidden. Even deceased kings had to undergo such an ordeal.
The priests, it is said, eulogised him, but the assembled people
either agreed, or expressed their dissent by a tumultuous noise, and
if the latter prevailed, the king was deprived of the customary
magnificent burial. This regulation, together with the priestly
control over the government, was probably the reason why few of
the Egyptian kings made any gross abuse of their power.

11. To be debarred from honourable burial could not but make
the deepest impression in a country where the greatest care and
large sums of money were bestowed upon the burial and preservation
of the bodies, which were embalmed and deposited in the chambers
of the catacombs. These mummies, as they are called, were embalmed in a more or less expensive way, according to the circumstances of the deceased and his relatives. The body was wrapped
up in fine linen or cotton, decorated with various ornaments, and
covered with hieroglyphic inscriptions, and finally placed in a coffin
or sarcophagus Such extraordinary care bestowed upon the preservation of the body, seems to be irreconcilable with the doctrine of
the migration of souls, as well as with that of a kingdom of the
dead, unless we assume that the preservation of the body was believed to be indispensable to the immortality of the soul. There
can be no doubt that the religion of the priests differed in many
essential points from that of the great mass of the people. We
have little information about the extent and amount of knowledge
possessed by the Egyptian priests, simply because the country had
no national literature. The god Thoth was regarded as the author
of all knowledge, and believed to have invented arithmetic, geometry, astronomy, and the art of writing. Geometry and astronomy
were cultivated by the Egyptians as a matter of necessity, in consequence of the annual inundations, by which the limits of the different lands and estates were swept away. The year of the Egyptians
consisted of twelve months of thirty days each, and five intercalary
days; such a year was by nearly a quarter of a day less than the
ordinary solar year, and in the course of fourteen hundred and sixty
years of this kind, the difference between it and the Julian year
amounts to a whole year. This fact was well known to the Egyptians, who called that period the dogstar period. Whether this
astronomical knowledge had been gained by the priests themselves,
or whether it was imported from Babylonia, cannot be determined;
but certain it is that the science made no progress in Egypt, but for
many centuries remained stationary at the point at which we first
meet with it. Such was the case with all the sciences and the arts
of the Egyptians, among whom everything continued to move
within certain fixed limits established by custom and lawgivers;
nay, a physician who adopted a new mode of treatment, was liable
to a capital prosecution, if his patient died under it.

The belief that the god Thoth had invented the art of writing, has received some illustration from the discovery of the nature of hieroglyphics, some of which are really phonetic, or a kind of alphabetic writing, and there can be no doubt that the alphabets of the Semitic tribes in Western Asia, such as the Hebrew and Phoenician, were only a farther development of the foundation which had been laid in Egypt. But here, too, the stationary and immovable character of the Egyptians did not allow them to complete what they themselves had invented, so that, in the end, they had to adopt the alphabet of their neighbours, who had learned the rudiments from them. The probability is, that the Phoenicians were the first who evolved a complete system of alphabetic writing from the rude beginnings they had learned from the Egyptians. Among the latter people, the want of a convenient alphabet no doubt contributed towards preventing the formation of a national literature, but their peculiar mode of thinking was probably a still more serious obstacle. Whatever literary productions the Egyptians possessed, may reasonably be supposed to have been nothing but dry records of facts and doctrines. Oratory and poetry, in particular, appear to have been quite foreign to them. The great number of musical instruments seen on their monuments, leads us to suppose that they possessed very considerable technical skill; but the state of music among all oriental nations, does not allow us to assume that they ever advanced beyond the simplest melodies.

12. The arts in which they were greatest, and which will secure to them the admiration of all ages, were architecture and sculpture. The character of the former is massive, grand, and earnest, and this character, combined with the gigantic dimensions of the temples at Thebes, produces an effect of sublimity which it is difficult to describe in words. The impression of solidity is enhanced by the fact that the outer walls rise slantingly instead of perpendicularly, while the roofs are completely flat. But all these temples are wanting in the unity of design which distinguishes the temples of the Greeks. The interior of the Egyptian temples is generally supported by numerous columns, whose capitals are of the greatest variety — the ornaments consisting mainly of productions of the vegetable kingdom. The uniformity of the strong walls is sometimes relieved by sculptures and paintings.

In middle Egypt, in the neighbourhood of Memphis, we meet with the celebrated pyramids, which do not occur in upper Egypt, and which were formerly regarded as among the greatest wonders of the world. They are structures of the simplest form, generally rising from a broad square base, and, gradually diminishing, end at the top in a point, or a small square surface. Their interior is almost a solid mass, being traversed only by a few narrow passages and chambers. They are found in groups on the elevated plains of

9 *

the Libyan hills, and the highest occur in the group of Gizeh. The loftiest among these, which is about four hundred and fifty feet high (each side at the base is about seven hundred and sixteen feet), is called the pyramid of Cheops — it being believed to be the one whose construction is ascribed by Herodotus to King Cheops. The height is about the same as that of the highest steeples in Europe, but in massiveness the pyramids are far more imposing. Originally the outer sides were covered with polished stones of different colours, but these coatings have been taken away by the Arabs, and at present not a vestige of decoration is left. Innumerable conjectures have been formed as to the purpose for which these structures were raised; but the general opinion at present is, that they were sepulchral monuments of kings, for they stand in the Necropolis of Memp' is, and are surrounded by numerous other tombs; and in every one of the pyramids which have been explored by Europeans, a sarcophagus has been found. The date of the foundation of these singular mausoleums, is probably more recent than that of the Theban tombs, which are entirely different.

13. Sculpture and painting are inseparably connected with the architecture of Egypt. The mechanical skill which the Egyptian artists possessed is really astonishing, for their statues and reliefs are all made of the hardest granite and porphyry, and wrought with a neatness and exactness which prove them to have been perfect masters. The forms of the bodies are strong and massive, and on the whole in accordance with nature, but the anatomy is not correct, and generally made according to a fixed type. The faces present a sort of transition from the Caucasian to the negro race, and some are by no means unhandsome; but they are stiff, without life or warmth, and are generally likewise of a fixed type. The statues in a sitting or striding attitude are likewise stiff, and nearly always the same. The historical reliefs and paintings have more life and animation, and in some of them national peculiarities are well expressed. The same may be said of the domestic scenes; but the highest objects of art appear not to have been aimed at. The Egyptian artists were more successful in their statues and reliefs of animals, than in their representations of the human form, and this arose probably from the fact that in the former they were less constrained by types and conventionalities. The gods are represented as beings with human bodies, but with the heads of animals, such as those of rams, hawks, ibises, and bulls. The sphinxes, on the other hand, have the body of a lion, with a human head. This combination was probably intended to indicate great strength, which in other cases was expressed by the superhuman size of the figure.

The character of Egyptian art is, on the whole, monumental — that is, its main object is to fix that which is conceived as a fact, and to transmit it to posterity. The true idea of art is neither aimed at nor attained; but the great mechanical and artistic skill, which might so easily have led to higher developments, remained stationary, like all other branches of Egyptian civilization.

14. The principal Greek writers on Egyptian history are Herodotus and Diodorus, both of whom visited Egypt themselves, and collected their information from the priests; but their accounts, though agreeing in many points, diverge in others so widely, that they almost appear like histories of two different countries. In the first half of the third century B. C., Manetho, an Egyptian priest of Heliopolis, at the request of king Ptolemy Philadelphus, wrote a history of Egypt in Greek. As he had no difficulty in gaining access to the records kept by the priests, and was also in a position to read and understand those documents for the explanation of which foreigners were dependent upon others, his work, if it had come down to us, would be a far more important and trustworthy source of information. But unfortunately the work is lost, with the exception of a few extracts, containing lists of thirty dynasties of kings with the years of their reigns; and even these extracts are so carelessly made, that in some cases they present almost insurmountable difficulties. The most authentic of all the records are the hieroglyphic inscriptions, which furnish us with many names and surnames of kings, their titles, the periods of their reigns, and their relation to the gods. The reading of these hieroglyphic records, in very many instances, confirms the statements of Manetho, and thus proves this historian to have derived his information from authentic sources. The statements of Herodotus and Diodorus, on the other hand, can scarcely be reconciled at all with the documentary history, and seem in most cases to furnish only a kind of popular traditions which those travellers heard in Egypt. Another very important source of information is the books of the Old Testament.

The chronology of Egyptian history has often been the subject of learned discussions. According to the chronology of Manetho, the foundation of the kingdom of Egypt belongs to the year B. C. 3892, and its founder, no doubt a mythical personage, was Menes. But it is impossible to take the early dynasties as historical.

15. The history of ancient Egypt is conveniently divided into four periods,—1. The Pharaonic period, during which the country was governed by native princes; it extends from the beginning to the conquest of Egypt by Cambyses in B. C. 526; 2. The Persian period, from B. C. 526 to the conquest of Egypt by Alexander the Great in B. C. 332; 3. The Macedonian or Greek period, from the foundation of Alexandria in B. C. 332, to the death of Cleopatra and the conquest by Augustus in B. C. 30; and, 4. The Roman period, from B. C. 30 to the capture of Alexandria by Khalif Omar in A. D. 640.

The Pharaonic period may again be divided into the periods of the old, the middle, and the new monarchy. The first extends from the beginning to the invasion of the Hycsos; the second is the period during which the Hycsos reigned in Egypt; and the third from the expulsion of the Hycsos until the conquest of the country by Cambyses.

16. The unhistorical character of the old and middle Pharaonic periods is sufficiently indicated by the circumstance that Egypt is said to have been first governed by gods, spirits, demigods, and the souls of the departed. After these there follow thirty dynasties of mortal kings, the first of whom was Menes. The number of these kings, according to some, was three hundred, and according to others five hundred. The earliest dynasties present in many respects as yet insurmountable difficulties, for it is uncertain whether they are to be taken as a series, or whether at least some of them were contemporary kings, ruling in different parts of Egypt. But the names found in hieroglyphic inscriptions, and identified with names of kings occurring as early as the fourth dynasty, seem to prove that the lists of the earliest human dynasties ought not to be rejected as altogether fabulous. The twelfth dynasty in Manetho, containing seven kings of Diospolis, seems to bear strong marks of historical authenticity; in it occurs the celebrated Sesostris or Sesortasen, who is said to have subdued all Asia and Europe as far as Thrace, and to have built the Labyrinth. But this dynasty has not yet been confirmed by any monuments, and Sesostris probably belongs to a much later period. The fifteenth, sixteenth, and seventeenth dynasties are those of the Hycsos or Shepherd kings, who are said to have ruled over Egypt for a period of five hundred and eleven years. From Manetho, as quoted by Josephus, we derive tolerably satisfactory information about these Hycsos. In the reign of an Egyptian king Timaus, he says, a foreign people (probably nomadic Arabs) invaded Egypt from the east, subdued the country without difficulty, killed or enslaved its inhabitants, and burnt cities and temples. In the Sethroite nome or district they built an immense earth-camp called Abaris, and their capital was Memphis. In the end, however, the Egyptians recovered their independence : the Hycsos were besieged at Abaris, and obtained a free departure from the country, whereupon they retired into Palestine. These Hycsos were no doubt a Semitic people, and akin to the Israelites; they must have been a warlike nation, which at first destroyed the traces of civilisation in Egypt, until afterwards they accommodated themselves to some extent to the manners and customs of the conquered people. It was, in all likelihood, during their reign that Joseph came to Egypt, and the reception which his people met with in Egypt is accounted for by the fact that the Hycsos were a kindred race. The new king who "knew

not Joseph," and oppressed the Israelites, was probably the first prince of the native dynasty after the expulsion of the Hycsos. The foreign rulers themselves have left behind no monuments in Egypt, but the struggles between them and the Egyptians are represented on several monuments, in which the Hycsos appear as defeated and fugitive barbarians. It was probably owing to the vanity of the Egyptians, who did not like to own that their country was ever subject to foreign rulers, that the priests gave no information about these occurrences to Herodotus and Diodorus.

17. The new monarchy extends from the expulsion of the Hycsos or the accession of the eighteenth dynasty down to the thirtieth or last, and there can be no doubt that this whole period is in all essential points historical. The expulsion of the foreign invaders was the commencement of the most brilliant period of Egyptian history. The eighteenth dynasty, which, like the nineteenth, had Thebes for its capital, was the period when Egyptian art reached its highest point. The names of its kings appear on many monuments at Luxor and Karnak, and also on the tablets of Abydos and Karnak. The great Rameses of the eighteenth dynasty was a conqueror who extended his dominions far and wide, and received the tribute of many subject nations. In the south, Egypt was extended to the second cataract of the Nile, in the west to the negro tribes of the interior of Africa, and the east was guarded by strong fortresses. Rameses is further said to have traversed Syria and Asia Minor as a mighty conqueror, and to have advanced as far as the frontiers of Persia and the shores of the Caspian sea. Such conquests required fleets, and Egypt itself must at that time have acquired a naval power, or else have compelled the tribes on the Syrian coast to furnish it. The conquests of Rameses in Asia can probably not be doubted, but appear not to have been lasting, as afterwards we hear nothing of a dominion of Egyptian kings in those parts. The struggles against the Hycsos seem to have braced the nation, and enabled it not only to crush its oppressors, but to plant its yoke upon the necks of others. The great Rameses is probably the same king as the Sesostris or Sesortasen of Herodotus and Diodorus. The period during which the eighteenth dynasty possessed the sovereignty of Egypt extended from B. C. 1655 to 1326.

The history of the nineteenth dynasty, which ruled from B. C. 1326 to 1183, is very confused; but Egypt still continued to enjoy a high degree of prosperity. Herodotus places the kings who built the pyramids, Cheops, Chephren, and Myarinus, several generations after Rameses (Sesostris); but although the names, as recent discoveries have shown, are historical, yet the historian was deceived in the time he assigns to them, for they belonged to the fourth dynasty.

18. After the nineteenth dynasty, the power and prosperity of

Egypt appear to have gradually decayed, and at the close of the twenty-fourth the country was subjugated by the Ethiopians, who furnish the twenty-fifth dynasty, consisting of three kings. Herodotus knows only the first of them, Sabaco or Sebichos, who, according to that historian, reigned over Egypt for fifty years and then quitted it of his own accord, whereupon the previous king Anysis, having concealed himself all that time, again came forward and occupied the throne. After him Sethos, a priest of Pthah (Hephaestus), usurped the sovereignty, and, as might be expected, reduced the power of the military caste to the advantage of that of the priests. The cause or occasion of this revolution is not mentioned anywhere, but must probably be looked for in the altered circumstances of the country, for it had to some extent become a maritime power, and the commercial part of the population may have supported the priestly against the military caste. It was in the reign of Sethos, that the Assyrian conqueror Sennacherib (about B. C. 712) threatened to invade Egypt with a large army. As the warrior caste bore the king no good will, he was in great difficulty in consequence of their refusal to serve against the invader. Trusting to a dream, it is said, he formed an army of merchants, artisans, and the populace, and went out against the enemy. But during the night a host of mice injured their bows, arrows, and shields so much, as to oblige them the next morning to take to flight. These occurrences, though apparently fabulous, must have some historical foundation; for we know from the Scriptures that, about the same time, Hezekiah, being hard pressed by Sennacherib, sought the assistance of Egypt, and that the Assyrian army perished before it was able to take Jerusalem. The Scriptures speak of an Ethiopian king Thirhaka, who marched out against the Assyrians, and this king is, according to Manetho, the third and last king of the Ethiopian dynasty, and identical with the one whose name appears in the Egyptian monuments as Tahraka. As Manetho does not mention either Sethos or Anysis, it is possible that these princes may have maintained themselves only in lower Egypt, while the upper part was in the hands of the Ethiopians.

19. If there be any truth in the story about a priest taking possession of the sovereign power in Egypt, it is evident that the ancient constitution of the kingdom must have been seriously shaken. The same truth is implied in the story of the dodecarchy, which, according to Herodotus, succeeded Sethos, and maintained the ascendancy for a period of thirty years, from B. C. 700 to 670. This dodecarchy was the government of twelve contemporaneous kings, whom the Egyptians themselves are said to have appointed; they formed connections with one another, and maintained justice in their administration of the affairs of the country. These twelve rulers are said to have built the Labyrinth, a little above lake

Moeris, which was intended to be their common place of burial. The remains of this gigantic building, which have recently been discovered, show that Herodotus' account of its three thousand chambers is by no means exaggerated. But he seems to be mistaken in ascribing to the dodecarchy a structure which can scarcely be of a later date than the time of the eighteenth dynasty. The dodecarchy is not mentioned by Manetho; but it would be hasty to infer from this, that our account of it is altogether a mere fable. The manner however in which Herodotus describes the end of the dodecarchy, clearly shows that he is relating only a popular legend. The twelve, he says, had received an oracle at the beginning of their reign, that the sovereignty of the country should in the end belong to him who should offer a libation in the temple of Hephaestus from a brazen vessel. Once the priest, instead of the usual twelve golden vessels, brought only eleven; Psammetichus, the ruler of Sais, then took off his helmet and offered the libation out of it. The other eleven princes, alarmed by what they saw, for they suddenly remembered the oracle, attacked Psammetichus and drove him into the marshy districts of lower Egypt. The banished prince, desirous to avenge himself on his colleagues, consulted the oracle of Buto, which returned the answer, that he should be avenged by brazen men coming from the sea. After a time, Ionian and Carian pirates were obliged during a storm to land on the coast of Egypt, and Psammetichus seeing their brazen armour concluded that they were the men promised by the oracle. He accordingly induced them by liberal promises to join him, and with their assistance he overthrew his enemies, and made himself sole king of Egypt, which he governed from B. C. 670 to 617.

20. The mere fact that a dynasty of princes acquired possession of the sovereignty by means of foreign support, opens a new period in the history of Egypt, which had hitherto shut itself jealously against all foreign influence. During this period, however, Egypt once more displayed, at least partially, its ancient power and greatness; but this revival was of short duration, for the nationality of the Egyptians had grown inflexible in its ancient forms, and was unable to assimilate the new elements introduced by Psammetichus. His object appears to have been the regeneration of Egypt by means of Greek civilisation, for to the Ionians and Carians who had assisted him he assigned lands on the Pelusiac branch of the Nile, and intrusted to them Egyptian boys to be instructed in the manners and language of the Greeks. He further intended to raise and strengthen his kingdom by encouraging the intercourse between it and foreign countries, by opening the ports to foreign merchants, and by extending commerce over the whole country. The native militia was superseded by regular Greek soldiers, and a portion of the military caste, offended at these and other measures,

emigrated into Ethiopia. He also formed a caste of interpreters or dragomans, to assist the natives in their intercourse with foreigners. The opposition which these measures called forth did not deter him from pursuing the path he had once struck into; and both he and his successors, who followed the same line of policy, were supported by their foreign mercenaries, who formed the real strength of the Egyptian armies. Neither Psammetichus, however, nor his successors, interfered with the religion of their subjects; we find them, on the contrary, as zealous in their religious observances and in maintaining and completing the ancient temples, as any of their predecessors.

21. Psammetichus was succeeded by his son Necho, or, as Herodotus calls him, Necos, who reigned from B. C. 617 to 601. We have already related that this king employed Phoenician sailors to circumnavigate Africa.[1] In his reign, Egypt came into conflict with Babylonia, which was then rising on the ruins of the Assyrian empire. Judah was at the time in alliance with Babylon, and its king Josiah, who opposed the army of Necho, was defeated in a great battle at Megiddo in B. c. 608. Necho then took Jerusalem, and having appointed Eliakim king of the country, and imposed an annual tribute upon it, he returned to his own kingdom; but four years later, when the war with Babylon was continued, and Necho had advanced as far as the Euphrates, he was completely defeated by Nebuchadnezzar in the battle of Carchemish or Circesium, on the eastern bank of the Euphrates, B. c. 604.

This catastrophe put an end to Necho's scheme of conquering Syria, which had already been partially carried into effect by Psammetichus. Both rulers had not only been attracted by the wealth and prosperity of the Phoenician cities, but were guided also by the conviction that Syria and Egypt were of the greatest importance to each other for mutual protection. Necho also knew that the two countries could not be maintained without a fleet, and accordingly had caused numerous ships to be built, both on the Mediterranean and on the Red sea. In this he must have been supported by the Phoenicians, with whom he seems to have kept up a good understanding. It was in consequence of these schemes that he attempted to connect the Mediterranean and the Red sea by a canal, which undertaking he is said to have left unfinished, because one hundred and twenty thousand men lost their lives while engaged in the work; but we know for certain, that in the reign of Darius, the canal was open for large vessels, and traces of it may be seen at the present day. It has now been neglected for upwards of a thousand years.

22. Necho was succeeded by his son Psammis, who reigned only

[1] See page 82.

six years, from B. C. 601–595, and Psammis by his son Apries (the Uaphris of the monuments, and Hophra of the Old Testament). The latter reigned from B. C. 595 to 570. Pursuing the same policy as his predecessors, he made war upon the Phoenicians, and subdued Tyre, Sidon, and Cyprus; but these acquisitions were not lasting, being snatched away by the Babylonian conquerors. In his reign, Egypt was for the first time assailed by its neighbours in the west, and the Greeks of Cyrene completely annihilated his army in a battle at Irasa. This defeat and the cruelties to which it gave rise, created great discontent among his subjects, especially the soldiers, who rose against him in arms. Amasis or Amosis, who was despatched by the king to pacify the malcontents, was raised by them to the throne, and then led the troops against his former master, who, being supported only by his brave Ionian and Carian mercenaries, while the native troops sided with Amasis, was defeated in battle, and afterwards murdered by the populace.

Amasis reigned from B. C. 570 till 526. He was a man of low origin, and his previous conduct was not of a kind to recommend him to the higher castes, for he is said to have been several times convicted of theft. But he possessed the affection of the soldiers and the people, and was thus enabled to disregard nearly all the rules and ceremonies of the priests. He displayed during his reign great shrewdness and prudence, and though he had dethroned the race of Psammeticus, he did not break off his connection with the Greeks, but, on the contrary, continued to confer considerable privileges upon them. His friendship with Polycrates, tyrant of Samos, is well known. In his reign Egypt enjoyed a prosperity such as it never after experienced under any of its native rulers. He died just in time, for his son Psammenitus had scarcely been six months in possession of the throne, when Egypt was invaded and conquered by the Persians under Cambyses, the son of the great Cyrus, B. C. 526.

23. Egypt thus became a satrapy or province of the Persian empire, though its internal affairs continued to be managed by native kings of the twenty-seventh, twenty-eighth, twenty-ninth, and thirtieth dynasties. The natural and religious aversion subsisting between the Persians and Egyptians, frequently caused the latter to rebel against their foreign oppressors, and this spirit of resistance was fomented by the numerous Greek and Jewish settlers in the country. The first great revolt broke out in B. C. 487, in the reign of Darius Hystaspis, who was thereby obliged to postpone his intended invasion of Greece for a period of three years. The rebellion, however, was suppressed by his successor Xerxes in B. C. 484. A second revolt, under Inarus, in which the Egyptians were aided by the Athenians, also proved unsuccessful, after having lasted from

B. C. 462 till 456.   Under Amyrtacus, the only king of the twenty-
eighth dynasty, Egypt, from circumstances that are not known to
us, regained its independence.   His sarcophagus, after many vicis-
situdes, is now deposited in the British Museum.   The last revolt
occurred during the thirtieth dynasty, in the reign of Nectanebus
II.; but in B. C. 350, Egypt was reconquered by the Persians, and
the last king of that dynasty withdrew as an exile into Ethiopia.
The country now remained subject to Persia, until, in B. C. 332, it
was conquered by Alexander the Great; after whose death it again
became an independent kingdom under the dynasty of the Ptolemies, until in B. C. 30 it was conquered by the Romans.   But of
its history under the Ptolemies and the Romans we shall have occasion to speak in a subsequent part of this work.

BOOK II.

HISTORY OF GREECE, MACEDONIA, AND THE GRAECO-MACEDONIAN KINGDOMS.

CHAPTER I.

GEOGRAPHICAL SKETCH OF GREECE.

1. In passing from Asia into Europe, we first meet, in the south-eastern peninsula of the latter continent, with the Greeks, or, as they were called by their native name, Hellenes. The civilisation of this small but illustrious people spread its mild and beneficent influence, more or less, over the whole of the ancient world, and in many respects has never been surpassed either by ancient or modern nations. Its literature and its arts are generally distinguished by the epithet classical — a term which also comprises the civilisation of the Romans, both Greeks and Romans being, so to speak, plants growing out of the same root, and belonging to the same sphere of intellectual development, though the Greeks reached a great and decided pre-eminence; for the civilisation of Greece was the model of that of Rome, and incomparably more refined and varied. In Greece we find man endowed with rare gifts and noble impulses, which are either wholly denied to oriental nations, or accorded to them only in an inferior degree. The Greeks were distinguished by a happy physical organisation, by extraordinary acuteness, flexibility, and versatility of mind, and by the power of developing within their own nationality a vast variety of specific forms; they felt the need, and possessed the ability ever to cast off that which had become obsolete and antiquated, and to assimilate to themselves that which was new and full of life; they had the full consciousness of the value of political liberty and independence, and were ever striving to obtain and preserve this blessing. Their outward eyes were no less keen in observing the forms and beauties of external nature, than their mental vision in tracing the relations subsisting between man and man, between man and nature, and between God and man. But as nothing human is quite perfect, we must be prepared to meet, in the character even of this gifted people, with features which cast a shade over their brilliant qualities, and fill our

(111)

hearts with sadness, in the contemplation of human infirmities.
First of all, the Greeks were pagans, and thereby deprived of that
blessed feeling afforded by the belief in one God, who embraces all
his creatures with love and care; they were agitated by strong passions and desires, which found vent in the disputes among political
parties, and among the numerous small states and independent
communities into which the country was divided. This want of
union brought about the downfall of their national independence
much earlier than might have been expected from their intellectual
superiority. But notwithstanding these and other drawbacks, the
history of the Greeks presents so much that is ennobling, elevating,
and instructive, that we may easily forget the darker sides of the
picture, and lovingly dwell upon its bright and wonderful phenomena.

2. The name Hellas, by which Greece was called by its own inhabitants, was originally confined to a small district of Thessaly,
whence, in the course of time, it was extended to all the countries
inhabited by Hellenes, both in Greece proper and in the numerous
colonies all around the Mediterranean. In a more restricted sense,
however, Hellas signified the country north of the isthmus of
Corinth, extending northward as far as the Ambracian gulf in the
west, and the mouth of the river Peneius in the east. These
boundaries of Hellas proper, as it is sometimes called, however, do
not mark the exact lines by which the Greeks or Hellenes were
separated from the non-Greek or barbarous tribes; for both Acarnania and Ætolia were inhabited by peoples which are expressly
said not to have been Hellenes, while, on the other hand, some
writers even excluded Thessaly from Hellas, extending its boundary
in the north-east only as far as the Maliac gulf. In the restricted
sense here described, the southern peninsula of Greece, called Peloponnesus, formed no part of Hellas; but being inhabited by Hellenes, it was of course as much a part of Hellas, in its wider sense,
as Attica or Bocotia. The Romans, for reasons not clearly ascertained, called Hellas *Graecia*, and its inhabitants *Graeci*, and from
these Roman names the modern *Greece* and *Greeks* are derived.

3. Hellas, then, is the southern portion of the easternmost of the
three great peninsulas which form the southern extremities of Europe, and among these three Hellas possesses the same advantages
that make Europe superior to the other continents; for although the
country itself is but small, in fact scarcely so large as the little
kingdom of Portugal, it has an enormous extent of coast, on account
of its numerous bays, gulfs, and creeks. In the north Hellas was
protected by a range of mountains running from west to east, under
the name of the Cambunian mountains, the eastern part of which
was the celebrated Olympus. In the west of Thessaly, which itself
forms a large basin, mount Pindus, the highest in Greece, runs from

north to south, and near its southern extremity branches off, forming the chains of Othrys and Œta. The heights of Phocis, Doris,
Bœotia, and Attica, also belong to the system of Pindus, which
even extends to some of the islands of the Ægean. Thessaly is
separated in the south from the rest of Greece by mount Œta, which
at the same time was a protection to the southern countries, so long
as the few passes of the mountains were well guarded. The most
celebrated of these passes is that of Thermopylae, consisting of a
road leading between the steep side of mount Œta and the sea.
This pass, about five miles in length, was of the highest importance,
as it formed the only road into the southern part of Greece for
armies coming from the north, and, being in some parts extremely
narrow, could easily be defended. At present the coast has been
extended by deposits from the sea; but the district can be easily
recognised, and the hot spring, from which the pass derived its
name, still sends forth its warm sulphureous water. The largest
rivers in all Greece are the Peneius in Thessaly, with its romantic
valley near the mouth, between mounts Olympus and Ossa, and the
Achelous in the west, between Ætolia and Acarnania.

In the south of Thessaly the peculiar conformation of Hellas is
most obvious and striking in the extraordinary variety of rugged
and romantic mountains, some of which are bare, while others are
clad with rich vegetation. Nature herself here seems to render
uniformity and the union of several tribes into one state impossible.
It may be said that this part of Hellas, between mount Œta and
the Corinthian gulf, is the country of the most striking contrasts,
for not only do sea and land, mountains and valleys, rugged rocks
and fertile plains alternate with one another in richest variety, but
two adjoining plains are sometimes so different, that in the one the
little rivers and streams are always filled with water, while in the
other they are nearly always dry. During the hot season of the
year, almost all are dried up, but the abundant dew makes up for
the want of water. The courses of the rivers are very short, the
country itself being narrow, and surrounded nearly on all sides by
the sea, which in many places enters deeply into the land, and forms
large bays. The very form of the country, with its indentations,
mountains, and valleys, appears to have stamped its character upon
the inhabitants, for it prevented their falling into sloth and effeminacy, while it braced them, and kept them in a state of activity and
watchfulness.

The climate of this part of Greece produced an equally salutary
effect; for while the fertility of the country produced everything
that was necessary to sustain life and to afford pleasure, yet the
exertion of man could nowhere be dispensed with, so that the love
of enjoyment could not be gratified without labour, the real condi-
ment of all pleasure. The heat, which during the summer season

10 *

would be oppressive, is tempered by the breezes from the sea and
the mountains, some of which are, during a great part of the year,
covered with snow. The transparency of the atmosphere and the
brilliancy of the sun present all the objects of nature to the eye in
a much purer and brighter light than in the northern parts of
Europe, and even more so than in Italy. The country produced in
most parts abundance of grain, wine, olives, and figs; but as it
yielded nothing without labour, nature herself prevented the Greeks
from falling into that state of listlessness and indolence which in
many Asiatic countries has so materially checked the progress of
civilisation.

4. Such is the general character of Hellas proper, and its different parts or provinces either combine all these features, or exhibit
some of them more prominently than others. In proceeding from
the south of Thessaly, through the pass of Thermopylae, we enter
the maritime country of the Opuntian Locrians, and thence on the
south-west we reach Phocis, with its renowned Parnassus, on the
southern slope of which was situated Delphi, celebrated for its
ancient oracle of Apollo, and regarded by the Hellenes as the centre
not only of their own country, but of the whole earth. On the
west of Phocis was the little country of Doris and the Ozolian
Locrians. Further west we have the rugged country of Ætolia,
which impressed its own character upon its inhabitants, and Acarnania, which, separated from Ætolia by the river Achelous, is
washed by the Ionian sea, and forms the last Greek country in the
west. On turning from Phocis eastward, we enter Bocotia, which
is divided by mount Helicon and its ramifications into two great
valleys. The northern one is a deep hollow shut in by mountains,
which is partly filled up by the lake Copais; this lake, however,
is more like a large swamp, especially in summer, for it is only
towards the end of winter that it really assumes the appearance of
a lake. It has outlets in the east towards the sea by means of subterranean passages called catabathra. Ancient Orchomenos was
situated on the border of this lake, which sometimes overflowed the
country far and wide, and was believed to have in very remote times
swallowed up entire cities. The second or south-eastern division
of Boeotia formed a fertile plain with its capital Thebes, whose
inhabitants were notorious for their fondness of good living. The
atmosphere of Boeotia was thick and heavy, and the Bocotians were
believed to be dull and unintellectual. Bocotia is bounded in the
south by the mountains Cithaeron and Parnes, on the other side
of which we have Attica, the most memorable region in regard to
the intellectual life of the Greeks, though its soil is by no means
as fertile and productive as many other parts of Hellas. Its extent
of coast is greater than that of any other province of Greece proper,
and was therefore particularly calculated to direct the attention of

its inhabitants to a maritime life. On its western side, where the sea forms the Saronic gulf, we have its capital Athens with the port-town of Piraeus. Attica is separated from Peloponnesus by the sea and by the small country of Megaris.

5. The great peninsula of Greece terminates in a smaller one, Peloponnesus, which, however, is an island rather than a peninsula, being connected with central Greece only by the narrow isthmus of Corinth. Nearly the whole of Peloponnesus is, like the rest of Greece, a mountainous country, and some of its mountains are of considerable height. Arcadia, the central part, is a high, uneven, and rough table-land, but contains excellent pasture, whence its inhabitants devoted themselves almost entirely to the feeding of flocks. The rough climate and their mode of life kept the Arcadians throughout the history of Greece in a more primitive state than any of the other Greeks. The plateau of Arcadia is surrounded on all sides by lofty mountains, which send their ramifications into the eastern and southern parts of the peninsula. All the mountains of Peloponnesus bear strong marks of great convulsions that have taken place in their formation, in some parts masses of rocks being piled upon one another, while others are distinguished by deep and wild ravines. The other countries or provinces of Peloponnesus are grouped around the central heights of Arcadia. The northern coast land comprises Achaia, Sicyon, and Corinth; in the east Argolis consists of a peninsula. In the south of Arcadia mount Taygetus extends southward as far as cape Taenaron, and divides Messenia from Laconia; while an eastern branch, mount Parnon, runs almost parallel, and terminates in cape Malea. Sparta, the capital of Laconia, was situated in the broad valley of the river Eurotas, at a considerable distance from the sea. The greater part of Laconia, being a rough mountainous country, admitted of little cultivation, though the valley of the Eurotas contained some very fertile districts. Messenia, on the other hand, which has many rich plains, was among the most fertile parts of Greece. On the western coast, between Messenia and Achaia, we have Elis with its fruitful plains and its mild delicious climate. Olympia, on the banks of the Alpheus, though it was not a city but only a mass of groves, altars, temples, a race-course, and other buildings erected for the convenience of the Hellenes assembling there every four years for the celebration of the Olympic games, was a place of far more importance than the capital, which bore the same name as the country.

6. The numerous islands by which Greece is surrounded belong to it in all essential points, for they are of the same physical and geological structure, and were at one time, no doubt, parts of the continent of Greece, from which they have been torn by volcanic or other agencies. The fertile island of Euboea stretches along

Phocis, Bocotia, and Attica; it is traversed by high mountains belonging to the chain of Pindus. The same chain is continued in the islands on the south-east of Euboea and Attica, and extends as far as Astypalaea; but Cos and the other islands in the north and south of it belong to Asia. The ancients called the European group of these islands the Cyclades (lying in a circle), and the Asiatic Sporades (the scattered). The Ægean sea, in which all these islands are situated, is closed in the south by Crete, the largest of all the Greek isles. As the navigation of the ancients consisted chiefly in coasting or sailing across narrow channels, these islands were of the greatest convenience to the Greeks in their intercourse with Asia, Africa, Italy, and Sicily, all of which countries accordingly were colonised by them at an early period.

CHAPTER II.

THE MYTHICAL PERIOD OF GREEK HISTORY.

1. THE history of Greece from its earliest dawn down to the migration of the Dorians, about B. C. 1100, is thoroughly mythical, for all the actions of individual men, as well as of whole communities, are described as influenced by and interfered with by an imaginary world of gods and beings of a higher order. But this very period, which in history is the most obscure, has been surrounded by the poetic and imaginative genius of the Greeks with a lustre quite unequalled in the legendary history of any other nation. It was to them the period of the great and mighty heroes whom they looked upon as their glorious ancestors; who were guided in their exploits by the gods, or struggled against their oppression and persecution; it was the period of which the events were immortalised by poets and artists, and in later times believed with the same firmness as the occurrences of well authenticated history. It would however be a serious mistake if we were to assume that the mythical lays of the ancient heroes had no other foundation than the fancy and imagination of the poets. Poets did not invent the substance of the lays, but derived it from the legends current among the people; and it was for this reason that the well-known stories, when clothed in poetic language, had such a charm, and exercised such an influence upon the Greeks, who derived from them their chief mental food and sustenance. Their faith in those legends was for a long time very intense, and the recollection of the heroes was kept alive

not only in poetry, but by relics shown in different places, by their tombs, and temples scattered over various parts of Hellas. We must further not be supposed to assert that after the Doric migration mythical legends all at once give way to history, for real history does not begin until the time of which we have contemporary records, and that time commences in Greece at a much later period than among the Asiatic nations which had a historical literature. Historians do not appear in Greece until about five centuries after the Doric migration, and during this intervening period between the mythical and truly historical ages the tendency to form myths was by no means extinct; on the contrary, the events handed down by oral tradition acquired more of a mythical than of a really historical character; but the mythical tendency no longer metamorphosed events in the same way as before; poets did not, until a very late period, take their subjects from that intermediate epoch, and consequently no deep interest in the occurrences of that period was felt or created. When, therefore, historians afterwards arose, the events of that period were either little known or known only as popular traditions.

2. It is the business of the historian to endeavour to discover that which constitutes the real groundwork of these rich and numerous legends and traditions about the early Greeks; but this task is beset with insurmountable difficulties. The immense variety of Greek legends so singularly interwoven with one another, and often contradictory, present at first sight an inextricable chaos, from which it seems impossible to extract anything of historical value. The stories about the heroes form the principal part of the mythical history, but some of them are so much interwoven with fables about the gods, that it is impossible to separate the one set from the other. So long as the legends about the gods were implicitly believed, no inquiries were made, but as soon as the faith in the gods disappeared among the better educated classes of the Greeks, several modes of explanation were devised. Some considered the myths to be mere allegories or symbols, embodying certain physical, ethical, or religious truths; others imagined that the gods had originally been great men, as kings and heroes, to whom their fellow-men paid divine honours for the benefits conferred upon their race. This latter view, though the most foolish and superficial of all, was adopted by some of the most eminent authors of antiquity, and has maintained its ground with many even in modern times.

3. Myths are never the result of an arbitrary or fanciful operation of the human mind, but are formed, in the early periods of a nation's history, instinctively and necessarily, in consequence of the manner in which men look at nature and the phenomena by which they are surrounded. The laws according to which this process

took place among the Greeks can still be ascertained with tolerable accuracy, from the numerous instances which speak for themselves, and from the rich literature which reveals to us the peculiar views and modes of thinking of that gifted people.   Ancient institutions and customs, of which no satisfactory explanation could be given, were accounted for by mythical stories, in which their origin was ascribed to certain occurrences; facts connected with the worship of the gods were metamorphosed into legends about their apparitions and interferences in human affairs; emigrants, taking with them from their former homes the worship of a particular divinity, would naturally form the belief, in the course of time, that the god himself had commanded them to quit their country, and had guided them to their new homes.   Legends, moreover, which the settlers found established in foreign lands, were eagerly caught up and combined with those which they brought with them.   These, and innumerable other circumstances, were the natural sources of mythical legends; but it is nevertheless often a matter of extreme difficulty in any given case to find the right key to the explanation of a myth; this will be easily understood if we remember that a simple legend has often been greatly modified and embellished by poets, so that we are required not only to divest the legend from these poetical additions, but to discover the true foundation of the simple legend itself.   After the time of Alexander the Great, when the creative genius of the Greeks had died away, they themselves undertook the task of collecting the ·mythical legends of their nation; and the rich stores of information accessible to them enabled them to reduce the whole mass to something resembling a continuous history; but they were ignorant in their notions about the nature of mythical legends, whence we cannot always place full confidence in their statements, nor can we distinguish the original materials which they collected, from the additions which they themselves devised as connecting links.

4. Thus, if we inquire after the primitive inhabitants of Greece, we meet with statements which have proved the greatest puzzle to all historians that have endeavoured to throw light upon the question.   The Hellenes, the name which subsequently belonged to the whole nation, appear in the earliest traditions as inhabiting only a part of Thessaly, whence they are said to have spread over the whole of continental Greece, and the islands surrounding it.   But while they were yet confined to a portion of Thessaly, they were surrounded on all sides by a great race commonly called Pelasgians. Who these Pelasgians were, is a question which the ancients themselves were unable to solve, and which modern writers have answered in the most different ways.   This much is certain, that in the remotest ages they occupied the north-western coasts of Asia Minor, and nearly the whole of Greece and Italy, and that in the historical

ages they had vanished everywhere, except in a few isolated places, where they maintained themselves and continued to speak their ancient language. It was this early disappearance of the Pelasgians that gave rise to the differences and contradictions in the traditions about them, for while some called them autochthones, that is, sprung from the earth itself, others state that they had immigrated from abroad, and had led a wandering life. The notion that they were autochthones implies no more than that they had inhabited the south-east of Europe from time immemorial, that is, probably from about the nineteenth century before Christ. The wandering character ascribed to them can scarcely be referred to the migrations that led them into Europe, but probably arose from the fact that, during the subsequent commotions in the countries occupied by them, they were expelled, and obliged to seek new homes in foreign countries, as, for example, during the changes which took place in Greece in and after the Trojan times. The most recent ethnological and philological inquiries have yielded the following results in regard to this intricate question, and we have no doubt as to their substantial correctness. The population of Europe emigrated from the East at a time which lies beyond all history. The first great body of immigrants was in all probability that which peopled the larger part of the south-east of Europe, and which we may call Pelasgians, for the name is of no consequence. They probably crossed the Hellespont, and occupied the countries to the south of mount Haemus and the Alps — one branch occupying the eastern peninsula of Greece, and the other the peninsula of Italy, in which countries they gradually proceeded from north to south. Some of these Pelasgians, however, appear to have remained in the north-west of Asia Minor, extending from the Hellespont to the river Maeander in the south. It is self-evident that many of the islands of the Ægean were likewise occupied by them. Some few parts of Greece appear about the same time to have been inhabited by tribes foreign to the Pelasgians. The races which at subsequent periods successively immigrated into Europe, and occupied the countries north of mount Haemus, were the Celts, Germans, and Slavonians, all of which must have proceeded from the same great parent stock, as their languages testify; but the affinity among the different tribes of the Pelasgians who took possession of Greece and Italy was much greater.

5. The Hellenes in Thessaly were probably only a distinct branch of the great Pelasgian race; at least we have every reason to believe that in language they differed no more than the Goths and Saxons, two tribes of the Germanic stock. This close affinity between Hellenes and Pelasgians also accounts for the fact, which would otherwise be inexplicable, that during the extension and conquests of the former, the latter so completely amalgamated and united

with them, that afterwards nearly all traces of the original differences disappeared — a result which could scarcely have followed, had the two races been quite distinct. As to the state of civilisation among the Pelasgians previous to their subjugation by, or amalgamation with the Hellenes, it has been asserted that they were little better than savages; but we have the strongest possible evidence that the whole race, even before the separation which led one branch into Greece and the other into Italy, had attained possession of at least the elements of civilisation. Many words referring to agriculture, the breeding of cattle, and human habitations, are common to the Sanscrit, Greek, and Latin, and thus prove that the things designated by such words must have been known to the nations before their separation and dispersion. The same fact is implied in various traditions, as, for example, that the first town on earth was built by a son of Pelasgus, that the most ancient towns and institutions in general are referred to the Pelasgians — that they invented a number of things required in agriculture, and lastly, that they were the first to make use of the alphabet which was introduced among the Greeks by the Phoenicians. Other evidences of the progress made in the arts of civilised life by those earliest inhabitants of Greece, exist at this day in many parts of Greece and Italy, in the gigantic remains of architectural structures, such as royal palaces, treasure-houses, and walls built of large square or polygon blocks. These we find in Italy, and in Arcadia, Argolis, and Epirus. Even large tunnels and dikes are ascribed to them.

6. Their religion consisted, no doubt, mainly in the worship of the powers of nature, many traces of which are visible also in the religion of the Hellenes, though they are more numerous in the purer religion of the Italians. Their principal god was Zeus, whose most ancient seat of worship was at Dodona in Epirus. He there also had an oracle which retained its celebrity for a very long period, until in the end it was eclipsed by that of Delphi. This male divinity had his counterpart in the female Dione, who was his wife, and the mother of Aphrodite, the goddess representing love and fertility. In some parts, such as the islands of Samothrace, Imbros, and Lemnos, in the north of the Ægean, a certain mysterious Pelasgic worship continued to exist down to a late period. The most remarkable branch of the Pelasgians were the Pierian Thracians, who inhabited the coast district of Macedonia north of mount Olympus, for mythology tells us that there the first poets flourished, such as Orpheus, Musaeus, Thamyris, Eumolpus, and Linus, all mythical personages who probably never existed; but the legends about them show that, according to the notions of the Greeks, poetry had been widely and enthusiastically cultivated by the Pelasgian Pierians, and had been employed by them for the exaltation and embellishment of their religious worship.

7. The civilisation thus commenced by the Pelasgians entered upon a new stage of development at the time when the Hellenes began to spread over central and southern Greece. The origin of the Hellenes is connected in the fabulous legends with the earliest period of the mythical ages, and their ancestral hero is called Hellen, a son of Deucalion and Pyrrha, the pair saved from the great flood. Hellen had three sons, Dorus, Xuthus, and Æolus, all of whom emigrated and took possession of the greater part of Greece. Xuthus, from whom no tribe derived its name, had two sons, Ion and Achaeus, to whom this honour was assigned. In this manner Greek mythology traced the four tribes into which the Greek nation was divided, viz., the Dorians, Ionians, Achaeans, and Æolians, to four descendants of Hellen. These heroes, like Hellen himself, and their stories, are neither historically nor poetically true; the heroes are nothing but ethnic symbols and artless personifications to represent the whole nation and the branches into which it was divided; and the story about them, in all probability, is one of those in which the later Greeks embodied their notions regarding the ancient state of things in their country, whence it cannot be regarded as a genuine ancient tradition. Other more ancient and more genuine traditions, as those in the Homeric poems, confine Hellen and the Hellenes to a part of Thessaly, and do not represent them as opposed to or distinct from the Pelasgians, but partially connect them, as, for example, when Poseidon is called the father of Achaeus and Pelasgus. Herodotus, so far from regarding Hellenes and Pelasgians as races opposed to each other, calls the Dorians a Hellenic and the Ionians a Pelasgian people, so that the Pelasgians are drawn into the circle of the Hellenes. The Æolians also are called Pelasgians. All this justifies the conclusion that not till several centuries after the Trojan times, when the Greeks had become conscious of their national unity, did the idea of deriving their origin from one common hero, and the several branches from his sons and grandsons, present itself to their minds. The reason why the Hellenes were privileged to give their name to the whole of Greece, is a subject on which we can only form conjectures.

8. At a time considerably more remote than the Trojan war, in which we find the Hellenes in the north, and the Achaeans in the south, the Hellenes, perhaps pressed on by neighbouring barbarians, quitted their Thessalian homes, and gradually spread over the whole of Greece, subduing, by their superiority in arms, the unwarlike tribes of the Pelasgians, and others with whom they came in contact. If we view the state of the country about the time of the Trojan war, we find in a part of Thessaly the Æolians, and along with them the Boeotians and Minyans, who were likewise Æolians; in another part of Thessaly, we find the Achaean Myrmidons or Hellenes, while other Achaeans occur in the east and south of Pelo-

ponnesus. The two races of the Achaeans and Æolians are the most prominent during the mythical period, while in the historical ages the Dorians and Ionians stand forth as the most conspicuous branches of the Hellenic race. The Dorians, during the legendary period, inhabited the small country of Doris, between mount Œta and Parnassus, while the Ionians were in possession of Attica, Euboea, and the north coast of Peloponnesus, which bore the name of Ægialeia. The manner in which the Hellenes became the masters of Greece, was not the same in all parts; in some instances the conquered Pelasgians were reduced to a state of servitude, in others, the conquerors and the conquered became completely united; and it may be assumed that in these latter cases, the old Pelasgian population was numerically far superior to the conquering Hellenes. This would account for the Ionians and Æolians being called Pelasgians, while the Dorians remained Hellenes. The civilisation which grew out of the Hellenisation of Greece was by no means a new one, but rather a continuation of that already commenced by the Pelasgians; a fresh impulse only was given by the Hellenes, themselves a branch of the Pelasgian stock, but "containing its best and purest blood, and destined to unfold the noblest faculties implanted in its constitution, and to raise the life of the nation to the highest stage which it was capable of reaching."

9. Such were the native elements constituting the nation of the Greeks. But there are also traditions stating that foreigners from distant countries immigrated into Greece, made its inhabitants acquainted with various arts and institutions of civilised life, and gave their names to cities and countries. The most celebrated among these alleged immigrants are Cecrops, reported to have come from Egypt, and built the Acropolis of Athens; Cadmus, the son of a Phoenician king, Agenor, who, when seeking his sister Europa, came to Boeotia, and there founded the Cadmea, the Acropolis of Thebes (he was also said to have introduced among the Greeks the arts of writing, and of melting and using metals); Danaus, who, with his fifty daughters, is reported to have come from Egypt, fleeing from his brother Ægyptus; and Pelops, lastly, a Phrygian or Lydian, a son of Tantalus, acquired dominion over a large part of Peloponnesus, and gave his name to the peninsula. Both the ancients and the moderns, until recent times, believed that these traditions were substantially correct, and that Greece received colonists, and some important religious and social institutions, from the east and from Egypt. But in our own days, very few men adhere to this antiquated belief. According to the genuine Attic tradition, Cecrops, the mythical founder of the Athenian state, was no foreigner at all, but an Attic autochthon, and the notion of his being an Egyptian did not become current until the fifth century B.C. It originated in the vanity of the Egyptian priests, who were anxious

to impress upon the Greeks that their institutions were all more or
less derived from Egypt. The story about Cadmus seems to have a
better foundation; not that a person of the name of Cadmus ever
lived, or did what tradition ascribes to him; but it cannot be denied
that in the earliest times there existed commercial relations between
the Greeks and Phoenicians, and it is an undoubted fact that the
Greeks derived their alphabet from the Phoenicians. The story of
Danaus can be shown to be of genuine Greek origin, and had originally nothing to do with Egypt; it may be traced to the same
source as the legend about Cecrops. The traditions about Pelops
are very contradictory, for Homer speaks of him not as a foreign
immigrant, but as a native prince, and others describe him as an
Achaean. The whole legend seems to be founded upon some vague
recollection of an ancient connection between Greece and a part of
Asia Minor.

10. But though we must reject these stories in the form in which
they have been transmitted to us, we need not on this account deny
that at some remote period adventurers, either singly or in bands,
immigrated into Greece and took up their permanent abode there;
we must, however, decidedly reject the idea that such adventurers
or exiles from foreign countries exercised any appreciable influence
upon the religious, social, or political institutions of the Greeks.
An original connection between the east and the earliest inhabitants
of Greece is an established fact, proved by ethnology and philology;
but the Greek language does not contain a trace of any influence
exercised by Semitic people or by the Egyptians. In most of the
traditions about foreign settlements in Greece, it is assumed that its
inhabitants lived in a state of wildness, and that they received the
first elements of civilisation from the foreign colonists; but we have
seen that these elements must have been known to the inhabitants
of Greece even before their separation from their kinsmen in India
and Italy. In matters of religion, on the other hand, it is equally
certain that the Greeks were much indebted to eastern nations, but
it is impossible to say how much of what they possessed in later
times was originally the common property of all the nations belonging to the same stock, and how much was imported at a subsequent
period, when the Pelasgians and Hellenes were already established
in Greece. Whatever we may think of these and similar matters,
certain it is that both the ideas and institutions which the Pelasgians brought with them from Asia, as well as those which were
subsequently imported to them from the same quarter, were in
Greece so much modified, and so changed in character, as to become
something quite different. Greek civilisation forms altogether a
striking contrast to that of oriental nations, by its freedom from
priestly thraldom, and by its active intellectual development in all
social and political relations.

11. If we follow the genealogies of the princely houses in the Greek legends, we find that the period from the sons of Hellen down to the fall of Troy embraces about six generations, or two hundred years, from B. C. 1400 to 1200, which form what may be properly termed the heroic age of Greece. This period is filled with accounts of the exploits of the heroes for the protection of the helpless and oppressed, against robbers, wild beasts, and monsters; it abounds in stories about adventures to satisfy ambition and the desire to possess what was deemed most precious. To ransack and destroy inoffensive towns, to roam about the sea for plunder, and carry away from the coast-districts cattle and men, and sell the latter as slaves, were not regarded as disreputable pursuits. But a right feeling of humanity, and a sense of awe for the gods, the avengers of all crimes, softened and subdued the violent passions of the Greeks of those days, who, during that period of chivalrous enterprise, strengthened their courage and were prevented by restless activity from sinking into barbarism and stolid insensibility. To refuse protection and support to a suppliant or beggar, to abuse the law of hospitality, was regarded as a grave offence against Zeus, the father of gods and men. Such were a few of the more prominent features of the Hellenes during the heroic period, which exhibit them in a light not unlike that of the chivalrous ages in the later history of Europe. Throughout that period the Hellenes appear as the ruling class, while the ancient conquered population was held in different degrees of subjection in the several parts of Greece.

12. None of the heroic families is more celebrated than that of Danaus in Argos, whose great grand-daughter Danae became, by Zeus, the mother of Perseus; from this latter was descended Heracles, the most illustrious of all the Greek heroes, a son of Zeus and Alcmena, the grand-daughter of Perseus. The numerous and gigantic exploits ascribed to him in the legends cannot have been performed by one man, or even by one generation of men. They may be divided into two classes, the first embodying all the labours and toils which mankind in its infancy has to sustain against nature; such are, for example, the stories of his having cleft rocks, turned the course of rivers, opened or stopped the subterraneous outlets of lakes, and cleared the land of noxious wild beasts. The second class of his exploits represents a state of society which is the natural result of the preceding one, when the different tribes have settled in fixed abodes, and are struggling with one another for possession and dominion. The hero accordingly appears as the protector of the weak and helpless, and as the chastiser of cruel tyrants. In all these rich and varied traditions, Heracles represents and embodies the history of two distinct phases in human progress. The exploits ascribed to him, especially those performed in foreign

lands, are probably of foreign, especially Phoenician origin, for the Heracles of that nation was worshipped in all their settlements round the Mediterranean, and the stories of his wanderings and exploits were incorporated by the Greeks with those of their own national hero.

13. Attica had its own hero in the person of Theseus, to whom, likewise, exploits are ascribed which can only have been the work of ages. His history, though rich and varied in detail, is as fabulous as that of the kings who are said to have preceded him. He is described as a son of Ægeus and Æthra, the daughter of a king of Troezen. To him are ascribed similar adventures and exploits as those related of Heracles, and which must therefore be viewed in the same light. But he is especially celebrated in Attic story as the hero who united the independent towns, or political communities of the country, into one state, who divided the people into three classes, and who laid the foundation of the political constitution of Athens. His story is closely connected with that of another hero, Minos, King of Crete, who ruled over the sea by his mighty fleets, and levied a heavy tribute upon Athens, from which Theseus delivered his country by slaying the monster Minotaurus. Minos is, like Theseus, described as a wise, political legislator, though the laws commonly ascribed to him belong to a much later period, being the work of Dorian settlers in Crete, who did not establish themselves in the island until the period between the fall of Troy and the occupation of Peloponnesus by the same race.

14. We might here enumerate a great many other heroes and their exploits, such as the tragic fate of the royal house of Thebes, and the story of the Calydonian hunt; but we must confine ourselves to a notice of two celebrated expeditions to foreign lands, which were conducted by confederate chieftains and their followers — we mean the expedition of the Argonauts, and that against Troy. The form in which the story of the former is usually related runs as follows :—Shortly before the outbreak of the Trojan war, Jason, a Thessalian prince, excited the jealousy of his kinsman, Pelias of Iolcos, who persuaded the prince to embark in a maritime expedition full of danger, in the hope that he might perish abroad. He was to sail to Colchis, on the eastern shore of the Black sea, thence to fetch the golden fleece there prepared. A vessel was built of unusual size, and, accompanied by a band of the most illustrious heroes from various parts of Greece, Jason set sail. After many adventures they reached Colchis, and not only gained their end, but Jason carried off Media, the daughter of the Colchian king Æetes, through whose assistance he had obtained the golden fleece. The return of the heroes was connected with as many adventures as their voyage to Colchis. The story of which this is an outline, seems to be almost wholly a poetical invention:

11 *

the adventure is incomprehensible in its design, astonishing in its execution, connected with no conceivable cause, and is attended with no sensible effect. It is impossible to conceive whence the Greeks at that age could have acquired a knowledge of Colchis, and still more that at that early period they should have ventured on a maritime expedition to so distant a region. The object of the undertaking is still more mysterious, and can be explained only by conjectures. The story about the fleece itself was, that Phrixus, having been rescued from his father's vengeance, had been transported by a ram across the sea to Colchis, and that on his arrival there he had sacrificed the ram to Zeus, and nailed the fleece to an oak in the grove of Ares, where it was carefully kept and guarded. The story about the Argonauts does not appear to have any historical foundation, nor to be connected with commerce, piracy, or discovery, unless it be that a series of maritime enterprises have been combined, extended, and embellished by the poets, for an audience always ready to listen to accounts of distant travels and voyages. It is also possible that the whole story merely indicates the beginnings of an intercourse between the northern Greeks and the inhabitants of the opposite coast of Asia; and it was perhaps not without reason that some of the ancients stated that the expedition of the Argonauts gave rise to the second of the above-mentioned expeditions, that against Troy.

15. The Trojan war is the noblest and most celebrated of all the enterprises of the heroic age, and this renown it owes to the immortal poem of the Iliad, the work of Homer. The story is briefly this :—Aphrodite, the goddess of love, had promised to Paris, the son of king Priam of Troy, the most beautiful wife, because he had adjudged to her the prize of beauty. This wife was no other than Helen, the daughter of Zeus and Leda, who was then married to Menelaus, king of Sparta, and brother of Agamemnon, king of Mycenae. Paris, when on a visit to Menelaus, violated the laws of hospitality by carrying off Helen with many treasures; and the Trojans, when called upon to surrender her, refused to comply with the request. Such conduct called for revenge; all the chiefs of Greece, looking upon the outrage as committed against them, united, under the supreme command of Agamemnon, for a common expedition against Troy. Although Agamemnon was the king of kings, swift-footed Achilles, the son of the goddess Thetis, surpassed him and all others in heroic courage and valour. In nearly twelve hundred ships the heroes and their followers sailed across to the coast of Asia, and besieged the city for a period of ten years. The Trojans, among whom Hector, a son of Priam, was the chief champion, defended themselves manfully, and sometimes threatened the Greeks with destruction. This happened during the time when Achilles took no part in the contest, because he thought himself wronged by

Agamemnon. The Trojans were assisted by auxiliaries from various parts of Asia Minor, and even from the far-distant east. The great gods also took part in the war, some favouring the Greeks and others the Trojans. But in the tenth year of the contest, Troy fell through the well-known stratagem of the wooden horse, according to the common belief, in the year b. c. 1184.

The story of the war of Troy and its conquest cannot be without some historical foundation, although its cause and the details related by the poet may be all fictitious. The Trojan war, as a general fact, cannot be denied. Attacks may have been repeatedly made upon Asia by the Hellenes for plunder, or more probably for the purpose of obtaining permanent settlements on the coasts, and it is not impossible that such expeditions may have given rise to a war which assumed, in the hands of poets, the form in which it has been handed down to us. Although Troy is said to have been destroyed at the end of the war, a Trojan state survived the fall of its capital, which was probably rebuilt, for we hear that it was destroyed a second time by the Phrygians, a Thracian people who entered Asia after the Trojan war.

16. The return of the heroes from Troy formed a distinct circle of epic poetry, of which the Odyssey forms only a small part, and which was full of tragic and marvellous adventures. The consequeuces of the war were no less disastrous to the conquering heroes than to the vanquished, for the former found their thrones occupied by usurpers, or their kingdoms in a state of anarchy, and many perished on their way homeward. In short, all the heroes disappear shortly after the Trojan war, and the heroic age comes to its close; we have arrived at the point which forms the transition from one period to another entirely new and different. A second consequence of the war was no doubt the acquisition by the Greeks of a more perfect knowledge of the eastern coasts and of the islands of the Ægean. It is not impossible that the Æolian colonies in Asia Minor, which are commonly said to have been planted about one or two generations after the Trojan war, consisted to a great extent of Greeks, who never returned from the Trojan expedition, for those colonies claimed Agamemnon as their ancestor. Certain, however, it is, that the foundation of the Æolian colonies, on the northwestern coast of Asia Minor, was the natural result of the Trojan war, and of the knowledge which the Greeks had acquired of those countries during the progress of the war.

17. We have already spoken in general terms of the more prominent characteristic features of the heroic age. We shall now endeavour to see what more we can learn from the Homeric poems about the government, social condition, religion, and arts during the same period; for it must be remembered that on these subjects the Iliad and Odyssey contain information as trustworthy as if they

were historical documents. Slavery existed in most parts of Greece ; slaves were chiefly employed in domestic service about their masters and mistresses, in gardening, and attending to the flocks and cattle. They were nearly in all cases persons taken prisoners in war or bought of pirates, or the children of such persons born and bred in the house of their master. We never hear of a whole population having been reduced to slavery by conquerors. Husbandry was carried on by freemen who served the wealthy landowners for hire. These latter formed a higher order, distinguished by birth, and generally by valour, wisdom, and a love of adventure. They were the nobles or the chiefs of the nation—one among whom was the head of all, and bore the title of king, for the kingly form of government was universally established in Greece during the heroic period ; but the king was only the first among his equals, who assisted him with their counsel. The people in every Greek state were divided into gené or clans, which were bound together by certain religious observances. Laws, in our sense of the term, did not exist—all rights and duties being fixed by ancient usage, and confirmed by successive precedents. The whole nation consisted of several tribes and numerous little independent states, and the legend of the Trojan war presents to us the first instance of a united national enterprise. The name Hellenes does not yet occur as a general designation of all the Greeks, who are generally called Achaei, Danai, or Argives.

18. The social relations in the heroic age were extremely simple. The conduct of women was under less restraint than at a later period, and maidens of the highest rank had to perform the ordinary domestic duties, down to fetching water and washing. A father had the absolute right of disposing of his daughter's hand, and at the marriage both parties made presents to each other. Many of the female characters in the Homeric poems command our respect and admiration, and are among the noblest conceptions of the poet, though we can hardly imagine that they are types of the whole sex at the time. The food of the Greeks, as at all subsequent times, was of the simplest kind, but singing and dancing were among the favourite amusements and ornaments of their social gatherings. Excessive drinking is hardly ever mentioned. Towards their inferiors the Greeks were kind and amiable, and their severity towards slaves was never wanton. In war, however, quarter was not given, unless it were to obtain a large ransom, and acts of ferocious cruelty were often indulged in. Great care, however, was taken to secure an honourable burial for the slain. Conquered cities were generally treated with merciless cruelty, the men being put to death, and women and children distributed among the conquerors as slaves.

19. The religion of the heroic age was only a further development

of that of the Pelasgians, and not essentially different from that which we find established during the historical ages. The Greek strongly sympathised with the outward world, and in all the objects around him he found life, or imparted it to them from the fulness of his own imagination. Every part of nature roused in him a distinct sentiment of religious awe, and everywhere he found divine powers to worship. The complicated system of mythology which arose out of this simple worship of the powers of nature, was formed partly by a process of personification, and partly by raising the local divinities of certain tribes to the rank of national gods, by connecting and uniting them into one great family. These processes were the work of the national mind of the Greeks, strengthened and guided by the poets. Each tribe and city, however, continued to worship one or more deities as its special patrons or protectors. All the gods were conceived as beings with human forms, and as subject to the same passions and frailties as mortals; but they were nevertheless believed to punish men for their offences, both in this world and in their future state. Prayers and sacrifices were employed to obtain their favour, and the more precious the offering was, the more pleasing it was thought to be to the deity. Hence the sacrifice of human life was the highest oblation. The gods were represented in statues and symbols, but we must not believe that these statues or symbols themselves were worshipped as the divine beings; such gross idolatry seems to have arisen only in later times, when the symbol was confounded with the power symbolised. The functions of the priests, both male and female, who were generally connected with the worship of some particular divinity, consisted mainly in offering sacrifices, though the kings and fathers of families might do the same on behalf of those whom they represented. The most important branch, however, of a priest's duties, consisted in his ascertaining the will of the gods, and those occurrences of the future which the faculties of man were unable to divine. The belief in the possibility of obtaining such knowledge gave rise to oracular places, the most renowned of which were Dodona and Delphi; but many other methods also were resorted to, to discover the will of the gods or the decrees of destiny. The awe and reverence for departed great men gradually led to hero-worship, which, common as it was in later times, is never alluded to in the Homeric poems.

20. In regard to the knowledge possessed by the Greeks during the heroic age, and the arts they cultivated, we find that their geographical information was almost confined to Greece, the islands of the Ægean, and the north-western parts of Asia Minor; all the rest of the ancient world was known only from vague rumours and reports, whence the poet's descriptions of foreign lands are full of most marvellous circumstances. The whole earth is conceived as a

plane surface, surrounded by the river Oceanus; the Mediterranean was only a depression of the earth's surface, the central point of which was Delphi. A vast pit in the earth, called Hades, was the receptacle of the departed spirits, and far below the earth lay the still more dismal pit of Tartarus. Mount Olympus, in Thessaly, was regarded as the highest mountain on earth, and as the habitation of the gods; and the vault of heaven was considered to be a solid vault of metal, supported by Atlas, who kept asunder heaven and earth.

Navigation was still in its infancy, and consisted mainly in coasting or sailing from island to island. The largest ships which sailed against Troy, are said to have carried one hundred and twenty men, though probably they did not really contain more than fifty. Engagements at sea are never mentioned. Astronomy as a science can hardly be said to have existed. All the Greeks, down to the time of Solon, divided the year into twelve lunar months, the defects of which were remedied by occasional intercalations. Commerce was indeed carried on, but was not held in great esteem by a nation which regarded the pursuit of war as more honourable, and piracy as more lucrative. Money is not mentioned by the poet, so that all commerce must have been carried on by barter. The wealthy heroes appear to have lived not only in rude plenty, but in a high degree of luxury and splendour; but we must remember that the poet, in descriptions of this kind, was not obliged always to adhere strictly to the real state of things. The arts amongst the Greeks, if compared with those of eastern nations, can scarcely be said to have advanced beyond a state of infancy.

The art of war was in a similar condition. In the Iliad we hear much of the combats of chiefs, but little or nothing of engagements of the masses; and the contests are decided by the valour of individual heroes, or by the interposition of the gods. The art of besieging a town seems to have been utterly unknown.

21. Although the poems bearing the name of Homer are the most ancient in European literature, yet they are by no means the first attempts that were made in poetry. The Homeric poems themselves furnish evidence of its having been cultivated before the Iliad and Odyssey were composed. The poet or minstrel, in the heroic age, was held in the highest honour by the chiefs and heroes; his presence was welcomed at all their feasts as that of a divinely inspired personage, for it was the poet who exalted and embellished the exploits of the heroes, whose deeds formed his principal themes. Another kind of poetry consisted of religious hymns to soothe the anger or win the favour of the gods. Music was always, and dancing occasionally, united with the recital of poetry. In connection with this early poetry, we must consider the art of writing which had been introduced among the Greeks at an early period by the

Phoenicians. Homer himself does not distinctly allude to it in any part of his poems, though it ought not to be inferred from this that it was unknown in his time. As to whether the Homeric poems were originally composed in writing, is a question which has been much discussed in modern times, though it is highly probable that at first they were not committed to writing, but composed by the poet, and retained in his memory, and that for a considerable time they were propagated only by oral tradition. No one now doubts that the Iliad is substantially the work of one genius; but it is more doubtful as to whether both the Iliad and the Odyssey are the productions of the same poet. The time in which Homer himself is believed to have lived, is separated by several generations from the Trojan war. Hesiod, some of whose productions have come down to our time, is a poet of a somewhat later period than Homer.

<hr>

CHAPTER III.

HISTORY OF THE DORIC STATES FROM THE RETURN OF THE HERACLEIDS, DOWN TO THE END OF THE SECOND MESSENIAN WAR.

1. ABOUT sixty years after the fall of Troy, during which period no change is recorded in the history of Greece, great commotions arose in the country in consequence of immigrations from the north. The first of these is the immigration of the Thessalians from Epirus into the country afterwards called Thessaly, in consequence of which the original inhabitants, as the Boeotians and Achaeans, were partly reduced to a state of servitude, and partly compelled to emigrate. The Boeotians took forcible possession of the country, subsequently called after them Boeotia. Here again the Cadmeans and Minyans being driven from their homes, and joined by Achaeans from Peloponnesus, are said to have crossed the Ægean, and established in the north-west of Asia Minor the settlements known under the name of the Æolian colonies. But it has already been remarked (p. 127) that these colonies probably were in a closer connection with the expedition against Troy than this tradition seems to indicate.

A much more important movement was that occasioned by the migration of the Dorians from their little country on the north of mount Parnassus to Peloponnesus, of which they conquered the fairest provinces. The fact of this migration, which is generally assigned to the year B. C. 1104, cannot be doubted, although there are questions connected with it which cannot be answered in a satisfactory manner. First of all, it is hardly conceivable that the little country afterwards known by the name of Doris should have sent forth bands conquering nearly the whole of Peloponnesus, although we may admit that the conquerors in this, as in many other cases were far less numerous than the conquered. Secondly, the manner in which the descendants of Heracles are mixed up with the migration is altogether fabulous. The consequence of this migration however was, that the population of the peninsula changed its character; the hardy Dorians either crushed the original inhabitants and reduced them to a state of servitude, or expelled them and forced them to seek new homes in foreign lands. The mountainous country of Arcadia, inhabited from time immemorial by Pelasgians, remained free, though its population, being surrounded on all sides by Dorian Hellenes, gradually lost their primitive character, and became Hellenes. The cause of the migration was intimately connected in the tradition with the story about the descendants of Heracles. They had, it is said, a legitimate claim to the succession to the throne of Argos, and made repeated attempts by force of arms to gain possession of it, until at length the three brothers Aristodemus, Temenus, and Cresphontes, supported by Dorians, Ætolians, and Locrians, crossed the entrance of the Corinthian gulf at Naupactus, and having conquered Tisamenus, a grandson of Agamemnon, divided the best portions of Peloponnesus among themselves.

2. Oxylus, an Ætolian chief who had guided the invaders, claimed and obtained as his share in the conquest the fertile country of Ellis, which he is said to have governed wisely and mildly, taking only a portion of the land for his followers, and leaving the remainder in the hands of the original inhabitants. Tisamenus, with many of his Achaean followers, attempted to obtain peaceful settlements among the Ionians on the north coast of Peloponnesus, but failing in this, he overcame them in a battle, and forced them to quit their country. Ionia henceforth bore the name of Achaia, and the exiled Ionians found refuge among their kinsmen in Attica; but as that country was too small, the Ionians, accompanied by numerous other adventurers, emigrated to the western coast of Asia Minor, where they founded what are called the Ionian colonies. In the meantime the Heracleid chiefs were engaged in dividing the conquest among themselves. Eurysthenes and Procles, the twin-sons of Aristodemus, obtained Laconia, Temenus, Argos, and Cresphontes Messenia. The conquest thus described in the traditions cannot possibly have been accomplished at once, or even within a short period. It is well known that Argos was not conquered until after a long protracted war. Pylos, in Messenia, even after the

conquest of the rest of the country, was for centuries ruled by the descendants of its ancient king Neleus. In Laconia the Dorian conquerors are said to have met with little resistance. Eurysthenes and Procles, who fixed their residence at Sparta, are reported to have allowed the conquered Achaeans the same rights as the conquering Dorians; but Agis, the successor of Eurysthenes, reduced the Achaeans to the condition of subjects, and all yielded except the inhabitants of the town of Helos, who, however, were compelled to submit, and lost not only their political independence, but their personal liberty, giving rise and name to the class of serfs called Helots. In this story also the vanity of the conquerors is but too apparent, and we know on very good authority that Amyclae, which is said to have capitulated at once, remained an independent little state in Laconia for a period of nearly three hundred years. Helos seems to have maintained its independence even later, and it is in short more than probable that the Dorians in Laconia as well as elsewhere had to struggle for a long period before they were complete masters of the countries once occupied by the Achaeans. A little later than the invasion of Peloponnesus, Corinth also was conquered by a Heracleid of the name of Aletes accompanied by Dorian adventurers, and the race of Sisyphus was dethroned. This event brought the conquering Dorians into conflict with Attica, which was then governed by Codrus, a son of Melanthus. The Dorians, in consequence of the wars and their devastations, it is said, suffering from scarcity in their newly conquered countries, resolved upon invading Attica, under the leadership of Aletes of Corinth. Accordingly they encamped in Attica, and the oracle of Delphi had promised them success, provided they spared the life of the Athenian king. This oracle had become known to the Athenians, and their king resolved to sacrifice himself for his country. Disguised in a woodman's garb, he went among the Dorians and killed one with his bill, whereupon he himself was slain by another. When the Dorians discovered what had taken place, they despaired of success, and withdrew their forces from Attica.

3. About the same time Megara, which had until then belonged to Attica, was separated from it, being occupied by a Dorian colony from Corinth, by which it was afterwards held in subjection. Ægina was likewise seized by Dorians from Epidaurus. But by far the most important Dorian colonies were those established in Crete during the third generation after the conquest of Peloponnesus. These colonies were founded by Dorians from Sparta and Argos, who during the broils and conflicts in Peloponnesus were induced to seek new homes elsewhere. Some of these emigrants, who cannot have been very numerous, established themselves in Rhodes, which henceforth became a Dorian island. The conquest of Crete is said to have been a matter of little difficulty, as the island had

12

been desolated by pestilence and famine; but it must nevertheless have taken some time before the Dorians became complete masters of it. The political institutions of Crete, greatly resembling those of Sparta, are said by some to have been introduced into the latter city from the island, while others maintain that the Cretan towns derived them from Sparta. The real truth, however, seems to be that neither place derived them from the other, but that they were the common institutions of the Doric race, which carried them with it wherever it formed settlements, though we do not deny that some of those institutions may have existed in Crete ever since the time of king Minos, to whom the Dorians of Crete were inclined to trace them, for the purpose of making them appear more ancient and venerable. All the inhabitants of Crete were divided into three classes, freemen, slaves, and periocci, the last of whom probably were the ancient proprietors of the soil, but were compelled to live in open towns and villages, and had to pay a certain tax to their Doric rulers, though they were personally free. The government, the administration, and the making of the laws, were in the hands of the Doric freemen, who also reserved other rights and privileges for themselves, though their rule does not appear to have been very oppressive. The slaves were either persons who had forcibly resisted the invaders, or such as had been slaves before. The land was partly left to its former owners, and partly taken possession of by the new colonists; but besides these portions, each state set apart a domain for itself which was cultivated by public slaves. All the land was tilled by the perioeci and slaves, while the Dorians knew no other pursuits but those of war, and lived by the toil of their subjects and slaves. The form of government was nearly the same in all the Doric colonies of Crete, which shows that it had a national character, and was not the result of accident. Kings are not mentioned, but their place was supplied by ten annual magistrates bearing the title of cosmoi, who were elected from among the most illustrious families by the body of free citizens. At the end of their year of office, the cosmoi might be elected into the senate, called geronia or bulé, of which they remained members for life. The number of senators in each state seems to have been thirty. This constitution was evidently thoroughly aristocratic. The assembly of the people, consisting of the free Doric citizens, might be convened by the magistrates whenever they thought it advisable, but its members seem to have had little power beyond giving their assent to the measures brought before them.

4. The most striking feature in the Cretan mode of life, though this too they had in common with most other Doric states, was the custom according to which all the citizens, old and young, took their meals together at public tables and at the expense of the state. These public meals, which were elsewhere called syssitia, bore in

Crete the name of andreia or andria. They kept up among the ruling class a feeling of unity and of superiority over their subjects, and bound together the citizens by close intimacy, while the young had opportunities of listening to the opinions and views of the older men. Besides this, however, the conduct of boys and youths was strictly watched by persons appointed for the purpose. Their training and education were conducted with the same severity and harshness as at Sparta. Institutions like these occur more or less in all the Doric states of Greece, a fact which shows incontrovertibly that they were not the work of any particular lawgiver, but the natural results of the character of the Doric race.

5. Although the history of the Doric states of Peloponnesus during the first centuries after their formation is extremely obscure, yet it is evident that Sparta was the chief among them, and that the Doric institutions there were more fully developed than in any other state. These circumstances, and the conquest of Messenia by Sparta, raised her in the course of time to the supremacy not only of Peloponnesus but of Greece, and the greatness and glory she thus acquired have shed a lustre over her whole history which in many respects is not well deserved. The constitution of Sparta is generally ascribed to Lycurgus, who is believed either to have devised it, or at least to have introduced it among his countrymen. But if we look to the nature of the Spartan institutions, and compare them with those of other Doric states, it becomes highly probable that they cannot have been the work of one particular mind, but that the ground-work at least was common to all the Dorians, so that Lycurgus, if he ever existed, cannot have done much more than systematise and supplement that which he already found in operation. The mythical character of the history of this renowned lawgiver is further confirmed by the different statements about his descent and the time when he flourished, for while some regard him as a contemporary of the Heracleid conquerors, others place him more than two hundred years later, that is, about B. C. 884. Sparta was governed by two kings descended from Aristodemus, whose two sons, Eurysthenes and Procles, ruled the kingdom in common, and Lycurgus was generally believed to have been connected with one of these royal houses. By an act of justice and generosity he secured the succession to a posthumous son of his brother; and as this involved him in unpleasantries with the infant's mother, who wished to marry him, he left his country and spent the best part of his life in foreign lands, though his countrymen often invited him to return. He is said to have gathered information in the most distant countries, and on his return he found Lacedaemon in a state of anarchy and political dissolution. The need of reform was generally felt, and having secured the favour of a large body of the leading men at Sparta, and been declared by the Delphic oracle to be wiser than ordinary mor-

tals, he successively procured the enactment of a series of ordinances, by which the civil and military constitution of the state, the distribution of property, the education of the citizens, and the regulation of their daily life and intercourse, were fixed as on a sacred and immutable basis. Having accomplished his great work in spite of violent opposition, he went to Delphi, having previously bound his fellow citizens by a solemn oath to make no change in his laws until his return. The lawgiver himself, however, never returned, and an oracle was transmitted to Sparta declaring that she should flourish as long as she observed his laws. When, where, and how he died was never known, but the Spartans honoured him as a god with a temple and annual sacrifices.

6. This story about the famous Spartan lawgiver was believed by nearly all the ancients, and one fact seems to be clear from their concurrent testimony, that the legislation, which is described as the work of Lycurgus, delivered Sparta from anarchy and the evils of misrule, and that it formed the commencement of a long period of tranquillity and order. The reforms which were introduced affected the whole country of Laconia, and the private as well as the public life of its inhabitants. The great object of the legislator seems to have been to maintain the sovereignty of Sparta over the rest of Laconia, and to unite the Spartans among themselves by the closest ties. The ancient usages and customs now assumed the character of strict law, sanctioned and hallowed by religion. In order to gain a basis for his new regulations, the lawgiver is said to have made an entirely new division of all the landed property in Laconia, thus removing the causes of discord, and facilitating the reform of abuses, which feuds and quarrels among the Doric rulers themselves seem to have produced.

7. Lycurgus, then, is said first of all to have divided Laconia, so far as it was then subject to Sparta, into thirty-nine thousand lots, of which nine thousand were assigned to Spartan families, and thirty thousand to the free Laconian subjects. As it is scarcely possible to conceive the existence of so many Spartan and Laconian families, we are perhaps justified in preferring another account, which speaks of only four thousand lots assigned to the Spartans by Lycurgus, and mentions that this number was doubled after the conquest of Messenia. There can be no doubt that in this distribution the ruling Spartans selected for themselves the most fertile and valuable portions of the country, to maintain their families and their numerous slaves. Some parts of the land, however, remained the property of the state, being its domain, while others continued, as before, to be the property of temples. How far these agrarian regulations were new, and how far the legislator only fixed by law what had been long established by custom, cannot be ascertained.

8. All the inhabitants of Laconia were divided into three ranks

or classes.—1. The Dorians of Sparta; 2. The serfs or Helots; and 3. The subject people of Laconia. The last were chiefly Achaeans, that is, the ancient inhabitants of the country, intermixed with strangers that had accompanied the Dorians at the time of the invasion. For the purpose of weakening them, the Spartans dispersed them over the country in open towns and villages. The ruling Dorians of Sparta always looked upon them with jealousy and a degree of fear. These Laconians had no political rights, but had to bear the heaviest public burdens, and to fight the battles, the main object of which was to gratify the pride and ambition of their rulers. Personally, however, they were free, and enjoyed the undivided possession of the trade and manufactures of the country; for the higher as well as the lower arts were looked upon as degrading to a Spartan. The Helots or serfs were probably the descendants of those Achaeans who, in consequence of their obstinate resistance to the invading Dorians, had been reduced to slavery. Their condition was most wretched; they were always feared and suspected by their masters, and atrocious violence was often resorted to, to reduce their strength or break their spirit. They were bound to the soil, and could not be torn from it, or sold into another country; some were employed in domestic, and others in public works; by zeal and industry, however, they might obtain their freedom. When a Spartan went out as a soldier in time of war, he was always attended by a number of Helots, who then had an opportunity of enriching themselves by the spoil. These advantages, however, which the Spartan slaves had in common with those of all other ancient nations, were more than counterbalanced by the inhuman cruelty with which they were treated by their masters; and on one occasion two thousand of them were murdered for no other reason than because they were brave men. It would seem also that in later times the condition of the Helots became worse than it had been originally. No wonder, therefore, that their masters lived in perpetual fear of them. The Spartans, that is, the ruling body of Heracleid and Doric conquerors, were entirely dependent upon their slaves, who cultivated their lands, and attended on them in time of war and during their stay at home; the Helot had to work and toil for his master, without ever enjoying the results of his labours. The ruling body of the Spartans had all equal rights, and formed a class like the Roman patricians, resembling, in many points, a modern aristocracy. They were the only real citizens of the state, all the rest being subjects and slaves. The Dorians at Sparta, as everywhere else, were divided into three tribes, just as the Ionians always formed four; their names at Sparta were Hylleans, Dymanes, and Pamphylians, and these three tribes were subdivided into thirty obae. It is not known whether the Hylleans, who claimed to be descended from Heracles, and to whom

12 *

the royal families belonged, had any privileges not shared by the two other tribes.

9. As all free Spartans, except the two kings, had equal rights, their constitution may be called a democracy, with two hereditary magistrates at its head; but in relation to the Laconians scattered over the country, it was a rigid aristocracy, which clung to the ancient forms of the constitution even at a time when its spirit had completely departed. The spirit of the Spartans was eminently conservative, so that in later times their constitution was in constant antagonism to the spirit of the age, which required reforms and improvements. The men who saw the evil and attempted reforms fell victims to their endeavours. The sovereign power at Sparta, as in all other ancient republics, resided in the assembly of the citizens, which was convened by the magistrates at stated periods, but could only accept or reject the measures brought before it—all discussion as well as the proposing of amendments being confined to persons in office. Such assemblies were no part of the legislation of Lycurgus, any more than the existence of a senate or council of elders, called gerusia, but had existed from time immemorial, and probably all that the lawgiver did, was to regulate and organise that which had existed as an ancient usage. The senate consisted of twenty-eight members, or, including the two kings, thirty, each representing one of the thirty obae. They were elected by the kings, without regard to anything except age and personal merit, and no one could become a member of the gerusia before he had completed his sixtieth year; but then they held their office for life. They had to prepare the measures that were brought before the assembly of the citizens, and in early times their authority must have been more extensive than afterwards, for the two kings had in the gerusia no more power than any other senator; but in later times, when part of their functions were assumed by the ephors, who bear some resemblance to the Roman tribunes of the plebs, the influence of both the senate and the kings was reduced to comparative insignificance.

10. It is remarkable that while the kingly dignity was abolished in all other parts of Greece, it was maintained at Sparta almost as long as it formed an independent state. Its powers, however, were in the course of time considerably reduced by the institution of the ephorate. The chief functions of the kings were to command the armies, of which they seem originally to have had the uncontrolled direction; besides this, they were the high priests of the nation, more especially priests of Zeus, and had a kind of jurisdiction which was afterwards greatly limited. However, although the power of the kings was not very great, the honours attached to their station were by no means insignificant, for they were revered as the chief magistrates and as connected with the gods

by their descent; and besides possessing extensive demesnes in various parts of the country, they received certain payments in kind which enabled them to maintain their household and to exercise great hospitality. The time when ephors were appointed is uncertain, some assigning the institution to Lycurgus and others to a later period, though the probability is that they too were an ancient Doric magistracy which had existed long before the time of the lawgiver. They were five in number, and were elected annually. They exercised from the first a kind of superintendence and jurisdiction over the civil affairs of the Spartans; but their political importance belongs to a later period.

11. The principle pervading the whole Spartan constitution was that a citizen was born and lived only for the state, that his substance, time, strength, faculties, and affections, were to be dedicated to its service, and that its welfare and glory should be his happiness and honour; and this principle was the necessary result of the circumstances under which a handfull of Dorians had become masters of a country with a population far more numerous than themselves. As the Spartans were a close aristocracy, their numbers continually decreased, and as their property could not be sold, but always descended to the eldest son, or in default of a male heir to the eldest daughter, the landed estates in the end accumulated in the hands of a few immensely wealthy proprietors, while a great many persons lived in extreme poverty. Money was not coined at Sparta even at the time when all the other Greek states had long adopted it as a convenience; the possession of precious metals was forbidden as dangerous, and bars or pieces of iron continued to be the only legal currency at Sparta down to the latest times. This prohibition of the precious metals, however, applied to the Spartans only, the Laconians not being affected by it, for they were free in their commercial dealings with other states. A regulation like this is always sure to defeat its own ends, and the Spartans in later times were notorious above all other Greeks for their avarice. The women, the mothers of the brave warriors, were much more respected and honoured at Sparta than in other parts of Greece, and some of them have acquired a renown in history which is scarcely inferior to that of the noblest Roman matrons. The education of young men for the service of the state was conducted with particular care. Its sphere was very narrow, for all that was aimed at was to train men who were to live in the midst of difficulty and danger, and who should be equally ready to command and to obey; the cultivation of the intellect and the feelings was totally neglected. Sickly or deformed infants were exposed in a glen of mount Taygetus. Warlike poetry and music, however, were much enjoyed by the Spartans, whence the Iliad became very popular among them at an early period, and Tyrtaeus was held in high honour. The other

amusements of the Spartans, young and old, were the palaestra or gymnastic exercises and the chase. They were soldiers from the age of maturity down to their sixtieth year.

12. All the institutions of Sparta were of a one-sided character, and the unlimited admiration bestowed upon them by both ancient and modern writers has in our time given way to a more correct estimate. In all their movements, the Spartans were cautious and slow; war was their element, and this spirit was maintained by their ancient system of tactics. The main strength of the army consisted in its heavy-armed infantry, the only mode of service which was thought worthy of a free Spartan. The cavalry never acquired any great efficiency at Sparta. The Helots formed the light infantry. Sparta, moreover, was never distinguished for its navy; its great strength always lay in its land force.

13. It was not till about a century after the time in which Lycurgus is commonly said to have lived, that all Laconia was subdued by its Dorian conquerors, and in the enjoyment of a period of repose. The institutions of Lycurgus made the Spartans strong and united; and having for centuries been accustomed to war with the ancient Achaean population of the country, they seem now to have been impatient for fresh enterprises. Jealousy appears to have sprung up between Argos and Sparta about the possession of the eastern coast of Laconia, which had originally belonged to Argos. Of this district the Spartans made themselves masters; and the result was a series of hostilities, in the course of which attempts were also made to conquer Tegea in Arcadia; they were often renewed, but always failed.

14. An easier and more inviting conquest offered itself in the west. It was probably not without jealousy and envy that the Dorians of Laconia observed that Messenia was a much fairer and more fertile country than their own, and a pretext for war was easily found. The Dorians in Messenia, moreover, had acted very differently towards the Achaean population, which, having submitted to the invaders without much resistance, had been treated with moderation and mildness by the conquerors. The first Dorian king, Cresphontes, is even said to have formed plans for uniting the Dorians and Achaeans into one people. The jealousy of his Dorian subjects, indeed, thwarted this scheme; but it was taken up again by his son Ægyptus, and carried His successors followed the same policy, and the country prospered, and the arts of peace flourished under it. The arts of war were probably not so much cultivated there as at Sparta, and this may have been another reason why the Spartans thought it an easy matter to conquer their neighbours. Such temptations rendered it easy for them to find a pretext for war.

15. Irritations and provocations are said to have occurred at different times; but the event which finally led to the outbreak of

war, was a private wrong committed by a Spartan against a Messenian. The result was, that in B. C. 743 the Spartans bound themselves by an oath not to cease warring against Messenia until the country should be made theirs by the right of conquest; and soon afterwards they invaded it, massacred the defenceless inhabitants, and established themselves in the fortified town of Amphea. Thus commenced the first Messenian war, which lasted from B. C. 743 to 724. The accounts which we have of it, as well as those of the second war, are little more than poetical lays or popular traditions. After the lapse of several years, during which the Spartans had constantly made ravaging excursions from Amphea, and the Messenians had suffered severely, the latter fortified themselves in the stronghold on mount Ithome. Victory was promised by an oracle to the Messenians, on condition of a pure virgin being sacrificed to the infernal gods; and when it became known to the Spartans that the sacrifice had been made, they were discouraged, until after several years their king, Theopompus, again led an army into the country, and fought a battle. The Messenian king was slain, and was succeeded by Aristodemus, whose daughter had been sacrificed for her country. He won the hearts of the people, governed them wisely, and formed an alliance with the Arcadians. The war continued in the form of petty inroads and ravages, which were renewed every year at the harvest season, and it was not till the fifth year of the reign of Aristodemus, that a pitched battle was fought at the foot of mount Ithome, in which the Spartans and their allies were defeated. But various oracles and successful stratagems of the Spartans, in the end reduced Aristodemus to despair, in which he made away with himself. The Messenians, upon this untoward event, lost their hopes, but not their courage. Damis, their commander, once more made a vigorous sally from Ithome; but when the bravest leaders had fallen, the people fled from the fortress, leaving their rich fields in the possession of the conquerors, and the war was at an end.

16. After this catastrophe, the main body of the Messenians dispersed from Ithome to their own homes, but many took refuge in foreign lands. Ithome was razed to the ground; and the Spartans, after taking all the other Messenian towns, disposed of the country at their pleasure. The Messenians who remained in their native land were reduced to the condition of serfs, and, like the Helots, had to pay to their masters half the produce of their fields; and the remaining portions of the land were distributed among the Spartans, or perhaps to the offspring of mixed marriages between Spartans and Laconians, who did not enjoy the full franchise, and were for this reason induced in B. C. 708 to quit Greece, and found a new home for themselves at Tarentum, in the south of Italy

It would seem that to this period also belongs the extension of

the powers of the ephors, who are commonly said to have been instituted by king Theopompus. Their superintendence of the execution of the laws must have brought them into frequent collision
with the kings; and a dexterous and enterprising ephor might by
this means easily raise his power above that of the kings themselves.
In later times, the ephors also had the power of convoking the
assembly of the people, of laying measures before it, and of acting
in its name. By this means they easily rose above all other magistrates, and exercised a power at Sparta not unlike that of the plebeian tribunes at Rome.

17. During the first Messenian war, Argos, probably under its
distinguished king Pheidon, had recovered the eastern coast of Laconia as far as cape Malea, and even conquered the island of Cythera. It seems at that time to have been a great power, but after
Pheidon's death all was lost again, and Sparta ruled over the south
of Peloponnesus from sea to sea. Caranus, a brother of Pheidon, is
said to have emigrated, and to have founded the dynasty of the
kingdom of Macedonia in the north. Sparta, however, was not to
enjoy her conquests undisturbed. The subjugated Messenians, and
still more their exiled countrymen, burned with indignation against
their oppressors. Aristomenes, a Messenian of noble descent and
surpassing valour, cheered on his countrymen and roused them into
action; alliances also were formed with Argos, Arcadia, and even
with Elis, and in B. C. 685 the Messenians took up arms to shake off
the yoke. The accounts of this war, which lasted till B. C. 668, are
still more mythical or fabulous than those of the first, though the
fact of the war itself is beyond all doubt. Aristomenes, it is said,
rallied his countrymen in the mountainous districts. A great battle
was fought before any assistance could come from Sparta; the victory was not decisive, but the Spartans were terror-struck by the
unexpected insurrection, and the Messenians conceived fresh hopes.
Aristomenes, who refused the proffered crown, is reported one night
to have boldly entered the city of Sparta, and to have dedicated a
trophy in the temple of Athena. The Spartans were advised by the
god of Delphi to seek an Athenian counsellor; and the Attic town
of Aphidnae sent Tyrtaeus, a martial poet, to their aid. They also
received auxiliaries from Corinth and other places, while the Messenians were supported by their exiled countrymen, and cheered on
by the soothsayer Theocles. Near Stenycleros a great battle was
fought, in which the Spartans were routed, so that for a time Messenia was freed from her enemies. After a while, however, Aristomenes again took up the offensive, ravaged the towns and villages
of Laconia, and was stopped in his progress only by an accidental
wound. In the third year Sparta again prepared for battle, in
which, assisted by the treachery of the Arcadians, she gained a victory. Aristomenes, nothing daunted, assembled his countrymen on

mount Eira, where they fortified themselves, and were besieged by the enemy. Aristomenes maintained himself by frequent sallies, and the Spartans, in order to prevent his obtaining supplies for his men, laid waste the surrounding country.

18. But all was in vain, for one night Aristomenes went as far as Amyclae, and returned laden with booty. In a second expedition of a similar kind, however, he was unsuccessful, and, with his companions, fell into the hands of his enemies, who, treating their captives like vile malefactors, threw them into a deep pit called the Ceadas. The life of Aristomenes is said to have been saved in a marvellous manner, and he soon again joined his men at Eira. But after many most extraordinary adventures and successes which the legend ascribes to him, he incurred the anger of the gods, who now turned against his country. The siege of Eira had lasted eleven years, when the fall of Messenia was brought about by treachery, B. c. 668. Guided by a herdsman who had learned the real condition of the enemy while concealed in the house of a Messenian, the Spartans attacked Eira, and, notwithstanding a most heroic defence of the besieged, which lasted for three days and three nights, there was no hope of success. Aristomenes, with a small band, forced his way through the besieging army, and went to Arcadia, where he was hospitably received. He afterwards made a last expedition into Laconia, where, with fifty of his companions in exile, he died sword in hand.

19. After this war, which had lasted for seventeen years, all the Messenians who remained in their country were reduced to the condition of Helots; but most of the people probably emigrated. Guided by sons of Aristomenes, a band of Messenians sailed to Rhegium in southern Italy, to join some of their kinsmen who had already settled there at the end of the first war. Afterwards they made themselves masters of the town of Zancle, on the opposite coast of Sicily, and called it Messene (Messina). The Spartan yoke was now fixed on the neck of Messenia for ever, and Sparta rapidly rose towards the supremacy in Greece. Tegea, the possession of which had been long coveted, was conquered about the middle of the sixth century B. c. Sparta, in many instances, interfered in the affairs of the other Greek states, and assumed a commanding tone, to which they were obliged to submit. The fame of the most powerful state in Greece spread so far, that even Croesus, the king of Lydia, sent ambassadors to court its friendship.

CHAPTER IV.

NATIONAL INSTITUTIONS OF THE GREEKS, AND HISTORY OF ATTICA DOWN TO THE PERSIAN WARS.

1. INDEPENDENTLY of the colonies established abroad in consequence of the migrations and conquests described in the preceding chapter, Greece herself also experienced many changes in her ancient national institutions. The Greeks at all times had no other bond of union but that of their common language and religion; in the expedition against Troy alone, they are said to have been also united under one military commander; but this union was only transitory, and produced no lasting effects. Greece remained divided into almost as many little states as it contained cities. There existed, however, from early times, certain associations for religious, and partly also for political purposes, some of which, in the course of time, assumed at least the appearance of national confederations. The most important among them were those called Amphictionies, or Amphictyonies, that is, unions among a number of places or tribes, with a common centre, which was always a religious one, such as a temple, at which the periodical meetings were held. One Amphictiony of this kind met at Onchestos in Boeotia, another in Calaurea, a small island of the Saronic gulf, and a third in Delos; but the most important and best known is that which held its meetings in the spring at Delphi, and in the autumn at Thermopylae. It was originally formed by twelve tribes, all of which belonged to the part of Greece north of the Corinthian isthmus; but afterwards, the Dorians of Peloponnesus also joined the association, so that its influence extended over the whole of Greece. But it nevertheless at no time assumed a really national character. The ordinary duties of the congress of deputies were chiefly connected with religion, and its main functions were to guard the temple of Delphi, and to restrain mutual violence among the states belonging to the league. This last object, however, was not always attended to; for we sometimes find members of the Amphictiony inflicting the worst evils of war upon one another, without any attempt being made to check them. The league was, in fact, powerless for good, and active only for unimportant or pernicious purposes; and it may be truly said, that one of the chief objects for which the league appears to have been originally formed, was afterwards completely disregarded. The only cases in which we find the confederacy actively interfering, are those in which the honour and interests of the Delphic temple were concerned, as, for

example, in the Crissaean or first sacred war, in B. C. 594. The inhabitants of Crissa were charged with extortion and violence towards strangers proceeding through their territory to Delphi. The Amphictions accordingly commenced a war against the town, which lasted for ten years, until B. C. 585. At the end of this period, Crissa was taken and razed to the ground, its harbour choked up, and its fertile plain changed into a wilderness. This war, the termination of which was a flagrant violation of one of the fundamental rules of the Amphictionic league, is said to have been brought to a close by a stratagem devised by Solon, the Athenian lawgiver.

2. Another class of national institutions consisted of the festive games celebrated at certain places, and at fixed intervals of time, and open to all true Greeks. The most important of these festivals was that celebrated every four years at Olympia, in Elis. The foundation of these Olympic games is extremely obscure; but after they had been neglected for a long period during the disturbances created by the Doric conquest of Peloponnesus, they were revived by Iphitus in concert with Lycurgus, but it was not till B. C. 776 that they were finally and permanently established, whence that year was employed as a chronological era. The Eleans presided at the games, and during their celebration there was a general suspension of hostilities, to enable the Greeks from all parts to go to Olympia without danger or hindrance. The contests at these games in honour of the Olympian Zeus, consisted of exhibitions displaying almost every mode of bodily activity; they included races on foot, and with horses and chariots; contests in leaping, throwing, wrestling, and boxing, and some in which several of these exercises were combined, but no combats with any kind of weapon. Towns and families regarded it as the highest honour for one of their members to gain a victory in any of the contests at Olympia. The prize consisted of a simple garland of the leaves of the wild olive. Athens and Sparta showered honours upon any of their fellow-citizens who had obtained a prize. The celebrity of these games led to the institution of several others of a similar nature, such as the Pythian, which were celebrated in the third year of every Olympiad —the Nemean and Isthmian, which were celebrated each twice in every Olympiad. These four contests were distinguished from all others chiefly by the nature of the prize, which was in all cases a simple garland. In regard to national unity, these contests had little influence, for they never induced the Greeks to merge their little local patriotism in the more comprehensive sentiment of a common country and nationality. The arts of poetry and sculpture, on the other hand, received strong nourishment at these exhibitions, for a victory gained often inspired the poet to the most sublime effusions of the lyric muse, and statues of the victors not only

13

adorned Olympia, but their native places, not to mention that literary productions were sometimes read by their authors to the assembled Greeks.

3. The form of government universally prevailing in the Greek states in the Homeric age, was a monarchy, limited by ancient custom as well as by the powerful chiefs, of whom the king was only the first, whence we may call it an aristocracy with a hereditary prince at its head. But owing to various causes which operated during the first centuries after the Trojan war, the title of royalty was abolished in nearly every part of Greece, and in all cases the power of the nobles increased at the expense of that of the kings. In our traditional history, the causes of this change are often quite fabulous; but the truth is, that it mainly arose out of the energy and versatility of the Greek mind, which prevented it from ever becoming stagnant like that of the Orientals, or from stopping short in any career which it had once opened, before it had passed through every stage. Royalty, however, was scarcely ever overthrown by violent revolutions; its title often long survived the substance, and the transition from monarchy to republicanism was generally brought about by a succession of reforms. The government substituted for monarchy was generally aristocratic or oligarchic — that is, the supreme power was assumed by the nobles, who had subdued the original inhabitants of the country, and distributed their landed property among themselves. In the course of time the commonalty, or the free subjects of the nobles, ever increasing in number and wealth, while the exclusive nobles became more reduced in numbers, put forward new claims, and became formidable opponents of the oligarchs, especially in large towns. Various means were devised by the nobles to check this progress of the commonalty, but to no purpose; and it often became necessary to make a compromise between the two parties, as for example in those cases where property was made the standard, instead of birth, to measure a citizen's rights and duties. Where the property standard was made low, the government at once became democratic instead of aristocratic. During the feuds between these two contending parties, it was sometimes found necessary to entrust unlimited powers to some individual who possessed the confidence of both, for the purpose of restoring order and tranquillity.

4. But the Greek oligarchies were sometimes also overthrown by a disastrous war, or by revolutions and dissensions within their own body; and it most commonly happened in such a case, that one of the nobles by skill and prudence conciliated the commonalty, and with its aid raised himself above his brother nobles. Such a usurper was designated by the name of tyrant, and his rule generally did not last long; or if he did succeed in maintaining his power until his death, his sons generally lost it by their own reck-

lessness or cruelty, which called forth a conspiracy or insurrection. It is worthy of remark that the Spartans were always ready to assist in overthrowing the power of a tyrant, though probably more from a desire to extend their influence over the Greeks, than from any desire to free them from a usurper; and this interference of theirs in the affairs of other states, greatly contributed to establish the so-called Spartan supremacy in Greece. The immediate object of the Spartans generally was, if possible, to introduce their own oligarchic form of government in the place of the one they helped to overthrow. But in this attempt they were frequently thwarted. The process which has here been described in general, will be illustrated in detail in the history of Attica; and what happened there, was more or less the same as what occurred in other states of Greece.

5. The early history of Attica is much less interesting than that of the Doric states; and it is in fact not till a comparatively late period that Athens begins to act a prominent part in Grecian history, though after it had once come forward, it soon eclipsed all the other states. The country of Attica is said to have been originally divided into a number of small independent states, governed by kings. The mythical king Cecrops is said to have united these states, and to have divided the country into twelve districts, or founded twelve towns. Athens, then called Cecropia, was at the head of this confederacy. The division of the country into twelve parts, seems to have been only a multiple of four, a number which we find in Attica no less than in other Ionian countries. Accordingly we hear of a division of the people of Attica into four tribes, which changed their names under several successive kings; the last set of names, which was traced to Ion, the founder of the Ionian race, continued to be used until a very late period, and is the most important of all. These names, Teleontes, Hopletes, Ægicores, and Argades, are descriptive of certain occupations, the second and third evidently signifying warriors and shepherds respectively; Argades probably referred to husbandmen, and the Teleontes were perhaps the nobles, who alone were entitled to hold the highest magistracies. These four divisions ought not to be regarded as castes, like those of India or Egypt; and to whatever circumstances they may have originally owed their names, the closer union among the people of Attica, and their intercourse with one another, in the course of time obliterated such primitive distinctions. The gradual union of these four tribes was promoted by their affinity of blood and language, and by the need of mutual assistance; and all were naturally disposed to look up to the people of Athens as their natural head and centre. The legends, however, describe this as the work of Theseus, who is said to have consolidated the national unity, and laid the foundation of the greatness of Athens, by collecting the scat-

tered inhabitants of Attica into one city, and putting an end to the perpetual discord among them. All that can be meant by this tradition is, that Attica became united as one state, of which Athens was the centre and seat of government, for it is inconceivable that all the population of Attica should have been collected into one city. In later times, several religious institutions, such as the Panathenaea, were believed to have been established to commemorate this union of Attica. Athens itself is said to have been enlarged on that occasion, and the lower city to have been added to the one existing on the Cecropian rock. The additional accommodation was probably required for the noble families which removed from the country to the seat of government.

6. In later times Theseus was regarded as the founder of all the great political institutions of Athens, which probably arose from a desire to represent those things that were endeared to all as venerable also by their antiquity. In the constitution which he was believed to have framed, all the nobles, called eupatridae, had an equal share in the government; they possessed all the offices of the state, with the power of regulating the affairs of religion, and of interpreting the laws, human and divine. The great body of the subject people consisted of husbandmen and artisans, who formed the commonalty, and were governed by the nobles and the king, whose rank, as in the Homeric poems, was only that of the first among his equals; but still the union of the commonalty in the one great state must have strengthened it so far as to resist any excessive harshness on the part of the eupatridae. In all the states of antiquity, the tribes were subdivided; in Attica each of the four tribes was divided into three *phratriae* or fraternities, and each phratria into thirty *gené*, *gentes*, or *clans*. It need hardly be observed that these political arrangements, though ascribed to Theseus, were the natural results of circumstances, and that it probably required a long period before they attained that development which the legend represents as the work of one man.

7. Notwithstanding, however, the absolute power exercised by the king and his officers, there existed at Athens, as in most ancient states, an assembly of the people, that is, an assembly of the burghers or nobles, for the commonalty had as yet no right to appear and vote in it. The power of the assembly was at first probably as limited as it was at Sparta. Hence the first contests of the nobles were not waged with the commonalty, but with the king. The legends about the kings of Athens cannot be accepted as history, but still even these legends represent the kings as conspired against by the nobles; and certain it is, that after the death of Codrus, the nobles, taking advantage of the disputes between his sons about the succession, abolished the title of king, and substituted for it the simple and less venerable one of archon or ruler. The office,

however, still remained hereditary in the house of Codrus and was held for life. Medon, a son of Codrus, was the first archon for life, and on his demise the nobles elected a successor from his family. This power exercised by the nobles, however, did not satisfy their ambition, for what they aimed at was a complete and equal participation in the sovereignty. Accordingly, after twelve archonships, ending with that of Alcmaeon, in B. C. 752, the duration of the office was limited to ten years, though it still continued to be held by the descendants of Medon. This change was followed in B. C. 683 by another, in which the term of the archonship was reduced to a single year, and at the same time the different powers which had until then been possessed by one, were distributed among nine archons. This reform is said to have been introduced in consequence of the misconduct of Hippomenes, the fourth of the decennial archons, and through it a large number of nobles obtained a chance of receiving at least a share in the sovereign power. The first of these nine mgistrates bore the title of *the* archon, and by his name the year was marked; the second had the title of king-archon, the name king being retained from religious scruples, as he had to perform the priestly functions which had formerly belonged to the king. The third archon was styled polemarch, and had the command of the Athenian army, until the time of the Persian wars, after which this duty was transferred to others, while the polemarch only retained a special kind of jurisdiction. The remaining six archons had the common title of thesmothetae, that is, legislators, or rather expounders of the law.

8. These successive changes are almost the only events that occur in the history of Athens from the time of Codrus down to the deposition of Hippomenes. The condition of the people of Attica, however, appears to have been anything but happy under the rule of their nobles, who seem to have abused their power as much as the Roman patricians, when freed from the control of the king. Their oppression was felt more especially in the administration of the law, of which they were the sole makers and expounders, and in regard to which they might indulge the greatest license, because there were no written laws. This circumstance led in B. C. 624 to the appointment of Draco for the purpose of drawing up a code of laws. We do not know what was the cause of the extraordinary severity to which his laws owe their celebrity, but as they were written, they necessarily limited the powers of the nobles, and hence we may infer that they had been compelled to make this concession to the growing discontent of the commonalty. The laws framed by Draco were so stern that they were said to be written in blood. All offences were in his eyes equally deserving of death as their punishment; and it is possible that it was owing to the un-

13 *

popularity of his laws that Draco was obliged to quit his native city and go to Ægina, where he died.

9. The discontent of the commonalty, instead of being allayed, now rose to such a pitch, that the people would readily have yielded to the rule of a tyrant in order to get rid of that of the nobles. In B. C. 612, Cylon, one of the nobles, formed a conspiracy to overthrow the government and make himself master of Athens. In this enterprise he relied upon the assistance of Theagenes, tyrant of Megara, and more especially on the general dissatisfaction of the people; but before entering upon it he consulted the Delphic oracle, the obscure answer of which led him to commence his operations at a wrong period. With the aid of a body of foreign troops furnished by Theagenes, he made himself master of the Acropolis; but his auxiliaries deprived him of the confidence and support of the Athenian people. His brother nobles called in the forces from all parts of the country and besieged him. During the blockade, Cylon and his brother made their escape, but their followers were in the end compelled to surrender to the archon Megacles, son of Alcmaeon, on condition that their lives should be spared. The archons, however, broke their promise, and not only slew their prisoners, but even killed some of them at the altars of Eumenides or Furies, at which they had taken refuge. As this crime was committed with the sanction of Megacles, he and all his house were henceforth looked upon as accursed persons, whose lives were forfeited to the gods, and the surviving partisans of Cylon did not fail to foster the belief that all the disasters which came upon Athens were the result of the divine wrath provoked by the sacrilege of Megacles. These superstitious alarms only increased the political ferment which was already going on, and it was evident that some extraordinary measure must be resorted to to prevent civil war, or even the ruin of the whole state.

10. The man who was thought by all parties the most fit to undertake the regeneration of his country, and who by his wisdom and moderation was likely to satisfy the reasonable demands of all, was Solon, son of Execestides, and a descendant of the house of Codrus. He had been long absent from his country on foreign travel, during which he had amassed treasures of knowledge and had formed friendships with the most illustrious men of his age. He returned soon after the suppression of the Cylonian conspiracy, and found his country in a most deplorable condition, and so weak as to be unable even to resist the Megarians, who had taken possession of the island of Salamis. The repeated vain attempts to recover it had completely broken the spirit of the Athenians; but Solon by a ruse once more stirred up their enthusiasm. He himself was appointed commander of the expedition, and in a single campaign drove the Megarians from the island, in B. C. 604. This

success raised his fame still higher. With the assistance of the moderate nobles he prevailed upon Megacles and his party to submit their case to the decision of a court of three hundred men of their own order. The court declared them all guilty, and in B. C. 597 all the Alcmaeonids were sent into exile, and even the remains of the dead were removed beyond the frontiers of Attica. In order to propitiate the gods completely, it was necessary to purify the city, and for this purpose Solon invited Epimenides of Crete, one generally regarded as a sage of superhuman wisdom, who had enjoyed personal intercourse with the gods. On his arrival he performed certain rites which pacified the superstitious minds of the Athenians, and having made some religious arrangements, he returned home with tokens of the warmest gratitude.

11. Their minds being now freed from religious fears, the Athenians were in a more suitable condition to consider their political affairs with calmness. Many of the agricultural population had been reduced to a state of absolute dependence; their political rights, if they had any, were merely nominal, and many when unable to pay their debts had been sold by their creditors as slaves into foreign countries; for the Athenian law of debt was as severe as that of Rome, empowering a creditor to seize his insolvent debtor and to sell him abroad as a slave. Those who groaned under such tyranny were eager only for a change, unconcerned about the means of effecting it. The eupatrids, being the owners of the fertile plains of the country, wished to keep things as they were. The inhabitants of the hilly districts, mostly shepherds and poor peasants, though less exposed to the rapacity and cruelty of the nobles than the lowland peasantry, were anxious for reforms which should secure them the same rights as those possessed by their lords. The men of the coast, chiefly merchants and traders, were averse to violent measures, but nevertheless joined with the rest in demanding reforms which should put an end to all reasonable complaints. Under these circumstances Solon was chosen, with the consent of all parties, to mediate between them, and under the title of archon he was invested, in B. C. 594, with full authority to frame a new constitution and a code of laws. His task consisted of two parts : the first and most pressing business was to relieve the present distress of the commonalty, and the second to prevent the recurrence of the same or similar evils, by regulating the rights and duties of the citizens on principles of justice and fairness. His first measure accordingly was a disburdening ordinance, which relieved the debtor without causing any great loss to the creditor. He then released the pledged lands and restored them to their owners, and, lastly, he abolished that part of the law of debt which authorised a creditor to seize and sell the person of his debtor.

12. When these most urgent affairs were settled, Solon entered

upon his second task by abolishing the laws of Draco, except those referring to murder; it would seem that by this measure, a number of exiles, and among them the family of Megacles, were restored to their country. Many foreigners also who had settled in Attica with their families, and had given up all connection with their own countries, were admitted as Athenian citizens. But the greatest change which he introduced, and which altogether changed the character of the Athenian constitution, was the substitution of property for birth, as the standard for determining the rights and duties of the citizens, although at first this change may have produced little effect, the nobles being naturally the wealthiest citizens; but the principle was changed, and the highest rights were placed within the reach of all. According to their property, then, Solon divided all Athenians, both the nobles and the commonalty, into four classes. The first consisted of persons whose estates yielded a net yearly income or rent of five hundred medimni (a medimnus is about six pints more than a bushel) of dry or liquid produce; the second of those whose income amounted to three hundred medimni, and who were called Knights, being able to keep a war-horse; the third of those whose annual revenue amounted to two hundred, or more probably one hundred and fifty medimni, and who were termed Zeugitae (yoke-men), from their supposed ability to keep a yoke of oxen for the plough; the fourth class, called thetes, comprised all those whose incomes fell below that of the third, and consisted mainly of free hired labourers. The highest offices of the state were accessible only to members of the first class, but minor offices were no doubt left open to members of the second and third. The duties of the citizens were determined by the classes to which they belonged; thus the members of the second formed the cavalry, the third the heavy armed infantry, and the fourth, being excluded from all offices, served only as a light armed infantry and were employed in later times in manning the fleets. In the popular assembly, the citizens of all the classes met on a footing of perfect equality, and its power from the first does not seem to have been limited to adopting or rejecting the measures laid before it by the senate, but the assembly might modify or amend the proposals at its discretion. The magistrates retained, in the constitution of Solon, their ancient powers, but became responsible for their exercise to the whole body of citizens. Their judicial functions also remained the same, but an appeal was left open against their verdicts to popular courts numerously composed of citizens of all classes indiscriminately. The democratic principle had thus acquired considerable strength even as early as the time of Solon, but the legislator had endeavoured to check its power by two great councils, the senate of Four Hundred, and the Areopagus.

13. The senate of Four Hundred, called bulé, is uniformly regarded

by the ancients as an institution of Solon ; at all events, it must be admitted that he fixed its number at four hundred, and that he gave it a more popular constitution by making it the representative of the clas-es, though the fourth was excluded. The qualifications for being elected a member of the bulé were a certain amount of property and a certain age, no one under thirty years being eligible. They held their dignity for only one year, after which they were liable to be taken to account for their conduct. The principal part of their business was to prepare the measures which were to be brought before the assembly of the people, and to preside at its deliberations. But the senate also had extensive powers connected with the finances and other subjects of administration. The second council, the Areopagus, is likewise called an institution of Solon, though according to the Attic legends it had existed from time immemorial. The functions of the Areopagus are involved in great obscurity; but we know that it took cognisance of cases of wilful murder, maiming, poisoning, and arson, and that besides these judicial functions, it also had political powers.

The ordinary assemblies of the people (ecclesiae) seem to have been held at most once in every month ; the votes were taken by show of hands, and without any distinction of classes, so that the vote of the humblest Athenian was as weighty as that of the wealthiest, and every voter was allowed to speak. The right to take part in the business of the assembly began at the age of twenty, but those who had passed the age of fifty were called upon to speak first.

The popular courts above alluded to consisted of a body of six thousand citizens, called the Heliaea, which was created every year by lot to form a supreme court. Every citizen, after attaining the age of thirty, might become a member of it. Solon's object seems to have been to make this court the guardian of the constitution rather than the minister of the laws. Hence we find it generally engaged in proceedings against illegal or unconstitutional measures, even when they had been sanctioned by the popular assembly.

14. Being convinced that no constitution, however wisely framed, could remain in force at all times and under altered circumstances, he made provision for periodical revisions and improvements of the laws; and this task was left to the citizens, for a class of men making the law a special object of their study, did not exist at Athens. His legislation, like that of most ancient lawgivers, inter-fered with the affairs of private and social life much more than the laws of modern states, but still Solon did not in this respect go so far as Lycurgus had gone. Up to the age of sixteen, the education of youths was left entirely to their parents or guardians ; during the next two years, they were trained in gymnastic exercises under public teachers, who kept them under severe discipline. At the

age of eighteen, they entered upon their apprenticeship in arms, during which they had to perform several duties for the protection of their country. At the end of these two years, they were admitted to all the rights of a citizen, for which the law did not prescribe a more advanced age; and until the age of sixty, they were liable to be called upon to perform military services. The regulations regarding the female sex were very stringent, and prevented their appearance in public as much as possible; their education was discouraged rather than otherwise, whence in later times they were generally ill-suited to make agreeable and useful companions to their husbands.

15. Solon was the first to perceive the advantageous position of Athens for becoming a maritime state, and it was he who laid the foundation of the Attic navy, by enacting that each of the forty-eight divisions called naucrariae, into which the four tribes were subdivided, should equip a galley; he also encouraged commerce and manufactures by inducing foreigners to settle in Attica, and granting them protection and certain privileges. These resident aliens (called metoeci), however, had to pay a small alien-tax, and to place themselves under the protection of an Athenian citizen, who acted as their patron. The condition of the slaves remained on the whole what it had been before, and although in Attica they were in better circumstances than in other parts of Greece, the law yet sanctioned certain things which are revolting to human nature; and Solon in this respect did not rise above the prejudices of his age and country.

16. The laws of Solon were inscribed on wooden tablets, and were at first kept in the Acropolis, but afterwards, for greater convenience, they were set up in the Prytaneum, the residence of the committee of the senate. After the completion of his legislation, Solon is said to have travelled for ten years; and during his peregrinations to have become acquainted with Croesus, king of Lydia, and Amasis, the ruler of Egypt, but these statements are irreconcilable with chronology. On his return to Athens, about B. C. 562, he found that faction had been busily engaged in attempting to pervert and undo his work. The three parties, of the plain, the highlands, and the coast, had revived their ancient feuds. The first was now headed by Lycurgus, the second by Megacles, an Alcmaeonid, and the third by Pisistratus, a kinsman and friend of Solon. The attempts of Solon to restore peace and union were of no avail; and Pisistratus, a man of great eloquence and liberality, had resolved to renew the attempt of Cylon. One day he pretended to have been attacked by his enemies: exhibiting his wounds to the people, and representing that they were the fruit of his attachment to the popular cause, he easily prevailed upon the multitude to grant him a body-guard for his personal safety. With

this force he made himself master of the Acropolis, and Megacles and his friends quitted the city. Solon, after having in vain made every effort against the tyrant, withdrew from public life, and Lycurgus and his party seem to have quietly submitted to the authority of Pisistratus, whose tyrannis commenced in b. c. 560. He avoided all display of power, being satisfied with the substance of it, and conducted himself outwardly as a simple citizen. Solon, whose advice the tyrant occasionally asked, died soon after, b. c. 559. But Lycurgus, who had only waited for an opportunity, formed a coalition with Megacles, and their united efforts compelled Pisistratus to quit Athens, his tyrannis having probably lasted not much more than one year.

17. The people do not appear to have been much pleased with their new rulers, and as each of the two was only thinking how he could get rid of his rival, Megacles, who was particularly disappointed in his expectations, entered into negotiations with Pisistratus, gave him his daughter in marriage, and promised to assist him in recovering his lost position. Pisistratus entered into the scheme, and was conveyed back to Athens in a manner which even struck the historian Herodotus by its childish simplicity. When Pisistratus was restored, he offended Megacles by not treating his daughter as a wife. Her father and his friends, indignant at the insult, once more made common cause with Lycurgus, and drove Pisistratus from the city. The exiled tyrant now went to Eretria in Euboea, and is said to have been inclined to give up all further attempts to recover what he had lost; but his eldest son Hippias urged him on not to despair. Accordingly he made preparations, and formed connections with powerful tyrants in other parts of Greece. Ten years were spent in these preliminaries, and at the end of this period he landed with an army of mercenaries at Marathon. The government of his adversaries had not been popular during his long absence; they assembled their forces, but want of care and circumspection brought about their defeat on the road from Athens to Marathon. Pisistratus immediately proclaimed an amnesty, on condition of his enemies quietly dispersing to their homes. This act disarmed his opponents, and Pisistratus once more was undisputed master of Athens.

18. He now endeavoured permanently to secure the possession of what he had so hardly won; and with this view he surrounded himself with a body of foreign mercenaries, and sent as hostages to Naxos the children of the nobles who had opposed him. At the same time he did all he could, by embellishing the city and extending its maritime power, to gain popularity among the Athenians; and his success was so complete, that he maintained his position without any further interruption for a period of fourteen years, until his death, in b. c. 527. The increased naval power of Athens is

evident from the fact that Pisistratus raised his friend Lygdamis to
the tyrannis in Naxos, and recovered for Athens the town of Sigeum
on the Hellespont, which was then in the hands of the Mytileneans,
with whom the Athenians had been at war about it for many years.
Pisistratus entrusted the keeping of Sigeum to a natural son, Hege-
sistratus, and thus secured for himself a place of refuge, if fortune
should ever again turn against him. At home he maintained the
laws of Solon, and gained popularity by his munificence towards the
poorer classes, while he removed some of them from the city, and
obliged them to engage in rural occupations. He adorned Athens
with many useful and ornamental works, such as a temple of Apollo,
and one dedicated to the Olympian Zeus, of which, however, he
had only laid the foundations when he died, and which was completed many centuries later by the emperor Hadrian. Among the
monuments combining splendour and usefulness, were the Lyceum,
a park at some distance from Athens, where stately buildings for
exercises of the Athenian youth rose among shady groves; and the
fountain Callirrhoë. The expenses of these and other works were
defrayed out of the revived tithe on the produce of the land, which
accordingly was a tax levied on the rich for the purpose of giving
employment to the poor. There is also a tradition that Pisistratus
first collected the Homeric poems, which were until then scattered
in unconnected rhapsodies; at all events, he certainly had a taste
for literature, for he was the first Greek that formed a library for
the good of those who wished to avail themselves of it. On the
whole, it must be owned that Pisistratus made most excellent use
of his usurped power, and Athens has had few citizens to whom
she owed a greater debt of gratitude than to Pisistratus. He died
at an advanced age, thirty-three years after his first usurpation.

19. The Athenians had become so accustomed to the mild rule
of Pisistratus, that his sons Hippias, Hipparchus, and Thessalus,
succeeded him without opposition. Hippias, the eldest, was at the
head of affairs, but the three brothers appear to have acted with
great unanimity. At first they followed in the footsteps of their
father, and Hipparchus, in particular, seems to have inherited his
father's literary taste, though they seem not to have been very
scrupulous about the means of getting rid of persons who had incurred their hatred or jealousy. But still the country was happy
and prosperous under them, and the Pisistratids might have governed Athens for many generations, had not an event occurred
which led to their overthrow and a complete change in the government. Harmodius, a young Athenian, had been grossly insulted
by Hipparchus, and, instigated by his friend Aristogeiton, he meditated revenge. The two friends resolved to overthrow the ruling
dynasty, and they and their comrades fixed on the festival of the
Panathenaea as the time for executing their design. Hipparchus

was killed during the procession, but Harmodius also fell in the fray. Aristogeiton was taken, and all those who were found to carry daggers were arrested. This happened in B. C. 514. Aristogeiton was tried and put to death, but took revenge by denouncing the most intimate friends of Hippias as conspirators. Henceforth fear and suspicion gained the ascendancy in the tyrant's mind, and he became stern and cruel. Executions were now things of common occurrence, and the taxes were increased, not for the public service, but to fill the tyrant's own coffers; and seeing that he was hated and detested at home, he endeavoured to strengthen himself by foreign alliances. Thus he gave his daughter in marriage to the son of the tyrant of Lampsacus, a protegé of Darius, king of Persia. But all this could not avert the storm which he was daily conjuring up against himself.

20. The exiled Alcmaeonids, perceiving the unpopularity of Hippias, and being abundantly supplied with money, resolved once more to try to effect their return and overthrow their rivals. Cleisthenes, who was then at their head, secured the favour of the Delphic oracle by extraordinary liberality, and hence, whenever after this the Spartans consulted the oracle, they received but one answer bidding them restore Athens to freedom, until at length they resolved to send an army into Attica to expel Hippias with his family. On their first landing at Phaleron they were defeated by the Thessalian auxiliaries of Hippias; but in a second expedition under Cleomenes, the Thessalians were routed, and Hippias alarmed sent his children out of the country. They fell, however, into the hands of the Spartans, who restored them to their father only on condition of his quitting Attica. Accordingly Hippias, in B. C. 510, left Athens, and for a time took up his residence at Sigeum. After his departure his friends and adherents were treated with great severity. A sentence of perpetual banishment was pronounced against the Pisistratids, and Harmodius and Aristogeiton received almost heroic honours.

21. After these events, Cleisthenes, following in the footsteps of Pisistratus, attached himself to the popular party in opposition to the nobles, and planned a great change in the constitution, which should for ever break the power of the aristocracy. Having gained the confidence of the commonalty, and the sanction of the Delphic oracle, he abolished the four ancient tribes, and made a new geographical division of Attica into ten tribes, each of which was subdivided into a number of districts called demi, each containing some town or village as its centre. Each of these townships was governed by a local magistrate called demarch, and every Athenian citizen was obliged to be enrolled as a member of some demos. At the same time Cleisthenes admitted many aliens and even slaves to the franchise, whereby he increased the strength of his own party.

14

These reforms changed the commonalty into a new body, furnished with new organs, and breathing a new spirit, which had shaken off all control of the old nobility. In accordance with the number of ten tribes, the senate was increased from four hundred to five hundred, fifty being taken from each tribe. The popular assembly henceforth was convened regularly four times in every month; the Heliaea was subdivided into ten lesser courts, but the number of the archons remained unchanged. Cleisthenes is also said to have instituted the famous process of ostracism, by which the people were enabled to get rid of any citizen who had made himself formidable or suspected, and that without any proof or even imputation of guilt.

22. The party of the nobles naturally detested the revolutionary proceedings of Cleisthenes as much as their author, and, urged on by their leader Isagoras, they contrived to win the Spartans over to their side. Cleomenes, the king of Sparta, accordingly demanded of the Athenians to banish the accursed race of the Alcmaeonids. Cleisthenes, either dreading the cry which had so often been disastrous to his family, or unwilling to expose his country to a hostile invasion, withdrew from Athens. The Spartan king, however, not satisfied with this, but bent upon raising his friend Isagoras to the tyrannis, invaded Attica with an army, and, acting as if he were sole master of the country, banished seven hundred families marked out by Isagoras, and then took steps to change the government of Athens into an oligarchy. But this attempt roused the spirit of the people, who besieged him and Isagoras in the Acropolis. After a few days they were obliged to capitulate; the Spartans and Isagoras were permitted to depart, but all their Athenian adherents were put to death, and Cleisthenes, with the seven hundred exiled families, triumphantly returned to Athens in B. C. 508.

23. Cleomenes having secured the alliance of the Corinthians, Boeotians, and Chalcidians, determined to wipe off the disgrace of the defeat he had sustained, by another invasion of Attica, which was now attacked on several sides; but some of his allies began to feel ashamed of what they were doing, and returned home, and as the two Spartan kings also could not agree as to their plan of operation, the enterprise was abandoned. In this distress, Athens had sent envoys to Sardis, to seek the protection of Persia, but the embassy had no effect, and is interesting only as the first occasion on which a Greek state had any dealings with Persia. After the Spartans had withdrawn, the Athenians set out to chastise the Boeotians, whom they defeated, and of whom they took seven hundred prisoners; they then crossed over into Euboea, where they were equally successful; they deprived the rich Chalcidian landowners of their estates, and distributed them among four thousand Attic colonists who settled there, but retained their franchise. Athens,

thus freed from internal as well as external enemies, became strong
and powerful in the enjoyment of political liberty. So long as she
had been ruled by her nobles, she had at times scarcely been able
to cope with the weakest among her neighbours, but now she advanced far ahead of them all. And this is the best proof of the
wisdom of Cleisthenes, who, no doubt, well understood the temper
and character of his countrymen.

24. But the foreign enemies of Athens were only hushed for a
time, and were secretly plotting against her. The Boeotians, burning to avenge their defeat, allied themselves with the Æginetans,
ancient enemies of Athens; and while they invaded Attica from
the north, the Æginetans, with their powerful navy, ravaged the
coasts. This war, in which Athens learnt the necessity of increasing her fleet, lasted, with various interruptions, for about fifty years,
and terminated in B. C. 456, in the subjugation of Ægina, and the
destruction of its navy.

The Spartans, in the meantime, had discovered that they had
been imposed upon by the Delphic priestess who had led them to
assist in the expulsion of the Pisistratids. This, and the fear of
the growing power of Athens, led them to invite Hippias to return
to Athens. He was to be supported by Sparta and all her allies,
and a congress of them was convened to consider the measures to
be adopted. At this congress the Corinthian deputy, Sosicles,
strongly objected to the scheme of setting up a tyrant among a free
people, and, encouraged by his eloquence, all the other deputies,
with one accord, declared against the proposal of the Spartans.
The design was accordingly abandoned, and Hippias soon afterwards
proceeded to the court of Darius, where he did his best to stimu-
late the barbarians to a war against his own country.

CHAPTER V.

GREEK COLONIES, AND THE PROGRESS OF ART AND LITERATURE FROM THE HOMERIC AGE TO THE PERSIAN WARS.

1. A MIGRATORY disposition, and a certain degree of restlessness,
often induced bodies of Greeks to quit their native land, and o
open for themselves new fields of enterprise in foreign countries.
All the shores of the Mediterranean and Black sea were covered
with their colonies in such numbers, that even about the year B. C.
600 they are said to have amounted to two hundred and fifty. But

while they thus established themselves in all parts round the basins
of those two seas, they at the same time possessed the talent of
maintaining and preserving their national character wherever they
went, and by this means they diffused the Greek language and
civilisation in all countries where they formed settlements. The
causes of their migrations were sometimes war and conquest, sometimes discord and party strife at home, sometimes over-population
and poverty, and in later times, also, commercial interests. On
quitting their native city, they took with them the sacred fire from
the public hearth, for colonies continued at all times to maintain
towards the mother city a relation similar to that of a daughter
towards a parent; they retained the customs, institutions, and religious observances of the mother city, showed it their respect on
certain solemn occasions, and never carried on war against it, unless
compelled by dire necessity. They did not, however, enter into a
relation of dependence on the mother state, but were entirely free
in their internal administration and government, though, when
visited by misfortunes from domestic or foreign enemies, a colony
naturally looked to the mother city for aid and protection.

2. We have already spoken[1] of the earliest or Æolian colonies,
which were founded immediately, or soon after the Trojan war.
The main body of the emigrants is said to have first landed at
Lesbos, where they founded six towns. Other detachments occupied the opposite coasts of Asia Minor, from mount Ida to the
mouth of the river Hermus. This part of the coast was until then
in the hands of Pelasgian tribes, which easily amalgamated with
the new settlers into one people. Cuma was the principal of the
eleven Æolian cities which thus sprang up on the Asiatic coast;
and Cuma and Lesbos founded thirty others in the territory called
Troas. It is not certain whether these Æolian colonies were united
by any religious or political bond like those by which the Ionian
and Dorian colonies on the same coast were kept together. The
coast country south of Æolis, from the river Hermus to the Maeander, was occupied by the Ionian colonies, consisting chiefly of
the Ionians who had been dislodged by the conquest of Peloponnesus by the Dorians.[2] On their passage across the Ægean, many
formed settlements in the Cyclades and other islands, and in the
course of time the little island of Delos came to be considered as
the common centre of the Ionian race. The Asiatic coast occupied
by these emigrants was inhabited by Pelasgians, Carians, and
Leleges, the last two of which tribes were expelled or exterminated.
Twelve cities or states were formed, of which Miletus occupied the
first rank; all claimed sons or kinsmen of Codrus, king of Athens,
for their ancestral heroes. Ten of the twelve Ionian cities had
existed before the arrival of the new settlers, but Clazomenae and

---

[1] See pp. 127, 131.   [2] Comp. pp. 132-3.

Phocaea were founded by the Ionians themselves Chios and Samos were likewise occupied by Ionians, and Smyrna was added to the confederacy at a later time, in the place of Melite, which was destroyed by the other members of the league.

3. The south-western corner of Asia Minor and the adjacent islands were occupied about the same time by colonists of the Doric race; for some of the Dorian conquerors themselves were drawn into the tide of migration, and led bands of their own race and of the conquered Achaeans to the coast of Asia Minor. The most celebrated of these expeditions was that of Althaemenes of Argos, who led colonists to Crete and Rhodes. Halicarnassus was founded by Dorians from Troezen, and Cnidus by others from Laconia, and a third band from Epidaurus took possession of the island of Cos. These six Dorian cities formed an association, and after the exclusion of Halicarnassus, they constituted what is called the Dorian pentapolis. There existed, however, many other Dorian towns, both on the coast and far inland, but they formed no part of this confederation. When the tide of these migrations had passed, and the affairs of Greece had become settled, a long period elapsed before fresh colonies were established in distant regions. The countries which next attracted the attention of the enterprising Greeks were the south of Italy (Magna Graecia) and the island of Sicily. The colonies founded on these western shores, like those in the east, were partly Æolian or Achaean, partly Dorian, and partly Ionian; but the Ionians of Chalcis in Euboea were the first who gained a permanent footing in the west, for the Ionian Cuma in Campania was by common consent the most ancient Greek settlement in those parts. It had existed, however, a long time before other adventurers followed in the same track, and it was not till B. C. 735 that Theocles, an Athenian, led a colony of Chalcidians from Euboea and Naxos to Sicily, and established the town of Naxos. After this commencement, a number of other Chalcidian colonies followed in rapid succession, such as Leontini, Catana, Messene, and Rhegium, on the opposite coast of Italy.

4. But the most powerful colonies of Sicily were of Doric origin. Of these, Syracuse was founded in B. C. 734 by Corinthians, who also established themselves in Corcyra, and in many other parts of the coast of the Adriatic. Syracuse, in its turn, became the metropolis of many other Sicilian towns, among which Camarina was the most important. Megara planted her most flourishing colonies on the coasts of the Propontis and the Bosporus, where, in B. C. 658, she founded Byzantium; but Megarian emigrants also founded Hybla in Sicily, which, in B. C. 629, became the parent of Selinus. Gela was founded in B. C. 690 by a body of Cretans and Rhodians, and in B. C. 582 sent out a band of settlers, who founded Agrigentum on the Acragas. Himera, on the north coast, was founded

by colonists from Messene, and Dorians who had been banished from Syracuse. Within half a century after the first Greek settlements in Sicily, most of the great cities in southern Italy were founded. Sybaris, Croton, Locri, Tarentum, and Metapontum, extended and secured the dominion of the Greeks in Italy by a number of new colonies, among which we need only mention Posidonia (Paestum), the ruins of which still attest its former greatness.

The country of Cyrene, on the north coast of Africa, possessed of inexhaustible wealth and a delightful climate, was colonised by the island of Thera, and the city of Cyrene itself founded four other towns in the same district. The Libyans of those parts seem to have yielded to the invaders without much opposition; and when at a later time they began to be alarmed about the growing power of the Greeks, they were defeated with terrible slaughter, and the dominion of the Greeks was firmly established in that part of Africa. Cyrene was governed for a time by kings, like the mother country; but about B. C. 637 there came an influx of additional settlers, and this seems to have made the people dissatisfied with their institutions. Demonax of Mantinea being invited to frame a new constitution, divided the people into three tribes, the first consisting of the descendants of the original settlers; the king was stripped of all his substantial powers; but afterwards a counter-revolution having been brought about, the government became a tyrannis.

5. The two groups of Greek colonies in Asia, the Ionian and the Dorian, formed each a kind of confederacy, though it was very loose, and far from uniting them into two compact political bodies. Each group had its periodical meetings for the celebration of festivals in honour of a tutelary divinity, but these meetings, at most, afforded an opportunity of discussing political matters in case of need. The meetings of Ionians were held at the foot of mount Mycale, on a spot called Panionium, and sacred to Poseidon; and those of the Dorians near a temple of Apollo, on the Triopian headland. None of the Greeks in Asia ever rose to the idea of a real political confederacy, like that subsisting among the Lycian towns, although the fact of their being exposed to the attacks of Asiatic barbarians ought to have induced them to strengthen themselves by union. Had they done so, their own history, and even that of the mother country, might have been very different from what it was. But this want of unity did not affect the prosperity of the several cities; on the contrary, in many respects their progress was so rapid that they outstripped the mother country itself. About the same time when the Greek states in Europe abolished royalty and established republican institutions, the same took place in the colonies of Asia. Miletus became a most powerful maritime state, and the parent of numerous colonies in Asia and on the coasts of the Euxine, which extended the empire of the Greeks to most distant regions.

In comparison with the active and enterprising spirit of the Ionians, the Æolians and Dorians remained stationary. But it was not only commerce and wealth that had charms for the Ionians; they also took the lead in the cultivation of the fine arts and of literature. The Euxine lost its terrors, when opened by the Milesians, while other Ionians turned their attention to the west. The Phocaeans founded Emporiae in Spain, and about B. C. 600 Massilia in Gaul, where they spread civilisation and the use of the Greek alphabet among the Celts. The Rhodians, who form an exception to the general character of the Doric colonies in Asia, also founded settlements in Spain and Gaul. We have already had occasion to mention that about the year B. C. 650 Psammetichus, king of Egypt, induced Greeks to go to his dominions, and allowed them to settle there.[1] This brief survey at once shows that there was not a country round the basin of the Mediterranean, that was not more or less influenced and benefited by the mild genius of Greek culture and civilisation.

6. While the Asiatic Greeks were flourishing in freedom, commerce, wealth, arts, and arms, the kingdom of Lydia gradually encroached upon their territory, and in the end crushed their independence. Gyges, the first Lydian king of the Mermnad dynasty, took Colophon, and invaded the territories of Smyrna and Miletus. Under his successor Ardys, Priene was subdued, while Sadyattes and Alyattes waged war against Miletus for many years, until in B. C. 612 a peace and alliance were concluded between Lydia and Miletus. Croesus conquered Ephesus, but treated it leniently; and in a short time all the Greek towns of the continent were compelled to acknowledge him as their master. Croesus, being an admirer of the Greeks, and a lover of their culture, treated them in such a manner that they felt his rule scarcely in anything else than in the necessity of paying tribute to him, for they were permitted to regulate their own internal affairs as they pleased. He is also said to have contemplated the subjugation of the neighbouring islands, but was cautioned against it, and confined himself to extending his kingdom towards the east. In this he succeeded so far as to make himself master of the whole of Asia Minor to the river Halys—Lycia and Cilicia alone maintaining their independence. The fame of Croesus resounded throughout Greece, and his liberality towards the Greeks was unbounded. In the end he became involved in a contest with Cyrus, who made Croesus his captive, and himself master of the kingdom of Lydia, including the Greek colonies, B. C. 546.[2] The Lydians were deprived of their arms, and compelled by their conquerors to devote themselves to the arts of peace and luxury, in consequence of which they lost their warlike character, and sunk into effeminacy. As Cyrus himself was obliged to return to his eastern provinces, he left the task of com-

[1] See p. 107.   [2] Comp. pp. 66 and 89.

pleting the conquest of the Greek colonies to his lieutenants.   The
Greeks were willing to submit to the Persians on the same terms
which had been granted to them by Croesus; but as unconditional
surrender was demanded, they prepared for resistance.   Envoys were
sent to Sparta for assistance, but in vain, and Mazares, a Median
general of Cyrus, took the towns of Priene and Magnesia.   Harpagus,
the successor of Mazares, vigorously pressed the Ionian cities.   The
inhabitants of Phocaea, finding that resistance was hopeless, emigrated to the western parts of the Mediterranean, where they had
already planted some colonies.   They first sailed to Alalia in Corsica,
but being attacked there by the Carthaginians and Etruscans, some
sailed to their countrymen in Massilia, and others to Rhegium in
southern Italy, where they founded Elea.   The example of Phocaea
was followed by Teos, whose inhabitants sailed to the coast of Thrace,
where they founded the city of Abdera.   In this manner all the
Ionian cities were conquered by Harpagus, and even some of
the islands endeavoured to avert greater calamities by voluntary
submission.

7. After the conquest of the Æolian and Ionian cities, Harpagus
advanced southward.   The Carians submitted without a struggle;
but Lycia determined to defend its ancient liberty.   The men of
Xanthus, when besieged by the Persians, burnt their city, together
with their wives and children, and then sallying forth died sword in
hand.   Other towns followed the same example, but whatever did
not bend to the will of the conqueror, was broken and ground to
dust, so that after a short time the whole of Asia Minor was obliged
to acknowledge the sovereignty of Persia.   The Persian rule was
perhaps not much more oppressive than that of Croesus had been;
but the misfortune was, that the Asiatic Greeks might be compelled
by their new masters to fight against their kinsmen in Europe.
However, during the reign of Cambyses, they remained quiet, and
the islands which had at first submitted were almost quite free, as
the Persians had no fleet to enforce their commands.   Samos was
then governed by the powerful tyrant Polycrates, and possessed a
fleet of one hundred galleys.   He became involved in a war with
Miletus which brought him into conflict with Persia.   In order to
avoid this, and at the same time gain a powerful ally in Cambyses
against secret enemies at home, he assisted the Persian monarch
with a portion of his fleet against Egypt, taking care to embark
those men whom he had most reason to fear.   But as the design
was discovered, the fleet turned against him, and being unsuccessful,
the men solicited aid from Sparta against the tyrant.   The Spartan
auxiliaries, though strengthened by a band of Corinthians, were
unable to effect anything, and the exiled Samians, after ranging for
some time as pirates in the Ægean, finally established themselves at
Cydonia in Crete.   Polycrates, now stronger than ever, resumed his

old plan of extending his dominion by the aid of Persia; but being treacherously enticed to go to Sardes, he was seized and hung upon a cross, B. C. 522. The Samians who had accompanied him were dismissed, and the satrap made an attempt to gain possession of Samos. The Greek cities of Asia continued, without much molestation from Persia, to live in peace and prosperity, until, in the reign of Darius, they allowed themselves to be enticed by an unprincipled adventurer into open rebellion against their rulers.

8. The cultivation of the arts kept pace with the advance of public and private prosperity, especially among the Ionians in Asia, who made more rapid progress even than the Greeks in the mother country. The same spirit which led the Ionians to commercial enterprises in distant lands, found employment at home in the cultivation of the arts which cheered and adorned their public and private life. Corinth and a few other Doric cities also could boast of early schools of art, but the Ionians surpassed them all, while Athens had as yet not emerged from its obscurity as a seat of art and literature. In Ionia and Samos temples of great splendour were erected at an early period, and the art of casting metal statues is said to have been invented in Samos. The progress which this and the sister arts made was extremely rapid. Sculpture in marble came into extensive use in consequence of its connection with architecture, the temples being sumptuously adorned with statues and figures in high relief. Statues intended for worship in the temples were generally of a typical character, and the artists were not allowed much freedom in their execution; but the case became different when sculptures were employed as ornaments for the outside of temples and other public buildings. The custom of honouring the victors in the public games with statues contributed still more towards the rapid development of the art—an art in which the Greeks have never been equalled, much less surpassed.

9. The same spirit which in art gradually brought about the union of truth and beauty also gave birth to new branches and forms of poetry. The first period of Greek literature is marked by the names of Homer and Hesiod, the former representing its beginning, and the latter its close; but we must not imagine that these poets were the only ones that adorned the first dawn of Greek literature; we have every reason to believe that the compositions and names of many others are lost, whose fame was eclipsed only by that of their great contemporaries. Hesiod was, like Homer, the head of a poetical school, and among the works which have come down under his name, some are undoubtedly the productions of others. He was a native of Ascra in Boeotia, but the time at which he lived is as uncertain as that of Homer, though it is generally assumed that he flourished after Homer, about B. C. 850. As Homer had been the poet of a conquering race of warriors, so Hesiod was the poet of

the peaceful peasantry of Bœotia, for in this character he appears in his "Works and Days," the only composition which has always been regarded as genuine.

10. Epic poetry, however, continued to flourish for two centuries after the beginning of the Olympiads, and the poets of this latter period are usually called the cyclic poets, because the subjects of their poems embraced a definite cycle or period of time. No subject, however, was excluded, from the origin of the world down to the close of the heroic age; but as the poetical interest in these compositions was subordinate to the desire to represent the events in their natural order of succession, these poems were the forerunners of history. We have no specimens of Greek lyric poetry as ancient as Homer, though we have no reason for believing that it was not cultivated at a very remote period; but it reached the summit of perfection at the time when epic poetry was dying away. Unfortunately, however, all the works of the Greek lyrists have perished, with the exception of the epinician odes of Pindar The few fragments of the other great lyric poets, however, are sufficient to justify the admiration of the ancients, and to show us how much we have to lament the loss of those masterpieces of the Greek muse. Lyric poetry was cultivated especially by the Dorians and Æolians, and with the former the themes were chiefly religious, martial, or political, while with the others they were more of a sentimental character. The grand choral poetry, which was peculiar to the Dorians, was brought to perfection by Arion and Stesichorus, and formed the element out of which afterwards the Athenian Thespis developed the Attic tragedy by the introduction of recitation by the performer. The most illustrious among the Æolian and Ionian lyrists are Archilochus, Hipponax, Alcaeus, on the one hand, and Anacreon, Ibycus, Mimnermus, and Sappho, on the other.

11 Prose was cultivated in Greece, as in all other countries, at a much later period than poetry, and Pherecydes of Syros, who lived about B. C. 550, is said to have been the first prose writer in Greece, and Cadmus of Miletus to have first applied prose to historical subjects. The first attempts in historical composition were mythological, and probably consisted of paraphrases in prose of portions of the epic cycle. Writers of this class could have no higher aim than to amuse and to gratify patriotic vanity, or the popular taste for the marvellous.

A certain spirit of philosophical inquiry manifests itself among the Greeks from the very earliest times, as their poetry and religion amply testify; but philosophy as a distinct branch of study does not appear until the middle of the sixth century B. C. That time was the period of the Seven Sages, all practical men, and actively engaged as statesmen, magistrates, or legislators. Their wisdom accordingly was derived from their intercourse with the world, rather than from deep meditation or speculation. But at the same time a few of the bolder spirits were led by the contemplation of the universe to inquire after a first cause of all the visible phenomena. The most ancient school of philosophy was founded by Thales of Miletus, a contemporary of Solon. He maintained that water or some liquid was the origin of all things. Half a century later, Anaximenes, likewise a Milesian, taught that air was the universal source of life, and Heraclitus of Ephesus attributed the same power to fire or heat. The mighty problem which those infant philosophers set themselves to solve cannot but fill us with wonder and amazement, and, however defective their solutions were, they gradually led to the recognition of one supreme mind, distinct from the visible world, to which it imparted motion, form, and order.

Nearly simultaneously with the Ionic school of philosophy, another sprang up at Elea or Velia, a Phocaean colony in the south of Italy. Its founder Xenophanes had emigrated from Colophon to Elea about B. C. 536. His system was based on the assumption of a supreme intelligence, which was identical with the world. His disciple Parmenides pursued his inquiries in the same direction, but set out from the idea of being, not from that of deity. His followers, Zeno and Melissus, were chiefly engaged in combating the opinions of other philosophers and of the vulgar.

It is not known whether Thales wrote an exposition of his doctrines, but his disciple Anaximander did so in a prose work, and his example was followed by all the philosophers of the Ionic school. Xenophanes and Parmenides, on the other hand, explained their systems in verse, a mode which was also adopted by Empedocles of Agrigentum. The remains of these works breathe a strain of oracular solemnity and obscurity.

12. The most celebrated of the western schools of philosophy was founded by Pythagoras of Samos, about B. C. 570. His history is very obscure, and partly mythical. It seems, however, certain that he gathered much information by travelling in foreign countries, such as Egypt. He is said to have been the first to assume the title of philosopher, that is, lover of wisdom. His mind appears to have been chiefly of a mathematical turn, and several discoveries in mathematics and astronomy are attributed to him. His fundamental doctrine was, that numbers represented the essence and properties of all things. He also taught the immortality of the soul in the form of a transmigration, similar to that maintained by the Brahmins and Egyptians.

On his return from his travels he went to the continent of Greece, being unable to endure the tyrannis of Polycrates, and then proceeded to Italy, fixing his residence at Croton. This city was distracted by the feuds between the nobles and the commonalty, but the influence of the former predominated, and Pythagoras proved a useful ally to them.　He formed an order or society consisting of three hundred of the noblest young men collected from the Greek cities in Italy, through whom he hoped to exercise an influence upon all his countrymen in the west.　This society seems to have been at once a philosophical school, a religious brotherhood, and a political association of an aristocratic or oligarchic character.　All the proceedings of this body were enveloped in great mystery. Neither Pythagoras himself nor his disciples appear to have intended to come forward as reformers or lawgivers, but rather to exercise a quiet and gradual influence on their countrymen by doctrine and example; but he became involved in a political contest in which he exerted himself to give support to the aristocracy. The popular party, roused by jealousy of the influence of the Pythagoraean fraternity, brought several charges against it.　At Sybaris the democrats compelled five hundred nobles to quit the city.　They took refuge at Croton, and when their surrender was demanded by the people of Sybaris, the Senate of Croton, by the advice of Pythagoras, refused to comply with the request, and prepared to repel force by force.　A war between the two cities was the result, and the Crotoniats, commanded by Milo, a disciple of Pythagoras, were victorious.　Sybaris was destroyed and swept from the face of the earth, the river Crathis being turned through its ruins, B. C. 510.　The aristocratic party at Croton wished to secure for themselves all the advantages of this victory, but the commonalty, indignant at such selfishness, rose against them, and more especially against the Pythagoraeans.　The house in which the latter were assembled was set on fire, B. C. 504; many of them perished, and the rest found safety only in exile.　Pythagoras himself is said to have died soon after at Metapontum.　The fall of the Pythagoraeans strengthened the commonalty not only at Croton, but in all the cities of southern Italy; but party feuds continued to disturb their peace and prosperity for many years afterwards.

CHAPTER VI.

THE PERSIAN WARS DOWN TO THE ESTABLISHMENT OF THE SUPREMACY OF ATHENS.

1. DARIUS, who ascended the throne of Persia in B. C. 521, came in contact with the Greeks through his conquest of Thrace and Macedonia, which he reduced during his great expedition against the Scythians; but even before that event, he had had to interfere

in the affairs of Samos, which, after the death of Polycrates, was governed by the tyrant Macandrius. Syloson, a brother of Polycrates, claiming the succession for himself, sought and obtained the assistance of Persia. An army under Otanes came across and succeeded indeed in restoring Syloson, but not until nearly the whole population was massacred, so that Syloson became the ruler of a deserted island. The cause, as well as the progress of Darius' expedition against the Scythians, who then occupied the plains between the Danube and the Don, is involved in great obscurity; and scarcely any fact connected with it is quite certain, except that it was conducted by Darius in person, and that it failed (about B. C. 507). An enormous army of nearly a million of men, it is said, was led by him across the Thracian Bosporus; and a fleet of six hundred sail, furnished by his Greek subjects, and commanded by their tyrants, was to sail up the Danube to a certain point, where it was to meet the land force. The king, with his army, without meeting much opposition, crossed the Danube, and then ordered the bridge, which had been constructed over the river, to be broken down. But being reminded that it might be wanted on his return, he ordered it to be left standing for sixty days. He then proceeded against the Scythians. The subsequent part of this enterprise is full of impossibilities and inconsistencies; and it is impossible to say more, than that the pursuit of the Persians was in the end changed into a retreat, in which they were obliged to abandon their baggage and the sick. When the sixty days had elapsed, and the bridge over the Danube was to be broken down, Miltiades, the Athenian, tried to persuade the Greeks to take it down, and thus at once to deliver themselves from the yoke of Persia; but, on the advice of Histiaeus, tyrant of Miletus, it was allowed to stand. Soon after, Darius returned, and his army was still large enough to enable him to leave eighty thousand men in Europe under Megabazus, to complete the conquest of Thrace and the Greek cities on the Hellespont. Darius, on returning to Asia, rewarded Histiaeus for his services with a district on the river Strymon, the tyrannis of Histiaeus over Miletus being intrusted to his cousin Aristagoras.

2. Megabazus reduced Perinthos, and having subdued all the Thracian tribes which had not yet submitted to his master, he made an expedition against the Paeonians, whom Darius wished to be transported into Asia. The great body of this people dispersed, but some of them were, by the king's command, located in Phrygia. When this matter was accomplished, Megabazus demanded of Amyntas, king of Macedonia, earth and water, the usual symbols of submission. Macedonia at this time was only a small kingdom, of which the ruling dynasty was believed to be of Hellenic origin, and descended from Heracles; but the people were a mixture of Illyrians and Pelasgians, and were always looked upon by the

15

Greeks as barbarians. King Amyntas consented to become the vassal of Darius, and a banquet was given to the Persian envoys; but their indecent and outrageous conduct roused the indignation of Alexander, the king's son, to such a degree, that he caused them all to be murdered in the banquet hall. No notice was ever taken of this occurrence either by Megabazus or by Darius.

3. In the meantime, Histiaeus founded in his Thracian principality a town called Myrcinus, and was collecting the elements of a power which roused the suspicion of Megabazus. The latter communicated his apprehensions to Darius, who at once resolved to make Histiaeus harmless, and, pretending that he wished to consult him, invited him to come to Sardes, where he was then residing. When he arrived, the king professed great friendship for him, declaring that he could not live without him, and took him to Susa, where he was to share his table and counsels. Histiaeus accordingly was kept in splendid captivity. The generals of Darius meanwhile completed the subjugation of the Greek cities in the north of the Ægean, and the islands of Imbros and Lemnos, so that about the year B. C. 505, all the nations from the banks of the Indus to the borders of Thessaly were subject to the king of Persia.

Meantime events were occurring in Naxos which were destined to become the source of a conflict between the colossal empire of Persia and the little states of Greece. The aristocratic party of the island of Naxos, being driven into exile by the democrats, solicited the aid of Aristagoras, tyrant of Miletus, and he, considering this a favourable opportunity for making himself master of the island, applied for assistance to Artaphernes, who had been appointed satrap of western Asia. Aristagoras represented the conquest of Naxos as an easy matter, and promised to defray all the expenses. A fleet of two hundred ships, commanded by a Persian admiral, was placed at his disposal, and having taken on board his own Ionian army, he sailed out. But a quarrel soon arose between Aristagoras and the admiral; and the latter, determined to thwart the Greek tyrant, warned the Naxians of their danger. The Naxians accordingly made most vigorous preparations to defend themselves, so that when they were besieged, the enemy was unable to make any progress. His means were soon exhausted, and in B. C. 501, he was obliged to return to Miletus without having effected anything. As he was unable to make good his promise to the Persian satrap, he was a ruined man, and saw no help for himself except in revolution. While pondering over this, he received a secret message from Histiaeus, who likewise saw no means of escaping from his captivity except by an insurrection of his countrymen. Aristagoras now assembled his most trustworthy friends whom he knew to be discontented with the rule of the barbarians, to deliberate upon a plan of action. Hecataeus, the historian, dissuaded them from it, but war was resolved upon, though the conspirators did not possess the means of carrying it on. In order to win the favour of the popular party, Aristagoras not only resigned his own tyrannis, but seized the other tyrants of the Asiatic cities who were stationed with the Persian fleet off Myus, B. C. 500.

4. Aristagoras now resolved also to apply to the Greeks in Europe to support their kinsmen in their attempt to shake off the Persian yoke. He first went to Sparta, with a map of the world engraven on a brass plate, to persuade king Cleomenes of the feasibility of his scheme. The money which he promised as the price for the assistance, was on the point of producing the desired effect, when the king, warned by his little daughter, declined to have anything to do with the matter. Aristagoras then proceeded to Athens, where his solicitations on behalf of oppressed Greeks were not made in vain, for they already knew that the Persian monarch had it in contemplation to re impose upon them their exiled tyrant Hippias. A decree accordingly was readily passed by the people of Athens to send a squadron of twenty ships to support the insurrection of their Ionian kinsmen in Asia. This squadron sailed in B. C. 499, accompanied by five galleys from Eretria in Euboea. After landing at Ephesus, the Athenians, strengthened by a large number of Ionians, straightway marched against Sardes. The Persian satrap took refuge in the strong citadel, and the lower city was plundered and set on fire. Satisfied with this achievement, and unable to take the citadel, the Greeks returned to Ephesus. But being pursued by the whole force which the Persian satrap had been able to muster, they were overtaken and beaten in a battle near Ephesus. The Ionians then dispersed, and the Athenians and Eretrians returned home.

5. When Darius was informed of these things, his rage knew no bounds; but he was more indignant at the obscure strangers who had dared to attack his dominions than at the Ionians themselves, and he charged one of his attendants daily to remind him of the Athenians. His first care, however, was to quell the insurrection of the Ionians, which was spreading farther and farther. The cunning Histiaeus obtained leave to go to Ionia, under the promise that he would soon put down the rebels. The Ionians in the meantime induced Byzantium and the other Greek cities in the north to assert their independence, and Caria and the island of Cyprus followed their example. The Persian generals were no less active in crushing the revolt. The cities on the Propontis and in Caria were reduced by Daurises, and Cyprus was overpowered by a Phoenician fleet. When this was accomplished, the Persians directed all their forces against the Ionian and Aeolian cities. When Clazomenae and Cuma had fallen, Aristagoras, having lost all hope of success, went to Myrcinus in Thrace, where soon after his reckless career

was cut short while he was besieging a Thracian town with a band of Ionians. Meanwhile Histiaeus arrived at Sardes, and it being hinted to him by the satrap Artaphernes, that he had had a hand in the revolt, he thought it advisable to make his escape to Chios. He would gladly have put himself at the head of the Greeks, but he was generally suspected and distrusted. He found himself a homeless adventurer, and withdrew to Lesbos, where he was more successful; he collected a small fleet, with which he sailed to Byzantium, and seized all the merchant-vessels of the cities which refused to recognise him as the sovereign of Ionia.

6. The insurrection of Ionia was in the meantime drawing to a crisis. Every effort was made against Miletus. A large fleet was brought together, consisting of six hundred ships. The fleet of the Ionians, amounting to three hundred and fifty-three triremes, was stationed near the little island of Lade, for the confederates had resolved to leave Miletus to defend himself. The Persians, notwithstanding their superiority in numbers, did not venture to attack the Ionians at sea, and had recourse to some unsuccessful stratagems. The Ionians, however, were careless, and this irritated some of those who saw the necessity of maintaining better discipline, to such a degree, that they made secret overtures to the enemy. When, therefore, the Persians at last made the attack, the Samians first withdrew from the fight, and their example was followed by others. Some of the Greeks, however, fought to the last, but their defeat was complete. This happened in B. C. 494, and the disaster was soon followed by the fall of Miletus; in the following year the other Ionian cities, and those in the north of the Ægean, likewise succumbed, and were treated with the utmost rigour. The terror which preceded the Persians everywhere induced the inhabitants of Byzantium and Chalcedon to quit their homes and found a new one at Mesembria, on the coast of the Euxine. Miltiades, who had been living on his large estates in the Thracian Chersonesus ever since the return of Darius from Scythia, also felt unsafe, and returned to Athens.

7. After the reduction of the Greek cities, they were made to feel the Persian yoke much more severely than before, and all traces of independence were effaced. Order and peace were restored at the expense of liberty; but still the cities in that happy climate soon revived and recovered from their calamities. Mardonius, the king's son-in-law, on being sent to succeed Artaphernes, allayed the discontent of the Greeks by deposing the tyrants who had been set up by his predecessor, and by restoring the democratic form of government. But at the same time he was accompanied by a large armament to chastise Athens and Eretria for their presumption, and to spread the terror of the king's name in Europe. A large was to sweep the Ægean, while Mardonius himself led an a

land through Thrace into Greece. The fleet was overtaken by a violent storm off mount Athos, and no less than three hundred ships and twenty thousand men are said to have been lost on that occasion. The land army was not much more fortunate, for one night the camp was attacked by a Thracian tribe, and the loss sustained was so great that Mardonius thought it prudent to return to Asia, B. C. 492.

8. But the determination of Darius was not shaken by these disasters; he renewed his preparations, and sent heralds to the principal cities of Greece to demand the customary signs of submission. Both at Athens and at Sparta these envoys were put to death, but many other cities, and Ægina with the other islands,,complied with the demand of the barbarians. The Athenians, still hostile to the Æginetans, sent ambassadors to Sparta to charge Ægina with high treason against the cause of Greece. Cleomenes, king of Sparta, advanced with a force against the Æginetans, who, being frightened, delivered up to him ten of their leading men, who were sent as hostages to Athens. The Æginetans retaliated, and a succession of acts of hostility continued to be committed from time to time by both states, while the Persians were making their preparations for invading Europe. In B. C. 490, a fleet of six hundred galleys with transports were assembled in Cilicia under the command of Datis and Artaphernes, ready to take the army on board. The fleet crossed the Ægean, subdued Naxos and the other Cyclades, and then sailed towards Euboea, taking in reinforcements from the islands during its progress. Eretria sent to Athens for succour against the impending danger, and the four thousand Athenians settled in Euboea were charged to defend that city; but as the Eretrians themselves were not agreed as to how to act, the Athenians returned to Attica. After the fall of Carystus, which had refused to admit the enemy, Eretria was besieged. Some traitors in the city opened the gates to the Persians, who plundered the temples, and then set fire to the place. The inhabitants were made prisoners, and afterwards transported to Asia as slaves. After this, the whole fleet sailed towards the coast of Attica.

9. Guided by the exiled tyrant Hippias, who had urged the Persians to this expedition against his own country, the army landed on the plain of Marathon, which is about five miles in length, and two in breadth. No sooner did the Athenians hear of the enemy's arrival, than they marched out to meet them, all serviceable citizens, and even slaves willing to earn their liberty, being armed. The Plataeans, the brothers and allies of the Athenians, obeyed the summons of Athens without delay. At the same time a messenger was despatched to Sparta in all haste, to give information of the danger, and request assistance. But the Spartans, not being themselves exposed to immediate peril, and having moreover some

15 *

religious scruples as to setting out about the time of the new moon, dismissed the messenger with promises of future succour. The Athenians, however, undismayed by this want of ready sympathy on the part of the leading state of Greece, resolved to attack the invaders. They were commanded, as usual, by ten generals, one of whom was Miltiades, who had recently returned from Chersonesus, but Callimachus as polemarch was at their head. The generals were divided in their opinions as to whether battle should be given to the Persians at once, or whether they should wait for the arrival of the Lacedaemonians. Miltiades, seeing the danger of delay, and fearing treachery, as Hippias had still some friends in the city, urged the necessity of attacking the enemy at once, and his colleagues gave way to his arguments. Accordingly, when the command came round to Miltiades, he drew up the little army in order of battle on a rising ground. At the signal of attack, they rushed on the enemy, who received them with scorn and contempt, as men hurrying to certain destruction. But before they were aware of it, the Persians found themselves engaged in close combat, and, owing to the skilful management of Miltiades, they were completely defeated. In the greatest confusion and disorder the barbarians rushed to their ships, but many perished in the marshes on the coast, and in their attempts to embark. The Persian fleet with the survivors then steered towards Sunion, to attack Attica on the opposite side, but they were prevented by the prompt movements of the Athenians, who arrived on the western coast before the Persians, and the latter, seeing that they had miscalculated, returned to Asia, without making any further attempts against the Greeks. So ended the great day of Marathon, in August B. C. 490.

10. The battle of Marathon was always looked upon by the Athenians as their most glorious achievement, and well might they be proud of it; for a small band of patriots had routed and defeated a countless host of barbarians, and thereby secured the independence of Greece and Europe. But what they had actually accomplished, was so much magnified in their heated imaginations, that in the subsequent reports about it, it became something altogether incredible and impossible. Athens, however, to whom the glory of this victory belonged almost exclusively, now for the first time became aware of her own strength. The Persian forces are said to have amounted to six hundred thousand men, while those of the Athenians and Plataeans are estimated at ten thousand; upwards of six thousand of the enemy lay on the field of battle, while the Athenians had lost only one hundred and ninety-two, but among them was Callimachus, the polemarch. The place where this glorious battle was fought is still marked by a tumulus, under which the Athenians are said to have been buried. The absence of the Spartans on the day of the battle was an event of incalculable

moment. They arrived after the battle was over with a force of only two thousand men, and having inspected the field strewed with the dead, they returned home, apparently feeling themselves that they had not done their duty towards their country.

11. Very soon after the battle of Marathon, Miltiades, somewhat elated by his success, requested a fleet of seventy sail, promising his fellow-citizens to increase their dominions. With this force, which was readily granted, he first sailed to Paros, where he had a private enemy. But the Parians repelled his attacks, and having received a wound in his knee, he returned to Athens without having accomplished anything. Xanthippus, the father of Pericles, brought an action against him for having led the people into useless expenses, and as public feeling was against him, he was sentenced to pay a fine of fifty talents. Being unable to raise this sum at once, he was thrown into prison, and soon after died of his wound. This verdict against their great commander has brought much censure upon the Athenians, but there are indications which seem to show that he had acted with disregard or even contempt of the laws of his country; and if so, the sentence pronounced against him, though severe, was not unjust.

12. The battle of Marathon ought to have taught the Persians a lesson which they stood much in need of; but instead of this, their anger was doubly inflamed, and thinking that his forces had been insufficient, Darius resolved to make the Athenians feel the whole weight of his arm. For three years preparations were made throughout his empire, and everything was furnished in abundance; but in the fourth an insurrection broke out in Egypt, and before he had made the necessary arrangements for its suppression, he died, B. C. 486. He was succeeded by Xerxes (B. C. 485—465), the favourite son of his favourite wife, who was urged by his friends and advisers to renew the enterprise, which, he was told, had failed only through mischance, and not through the inability of the Persians. Mardonius was foremost among these advisers, and he was eagerly supported by treacherous Greeks, who had gone to Susa for the purpose of accomplishing their selfish ends. A fresh invasion of Greece accordingly was resolved upon; but before proceeding, Xerxes had to reduce Egypt, which was effected in the second year of his reign. After this, the whole of Asia was ransacked for a period of four years, and all available resources of his empire were collected to be turned against Greece. To facilitate the progress of the army and fleet, a bridge of boats was thrown across the Hellespont, and a canal dug through the low isthmus which connects mount Athos with the mainland, in order to avoid the dangerous doubling of that promontory, where the fleet of Mardonius had been destroyed.

13. When all this was completed, Xerxes in the spring of B. C. 480 set out from Sardes with an army consisting of nations of all

colours, costumes, arms, and languages. When they had crossed the Hellespont at Abydos, they proceeded from Sestos up the Chersonesus towards Doriscos, where the whole motley host was reviewed; it is said to have consisted of one million seven hundred thousand foot and eighty thousand horse. The fleet, which had arrived off the coast of the same place, numbered one thousand two hundred and seven triremes and three thousand smaller vessels. From Doriscos the army, accompanied by the fleet, marched along the coast through Thrace and Macedonia towards the south.

The Greeks had at first been slow in making preparations for the common danger, but when it became known what Xerxes was doing, the leading states and those breathing the same spirit of independence began to feel that their safety depended upon union. But unanimity was a thing difficult to attain in Greece. The people of Thessaly were obliged by the ruling family of the Aleuadae to yield when the Persians demanded of them earth and water, and their example was followed by all the tribes between them and mount Œta. The Phocians refused compliance with the demand, but the Dorians and Boeotians yielded; Thespiae and Plataeae alone remained faithful to the cause of Greece. Selfishness and pusillanimity thus prevented a coalition among the northern Greeks. The Peloponnesians, so far as the influence of Sparta reached, were unanimous, but Argos and Achaia, from enmity towards Sparta, resolved to remain neutral. Athens and Sparta, however, exerted all their power to meet the impending danger. The leading man at Athens, and the soul of all her counsels, was Themistocles, whose object was to make Athens great and powerful, that he himself might move and command in a large sphere. He was most distinguished for extraordinary quickness of perception as to what was the real state of affairs at any given time, and what was required therein to ensure a definite end. But by his side stood Aristides, a man somewhat older than he, and who had already reached the height of popularity by his extraordinary honesty and disinterestedness, which procured him the honourable surname of the Just. He, like Themistocles, to whom he was inferior in abilities, had the welfare of his country at heart, but simply and singly, not as a means, but as an end. Men like these could not but come into frequent collision, and by the contrivance of Themistocles Aristides was sent by ostracism into honourable exile, B. C. 483. By the removal of his rival, Themistocles was left in the undivided possession of the popular favour. He saw the necessity for Athens to enlarge her naval force, and prevailed upon the people to devote the profits they had hitherto derived from the silver mines of Laurion to the increase of their navy. The Athenians thus raised their fleet to the number of two hundred ships, and became a maritime people, for which nature had in fact destined them by the situation of their city.

14. Even before Xerxes had left Asia, the Greek states favourable to the cause of independence had held a congress on the isthmus of Corinth, with the view of bringing about a union; but they met with little or no success. Envoys were even sent to Gelo, tyrant of Syracuse, who promised his support, if the Greeks would intrust to him the command of all their forces. This embassy had probably been sent, because it was known that Xerxes had instigated the Carthaginians, through his Phoenician subjects, to attack the Greek cities in Sicily. The proposal of Gelo, however, was rejected. Meanwhile Themistocles did all he could, not only to allay animosity and silence disputes among the Greeks, but also to brace the energy of his fellow-citizens. The enthusiasm thus infused into the friends of liberty is clear from the fact that the Greeks assembled at Corinth, bound themselves by an oath to consecrate to the god at Delphi a tenth of the substance of every Greek people, which had surrendered to the Persians without being compelled by necessity. It was also resolved at the congress that the progress of the Persians should be opposed at the pass of Thermopylae, whither a small body of Peloponnesians was sent at once, and that the fleet should guard the northern entrance of the Euboean channel. The whole fleet consisted of two hundred and seventy-one triremes, of which Athens furnished by far the greater part. The Spartan Eurybiades had the command of the fleet.

15. When the Persian armada in its course southward came near cape Sepias, it was overtaken by a storm, which burst upon it with irresistible fury, and lasted for three days and three nights. The coast for many miles was covered with wrecks and corpses; four hundred ships and innumerable lives were lost, and the remainder of the fleet took shelter in the gulf of Pagasae. The Greeks, rejoiced at this disaster of the enemy, returned to their station at Artemisium, which during the first alarm they had abandoned, and at once captured fifteen of the enemy's ships, which had been detained. But when it became known that the loss of the Persians, great as it was, was scarcely felt by them, the Greeks again began to despond, and Themistocles had great difficulty in keeping the fleet together. At length, however, when the Persians had sustained another loss from a storm, the Greeks took courage and boldly sailed out to attack the enemy. A small squadron of Cilician vessels was taken and destroyed. This led to a general engagement, in which the unwieldy armament of the Persians was thrown into confusion and sustained great loss. But one half of the ships of the Greeks were likewise disabled, and they now resolved to retreat, partly on this account, and partly on account of tidings which had just reached them from Thermopylae.

16. The small band of Peloponnesians which had been sent to bar the progress of the Persians in the pass of Thermopylae was

commanded by the Spartan king Leonidas. It consisted of three hundred Spartans, five hundred Tegeatans, and about two thousand from other Peloponnesian cities; and these had been joined by one thousand Phocians and seven hundred Thespians. It was believed that this force was sufficient to prevent the enemy from making his way through the pass—it being unknown that there was a path across the mountain by which the pass could be evaded. But when its existence was discovered, Leonidas sent the Phocians to occupy the heights. When the Greeks became aware of the countless hosts by which their small force was to be assailed, Leonidas could scarcely keep his men together, and he sent envoys to the south to ask for speedy reinforcements. Xerxes, who had hoped to scare them by his mere presence, was astonished when he heard that they were awaiting his attack in all composure. After a few days he ordered his men to bring the Greeks captive before him; but attack after attack proved fruitless, and the slaughter on the side of the barbarians was great. Xerxes began to despair of success, when the path across the mountain was betrayed to him by a base Greek of the name of Ephialtes. A detachment of the king's troops accordingly followed the infamous traitor up the mountain. The Phocians, unable to drive the enemy back, retreated, and the barbarians, unconcerned about them, pursued their course. When the Greeks in the pass heard what had happened, Leonidas declared for himself and his Spartans the determination to defend his post to the last, but allowed those of his allies who wished to save themselves to withdraw. All availed themselves of this permission except the Thespians and four hundred Thebans. When the detachment guided by Ephialtes arrived at the southern entrance of the pass, the Spartans were at once attacked on both sides. Leonidas, knowing his hopeless condition, sallied forth, determined to sell his life and those of his countrymen as dearly as possible. Four times the Persians were driven back, until at length the Spartans being surrounded on a hillock, were all slain. Leonidas had fallen at an early part of the day; all were subsequently buried on the spot where they had fallen, and an inscription on their tomb bade the passenger go to Sparta and tell their countrymen that they had fallen in obedience to the laws of their country. The battle of Thermopylae was fought in the summer of B. C. 480, and the Persians are said to have lost there no less than twenty thousand men.

17. Xerxes having now gained the entrance into Greece, advanced through Doris against Phocis, whose inhabitants took refuge in the mountains. The Persians poured undistinguishing ruin upon everything that came in their way. The main body of their army proceeded through Boeotia against Attica, while a small detachment was sent to strip the temple of Delphi of its treasures. The

Delphians had left their city to the protection of Apollo, who in the hour of danger did not forsake it. For when the barbarians advanced, a fearful thunderstorm is said to have burst upon them, and huge rocks falling from the precipices of Parnassus to have crushed many; and the Persians, terror-stricken, retraced their steps, and were pursued by the Delphians with unresisted slaughter. The Athenians had hoped that the Peloponnesians would throw an army into Boeotia for the protection of Attica, but it soon became evident that they were bent upon defending only the entrance to Peloponnesus, and leaving Attica to its fate. The Athenians asked the Delphic god for advice, and the priestess, probably at the suggestion of Themistocles, told them that they must defend themselves behind their wooden walls. Themistocles, of course, had no difficulty in explaining the mysterious import of the oracle, and convinced them that they must rely for safety upon their navy. This being approved of, the Athenians begged their allies to sail with them from Artemisium to Salamis, there to provide for the safety of their wives and children, and deliberate upon their mode of action.

18. Meanwhile the Persians advanced through Boeotia towards Athens, Thespiae and Platacae being reduced to ashes, while all the other Boeotian towns admitted Persian garrisons, the Athenians, by the advice of Themistocles, abandoned their city to the protection of its tutelary divinity, and transported their families and movable property to Salamis, Ægina, and Troezen, where they were received with great kindness. A few men only remained in the Acropolis. The Greek fleet, assembled at Salamis with its recent reinforcements, amounted to three hundred and eighty ships. In their council of war the Greeks were almost unanimous that the fleet should quit Salamis, and move nearer the isthmus, where it might co-operate with the Peloponnesian army. While these consultations were going on, it was announced that Xerxes had overrun Attica, and that he was spreading desolation over the whole country. The lower city was taken and destroyed, and the small band in the Acropolis was overpowered by surprise. The temples were then plundered, and the whole Acropolis set on fire. These terrible occurrences greatly alarmed the commanders of the Greek fleet, and there seemed little prospect of their remaining united at Salamis; but Themistocles was now more than ever convinced that the only hope of safety consisted in their meeting and engaging the hostile fleet in the straits of Salamis. As his arguments had no effect, he had recourse to threats, declaring that if the allies persisted in their design, the Athenians would sail away with their families and all their property, and seek a new home in Italy. These words produced the desired effect.

19. But as there was still danger lest the Peloponnesians should change their minds, Themistocles, assuming the mask of a traitor to

his country, sent a trusty slave to the Persian admiral with the
message that the Greeks were on the point of fleeing and dispersing,
and that, if he attacked them at once, this would ensure a complete
and easy victory, whereas, if he allowed them to disperse, he would
have to fight against them one by one. This advice, agreeing as
it did with the wishes of the Persians themselves, was followed at
once.   In the night the Persian fleet blocked up the narrow channels by which Salamis is separated from Attica and Megara. When
the morning dawned, the whole sea was seen covered with the
enemy's ships, and the Attic coast lined with troops, while Xerxes
himself intended to view the great naval engagement from a lofty
throne erected on a height. As soon as the gigantic fleet had
entered the narrow channels, and was pent up in such a manner
that movements and evolutions were utterly impossible, the Greeks
attacked them.   The damage done by the Persian ships to one another during the confusion which soon ensued was almost as great
as that inflicted by the valiant Greeks with their nimble triremes.
The event of the battle was in reality decided at the first onset;
but the fight continued all day, until towards evening the remainder
of the hostile fleet withdrew towards Phaleron, whither the Greeks
did not pursue them. This glorious victory was completed by
Aristides, who though in exile had joined the fleet of his country
in the hour of danger. The barbarians are said to have lost on
that day five hundred ships, and the Greeks only forty. Xerxes,
though he still had a sufficient force to renew the contest, felt that
such another defeat would expose him to the greatest danger, and
at once resolved to retreat. In this resolution he was confirmed by
Mardonius, who told him that the land army was still unconquered,
and asked for three hundred thousand men, with whom he promised
to subjugate the whole of Greece. Xerxes, satisfied with the proposal, made preparations for his return across the Hellespont.

20. As the hostile fleet quitted the Saronic gulf, and sailed northward, many of the Greeks burned with the desire of pursuing the
enemy; but Eurybiades thought this dangerous, and even Themistocles gave way to his remonstrances. As the enemy's fleet had
already advanced as far as the Cyclades, the Greeks contented
themselves with chastising those islanders who had supported the
Persians. It is even said that Themistocles hurried the king's
flight, by sending a messenger to inform him that the Greeks
meditated breaking down the bridge which had been constructed
across the Hellespont; and that Xerxes, terrified by this information,
made with all possible speed for the Hellespont. Mardonius accompanied his master as far as Thessaly, where he himself intended to
take up his winter quarters. The sufferings which the king's army
had to endure during this retreat were terrible, and when he arrived
at Sestos, he found the bridge destroyed by the waves, but the fleet

was in readiness to carry him and the wreck of his army across to Abydos. Several of the Greek towns in the north of the Ægean now shook off the Persian yoke, though the king's generals made every effort to prevent it. Themistocles continued his proceedings among the Cyclades, where he tarnished his fame by accepting large bribes, with which some of the islanders purchased their impunity. But the praise of his wisdom and prudence, nevertheless, now resounded through all Greece, and even the Spartans bestowed on him the same honours as upon their own admiral Eurybiades.

At the same time when the battle of Salamis was fought, the Sicilian Greeks gained a most memorable victory over the Carthaginians at Himera, where they fought against an army of three hundred thousand men, commanded by Hamilcar.

21. Shortly after the battle of Salamis the Athenians returned to Attica to rebuild their homes and cultivate their fields, and in the following spring they made active preparations, for they knew that Mardonius was in Thessaly, and a Persian fleet of three hundred sail was still in the Ægean to watch the movements of the Ionians, whom the Persians could not trust. Mardonius, who had by this time become convinced of his difficulties, formed the plan of detaching Athens from the interest of the other Greeks, and engaged Alexander of Macedonia to negotiate a peace and alliance between Athens and Persia. But the manly answer of the Athenians, that, so long as the sun held on its course, Athens would never become the ally of Persia, at once destroyed the hopes of Mardonius and the fears of the other Greeks. Mardonius now set out without delay to make himself master of Athens, and the treacherous Thessalians and Bœotians displayed great zeal in the service of the barbarians. When he arrived at Athens, he found nothing but the deserted walls, for the inhabitants seeing that no aid could be expected from the Peloponnesians, notwithstanding their many promises, had withdrawn with their families to Salamis, B. C. 479. Mardonius now renewed his proposals of peace, but with no better success than before. The Spartans were in the mean time only busied about protecting themselves in their peninsula, by fortifying the isthmus of Corinth. Complaints and even threats were resorted to by the Athenians, Megarians, and Plataeans, when at length the ephors ordered Pausanias, the guardian of the young king Pleistarchus, to lead an army of five thousand Spartans, each attended by seven Helots, into Bœotia. Mardonius, not being inclined to fight a battle in Attica, threw himself into Bœotia, where he hoped to be supported by the Thebans and other Bœotians; but before leaving Attica he destroyed everything which had been left untouched during the previous invasion. He pitched his camp in Bœotia, between Erythrae and the river Asopus, expecting that Pausanias would give him battle there.

22. Pausanias on his march northwards was strengthened by rein-

forcements from the Peloponnesians, and an army of the Athenians
commanded by Aristides. The whole force, amounting, it is said, to
one hundred and ten thousand men, encamped near Erythrae, at the
foot of mount Cythaeron. In a first engagement the Greeks were
successful against the cavalry of the Persians, but for the sake of
greater safety Pausanias descended into the territory of Plataeae,
which still lay in ruins. Mardonius advanced against him with all
his forces, but for ten days the armies faced each other without
coming to any engagement, the signs in the sacrifices being unfavourable, when at length Mardonius resolved to wait no longer. In the
night before the battle, Alexander of Macedonia rode up to the
Athenians, informed them of the determination of the enemy, and
exhorted them to keep their ground. Pausanias made his arrangements accordingly. Mardonius, mistaking the enemy's movements
for signs of fear, attacked them with great vehemence, and the
Greeks were thrown into an unfavourable position. In the following
night, therefore, they moved off towards a more convenient place,
close to Plataeae. Mardonius again imagining that his opponents
had taken to flight, attacked them without delay. He and his Persians fought bravely; but he was mortally wounded, and his fall
decided the issue of the battle. The Persians and all the other
barbarians gave way at once. Artabazus, who commanded forty
thousand men, now came up to reinforce the Persian army, but
finding that it was too late, he returned through Phocis hoping to
reach the Hellespont. The Greek auxiliaries of the Persians immediately dispersed, the Thebans alone continuing to fight against
the Athenians, while the survivors of the barbarians shut themselves
up within their camp. The Athenians were the first to break into
it, and the Asiatics having lost all hope of defending themselves
successfully, allowed themselves to be slaughtered without a struggle,
like sheep in a fold. Out of the whole multitude of barbarians only
three thousand are said to have escaped from the carnage. The
booty and the treasures found in the camp were immense, and
Pausanias ordered the Helots to collect them, that both gods and
men might receive their due share. A tenth part was dedicated in
the form of tripods and statues to Apollo, Zeus, Poseidon, and
Athena; and a magnificent present was selected for Pausanias, to
whom the glory of the victory of Plataeae was justly ascribed.

23. Artabazus, after the loss of many men from famine and
through the attacks of the Thracians, reached Asia in safety; and
Alexander of Macedonia was rewarded for his services with the
Athenian franchise. Greece was now completely and finally
delivered from the Persian invaders. The Greeks before quitting
Boeotia, endeavoured, under the direction of Aristides, to secure
for the future unity among their countrymen against foreign aggression, and resolved upon carrying out the threat against those Greeks

who had supported the Persians. The Thebans had forfeited every claim to leniency, but it was nevertheless agreed to punish only the guilty few and not the whole population. The army accordingly appeared before the gates of Thebes, demanding the surrender of the traitors to their country. As the demand was refused, the city was blockaded for twenty days, after which the offenders themselves consented to be delivered up. Most of them were carried off by Pausanias, and put to death by him without any trial.

24. On the same day on which the Persians were defeated at Plataeae, they also suffered a severe blow on the coast of Asia. The Greek fleet, commanded by the Spartan king Leotychides, was stationed at Delos watching the movements of the enemy, when envoys from Samos solicited its aid against their own tyrant, who was a zealous supporter of Persia. Leotychides accordingly sailed to Samos. The Persian fleet, instead of protecting the tyrant, withdrew towards the mainland to seek the assistance of the land army of sixty thousand men, which was stationed near mount Mycale to keep Ionia in subjection. The Persian ships accordingly were drawn up on the beach, and protected as well as they could be in the hurry. The Greeks, seeing the fear of their enemies, resolved to cross over from Samos, give them battle, and issue a proclamation to the Ionians, calling upon them to remember their liberty. At the same time a rumour reached the Greeks of a victory gained by their countrymen in Boeotia over Mardonius, and this report at once roused their courage and confidence. The Persians were drawn up at the foot of mount Mycale. The Athenians and Spartans made the attack and drove the enemy into the enclosure surrounding their ships; but when the barbarians found that the pursuers had entered the enclosure with them, they betook themselves to the mountain passes, and the Persians themselves, after maintaining the contest for a while, were completely routed. The Samians and the other Ionians joined the Greeks as soon as they were able, and the carnage among the Asiatics was fearful. A few only escaped to Sardes, where Xerxes was still watching the course of events, and the Greeks, after collecting the booty and burning the ships of the enemy, returned to Samos.

25. As Europe and the islands of the Ægean were now safe, it only remained to be decided in what way the Ionians should be permanently protected against their oppressors; it was resolved to return to Europe, and to leave the Ionians to make the best terms they could with Persia for themselves. Xanthippus, the father of Pericles, however, wished to recover the principality of Miltiades in Chersonesus, and as the Spartans had no interest in this matter, it was left to the Athenians alone, while Leotychides and the Peloponnesians sailed home. Xanthippus and the Athenians laid siege to Sestos, where many Persians of rank had sought refuge. The

fortress was very strong, but Xanthippus would not give up the
enterprise, and blockaded the place during the winter, until in the
spring of B. C. 478 famine induced the Persians to try to make their
escape by night.   Many of them, however, were overtaken and put
to death, and the Greek inhabitants of Sestos opened their gates
to the Athenians.   After this Xanthippus and his fleet also sailed
home.

26. On their arrival, the Athenians found their country a wasted
land, and their city a heap of ruins.   The restoration of the private
dwellings was left to their owners, who rebuilt them as well as they
could under the circumstances, and without any system or plan;
the rebuilding of the temples was left for another season, the
thoughts of Themistocles and Aristides being engaged in providing
for the immediate security and permanent strength of the city.
The walls of Athens were restored and extended; but this was
viewed by her allies with fear and jealousy, for they seem to have
forgotten what she had suffered and what she had done for their
common liberty.   Envoys, accordingly, were sent from Sparta, who,
under the disguise of friendship, advised them not to fortify their
city, as it would only strengthen any invading enemy, adding that
Peloponnesus would always be a sufficient refuge for all Greeks.
Themistocles, who saw through their selfish and jealous scheme,
deceived the Spartans, and carried on the work of fortification with
increased activity; and when at length the city was sufficiently
strong, Themistocles, who had himself gone to Sparta, bade them
in future treat the Athenians as reasonable men, who knew what
was due to their own safety as well as to Greece.   The Spartans,
with their usual skill, disguised their vexation, and the fortifications of Athens were quietly completed.   When this was done,
Themistocles, who thoroughly understood the vocation of Athens,
proposed to fortify its three harbours of Phaleron, Munychia, and
Piraeus, by a double range of walls, for hitherto Athens had used
only Phaleron as its port.   At the same time, a plan was formed
of making Piraeus a port town; the success was complete, and
Piraeus became the seat of numerous merchants and tradesmen of
every description, especially aliens who settled there under the protection of Athens.

27. Athens was now strong, and conscious of her position and
power.   In the spring of B. C. 477, the allied fleet, commanded by
Pausanias, again put to sea, the contingent of the Athenians being
under the command of Aristides and Cimon, the son of Miltiades.
They first sailed to Cyprus, which they wrested from the hands of
the Persians; then, having proceeded to the north, they laid siege
to Byzantium, which was still occupied by the Persians, but was
soon taken.   The mind of Pausanias seems to have become perverted by the victories he had gained, for he now adopted the

manners of the barbarians, and began to treat his allies with a haughtiness as if they were his subjects; his ambition was unbounded, and he was blind to the dangers to which he exposed himself. In this state of mind he formed the scheme of betraying Greece into the hands of the Persians, in the hope that he might be made the ruler of his country, as a vassal of the great king. He accordingly made overtures to this effect to Xerxes, asking for his reward the hand of the king's daughter. Xerxes eagerly caught at the proposal, and Pausanias, on discovering this, no longer dissembled his intentions, but at once assumed the pomp and state of a Persian satrap. The Ionians soon found that the treatment they experienced from him was no better than from the Persians. The conduct of the Athenian generals, on the other hand, was all the more winning, from its contrast to that of the Spartans; and hence the allies began to consider how much happier they would be under the command of Aristides and Cimon. The wish gradually ripened into a resolution, and all the allies, with the exception of those from Peloponnesus and Ægina, offered to Athens the supremacy in all their common affairs. Aristides, to whose wise conduct his country owed her present proud position, now undertook the task of regulating the laws of the confederacy, and of its relation to Athens as its head. The great object was to protect the Greeks against the barbarians, and to weaken and humble the latter as much as possible. All were to contribute towards this common end, and Athens, as the organ of the public will, was to collect and direct their forces. Each separate state, however, was to remain perfectly independent in its own affairs. A common fund was established from annual contributions, Delos was chosen as the treasury of the confederates, and in its temple of Apollo the deputies of the several states were to hold their meetings.

28. Through the folly and treachery of one man, Sparta had lost a position which it had maintained for centuries. Pausanias was recalled, but it was too late, and the new generals who were sent out had to be content with a subordinate rank. Sparta, unable to brook this, withdrew from the scene of action, leaving her rival triumphant. She still remained, however, the head of her Peloponnesian allies, who now rallied all the more closely around her, so that henceforth Greece is divided between two great confederacies. The supremacy of Athens lasted until the end of the Peloponnesian war, B. C. 404. But before proceeding to describe the glorious career upon which she now entered so honourably, we shall briefly notice the later occurrences in the lives of the men who had brought about this great change.

29. Aristides, whose last and noblest work was the regulation of the Athenian confederacy, was also the author of some important reforms in the political constitution of his native country, for he is

16 *

said to have opened the archonship and the council of the Areopagus to all Athenian citizens, irrespective of any property qualifica-
tion. Such a change had become necessary by the course of events.
Aristides died in the full enjoyment of the confidence which his
countrymen had placed in him throughout his life.

Pausanias, after his recall to Sparta, was subjected to a severe
inquiry, but as no satisfactory evidence of his treacherous designs
was produced, the accusation was dropped. Without leave from
the ephors he went to Byzantium, and there renewed his criminal
intrigues so openly, that they reached the ears of the authorities at
home. He was summoned to return, and, though tried again, he
could not be convicted, and was restored to liberty. He now planned
an insurrection of the Helots, hoping, with the aid of Persia, to
rise to the head of the state; at the same time he continued his
correspondence with Persia, until one of the messengers entrusted
with a letter, found that he, like all his predecessors, was to be put
to death in Asia to prevent his divulging the scheme. His fear
and resentment were roused, and he revealed the whole affair to the
ephors; but they, not satisfied even with this, contrived, by a cunning device, to hear the truth from Pausanias' own lips. The
ephors then tried to arrest him; but he fled into a temple of
Athena, and as they feared to pollute the sanctuary with his blood,
the roof was taken off and the entrance walled up. In this condition he was left until he was on the point of expiring. He was
then carried out of the temple, and expired as soon as he had
crossed the bounds of the sacred ground. But although he had
not died in the temple, still the minds of the Spartans were often
disturbed by religious scruples.

30. The fate of Pausanias involved that of Themistocles. He
too had become proud and indiscreet, but never acted the part of a
traitor to his country. When his selfishness and avarice became
known, numerous enemies rose against him at home, and he was
gradually supplanted in the popular favour by younger men. Under
these circumstances it was not difficult to persuade the Athenians
that his presence was dangerous to the liberty of the state, and he
was exiled by ostracism. He withdrew to Argos, where he was
residing in B. C. 471, when Pausanias was convicted. The Spartans
had never forgiven Themistocles for the manner in which he had
eluded their scheme of preventing the fortification of Athens; it
was now said that the inquiry into the crime of Pausanias had led
to discoveries showing that Themistocles also had been implicated
in the plot; and it was demanded that the Athenians should punish
him as the accomplice of the Spartan. Although no evidence
whatever was then, or ever after, produced of his guilt, his enemies
at Athens rejoiced at the opportunity, and officers were forthwith
sent out to arrest him. Themistocles, foreseeing this, had fled to

Corcyra, and thence to Epirus, where he was protected in the house
of king Admetus. Being supplied with all necessaries by his host,
he proceeded to Pydna, and there embarked for Ephesus, which he
reached not without danger. Very soon after his arrival in Asia
Xerxes died, B. C. 465, and was succeeded by Artaxerxes. Themistocles went to the king's court, and in a letter endeavoured to
persuade him that he had claims upon his gratitude, and that his
present misfortunes were the consequence of his zeal for the interest
of Persia. This scheme succeeded, and Themistocles won the favour of Artaxerxes to such a degree, that even the courtiers are
said to have envied him. After some time the king sent him to
Asia Minor, assigning to him three flourishing towns for his maintenance, Magnesia having to provide him with bread, Myus with
viands, and Lampsacus with wine. He thus spent the latter part
of his life at Magnesia in princely splendour. He is generally said
to have made away with himself, because he had promised the king
more than he was able to perform; but this account is at least
doubtful.

CHAPTER VII.

THE SUPREMACY OF ATHENS DOWN TO THE COMMENCEMENT OF THE PELOPONNESIAN WAR.

1. As all fear of Greece being again invaded by the Persians
was now removed, the Greeks, who had hitherto acted mainly on
the defensive, resolved to assume the offensive; and the situation
of their colonies in Asia offered a fair pretext for this. Cimon of
Athens, the son of Miltiades, was foremost in directing the attention of his countrymen to that quarter. He had no particular talent
as an orator or statesman, but had given early proofs of ability on
the field of battle. He moreover belonged to the aristocratic party,
though he did not disdain to employ the means of a demagogue for
the purpose of gaining popularity. He first distinguished himself
in the battle of Salamis, and many then began to look upon him as
a worthy rival of Themistocles. While the popularity of the latter
was on the decline, Cimon was rapidly rising in popular favour in
consequence of several successful enterprises, such as the capture
of Eion on the Strymon, in B. C. 476, the reduction of Scyros for
the Amphictions, and that of Carystus in Euboea. But the conquest of Naxos, in B. C. 466, was a far more important event. That
island began to repent of its alliance with Athens, and the latter
then exacted by force what was no longer cheerfully given. The

Naxians were reduced by Cimon after a hard siege, and having become the subjects of Athens instead of its allies, they were treated with a severity which they could scarcely have expected from Persia. But their example did not deter others from attempting to get rid of the Athenian alliance; one state revolted after another, and all were punished with the loss of their independence. Many also commuted their personal services in the endless expeditions for stated payments in money, and by this means lost their warlike spirit, while Athens acquired more and more power over those who were nominally her free allies. But their feeling of discontent arose from their notion that the time of danger was passed, and that they needed no further protection.

2. In the year B. C. 465, a large Persian fleet of about three hundred and fifty sail was assembled at the mouth of the river Eurymedon, in Pamphylia. Cimon, who had increased the number of his ships to two hundred and fifty, provoked the enemy to an engagement, and gained a complete victory. Having sunk two hundred of the enemy's vessels, he sailed up the river, and also defeated the Persian land-army. On his return he met a squadron of eighty galleys which was intended to strengthen the Persian fleet, but was utterly destroyed by him. After this treble victory, he sailed northward, where he expelled the remnants of the Persian forces in the Thracian Chersonesus. About B. C. 464, the Athenians became involved in a contest with the island of Thasos, regarding the gold-mines in Thrace, which were claimed by Athens. The Thasians were first defeated at sea, and then closely besieged by Cimon. In this distress they applied to Sparta for assistance; and the Spartans delighted at the opportunity, were making preparations for invading Attica, when suddenly, in B. C. 464, the whole of Laconia was shaken by an earthquake, during which immense blocks of stone rolled down from mount Taygetus, spreading terror and destruction all around. At Sparta itself only five houses were left standing, and upwards of twenty thousand persons were killed. Helots from all parts hastened to the city to take advantage of the misfortune of their masters, and it was only owing to the presence of mind of king Archidamus that the citizens were saved from the hand of revengeful slaves. But this was not all, for the Messenians also rose against their detested rulers, and fortified themselves at Ithome. The Thasians, who were thus left to themselves, became subjects of Athens, and the Spartans, being unable to reduce the revolted Messenians, did not blush to send for assistance to the Athenians, against whom they had just been planning an expedition. But the aristocratic party, with Cimon at its head, happened just then to be all-powerful at Athens, and as that party was at all times favourable to Sparta, Cimon himself was sent with a large force to besiege Ithome. But when the Athenians made no greater

progress than the Spartans had made before, the latter, judging of others by themselves, began to suspect Cimon, and dismissed him and his army. The Athenians, understanding the real motive, were exasperated in the highest degree, and all connection with Sparta being broken off, an alliance was entered into with Argos, her ancient rival and enemy. The Messenian war was in the meantime carried on until B. C. 455, when the brave defenders of their liberty surrendered, on condition of leaving Peloponnesus with their families for ever. The Athenians kindly gave to the unfortunate Messenians the town of Naupactus, where they settled, waiting for a day of retribution.

3. The democratic party at Athens was then headed by a most promising young man, Pericles, the son of Xanthippus, and a descendant of Cleisthenes. He had from his earliest days devoted himself to intellectual pursuits, and enjoyed the intimacy of the first men of the age; he had enriched his mind with all the stores at his command, that they might become instruments for managing the affairs of his country. During the period that Cimon was engaged in his military expeditions, Pericles had taken a prominent part in the discussions of the popular assembly, where his majestic appearance and his powerful eloquence, combined with his great wisdom and prudence, made him the acknowledged leader of the democracy and the most formidable opponent of Cimon. The latter had made munificent use of his wealth, and though opposed to the popular interest, he did everything which his ample means enabled him to do, to win the favour of the people, that he might use them as a means for his ends; for he and his brother nobles were bent upon retaining the few privileges they yet possessed, and of putting a stop to the progress of popular liberty. Pericles was not able to rival Cimon in his reckless liberality, and probably would have disdained it if he had had the means. He conceived that it was more honourable for the poorer classes to be supplied with the means of enjoyment out of their own, that is, the public funds, than to depend upon the liberality of wealthy individuals. With this view he carried a series of measures, partly himself and partly through his friends, the most prominent among whom was Ephialtes, a man of rigid integrity, earnestness, and fearlessness. Pericles' own conduct also was such that though he courted the people, he yet, from never descending to low means, always retained the respect of the citizens, though they might differ from him in their political views.

4. The struggle between the aristocratic and democratic parties had been going on for some time, and on one occasion Cimon was in danger of being exiled; but the contest came to a head when Pericles and Ephialtes extended their reforms even to the Areopagus, the ancient stronghold of the aristocracy. The object of Pericles and his friends was to narrow the functions of the Areopagus

so much as to leave it nothing but its venerable name. The aristocracy left no means untried to thwart their opponents; but it fortunately happened that at this very time the Athenians were slighted by the Spartans for their want of success against Ithome, and this made Cimon and the whole aristocracy extremely unpopular. Under these circumstances, Ephialtes without much difficulty carried a decree by which the Areopagus seems to have been shorn of all its political power. Soon after this, Cimon was exiled by ostracism, probably for the purpose of preventing any popular outbreak in the city.

5. About this time, B. C. 460, Inarus, king of some Libyan tribes in the west of Egypt, revolted against the Persians, and his authority was acknowledged in his own country and in the greater part of Egypt, which joined him. Artaxerxes sent a large army commanded by his own brother against the rebels. An Athenian fleet of two hundred sail happened at the time to be lying off Cyprus, and Inarus sent for its assistance. The armament immediately sailed southwards and enabled Inarus to defeat the Persians. The Athenian fleet then sailed up the Nile as far as Memphis, which was besieged, as a portion of the city was in the hands of the Persians. This siege lasted more than five years; and the Athenians, being in the end pressed by a very numerous army, were not only obliged to raise the siege, but were themselves surrounded by the enemy on an island in the Nile. All of them perished except a few who escaped to Cyrene and thence returned home. Inarus himself fell into the hands of the Persians, and was put to death B. C. 455.

6. Owing to the rupture with Sparta, Athens lost the friendship of the Corinthians, but for this she was indemnified in some measure by gaining possession of Megara. This, however, roused the enmity not only of Corinth, but of Ægina and the maritime towns of Argolis, and war was declared in B. C. 457, while the Athenian armament was still in Egypt. But the Athenians with most undaunted courage attacked their enemies and defeated them in several engagements. Myronides was then at the head of the Athenian forces, and gained a most complete victory, in which every Corinthian soldier perished. During this war between Corinth and Athens, Artaxerxes sent an envoy to Sparta, endeavouring to induce the Spartans by bribes to attack the Athenians, in order to compel them to withdraw their forces from Egypt. Sparta was then still engaged against Ithome, and could not comply with the king's request, but Pericles, apprehensive of danger, completed the long walls connecting Athens with its port-town, which had been commenced some time before. He well knew that there was a party in the city ready at any moment to sacrifice their country, if thereby they hoped to recover any of their lost privileges This

became evident during an expedition of the Spartans against the Phocians, when the former were preparing to strike a blow at Athens, and the oligarchical faction in the city promised them their co-operation. But the scheme was suspected and thwarted, though in the battle which was fought near Tanagra in Bocotia, B. C. 457, the Athenians were defeated in consequence of the treacherous conduct of the Thessalians, who were allied with them. This defeat was keenly felt by the Athenians, and hence in the following year, B. C. 456, they took the field again under the command of Myronides, who at that time was the soul of all their military undertakings. This time their arms were successful, and at Œnophyta they gained a complete victory over the Bocotians, and razed the walls of Tanagra to the ground. Henceforth their influence predominated both in Phocis and in Boeotia, and soon after Ægina also capitulated, and became subject to Athens.

7. The news of the disaster of the Athenians in Egypt does not seem in the least to have discouraged their fellow-citizens at home, who continued the war against Sparta and her allies as vigorously as before. Landings and ravages were made on the coasts of Peloponnesus, both in B. C. 455 and 454, though no great advantages were gained. In the year B. C. 453 Cimon was recalled from exile, on the proposal of Pericles himself, who had probably become convinced of the necessity for all good citizens to co-operate against the schemes of the unprincipled oligarchical faction, which would have delivered Athens into the hands of a foreign enemy in preference to seeing the democratic party prosperous. About that time the honest Ephialtes was assassinated by aristocratic emissaries; and it was this and similar occurrences that suggested to Pericles the desirableness of forming a coalition with Cimon. The result was as had been anticipated, for during the three years after Cimon's return Greece was in the enjoyment of peace; and this pause was followed by a truce of five years, during which Cimon undertook his last expedition against the Persians.

8. In Egypt, another pretender, Amyrtaeus, had arisen in the meantime, and, like his predecessor, solicited aid from Athens. The Athenians complied with the request, and Cimon, with a fleet of two hundred galleys, sailed to Cyprus. Thence he sent a squadron to Amyrtaeus, while he himself laid siege to Citium. He died there in B. C. 449, and his army was soon after compelled to raise the siege from want of provisions. On their return home, the Athenians fell in with a large fleet of Phoenician and Cilician galleys, and having completely defeated them, they followed up this victory by another which they gained on shore. Soon after this, they were joined by the squadron from Egypt, which had accomplished its main object there, and all sailed home. In later times, it was generally believed that, during his last campaign,

Cimon had compelled the king of Persia to accept a peace, which obliged him to abandon the military occupation of Asia Minor to the distance of three days' journey from the western coast. But subsequent events show that such an arrangement did not exist, and the whole story about the peace of Cimon is probably a fabrication originating in the vanity of the later Greeks.

9. The peace of Greece was again disturbed in the year after Cimon's death, B. c. 448, by a quarrel between the Delphians and Phocians about the guardianship of the Delphic temple and its treasures, which was wrested by the Phocians from their opponents, to whom it had belonged from time immemorial. A spartan army recovered for the Delphians what they had lost, and several privileges were conferred at Delphi on the Spartans. But no sooner had the Spartan forces withdrawn, than Pericles advanced with an Athenian army, and undid their work. In the year following, the ascendancy of the Athenians in Boeotia was broken by a revolution, in which the party hostile to Athens completely gained the upper hand. The consequences of this soon became manifest on every side, for in B. c. 445, when the five years' truce expired, Euboea revolted; and no sooner had Pericles crossed over to quell the insurrection, than he was informed that another had broken out at Megara, and that most of the soldiers of the Athenian garrison had been put to death; at the same time, he learned that a Peloponnesian army was on its march against Attica. Pericles, therefore, returned, and found the Peloponnesians already ravaging the plains of his country; but, by means of bribes, he prevailed upon the Spartan commanders to give up their undertaking. Having thus got rid of this enemy, he returned with a large force to Euboea, and soon overpowered all resistance. But notwithstanding this success, the people of Athens were disposed to make peace. The Spartans also did not feel inclined to continue the war; and accordingly, a truce was concluded for thirty years, in B. c. 445, by which the Athenians were required to give up all their possessions in Peloponnesus—that is, Troezen, the ports of Pegae, and Nisaea—and their connection with Achaia. After these concessions, Athens still remained mistress of the sea, and her maritime empire was untouched. The aristocracy, now headed by Thucydides, had opposed this truce, but Pericles bore down all opposition, for his influence at Athens was now greater than ever, and remained so till the last day of his life.

10. During this time, Pericles was enabled to carry out his views into action. Throughout his life he had mainly two objects; first, to extend and strengthen the Athenian empire; and secondly, to raise the confidence and self-respect of his countrymen to a level with their lofty position. The Athenian confederacy had undergone considerable changes since its regulation by Aristides; and ever in his lifetime the treasury had been transferred from Delos

to Athens. Cimon had afterwards reduced the weaker states of the league to a defenceless condition, so that little remained to be done to change the confederacy into an empire, over which Athens ruled with almost despotic power. Pericles raised the annual tribute from four hundred and sixty to six hundred talents. All the subject states had a democratic form of government imposed upon them, whether they liked it or not; but what was worse than all, was the fact that all important trials were transferred from the cognizance of the local courts to the tribunals at Athens, which caused to the allies the greatest inconvenience and annoyance.

11. In B. C. 440, an event occurred which seemed likely to interrupt the truce, but in reality consolidated the Athenian empire, and gave Pericles an opportunity of displaying his brilliant qualities as a military commander. The island of Samos had an aristocratic form of government, which the popular party were anxious to overthrow with the aid of Athens. Pericles was sent with a squadron of forty galleys to assist the popular party. On his arrival, he established a democratic form of government, and took one hundred members of the aristocracy, who were sent to Lemnos as hostages. Leaving only a small garrison behind, he returned home. During his absence, some of the nobles entered into negotiations with the Persians, and with an army of mercenaries overpowered the Athenian garrison, restored the old form of government, and having also rescued the hostages, they openly renounced their connection with Athens. Sparta and her allies were applied to for assistance, but to no purpose, for they were not inclined to break the truce. As soon as these proceedings became known at Athens, Pericles again set out with his fleet; he soon drove the Samians into their town, and surrounded it with entrenchments. As he expected the approach of a Phoenician fleet which was said to be on its way, he sailed out to meet it; but it did not make its appearance. During his absence, the Samians gained considerable advantages, but his return changed the aspect of things. They were obliged to confine themselves to the defensive; and after the war had lasted nine months, they were compelled by famine to capitulate, and become subjects of Athens. Byzantium, which had sided with Samos, was soon afterwards reduced to the same condition

12. Pericles on his return was received at Athens with extraordinary honours, and the whole success was ascribed to him. The conquest of Samos completed and consolidated the Athenian empire, over which Athens henceforth ruled without opposition and without restraint. The Athenians were now in a condition, by means of colonies in places where they seemed to be useful, both to strengthen themselves and to provide for the poorer classes. Settlers accordingly were sent to Oreus in Euboea, to Naxos, and Andros, and colonies were established at Amphipolis and Thurii. To this

17

last colony, which was founded in B. C. 443, the Athenians invited
foreigners from all parts of Greece, and among them were the historian Herodotus and the orator Lysias. Every Athenian citizen
at this time must have felt his position raised, and Pericles endeavoured to enhance the value of the franchise, by rigorously excluding all those who were not entitled to its exercise; at the same
time he took care to provide useful employment for those who had
little or no means of subsistence, partly by sending out every year
a squadron of sixty galleys, in which the men were trained, and
partly by the great architectural works which he planned for the
defence and embellishment of the city. Among these works we may
mention a third wall connecting the city with Piraeus, which ran
between the two already completed; the temples which crowned
the Acropolis, the most magnificent of which were the Parthenon
or Virgin's temple, adorned by the sculptures of Phidias, and the
splendid approach to it called Propylaea. These and many other
works gave employment to the genius of the artist as well as to the
skill of the artisans; and during that period of extraordinary
activity, there must have been a comparative scarcity of hands at
Athens.

13. But not only upon architectural works and their embellishment did Pericles spend the public treasures; he also devoted a
considerable portion to spectacles and amusements of the people.
A taste for them had always existed, and Pericles made them accessible to all, poor as well as rich. In this way the poorer classes
were provided out of the public funds with the means of attending
the theatre, and taking part in other public festivals. In like
manner he introduced the practice of paying the jurors for their
attendance in the courts of justice. These regulations, at first quite
harmless, and perhaps no more than fair and just, afterwards
became very detrimental to the welfare of the state, especially when
the payments were increased to twice or thrice the original amount.
Pericles is also said, though erroneously, to have introduced the
payment for attendance in the popular assembly, which we afterwards find established.

14. The period during which Pericles guided the Athenians is
justly called after him the age of Pericles, and forms the most
brilliant epoch in Athenian history. Down to the time of the
Persian wars, Athens did less for the intellectual and artistic progress of Greece than many other cities both in Europe and Asia;
but her peaceful glories quickly followed, and outshone those of her
victories and conquests. Literature and the arts were now cultivated there with greater success and rewarded with more distinguished honours than anywhere else. Architecture and sculpture
rose to the highest perfection, and Athens enriched literature with
the drama, the highest and noblest of all poetical compositions.

The drama grew out of the Doric choral poetry, whence the chorus continued for a long time to form a very prominent part in it. At the time when it reached its highest point, lyric poetry was gradually dying away, and Simonides of Cos, Bacchylides, and Pindar, were the last, and at the same time the greatest among the lyric poets of Greece. The greatest dramatists, at least in tragedy, belonged to the age of Pericles. Phrynichus, the first, whose works have perished, is highly praised by the ancients; and even Æschylus spoke of him as a worthy rival. But the way in which Æschylus developed and displayed the capabilities of the art, entitles him to be regarded as the father of Attic tragedy. He introduced the dialogue, and thereby raised the really dramatic portion of the composition to the principal rank, while the choral part became subordinate to it. He always exhibited three tragedies together, which were indeed distinct, but in reality constituted only one great drama, called a trilogy. Out of seventy pieces ascribed to him, seven only have been preserved, and among them there is only one complete trilogy, the Oresteia.

15. Sophocles, a younger contemporary of Æschylus, surpassed him in the general harmony of his conceptions, in the equal distribution of grace and vigour, and in the unsurpassed charm of his language; though in some respects Æschylus was perhaps a genius of a higher order. He was held in the greatest estimation by the Athenians, and the Antigone, one of his seven extant dramas, filled them with such admiration, that they appointed him, in B. C. 440, one of the generals who accompanied Pericles in the war against Samos. He himself, however, experienced the mutability of popular taste, when he saw himself supplanted by Euripides, a poet of a much lower order. Attic tragedy in the hands of these three great masters of the art was not an idle amusement, but a means employed for religious, moral, and sometimes even for political purposes; this, however, was the case more especially with comedy, for while tragedy took its subjects from the mythical history of Greece, the sphere of comedy lay within the walks of daily life, and its main business was with the immediate present, whence it supplied in some respects the place which is occupied in modern times by a free press. All theatrical performances were connected with the celebration of the festivals of Dionysus, under whose protection the comic poets enjoyed unbounded freedom and license. With this power the comic poets assailed every kind of vice and folly, if it was sufficiently notorious to render their ridicule intelligible, and men in the highest positions did not escape this kind of castigation. Comedy was raised to its highest perfection during the period of the Peloponnesian war by the genius of Aristophanes.

16. The mere fact of Pericles possessing unbounded influence with the people, and being their acknowledged leader, could not

fail to call forth envy, jealousy, and hatred; and suspicions were raised and circulated not only regarding his private life, which indeed presented some vulnerable points, but also in reference to his public actions. The first attacks, however, were not made directly against himself, but against his friends, through whom his enemies hoped to wound him. First of all, Phidias was charged with having embezzled a portion of the gold destined to be employed in his magnificent statue of Athena in the Parthenon. Fortunately the gold had been applied in such a manner that it could be taken down and weighed, and this circumstance silenced the accusers, when called upon to prove their assertion. Another attack upon the artist, for having introduced his own portrait among the figures on the shield of the goddess, was more successful. Phidias was thrown into prison for impiety, and died there. Having gained their object in this matter, the enemies of Pericles began their manœuvres against Aspasia, the most beautiful and accomplished woman at Athens, in whose safety the great statesman felt as much concern as in his own. His most intimate friends were the most illustrious philosophers of the time, whose creed certainly was very different from the superstition of the multitude. These and other circumstances furnished materials for a prosecution against Pericles. But all machinations failed, and their failure at length induced his enemies to drop their proceedings. Pericles, with one brief interruption, never again saw himself assailed in his high position, which he maintained down to the end of his life. We cannot indeed wonder that both ancient and modern historians have brought charges against him; but a closer examination shows that they are based upon nothing but vulgar gossip and scandal, which are always ready and glad to detract from real and genuine greatness.

CHAPTER VIII.

THE PELOPONNESIAN WAR.

1. THE prosperity of Athens, and her ever-increasing power and glory, could not but excite the hatred and alarm of the other Greek states, and especially of Sparta, which saw itself humbled in proportion as Athens rose. While the former and her allies were united in their jealousy of Athens, the Athenian confederacy could not be entirely relied upon, for many of the allies submitted only with great reluctance to their mistress, who seemed, and in many instances actually was, more concerned about her own aggrandisement than

about the welfare of those whom she professed to protect. But there were other ingredients which increased the hostile feelings between Athens and Sparta: Athens was the representative of the Ionian race, and everywhere introduced or supported a democratic form of government, while Sparta, the representative of the Dorians, favoured aristocratic or oligarchic institutions. These feelings and animosities were the real causes of the Peloponnesian war, which for twenty-seven years disturbed the peace of the whole Greek world, and terminated in the downfall of Athens. Both parties seem to have been aware of what such a war would lead to, and avoided its outbreak as long as they could, until at length several circumstances concurred which made the continuance of peace a matter of impossibility.

2. Epidamnus, a colony of Corcyra, on the coast of Illyricum, was at that time distracted by internal feuds, during which the aristocratic party was expelled from the city. With the assistance of the neighbouring barbarians, the exiled nobles pressed the town closely. The Epidamnians applied for succour to their mother city of Corcyra, and as the Corcyraeans did not listen to the request, the Epidamnians addressed themselves to Corinth, the mother-city of Corcyra, which had likewise taken a part in the establishment of the colony of Epidamnus. Corinth gladly seized the occasion, because it afforded her an opportunity of curbing the spirit of Corcyra, which had become very powerful, and neglected the performance of the ordinary duties of a colony towards the mother-city. A Corinthian army accordingly proceeded by land to Epidamnus, and the Corcyraeans, on being informed of this, went with a fleet to Epidamnus, demanding of its citizens to restore the exiles and to dismiss the Corinthian garrison. When this was refused, the Corcyraeans, joined by the exiles and others, blockaded Epidamnus by land and by sea. The Corinthians then sent out a large force to raise the siege of Epidamnus, and at the same time declared war against Corcyra. A naval engagement took place between the Corinthian and Corcyraean fleets near the mouth of the Ambracian gulf, in which the Corcyraeans gained a complete victory. On the same day, Epidamnus was obliged to surrender to the besiegers, who sold all its inhabitants as slaves, while the Corinthians were kept in captivity. This happened in B. C. 434.

3. After this defeat, the Corinthians made great efforts to protect their own colonies on the Ionian sea, and to strengthen themselves for the continuation of the war, while the Corcyraeans, on the other hand, applied for assistance to Athens. Corinth also sent envoys to Athens to counteract their influence. The Athenians took the affair into serious consideration, and were at first inclined to side with Corinth, but afterwards concluded a defensive alliance with Corcyra for the protection of their respective territories. But at

17 *

the same time they did not declare war against Corinth. In accordance with this treaty of alliance, Athens sent ten galleys to Corcyra, with orders not to engage in any contest, unless Corcyra should be attacked. The Corinthian fleet of one hundred and fifty ships soon after fell in, near Sybota, with that of the Corcyraeans, which consisted of one hundred and ten, the Corcyraean land army being drawn up on the coast. In the ensuing sea fight, neither party gained a decisive victory. The ten Athenian galleys, however, seeing their allies hard pressed, took part in the contest. In the meantime, twenty more ships had come from Athens, and when they in conjunction with the Corcyraeans again offered battle, the Corinthians withdrew, merely charging the Athenians, through the mouth of a herald, with having violated the peace. These occurrences belong to the year B. C. 432, and are the first acts of open hostility between Athens and Corinth.

4. At the same time the Athenians were involved in a war with Perdiccas, king of Macedonia, who tried to ally himself with Sparta and Corinth, and did all he could to induce the cities in the north of the Ægean to shake off their alliance with Athens. Potidaea, one of those towns, was a colony of Corinth, and the Athenians, in order to be beforehand, ordered the Potidaeans to destroy their fortifications, to give hostages, and to dismiss the Corinthian magistrates. As Sparta had openly declared its determination to protect the Potidaeans, they were emboldened to assert their independence of Athens, and other towns in those parts followed their example. Meantime an Athenian fleet arrived to enforce the orders of the sovereign city; but the admiral Archestratus finding his armament too small to carry on the war against the revolted cities, sailed to the coast of Macedonia, and commenced hostilities against Perdiccas. The Corinthians now also sent one thousand men to support Potidaea, and the Athenians despatched a second squadron, under the command of Callias, who, finding Archestratus engaged in the siege of Pydna, prevailed on him to make peace with Perdiccas, that they might be able to direct all their forces against the Corinthians and their friends. Accordingly they proceeded by land to Potidaea. On the isthmus near Olynthos they encountered their enemies and defeated them, notwithstanding the treacherous desertion of Perdiccas, B. C. 432. The Peloponnesians and Corinthians, however, succeeded in throwing themselves into the town of Potidaea, which the Athenians forthwith began to besiege both by land and by sea.

5. As it was evident that these disputes could not be easily settled, a congress of the Peloponnesian allies was summoned to Sparta, and all states which believed themselves to be wronged by Athens were invited to send deputies to the meeting. Many complaints were brought forward by Ægina and Megara, but above all by

Corinth. Athenian envoys, who happened to be at Sparta on other business, manfully defended the conduct of their city. But war was decreed, notwithstanding the cautious advice of the Spartan king Archidamus, who wished to settle the disputes by negotiation. This declaration of war belongs to B. C. 432, but the Spartans, with their usual slowness and caution, did not proceed to action at once, and a whole year passed away before they were ready to take the field. In the meantime, however, they did all they could to justify the war in the eyes of Greece, and to show that its declaration was a matter of necessity rather than choice. Nay, Sparta went so far as to declare that she went for peace, and was prepared to keep it, if the Athenians would raise the siege of Potidaea, and make Ægina and Megara independent. The Athenians, guided by Pericles, declared themselves willing to refer their differences to impartial judges, but added that they would always be ready to repel any attack. After this, no further negotiation was attempted.

6. Before the general war commenced, an outrage was committed by the Thebans upon Plataeae, the ally of Athens, which, in the spring of B. C. 431, they surprised by night. But nearly all the invaders were taken prisoners by the Plataeans, and one hundred and eighty were put to death. Athens provided Plataeae with a military force to defend itself, and with supplies, at the same time inviting those who were unfit for service during the siege which was anticipated, to come to Athens. In the meantime, active preparations were made both by Sparta and Athens. The sympathies of most of the states of continental Greece were in favour of the Spartans, who declared themselves the champions of the liberty and independence of all the Greeks. But still all Greece looked forward with sad forebodings to the real outbreak of the war. The allies of Sparta included all the Peloponnesians except the Argives, who remained neutral; beyond the Isthmus she was supported by Megara, Phocis, Locris, Boeotia, and the cities of Ambracia, Leucas, and Anactorium; Sparta further courted the friendship of Persia, and called upon the Dorian colonies in Sicily and Italy for assistance. The allies of the Athenians, on the other hand, were Chios, Lesbos, Plataeae, the Messenians at Naupactus, the greater part of Acarnania, Zacynthos, and Corcyra, while they received tribute from the following towns and countries which were subject to them: — Caria, the Dorian cities in Asia Minor, Ionia, the cities on the Hellespont, the coast of Thrace, all the islands between Peloponnesus and Crete, and the Cyclades, with the exception of Melos and Thera. All Greece was thus divided into two great hostile camps, only few states maintaining a position of neutrality.

7. When all preparations were completed, king Archidamus assembled the Peloponnesian allies on the isthmus of Corinth, and in the summer of B. C. 431 invaded Attica. He confined himself,

however, to the north about the town of Œnoe, so that the Athenians, who maintained the defensive, had time to gather their movable property within the fortifications of the city. Archidamus then made attacks upon several country towns, and ravaged the fields, for his object was to draw the Athenians out to battle. But Pericles was immovable, and with the greatest firmness adhered to the plan of operation he had once adopted. Archidamus, finding at last that he could not tempt his enemy, returned home and disbanded his army. In the meantime, an Athenian fleet of one hundred galleys had been retaliating upon Peloponnesus, the coasts of which they ravaged; another squadron devastated the coast of Locris; the Æginetans were driven with their wives and children from their island, and the Athenian fleet in the western seas continued its operations against the confederates of Sparta. The alliance which the Athenians in this year formed with the Thracian chief Sitacles, was of great service to them in the war against the Chalcidian towns and Macedonia. Late in the autumn of the same year the Athenians, commanded by Pericles himself, made a ravaging incursion into Megara, which was afterwards repeated year after year, just as the Peloponnesians, during the first five years of the war, repeated their invasion of Attica, neither party being apparently inclined to bring the war to a close by a decisive battle. The war, however, was carried on during that period in several parts of Greece; and on the whole, the Athenians had generally the advantage over their enemies.

8. In the second year of the war, just when Archidamus had entered Attica early in the summer, Athens was visited by a fearful pestilence, which, with few interruptions, continued to rage for two years, and carried off four thousand four hundred citizens, and no less than ten thousand slaves. The city was at the time overcrowded with country people and their cattle from all parts of Attica, and this state of things naturally aggravated the evil. The loss of lives was perhaps a minor calamity, compared with the moral effects produced by the plague; for the people in their despair became reckless, and regardless of all laws, human and divine, thinking that, after all, their life was not safe for a single hour. The Lacedaemonians, notwithstanding this, ravaged Attica both in the north and in the south for a period of forty days, and then returned home. The Athenian fleet, as in the first year, made its ravaging tour round Peloponnesus; another squadron destined for Potidaea was obliged to return, in consequence of the plague having broken out among the crew. Potidaea continued to be beseiged until about the end of the second year of the war, when the inhabitants were compelled to surrender by famine. The fearful and deadly hatred which had already sprung up among the belligerents was displayed by the merciless cruelty shown by the Spartans against inoffensive merchants,

who were invariably killed, unless they declared themselves in favour of Sparta; and Athens retaliated by murdering some Peloponnesian ambassadors who had been intercepted.

The most memorable event of the third year of the war, B. C. 429, was the death of Pericles by the plague, which had previously bereft him of his children and dearest friends. The loss of Pericles at this time was irreparable, and the Athenians, to their cost, soon found out what he had been to them. His successors were men swayed by ambition, avarice, and envy. Pericles had ruled the democracy with a gentle, yet mighty hand; but those who succeeded him courted the favour of the people by humouring its evil passions, and thus leading it to acts which, both morally and materially, undermined its power. Another remarkable event of the same year is the heroic and almost miraculous defence of the little town of Plataeae against the united efforts of the Peloponnesians; for this year Archidamus, instead of invading Attica, directed all his forces against Plataeae. In the end of the summer, he returned to Peloponnesus, but the siege of Plataeae lasted until B. C. 427, when, after the loss of half its defenders, the survivors were obliged to capitulate. By the desire of the Thebans, the most inveterate enemies of the Plataeans, they were butchered one by one, and all the women were made slaves. The town itself was afterwards razed to the ground. It is not known, though it may easily be conjectured, what circumstances prevented the Athenians from sending active support to their ancient and faithful allies. In the year in which Pericles died, no exploit of any consequence was performed on land, but Phormio, the commander of the fleet in the western sea, gained a complete victory over the Lacedaemonians, who had advanced to support the Ambracians in an attempt to conquer Acarnania. In a subsequent engagement near Naupactus, he was equally successful, and the Peloponnesian fleet retreated to Corinth. But, on the whole, the Athenians were unable, during this year, to make any great efforts abroad, in consequence of the loss of their great leader, and the continued ravages of the plague.

9. The fourth year of the war, B. C. 428, began with the usual invasion of Attica by king Archidamus. The Athenians, also, still adhered to their former tactics, only preventing, by their cavalry, the enemy from approaching too near the city. The most important event of this year was the revolt of Lesbos, a wealthy and powerful island. There, as in other allied states, the aristocratic party was favourable to Sparta, while the popular party clung to the alliance with Athens. The city of Mytilene, which took the lead in the revolutionary movement, had sometime before made overtures to Sparta, which had been rejected. Information of the design, however, was carried to Athens, and the Mytileneans were thus driven into open rebellion before they were sufficiently prepared. The

Athenians at first endeavoured, by persuasion, to induce the islanders to remain faithful to them; but as they failed, a fleet was dispatched against them, and hostilities were commenced. As the Mytileneans did not feel strong enough to engage in the contest, they, for the purpose of gaining time, concluded a truce with the Athenian admirals, but at the same time sent envoys to solicit the support of Sparta. The people of Athens, however, refusing to negotiate with the rebels, ordered hostilities to be recommenced. The Spartans in the meantime admitted the Lesbians into the Peloponnesian league, and promised to protect them, for it was believed that Athens had fallen into a helpless condition. But they miscalculated, for Athens in that year had a more powerful navy than ever before, and took the greatest precautions in guarding Attica, Salamis, and Euboea. The Spartans had resolved to attack Athens, both by land and by sea; but the promptness of the Athenians, whose fleet even threatened the safety of Sparta itself, compelled the enemy to relinquish their undertaking. It was, however, decreed that a fleet should be sent to the relief of Lesbos. In the meantime, the Athenians, under Paches, invested Mytilene both by land and by sea, and the promised fleet from Peloponnesus did not make its appearance until the year following, B. C. 427. In the beginning of this year, the Peleoponnesians, commanded by Cleomenes, again invaded Attica, and ravaged the country in all directions. Their stay was prolonged, in the expectation of receiving favourable tidings from Lesbos. But the Mytileneans had been forced to surrender before the Peloponnesian fleet arrived. Paches then became master of the island, and many of those who had favoured the revolt were first sent to Tenedos and then to Athens. The Peloponnesian fleet, after having made a descent upon the coast of Ionia, returned home, but was dispersed by a storm before it reached the coast of Peloponnesus. Paches remained in Lesbos for the purpose of regulating its affairs; but it was for the people at home to decide what punishment was to be inflicted upon the Mytileneans. On the advice of the bloodthirsty Cleon, a leather-merchant, who was then the most popular man at Athens, it was decreed that all the men should be put to death, and the women and children sold as slaves. Orders to this effect were immediately sent to Paches. But on the following day, the Athenian people, repenting of the bloody decree, reversed their previous resolution, and on the proposal of Diodotus, it was decreed that only the most guilty among the rebels should be put to death. A second ship was accordingly sent off to prevent the execution of the first order, and it arrived just in time to save the unfortunate Mytileneans. One thousand of the leaders in the insurrection, however, were put to death, and Mytilene lost its ships and walls. Lesbos, instead of a free ally, now became subject to Athens. This year is also marked by a civil war between the aristocratic and democratic parties in the island of Corcyra, which in cruelty and ferocity is scarcely equalled by any similar occurrence in ancient history, and in which the Corcyraeans destroyed their own prosperity for ever.

10. The same epidemic which in Greece set Dorians against Ionians, and the nobles against the demos, had in the meantime also spread to Sicily, where Syracuse headed the Doric cities, while the Chalcidian or Ionian towns supported Leontini, which was at war with Syracuse. The Leontine envoy Gorgias prevailed upon the Athenians to send a fleet to Sicily, which was intended partly to prevent supplies being conveyed from Sicily to Peloponnesus, and partly to try to reduce Sicily to a state of dependence upon Athens. This squadron was sent in B. C. 427, and took its station at Rhegium in the south of Italy, from which point it made some ravaging expeditions.

11. In the beginning of the year 426 a Peloponnesian army again assembled on the Isthmus, but a succession of earthquakes terrified the Spartans so much that they abstained from entering Attica, and the Athenians being thus unmolested at home, were enabled to take the offensive in several successful enterprises in Boeotia, Locris, and Ætolia. In Sicily, too, the Athenians made some progress, for they compelled the owns of Mylae and Messene to surrender, and gained possession of a fortified place on the river Halex in southern Italy. In the following year, B C. 425, the war between the Syracusans and the allies of Athens was continued, though the Athenians themselves took no active part in it. In Greece itself the campaign of this year was again opened by an invasion of Attica under King Agis, but bad tidings from Peloponnesus obliged him to quit Attica, after a stay of only fifteen days. This invasion, the fifth, was the last that Sparta attempted. The news by which Agis was induced to return was, that Demosthenes, a distinguished general of the Athenians, had gained a firm footing at Pylos in Messenia. Demosthenes had accompanied in a private capacity the fleet sailing to Corcyra, under the command of Sophocles and Eurymedon, but had permission to land on the coasts of Peloponnesus and harass the enemy. Pylos was then a deserted place, but Demosthenes, perceiving the advantages of the position, resolved to fortify it and to establish himself in it. With the assistance of the fleet, which was obliged by stress of weather to take shelter in the excellent harbour of Pylos, the object was soon attained. The Spartans, who had at first looked on with indifference, became alarmed; the army was recalled from Attica, and attacks were made upon Pylos, but to no purpose; for Demosthenes acted with great prudence, and was reinforced by runaway Helots and Messenians, as well as by a squadron of Athenian galleys. The Spartans then took possession of the uninhabited island of Sphac-

teria, situated in front of the harbour, with a body of heavy-armed men commanded by Epitadas, with a view to block up the harbour. All attacks of the Lacedaemonians were repelled, and the Athenians then blockaded the Spartans shut up in Sphacteria, who would have been starved to death had they not been supplied with provisions by the desperate daring of some Helots, who thereby hoped to win their liberty. Under these circumstances Sparta would gladly have come to an understanding with Athens; but in the latter city Cleon had the popular ear, and the terms proposed were of such a nature that Sparta could not accept them. In the meantime the Athenians, who were besieged in the fortress of Pylos, likewise began to suffer from want of provisions, and the protracted siege in the end made the people at Athens repent of not having accepted the offers of Sparta. Cleon, however, with his usual energy and boastfulness, went so far as to intimate, that if he had the command he would bring the Spartans from Sphacteria captive to Athens. Upon this the people, half in joke and half in earnest, appointed him commander. Cleon accordingly embarked, and on his arrival Demosthenes' skilful management and other circumstances had just brought the state of matters to a crisis. An attack was made upon the island on all sides, and with the aid of Messenians acquainted with the locality, and favoured by the accidental conflagration of a forest which had shortly before covered the island with ashes, the Athenians drove the Spartans into a fort in a corner of Sphacteria, and then forced them to surrender at discretion. Of the original number of four hundred and twenty Spartans, two hundred and ninety still survived and were carried as prisoners to Athens. What Cleon had rashly promised was thus made good by accident.

12. Pylos remained in the hands of the Athenians, who were joined by many Messenians and Helots, and proved a source of great annoyance to Sparta. The Spartans made several attempts to recover their prisoners by negotiation, but the Athenians, elated with their success, made too exorbitant demands, and in the end declared that they would put all the prisoners to death, if the Peloponnesians again invaded Attica.

During the same year the Athenians were victorious also in other parts, especially in an undertaking conducted by Nicias against Corinth. In B. c. 424 they reached the highest point of their good fortune, and nothing seemed to check their unbounded spirit of enterprise. Among other conquests, they made themselves masters of the island of Cythera, a point of the greatest importance to Laconia. These events were extremely discouraging to the Spartans, and in their despondency they confined themselves to defending the most important places, leaving the Athenians to continue their ravaging expeditions. While the Athenians were thus flushed with success and victory at home, the commanders of their fleet in

Sicily concluded peace with the Sicilians without having made any conquest in those quarters. The Sicilians, under the wise guidance of Hermocrates, had come to the conviction that by fighting against one another, they were only weakening themselves and paving the way for foreign conquerors. A peace was accordingly concluded at a congress held in Gela, and the allies of the Athenians dismissed their friends because they no longer needed their assistance. The people at Athens were so ill satisfied with this that they punished some of the generals, on the alleged ground that they had been induced by bribes to quit Sicily.

13. There had latterly been rising at Sparta a man not only distinguished for his valour, but possessed of qualities which few Spartans ever displayed, either in public or in private life—genuine kindness and affability. This was Brasidas; he had already signalised himself during the siege of Pylos and elsewhere. He now checked the undertakings of the Athenians against Megara, compelled them to give up that city, and confine themselves to the port-town of Nisaea, whereupon an oligarchy was established at Megara. But this loss was insignificant in comparison with those which were to be inflicted on Athens by the same hand in the north of the Ægean, whither he was then proceeding. Before he exerted his influence there, however, the Athenians suffered a serious defeat in Boeotia, whither they had been invited by a party favourably disposed to them. The battle of Delium, a sanctuary of Apollo, cost the Athenians a loss of one thousand heavy-armed men, besides a large number of light-troops and others. This defeat was the most serious and the most bloody that the Athenians sustained during the first fourteen years of the war, but it was only the beginning of greater disasters. The Spartans resolved to transfer the seat of the war to Chalcidice and the coast of Thrace, hoping thereby to compel the Athenians to abandon Pylos and Cythera; and Brasidas was the man chosen to conduct the operations in that quarter. He proceeded to the north by land, and on reaching Macedonia he was joined at once by the fickle king Perdiccas. After spending some time in endeavouring to settle a dispute between the king and Arrhibaeus, king of the Lyncestians, he advanced to Chalcidice, and proclaimed himself the deliverer of the Greek towns from the yoke of the Athenians. His kindness and frankness won all hearts; the name of the Lacedaemonians through .
him became popular among the Athenian allies, and many of them wished to become connected with Sparta. Acanthos and Stagiros at once revolted from Athens, and admitted Lacedaemonian garrisons. During the ensuing winter he induced Amphipolis on the Strymon to surrender, but the historian Thucydides saved Eion at the mouth of the river for the Athenians. The surrender of Amphipolis was followed by that of several smaller towns. Brasidas,
18

though ill supported by Sparta, was thus making rapid progress, while the Athenians undertook scarcely anything worthy of notice, so that the advantages they had gained in and about Peloponnesus were now counterbalanced by the conquests of Brasidas in the north. The Lacedaemonians, however, never lost sight of their fellow-citizens who were kept in captivity at Athens; both parties in fact were anxious to come to terms, and a truce was concluded at the beginning of the ninth year, B. C. 423. During this truce, which was to last for one year, negotiations for a permanent peace were to be conducted.

14. When the terms of the peace were on the point of being settled, an event occurred in Chalcidice,. which induced the Athenians to break off all negotiation, and commence hostilities against the revolted towns in that district. Brasidas, on his return from Macedonia, whither he had gone to assist Perdiccas a second time, found the Athenians engaged in active hostilities, and the truce was evidently broken in the north, though in Greece proper it continued to be observed, probably from the general desire for peace. While the Athenians were besieging Scione, Perdiccas again allied himself with them, and prevented the passage of reinforcements which were on their way to Brasidas. In the beginning of B. C. 422, when the truce expired, Cleon undertook the command of the Athenian forces in the north, and proceeded to Scione, which was still besieged. He at once succeeded in taking Torone during the absence of Brasidas, and then sailed towards Amphipolis. There he was met by the Spartan commander, who had in the meantime received considerable reinforcements. As soon as Cleon saw that the enemy was ready to engage in a battle, he began to retreat; but Brasidas perceiving this fell upon the Athenians and soon routed them. Brasidas himself received a mortal wound while rushing against the enemy, and was carried from the field by his soldiers. Cleon had from the first thought of nothing but flight, and being overtaken by a common soldier he was slain, while the Athenians made a long and brave resistance, until in the end they were put to flight. They lost six hundred men, while the Lacedaemonians had only seven dead, and those who had escaped returned home. The memory of Brasidas was honoured at Amphipolis, where he died, with annual games and a festival called the Brasideia.

15. The plans which had been formed by the great Brasidas were not carried out by his countrymen, who were bent upon making peace and obtaining the liberation of their prisoners. The pride and arrogance of the Athenians had been considerably lowered by their recent losses, and Cleon, the principal advocate of the war, was no more. Nicias, who now guided the councils of the Athenians, though a brave and able general, was in favour of peace. Negotiations, accordingly, were commenced, and continued during

the ensuing winter. At length, in the spring of B. C. 421 the basis of a peace was settled, and it was agreed that each of the belligerent parties should restore what they had conquered during the war. This peace was agreed to by Atheus and Sparta and their respective allies, with the exception of the Boeotians, Corinthians, Eleans, and Megarians. All the Athenian and Lacedaemonian prisoners were, of course, returned without ransom. This peace commonly called the peace of Nicias, was concluded for a period of fifty years. The Spartans were to commence carrying the terms of the peace into effect, and the Athenians to follow. Early in the same year in which this peace was concluded, the Spartans entered into an offensive and defensive alliance with Athens, in which it was stipulated that each should be entitled to increase or diminish the number of its allies. This plan had been devised by Sparta, because her thirty years' peace with Argos had just expired, and she wished to strengthen herself for the event of a war with that state. But the measure at once roused the fear and opposition of the smaller states, and it was evident from the first that the peace could not be of long duration.

16. For nearly seven years after the conclusion of the peace of Nicias, the Athenians and Lacedaemonians indeed abstained from invading each other's territories, but Greece was nevertheless not in the enjoyment of peace, for neither Athens nor Sparta strictly adhered to the terms agreed upon, and each was anxious to increase the circle of its allies. Meantime Argos put itself at the head of a new confederacy, which might embrace all the Greeks except the Athenians and Spartans, and was joined by the Mantineans, Eleans, Corinthians, and Chalcidians, while others were only wavering. Sparta came to a separate understanding with Bocotia, and Argos declared itself in favour of Athens. Amid these difficult complications, the warlike dispositions of the Athenians were fanned by Alcibiades, who was still a young man, but was honoured by the people on account of his ancestors. He was an extraordinary man, and perhaps the most perfect image of the Athenian people themselves. The consciousness of his powers, and his reckless ambition, impelled him on all occasions to claim the foremost place; he was naturally of an aristocratic temperament, and whenever he appeared as a popular leader, it was for the purpose of gaining some personal object. It was this man who brought about the conclusion of an alliance between Athens, Argos, Elis, and Mantinea; it was to be both offensive and defensive, and to last for one hundred years. The Corinthians soon after returned to their alliance with Sparta. All this occurred in B. C. 420, and in the following year symptoms of a great and general struggle appeared in Peloponnesus, for a war between Argos and Epidaurus furnished opportunities to the Athenians of annoying Sparta. But peace was formally still main-

tained. In B. c. 418, however, the Argives, stimulated by Alcibiades, went so far in their provocations, that Sparta could endure it no longer. The Lacedaemonians with a considerable force entered the territory of Mantinea, and in a battle fought against the Argives gained a decisive victory. This battle of Mantinea at once restored the military glory of Sparta, which was further strengthened by the fact that a party at Argos, hostile to its democratic constitution, brought about a peace with Sparta, in spite of the efforts made by Alcibiades to thwart it. Argos renounced her former allies, and discontinued her hostilities against Epidaurus. Argos and Sparta then endeavoured to draw into their alliance as many states as possible, and Sparta in particular was busily engaged in establishing oligarchic forms of government wherever her influence enabled her to do so.

17. But in B. c. 417, the democratic party at Argos recovered its former position, and the aid sent by Sparta to support the oligarchy came too late. The victorious party formed connections with Athens, and provided for the safety of the city in case of an attack. In B. c. 416, Alcibiades sailed with a squadron of twenty galleys to Argos, where he took on board three hundred of the leading oligarchs, and then deposited them in the neighbouring islands, where they were guarded as prisoners by the Athenians. The Doric isle of Melos was the only island that did not belong to the Athenian confederacy; attempts had previously been made to gain it over, but without effect. The Athenians now thought circumstances favourable, and sent out a fleet under Cleomedes to reduce Melos. Negotiations were first tried, but the Melians rejected them, and all they were ready to agree to was to remain neutral. The Athenians accordingly began to besiege the town. The courage and perseverance of the Melians protracted the siege until the following winter, when, finding resistance no longer possible, they surrendered at discretion. The ravages of the Athenians reduced the island to a wilderness, which was peopled again by five hundred settlers sent by the conquerors. The Spartans, still adhering to existing treaties, had sent no assistance to their Melian kinsmen; but still a number of otherwise trifling occurrences foreboded more important events.

18. The desire to establish themselves in the western seas, and to gain possession of Sicily, had long since been awakened in the Athenian people and its demagogic leaders after the death of Pericles. The first attempt to realise this desire had been made some years before, during the war between Leontini and Syracuse; but the peace of Gela had checked their designs for a time. The Athenians were now in a state of mind when anything grand and adventurous had a particular charm for them, and not being willing to be the first to break the peace with Sparta, they eagerly listened to the advice of Alcibiades and other men of the war party. Their

opponents were as anxious to maintain peace at any price. Under these circumstances, ambassadors from Egesta in Sicily appeared at Athens, B. C. 416, soliciting aid against the neighbouring town of Selinus, and pr mising to support the Athenians with large sums of money against their enemies, especially the Syracusans. Athenian envoys were forthwith sent to Sicily to look into the state of affairs there. On their return in the spring of B. c. 415, they brought with them sixty talents, and gave the most rapturous description of the wealth of Egesta. The Athenians forthwith decreed to send out a fleet under the command of Alcibiades, Nicias, and Lamachus, the first of whom thus saw the realisation of his most ardent wishes. Nicias was in his heart opposed to the undertaking, but his warnings were not listened to. Every effort was made to send out an expedition worthy of the name of Athens, and as the peace party were unable to prevent the undertaking, they devised a scheme by which they intended to ruin Alcibiades; but in doing this they deprived themselves of the only man capable of conducting the enterprise to a glorious end, and brought the greatest calamity upon their country.

19. When the fleet was in the port ready to sail, it happened that one morning nearly all the numerous busts of Hermes which adorned the streets of Athens were found mutilated. This act of wantonness on so large a scale filled the minds of the Athenians with alarm; it was believed that it was the work of a conspiracy against the constitution, and great rewards were offered to any one who could give information about the perpetrators. Informers of all ranks came forward, and those who were denounced thought it safest during the general excitement to take to flight; but they were sentenced to death, and their property confiscated. No ancient writer has given an explanation of this mysterious affair, but it seems probable that it was a scheme devised by the peace party, in conjunction with the personal enemies and rivals of Alcibiades, for the purpose of getting rid of him. His name however was not mentioned by any of the informers, until the expedition had actually sailed. The splendid armament which left the port of Piraeus consisted of one hundred and thirty-four galleys, five thousand one hundred heavy-armed men, four hundred and eighty bowmen, and seven hundred slingers; and the fleet was accompanied by thirty transports and one hundred boats. Upon this magnificent force Athens rested her boldest hopes. It first sailed to Ægina and thence to Corcyra, where it was to meet the contingents of the allies.

20. The fleet sailed from Corcyra to the south of Italy, and halted at Rhegium, while three ships sailed to Egesta to reconnoitre. When these ships returned, they brought the discouraging news that thirty talents was all the money they had been able to

18 *

obtain, and that Egesta was far from being the wealthy town which it had been represented to be. But Alcibiades and Lamachus were nevertheless determined to proceed, and not only to assist the Egestaeans, but to gain as many allies as possible, and make a vigorous attack upon Syracuse. This plan being finally adopted, several Sicilian towns were taken, and the fleet appeared before Syracuse. At this moment an Athenian state-vessel arrived to recall Alcibiades from the command of the army, and to take him back to Athens to defend himself against the charges which his enemies had in the meantime brought forward. Alcibiades departed without remonstrance from Sicily in his own galley, accompanied by the Athenian state vessel. But when he approached Thurii, he landed and made his escape. Soon afterwards he crossed over to Peloponnesus; but the Athenians not only condemned him to death, but confiscated his property, and pronounced an awful curse against him. When Alcibiades was gone, the soul of the Sicilian expedition was lost; the war was carried on in a slow and tedious manner, and the Syracusans seeing the enemy engaged in distant parts of the island soon recovered from their first fright. Thus things went on until the winter set in, and then the Athenians resolved upon besieging Syracuse. Guided by a treacherous Syracusan, they effected a landing at a point called Olympian on the south-west side of the city, where they pitched their camp in a very favourable position. The Syracusans came out, and a battle was fought at once, in which they were saved only by their cavalry. As, however, it was winter, the Athenians, without making any further attempts, withdrew to Catana, which had joined their alliance.

21. Hermocrates, still the soul of the councils at Syracuse, did all he could to train and cheer his fellow-citizens for the contest, and sent envoys to Sparta and Corinth for succours. The Athenian armament also was expecting reinforcements from Athens The Syracusans extended their city for the purpose of rendering a blockade difficult, and endeavoured to increase the number of their allies. Their example was followed by the Athenians, who sent round envoys to the towns of Sicily, and even to Carthage and the Tyrrhenians. The Greek towns in Sicily were lukewarm in their support of Syracuse, but assistance came from a quarter from which they had least expected it. Alcibiades had gone to Sparta, where he was received with great honours. While he was staying there, the Syracusan envoys, accompanied by others from Corinth, arrived, for the Corinthians were quite willing to support their kinsmen in Sicily. Alcibiades strongly advised the Spartans to send a large force and an able general to Syracuse, and establish themselves at the same time at Decelea in Attica; and his advice was at once acted upon. Gylippus, one of their ablest men, was sent with a small force to Syracuse, and further assistance was promised.

22. In the spring of B. C. 414, the Athenians renewed the siege of Syracuse, but a long time elapsed before the city could be invested. The first conflict occurred at the heights called Epipolae, where the Syracusans were defeated. The Athenians then advanced against the quarter of the city called Tyche, and began the work of circumvallation. Various engagements took place in which the Syracusans were worsted, but in one of them Lamachus was killed, and this somewhat encouraged them. The Athenian fleet in the meantime had entered the great harbour of Syracuse, and the whole army of the besieged threw itself into the city, which was now wholly blockaded. The despondency in Syracuse was so great, that the people began to think of peace, and deposed Hermocrates, their best and most patriotic adviser. The Athenians, on the other hand, were now joined by many of the Sicilian towns, and even by some of the Tyrrhenians; the army, now commanded by Nicias alone, was filled with hopes of victory. Under these circumstances Gylippus arrived and landed near Himera, on the north coast of Sicily. His mere arrival inspired the Dorian towns with fresh confidence and the hope of a vigorous support from Sparta, and numbers flocked to his standard. The Syracusans also felt their spirits reviving, and banished all thoughts of peace from their minds. Gylippus succeeded in gaining the heights of Epipolae, and being joined by the Syracusans, attacked the fortifications of the Athenians, which were nearly completed.

23. The arrival of Gylippus completely changed the aspect of affairs. The Athenians were not only prevented from completing their fortifications, but lost their stores, and it was evident that their operations by land would not lead to the desired issue. Gylippus devoted all his attention to the safety of the city and the training of his troops. The success which he met with in this respect, and in some skirmishes with the Athenians, induced both the natives of Sicily and the Greek towns to embrace the cause of Syracuse, while the Athenians had scarcely any allies except Naxos and Catana. Syracuse, moreover, had received reinforcements from Greece, and was expecting more. Nicias was in a most difficult and dangerous position, for instead of besieging Syracuse, he himself was besieged. He accordingly wrote to Athens for reinforcements, and desired to be recalled on the ground of his ill health. This last request was refused, but Demosthenes and Eurymedon, being appointed his colleagues, were sent with fresh troops to Sicily. The report of these preparations induced the Lacedaemonians, in the beginning of B. C. 413, to invade Attica under the command of Agis, for the peace had been openly broken in Greece the year before, when Athens, to assist Argos, ravaged some Laconian towns. After laying waste some parts of Attica, Agis, as Alcibiades had advised, fortified himself at Decelea, whence he was enabled to

annoy the Athenians by devastating their fields, and thus to become
a most troublesome enemy. Athens now had to carry on war in two
quarters; her expenditure was increased, while her revenues were
diminished, and outward misfortunes could not fail to call forth
discontent and a revolutionary spirit at home.

24. Gylippus and Hermocrates prevailed upon the Syracusans to
attack the Athenians by sea, before the new commanders with their
additional forces arrived, and a battle was fought at the entrance of
the great harbour of Syracuse, in which the Athenians were victorious, but when they returned to their station on the coast, they
found it already occupied by the land-army of Gylippus. This emboldened the Syracusans to harass the enemy, who from want of
provisions became more and more reduced, in every possible way,
and they even fought a second naval battle, which lasted for several
days, and in which the Athenians were obliged to retreat. This at
once destroyed the prestige of the Athenian name, for they had
until then been believed to be invincible at sea. At this critical
juncture Demosthenes and Eurymedon arrived with strong reinforcements. They were larger than the Syracusans had anticipated,
and created great alarm among them, while the hopes of the Athenians revived. Demosthenes, impatient of delay, resolved to recover
Epipolae, and in a nocturnal and unexpected attack, he was at first
very successful; but various circumstances then combined to throw
the Athenian forces into confusion, and they were completely
defeated; great numbers were cut to pieces in the darkness of the
night, and the rest escaped to the camp. The Athenian generals
were disheartened by this misfortune, which was aggravated by disease among the troops. Demosthenes even went so far as to propose
to give up Sicily altogether. Nicias had the same feeling, but he
was also aware of the dangers connected with a withdrawal. At
length, however, he gave way, and it was agreed that the Athenian
forces should withdraw in secret, without the knowledge of the
enemy. But an eclipse of the moon made so strong an impression
upon their excited and superstitious minds, that the departure was
deferred. In the meantime the Syracusans, having received reinforcements and information about the design of the Athenians,
advanced at once with seventy-six galleys against the naval station
of the Athenians, whilst the land army marched against their fortifications. The Athenian fleet, consisting of eighty-seven ships, was
completely defeated, Eurymedon's retreat was cut off, and he himself was slain. The ships which made their escape gallantly resisted
a subsequent attack of Gylippus and repelled the enemy. But the
loss of the Athenians was very great, and the spirits of the Syracusans were raised to such a pitch that they aimed at nothing short
of annihilating the army of their opponents.

25. Meantime they made preparations for another great sea-fight;

the Athenians knowing that the decisive moment was approaching, made their arrangements accordingly. All the fleet, amounting to one hundred and ten vessels, was soon made ready for the contest, but Gylippus, who knew all the enemy's plans, contrived to neutralize them. Nicias remained with the land-army, which was drawn up on the coast. When the naval engagement commenced, the contest was carried on with the greatest exasperation on both sides. At length the Athenians retreated towards the coast, and the land army broke up in utter confusion, and most of the men fled in terror. Nearly half their fleet was destroyed; everything was neglected, and all they thought of was flight. The fleet was abandoned, and it was agreed to retreat by land to some place of safety. The Syracusans, on being informed of this, occupied all the roads and passes. The Athenian army, when commencing its retreat, still amounted to forty thousand men. The sick, the wounded, and the dying were left behind. Nicias commanded the van, and Demosthenes the rear. Throughout their march they were harassed by the Syracusans, who after some days forced them to prepare for battle in a narrow position. When the fight had lasted for some time, Demosthenes and his troops were summoned to surrender their arms, on condition that none should suffer a violent death. The demand was complied with by all, six thousand in number. On the following day Nicias also was overtaken by Gylippus, and heard of the fate of his colleague; but not believing it, he refused to listen to any proposals, and continued his march amid the most extraordinary difficulties, until in the end he was obliged to surrender at discretion. The Athenian army had by this time been greatly reduced; the captives, amounting to seven thousand, were sent into the quarries near Syracuse, and their treatment was inhumanly cruel, for they lived crowded together in a pestilential atmosphere, and their scanty food only increased their torments. After spending seventy days in that fearful dungeon, in the midst of the corpses of their fellow-soldiers, the survivors, except the Athenians and the Sicilian and Italian Greeks, were sold as slaves. Nicias and Demosthenes, notwithstanding the promises of Gylippus, were put to death. Thus ended an undertaking which, in the opinion of Thucydides, was the greatest, not only in the Peloponnesian war, but in any war that had ever been carried on. The loss of the Athenians was fearful, and far greater than any they had yet sustained. The heartless cruelty displayed by the Syracusans on that occasion must ever be held in the greatest detestation.

26. The blow which Athens had received was fatal, and forms the beginning of her gradual decline. The news on reaching Athens was at first disbelieved, but when at length it was found to be but too true, the people became desponding and disheartened, and vented their feelings against those who had induced them to

send out the expedition. But the depression did not last; the Athenians soon roused themselves, and resolved to continue the war, and preserve the power they still possessed. The Spartans, by a bold stroke, might have put an end to the war; but the moment for action was neglected, and the war continued nine years longer— a period commonly called the Decelean war, because the Spartans retained possession of Decelea in the very heart of Attica, though the principal seats of the war were the sea and the coast of Asia Minor; for, through the Sicilian expedition, Sparta had become a maritime power, which rose to its height under the command of Lysander. The allies of Athens, now thinking her too weak to make any great effort, commenced negotiations with Agis about their revolt. The first that came forward were Euboea and Lesbos; the Persian satraps of Western Asia also sent envoys to Sparta, to gain her over to the interests of Persia, and to deprive Athens of her possessions in Asia Minor and on the Hellespont. The Spartans were ready with their promises, but it was not till B. C. 412 that anything was done. Alcibiades, who had urged the Spartans on, was then sent with five ships, commanded by Chalcideus, to Chios, and induced the people to renounce the alliance with Athens. Erythrae and Clazomenae soon followed the example. The Athenians sent out two squadrons to pursue the Lacedaemonians, and prevent the spreading of the revolt; but they were unable to check the skilful management of Alcibiades; and while he was pursuing his successful undertaking, a treaty was concluded between the king of Persia and Sparta, in which the Greek towns in Asia were delivered up to the barbarians.

27. The Chians, though put to flight by an Athenian fleet, tried to induce as many as possible to join the revolt, but the Athenians having gradually assembled a large force in those parts, compelled most of the revolted towns to return to their allegiance, and the Spartan admiral, Chalcideus, was slain near Miletus. Chios was laid waste, and the islanders were beaten in several engagements. Late in the summer of B. C. 412, a large Athenian reinforcement, commanded by Phrynichus and others, arrived at Samos, and forthwith proceeded to attack Miletus. A battle was fought, in which Tissaphernes and Alcibiades took part, but no decisive victory was gained by either party, when suddenly an auxiliary fleet arrived from Syracuse. Phrynichus, therefore, wisely retreated to Samos, and his allies, the Argives, being dissatisfied with this movement, returned home. The Spartans thus remained in possession of Miletus, and also gained over some other places; but at sea the Athenians remained, on the whole, in the ascendancy. Tissaphernes became dissatisfied with the conduct of the Spartans, and Alcibiades, who had for some time been suspected by the Spartans, and hated by their king Agis, now went over to him, and persuaded him to

reduce the support which till then he had given to the Spartans, showing him that it was for the interest of Persia to allow Sparta and Athens to weaken each other. The advice was adopted by Tissaphernes, and caused no small loss to the Spartans.

28. But Alcibiades had not intended to benefit the king of Persia more than Athens and himself, for he had only wished to weaken his countrymen so far as to induce them to recall him from exile. At the same time he had thrown out several hints to the Athenians at Samos, such as, that he would gain over Tissaphernes to their side; that he was willing to return to Athens if an oligarchical government were instituted, and the like. The Athenians at Samos, and especially the nobles, were taken with the scheme. Phrynichus alone set himself against it; but it was without avail. Pisander went to Athens with the proposals of Alcibiades, and Tissaphernes was induced at once to side with the Athenians. Pisander met a stronger opposition at Athens than he had anticipated; but he persevered, and at last the people yielded. Pisander and ten envoys were then sent to Alcibiades and Tissaphernes. Immediately on their arrival, they made Cos their head-quarters for the negotiation. But the demands of Alcibiades were so exorbitant, that the Athenian commissioners broke off all negotiation, and returned to Samos. At Athens, however, the promoters of the scheme had been very active, and at the beginning of B. C. 411, the oligarchical government was established. In many of the allied states the same change was successfully accomplished. The leaders of the revolution at Athens, with Pisander at their head, prevailed upon the people to elect ten men with unlimited power, who were to prepare a series of new laws. A body of four hundred men was then elected, and the franchise limited to five thousand citizens, all others being deprived of it. The council of Four Hundred had almost unlimited power. The chief promoters of this oligarchical scheme were Pisander, the orator Antiphon, and Theramenes. All the thoughts of the new government were directed towards a speedy conclusion of peace with Sparta. At the same time deputies were sent to Samos to gain over the army to the new order of things. But the popular party in Samos itself, and the Athenian generals, among whom was Thrasybulus, defended the rights of the people. The Samian oligarchs were overpowered by the people, and when the Athenian army was informed of the tyrannical and cruel proceedings of the oligarchs at home, both the fleet and the army bound themselves by an oath to maintain the old democratic constitution, and, in case of need, even to renounce Athens, and seek a new home elsewhere.

29. During the time of these disturbances in Samos and at Athens, the Peloponnesians remained inactive and wasted their time, and the support they had expected from Persia did not come

But still the Athenians sustained many losses, for Abydos, Lampsacos, Thasos, Byzantium, and many other towns, revolted, and even Euboea, which was of the greatest importance to Athens, was lost. Things, however, were preparing which were to be ample compensation for these reverses. For Thrasybulus had at length prevailed upon the army in Samos to recall Alcibiades. When he arrived, he made a great display of his patriotism and his influence with Tissaphernes, and the soldiers elected him their commander along with Thrasybulus and Thrasyllus. He now tried to inspire Tissaphernes with the most exaggerated notions of his new position and power, for the satrap had not yet made up his mind openly to support the Athenians and break with the Spartans, whose fleet was now commanded by Mindarus. In the meantime, envoys from Athens arrived at Samos and endeavoured to exculpate and justify the oligarchic rulers of Athens. But the soldiers would not listen to them, and had it not been for the moderation of Alcibiades, they would have returned home at once to re-establish the democratic form of government. This change, however, was not brought about by the army, but by the quarrels and disputes among the leaders of the oligarchy itself; and it was more particularly Theramenes who placed himself at the head of a counter-revolution. But many other Athenians also suspected that the oligarchs were secretly plotting with the Spartans; and when a Lacedaemonian fleet actually appeared off the coast of Attica, the people rushed to their ships and fought a battle, in which they lost twenty-two galleys, and Euboea was taken by the enemy. For a moment this loss filled the people with despair, but they soon recovered, and in the assembly, which was immediately summoned, the Four Hundred were deposed, and many other useful measures were carried with great moderation. Envoys were forthwith despatched to Samos to recall Alcibiades. Pisander and some of his friends took refuge among the Lacedaemonians at Decelea.

30. Mindarus, the Spartan admiral, growing at length tired of waiting in vain for reinforcements from Tissaphernes, contrived to elude the vigilance of the Athenians, and sailed to the Hellespont, where he hoped to succeed better with Pharnabazus. But the Athenian fleet followed the enemy, and near Cynossema they gained a great victory, which, though dearly purchased, roused their courage and confidence. A second great naval battle was fought near Abydos, in which the appearance of Alcibiades decided the victory. Tissaphernes had by this time come to the Hellespont, and as Alcibiades was trying finally to win im over to the side of Athens, the satrap seized him and sent him as a prisoner to Sardes, on the ground that the king wished to continue the war against Athens. About a month later, however, Alcibiades made his escape, and returning to the fleet, he determined to fight a decisive

battle against Mindarus. He accordingly sailed to Cyzicus, and coming unexpectedly upon the enemy he drove them on shore and an engagement ensued on land in which Mindarus fell. The army fled, and the entire fleet became the prize of the Athenians. These events occurred in B. C. 410. The condition of the Peloponnesians after this defeat was quite hopeless, while the Athenians advanced unchecked in their victorious career, and recovered all that was lost on the Hellespont. In Attica also the Athenians successfully repelled an attack made by Agis from Decelea, in which he sustained great loss. Thrasyllus, who had gained this victory easily, obtained large reinforcements, with which he sailed towards the west coast of Asia, and finally joined the fleet at Sestos, which continued the contest against Pharnabazus.

31. In the beginning of B. C. 409, Alcibiades besieged Chalcedon and compelled it to surrender. Byzantium was delivered up to the Athenians by traitors, and Pharnabazus concluded a treaty with them, in which he promised them twenty talents. This treaty, however, was never ratified by the king, who continued to side with Sparta, and sent his son Cyrus as commander of his forces in Asia Minor, with orders to support the cause of the Peloponnesians. These things happened in the beginning of the year B C. 408, and the time had now come for Alcibiades to return to his country as the victorious and admired conqueror of its enemies. His reception at Athens was enthusiastic — every charge which had been brought against him was forgotten, and for a time he was again the favoured darling of the people. He had been in Athens scarcely three months, when he was made commander of a fleet of one hundred galleys, and sailed against Andros, which had revolted from Athens. But he was unable to reduce the island, and this furnished his enemies with a fresh handle against him, for the people of Athens had such an exalted opinion of him as to believe that he could accomplish everything, and consequently to regard any failure as owing to his want of good will.

32. The Peloponnesians, too, were now commanded by a great general, Lysander, the successor of Mindarus, and a worthy adversary of Alcibiades. He was then waiting at Ephesus for the arrival of Cyrus, who was a zealous friend of the Spartans, partly from hatred of Tissaphernes, and partly from a hope to be assisted by the land forces of the Spartans in his own undertakings. Lysander's fleet had been increased to ninety ships, and Antiochus, one of the officers of Alcibiades, although forbidden by his commander to attack Lysander, sailed into the harbour of Ephesus to challenge the enemy. The general engagement which arose out of this, ended unfortunately for the Athenians, who lost seventeen ships Alcibiades was unable to repair the loss, and returned to Samos. There the army, ascribing the discomfiture to his carelessness, was

19

so indignant as to depose him, and appoint ten generals in hi
stead, B. C. 407. Alcibiades, knowing the fickleness of his coun
trymen, went as a voluntary exile to Chersonesus, and never saw
his country again. Three years later, he showed that his patriotism
was undiminished; after the downfall of Athens, he went to the
satrap Pharnabazus, who abandoned him to the implacable hatred
of the Spartans. Conon, the ablest among the successors of Alcibiades, remained at the head of his forces about Samos. In B. C.
406, Lysander was succeeded by Callicratidas, a young hero of a
disposition similar to that of Brasidas; he took Methymna in
Lesbos by storm, put Conon to flight, and compelled him to engage
in a fight in which the Athenians lost thirty ships. The Athenians, on hearing of this and other reverses, equipped with the
utmost speed a fleet of one hundred and ten sail, which was increased at Samos to one hundred and fifty. Near the group of
islands called Arginusae, this armament was attacked by Callicratidas. The young Spartan hero fell in the battle, and the victory
was gained by the Athenians. The Lacedaemonians lost upwards
of seventy ships. Immediately after the battle, a storm arose which
rendered it impossible for the Athenian generals to collect the
wrecks, the shipwrecked, and the corpses. This apparent neglect
was seized upon at Athens by their enemies, and the generals were
summoned to return and take their trial. Six of them obeyed the
command, and went to their own destruction, for the people, goaded
on by its democratic leaders, condemned them all to death. Theramenes, who was one of the generals, acted the part of an accuser of
his colleagues to save himself, and Socrates was one of the few who
condemned the proceedings as unjust. But the eyes of the people
were soon after opened, and its evil advisers had to pay for their
crime with their lives.

33. After the death of Callicratidas, Lysander was again placed
at the head of the Peloponnesian forces, and in B. C. 405 he joined
the fleet at Ephesus, with reinforcements and subsidies from various
quarters, especially from young Cyrus, who was then plotting against
his brother Artaxerxes. Soon afterwards Lysander sailed towards
the Hellespont and took Lampsacos. He was followed by the
Athenian fleet, which took its station at Ægospotami, opposite
to Lampsacos, in a position where the men had to leave their ships
in order to obtain provisions. Alcibiades, who was living in the
neighbourhood, cautioned his countrymen, but his advice was
scorned. After some days, when the Athenians had been lulled
into security, and were as usual scattered on the shore, Lysander
attacked them. Conon, seeing the impossibility of gathering his
forces, fled with a few ships; all the remainder were captured, and
the crews were cut to pieces on shore or taken prisoners. Conon
escaped to Evagoras in Cyprus, but two of his colleagues were put

& death at Lampsacos. Lysander now proceeded to subdue the
allies of Athens one after another, but sent the garrisons of the
cities to Athens, where he hoped by this means to create want and
famine. At the same time all the Peloponnesian land forces assembled in Attica, and encamped close to the gates of the city; and
Lysander, who approached with his fleet, ravaged Salamis, and appeared before Piraeus. Athens was thus attacked by land and by
sea; but although the people were without means of defending
themselves, they yet refused to surrender at once, for they knew
the fate that was awaiting them. When at length famine had
reached a fearful height, they offered to treat with the Spartans, if
they would promise to spare the city and the long walls. They were
referred to the ephors at Sparta, but finding that negotiation was
impossible with the exasperated enemy, they were obliged to submit
on the following terms:—that the long walls and the fortifications
of Piraeus should be pulled down; that all ships, with the exception
of twelve, should be delivered up; that all the exiles of the oligarchical party should be recalled; that henceforth Athens and Sparta
should have the same friends and the same enemies; and lastly, that
Athens should recognise the supremacy of Sparta both by land and by
sea, and that all her allies should be restored to independence.
Theramenes, who had acted a very equivocal part in obtaining this
peace, advised the desponding people to accept it. All the terms
were at once complied with, and Lysander, having entered Piraeus,
commenced the work of demolition, B. C. 404. Thus ended the
Peloponnesian war, which had lasted for twenty-seven years, and in
which more Hellenic blood had been shed than in all the previous
wars together.

CHAPTER IX.

**FROM THE CLOSE OF THE PELOPONNESIAN WAR TO THE PEACE
OF ANTALCIDAS.**

1. As soon as the fortifications were demolished, the people of
Athens, by command of Lysander, elected thirty men, commonly
called the Thirty Tyrants, who were to rule the state according to a
constitution to be newly framed. The most conspicuous among them
was Critias, but Theramenes also was one of the Thirty. When
the election was completed, the Peloponnesian army and fleet departed. But Lysander, before disbanding his fleet, sailed to Samos,
where he likewise instituted an oligarchy, and then returned home

with immense booty and the tribute he had levied on the former allies of Athens. The Thirty at first directed their rigour chiefly against the leading demagogues; this rule, however, was soon forgotten, or made a mere pretext for getting rid of the noblest and wealthiest men, to satisfy the avarice and cupidity of the tyrants. But the number of exiles was greater than that of those who were put to death. The reckless cruelty of the tyrants knew no bounds. They were assisted in their deeds of blood by a band of mercenaries sent by Lysander. From among the citizens three thousand were selected, who alone were to have the franchise, and to be permitted to bear arms. All the rest were placed beyond the protection of the law, and their lives depended upon the pleasure of the Thirty. About one thousand four hundred Athenians fell victims to the blood-thirsty oligarchs during that fearful year, called in Greek history the year of anarchy, and five thousand emigrated, leaving behind all that they possessed. The rule of terror was so great, that even cities hostile to Athens took pity upon the unfortunate exiles. Theramenes in the end also began to feel that he could not co-operate with his colleagues, and remonstrated with Critias, in return for which Critias charged him with treason, effaced his name from the list of citizens, and thereby declared him an outlaw. He was thrown into prison, and had to drink the deadly hemlock. He submitted cheerfully to his fate, and thus in a measure atoned for the offences of his more than equivocal life.

2. But the more reckless the tyrants became, the more they accelerated the day of retribution. One of the exiles was Thrasybulus, who had so often signalised himself during the war. He had at first gone to Thebes, but being joined by a band of seventy fellow-exiles, he had taken possession of the small fort of Phyle, in the north of Attica. The Thirty, unable to dislodge him, stationed a small corps in the neighbourhood to watch his proceedings. The number of exiles flocking to him soon increased to seven hundred, with whom he put the enemy to flight, and then proceeded to Piraeus. The Thirty, feeling unsafe at Athens, murdered three hundred horsemen whom they suspected of favouring the exiles. A battle was then fought in the streets of Piraeus, in which the exiles gained the victory. Critias himself fell, and many of his followers. The conquerors behaved with exemplary moderation, and the vanquished retreated to the city, from which the survivors of the Thirty withdrew to Eleusis. Their partisans at Athens endeavoured to make a compromise; but failing in this, both they . and the Thirty sent to Sparta for assistance. Lysander accordingly came with an army, and his brother blockaded Piraeus with a fleet. The Spartan king Pausanias, however, being jealous of the exploits of Lysander, advanced with another army, but was anxious to save Athens, and to restore peace. An understanding was easily come

to, and a general amnesty was proclaimed by Thrasybulus, from which the Thirty and their official tools alone were exempted. Thrasybulus then marched up into the city, advising his fellow-citizens to maintain peace and union, and to return to their old constitution. The advice was strictly followed; but when it became known that the Thirty at Eleusis were making preparations for a fresh struggle, the people marched out in a body, and inflicted summary punishment upon them. Their followers, however, and even their children, were pardoned and allowed to avail themselves of the general amnesty. Such was the end of the tyranny of the Thirty in B. c. 403. The ancient constitution was restored, and a commission of five hundred men appointed to revise the laws and put them together in the form of a code.

3. Athens, which at the beginning of the Peloponnesian war had been at the head of a powerful empire, had now, according to all appearance, suuk down to the rank of a second-rate state, but nevertheless, as throughout the war it had been the place in which the greatest interest was centred, so it remained, even after its great reverses, a state possessing more vitality than any other. Its intellectual vigour and activity were progressing as actively as if the late calamities had passed by without any disastrous effect, and during the period which now followed, Athens was so rich in the productions of art and literature, that in some respects she rose higher even than in earlier and happier times, though it must be owned that fancy and imagination gradually gave way to thought and reflection, and that, accordingly, poetry was supplanted by learning. The loss of the supremacy of Athens and the change in her constitution were only transitory; but the changes which were produced by the war on Sparta were of a more serious character. Sparta had become a maritime power, which was incompatible with the character of its aucient laws and institutions, whose object was to make it a powerful continental state. One of the consequences of this change was, that foreign manners, luxuries, and effeminacy, easily found their way into Sparta, although the ancient forms continued to be observed most scrupulously; the spirit of the constitution and the altered circumstances formed a most glaring contrast. In the course of the war, the power of the ephors had risen to such a point, that the executive was mainly in their hands, and the perpetual quarrels between the two kings contributed not a little towards making the ephorate a despotic power in the state. The extended intercourse with foreign countries rendered the introduction of money among the Spartans necessary, and Sparta soon became the richest among the Greek states, that is, Spartan citizens were richer than those of any other state; but the wealth was accumulated in a few families, which were thus enabled to exercise an uudue influence on all public matters. The number of uine thou-

sand Spartan citizens mentioned in the tradition about the legislation of Lycurgus was now reduced to seven hundred ; of these only
one hundred were in the enjoyment of all civic rights, and these
few lived in proud and haughty seclusion from the rest of the
population.

4. Athens came forth from the long struggle outwardly humbled,
but not internally broken ; and the Athenians then, as at all other
times, displayed a high degree of skill in accommodating themselves
to new circumstances, or, in case of need, returning to their ancient
institutions.   The number of Athenian citizens was not materially
diminished, notwithstanding all the calamities of the war and the
pestilence, for they were liberal in bestowing the franchise upon
aliens and slaves who benefited the state by their commerce and
industry.   The Athenian people were often led by unprincipled
demagogues into acts of injustice and cruelty, and were prevailed
upon by them to squander, on pleasures and amusements, the
money from the public treasury which ought to have been devoted
to the public service.   Large sums were thus spent for the purpose
of enabling the poorer citizens to take part in the popular courts
and the assembly, and to spend a holiday in the theatre, or amuse
themselves on other festive occasions.   Such measures, again,
created an inordinate love of pleasure and idleness.   But notwithstanding all this, the mass of the people on all occasions displayed
a peculiarly noble character; were always more honest, virtuous,
and merciful than the oligarchical party, which could not sate
itself with blood whenever circumstances raised it into power.   The
misfortunes which the war and their own party spirit had brought
upon the Athenians led them, under the wise guidance of Thrasybulus, to reform their constitution, and make it a moderate democracy, which was again placed, as of old, under the superintendence
of the Areopagus.   For one generation at least, the Athenians
lived happy under their new, or rather their ancient, constitution,
and it was not till the time of Philip of Macedonia that party animosities appeared again to disturb that happiness.

5. The golden age of Attic art and literature extends from the
beginning of the Persian wars to the death of Alexander, and
accordingly lasted for a period of about two hundred years. During
the first of these two centuries poetry and art were cultivated with
care and enthusiasm, and the drama, the highest and most complicated of all poetical productions, reached the highest degree of
perfection and popularity.   The latter century is the period in
which Attic prose, in oratory and philosophy, attained its full
development.   The time of the Peloponnesian war was the most
flourishing season of the long golden age, for to it belong Sophocles
and Euripides, Aristophanes, Thucydides, and Socrates.   The last
of these great men, though he did not write any work himself, has

been immortalised by his disciples Plato and Xenophon. He is truly said to have drawn down philosophy from heaven, and to have introduced it into the habitations of men; for before his time outward nature alone had been the object of speculation and observation with philosophers, whereas he directed attention to the moral nature of man and his duties to his fellow-men. But he had to pay the penalty which almost all the great authors of new ideas have to pay. He was accused of disregarding the publicly recognised gods, of introducing new divinities, and of corrupting the young. He defended himself manfully, but disdained to employ any illegal means to obtain his acquittal, and when he was condemned to death, he cheerfully drank the fatal cup, in B. c. 399, after a long and useful life of seventy years.

6. Ever since the wars with Greece, Persia had become weaker and weaker; and its history consists of a succession of revolts in Egypt and other provinces, of court intrigues and cruel punishments. Xerxes was murdered in B. c. 465 by Artabanus, who occupied the throne only for a period of seven months, and was succeeded by Artaxerxes I., surnamed Longimanus, from B. c. 465 to 425. His successors, Xerxes II., reigned only two months, and Sogdianus seven. The throne was then occupied by Darius II., surnamed Nothus, who died in B. c. 405, leaving behind him two sons, Cyrus and Artaxerxes, surnamed Mnemon, who, being the elder, naturally succeeded his father on the throne. Cyrus, as we have already seen, had been appointed by his father governor of the maritime districts of Asia Minor, and having formed the plan of placing himself on the throne, with the aid of his mother Parysatis, he had formed connections with Sparta, and enlisted in his service malcontents and exiles from all parts of Greece; for matters had now come to this, that Greeks lent their swords and arms for money even to the arch-enemy of their own country. Strengthened by such Greeks, and being plentifully provided with money, he undertook an expedition against his brother, who had already for some years occupied his throne; but only his most intimate friends knew the object of the expedition—Cyrus making the army believe that he was marching against the rebellious Pisidians. In the summer of B. c. 401 he set out from Sardes. At Thapsacus, on the Euphrates, the army was informed that they were marching against the king of Persia, and the reluctance of the soldiers was overcome only by increased pay and liberal promises. In the battle of Cunaxa, where Artaxerxes himself commanded an army of one million two hundred thousand men, Cyrus was slain and the king wounded. The Greek mercenaries, however, were unconquered, and offered the command to Ariaeus, a friend of Cyrus, who afterwards faithlessly deserted them. As they refused to surrender, they were under various pretexts drawn into the interior of the enemy's country, where their

commanders were put to death. Xenophon, to whom we are indebted for a detailed account of this memorable enterprise, restored their sinking courage, and exhorted them to return home under all circumstances. The retreat was then commenced — the Spartan Cheirisophus commanding the van and Xenophon the rear. They proceeded northward through unknown mountainous countries, and after encountering the most untoward difficulties, being pursued by Tissaphernes, the Persian satrap, and attacked by the fierce and warlike Carduchi, they at length reached the Greek city of Trapezus. Their number, which had originally amounted to nearly thirteen thousand, was then reduced to eight thousand. From Trapezus they proceeded partly along the coast and partly by sea to the western coast of the Euxine. Five thousand of them there engaged in the service of a Thracian prince, but were afterwards recalled to Asia, where hostilities had in the meantime broken out between the Spartans and Tissaphernes. This retreat of the Greeks is one of the most memorable in all military history, and shows the superiority of a small band of well-disciplined soldiers over hosts of untrained barbarians. The whole expedition lasted no more than fifteen months, ending in the autumn of B. C. 400.

7. The death of Cyrus had changed the relation subsisting between Sparta and the king of Persia. Tissaphernes, who had remained faithful to his master during the insurrection of Cyrus, was rewarded with the satrapy of Asia Minor; but on his return the Greek cities refused to obey him. Many of them had, during the late war in Greece, become subject to Persia, and those which were yet free now invoked the assistance of Sparta. Thimbron accordingly was sent with a large force into Asia; but though reinforced by the Athenians, as well as by the Asiatic cities, he effected little, and his successor Dercyllidas, being personally hostile to Pharnabazus, entered into negotiations with Tissaphernes, B. C. 399. By this means he gained over many of the Æolian cities, and then went to Chersonesus to protect the Greek towns there against the inroads of the Thracians. The liberation of the Greek cities in Asia was carried on vigorously, but at the same time Pharnabazus and Tissaphernes became reconciled, and their united forces met the Greeks on the north of the Mæander. No battle, however, was fought, and a truce was concluded in B. C. 397, to enable both parties to consider the terms of peace proposed by Dercyllidas, who demanded the independence of the Greek towns. The satraps consented to this, on condition that the Greek armies and governors should be withdrawn from them.

8. While Thimbron and Dercyllidas were engaged on the coasts of Asia, the Spartan king Agis was carrying on a war against Elis, which lasted for two years, B. C. 399 and 398, and at the end of which Elis was compelled to demolish its fortifications, to recognise

the independence of the towns in Triphylia, and to enter into an alliance with Sparta. Soon after the conclusion of this peace Agis died, and was succeeded by his brother Agesilaus, the most intelligent ruler in the whole history of Sparta, B. C. 398. In the very beginning of his reign a conspiracy of the poor, headed by one Cinadon, was formed against the few wealthy Spartans. It was thwarted solely by the prudence and circumspection of Agesilaus, but the causes which had led to it were not removed, and the evil continued to increase. Soon after this, information was received at Sparta of fresh preparations of Persia against the Greeks, and Agesilaus, accompanied by Lysander, set out with a large force for Asia, and arrived at Ephesus. Tissaphernes, not yet feeling sufficiently prepared, concluded a truce with Agesilaus, promising to ask for the king's sanction to the independence of the Greek cities; but his real object was to gain time and to collect his forces. Lysander, whose ambition became offensive to Agesilaus, was sent to the Hellespont. When at length Tissaphernes threw aside the mask, Agesilaus also obtained reinforcements and marched into Phrygia, a portion of which he laid waste; but nothing of importance was achieved. During a second invasion, a battle was fought in the neighbourhood of Sardes, in which Agesilaus gained a complete victory. In consequence of this, Tissaphernes was deposed, and his successor Tithraustes put him to death. The new satrap then concluded a truce with the Spartan king, and by a large bribe induced him to direct his arms against Pharnabazus. Agesilaus was also commander-in-chief of the Spartan navy, which was furnished by the Asiatic cities, and amounted to one hundred and twenty galleys, but he transferred this office to Pisander, his wife's brother, a bold but inexperienced man, B. C. 395. Agesilaus was very successful in his operations against Pharnabazus, and advanced so far into the interior, that he began making preparations for an expedition into the heart of the Persian empire. But this plan was not carried into effect, for in the midst of his preparations he was summoned to return to Greece, B. C. 394.

9. During the successful enterprises of Agesilaus in Asia, Tithraustes had contrived, by means of Persian gold, to stir up the Greeks against Sparta, in the hope that this might be the means of getting rid of so dangerous an enemy as Agesilaus. The plan succeeded, and Thebes, Corinth, Argos, and Athens, formed a league against Sparta, which had rendered itself odious to all the Greeks, because its harmosts, or governors of cities, everywhere acted like tyrants, although the Spartans boasted of being the deliverers of Greece from the tyranny of Athens. Hostilities were commenced between the Locrians and the Phocians, the former of whom were supported by Thebes, while the latter applied to Sparta for assistance. A Spartan army, commanded by Lysander, proceeded to the

scene of the war, and on its passage through Bocotia made an attack upon Haliartos, B. c. 395. The Thebans came to the rescue of the town, and Lysander was slain. This was the first battle in the war, commonly called the Bocotian or Corinthian war. Soon after the battle, the Spartan king Pausanias also arrived, but on finding what had happened, he retreated — a step which brought upon him a capital charge, and obliged him to spend the remainder of his life in exile at Tegea. The confederates now held a congress at Corinth to deliberate about the future management of the war; and the alliance was readily joined by the Euboeans, Leucadians, Acarnanians, Ambracians, and Chalcidians. Several important places were wrested from Sparta, or induced to revolt. While the power of Sparta was thus sinking in Greece, the king of Persia intrusted Conon, an able Athenian exile, with unlimited power to equip a fleet against her. It was at this moment that Agesilaus was ordered to return home from Asia. He obeyed with a heavy heart, and in thirty days reached Greece by the same road which Xerxes had once traversed. Before his arrival in Bocotia the war had already broken out. The Corinthians and their allies, preventing the Spartan army from marching northward, were assembled at Nemea, and a battle was fought there in which the Spartans gained the victory. Agesilaus, having received information of it at Amphipolis, continued his march southward amidst great difficulties. Late in the summer of B. c. 394 he reached Bocotia, and there was met by the distressing news of the entire defeat of the fleet, and the death of Pisander. This defeat had been sustained off Cnidos, and its consequences were of immense advantage to the reviving power of Athens. A few days later a battle was fought between Agesilaus and the confederates on the banks of the Cephissus, in the plain of Coronea. The contest was carried on with rage and hatred, each party being bent upon destroying the other; but in the end Agesilaus was victorious, and having dedicated to the Delphic god one hundred talents of the booty made in Asia, he went home and disbanded his army.

10. After this the war was continued by means of ravaging incursions into the territory of Corinth, where the exasperation rose to such a pitch that all who were known to wish for peace were massacred. But a few who had escaped opened the gates of Lechaeon, the Corinthian port-town, to the Lacedaemonians, who forthwith demolished a part of its walls, B. c. 393. The war continued to be carried on in the Corinthian territory, but Corinth, with the aid of the Athenian Iphicrates and his peltasts, maintained itself successfully against the Spartans under Agesilaus, and even recovered several places which had been lost. In the meantime, the Greek cities in Asia Minor were delivered from their Spartan governors, and joined Pharnabazus and Conon, both of whom in

the spring of B. C. 393 sailed with a fleet to the coast of Laconia, spreading devastation wherever they landed, and making themselves masters of Cythera. Pharnabazus supplied the Greeks with subsidies against Sparta, and even consented to Conon's plan to rebuild the walls of Athens. The work of restoration was carried on with such vigour, that in the spring of B. C. 392 it was completed. The maritime power of Sparta was at an end, and Athens was fast recovering her former supremacy. But the Spartans resolved to neutralize the influence of Conon, or, if possible, to ruin him by intrigues. The crafty Antalcidas accordingly was sent to propose terms of peace to Tiribazus, a Persian satrap, by which the Asiatic cities were to be sacrificed to the king of Persia; but the islands and the cities in Greece were to be free and independent. The satrap was pleased with the scheme, though it was opposed by Conon and other envoys, who had likewise gone to Asia. In order to enable the Spartans to compel the other Greek states to yield, Tiribazus advanced them money to build a fleet, and Conon was taken prisoner by the Persians. He made his escape soon after, but took no further part in the war, and died in Cyprus. But after a short time quarrels among the Persian satraps induced them to change their policy, so that Sparta had to continue the war against the Persians, while Athens was favoured by them.

11. Meanwhile, the Spartans gained some advantages in Acarnania, which country they compelled to enter into an alliance with them, B. C. 390; and the Spartan Teleutias was successful in preventing the Athenians from reaping benefit from a revolution which had taken place in the island of Rhodes, and in which the popular party had gained the upper hand. These circumstances alarmed the Athenians not a little, and they once more sent out the aged Thrasybulus with a fleet. He first gained considerable advantages on the coast of Thrace and in the Ægean, and then proceeded to Rhodes, but was taken by surprise in his camp at Aspendos and killed. Owing to the fall of this brave man, whose place was supplied by the reckless and effeminate Agyrrhius, the Spartans recovered their losses on the coasts of the Hellespont, until they were defeated in B. C. 389 by Iphicrates at Abydos. In the year following they made themselves masters of Ægina, and harassed the Attic territory. While these things were occurring in Greece, Antalcidas again went to Asia, determined to conclude a peace with Persia, in spite of all opposition. At the same time he increased the naval power of Sparta, and did much injury to the commerce between Athens and the Euxine. These circumstances led the Athenians also to turn their thoughts to peace, and their allies, the Argives and Corinthians, being tired of the war, likewise sent envoys to Tiribazus. With the consent of these ambassadors a peace was concluded on the following terms:—That the cities in Asia and the

islands of Clazomenae and Cyprus should belong to the king of Persia; but that all other Greek towns, large and small, should be independent, with the exception of Lemnos, Imbros, and Scyros, which should, as of old, belong to the Athenians. This peace, called the peace of Antalcidas, was concluded in B. C. 387. The Thebans and Argives were not inclined to comply with its terms, according to which they ought to have set free the towns in their respective territories, over which they had hitherto exercised the supremacy. But they were compelled by threats to yield. Sparta, however, which ought to have been foremost in emancipating the towns of Laconia and Messenia, retained its sovereignty over them, while it sacrificed the independence of the Asiatic Greeks, to secure which so many battles had been fought against the barbarians during the last hundred years.

CHAPTER X.

FROM THE PEACE OF ANTALCIDAS TO THE BATTLE OF CHAERONEIA.

1. THE object of the peace of Antalcidas was to divide all Greece into a large number of small independent states; but that object was never completely attained. Sparta itself not only refused to resign its supremacy over Laconia and Messenia, but openly aimed at the sovereignty of all Greece. The small towns, moreover, in the course of a short time were naturally subjugated by their more powerful neighbours. In the quarrels which thus arose, Sparta took a dishonest part, and fostering dissension, turned it to its own advantage by subduing both small and great. In this manner the Mantineians became subject to Sparta. The city was destroyed and its inhabitants were distributed among four open villages, B. C. 385. In B. C. 384, Philus experienced a similar fate, and Sparta by violence established her supremacy in Peloponnesus, Argos alone maintaining its independence. But not satisfied with this she assumed the right of interfering in the affairs of the most distant parts of Greece. A coalition was then forming in the north, of which Olynthos was the head; and a report that Athens and Boeotia purposed to join it, induced the Spartans at once to send out Eudamidas with two thousand men, who took possession of Potidaea. The war, of which this was the commencement, is called the Olynthian, and lasted from B. C. 383 to 379. Soon after the departure of Eudamidas, the great army of the Peloponnesian allies

followed under Phoebidas. On his arrival at Boeotia, the oligarchical party of Thebes betrayed the city into the hands of Phoebidas, and Ismenias, the leader of the popular party, was arrested. Sparta sanctioned this act of base treason, and Ismenias was put to death. But about three hundred men of the popular party escaped to Athens, one of whom was Pelopidas, the future deliverer of his country. Epaminondas, the friend of Pelopidas, though belonging to the same party, was left unmolested, because he had neither wealth nor rank to make him formidable.

2. The war against Olynthos was at first unsuccessful, until in B. C. 381, Agesipolis, with a fresh army and numerous reinforcements, gave a different turn to the state of affairs, and compelled the Olynthians to confine themselves within their walls. But Agesipolis died the year after, and was succeeded in the command by Polybiades, who continued the siege, and in the end forced the Olynthians by famine to sue for peace. A treaty was accordingly concluded, in which the supremacy of Sparta was recognised, B. C. 379. Sparta had now reached the height of her power; all opposition was crushed, and Argos and Corinth were as yet too exhausted to venture upon a fresh war. But this year of Sparta's greatest prosperity was at the same time the beginning of her downfall.

3. Pelopidas in his exile had been forming plans of delivering his country, and with a small number of fellow-exiles he entered Thebes by night in disguise; and being there joined by Charon, they proceeded to the houses of the leaders of the oligarchy and put them to death. The citizens were then called out to assert their freedom. At daybreak all the Thebans assembled in arms, and an Athenian army, which had been waiting on the frontier, hastened to Thebes to assist the popular party. The Spartan harmost withdrew to the Cadmea, but was soon obliged to capitulate; he and his garrison were allowed to depart unhurt, but those Thebans who had been instrumental in betraying the city into the hands of the enemy were put to death. The Spartans on hearing the tidings of these events, resolved to reduce Thebes by force of arms, and thus commenced the Theban war, which lasted for many years, from B. C. 378 to 362. During this war, in which all Greece took part, Thebes recovered the supremacy of Boeotia, and under Epaminondas even gained that of all Greece; while Athens recovered her maritime ascendancy. By this war, too, Greece weakened herself so much, that subsequently she became an easy prey to the Macedonians.

4. In the beginning of B. C. 378, Cleombrotus invaded Boeotia, but committed no act of hostility against Thebes; and the Athenians, who from fear began to think of renouncing their alliance with Thebes, were induced only by a stratagem to remain faithful.

20

They then earnestly prepared for war against Sparta, and concluded alliances not only with the Bœotians, but with the most powerful maritime towns, such as Chios, Byzantium, Rhodes, Mytilene, and a large number of others. Athens was at the head of this new confederacy, and had the supreme command in the war; but every allied state had a separate vote. The Athenian navy was gradually increased to three hundred sail, and the moderation and wisdom displayed by the Athenians in their new position secured to them the confidence of the confederates. During the first two years of the war, the Lacedaemonians invaded and ravaged Bœotia, but nothing of any consequence was effected, for the Thebans remained behind their fortifications; in the third year the Lacedaemonians were repulsed by the Athenians in attempting to march through the passes of Cithaeron. Meanwhile, Pelopidas had formed and trained an excellent army at Thebes, the most illustrious part of which, the sacred band, consisted of a body of the most patriotic young men. The Spartans, after being baffled by the Athenians, built a fleet partly to operate against Athens, and partly to transport their troops into Bœotia, but it was destroyed off Naxos by the Athenian Chabrias in B. C. 376; and to prevent the Peloponnesians from sending forces against Bœotia, the Athenians, sending Timotheus with a fleet round Peloponnesus, gained possession of Cythera, and induced Cephallenia, Acarnania, and several Epirot tribes to join the Athenian confederacy. By this means Bœotia escaped being again harassed and ravaged by the Lacedaemonians, and Thebes established her supremacy over the Bœotian towns, which was completed in B. C. 375, when the influence of Sparta was broken in a battle near Orchomenos.

5. The success of Thebes excited fears and alarm at Athens, and led to a peace between Athens and Sparta, on the understanding that the terms of the peace of Antalcidas should be carried into effect. Thebes, guided by Pelopidas and Epaminondas, refused to become a party to this peace, and the Bœotian towns which still asserted their independence, such as Plataeae, Thespiae, and Orchomenos, were razed to the ground. The peace between Athens and Sparta did not indeed last long, but Athens pursued an independent course, leaving Sparta to continue the war against Thebes. In the other parts of Greece the intestine struggles between oligarchy and democracy were continued or recommenced with the same fierceness as during the Peloponnesian war, and as the oligarchs were no longer supported by Sparta, the democratic party almost everywhere gained the upper hand. At Zacynthos, where the popular party was aided by Timotheus, the Spartans were unsuccessful in attempting to support the oligarchs; they were at the same time besieging Corcyra likewise in aid of their partisans, and before Iphicrates, who succeeded Timotheus, could reach the island, the Spartans had

been defeated, and their fleet, from fear of the Athenians, had retreated to Leucas, B. C. 373. But Iphicrates nevertheless continued the war with great success, and was on the point of beginning operations against Peloponnesus, when negotiations for peace were again commenced. The terms proposed by the king of Persia, who now acted the part of a mediator among the Greeks, were again those of Antalcidas, and were accepted by both Athens and Sparta, but Thebes was excluded because it refused to set the Bocotian towns free.

6. Immediately after the conclusion of this peace, the Spartan king Cleombrotus marched into Bocotia, and in B. C. 371 the Thebans, without any allies, fought the great battle of Leuctra against an army far more numerous than their own. But they were commanded by Pelopidas and Epaminondas, and gained a brilliant victory, for Cleombrotus was killed, and with him four hundred Spartans and upwards of three thousand Laconians. The victory was owing to the prudence and courage of Epaminondas, who on that day gave the first signal proof of his skill as a military commander. Sparta in this battle lost her military glory and her power; her supremacy in Peloponnesus was gone, and the Arcadians were the first that began to assert their independence. Mantinea was rebuilt; all the Arcadian states united themselves into one, and it was resolved to found a capital, which was forthwith commenced, and received the name of Megalopolis. The Spartans indeed endeavoured to check the growth of this new state, but to no purpose. The Arcadians expected support from Thebes, which strengthened itself by alliances with the Phocians, Euboeans, Locrians, Acarnanians, and others, and then invaded Peloponnesus, in B. C. 369, under the command of Pelopidas and Epaminondas. In Peloponnesus they were joined by the Arcadians, Argives, and Eleans, and an army of seven thousand men marched against Sparta. Never had an enemy been so near the gates of the city, and in their alarm the Spartans would even have enlisted their slaves, had they not been afraid of them. As the first attack on the city produced no effect, Epaminondas proceeded southward as far as Helos and Gythion, which he set on fire. Large numbers of Helots and Spartan subjects flocked to his standard. But the severest blow he inflicted upon his enemies consisted in the restoration of the independence of Messenia. He invited the Messenians from all parts of Greece to return to their ancient homes, and began building the capital of Messene at the foot of Ithome, which became its citadel. All this was accomplished in less than three months, after which Epaminondas returned to Bocotia, in the autumn of B. C. 369.

7. Sparta in her distress applied to Athens for assistance, and the Athenians, with their wonted generosity, sent Iphicrates into Peloponnesus; a treaty was at the same time concluded between the

two cities, according to which the supreme command should belong
to each alternately. But Iphicrates was not able to cut off the
returns of Epaminondas from Peloponnesus, as he had hoped. In
the year B. C. 368 Epaminondas made a second expedition against
Sparta. The Isthmus was occupied by Athenian and Peloponnesian forces, but Epaminondas defeated them and forced his way into
the peninsula, where, being joined by his allies, he ravaged the
territories of several towns attached to Sparta, and compelled others
to surrender. In the meantime Sparta received succour from Dionysius, the tyrant of Sicily; and Arcadia, in consequence of its
ambition or arrogance, found itself forsaken by Thebes. While
the condition of Sparta was thus somewhat improved, proposals of
peace arrived from the king of Persia; but they were not listened
to, and Thebes peremptorily declared that she would not give up
her supremacy over Bœotia. The war therefore continued,
although another enemy had arisen in the north, against whom
Thebes had to direct a part of her forces. Jason of Pherae in
Thessaly, being commander-in-chief of the Thessalian towns, and
seeing the distracted state of Greece, formed the scheme of raising
himself to the supremacy of all the Greek states. With this view
he interfered in the war between Thebes and Sparta; but soon
after the battle of Leuctra, in B. C. 370, he was assassinated. His
two successors were likewise murdered in rapid succession. Alexander, who then succeeded to the tyrannis of Pherae and to the
command of the Thessalian towns, attacked Macedonia, and concluded a treaty with king Alexander, whose brother Philip he
received as a hostage. In B. C. 368 Pelopidas invaded Thessaly,
but was made prisoner. It was in vain that the Thebans sent an
army into Thessaly to obtain his liberation, for Alexander of
Pherae was assisted by the Athenians; but Epaminondas in a second
campaign gained his end. Some years later, Pelopidas again
entered Thessaly to assist the towns against their cruel tyrant, but
he fell in a bloody battle at Cynoscephalae; the Thebans, however,
gained the victory, and compelled the tyrant to restore independence to the Thessalian towns, and to enter into an alliance with
Thebes, B. C. 364.

8. Meanwhile the Arcadian state had come to an untimely end;
it had carried on the war against Sparta single-handed; but the
Spartans, with the reinforcements from Syracuse, defeated the Arcadians in B. C. 367, in a battle in which ten thousand Arcadians
are said to have fallen, while the Spartans did not lose a single
man. In the year after this battle, B. C. 366, Epaminondas invaded
Peloponnesus for the third time; but the few advantages he gained
were soon lost again. In the year following the Arcadians, at the
suggestion of their brave leader, entered into an alliance with
Athens against Thebes, and this led several of the minor states to

think about peace, but a war, which broke out in B. C. 365, between Arcadia and Elis, destroyed all hopes of it. The Arcadians invaded and ravaged the country of Elis; but Sparta then allied herself with Elis, and in the next year, when the Arcadians renewed their inroad, the Lacedaemonians appeared with an auxiliary force. The Arcadians, by their superiority in numbers, defeated both hostile armies, and even took possession of Olympia. The treasures of its temple, however, soon led the Arcadians to quarrel among themselves, some wishing to employ them in paying the armies, while others were unwilling to give them up. But both parties appeared to be willing to come to an understanding and arrange matters amicably, when suddenly the Theban commander, who was present, arrested a number of the most distinguished persons who had supported the opinion, that the treasures should be spent upon the army. Mantineia, which had been at the head of that party, keenly felt the insult, and called on all the Peloponnesians to assert their independence of Thebes. But Epaminondas was already approaching with an army. He was accompanied by the Euboeans and Thessalians, and in Peloponnesus he was joined by the Messenians, Argives, and the inhabitants of several Arcadian towns. The army of the Lacedaemonians and their allies was encamped at Mantineia. After several petty and unsuccessful skirmishes, Epaminondas resolved to venture upon a decisive battle, which was fought in the summer of B. C. 362 in the neighbourhood of Mantineia. His attack was so vehement that the enemy was overpowered at the first onset, and put to flight. But Epaminondas himself was mortally wounded, a spear having pierced his breast: he would not allow the weapon to be extracted from the wound, until he was assured that the victory was won. After this was done, he expired. The consequence of this battle, one of the greatest in Greek history, was that Thebes sank from the lofty position she had for some time occupied, for her greatness had been owing solely to Pelopidas and Epaminondas; but the power of Sparta was likewise broken. Both parties were weakened and exhausted, and remained quiet for a time; but peace was not concluded until the year following, B. C. 361, when independence was secured to the Messenians. Sparta alone could not bring herself to be a party to it. In the same year she was deprived of her great hero Agesilaus. He had gone with an army to Egypt to support a rebellion against the king of Persia, and on his return, laden with booty, he died at a place on the Libyan coast.

9. During the period which had just elapsed, a great change had taken place in the affairs of Greece. Formerly the citizens of every little state had joyfully tendered their service whenever their country stood in need of it, but it had now become a regular custom to engage mercenaries to fight the battles, while the citizens

20 *

remained at home and enjoyed the pleasures and luxuries of life. This new system was accompanied by all the evils that usually follow in its train, especially when a state is poor, as was then the case with nearly all the Greek republics. Athens, however, although in many respects she was not better than other states, still retained a vitality, and at times displayed an energy, which are truly astonishing, and show that her citizens had not become quite unworthy of those ancestors who fought the battles of Marathon and Salamis. But though we must admit this, it cannot be denied, on the other hand, that the ancient feeling of national honour had disappeared at Athens, for the demagogues betrayed and sold their country, fully knowing what they were doing, and the people looked on with indifference, being bent only on pleasure and amusement. While all the states of Greece were more or less in this condition, a power was rising in the north and emerging from a state of barbarism, which in the end crushed the liberty of Greece. That power was Macedonia.

10. Ancient Macedonia, about the time of Philip, extended in the south as far as mount Olympus and the Cambunian range of mountains, in the east to the river Strymon; in the north and west the boundary line cannot be accurately marked; but Philip, the father of Alexander, greatly extended his kingdom. The country forms a plain somewhat resembling an amphitheatre, surrounded on three sides by high mountains, but intersected by lower ranges of hills, which form wide valleys stretching from the sea-coast to a considerable distance in the interior. These valleys were as fertile as the best parts of Greece; the heights were richly wooded, and well adapted for pasture land; and several of them were rich in metals of every description. It has already been remarked, that the great body of the people were in all probability Pelasgians, mixed with Illyrians, and that the Greeks usually called them barbarians. The ruling dynasty, however, claimed to be of Hellenic origin, and traced their descent to Caranus, a brother of the Heracleid king Pheidon of Argos. The kingly dignity was never abolished in Macedonia, but maintained itself from the earliest to the latest times. The history of the kingdom, from its foundation down to the accession of Archelaus in B. C. 413, is almost buried in obscurity. The country appears to have been governed by several princes who were frequently at war with one another. Archelaus, who reigned from B. C. 413 to 399, laid the foundation of the greatness of Macedonia, by building fortresses, making roads, and increasing the armies. He was also a great admirer of art and literature, and did much to introduce Hellenic culture among his subjects. He appears to have been murdered by his own friend Craterus, and was succeeded by his son Orestes, who, being a minor, was under the guardianship of Aëropus. During the first

four years Aëropus was faithful to his ward, but during the last two he reigned alone, and was succeeded in B. c. 394 by his son Pausanias, who was assassinated the very year of his accession by Amyntas II. This last occupied the throne for a period of twenty-four years, from B. c. 393 to 369. Amyntas sided with the Spartans in their war against Olynthos and its confederacy. He also connected himself with Jason, the tyrant of Pherae, and cultivated the friendship of the Athenians, with whom he sympathised in their hatred of Olynthos and of Thebes. Under him the seat of government seems to have been transferred from the ancient capital of Ægeae (Edessa) to Pella. He died at an advanced age in B. c. 369, leaving behind him three legitimate sons, Alexander, Perdiccas, and the great Philip. Alexander, the eldest, seems to have reigned for two years; and while he was engaged in a war against Alexander of Pherae, a usurper of the name of Ptolemy Alorites arose. Pelopidas the Theban being called upon to mediate between them, left Alexander on the throne, but took several hostages with him to Thebes. One of these hostages is said to have been the king's youngest brother Philip. But no sooner had Pelopidas left Macedonia than Alexander was murdered, B. c. 367. Ptolemy Alorites now took possession of the supreme power; but Pausanias, a new pretender, brought him into great difficulties, from which he was rescued by the intervention of Iphicrates, who established Perdiccas, the second son of Amyntas, on the throne, while Ptolemy retained the substance of power under the title of regent. The partizans of the late king again invoked the interference of Pelopidas against him, but he maintained himself in his position, and concluding a treaty with Thebes, he gave up the alliance with Athens. He continued in the exercise of his power until B. c. 364, when he was assassinated by the young king Perdiccas, who now reigned in his own name until B. c. 359. The history of this latter period of his reign is very obscure, and we only know that he was engaged in hostilities against Athens on account of Amphipolis, and that he patronized and invited to his court the most eminent Greek philosophers and men of letters. He was killed in a war against the Illyrians.

11. Philip, his brother, who was living at Thebes as a hostage, now made his escape to Macedonia, to establish his claims to the throne. The kingdom was in a most perilous condition: it was threatened by the victorious Illyrians, who had destroyed a great part of the Macedonian army, and by other neighbouring tribes. In addition to this, Philip was opposed by two pretenders, Pausanias and Argaeus, the former of whom was supported by the Thracians, and the latter by the Athenians. Pausanias was induced by Philip's liberality to give up his claims, and Argaeus with his allies was defeated near Methone. The towns on the Thracian coast

were the cause of the first conflict between him and the Athenians, who had been endeavouring to maintain or increase their maritime power.   But their successful days were gone; their fleet under Leosthenes was defeated by Alexander of Pherae, and they were unable to prevent their ancient colony of Amphipolis from falling into the hands of the Olynthians, B. C. 359.   This was what Philip had wished, for his object was to drive the Athenians from the coast of Thrace, and to add it to his own empire.   The year after this he also subdued the Paeonians, and all the country as far as Lake Lychnitis.   During his residence at Thebes, Philip had become acquainted with the civilisation of the Greeks ; and although he preserved the manners and customs of his own country, he always favoured and cherished Greek culture.   With the prudence, cunning, and adroitness of an expert politician, he combined the talents of a general, the energy and perseverance of a soldier, and the generosity and liberality of a king.   He did not interfere with the customs and institutions of the nations he conquered, whence they felt the loss of their political freedom less painfully.   His army, consisting of heavy-armed infantry, well-trained cavalry, and his brave body-guard, was far superior to the mercenary troops employed at that time by the Greek states, and fought for the honour and glory of their own nation.   His heavy-armed soldiers formed the phalanx, which, though somewhat awkward, was irresistible.   Being in possession of great wealth, he practised the art of bribery as successfully as that of arms.   Promises and oaths were no obstacle to him, if by their violation he could gain his own ends.   Unfortunately for Greece, Philip had at his command the forces of a united and compact kingdom, while Greece was torn to pieces by party spirit, weakened by the want of unity against the common enemy, and betrayed by unprincipled demagogues and orators.

12. At the time when Philip was extending the frontiers of his kingdom in the west and in the east, Athens was unable to check his victorious progress, for she was already engaged in what is called the Social War, against her revolted allies, from B. C. 357 to 355.   The allies were headed by Chios, and with a fleet of one hundred galleys they ravaged Imbros, Lemnos, and Samos.   Athens had able commanders in Timotheus and Iphicrates, but the enmity and short-sightedness of Chares, a man less able than either of them, drove them into exile, and the command passed into his hands.   Owing to the negotiations he had entered into with a revolted Persian satrap, king Artaxerxes II. threatened to support the allies with a large fleet.   Athens therefore ordered Chares to suspend hostilities, and concluded a peace, in which she lost her most powerful allies, and with them the best part of her revenue. While these things were going on, Philip of Macedonia had inter-

fered in the affairs of Thessaly, where his assistance had been requested against the tyrant Lycophron of Pherae, the murderer and successor of Alexander. Philip acted with energy, and recovered freedom and independence for all the Thessalian towns, in consequence of which, they supported him in his schemes for a long time. But he did not abolish the tyrannis at Pherae, as he saw that the tyrants also might be useful to him; and it was his connection with Pherae that opened to him the road to Greece, as Pherae supported the Phocians in the war in which they were soon afterwards engaged, and which is commonly called the Sacred, though it was in reality only a continuation of the Theban war. It lasted for ten years, from B. C. 355 to 346, and was carried on with unparalleled exasperation on both sides.

13. The Thebans had resolved to avail themselves of the position they still occupied among the Greek states for the purpose of conquering the Phocians. The ancient and obsolete council of the Amphictions was thought a fit instrument to accomplish this end, and an accusation was brought before it against the Phocians for having taken into cultivation a tract of land which had been regarded as an accursed district, and had until then been a waste. The council of the Amphictions, according to the wishes of the Thebans, declared the Phocians guilty, and, demanding an exorbitant fine, ordered them to destroy the work of their own hands. As the Phocians refused to obey the command, the Amphictionic states forthwith commenced hostilities against them. The Phocians, however, who had foreseen what now happened, had taken possession of the Delphic temple and its treasures. The Thebans and Locrians were the first to commence the war to vindicate the honour of Apollo. The brave Philomelus was the soul of all the undertakings of the Phocians, and it was by his advice that they seized the treasures of the Delphic temple, and coined the enormous sum of ten thousand talents to defray the expenses of the war. For a time Philomelus and his mercenaries were successful, but in the end he was defeated in a bloody battle near Neon, B. C. 353, whereupon his brother Onomarchus undertook the command, for the Phocians were resolved to fight to the last. Onomarchus scrupled at nothing, and the sacred treasures were lavishly employed in bribing as well in meeting the necessary expenditure. He subdued several Locrian towns, and even entered Boeotia, where he conquered Orchomenos.

14. Lycophron of Pherae had been gained over by the bribes of Onomarchus, and in the struggles between the Thessalians and their tyrant, the Phocians had sent an auxiliary force to support Lycophron, but had been defeated by Philip. Onomarchus, however, soon after followed in person and routed Philip and the Thessalians in two battles. Philip then returned to Macedonia to

collect a fresh army, with which shortly after he re-appeared in Thessaly. Onomarchus again went to the assistance of Lycophron with a large army. A bloody battle was fought near Magnesia, in which the Macedonians proclaimed themselves the champions of Apollo and gained the victory. Athens and Sparta were allied with the Phocians, and Onomarchus perished in attempting to reach the Athenian fleet which was stationed near Thermopylae. He was succeeded by his brother Phayllus, whom Lycophron, when obliged to give up Pherae, joined with a large band of mercenaries. Philip attempted to penetrate into Greece by Thermopylae, but being prevented by the Athenian fleet, returned to Macedonia. He had, however, gained a right to interfere in the affairs of Greece, and the great Athenian orator Demosthenes, who already saw through the king's schemes, directed the attention of his countrymen to them in his first Philippic speech, which he delivered in B. C. 352. Meanwhile Phayllus continued the war with great vigour; but he was repeatedly beaten in Boeotia, and at last, in B. C. 351, an illness terminated his life. Phalaecus, his successor, was at first likewise unsuccessful; but Boeotia suffered fearfully from the repeated inroads and devastations of the Phocians, and notwithstanding the Persian subsidies which Thebes received, the Phocians in the end defeated the Boeotians in a great battle at Coroneia, B. C. 346, in consequence of which many Boeotian towns fell into the hands of the enemy.

15. In this distress the Thebans sought the assistance of Philip, who rejoiced at the opportunity thus offered to him. As early as the year B. C. 358, the Olynthians and the other Chalcidian towns had concluded an alliance with Athens, to protect themselves against the encroachments of Philip, who, shortly after his return from Thermopylae, thinking the Athenians sufficiently careless about their allies, marched with a large army against Olynthos. The terrified Olynthians sent three successive embassies to Athens, and the eloquence of Demosthenes roused his countrymen to send auxiliary forces, and even to attempt the formation of a confederacy of all the Greeks against Macedonia. However, nothing was able to check the king's progress. The Chalcidian towns were conquered one after another, and Olynthos itself was treacherously delivered up into his hands, and, like many other places, razed to the ground, B. C. 347. To lull Athens into security, Philip carried on negotiations for peace, while at the same time he continued his conquests on the coasts of Thrace. Demosthenes exerted himself in vain to open the eyes of the Athenians to the designs of Philip, and even the great orator himself was deceived in the end. It was at this juncture that the Thebans invited Philip to bring the Sacred War to a close. The Athenians, who were likewise tired of the war, and unable to sustain any further losses, sent ambassadors to Philip to

conclude a peace with him. The king excluded the Phocians from the negotiations, in order not to offend the Thebans, and also retained possession of the Athenian colony of Amphipolis. The peace was accepted at Athens, and another embassy went to Pella to obtain the king's signature. But the ambassadors were purposely detained while Philip continued his conquests in Thrace and made fresh military preparations. At length, however, he signed the peace at Pherae, whither the ambassadors had followed him. But as soon as they left him, he passed through Thermopylae without meeting with any opposition. Phalaecus now despaired of his country's cause, and, concluding peace with Philip, took his departure for Peloponnesus. The Phocians, thus forsaken by their leader, surrendered, on the understanding that Philip would exercise his influence with the Amphictions in their behalf; but they were bitterly disappointed, and the verdict against them was most merciless: the Phocians were for ever excluded from the league, their arms had to be delivered up, their towns were destroyed, and the people were to live in open villages, and to pay annually sixty talents to the temple of Delphi, until the god should be indemnified. This sentence was carried into execution by Theban and Macedonian soldiers, and ten thousand Phocians were transported to colonies which Philip had established in Thrace. Many Boeotian towns which were hostile to Thebes were given over to that city, and deprived of their walls, while a great number of their inhabitants were reduced to slavery.

16. Philip had now gained one important step towards the supremacy of Greece, which was the object of his ambition, for he stepped into the place of the Phocians in the Amphictionic league, and obtained the superintendence of the Delphic temple with the presidency at the Pythian games. The terrible fate of the Phocians alarmed the Athenians in the highest degree, but their fears were allayed by the fair intentions which the bribed Æschines ascribed to Philip, and as Athens was not in a condition to commence hostilities, even Demosthenes, in the end, advised his countrymen to keep peace, and give in their adhesion to the decree of the Amphictions. During the whole period of the Sacred War, Sparta had been engaged in a contest in the hope of recovering her supremacy in Peloponnesus. With this view she waged war against Megalopolis and Argos; and against the latter city, which was supported by Thebes, she was very successful. At the close of the Sacred War, in B. C. 346, hostilities were still going on; Philip's gold had found its way even into Peloponnesus, where a Macedonian party was formed in several cities, and Sparta apprehended an invasion of the peninsula. Athens, also dreading this, endeavoured to deprive the king of every pretext for interfering by bringing about a peace among the Peloponnesian states. In the meantime, Demosthenes

convinced the Athenians that Philip had never honestly wished for peace, and that all his pretensions were mere blinds, his object being to crush the democratic constitution of Athens, and to make himself master of Greece. As the king had his agents scattered over all parts of the country, he was enabled for a time to turn his attention to other matters, and not only established colonies, embellished his capital, and vigorously worked the mines in Macedonia and Thrace, but subdued Illyricum and Thessaly. He then made himself master of Ambracia, but was prevented from advancing further south in that quarter by the precautions of Athens. He continued, however, his conquests on the coast of Thrace, where again he came into conflict with the Athenians, but nothing was able to rouse them to vigorous action against the intriguing Macedonian, who, while professing to be concerned about the maintenance of peace, was doing all he could to stir up a war in Greece, in order that he might have an opportunity of interfering.

17. Meanwhile Phocion was counteracting the influence of Philip in Euboea and Megara, and even recovered Euboea for Athens. The events on the coast of Thrace at length began to rouse the slumbering energies of Athens, though not until even the king of Persia had shown symptoms of alarm. When Philip in B. C. 34 laid siege to Perinthos and Byzantium, the Athenians prevailed upon Cos, Rhodes, and Chios, to support Byzantium, and the Persian king also sent an auxiliary force. Athens in vain endeavoured to bring about a general coalition among the Greek states against the aggressor. Phocion, who now undertook the command, succeeded in repelling him, and the Athenians in their new ardour annihilated, in B. C. 339, all traces of peace and friendship with Macedonia. In the same year, Philip made an unsuccessful expedition against a Scythian tribe about the mouths of the Danube, and on his return he was met by envoys from the council of the Amphictions, who informed him that he was appointed commander-in-chief of the Amphictionic army in a war against the Locrians of Amphissa, who were charged with having taken into cultivation the plain of Cirrha which was sacred to Apollo. Philip himself had through his agents and hirelings stirred up this Sacred War. He of course readily accepted the new office, and at once proceeded southward with an army much larger than was required against the single town of Amphissa. At the same time he tried to thwart the attempts of the Athenians to bring about a coalition against him, and stirred up the ancient animosity between Thebes and Athens. Amphissa was soon reduced, but as he nevertheless remained with his army in Locris, and at the beginning of the following year suddenly took possession of Elateia and Cytinion, the astonished Greeks at once perceived his real object. Demosthenes' prophecies were now seen to be true, and under his guidance Athens concluded an

alliance with Thebes. The Athenians were ready to do anything and to make any sacrifice to secure the independence of Greece. They were reinforced by a considerable number of troops from other states, which were at length roused to a sense of duty. The army of the Greeks was about equal in number to that of the Macedonians. The Greeks at first were successful, and Philip being defeated in two battles, began to despair, but in the autumn of B. C. 338, a decisive battle was fought in the plain of Chaeroneia. The Greek commanders were not men of any great abilities, while the Macedonians, independently of Philip himself, were commanded by the experienced Antipater and the bold young Alexander, Philip's son. The issue of the battle was for a long time undecided, but in the end the Macedonians gained the victory. One thousand Athenians lay dead on the field of battle, and two thousand were taken prisoners; the Thebans also sustained great loss.

18. The battle of Chaeroneia decided the fate of Greece. On the whole, Philip showed great moderation, for he treated the prisoners humanely, and restored them to liberty without ransom. He refused to inflict any severe punishment on Athens, and even offered peace on conditions which did not interfere with their political constitution. But the Athenians, when recovering from the first consternation, refused to listen to any proposals of peace, and were resolved to continue the struggle. Demosthenes and other patriots fanned the flame. But on cool reflection, it was found that their enthusiasm lacked the means of giving it effect; and an embassy was sent to Philip to accept and ratify the peace on the terms proposed by him. The Athenians had to give up Samos, for which they received Oropos, and promised to send deputies to a congress which was to meet at Corinth in the spring of B. C. 337. It was Demosthenes who had urged his countrymen to the last struggle; but though it had been undertaken in vain, the people of Athens honoured his patriotic zeal, by commissioning him to deliver the funeral oration on those who had fallen in the battle. The king of Macedonia henceforth was the real master of Greece; but the administration of Athens was, during the unfortunate period which now followed, in the hands of men like Phocion, Demosthenes, and Lycurgus, who by their honesty and patriotic zeal kept Athens at the head of the Greek states, and raised her, comparatively speaking, to a high degree of prosperity. The Thebans were severely chastised for having abandoned the alliance with Philip; the Cadmea was occupied by a Macedonian garrison, and Thebes lost her supremacy over the Bocotian towns. In Peloponnesus, the Corinthians, Achaeans, Eleans, and the towns of Argolis submitted to him as their acknowledged sovereign. Even Sparta yielded, for she was weak and helpless.

19. In the spring of B. C. 337, the congress of the deputies from
21

all the Greek states met at Corinth by command of Philip. Sparta alone kept aloof. There the king announced the final object of his undertakings to be the subjugation of Persia, and he himself was appointed commander-in-chief for the national war with unlimited power. The contingents to be furnished by the Greek states were fixed, and Philip made preparations on the largest scale. Some detachments of troops under Attalus and Parmenio were sent at once into Asia; but Philip himself was yet detained in Europe to settle some family disputes, and to quell an insurrection in Illyricum. His wife Olympias, the mother of Alexander, had spent some time away from the court, and when a reconciliation was effected, Philip endeavoured to strengthen it by giving his favourite daughter Cleopatra in marriage to Alexander of Epirus, a brother of Olympias. In the autumn of B. C. 336, brilliant festivals were celebrated at Ægeae in honour of this marriage. In the midst of these festivities Philip was murdered at the entrance of the theatre by one Pausanias, who had a private grudge against him. His son Alexander was only twenty years old, but the people and the army demanded his succession. He had already distinguished himself on several occasions; and his energy and genius peculiarly qualified him to rescue the kingdom from its perilous condition, for Greece was in commotion to assert its independence, the barbarous nations in the north and west were trying to shake off the recently imposed yoke, and at the court itself there were conspirators aiming at the life of the young king. His genius, however, overcame all dangers and difficulties.

CHAPTER XI.

THE REIGN OF ALEXANDER THE GREAT.

1. PHILIP'S son Alexander, surnamed the Great, had received the most careful education under the superintendence of Aristotle, the greatest of all ancient philosophers. Under his training the young prince had become a perfect Greek, and a lover and admirer of Greek art and literature. When the news of his father's death and his own accession reached Athens, the patriots, among whom Demosthenes was foremost, exerted themselves once more, and a decree was forthwith passed, to honour the king's murderer with a crown, and to protest against his son's assuming the supremacy in Greece, for it was imagined that the young king might easily be kept at bay; but they knew not his energy and his spirit. His first care was to get rid of those who were inclined to dispute his succession.

Attalus, who had already been sent into Asia, and claimed the throne of Macedonia for a son of Philip's second wife Cleopatra, was despatched by an assassin; and when Alexander had secured himself against all pretenders, he marched into Thessaly to assert his supremacy over Greece sword in hand. The Thessalians after some slight resistance gave way, and recognising his claims at once promised to furnish their contingents whenever he should require them. With unexampled rapidity he proceeded southward, where no one expected him. At Thermopylae the Amphictions did homage to him, but as deputies from Thebes, Athens, and Sparta did not appear there, he marched into Boeotia, and encamped before the gates of Thebes. This at once convinced the Athenians that they had judged him wrongly, and an embassy was forthwith sent to sue for pardon, which was granted on condition of Athens sending deputies to the congress at Corinth, whither Alexander himself went from Euboea. There all the Greek states, with the exception of Sparta, accepted the king's "peace and alliance." He himself was appointed, in the place of his father, commander-in-chief of the Greeks against Persia, and all the states promised their contingents. The congress of Corinth, which had the superintendence of all the national affairs of Greece, remained assembled until Alexander's death.

2. The submission of Greece being thus secured, the young king returned in B. C. 335 to Macedonia, and immediately proceeded, with the most extraordinary rapidity and energy, against the northern and western barbarians, who threatened his kingdom. He humbled the Triballi between mount Haemus and the Danube, and even crossed that river to strike terror into the Getae who dwelt on its eastern banks. On his return thence he directed his arms against the Illyrians, in whose mountainous country his army was often in most perilous positions; but his quickness and personal bravery overcame all difficulties, and the conquered chiefs were compelled to do homage to him. He was, however, detained in Illyricum longer than had been anticipated, and reports were spread in Greece of his being defeated and killed. These rumours were eagerly caught up by the parties hostile to Macedonia in the different states of Greece, and a large sum of money which the king of Persia caused to be distributed among them produced the desired effect. Several states at once rose in arms, but Athens and Thebes distinguished themselves above all others by their zeal. Demosthenes and Lycurgus induced the Greeks to decree war against Macedonia and defend their independence. At Thebes the Macedonian garrison was besieged in the Cadmea and two officers were put to death. Suddenly, while the siege was still going on, Alexander appeared in Boeotia with an army of twenty-three thousand men, with whom he had come from Illyricum in an incredibly short period Every offer

of reconciliation was rejected by the Thebans, and, after a brave defence, the city was taken by Alexander. Fearful vengeance was now inflicted upon the place; the Cadmea was saved, but the city, with the exception of the temples and the house of the poet Pindar, was razed to the ground; the inhabitants, with the exception of the priests, were sold as slaves; their number amounted to twenty thousand, while six thousand had fallen in battle. This fearful fate of Thebes was not wholly undeserved, for she had at times acted with the same merciless cruelty towards her weaker neighbours.

3. The fall of Thebes made a deep impression upon all the Greeks, and the Athenians, being again the first to change their minds, sent ambassadors to implore the king's mercy. The request was granted on condition that they should deliver up to him the leaders of the party hostile to him, especially Demosthenes and Lycurgus. This demand, however, was not insisted upon, for Alexander, being anxious to win the affections of the Athenians, even condescended to flatter them. It may be said in general that he was desirous by kindness and benevolence to secure tranquillity among the Greeks during his Asiatic expedition, upon which his mind was bent. In the autumn he quitted Greece, and during the ensuing winter made his preparations against Persia. In the spring of B. C. 334, he set out with an army of thirty thousand foot and five thousand horse for Amphipolis and thence proceeded to Sestos, where a fleet was in readiness to transport his forces into Asia. Although his army was small, he felt sure of victory, for he knew the inefficiency of the myriads which the king of Persia had to oppose to him. Antipater was left behind as regent of Macedonia during his absence. His army consisted chiefly of Macedonians and other subject nations, for the Greek states are said to have furnished only about seven thousand men. But a far larger number of Greeks, unable to bear the Macedonian yoke, had left their country to serve under the king of Persia, and among them were some men of great military talent, such as Memnon the Rhodian, who commanded all the naval forces of Persia, and kept up connections with the Greeks in Europe. His death in B. C. 333 was a great relief to Alexander.

4. "The Persian empire, which was at this time governed by Darius, surnamed Codomannus, had been in a state of decay ever since the time of Artaxerxes II., who reigned from B. C. 405 to 359. The voluptuous and licentious court, with its intrigues of women and its cruelties, presents a revolting picture of oriental baseness. In the interior of the empire we find the unbridled despotism of the ruler, along with anarchy and insubordination in the provinces, which produced revolts and bloody oppression. Some provinces made themselves independent, and the great king at Susa did not possess the power to reduce them to obedience; in others, the satraps ruled at their own discretion, and oppressed their sub-

jects with impunity, if they did but pay their tribute to the sovereign. The whole empire became like a rotten building which only required a strong shock from without to crumble into ruins. When Artaxerxes II. was despatched by poison he was succeeded by his son Ochus, from B. C. 359 to 338, under whom the eunuch Bagoas, a monster in human form, had all the power in his own hands. Under his administration the empire would have broken to pieces, had not the blood-thirsty king and his terrible eunuch, by means of hosts of mercenaries, crushed the insurrections that broke out in various parts of his empire. Phoenicia threw off the Persian yoke, and, restoring its ancient federal constitution, made Tripolis its capital, B. C. 350; but the fall of Sidon, when forty thousand men killed themselves, that they might not be tortured to death by the Persians, and the city was reduced to a heap of ashes, made the other cities yield, and the Persian rule was once more established in the countries about mount Lebanon. In Egypt matters took a similar turn ; for Nectanebos, after several successful contests, was defeated by the superior tactics of the Persian mercenaries in B. C. 347, and was obliged to fly into Ethiopia, whereupon Ochus and Bagoas raged with even greater fury and cruelty than Cambyses had done at the first conquest of the country. After a reign of twenty-two years, Ochus and his whole house were murdered by Bagoas, and after an interval of two years the throne was ascended by Darius Codomannus, B. C. 336, a man of mild and affectionate character, but unfit to govern such an empire as Persia then was. As his life was not safe against the attacks of Bagoas, he got rid of the eunuch by poison, and afterwards displayed as much moderation and justice as was possible under the deplorable circumstances of the empire; but Darius had to pay the penalty for the crimes of his predecessors.

5. When Alexander, in the spring of B. C. 334, crossed the Hellespont, he was accompanied by poets, historians, and philosophers, who were to immortalise his deeds, as those of Achilles had been immortalised by Homer; but in this anticipation he was disappointed, for among all those who have written about Alexander there is none that approaches the ancient bard of Greece. His generals, Cleitus, Parmenio, Hephaestion, Craterus, Ptolemy, Antigonus, and others, were the first of the time, and two of them, Ptolemy and Aristobulus, subsequently wrote accounts of their master's expedition, but their works are lost. On his arrival in Troy, Alexander celebrated games and offered up sacrifices in honour of the heroes of the Trojan war, among whom Achilles was the ideal which he is said to have striven to imitate. He delighted the Greeks by his love and admiration for their great heroes, while he cheered on the Macedonians by his chivalrous courage, his valour, and his adroitness. What such an army under such a leader was

21 *

capable of effecting, became manifest in the very first encounter with the enemy on the little river Granicus, B. C. 334, where the Persians were defeated, although their numbers far surpassed those of the young Macedonian. The result of this victory was the submission of nearly all Asia Minor, as far as Mount Taurus. Halicarnassus, which was bravely and skilfully defended by Greek mercenaries, was taken by assault, and the other Greek cities, submitting, for the most part of their own accord, welcomed the hero who boasted of being a Greek like themselves, and promised to restore their ancient democratic constitutions. The most important islands of the Ægean fell into his hands, at the time when the enterprising Memnon of Rhodes, who had stirred up Sparta and other Greek states with Persian gold, suddenly died. In consequence of this, the Lydians, Carians, and Pamphylians likewise acknowledged his supremacy, and retained their ancient institutions. At Gordium Alexander cut with his sword the famous knot at the ancient royal carriage, the untying of which was connected by an oracle with the dominion of all Asia. After this he marched through the dangerous mountain country of Cilicia, where, by bathing in the icy waters of the river Cydnus, he brought on a serious illness, from which he was saved only by the skill of his Greek physician Philip, and by his own faith in human virtue; for he had been cautioned in an anonymous letter against Philip, who was said to have been bribed by the Persians to poison him; but without giving way to suspicion, Alexander took the draught prepared by Philip, and, while drinking it, handed the anonymous letter to him.

6. Darius, who had hitherto remained unconcerned in his capital of Susa, and had neglected to guard the mountain passes, now advanced with a large army to meet the enemy near the passes leading from Cilicia into Syria, but was completely defeated, in B. C. 333, in a great battle near Issus. The unfortunate king fled with the remains of his cowardly army into the interior, while Alexander made preparations for subjugating Palestine and Phoenicia, for he could not with safety leave these countries unsubdued in his rear. His general, Parmenio, in the meantime conquered the wealthy city of Damascus with its royal treasures. The booty which Alexander made at Issus was immense, and among his numerous prisoners were the mother, wife, and two daughters of Darius, whom the conqueror treated with kindness and generosity. Palestine and Phoenicia offered no resistance, but the city of Tyre in its proud feeling of greatness and of its insular security, haughtily spurned the demand to surrender. Alexander now undertook the memorable siege of Tyre, which detained him seven months. He constructed a causeway fortified with towers from the mainland to the island; from it his soldiers attacked the city with all the means

which the military art could then devise, while his fleet, which had been increased by those of Rhodes and Cyprus, blockaded the city by sea. But the Tyrians thwarted all his plans by skilful counter-operations, and offered a most desperate resistance. At length, however, they had to succumb, and experienced the same merciless fate as Thebes, for all the inhabitants who were unable to escape, were massacred or sold into slavery, and the city was razed to the ground, B. C. 332. The commerce of which Tyre had until then been the centre, was afterwards transferred to Alexandria, which Alexander, after his conquest of Egypt, caused to be built at the mouth of the Nile, in the most convenient situation for connecting the eastern with the western world. Gaza, a well fortified and bravely defended frontier town, experienced a fate similar to that of Tyre. Egypt, on the other hand, where the Persians were hated and detested, welcomed the Macedonians as its deliverers, and Alexander treated their national and religious feelings and peculiarities with a consideration which the Persians had never shown them. From Egypt he marched to the famous Oasis of Siwah with its celebrated oracle of Ammon, the priests of which declared him a son of the god: this, with the superstitious and imaginative nations of the East, greatly increased his authority, and made him appear in their eyes as a being of a higher order.

7. While Alexander was engaged in Egypt, Darius had time to assemble fresh forces and prepare for a great struggle, which was to decide the fate of his empire. But before venturing upon this final step, he endeavoured, by certain concessions, to make peace with Alexander. The Macedonian's mind, however, was not set upon peace, and quitting Egypt with his army, which had been increased by fresh reinforcements, he advanced towards the Euphrates and Tigris, which he crossed, and in the plains of Gaugamela, he defeated, in B. C. 331, the hosts of the Persians which had assembled from the eastern parts of the empire, and are said to have been twenty times as numerous as the army of Alexander. The consequence of this great victory was, that the Macedonians became masters of Babylon and its fertile territory, and of the ancient capitals of Susa, Persepolis, and Ecbatana, with their vast treasures. Persepolis was recklessly destroyed by fire, but its ruins, with their sculptures and inscriptions, still attest the greatness and magnificence of the ancient residence of the kings of Persia. Darius, after his defeat, fled from Ecbatana into the mountainous country of Bactria, where he was killed by the treacherous hand of his own satrap Bessus, who now assumed the title of king of Persia; but soon afterwards, the traitor was overtaken and captured by the Macedonians, who nailed him to a cross.

8. During the years B. C. 329 and 328, Alexander, by the boldest marches through the snow-covered mountains of the Indian Cau-

casus, where his soldiers almost perished with hunger and fatigue, succeeded in making himself master of the countries on the south-east of the Caspian, and about the rivers Oxus and Jaxartes (Aria, Hyrcania, Bactria, Sogdiana, and others), which were inhabited by hardy and warlike tribes. At this stage of his progress, he appears to have aimed not merely at making conquests, but civilising the wild and barbarous tribes of Asia; for four new towns, all bearing the name of Alexandria, were founded by him in the distant East, as centres of Greek civilisation and of commerce. Some of these cities, as Herat and Candahar, exist even at the present day under altered names. At Bactra, Alexander, in B. C. 328, solemnized his marriage with Roxana, the daughter of a Bactrian chief, "the pearl of the East," who had fallen into his hands during the conquest of a strong mountain fortress, into which the natives had carried their women and treasures. As he still continued to advance eastward, the Macedonians repeatedly expressed their discontent with the insatiable ambition of their king; but he nevertheless pushed onward, for the wondrous country beyond the Indus, about which so many marvellous tales were current, seems to have had irresistible attractions for him. He crossed the Indus in B. C. 327, not far from the modern town of Attok. But the warlike inhabitants of the Punjaub, excited by their priests, offered a more vigorous resistance than the cowardly subjects of the king of Persia had done, and Alexander was more than once in imminent danger, as he was always foremost in the assaults upon the fortified strongholds of the natives. But the mutual jealousy of the petty chiefs facilitated the conquest of the country by the Macedonians. Several, and among them Taxiles, whose dominion was situated on the east of the Indus, allied themselves with Alexander against Porus, the most powerful of the Indian princes on the east of the Hydaspes. The passage of this river, under the very eyes of the enemy, and the subsequent battle, in which the brave Porus was wounded and taken prisoner, while twenty thousand Indians covered the field of battle, are among the greatest military feats in all ancient history. Two newly-founded cities, Bucephala, so called in honour of Alexander's charger Bucephalus, and Nicaea, were intended to spread Greek civilisation even in India. Alexander then continued his march to the river Hyphasis, on the frontiers of the Punjaub, and was making preparations for penetrating into the country of the Ganges, which he intended to add to his empire. But now the discontent of the Macedonians was expressed so loudly and unreservedly, that Alexander, though with great reluctance, resolved to return. Twelve stone altars which he erected on the banks of the river, were designed to mark the eastern boundary of his gigantic empire. He restored to Porus and the other princes who had entered into alliance with him their territories, on condition of their recognising his supremacy; and after having undertaken a bold expedition against the Malli, and founded a town, Alexandria, at the junction of the Hydaspes with the Indus, he sailed down with a fleet built on the Hydaspes, in order to examine the mouth of the Indus and the ocean.

9. The result of this voyage of discovery was, that Alexander's admiral, Nearchus, was ordered to sail with the fleet along the coast of the modern Beloochistan, while the king himself with his army returned through the fearful Gedrosian desert, where the burning heat of the sun, and the want of water in a sea of dust and sand, combined with hunger and fatigue, in the course of two months, B. c. 326, destroyed three-fourths of his army. The warriors who in so many battles had braved every peril, there died a miserable death in the desert. Alexander, it is true, shared all hardships and dangers with the meanest of his soldiers, and cheered the survivors with presents and festivals when they had escaped from the desert; but the undertaking had nevertheless been reckless in the highest degree, and the excess in which his men indulged after their escape, was almost as fatal as had been their previous want.

10. When Alexander reached Persia, B. c. 325, he dismissed the Macedonian veterans who had become unfit for further service, with rich presents, under the command of Craterus, who led them back to Europe. Many of the men whom he had appointed satraps before going to India had committed various acts of oppression, in the belief that Alexander would never return; but all these were now taken to account and punished, and the king set about the task of uniting the conquered nations with the conquerors into one great nation, to be kept together by the bond of Greek civilisation. With this object in view, it is said, he did not treat the Persians as a conquered people, but endeavoured to win them by mild treatment, and by respecting their national customs and ideas. It may, however, be doubted whether the means he adopted were calculated to produce the desired effect, and whether his object was not rather to change his Macedonians and Greeks into obedient and servile Asiatics. At all events, his adopting the style and pomp of an eastern monarch, his surrounding himself with Persian attendants, and his exacting from the Macedonians the prostration and adoration which eastern nations were, and still are in the habit of showing to their rulers, can scarcely be called a means of hellenizing the Orientals. The union between the East and the West was consolidated by intermarriages. Alexander himself set the example, by taking a second wife, Barsine, the eldest daughter of Darius; about eighty of his generals received Asiatic wives, assigned to them by their king, and ten thousand other Macedonians chose Persian women for their wives, with whom they received rich

dowries from the king. The solemnities of these marriages occupied five days, and were accompanied by the most brilliant festivities and amusements. But these measures, while no doubt they pleased some, at the same time offended the feelings of many Macedonians and Greeks, who could not brook the idea of the conquered barbarians being raised to an equality with themselves. A mutiny broke out in B. C. 324, during a review of the troops at Opis; but the king quelled the rebellion, partly by severity and partly by prudence. Philotas, the head of the malcontents, was put to death, and his aged father Parmenio was murdered at Ecbatana.

11. Whatever may have been Alexander's motives when he first adopted the Persian court ceremonial, certain it is, that afterwards he retained it because it gratified his personal feelings to see himself worshipped as a demigod, and to be approached with servile prostration. In these feelings he was confirmed by base flatterers and sophists, while more honest men, such as the philosopher Callisthenes, who openly rebuked the king for his conduct, were treated with revolting cruelty. His court at Babylon, which he chose as the capital of his empire, in B. C. 324, was of the most brilliant kind, and ambassadors appeared before him from the remotest parts of the world to do homage to the conqueror of Asia. Among other nations of western Europe, the Romans also are said to have honoured him with an embassy. His name must at that time have been familiar to all nations, from the borders of China to the shores of the Atlantic. Banquets and drunken riots followed one another in rapid succession, and under such exciting influences the king sometimes committed acts of which he afterwards bitterly repented, such as the murder of his brave general Cleitus, who had saved his life in the battle on the river Granicus, but had now provoked the king's anger during a banquet, by ridicule and scorn. Alexander did not intend to rest satisfied with the conquests he had already made; he was engaged at Babylon with vast schemes for fresh enterprises, as well as with the establishment of useful institutions in various parts of his enormous empire. He contemplated the conquest of Arabia, Africa, Sicily, Italy, and Spain. But his body sank under the excitements and exertions required for the superintendence of his great preparations. About the middle of the year B. C. 323, he was attacked by a fever, which terminated his life in the course of eleven days, at the early age of thirty-two years. He died without having appointed a successor, but is said to have given his seal-ring to Perdiccas, and when asked to whom he left his empire, to have replied, "to the most worthy." His body was embalmed, and in B. C. 321, it was conveyed to Alexandria in Egypt, the greatest and most important of all his colonies.

12. Alexander does not belong to the history of Macedonia or Greece only; from China to the British islands, his name appears

in the history or early poetry of every country. In the East he is still the hero of ancient times, and the tales of the exploits of Iscander are still listened to with delight by the people of Asia. Upon that country in particular his conquests made a lasting impression; for although his empire was dismembered after his death, the Greek colonies he had founded there long survived him; and from the ruins of his empire, kingdoms were formed as far as India, which maintained themselves for centuries. New fields were opened to science and discovery, and it is mainly due to him that eastern Asia became accessible to European enterprise. Asia Minor, and Egypt in particular, became the centres of all intellectual and literary life, as well as of commerce and industry. Geography and ethnology were extended and corrected; the military art was improved by the assistance of mathematical science, though the use of elephants in war, which was imported into Europe from the East, was rather a step backward towards the clumsy method of eastern warfare. The practical sciences, especially mathematics, mechanics and natural history, upon the extension of which Alexander had spent large sums, received new forms and a broader basis. The fine arts and literature, on the other hand, sank more and more; the age was one of reflection rather than production, and the influence of the East soon became manifest in the colossal and fantastic productions of art.

13. While Alexander was engaged in the conquest of Asia, Agis III., king of Sparta, in B. C. 333, put himself at the head of a Peloponnesian confederacy, to throw off the Macedonian yoke, and connections were formed with the satraps Pharnabazus and Autophradates, the successors of Memnon, who furnished the Greeks with ships and money. The Athenians also resolved to support the insurgent Greeks with a fleet of one hundred galleys; but the decree was cancelled, on the suggestion of Demades, because the money was wanted for the amusement of the people. Athens accordingly remained quiet, and Alexander on several occasions showed his respect to the Athenians by sending them reports of his victories, presents of suits of Persian armour, and the statues of Harmodius and Aristogeiton, which had been carried away from Athens by the Persians. Agis gained a victory in B. C. 331 over the Megalopolitans, who had refused to join the confederacy, and this gave fresh courage to the Greeks. But Antipater, the regent of Macedonia, who had in the meantime received large sums of money from Asia, invaded Peloponnesus with an army of forty thousand men. A great and decisive battle was fought near Ægae, not far from Megalopolis, in which the Spartans notwithstanding their great valour, were overpowered and lost not only their king, but upwards of five thousand brave soldiers. Sparta, thus humbled, sued for peace and pardon; and the congress of Corinth, to which

her requests were referred, decreed that she should join the Greek confederacy, and pay one hundred and twenty talents as an indemnification to Megalopolis.

14. Greece now remained quiet for some years, until the news of Alexander's death was the signal for fresh struggles in all parts of the empire. Shortly before his death, in B. C. 324, Alexander himself had thrown a firebrand into Greece, by a proclamation which he caused to be made at the Olympic games, ordering that all the exiles should be restored to their respective homes in Greece. The Thebans alone were excepted from this apparent amnesty—the real object of which, however was to strengthen the Macedonian party in those states of Greece, the fidelity of which could not be trusted. The property of the twenty thousand exiles to whom the proclamation referred, had in the meantime passed into other hands, and the message accordingly created great exasperation and opposition. An embassy sent to Babylon to remonstrate with the king produced no effect, and open resistance was thought of. This feeling was fostered by Harpalus, Alexander's treasurer, who a little before had secretly quitted Asia with a large sum of money, thirty ships, and six thousand mercenaries. Leaving the greater part of his treasures at Taenaron in Laconia, he proceeded to Athens, where many were found willing to avail themselves of his money against Macedonia. But as Antipater demanded his surrender, Harpalus made his escape, and taking with him his treasures from Taenaron, he went to Crete, where he was slain by a Lacedaemonian, who fled with his money to Cyrene. The Athenians, alarmed by the threats of Antipater, instituted inquiries to discover who had accepted money from Harpalus. Many men of note became implicated, and among them was Demosthenes, who was sentenced to pay a fine of fifty talents, and, being unable to raise that sum, fled to Ægina, and thence to Troezen, where he remained in exile until, soon after, he was recalled by his fellow-citizens, but he never ceased to exert himself for the independence of Greece.

15. When at length the news arrived that Alexander had died at Babylon, the Athenian people in their delight disregarded the warnings and admonitions of men of experience and property, who were, on the whole, favourable to Macedonia, because peace was maintained under its supremacy, and peace at any price seems to have been their motto. Just at this time Leosthenes, an Athenian of great military renown, happened to arrive from Asia with a body of eight thousand mercenaries, and by the request of the Athenians retained them, until the necessary preparations for open war could be completed. The friends of Macedonia were expelled, and on the recommendation of the orator Hyperides and a few other enthusiastic patriots, the Athenians resolved to equip a large fleet, and all Greeks were called upon to assert their independence. Many

refused to join from jealousy of Athens, but an army was nevertheless raised, amounting to thirty thousand men, to which Athens and
the Ætolians furnished the largest contingents. Leosthenes was
appointed commander of the allied troops, and after having forced
his passage through Bocotia, he took possession of the pass of
Thermopylae. Antipater was in a difficult position, for the Illyrians
and Thracians were likewise rising against Macedonia; but he
quickly invaded Thessaly, and at the same time sent to Asia for reinforcements. When the hostile armies met near the Trachinian
Heraclcia, the Thessalian cavalry went over to Leosthenes, and
Antipater was obliged to retreat. He threw himself into the town
of Lamia, and being besieged by Leosthenes, made proposals of
peace. The Athenians, flushed with their success, demanded the
unconditional surrender of the regent. This, however, was refused,
and events immediately occurred which changed the aspect of
affairs. The Ætolians left the allied army, because they had to look
after their own affairs at home, and Leosthenes died in consequence
of a wound he had received at Lamia. He was succeeded in the
command by the youthful Antiphilus. Meantime Leonnatus having
arrived with a large force from Asia, and entered Thessaly, Antiphilus raised the siege of Lamia and fought a pitched battle against
the troops of Leonnatus, who was himself slain. Antipater escaping
from Lamia, rallied his troops in Thessaly, and being joined by
Craterus, who had likewise arrived from Asia, he fought a great
battle near Crannon, B. C. 322. The Macedonians gained the day,
and the Athenian army was twice defeated by that of Macedonia.
The towns of Thessaly surrendered at once, the allied forces dispersed, and each state concluded peace for itself. The Ætolians
and Athenians alone remained in arms.

16. Antipater now advanced into Boeotia, demanding of the
Athenians to surrender the enemies of Macedonia. Demosthenes,
Hyperides, and other patriots took to flight. Several embassies
were sent to Antipater to obtain favourable terms, but the conqueror
insisted upon Athens surrendering at discretion, delivering up the
leaders of the anti-Macedonian party, paying the expenses of the
war, and receiving a Macedonian garrison in Munychia. The Athenians were obliged to submit, and after the garrison had entered
Munychia, their democratic form of government was changed into
a timocracy, in which only nine thousand citizens retained the
franchise. Many thousands quitted the city and went into exile.
The patriots who had taken to flight were in their absence sentenced
to death. Demosthenes, the noblest and purest of them, had taken
refuge in the temple of Poseidon, in the island of Calaurcia, where,
on discovering that he was no longer safe, he took poison which he
had for some time been carrying about with him. The war which
was thus brought to a close is generally called the Lamian; in it

22

Athens lost her freedom and her constitution. After having humbled Athens, Antipater and Craterus set out against the Ætolians; but before they could effect anything, they were obliged to give up the undertaking, in consequence of the disturbances, which had broken out in Asia.

CHAPTER XII.

THE SUCCESSORS OF ALEXANDER, UNTIL THE TIME OF THE ACHAEAN LEAGUE.

1. As Alexander had left no heir capable of filling the throne, there being only his weak-minded brother Arrhidaeus, and two infant sons, the youngest of whom was not born till after the king's death, his vast empire broke to pieces more rapidly than it had been conquered. After many and bloody wars, in the course of which the whole family of Alexander was extirpated, and the most sacred ties of nature rent asunder and trodden under foot, his generals took possession of the separate countries of which the empire was composed, and raised them to the rank of independent kingdoms. At first Perdiccas, to whom Alexander is said to have given his seal-ring, enjoyed the highest authority, and undertook the office of regent of the whole empire for Arrhidaeus. But when, in conjunction with the brave and prudent Eumenes, he made war upon Ptolemy, the governor of Egypt, he was murdered by his own soldiers at Memphis in B. c. 321. After this, Antigonus, a warlike and very talented general, acquired the greatest power in Asia Minor, and undertook a new division of the empire, while the rough but honest Antipater, and his domineering son Cassander, kept Macedonia and Greece in their hands. Antipater died in B. c. 318, having appointed the aged Polysperchon, an Epirot prince, his successor and guardian of the royal family, who were kept at Pella in a sort of splendid captivity. But Cassander, Antipater's son, in B. c. 315. deprived Polysperchon of his position, and caused Alexander's mother Olympias, who had in B. c. 317 murdered Archidaeus and his wife Eurydice, to be stoned to death; some years later, B. c. 311, he put to death Roxana with her young son Alexander, and in B. c. 309, caused Heracles, a son of Alexander by Barsine, to be strangled during a banquet. Thus every member of the family of the great conqueror died a violent death, and the fate of some was truly tragic.

2. Meanwhile, the armies of Antigonus were fighting in Asia against Eumenes, and the power of the former was still on the increase, when Eumenes, after a fierce struggle of several years, in which the chivalrous Craterus also had fallen, was taken prisoner by him, and died in a dungeon, B. C. 316. Antigonus now took possession of the treasures at Susa, and increased the number of his mercenaries so much, that he was able to bid defiance to all the other generals, and to compel them to acknowledge him as regent of the empire, and as their master. But as it soon became evident that he aimed at nothing short of the empire of Alexander, and as he deprived his ally Seleucus of the governorship of Babylonia, the four most powerful generals, Ptolemy, Seleucus, Lysimachus (who had put himself in possession of Thrace), and Cassander, allied themselves against Antigonus and his son Demetrius, who afterwards obtained the surname of Poliorcetes. This led to a general and long protracted war against Antigonus, B. C. 315, which was carried on with varying success in Asia and Europe, and terminated in B. C. 311. Towards the close of it, in B. C. 312, Seleucus, after a victory over Demetrius at Gaza, succeeded in establishing himself in Babylonia and the, eastern provinces, and this year accordingly is the first of what is called the era of the Seleucidae, who governed the Syrian empire until B. C. 65. In the peace concluded in B. C. 311, the whole empire of Alexander was parcelled out among the competitors. Some years later, a fresh war broke out, in which Ptolemy suffered a great defeat near Salamis in Cyprus, B. C. 306, whereupon Antigonus and Demetrius assumed the title of king in their dominions. Their opponents, Cassander, Ptolemy, and Lysimachus did the same. But an unsuccessful attack made by Antigonus upon Egypt, and the heroic defence of Rhodes against Demetrius, who, although a master in all the arts of besieging, was unable to conquer the city, kept matters for some years in a state of uncertainty, until, in B. C. 301, the great battle of Ipsus in Phrygia decided the case in favour of the three adversaries of Antigonus, who himself fell at the advanced age of 80, while his son Demetrius was obliged to take to flight. In the peace which was then concluded, Macedonia, Thrace, Syria, and Egypt, were recognised as four independent kingdoms.

3. During these wars among the successors of Alexander, Greece was not in the enjoyment of peace, and Athens in particular experienced several times a change of masters. During the quarrel between Polysperchon and Cassander, the former, in order to attach the Greeks to himself, proclaimed the freedom of the Greek states, the restoration of democracy, and the recall of the exiles. Nicanor, who had been appointed by Cassander commander of the Macedonian garrison at Munychia, refused to evacuate the place, and was supported by the aristocratic party at Athens, who were favourable

to Macedonia. Phocion also assisted him. Polysperchon at length sent his own son Alexander with an army against Nicanor, but without effect. The democratic party at Athens naturally favoured Polysperchon, and its leaders accused Phocion and his friends of high treason, in consequence of which he was sentenced to death, and in B. C. 317 cheerfully drank the fatal hemlock. Soon afterwards Cassander, who had in the meantime collected money, ships, and mercenaries in Asia, entered Piraeus. Polysperchon also appeared, but, leaving his son Alexander to carry on the operations against Cassander, he marched into Peloponnesus with an army of twenty thousand men, and conquered the whole of the peninsula, with the exception of Megalopolis. The Athenians being pressed by two hostile armies, concluded peace with Cassander, in which their independence was secured, and their franchise extended. At the same time, however, Cassander appointed Demetrius of Phaleron, a celebrated and popular orator. governor of Athens. His administration lasted from B. C. 318 till 307, during which period the prosperity of Athens visibly revived. The popularity and admiration which he at first enjoyed, is manifest from the fact, that the people erected three hundred and sixty statues to him; but his subsequent extravagance made him more odious even than a tyrant.

4. During the struggles among the generals of Alexander, Greece was always the bone of contention. Antigonus, like Polysperchon, was anxious to win the favour of the Greeks, and with this view declared himself the champion of the independence of Greece, and of the members of the royal family; in B. C. 314, Ptolemy also declared the Greeks to be free. But such proclamations were mere words, as none had the power of giving effect to them. Cassander, however, by ordering, in B. C. 315, Thebes to be rebuilt, gained more popularity than the others did by their high-sounding but empty proclamations. He also reconciled himself with Polysperchon, after the death of his son Alexander, by assigning to him the supreme military command in Peloponnesus, where the Macedonian power was weakened by Antigonus. While the struggle was thus going on in Peloponnesus, Ptolemy appeared in Greece, B. C. 312, and took Euboea, Boeotia, Phocis, and Locris from Cassander, who was thus obliged to abandon Greece, and return to Macedonia. In the general peace of B. C. 311, the independence of Greece had been guaranteed; but the terms of that peace were kept only so long as it suited the interest of the contracting parties. Cassander, however, being ruler of Macedonia. possessed great influence in the affairs of Greece, until, in B. C. 308, he came to an arrangement with Ptolemy, in which it was agreed that both parties should remain in the undisturbed possession of those parts of Greece which they had conquered.

5. When Demetrius of Phaleron had governed Athens for about ten years in the name of Cassander, and had by his reckless conduct become as detested as he had before been admired, Demetrius, the son of Antigonus, suddenly appeared with a large fleet before Piraeus, proclaiming himself the champion of freedom, and promising to restore to the Athenians their democratic form of government, B. C. 307. He was received with great enthusiasm, and Demetrius of Phaleron, who was allowed to depart in safety, went to Thebes, and afterwards to Ptolemy, in Egypt. Munychia, however, had to be conquered by force of arms. Demetrius now restored to the Athenians their ancient democratic constitution, and caused vast quantities of corn to be distributed among the people. The grateful Athenians overwhelmed both father and son with the most extravagant honours, and even proceeded to worship them as gods. But this joyous enthusiasm did not last long; Demetrius soon after quitted Athens, the scene of his great triumph, and hurrying from one enterprise to another, was in the end taken prisoner, and died as an exile in Syria. When Athens had recovered her popular government, the democratic and Macedonian parties immediately renewed their struggles. The popular or patriotic party was headed by Demochares, a son of the sister of Demosthenes, a sincere and honest lover of his country and its constitution. Severe measures were adopted to protect the liberty of the people against unpatriotic influences, but it was to no purpose : the dream of freedom soon vanished. While Demetrius Poliorcetes was engaged in the East, the Macedonians recovered their ascendency in Greece. Polysperchon, who had been kept employed in Peloponnesus by Cassander, conquered the greater part of the peninsula, and Cassander invading Attica, laid siege to Athens. The city was ably defended by the noble Demochares; but in the meantime Demetrius Poliorcetes, after concluding peace with the Rhodians, arrived with a large fleet at Aulis, and by a rapid succession of victories, put an end to the government of Cassander in Greece. The towns thus delivered from the Macedonian yoke vied with one another in showering honours upon Demetrius, and at a congress held in Corinth he received the supreme command over all Greece. But he had by this time become an insolent and voluptuous tyrant, and his short stay at Athens, during which he exiled the patriotic Demochares, was not calculated to regain for him the affections of the people.

6. Just at the time when Demetrius was proceeding northward against Cassander, he was recalled to Asia by his father Antigonus, against whom, as has been already noticed, a coalition had been formed by Cassander, Ptolemy, Seleucus, and Lysimachus. The result of this was the decisive battle of Ipsus, B. C. 301, in which Antigonus lost his life, and his kingdom was divided between Lysimachus and Seleucus. Demetrius fled to Greece, where he hoped

22 *

to establish a new kingdom for himself; but as the Athenians refused to admit him within their walls, and as nearly all Peloponnesus had declared in favour of Cassander, he went to Thrace, where he took the Chersonesus from Lysimachus, and allied himself with Seleucus of Syria, by whose aid he gained several advantages in Asia. In the meantime Leochares, supported by Cassander, had set himself up as tyrant at Athens, and was conducting himself with unexampled fury and cruelty. When Demetrius was informed of this, he quickly hastened to Athens, and took the city by storm. Ptolemy, who had come to assist the tyrant, was obliged to retreat. This happened in B. C. 295; and Demetrius, on entering the city, to the great astonishment of all, pardoned their past conduct, and distributed one hundred thousand bushels of grain among the famishing people. But to secure himself for the future, he placed strong garrisons at Munychia and Piraeus, and fortified the hill of the Museum. He then marched into Peloponnesus, and appeared before the gates of Sparta, when again he was suddenly obliged to turn his attention in a different direction. Cassander of Macedonia died in B. C. 296, and was succeeded by his son, Philip IV., who, however, died the year after, leaving the succession disputed by his two brothers, Antipater and Alexander. Antipater, the elder, killed his mother Thessalonice, a daughter of king Philip, because he believed her to favour his brother. Hereupon Alexander applied for assistance to Pyrrhus, king of Epirus, and to Demetrius. In the meantime, Antipater, who had fled to Lysimachus for support, was murdered, and Alexander, finding the presence of Demetrius in Macedonia inconvenient, tried to get rid of him. But Demetrius anticipated him; he slew him, and ascended the throne of Macedonia himself, B. C. 294. He then drove Pyrrhus back into his own kingdom, and reigned for a period of seven years, during which nearly all Greece paid homage to him and his son Antigonus Gonatas. Not satisfied with his empire, he formed the plan of reconquering what he and his father had lost in Asia. Pyrrhus was induced to make war against him by the princes whose dominions were threatened by Demetrius; and when the armies met, the troops of Demetrius went over to Pyrrhus, who was extremely popular in Macedonia. Pyrrhus now took possession of the throne, B. C. 287; but after the lapse of seven months, he too was expelled by Lysimachus, who then ruled over Macedonia for five years, from B. C. 286 to 281. Demetrius never returned to Macedonia; but after various misfortunes, he died as a prisoner of Seleucus in Syria, B. C. 283.

7. At the time when Pyrrhus was raised to the throne of Macedonia, Athens again rose to assert her freedom. The Museum was stormed, the garrisons were expelled from the port-towns, and the Macedonians were defeated near Eleusis. Pyrrhus, who was well

disposed towards the Athenians, allowed them the enjoyment of their ancient freedom. Demochares, returning from exile, managed the affairs of his country till about B. C. 280, in the most admirable manner, and for a time Athens once more enjoyed the happiness of former and better days. Lysimachus concluded a treaty of friendship with her, and did not interfere with her administration, in which law and order had been restored. After expelling Pyrrhus, he united Macedonia with his dominions in Thrace and Asia, but domestic misfortunes brought about his downfall. At the instigation of his second wife Arsinoë, he put to death his excellent son Agathocles, whose wife Lysandra fled to Seleucus imploring him to avenge the death of her husband. In the ensuing war, a decisive battle was fought, in B. C. 281, at Cyrupedion near Sardes, in which Lysimachus was defeated and killed. Seleucus was now anxious to gain possession of Macedonia and Thrace, but was assassinated near Lysimachia on the Hellespont by Ptolemy Ceraunus, a son of Ptolemy Soter, who had been deprived of the succession in Egypt by the intrigues of his mother Berenice. Ptolemy Ceraunus now ascended the throne of Macedonia, compelled the widow of Lysimachus to marry him, and caused her children to be murdered before her own eyes. But he did not enjoy his bloody supremacy more than two years.

8. This was the time of a great migration of the Celts, some of whom came down upon the plains of Lombardy, while others descended into the peninsula south of mount Haemus. In B. C. 280 a swarm of them invaded Macedonia, and in an engagement with them Ptolemy Ceraunus lost his life; but Sosthenes, the brave Macedonian general, checked their victorious progress. Another army, however, of the same race of barbarians marched southward with the intention of plundering the temple of Delphi, while one detachment marched into Ætolia. The Greeks were resolved to defend themselves against the invading hordes. When the barbarians approached Delphi, in B. C. 279, they are said to have been terror-struck by the same miraculous phenomena which had saved that city during the invasion of Xerxes. They suffered immensely, their king Brennus fell, and the remaining hosts dispersed, some settling on the Danube, others in Thrace, and others again crossing over into Asia Minor, where in after times they were known by the name of the Galatians.

9. After the fall of Ptolemy Ceraunus, in B. C. 280, Antigonus Gonatas ascended the throne of Macedonia, of which he maintained possession until his death in B. C. 239, with the interruption of a period of two years (B. C. 274–272), during which Pyrrhus, after his return from Italy, occupied it; but when Pyrrhus had fallen at Argos, Antigonus remained the acknowledged ruler of the kingdom and of Greece, though in the latter country his authority had to be

established by force of arms, and even this succeeded only partially.
As soon as peace and order were restored in Macedonia, he had to
undertake a war against Athens, which had recovered its independence during the first reign of Pyrrhus. The war broke out in
B. C. 269, apparently because the Athenians refused to admit a
Macedonian garrison. Although they were supported by Sparta
and the king of Egypt, they were compelled, in B. C. 262, after a
siege of seven years, to surrender, and Macedonian garrisons again
entered Munychia, Piraeus, and the Museum. But Antigonus
treated the city with comparative mildness, for he did not interfere
with its democratic constitution, and soon afterwards even evacuated
the Museum. The presence of the garrisons in the port-towns,
however, daily reminded the Athenians of their real condition.
This state of things lasted until B. C. 229, when Aratus, then at the
head of the Achaean league, prevailed upon the Macedonian commander, by means of a bribe, to evacuate the port-towns. Athens
then, though free, was politically too weak to join the Achaean
league, as Aratus wished But she nevertheless remained the intellectual centre of Greece, and it was owing in a great measure to
her influence that Rhodes, Alexandria, Antioch, and Pergamus
began to foster and cherish the arts and literature of Greece.

CHAPTER XIII.

MACEDONIA AND GREECE DOWN TO THEIR CONQUEST BY THE ROMANS.

1. AFTER her struggle with Antigonus Gonatas, Athens withdrew from the scene of great political events; but Sparta had still
to pass through a succession of violent changes and revolutions,
which both darken and brighten the last period of her history.
The ancient constitution of Lycurgus was still preserved, but its
observance was a mere matter of form ; its spirit had long ceased
to exercise any influence upon the Spartans. The ephors had
become the highest authority in the state, and the kings, who were
little more than the representatives of two ancient families, sometimes went out as commanders of bands of adventurers, and sold
their services to foreign states. The number of Spartan citizens
had become enormously reduced, and all the wealth of the country
was possessed by a few families, and in some instances had fallen
into the hands of women, who, as wealthy heiresses, attracted more
attention and exercised more influence than was compatible with

the good of the state. Although, throughout the Macedonian period, Sparta had with a considerable degree of firmness resisted the demands of the Macedonian rulers, still she did nothing for the liberation of Greece, and in the time of Demetrius, she escaped being conquered by him only by an accident. Sparta was then surrounded by walls, which alone shows that the ancient spirit of its citizens was gone. Once only, during the invasion of Peloponnesus by Pyrrhus, the Spartans showed that their ancient valour had not quite vanished.

2. This wretched condition of the state induced king Agis IV. (B. C. 244–241) to attempt a thorough reform of the constitution. Supported by the ephor Lycurgus and the younger generation of the Spartans, he carried several laws to relieve the poor, who were overwhelmed with debt; a fresh division of the land was to be made ; four thousand five hundred lots were to be set apart for the Spartans, whose numbers were to be supplemented by Laconians, and fifteen thousand for the Laconians. This and other measures were meant to revive the spirit of the ancient constitution. His colleague Leonidas, who opposed the reforms, was deposed, and sent across the frontier, and all obstacles seemed to be removed. But during an expedition which Agis undertook against the Achaeans, Leonidas was recalled by a party at Sparta, and Agis on his return was treacherously seized and put to death, together with his mother and grandmother. His wife Agaitis, who was as enthusiastic for reforms as her husband had been, afterwards married Cleomenes III. (B. C. 236–220), the last Heracleid king. Cleomenes now completed by force the work commenced by Agis. He began by causing the ephors to be murdered, and then carried the cancelling of debts and the distribution of the land without opposition Everything went on successfully and promised the return of a happy age, when a war with the Achaean league brought about the downfall of Cleomenes and of Sparta.

3. Throughout the historical period of Greece, the Achaeans had acted a subordinate part; but at the time of the Macedonian domination they appear to have conceived the idea that union alone could save Greece, and prevent the country from becoming a mere province of Macedonia. Twelve towns of Achaia had from early times formed a sort of loose confederacy; but in B. C. 280 four of them drew more closely together for the express purpose of driving the Macedonians from Peloponnesus. In B. C. 275 other towns joined the league, the importance of which continued to increase, until it reached its most flourishing point in B. C. 251, when Aratus became its strategus, and united his native city of Sicyon with the confederacy. According to the constitution of the league, all the members formed one state, at the head of which was a strategus, the central government being at Ægion. The cities composing the

league, both large and small, had one vote each, and sent their deputies annually. The strategus, who had the executive and the supreme command in war, was assisted by two other officers, the hipparchus and the secretary, and by a senate, in which each town was represented by one deputy. This league and its constitution, though it was not free from serious defects, yet through the wise conduct of the best of its strategi, continued for a comparatively long period to enjoy the respect of foreign powers as well as of the Greeks themselves.

4. A similar league was formed among the Ætolians about the same time; but its objects were not so patriotic, for the Ætolians did not look beyond the promotion of their own interests. The Ætolians were distinguished for their bravery and energy; but had remained behind in the career of Greek civilisation, and were in fact semi-barbarians. The constitution of their league resembled that of the Achaeans, and was essentially democratic; its annual meetings were held at Thermos. The power of this league rose very rapidly, for Phocis, the Ozolian Locrians, the Cephallenian islands, and portions of Acarnania, Thessaly, and Peloponnesus, belonged to it. The Ætolians, like the Achaeans, pretended indeed to fight against foreign influence and on behalf of the independence of Greece; but they were rude, quarrelsome, faithless, and, above all, bent upon plunder and rapine.

5. From the year B. C. 251, Aratus was the soul of the Achaean league, even when he was not invested with the office of strategus, to which he was elected twelve times. The object which he steadily pursued was to destroy the power of the tyrants who, during that period, set themselves up in nearly all the Greek cities under the protection of Macedonia, and to unite all Peloponnesus under one democratic constitution. He effected much as a statesman by his prudence and eloquence, but he was wanting in resolution and personal courage. In B. C. 243, when he was strategus for the second time, he expelled the Macedonian garrison from Acrocorinthus, and prevailed upon the Corinthians, and soon afterwards upon the Megarians, to join the Achaean confederacy. About the year B. C. 226, when Aratus was strategus for the eleventh time, the league had gained, besides, the towns of Troezen, Epidaurus, Phlius, Hermione, and Argos. Three years before, he had delivered Athens from its Macedonian garrison, though that city was not able to join the confederacy. During this period, the Ætolians evinced a spirit hostile to the Achaeans, and even went so far as to conclude a treaty with Antigonus Gonatas about a division of Achaia. In the meantime, the reforms of Cleomenes not only strengthened Sparta internally, but increased her power and influence among the neighbouring states of Peloponnesus. Argos and Mantineia were subdued, and Cleomenes strove to recover for Sparta her ancient

supremacy in the peninsula. Sparta thus aimed at the same object as Aratus, and a conflict was unavoidable.' Neither party was willing to give way, and in B. C. 224, the Achaeans not only resolved upon war against Sparta, but Aratus so far forgot the objects of the Achaean league as to solicit the aid of Macedonia.

6. Antigonus Gonatas, king of Macedonia, had died in B. C. 239, and had been succeeded by his son Demetrius, who reigned until B. C. 229. At his death, his son Philip was still under age, and the guardianship was undertaken by Antigonus Doson, who faithfully discharged his duties as regent and guardian until B. C. 220, when Philip ascended the throne. Aratus had been in negotiation with Antigonus Doson even before war was declared against Sparta, and the king had readily promised his assistance. When the war broke out, Cleomenes was eminently successful, and defeated the Achaeans in three battles. Many towns fell into his hands, and he then laid siege to Acrocorinthus. He neglected no opportunity of offering to enter into negotiations for peace; but Aratus was short-sighted enough to surrender Acrocorinthus to Antigonus Doson, who demanded that fortress as a pledge and as a point from which he might carry on his military operations. As the Ætolians were in the possession of the pass of Thermopylae, Antigonus had to take a circuitous route, but when he arrived on the Isthmus, his presence changed the whole aspect of things. Cleomenes offered a brave resistance, but was obliged to return to Sparta in consequence of his wife's death. In the spring of the following year, B. C. 223, Antigonus set out for Arcadia, and being joined by the Achaeans, he took possession of several important towns without Cleomenes being able to prevent it. In the following winter, however, the Spartan king gained some advantages, and in the spring of B. C. 222, he advanced up to the very gates of Argos. But soon after, Antigonus invaded Laconia with an army of thirty thousand men. Cleomenes had pitched his camp at Sellasia, north of Sparta, and here a great battle was fought, B. C. 221, in which Philopoemen of Megalopolis, then serving in the army of the Achaeans, decided the victory. Cleomenes escaped with only a few horsemen to Sparta, but not feeling safe, he sailed to his friend, king Ptolemy III. at Alexandria, by whom he expected to be supported in continuing the war; but Ptolemy died soon after, and his successor, a voluptuous libertine, kept Cleomenes like a prisoner. An attempt to excite the people of Alexandria against their contemptible ruler failed, and Cleomenes and his friends in despair made away with themselves, B. C. 220. His mother and children, who had followed him to Alexandria, were put to death, and died in a manner worthy of Sparta. After the victory of Sellasia, Antigonus took Sparta without resistance. Respect for its past glory induced the conqueror to treat it with moderation. The ancient constitution was

restored, and the ephoralty revived; but the line of Heracleid kings had become extinct, and Sparta had to keep a Macedonian garrison. Immediately after this, Antigonus was recalled to Macedonia, which had in his absence been attacked by the Illyrians.

7. The battle of Sellasia had indeed broken the power of Sparta, but the independence of the Achaean league was likewise gone, for Acrocorinthus, one of the three fetters of Greece, remained in the hands of the Macedonians, and the Achaeans could undertake nothing without their sanction—and all this was the work of the short-sighted policy of Aratus. Antigonus Doson died in B. C. 220, and the throne was then occupied by Philip V., the son of Demetrius, who was only seventeen years old. He was a quick and enterprising young man, who, in the course of his long reign, from B. C. 220 to 179, displayed great military abilities. The beginning of his reign is marked by the outbreak of what is called the Social War, which was occasioned by Sparta. Lycurgus obtained by purchase from the ephors the dignity of king, and after having got rid of the last member of the Heracleid family, and constituted himself sole king of Sparta, he entered into an alliance with the Ætolians against the Achaeans and Macedonians. Aratus took the field against the Ætolians, who had already invaded Arcadia, but was defeated, and the Ætolians, meeting with no further opposition, returned across the Isthmus, ravaging the country as they advanced. This happened in B. C. 220, and was the beginning of the Social War, in which the Achaeans, supported by Philip, the Bocotians, Phocians, Epirots, Acarnanians, and Messenians, fought against the Ætolians, Spartans, and Eleans, for a period of three years. In B. C. 219, Philip himself entered Ætolia with an army, and ravaged the country as far as the mouth of the Achelous. In the following winter, he invaded Elis and Arcadia, where he destroyed the strongholds of the Ætolians, while they made inroads into Epirus and Achaia. In the spring of B. C. 218, Philip again entered Ætolia, and having taken Thermos, its capital, traversed Peloponnesus to its southernmost point. But when he left the penisula, the Ætolians reduced the Achaeans to great straits; and in addition to this, Philip, whose attention was attracted by the Hannibalian war in Italy, was anxious to get rid of the petty disputes among the Greeks, and concluded, in B. C. 217, a peace with the Ætolians, who were to surrender to him Acarnania, but retained the undisturbed possession of all other places they had conquered. The Achaeans, who were thus abandoned to their fate, were naturally displeased with the king's measure. Aratus remonstrated with him for his conduct, but was soon after silenced for ever by being poisoned by Philip's orders, B. C. 213.

8. Philip's warlike disposition was stimulated by Demetrius of Pharos, who, considering himself wronged by the Romans, had

gone to the court of Macedonia. After the battle of Cannae, in B. C. 216, Philip concluded a treaty with Hannibal, in consequence of which a Roman fleet was stationed at Tarentum, to protect Italy against an invasion from Macedonia. In the following year the Romans gained possession of several towns of Illyricum, though the country still remained subject to Macedonia. The Romans being too much occupied at home to make any great exertions against Philip, stirred up an enemy against him in Greece, by concluding a treaty with the Ætolians, B. C. 211. In this new alliance they were joined by the Eleans, Messenians, Lacedaemonians, and by the kings of Illyricum, Thrace, and Pergamus, while Philip was supported by the Achaeans, Boeotians, Thessalians, Acarnanians, Epirots, Euboeans, Phocians, Locrians, and by king Prusias of Bithynia. Greeks were thus once more arrayed against Greeks, and fighting for the interests of foreigners, who took part in the war only when it suited their convenience. This was the work of the Romans, who gained several advantages for the Ætolians, and urged them on to continue the war, so that the attempts of the Athenians, Rhodians, and others to bring about a peace led to no results. After the year B. C. 206, the Romans themselves ceased to take part in the war; and the consequence was that the Ætolians found themselves obliged to conclude peace with Philip on his own terms, B. C. 205. At length, B. C. 204, a peace was also brought about between Philip and the Romans, who received some portions of Illyricum, and it was stipulated that neither party should attack the allies of the other.

9. While this war was going on in the north, hostilities had also been continued in Peloponnesus. In B. C. 208 Philopoemen was strategus of the Achaeans; he was distinguished both as a statesman and as a general, and acquired extraordinary influence over the Achaeans, who were becoming weary and indifferent. His first operations were directed against Sparta, where, after the death of the usurper Lycurgus, in B. C. 211, Machanidas had set himself up as tyrant; he had from the first indulged in hostilities against the Achaeans, but in B. C. 207 Philopoemen defeated him in a great battle near Mantineia. In the same year, Nabis, a bloodthirsty monster, usurped the tyrannis at Sparta, and made the city feel all the horrors for which the tyrants of that period are notorious in Greek history.

10. The peace which Philip had concluded with the Romans does not appear to have been made by him with the intention of keeping its terms; for he deprived the young Egyptian king Ptolemy Epiphanes of his possessions in the north of the Ægean, although he was under the protection of Rome, and not long afterwards he laid siege to Athens, in consequence of the following circumstances: —Two Acarnanian youths, who were staying at Athens, and were

23

believed to have profaned the Eleusinian mysteries, were murdered during the religious excitement of the people. The Acarnanians thereupon, supported by Macedonia, invaded Attica, and ravaged the country. The Athenians, being allied with Attalus, king of Pergamus, and with the Rhodians, declared war against Philip, who forthwith proceeded with a fleet to blockade Athens. Assisted by a Roman squadron, the Athenians succeeded in repelling him, in revenge for which he destroyed everything he could reach in Attica. The aid of Rome, when formally solicited by the Athenians, was not withheld, and in B. C. 200 the consul Sulpicius Galba commenced the second war of the Romans against Macedonia. The two belligerent parties had the same allies as before. During the first years the Romans carried on the war without energy, but in B. C. 198 T. Quinctius Flamininus undertaking the command, at once succeeded in gaining over the Achaeans, so that now both the Ætolians and Achaeans fought on the same side. Flamininus advanced from Epirus into Thessaly, while Philip withdrew from Macedonia. Negotiations were commenced, but as they led to no results, the great battle of Cynoscephalae was fought in B. C. 197, which ended in the total defeat of Philip — a result mainly owing to the valour displayed by the Ætolians during the engagement. Peace was then concluded and sanctioned by the Roman senate, in B. C. 196, on condition that Philip should withdraw all his garrisons from the Greek cities, the most important of which, Acrocorinthus, Demetrias, and Chalcis, were to be occupied by the Romans. The Athenians received the islands of Paros, Imbros, Delos, and Scyros, but Ægina was given to Attalus. The Ætolians made no secret of their dissatisfaction with these arrangements, but openly declared that the fine promises of Flamininus about the freedom of Greece were without meaning so long as the Romans kept garrisons in the three most important fortresses.

11. In B. C. 196 the Isthmian games happened to be celebrated, and Flamininus on that occasion solemnly proclaimed before the assembled Greeks the freedom and independence of their country. The announcement was received with the most extravagant joy and enthusiasm. Flamininus, however, remained in Greece, for Antiochus the Great, king of Syria, being stirred up by Hannibal, was making great preparations for war, and Nabis, the tyrant of Sparta, refused to give up Argos. Flamininus, in conjunction with the Achaeans, soon succeeded in liberating Argos, and even attacked Sparta, while the Rhodian and Pergamenian fleets took possession of the maritime towns of Laconia. These losses obliged Nabis to submit to a peace, dictated by Flamininus, B. C. 195. He was deprived of the maritime towns, which were declared free, and had to pay a heavy sum of money, but he nevertheless remained tyrant. As he was always hostile to the Achaeans, who had assisted in con-

quering him, they complained of the leniency of Flamininus towards him, and in this sentiment they were joined by the Ætolians.   In B. c. 194 the Romans indeed evacuated the three fortresses, but the Ætolians nevertheless urged Nabis on to recover the maritime towns which had been ceded to the Achaeans.   A war thus arose between the tyrant and the Achaeans, and the latter being commanded by Philopoemen, blockaded their enemy in the city of Sparta.   The Ætolians, who ostensibly came to his succour, murdered him, and took possession of the citadel; but the Spartan recovered it by storm, and nearly all the Ætolians were cut to pieces.   During the confusion Philopoemen made himself master of the city and of Laconia, and in B. c. 192 added both to the Achaean league, which now embraced the whole of Peloponnesus.

12. The Ætolians entertaining an implacable hatred against the Romans, invited Antiochus, king of Syria, to come to Greece, the conquest of which they represented to him as a matter of no great difficulty.   In B. c. 192 Antiochus arrived, and many of the Greeks at once joined him; but he was not provided with a sufficient army, nor did he act with sufficient quickness and decision.   In the spring of B. c. 191 he was defeated by the consul M. Acilius Glabrio at Thermopylae, and immediately returned to Chalcis, whence he crossed over into Asia.   But the Romans did not allow his invasion of Greece to pass with impunity, as we shall see in the history of Rome.   Another victory was soon gained over the Ætolians, who were thus compelled to sue for peace.   A truce was at length, B. c. 190, granted to them for six months; and when at the expiration of it they recommenced hostilities, the Romans at last, in B. c. 189, compelled them to accept the following terms:—To recognise the supremacy of Rome, to conclude an offensive and defensive alliance, to dismiss from their confederacy all the towns out of Ætolia, and to pay a heavy sum of money to defray the expenses of the war. The power of the Ætolian confederacy was thus for ever annihilated, though the league continued a weak and helpless existence a long time afterwards.

13. In B. c. 188, a few years after the capture of Sparta by Philopoemen, a fresh war broke out between the Achaeans and Spartans, because the latter had taken forcible possession of one of the coast towns.   Both parties referred the case to Rome, but received equivocal answers, until in the end Philopoemen restored a number of persons who had been exiled by Nabis, put the leaders of the anti-Achaean party to death, and made several violent reforms, going even so far as to compel the Spartans to abolish the ancient constitution of Lycurgus, and establish a democracy.   The Spartans bore these wanton insults with deep but suppressed indignation, as they were unable to offer resistance, or to obtain aid from the Romans.   In B. c. 183, the Messenians revolted against the

Achaeans. Philopoemen marched against them ; but on his way he was surprised and overpowered by some Messenian horsemen, who conveyed him in a dying state to Messene. The enraged Messenians ordered him to be put to death, and he drained the poison-cup with calmness and intrepidity. He was succeeded in the office of strategus by Lycortas, father of the historian Polybius, under whom the Achaeans reconquered Messene, and took revenge for the murder of Philopoemen, by putting to death the most conspicuous among the Messenians. But peace and order were not restored by such measures, and the time was fast approaching when the mighty hand of Rome was to silence all disputes, by depriving the several states of all power of action.

14. Philip of Macedonia had for a time quietly submitted to the humiliating peace dictated to him by the Romans; but towards the end of his life he resolved once more to try the fortune of war, and made active preparations. He was, however, prevented from taking decisive steps by a quarrel between his two sons, Demetrius and Perseus. The latter persuaded his father that Demetrius was conspiring against him, and the king was induced to consent to Demetrius being put to death. When the king discovered the deceit which had been practised upon him, he was seized with the deepest grief, and died shortly after, B. C. 179, leaving the kingdom to his only surviving son Perseus. The new monarch continued the preparations which had already been commenced, for he hated the Romans even more intensely than his father; but seven years elapsed before hostilities were actually begun. Perseus was a man of considerable talent, but trusted too much to himself, and could not be prevailed upon to part with his money when it was required, and these circumstances brought about the final overthrow of his kingdom. He had formed connections with the kings of Illyricum, Thrace, Syria, Bithynia, with the princes and towns of Epirus and Thessaly, and even with Carthage and the Celtic tribes on the Danube. His plans were admirable. The Greeks, except the Boeotian towns, had not the courage to join the alliance against Rome. The first three years of the war which broke out in B. C. 171, passed away without any great advantage being gained by either party, though fortune seemed to favour Perseus. This circumstance, and the fact that the war was protracted so long, at last excited among the Greeks a general feeling in favour of Macedonia; but his niggardliness deprived him of his most valuable allies, and obliged him to fight single-handed. In B. C. 168, L. Æmilius Paullus defeated Perseus with great loss in the decisive battle of Pydna. The vanquished king fled with his treasures to the island of Samothrace, but was overtaken and surrendered. Paullus treated him mildly, but afterwards took him to Italy, where he adorned the triumph of his conqueror, and spent the remainder of his life in honourable

captivity. Macedonia was now divided into four independent districts for the purpose of weakening the country; the people had to pay tribute, but their form of government was democratic.

15. During this last Macedonian war, the Achaeans, though reluctantly, had fought on the side of the Romans. But the miserable party spirit among them induced some of their number to denounce a great many as having openly or secretly favoured Perseus. These denunciations led to a regular inquisition in the Achaean towns, and upwards of one thousand Achaeans, one of whom was Polybius, the historian, were sent to Rome to answer for their conduct. But instead of being tried they were kept as hostages in Italy, until in B. C. 151 the surviving three hundred were allowed to return to their country. The Ætolians, who were likewise suspected of having favoured Macedonia, were treated with still greater severity, for five hundred and fifty of the most distinguished were put to death, and many were carried away into captivity.

16. The final decision of the fate of Greece was brought about by Athens. From mere want and poverty, the Athenians plundered Oropos, a town in their own territory. A complaint against them was brought before the Roman senate, which appointed a commission of Sicyonians to inquire into the matter. As the Athenians refused to appear before the commissioners, they were sentenced to pay a fine of five hundred talents. Being unable to raise this heavy sum, they sent ambassadors to Rome petitioning the senate to cancel the sentence; and the fine was actually reduced to one hundred talents. This happened in B. C. 155. Soon afterwards the Athenians renewed their outrage on Oropos, which now applied for redress to the Achaeans. A threatening decree passed against Athens by the Achaeans at length secured Oropos from further attacks of the Athenians. About the same time the possession of the town of Belmina became the cause of fresh hostilities between the Achaeans and Lacedaemonians. The Spartans would have sustained serious losses had it not been for the treachery of the Achaean strategus Democritus, who was succeeded by Diaeus, a most implacable enemy of the Romans. In B. C. 149, Andriscus, a Thracian of low origin, came forward as a pretender to the throne of Macedonia, assuming the name of Philip, and declaring himself to be a son of the late king Perseus. The man succeeded in making the Macedonians believe his story, and, tired of the Roman yoke, they flocked around his standard. At first he was successful against the Romans; but in B. C 148 he was conquered by Caecilius Metellus, whose triumph he afterwards adorned at Rome. Macedonia was now constituted a Roman province. While this war against the Pseudo-Philip was going on, the Greeks continued their petty but bitter hostilities; and Metellus, who wished them well, desired

23 *

them to keep peace, and promised that their affairs should be inquired into by a Roman commissioner. But when the Roman ambassadors appeared before the assembled Achaeans at Corinth, their demand was received with scorn and insolence. A second embassy sent by Metellus fared no better, and the thoughtless Achaeans declared war against the Romans. Metellus, in B. C. 147, after the reduction of Macedonia and Thessaly, marched with his army into Boeotia. The Achaean strategus Critolaus had intended to occupy Thermopylae, but arrived too late, and was routed near Heracleia. He rallied again in Locris, but was defeated a second time, and perished in endeavouring to escape.

17. The Achaeans were in despair; but the time had now come when they had to atone for their rash and inconsiderate mode of acting. While Metellus was advancing from the north, a Roman fleet landed a force in Peloponnesus, which laid waste the country. Diaeus assembled the last forces of the Achaean league in the neighbourhood of Corinth, and even armed a body of twelve thousand slaves. Metellus remained some time in Boeotia, where he punished the Thebans for having taken part in the war, by destroying their city. He then advanced towards Megara, and once more tried what peaceful means would do. But the infatuated Diaeus rejected all proposals. During this interval the command of Metellus passed into the hands of L. Mummius, a rude soldier who had no sympathy with the Greeks. He at once, in B. C. 146, occupied the Isthmus with an army of twenty-three thousand foot and three thousand five hundred horse; and in the battle of Leucopetra, in the neighbourhood of Corinth, the fate of Greece was decided for ever. When Diaeus, who had fought with the courage of despair, found that all was lost, he fled with a small band to his native city of Megalopolis, where he killed his wife, took poison, and then set fire to his house. Three days after the battle, Mummius entered the city of Corinth, which he ordered to be sacked and destroyed by fire; all the male inhabitants were massacred, and the rest of the population sold as slaves. The Roman commissioners declared the Achaean and all other confederacies in Greece to be dissolved, and the territory of Corinth became domain land of the Roman republic. The ravages and devastation caused by the Roman soldiers in Peloponnesus after the fall of Corinth were fearful, and many a town shared its fate. Greece, however, was not at once constituted a Roman province; indeed this step does not seem to have been taken until the time of Sulla. Many of the severe measures which were adopted at first were afterwards relaxed, and a number of Greek cities enjoyed a kind of freedom even under the supremacy of Rome. The political life of Greece, however, was now extinguished, and whatever advantages it continued to enjoy, were owing

to the reverence with which civilised nations viewed it, and to its pre-eminence in arts and literature, which to some extent continued to flourish in the country in which they had first reached their highest perfection.

CHAPTER XIV.

ASIA AND EGYPT UNDER THE SUCCESSORS OF ALEXANDER THE GREAT.

1. AFTER the battle of Ipsus, in B C. 301, the whole of the vast empire of Alexander the Great was finally broken up into four great monarchies: Macedonia, of which we have already given the history; Syria under Seleucus and his successors; Egypt under the Ptolemies; and Thrace under Lysimachus; while in Asia Minor there were formed a few less important kingdoms or principalities, such as Pontus, Pergamus, Bithynia, and Cappadocia. The Thracian kingdom of Lysimachus, as we have seen, was of very brief duration, while the kingdoms of Syria and Egypt continued their independent existence longest, until, with the rest of the ancient world, they were swallowed up by the all-absorbing power of Rome.

2. The founder of the Syrian dynasty was Seleucus, surnamed Nicator; its era is commonly dated from the year B. C. 312, when Seleucus recovered Babylon. After long and successful wars, he succeeded in uniting under his sceptre all the countries from the Indus to the Hellespont. The ancient country of Syria, however, was the seat of government; he there built the magnificent capital of Antioch on the river Orontes, which was rivalled in splendour only by Seleucia on the Tigris. These and about forty other cities founded by Seleucus and his successors tended to spread and establish Greek civilisation in the East. We have already seen (p. 259) that when attempting to make himself master of Macedonia, he was assassinated in B. C. 280, by Ptolemy Ceraunus, at Lysimachia.

He was succeeded by his son Antiochus Soter (B. C. 280–261), under whom we already meet with the usual horrors of an eastern court, which continued ever after to disgrace these Hellenistic rulers of Asia. The immense wealth accumulated in Syria from the wealthy provinces of the East, also created oriental luxury and effeminacy, which again fostered an abject and servile spirit among the people, manifesting itself in the basest flatteries towards their degenerate rulers, who were addicted to all the vices of eastern despots. Acts of bloody cruelty, the dominion of women and favourites, general moral corruption, together with disastrous wars against Egypt and the nations of Asia Minor, form the main topics of the history of the Syrian empire. Antiochus Soter fell in a battle against the Celts of Asia Minor, and was succeeded by his son Antiochus Theos (the god), who reigned from B. C. 261 till 246, carried on a war against Egypt, and was murdered by his own wife. In his reign, about B. C. 250, Arsaces founded the Parthian empire, and Bactria also became an independent kingdom, whereby the Syrian monarchy was considerably reduced. Antiochus was succeeded by Seleucus II., surnamed Callinicus, from B. C. 246 till 226, who began his reign by murdering his step-mother and her infant son. This involved him in a war with Ptolemy Euergetes of Egypt, who not only made himself master of all Syria, but carried his arms beyond the Tigris. Ptolemy however was obliged to return to his own kingdom, and this enabled Seleucus to recover the greater part of what he had lost. His brother Antiochus Hierax attempted to establish an independent kingdom for himself in Asia Minor; this led to a war between the brothers, in which Antiochus was defeated. Seleucus then endeavoured to subdue Parthia and Bactria, but was unsuccessful, and those kingdoms afterwards dated their independence from this time. Attalus of Pergamus, in the meantime, likewise extended his principality at the expense of Syria. Seleucus died by an accidental fall from his horse, and was succeeded by Seleucus III. (Ceraunus), from B. C. 226 to 223, who was an imbecile both in body and mind, and was murdered by two of his own officers.

3. The Syrian throne was now occupied by a brother of Seleucus III., Antiochus III., surnamed the Great, who reigned from B. C. 223 till 187. He is the only one among the Seleucidae who was not quite unworthy of the throne he filled. As he was only fifteen years old at his accession, attempts were made in various parts of his empire to throw off the yoke and gain independence. His first undertakings were directed against the revolted satraps, who were subdued; but an attempt to wrest Phoenicia and Palestine from Egypt was unsuccessful, and he had to give up those countries in consequence of his defeat at Gaza, in B. C. 217. In Asia Minor he had to combat Achaeus, who had for a time maintained himself as an independent ruler, but was finally conquered by Antiochus, B. C. 214. His most important undertaking, however, was a seven years' war, from B. C. 212 to 205, in which he endeavoured to recover the revolted provinces of eastern Asia. He met indeed with great success, but found it impossible to subjugate the Parthian and Bactrian kingdoms, and accordingly concluded a peace with them, in which their independence was finally recognised. On his return he renewed the war with Egypt, and this time he was more successful, for he conquered Coelo-Syria and Palestine. In B C. 196 he crossed over into Europe and made himself master of

the Thracian Chersonesus. The Romans indeed demanded of him to restore this conquest to Macedonia; but Antiochus, being urged on by Hannibal, who in B. C. 195 arrived at his court, refused, and began to think of attacking the Romans themselves. The execution of this plan, however, was delayed until B. C. 192, when on the invitation of the Ætolians he again crossed over into Europe. However great he may have been in his eastern campaigns, it is certain that during his invasion of Greece, from which he was driven by a defeat at Thermopylae in B. C. 191, and the whole of the remainder of his reign, we are not informed of any action that could raise him above the ordinary range of eastern despots. His fleet also suffered two defeats, and he himself was finally conquered by the two Scipios, in B. C. 190, in a battle near Magnesia, at the foot of mount Sipylus. This battle broke the power of the Syrian empire for ever, for the king had to give up all his dominions west of mount Taurus, to surrender his elephants and ships of war, and to pay the heavy sum of fifteen thousand talents. He was killed a few years later during his attempt to rob a wealthy temple of its treasures, and was succeeded by his son Seleucus IV., surnamed Philopator, who reigned from B. C. 187 to 175.

4. The Syrian empire, thus reduced within narrow limits, continued to exist for more than a century under a long succession of contemptible rulers, whose history is full of atrocious crimes, and who continued from time to time to be involved in wars with Egypt about the possession of Phoenicia and Palestine, the eternal bone of contention between Egypt and Syria. After the time of Antiochus the Great, the power and influence of Rome in the affairs of the kingdom increased from year to year, until in B. C. 65 Pompey made the kingdom a Roman province, and deposed its last king Antiochus XIII., surnamed Asiaticus. The kingdom, composed as it was of most heterogeneous elements, without any internal bond of union, could be kept together by the sword alone, and as the warlike character of the Syrian rulers began to disappear soon after the foundation of the empire, its fate could not possibly have been other than that which history reveals to us; the provinces which felt strong enough, asserted and maintained their independence as distinct states, and the remainder fell an easy prey to the Romans.

5. Independently of the eastern kingdoms of Parthia and Bactria, which were formed out of provinces of the Syrian empire, some minor states sprang up in Asia Minor. The greater part of that vast peninsula had been united by Lysimachus with his kingdom of Thrace; but during the wars in which he was involved during the later years of his life, a large portion of it fell into the hands of Seleucus, while in other parts independent principalities arose, such as—(1.) The state of the Galatians, formed by bands of Celtic tribes, which, after ravaging Macedonia and Greece, had migrated

into Asia Minor, and established themselves there by their victory over Seleucus near Ancyra, in B. C. 280. (2.) The kingdom of Pergamus; its first rulers, Attalus and Eumenes, were wise and brave, and extended their dominion in all directions. The Pergamenian court was on a small scale what the Alexandrian was on a large scale. The kings watched over the material interests of their subjects, and patronised the arts and literature by a liberal application of the public money. The library of Pergamus was, next to that of Alexandria, the most celebrated in the ancient world. The kingdom was allied with Rome at an early period, and its last two kings, Attalus III. and IV., stooped to the lowest flatteries towards the Romans, who obliged the last king to bequeath his kingdom to them. (3.) The kingdom of Bithynia was formed about the same time as that of Pergamus, and continued its existence until B. C. 74, when Nicomedes III. bequeathed his kingdom to the Romans. (4.) Armenia became an independent kingdom during the later years of Antiochus the Great. Pontus and Cappadocia had been formed at an earlier period, out of hereditary satrapies of the Persian empire, and their dynasties were connected with the family of the kings of Persia.

6. Egypt had been assigned as a province to Ptolemy, the son of Lagus, surnamed Soter, in B. C. 323. After the murder of Perdiccas, he enlarged his dominions by the conquest of Coelo-Syria and Phoenicia. In his defeat by Demetrius off Salamis in Cyprus, Ptolemy lost that important island; but notwithstanding this reverse, he following the example of Antigonus and Demetrius, assumed the title of king of Egypt, B. C. 306, and this kingdom ever afterwards remained hereditary in the dynasty of which he was the founder. After the battle of Ipsus, in which he seems not to have taken a prominent part, he devoted himself almost entirely to promoting the internal prosperity of his kingdom, and the cultivation of the arts and sciences, objects which were pursued with equal zeal by his two successors. He made Egypt a great military and maritime state. His capital Alexandria became the great centre of commerce and Greek culture for the eastern and the western world. His most celebrated institution was the Museum, which was connected with the royal palace, and contained the well-known Alexandrian library, and residences for scholars, philosophers, and poets. But he and his two successors, who thus nobly exerted themselves, were, after all, foreigners to the country; and the men whom they employed to carry out their designs were likewise foreigners—Greeks and Jews. The native Egyptians, though they must to some extent have become hellenized, continued to cherish their inflexible and stubborn hatred to foreigners and foreign institutions, and bore their yoke in sullen seclusion. The splendour of the court of the Ptolemies therefore was, and always remained, an

exotic plant, which could not take root in the foreign soil; and consequently it cannot much surprise us to find that the later Ptolemies abandoned the high objects aimed at by the founders of their dynasty, and employed the treasures of their kingdom in satisfying their sensual pleasures and passions, until in the end the Alexandrian court became as notorious for its immoralities and its horrors, as it was distinguished for its wealth and splendour.

7. In B. C. 285, Ptolemy Soter abdicated in favour of his youngest son Ptolemy Philadelphus, who reigned from B. C. 285 to 247, to the exclusion of his two elder brothers, Ptolemy Ceraunus and Meleager. His father died in B. C. 283. The long reign of Philadelphus was marked by few events of importance, except the usual hostilities with Syria, and the conclusion of a treaty with the Romans. His chief care was directed to the internal administration of his kingdom, and to the patronage of literature and the arts. The institutions founded by his father attained, under his fostering care, the highest prosperity. Natural history, in particular, was studied at Alexandria with great ardour, and many important works on science were produced. In his reign the Egyptian priest Manetho wrote a history of Egypt in Greek; and it is said to have been by the king's command that the sacred writings of the Jews were translated into Greek (the Septuagint). Under him the power of Egypt rose to its greatest height, for his dominions comprised, besides Egypt itself and portions of Ethiopia, Arabia, and Libya, the important provinces of Phoenicia, Coelo-Syria, Cyprus, Lycia, Caria, and the Cyclades; and in most of these countries he established numerous colonies. Cyrene also became united with his kingdom through a marriage. In his private character, however, Philadelphus does not appear in a favourable light, and his court already exhibited many scenes which show that he and those who surrounded him were becoming demoralised and degraded orientals.

8. He was succeeded by his eldest son Ptolemy Euergetes, from B. C. 247 to 222. This king was successful in his wars against Syria; and the Asiatic provinces of that empire, as far as Bactria and India, submitted to him. From this great expedition he was recalled by news of an insurrection in Egypt. At the same time, his fleet was actively and successfully engaged in the eastern parts of the Mediterranean. His eastern conquests, however, appear to have again fallen into the hands of Seleucus of Syria, and he retained only the maritime parts. Like his father, he maintained friendly relations with Rome, and largely added to the treasures of the Alexandrian library. He was succeeded by his son Ptolemy Philopator, from B. C. 222 to 205, whose reign was the commencement of the decline of the Egyptian empire. Its very beginning is stained with crimes of the darkest hue. The monarch gave him-

self up to indolence and luxury, leaving the whole administration in the hands of his ministers. The kingdom rapidly decayed, and Antiochus the Great of Syria, not slow to profit by this state of things, for a time made himself master of Phoenicia and Coelo-Syria; but in the end he was defeated and obliged to conclude peace with Egypt. After this Ptolemy, without any restraint, indulged in every vice and debauchery, and his mistresses and favourites were allowed to manage the affairs of the state in whatever way they pleased. But he still continued to some extent to patronise letters, and supported the Romans with supplies of grain during their second war with Carthage. Philopator was succeeded by his son Ptolemy Epiphanes, from B. C. 205 to 181, who was only five years old at the time of his father's death. The king of Syria and Macedonia, availing themselves of this opportunity, wrested from Egypt Coelo-Syria, the Cyclades, and its possessions in Thrace. The ministers of the young king solicited the intervention of Rome in behalf of their master. The Romans demanded of the conquerors to restore to Egypt its possessions, but the demand was evaded by private arrangements among the different courts, and in B. C. 193 king Ptolemy married Cleopatra, a Syrian princess. So long as he was under the guidance of wise men things went on pretty fairly, but he soon became tired of such advisers, and having removed them by poison, followed the example set him by his father, until he himself too was cut off by poison.

9. At his death he was succeeded by his infant son Ptolemy Philometor, who reigned till B. C. 146. His mother Cleopatra undertook the regency, and maintained order and tranquillity in the kingdom; but after her death in B. C. 173, the administration was left to unworthy and unprincipled favourites. Henceforth the history of Egypt, whose kings were under the almost absolute control of Rome, consists of a succession of disgusting details, and it may safely be asserted that a more contemptible set of rulers never disgraced a throne than the later Ptolemies. Under their wretched rule the state continued its miserable existence until the year B. C. 30, when the dissolute Cleopatra made away with herself, and Egypt became a Roman province.

10. After the overthrow of the independence of Greece in the reign of Philip, the father of Alexander, a great change gradually took place in the minds of the Greeks. Their stern notions about the sovereignty of the people, and the position of the citizens, had to undergo considerable modifications. Until then a citizen had been not so much a free individual agent, as a member of a political community, in which the person was absorbed, while every stranger not belonging to the same community was regarded as a being beyond the protection of the law, or even as an enemy. But under the Macedonian and Roman supremacy, the individuality of

every man became more important in proportion as his character of
citizen lost in value and dignity. With this feeling the undivided
interest in the welfare of the state and the all-powerful patriotism
of former days likewise disappeared. The narrow democratic communities of single cities were broken up, and enlarged into confederacies; these and the great monarchies which were formed out
of the empire of Alexander, and with which many of the scattered
Greeks were incorporated, gradually accustomed them to live at
peace with their neighbours, to regard themselves as members of
one large state, and to sacrifice the right of governing themselves
in petty and turbulent states to the idea of larger political bodies.
Even the national feeling of the Greeks, and the strong contrasts
between hellenism and barbarism, were softened down by the amalgamation of the Greeks and Orientals in the monarchies of the
successors of Alexander, whence the exclusive Greeks of former
times now became to some extent cosmopolites.

11. Their notions about religion had experienced a similar change.
The undoubting and child-like faith of the early times, when the
gods were conceived as beings that took an interest in the joys and
sorrows of mortals, had long since vanished among the higher and
educated classes, and was despised as superstitious. The philosophical inquiries, from the time of Socrates downwards, had shaken
polytheism to its foundations. Governments attempted to interfere,
declaring themselves the defenders and upholders of the ancient
national religion, and some philosophers were even punished or
banished on the ground of atheism. But it was of no avail; ancient polytheism could not maintain its ground, and was gradually
making way for a purer and holier religion, which was intended to
extend its blessings over all mankind, and teach them that they are
all governed by one God, whose loving-kindness towards all knows
no bounds.

24

BOOK III.

HISTORY OF ROME, CARTHAGE, AND THE NATIONS OF WESTERN EUROPE.

CHAPTER I.

ITALY AND ITS INHABITANTS.

1. ITALY is the middle one of the three peninsulas in which southern Europe terminates; it extends from the foot of the Alps to the straits of Sicily, which island itself seems at one time to have formed its southernmost part. The whole peninsula is traversed by the chain of the Appenines, which, commencing at the western extremity of the Alps, run in a south-eastern direction, in such a manner as to constitute as it were the spine of Italy. These mountains, however, do not form a mere ridge rising between the two sides of the peninsula, but form broad plateaus connected by passes. The broad low lands in the north between the Alps and the Appenines, however, do not, either geographically or historically, belong to ancient Italy. The eastern part of the peninsula which sinks down towards the basin of the Adriatic has few and unimportant rivers, and few harbours; the western part, on the other hand, has many navigable rivers, and is a hilly country with many harbours and bays, which sinks down towards the west and south, to the point where the fertile plain of Campania begins. The Italian peninsula has, on the whole, the same temperate and genial climate as Greece; it is healthy in the hills, and, generally speaking, also in the plains; but the coasts of Italy are not so richly articulated as those of Greece; and the sea around it is not studded with those numerous islands, which made the Greeks a maritime nation. Italy, on the other hand, has superior advantages in its rich broad valleys traversed by rivers, and in the fertile slopes of its hills, which are fitted both for agriculture and for pasture. The vast plain in the north between the Appenines and the Alps, which was not regarded as a part of Italy, until a very late period, is watered by the river Po and its numerous tributaries.

2. It has already been observed that, when at some remote

period of which history furnishes no information, the nations of the
Indo-Germanic family migrated into Europe, one branch of it descended from the north upon Italy, and continued its migration
southward so long as nature set no insuperable barrier to their progress.   The tribes therefore which occupied Italy were akin to
those which settled in Greece.   This assumption is fully borne out
by the languages of the Greeks and Italians, the roots and inflec-
tions of which are so much alike, that their original identity cannot
be mistaken.   This original identity of the nations of Italy and
Greece is perhaps most appropriately expressed by the name of Pelasgians, which is given to most of the primitive inhabitants of
both Greece and Italy, and may be viewed as the appellation common to all the tribes of the Indo-Germanic stock which ultimately
fixed their abodes on the coasts of Asia Minor, the islands of the
Ægean, Greece, and Italy.   The time when the immigration into
the Italian peninsula took place belongs to so remote a period, that
not even a tradition about it has been preserved; and the Italian
nations, like most other ancient peoples, regarded themselves as
autochtons or earthborn.

3. But, although all the original inhabitants of Italy belonged
to the same stock, yet in the course of time the languages, the
chief criterion of nationality, of the different tribes, underwent
changes and modifications so great that to the untrained mind they
assume the appearance of different languages, while in reality they
are only different dialects of the same primitive tongue.   So far as
our knowledge at present goes, we are enabled to distinguish three
original Italian languages, the Iapygian, the Etruscan, and the Italian proper, as we may call it, the last of which embraces the dialects of the Latins, Umbrians, Marsians, Volscians, and Sabellians.
The languages spoken by all these tribes are but dialects of one and
the same branch of the Indo-Germanic stock.   That which presents
the greatest peculiarities is the Iapygian in the extreme south-east
of Italy; it exists in numerous inscriptions which have not yet been
deciphered, though it is evident that the language is Indo-Germanic,
which also accounts for the facility with which the people in that
part of Italy afterwards became hellenized.   The Iapygians were no
doubt the most ancient inhabitants of Italy, and had been pushed
into the south-eastern corner by other immigrants pressing upon
them from the north.   The central part of the peninsula was
inhabited by those nations whose history determines that of the
whole, and which may therefore be termed *the* Italians.   They are
divided into two main branches, the Latins and Umbrians, to the
latter of which belong the Marsians and all the Samnite or Sabellian tribes.   The languages spoken by these tribes formed one distinct group of the Indo-Germanic family, and it was at a comparatively late period that it branched out into the different dialects,

which we now know partly from inscriptions and partly from the literature of the Romans.

4. The Etruscans, Tuscans, or Tyrrhenians form the strongest possible contrast to the Latin and Sabellian tribes as well as to the Greeks, and all we know of their manners and customs leads us to infer that they were widely different from all the branches of that family which we have called Pelasgian. This is more particularly striking in their religion, which was of a gloomy and fantastic character, delighting in mysteries, and wild and savage notions and rites. The same striking peculiarities are exhibited in the language of the Etruscans, the numerous remnants of which in inscriptions stand so isolated, that as yet no one has been able to decipher them, or to assign to the language, with any degree of certainty, the place which it occupies in the classification of languages. It is equally impossible to determine from what quarter the Etruscans migrated into Italy, though it is highly probable that they came from the valleys of the Raetian Alps, the native name of the Etruscans being Rasena, which may possibly be connected with Raetia. That they immigrated from the north, not by sea, is rendered further probable by the fact that all their great towns were built in the interior of the country. There was, however, a tradition in antiquity, according to which the Etruscans were Lydians, who had migrated into Italy from Lydia. But even ancient critics saw the absurdity of this tradition, inasmuch as the religion, the laws, the manners, and the language of the Etruscans did not bear the slightest resemblance to those of the Lydians. It is possible that some band of Asiatic adventurers landing in Italy may have given rise to the story, but it is more probable that the whole is based upon some mistake or some etymological speculation, for there existed in Lydia a town called Tyrrha and a tribe called Torrebi. But before the Etruscans immigrated into the country which to this day bears their name, it was probably inhabited by a race more closely akin to the Latins and Sabellians, that is, a people belonging to what we have called the Pelasgian race.

5. It is historically certain, that previously to the great Celtic immigration into Italy, the Etruscans occupied the country north of the river Po, and extended eastward as far as the Adige. The country south of the Po was occupied by Umbrians. When the Celtic hordes poured down from the Alps upon the fertile plains of Lombardy, the Etruscans being pushed forward pressed upon the Umbrians, and finally settled in Etruria on the south-west of the Appenines. There they completely subdued the previously established race or races, and maintained their own nationality, in spite of the influence of their southern neighbours, down to the time of the Roman emperors. In the south the river Tiber separated the Etruscans from Rome, though they are said at different

times to have advanced beyond that river, and even into Campania. Bodies of Etruscans also are said to have received settlements at Rome, and it can hardly be doubted that the dynasty of the Tarquins, to which the last kings of Rome belonged, was of Etruscan origin; though it is singular, that during the regal period Etruria exercised no important influence upon either the language or the customs of the Romans. The Etruscans from very early times applied themselves to navigation, commerce, and industry, in consequence of which their cities rose to a high degree of prosperity and independence; and this was probably the reason why they were less warlike than the Romans and Sabellians, and began at an early period to avail themselves of the services of mercenaries. The earliest constitution of the Etruscan cities seems to have been, on the whole, like that of Rome. Twelve cities, each governed by a lucumo or king, formed a confederacy, which, however, appears to have been very loose; and in each city the nobles and the commonalty were as fiercely opposed to each other as at Rome.

6. The last immigration into Italy from the north is that of the Celts or Gauls, who, expelling the Etruscans and Umbrians, took possession of the extensive country between the Alps and Appenines, and advanced southward as far as Picenum. The country thus occupied by them bore the name of Gallia Cisalpina, to distinguish it from Gaul beyond the Alps. The time when the Gauls made their first appearance in Italy is not quite certain, though it was probably about the period of the Tarquins. They did not, however, rest satisfied with the country on the north and east of the Appenines, but made frequent attempts upon Etruria and Rome itself, which was once conquered and destroyed by them; but they never succeeded in permanently establishing themselves on the south or west of the Appenines.

7. The coasts of southern Italy were occupied at an early period by Greek colonies, whence that country is generally designated by the name of Magna Graecia or Great Greece. In the Homeric poems Italy seems to be unknown to the Greeks; but at the time when the Theogony of Hesiod was composed, they appear to have been well acquainted with the coasts of Italy, and it was probably not long after that the Greeks commenced to establish their colonies there. The most ancient of these settlements was Cumae in Campania, founded by Asiatic merchants as a commercial factory. It is said to have been three hundred years older than Sybaris, which was founded in B. C. 723. But the earliest Greek colony in Italy of which the date is known, is Rhegium, which was founded in B. C. 746; this is the most ancient fact in the history of Italy that is chronologically certain. But the foundation of these colonies was followed in rapid succession by that of many others; and during the same period the coasts of Sicily also were occupied by

24 *

Greek settlements. The influence exercised by these colonies upon the civilisation of Italy was immense, and the whole of the south of Italy in particular became completely hellenized, in consequence of the facility with which the Greek language and Greek customs were adopted by the natives.

CHAPTER II.

THE BEGINNINGS OF ROMAN HISTORY, DOWN TO THE ESTABLISHMENT OF THE REPUBLIC.

1. The Latin branch of the Italian nations probably occupied at one time the western coast of Italy, from the Tiber to the straits of Sicily, and even a portion of Sicily itself. They appear in history under different names, such as Siculi, Latini, Ausones, and Opici. In the southern parts, as well as in Sicily, their nationality was overpowered by the Greek colonies, in consequence of which they were completely hellenized; in Campania they were early conquered and subdued by a branch of the Sabellian nation, which established itself in the country, and in conjunction with the Greek colonists modified the national character of the original inhabitants. Hence the Siculi, Ausones, and other southern branches of the Latin race, cannot be expected to act any prominent part in the history of Italy. But in Latium the case was different; there no Greek colonies were founded, and the Latins, after hard struggles with their northern and eastern neighbours, the Etruscans, and Sabines (the Sabellians), succeeded in maintaining their independence. Thirty of the towns of Latium formed a political confederacy, of which Alba Longa was the head. The confederates, called *populi Albenses*, annually celebrated a common festival in honour of Jupiter Latiaris. Another similar confederacy was that which held its meetings in the grove of Diana at Aricia. In later times the Latins, who had formed these ancient confederacies, called themselves *Prisci Latini*, the ancient Latins, to distinguish themselves from the Latin colonies established out of Latium, in different parts of Italy. Rome itself was in all probability originally no more than one of the thirty Latin towns belonging to Alba, for which reason it is sometimes called a colony of Alba.

2. The most ancient part of the city of Rome was situated on the Palatine, one of the many hills which rise on both banks of the Tiber, at a distance of about twenty English miles from its mouth. The time of its foundation is unknown, though it was in antiquity,

and still is generally assumed, for the sake of convenience, that it was built in the year B. C. 753. But there can be no doubt that Rome as a Latin town had existed long before that time. According to a story which arose in Italy at an early period, and probably owed its origin to the mere fact that the Romans ethnologically belonged to the same race as the Trojans, the founders of Rome were descended from the Trojan Æneas, who, after the destruction of Troy, had landed with a few followers on the coast of Latium. Numitor, king of Alba Longa, and a descendant of Æneas, says the story, was deprived by his brother Amulius of his throne, and his daughter Rhea Silvia was made a priestess of Vesta, to remove all apprehensions for the future, since, as a vestal, she was not allowed to marry. But the uncle's design was thwarted, for Rhea Silvia became by Mars the mother of twins, Romulus and Remus. Amulius endeavoured to get rid of the infants by exposing them in a basket on the banks of the Tiber, which happened to have overflowed the country; but the basket was thrown on dry land, and the babes were suckled by a she-wolf, and afterwards brought up by a shepherd. When they had grown up to manhood, they became through an accident acquainted with their history, and the injustice done to their grandfather. With the aid of their comrades they restored Numitor to the throne of Alba Longa, and built the town of Rome on the Palatine hill, on the left bank of the river Tiber. In a dispute about the name to be given to the new town Romulus slew his brother Remus. This legend is evidently a pure fiction, and Romulus himself a mere invention to account for the name of Rome, like those we meet with, in innumerable instances, both in Greece and in Italy.

3. The history of Rome, from its foundation to the establishment of the republic, and in many respects down to its destruction by the Gauls, is so much mixed up with poetical and other legends, that it is impossible to say what is historical and what not. The few facts which can be gleaned are derived partly from ancient monuments, and partly from the institutions of later times, which occasionally allow us to catch a glimpse of what must have been the original state of things. We are told that Rome was governed by seven kings before the abolition of royalty; each king has a fixed number of years assigned to his reign, and certain political, social, and religious institutions are ascribed to him; but historical criticism has shown that not the slightest reliance can be placed upon these details, for almost everything is arranged symmetrically, whence it is evident that the early history was in later times made up artificially from slender and vague traditions. For, during the Gallic conflagration, about B. C. 390, nearly all the historical monuments perished. This being the case, it would hardly be necessary here to repeat the stories of the several kings, some of whom are purely mythical,

were it not that these stories are so often alluded to by writers of all ages and countries. For this reason we shall give a brief outline of them all, accompanying each with a few critical observations to show how much of truth may be contained in it.

4. When the little town on the Palatine hill was built, and surrounded by a ditch and a rampart, Romulus, as the story runs, opened an asylum for people of every description, in order to increase the number of inhabitants. Everybody found a welcome reception; but as few or no women were to be found in the new town, the population would have died out after a short time. Romulus made applications to the neighbouring communities to obtain wives for his subjects, but his proposals being treated with contempt, he resolved to obtain by stratagem what was refused to his honourable request. He invited the neighbouring Sabines and Latins to come to Rome to witness certain festive games; and when they were assembled his Romans fell upon the daughters of their guests, and carried them off by force. In consequence of this, Rome became involved in a war with the Sabines, which, however, was brought to an amicable conclusion by the intervention of the women, who threw themselves between the two armies, and declared themselves willing to share the fate of their new husbands. Peace was then concluded, in which it was agreed that the Romans and Sabines should be united in one state, on condition, however, that each nation should have a king of its own. The Sabines, under their king Titus Tatius, then built a new town for themselves on the Capitoline and Quirinal hills, T. Titius dwelling on the Capitoline, and Romulus on the Palatine. This happy union, however, did not last long, for after some years T. Titius was slain at Laurentum, and Romulus thenceforth ruled as sole king of Rome, over both the Romans and Sabines.

5. After this Romulus is said to have waged successful wars against Fidenae and the Etruscan town of Veii, the latter of which he compelled to give up a portion of its territory. His reign extended over a period of thirty-eight years, from B. c. 753 to 716, and his death was as marvellous as his birth, for while he was reviewing his people, his father Mars descended in a tempest, and bore him up to heaven. It was afterwards believed that he himself had become a god like his divine father, and that, under the name of Quirinus, he watched over the interests of the state he had founded. The Romans of later times naturally entertained the opinion that Romulus, the founder of their state, was the author of the ground-work of their political constitution. Hence he is said to have divided the whole people into three tribes, the Ramnes, Tities, and Luceres, each tribe into ten curiae, and each curia into a number of gentes. The original senate of one hundred members s said to have been increased to two hundred at the time when

the Sabines united with the Romans in one state. The Ramnes in this division are the original Romans (Ramnes being in fact identical with Romani), the Tities are the Sabines, so called from their king T. Tatius. But who the Luceres were is uncertain, nor do we know the exact time when they became incorporated with the other two tribes. Besides the people contained in the three tribes and their sub-divisions, who constituted the sovereign people, we hear in the very earliest times of clients and slaves. The clients may be regarded as the retainers of certain families or gentes, and the person to whom a client was attached was called his patron (from *pater*, a father)—a name which seems to indicate that the relation subsisting between a patron and his client resembled that between a father and his son. The plebeians, or the commons of Rome, did not exist in the earliest times, unless we regard the clients as plebeians.

6. After the ascension of Romulus, a whole year is said to have passed away without a successor being elected, until at length the Romans chose, from among the Sabines, the wise and pious Numa Pompilius, who did for religion and the worship of the gods what Romulus had done for the political organisation of the state. His long reign of forty-three years, from B. C. 715 to 672, is described as a period of uninterrupted peace, during which the king was chiefly occupied in establishing the priesthood and the ceremonies connected with the worship of the gods. He first regulated the calendar by the institution of a lunar year of twelve months or three hundred and fifty-five days, of which some were set apart for religious purposes; and then instituted the various orders or colleges of priests, as the flamines, or priests of Jupiter, Mars, and Quirinus; the vestal virgins, the salii of Mars, the pontiffs who possessed the most extensive powers in all matters connected with religion; and lastly, the college of augurs, whose business it was to ascertain the will of the gods by observing the flight of birds in the air and their manner of feeding. Numerous temples and altars also were built to the gods, and in all these matters Numa is said to have been guided by the counsels of a divine being, the nymph Egeria, who favoured him with her presence in a sacred grove. Amid these pious operations his reign glided away in profound peace, and the temple of Janus, which was built by Numa Pompilius, remained closed throughout the king's reign—a sign that Rome was not at war with any nation. There can be no doubt that many of the institutions ascribed in the legend to Numa, had existed from time immemorial among the Latins and Sabines; his history seems, in fact, to be scarcely less mythical than that of his predecessor. The religion of the Romans, which is almost described as a device of Numa, was in all essential points the same as that of the Greeks— a worship of nature and her various powers personified, but with this difference, that the Greeks, being a more poetical nation, clothed

their conceptions and ideas in the form of numberless stories, of which the Roman religion, in its ancient and pure state, is perfectly free.

7. After the death of Numa Pompilius, the Romans chose Tullus Hostilius for their king from among the Ramnes. His reign, extending from B. C. 672 to 640, was totally opposed in character to that of his predecessor, for he is said to have neglected the worship of the gods, and to have carried on serious wars with his neighbours. The first war was that with Alba Longa, the alleged mother-city of Rome. The two little states had indulged in mutual acts of violence, and as reparation was refused, arms were resorted to. The contest was for a long time doubtful, till at length the commanders on both sides agreed that the dispute should be decided by a combat of three brothers who were serving in the Roman army, and bore the name of Horatii, with three brothers, called Curiatii, in the army of the Albans; and it was further agreed, that the victorious party should rule over the vanquished. The three champions now came forward on both sides; and two of the Horatii were soon slain, but the remaining one was unhurt, while the three Curiatii were wounded. Horatius then took to flight, and the three Albans pursued him at intervals from one another. Horatius, who had foreseen this, turned round and slew them one after another. When the Romans were returning home in triumph, Horatius met his sister, who burst into tears when she saw her brother carrying among the spoils a garment she had woven with her own hands for one of the Curiatii, to whom she had been betrothed. Horatius, enraged at her conduct on such an occasion, ran her through with his sword. For this outrage he was tried and sentenced to death; but he obtained his acquittal by an appeal to the people, who were moved by the thought of what he had gained for his country, and by the entreaties of his father. This beautiful story, so much cherished by the Romans of all ages, is unquestionably no more than a popular tradition or poetical fiction, though the fact of Alba being overpowered by the Romans need not on this account be doubted.

8. Alba was bound by the terms agreed upon to recognise the supremacy of Rome, but the yoke was borne with reluctance. During a war between Rome and Fidenae, in which the Albans ought to have assisted the Romans, they formed a treacherous design. When this was discovered by Tullus Hostilius, he, after the enemy was defeated, ordered the commander of the Albans to be put to death, and their city to be razed to the ground. His orders were immediately carried into execution. The people of Alba are said to have been transferred to Rome, where the Caelian hill was assigned to them as their habitation; some of the noble Alban families obtained the full Roman franchise, while the great

body of the people entered into a relation which was neither that of full citizens nor of clients, but was designated by the name of *plebs* as opposed to the *patres, patricii* or *populus Romanus*, by which names the old citizens were henceforth designated. The strength of Rome was thus doubled by the fall of Alba, which may be regarded as an historical fact, though it is not likely to have taken place under the circumstances related in the legend. After the destruction of Alba, the Roman king waged war against the Sabines and Latins, over the latter of whom he claimed the same authority as that formerly exercised by Alba. Towards the end of his reign, the displeasure of the gods at the neglect of their worship manifested itself in various ways, and in the end Tullus Hostilius and his whole house were destroyed by Jupiter with a flash of lightning.

9. After his death the Romans elected Ancus Marcius, a Sabine, from among the Tities, to the throne (B. C. 640–616). He was a relation of Numa, in whose footsteps he followed, though he did not give himself up wholly to religious duties, for when occasion required, he displayed as much valour in the field as piety at home. The Latins, who had concluded a peace with his predecessor, now rose in arms to assert their independence of Rome; but in vain: many of their towns were taken, and the whole body of them was defeated in a pitched battle. Many thousands of them were transferred to Rome, where, being settled between the Aventine and Palatine, they entered into the same relation as that of the conquered people of Alba, that is, they became plebeians, whose number now probably far surpassed that of the old citizens or patricians. We must not, however, suppose that all or even the greater number of the Latins were transferred to Rome, for the majority must no doubt be conceived to have remained in their towns and on their farms or estates. Ancus Marcius extended the dominion of Rome as far as the mouth of the Tiber, where he built Ostia, the port-town of Rome, and established salt-works.

10. The reigns of Tullus Hostilius and Ancus Marcius are most remarkable, because they form the period during which Rome obtained its commonalty, henceforth the most interesting part of its population, on account of its persevering struggles to remove the wrongs under which it suffered, and to obtain as much power as was necessary to protect itself against the oppressive tyranny of the patricians. These plebeians were personally free, but, being excluded from the political organisation of the patricians, they had no political rights, but only duties. The law, moreover, declared marriages between patricians and plebeians illegal. The plebeians formed, in fact, an irregular mass without any organisation among themselves, except that they were divided, like the other Italians, into gentes or clans. It is further remarkable that the legends

represent the first four kings of Rome as alternately belonging to the Ramnes and Tities, that is, to the Latin and Sabine tribes — no king of the Luceres being mentioned. As to the remaining kings, Tarquinius Priscus and Tarquinius Superbus, the legends point to Etruria as the country from which they came, though they are not described as Etruscans, but as descendants of a Corinthian Demaratus, who is said to have settled at Tarquinii in Etruria. Servius Tullius, the sixth king, who in some traditions is described as an Etruscan, is said by others to have been a Latin, which latter supposition is more in accordance with the political reforms that are ascribed to him. It further deserves to be noticed that the Roman state, which, in the reign of Ancus Marcius, is described as comprising only a small portion of Latium, suddenly appears under his successor as a powerful monarchy, under which architectural works were constructed, challenging in grandeur and durability a comparison with the immortal structures of the Egyptians.

11. The fifth king of Rome, Tarquinius Priscus, who is said to have reigned from B. C. 616 till 578, is represented in all the traditions as a foreigner, who by his wealth and wisdom gained the favour of Ancus Marcius, and after his death was elected king of Rome. After a successful war against the Sabines he began the building of the great Capitoline temple, which was dedicated to Jupiter, Juno, and Minerva, and was not completed until the reign of the seventh king. After peace had been concluded with the Sabines, he carried on a war with the Latins, whose towns he conquered one after another, so that the whole country became subject to him. From some traditions it would seem that in the reign of Tarquinius Priscus the sovereignty of Rome was acknowledged by all the Latins, the Sabines, and the Etruscans. But what makes his reign still more illustrious than these conquests, is the great and useful architectural works which he is said to have executed, such as the great sewer (*cloaca maxima*), by means of which the Forum and the other low grounds were drained and secured against inundations of the river; and the great race-course for horses and chariots (*circus maximus*). The religion of the Romans, which had before been of a simple and rustic character, is said through his influence to have become more pompous and showy; the gods were then first represented in human forms. He is also said to have increased the number of senators from two hundred to three hundred, which seems to suggest that the third tribe, the Luceres, were then incorporated with the Roman state. Tarquinius Priscus is reported to have intended to give to the plebeians some kind of organisation, and to surround his extended city with a stone wall; but he was prevented from executing these plans, which were reserved for his successor. Tarquinius was murdered by the sons

of his predecessor, who looked upon him as a usurper that had interfered with their legal claims to the succession.

12. Tarquinius Priscus was succeeded by Servius Tullius, who reigned from B. C. 578 to 534. He is described as a foreigner who was married to a daughter of Tarquinius, but his origin is uncertain. His reign is celebrated in history for three great measures; first, for the organisation he gave to the plebeians; secondly, for his political reforms; and thirdly, for the fact that he surrounded the city with a stone wall in those parts where it needed such protection. He divided the whole body of the plebeians into thirty local divisions, four of which belonged to the city, and the remaining twenty-six to the country around it. Each of these divisions, called *tribus*, was headed by its own magistrate, and all the thirty tribes might meet for discussion in assemblies called *comitia tributa*, as distinguished from the meetings of the patricians, the *comitia curiata*. His political reform consisted in his making property instead of birth the standard by which the rights and duties of the citizens were to be determined. For this purpose he instituted a census, and divided all the people into five property classes, and these again into one hundred and ninety-three centuries or votes, which, however, were distributed in such a manner that all political power was virtually vested in the wealthy classes, so that for the moment the change was probably not a very violent one. A sixth class, consisting of the proletarians, or *capite censi*, had no political rights, but were at the same time exempt from military service. The assembly of the one hundred and ninety-three centuries (*comitia centuriata*) embracing both patricians and plebeians, henceforth truly represented the whole body of the Roman people, and to it were transferred all the more important functions which until then had belonged to the assemblies of the patricians in their curiae. This reform, which was intended to place the plebeians on a footing of equality with the patricians, and to establish the king's power on the broad basis of the whole people, drew upon Servius Tullius the hatred of the patricians, who, headed by Tarquinius, his own son-in-law, created a revolution, in which the aged Servius was murdered, and Tarquinius ascended the throne.

13. Tradition represents this revolution in the following tragic story. In order to propitiate the sons of his predecessor, Servius had given his two daughters in marriage to the two sons of Tarquinius, Lucius and Aruns. The former, a man capable of criminal actions, though not naturally disposed to crime, was married to a mild and virtuous woman, while the wife of his gentle brother Aruns was the very essence of wickedness. Enraged at the long life of her father, and at the indifference of her husband, who seemed to be willing to leave the succession to his more ambitious brother, she planned destruction for both. An agreement was entered into
25

between her and Lucius, that he should kill his wife, and she her husband, and that then she and Lucius should be united in marriage. When these crimes were accomplished, Lucius, stimulated by his fiendish wife, entered into a conspiracy with discontented patricians, with the view of destroying the aged king Servius. About the harvest season, when many of the people were engaged in the fields, Lucius Tarquinius appeared in the senate with the ensigns of royalty, and a band of armed followers. The king, when informed of these proceedings, hastened to the curia, and called Tarquinius a usurper. The latter, then seizing the king, threw him down the stone steps. He was picked up bleeding and bruised, by his faithful adherents, who endeavoured to carry him home; but before reaching the palace, they were overtaken by the emissaries of L. Tarquinins. The king was murdered, and his body left lying in the street. Meantime Tullia, the wife of Tarquinius, impatient to receive the news of her husband's success, hastened to the senate, and saluted him as king. This unnatural conduct was too much even for L. Tarquinius, who bade her return home. When on her way back, the chariot drove through the street in which her father's body was lying; the mules on approaching it reared, and the driver stopped; but Tullia ordered him to go on, and the chariot passed over the king's body, the blood of which stained the garments of the unnatural daughter. The street in which this happened bore ever after the name of *vicus sceleratus*, or the accursed street.

14. L. Tarquinius, surnamed Superbus, now ascended the throne, on which he maintained himself from B. c. 534 to 510. The constitutional reforms of Servius Tullius were abolished at once, and the labours of that king seemed to have been spent in vain. The acts of oppression ascribed to Tarquinius are almost incredible; but it cannot be denied that he was a man of great military skill, for he enlarged his kingdom more than any of his predecessors, and embellished the city with great and useful architectural structures. The Latin towns were compelled to conclude a treaty with him, in which Rome was recognised as the head of them all; he conquered Suessa Pometia, the wealthy town of the Volscians, and strengthened and extended the dominion of Rome by the establishment of colonies, such as Signia and Circeii, thus laying the foundation of Rome's dominion, for it was through such colonies, both Roman and Latin, that the power of Rome was established, and her language and civilisation were diffused over all parts of the peninsula. But in spite of his military achievements, even the patricians began to show symptoms of discontent, for it was but too evident that he aimed to do away with the senate, and establish himself as an absolute ruler. His acts of oppression towards the senate and the patricians, the heavy taxes and task-work demanded of the plebeians, called forth feelings among his subjects which could not be

mistaken. The king, it is said, was harassed by dreams and threatening prodigies; in this distress he sent two of his sons, Titus and Aruns, to consult the oracle of Delphi. To amuse them on their journey, he sent along with them a cousin, L. Junius Brutus, who had assumed the character of an idiot to escape being put to death by the king. When the princes had executed their orders at Delphi, their curiosity prompted them to consult the god about themselves also, and the answer given was that the throne of Rome should belong to him who, on returning home, should be the first to kiss his mother. Upon this it was agreed that the brothers should kiss their mother simultaneously, and that thus they should reign in common. But on their landing in Italy, Brutus, as if falling by accident, without being observed, kissed the earth, the mother of all.

15. Some time after this the Romans were besieging Ardea, the fortified town of the Rutulians. As the siege was protracted, it one day happened that while the king's sons and their cousin Tarquinius Collatinus were discussing in their tent the virtues of their wives, it was agreed that the three should return home by night to surprise them, and see how they were spending their time. At Rome the princesses were found revelling at a luxurious banquet, but on coming to Collatia, they found Lucretia, the wife of Tarquinius Collatinus, engaged with her maids in spinning. In this occupation she appeared so beautiful and lovely, that one of the princes, Sextus Tarquinius, a few days later, returned to Collatia, where as a kinsman he was hospitably received. But in the dead of night he entered her chamber, and threatened to kill her, to lay a dead slave by her side, and to declare that he had detected her in adulterous intercourse with him, if she would not consent to gratify his lust. By the combination of these terrors he gained his end. But on the following morning she sent for her father and her husband. Both came, accompanied by P. Valerius and L. Junius Brutus. The disconsolate Lucretia related to them what had happened, and having called on them to avenge the wrong, plunged a dagger into her breast The moment had now come for Brutus to throw off the mask; he drew the dagger from her breast and vowed destruction to the royal house of the Tarquins. In this vow he was cordially joined by his friends who stood round the body of Lucretia, which was then carried into the market-place of Collatia. The people there at once took up arms, and promised to obey the commands of the liberators. Brutus then proceeded to Rome, where the sad tale produced the same effect as at Collatia. Brutus, who held the office of *tribunus celerum* (commander of the cavalry), summoned a meeting of the people in the Forum, and it was unanimously decreed that king Tarquin should be deposed and banished, with all his family. Lucretia's father remained behind as commander of the garrison at

Rome, while Brutus set out for Ardea to attack the king. When he arrived in the camp, the soldiers confirmed the decree of the people, and the king, who had gone to Rome by a different road, finding the gates closed against him, took refuge at .Caere in Etruria.

16. Such is the legendary story of a revolution which for ever put an end to the kingly government at Rome. How much there is of real history in it cannot be ascertained, though it scarcely admits of a doubt that Tarquinius Superbus was the last king of Rome, and that his rule had been very tyrannical, whatever allowances we may make for exaggeration. But whether the revolution was accomplished in the quiet and rapid way in which the legend describes it, is more than doubtful. During the period which is closed by it, Rome was an elective monarchy, and it is only under the later kings that we hear of sons claiming the right to succeed their fathers on the throne. The king, elected by and from among the patricians, was the supreme magistrate, and as such commander of the armies, supreme judge, and the high priest of the nation. His power was not absolute, for he had to consult the Senate, or council of elders, which existed at Rome as in most ancient states. Its members were indeed chosen by the king himself, but their number, three hundred, seems to suggest that the Senators were the representatives of the three tribes and the thirty curiae; at all events the king was obliged, by custom, to listen to the advice of the senate, at whose meetings either he himself or his representative (the *praefectus urbi*) presided. Independently of the senate, the king's power was limited by the assembly of the people, that is, the old citizens or patricians, in their *comitia curiata*, until, by the reforms of Servius Tullius, the great national assembly, the *comitia centuriata*, stepped into the place of the former. All matters which had to be brought before the assembly of the people, such as those connected with peace and war, the election of magistrates and proposals of new laws, were first discussed and prepared in the senate, and if sanctioned by that body, were then laid before the people, who might either adopt or reject them.

17. As to the state of civilisation among the Romans during the regal period, we have every reason to believe that they were not very far behind our own ancestors during the middle ages; for they had a regularly organised form of government, lived in towns surrounded by fortifications, had regular armies, and above all, loved and cherished agriculture, and constructed architectural works, which still attract the admiration of travellers. The legends contain many traits revealing to us the ways of living among the early Romans. The art of writing, which was, no doubt, introduced among the Romans by the Greeks settled in southern Italy, was known during the regal period, but was not employed for literary

purposes. King Servius Tullius is said to have coined the first brass, and to have marked it with the figure of some animal, whence the name *pecunia* for money.

CHAPTER III.

FROM THE ESTABLISHMENT OF THE REPUBLIC UNTIL THE DECEMVIRAL LEGISLATION.

1. AFTER the expulsion of the Tarquins, B. C. 509, the people assembled in the comitia abolished the kingly dignity for ever, restored the laws of Servius Tullius, and elected two magistrates from among the patricians, L. Junius Brutus and Tarquinius Collatinus, who, under the title of praetors (afterwards consuls) were to conduct the government for one year. These magistrates had the same power and the same insignia as the kings, except that the priestly functions of the king were transferred to a new dignitary, called *rex sacrorum*. The power of the patricians was virtually increased, inasmuch as two of their order might every year be raised to the highest magistracy. The senate and the comitia centuriata retained the powers assigned to them by Servius Tullius. The plebeians, being completely under the dominion of the patricians, were probably in a worse condition than they had been under the monarchy, as the king would naturally favour the great body of the plebs, to have in them a counterpoise to the arrogant and ambitious nobles. The plebeians were excluded from all the public offices and from the right of contracting legal marriages with patricians. In the great national assembly the patricians carried every measure by the overwhelming numbers of their votes, so that the plebeians exercised scarcely any influence upon the elections and the passing of laws. The administration of justice, moreover, was completely in the hands of the patricians. Under such circumstances a conflict between the two orders could not be far distant.

2. The young republic had from the first to maintain very serious struggles against both domestic and foreign enemies. Even under the very first consuls a number of young patricians formed a conspiracy, the object of which was to restore the exiled king. When it was discovered, Brutus, with a sternness peculiarly characteristic of a Roman, ordered the guilty parties, and among them his own two sons, to be put to death. But the greatest danger came from Etruria, where Tarquinius, the exiled king, had solicited and ob

tained the aid of Porsenna, lars or lord of Clusium. The Etruscan chief marched against Rome and established himself on the hill Janiculum, on the right bank of the Tiber. The war with this powerful colony was afterwards greatly embellished by tradition and popular lays, in which the glory and valour of the republican Romans appear in most brilliant colours. Once, it is said, the Romans crossed the Tiber for the purpose of driving the invader from his stronghold, but were repulsed and obliged to return to the city. The enemy would have followed them across the river, had not Horatius Cocles, a valiant and powerful Roman, who was intrusted with the guarding of the wooden bridge (*pons sublicius*), with two comrades kept the whole hostile-army at bay, while the Romans were engaged in breaking down the bridge. Soon he even dismissed his two companions and alone resisted the attacks of the foe, until the crashing of the timber and the shouts of his fellow-citizens announced to him that the work of demolition was completed. He then prayed to Father Tiber to receive him and his arms in his sacred stream, and leaping into the river safely swam across amid showers of darts sent after him by the Etruscans. His grateful countrymen rewarded him with a statue in the comitium and with as much land as he could plough round in a day. A similar reward was given to Mucius Scaevola; for when during the protracted siege Rome was suffering from famine, that heroic youth, with the sanction of the Senate, undertook to deliver the city by murdering the chief of the Etruscans. He secretly made his way into the enemy's camp, and being acquainted with the Etruscan language contrived to reach the tent of Porsenna. But by mistake he killed the king's scribe instead of the king himself. He was seized, and as the king was endeavouring by threats to extort his confession, Mucius thrust his right hand into the fire which was burning on an altar close by, to show that he dreaded neither death nor torture. From this circumstance he derived the surname of Scaevola, that is, left-handed.

3. But however fascinating the stories are in which the Romans have clothed the first struggles of their republic for freedom and independence, we know on good authority that Porsenna made himself master of Rome, and obliged the Romans to purchase his departure by giving him hostages, and ceding to him one-third of their territory, that is, ten out of their thirty local tribes. It deserves to be noticed, that throughout this war, which is said to have been undertaken on behalf of the exiled Tarquinius, he himself is never once mentioned as taking part in it. After the war, Porsenna also disappears, and is no more heard of. About the same time. B C. 505, the Romans had to carry on war against the Sabines, and some revolted towns of the Auruncans, against both of whom their arms were successful. A more formidable war, however,

broke out in B. c. 501 with the Latins, whom Tarquinius, through the influence of a kinsman, is said to have stirred up against Rome. Thirty Latin towns conspired against Rome, and, under these alarming circumstances, the Romans, thinking it safer to place the supreme power in the hands of one man, appointed, in B. c. 498, T. Larcius dictator, an office which existed in several Latin towns. This step kept the enemy in awe, and the plebeians at home in quiet submission. The war lasted for several years, until it was brought to a close in B. c. 496, by the famous battle of lake Regillus, on the road from Rome to Praeneste. The victory was gained by the Romans, in whose ranks the gods Castor and Pollux were seen fighting. The whole account of this battle, which forms the close of the mythical period in Roman history, is thoroughly fabulous; the victory over the Latins cannot be true, as three years later, B. c. 493, they concluded a treaty with Rome, under Spurius Cassius, in which they were placed on a footing of equality with her, without any previous dispute or feud being mentioned. King Tarquinius is said to have been wounded in the battle, and to have withdrawn to the Greek tyrant of Cumae, where he soon after died in B. c. 495.

4. As long as Tarquinius was alive, and Rome was threatened by foreign enemies, the patricians did their best to keep the plebeians in good humour, as they required their aid in the battles, for the main body of the Roman armies consisted of plebeians, and without them it would have been impossible for the republic to maintain itself. But no sooner had the dangers passed away, than the patricians, disregarding everything but their own interests and privileges, gave the rein to their avarice and domineering spirit. The plebeians were free landed proprietors, without possessing the franchise; but they were obliged to pay the tributum or land-tax, and serve in the armies without pay. During the time of their military service, their fields, if they were not overrun or taken by the enemy, were at all events neglected. The harvest time generally manifested the deplorable consequences of this state of things, and the small landed proprietors, to escape from momentary distress, had to borrow of their wealthy neighbours, who were generally patricians, at an exorbitant rate of interest of from ten to twelve per cent. The law of debt at Rome, as in many other ancient states, was extremely severe, and if the debtor did not pay back the borrowed money at the stipulated time, his person and estate were forfeited to the creditor, who might seize and employ him as if he were his slave, while his family sank deeper and deeper into misery. The patricians, who alone were entitled to occupy the public or domain land conquered in war, and had it cultivated by their clients, who did not serve in the armies, were to a great extent exempted from the misfortunes which might befal

the plebeians, and which appear to have become more serious every
year from the time of their incorporation with the Roman state.
The oppression exercised by the patricians became in the end
unbearable, and as the law was all in favour of the hard-hearted
creditors, the plebeians in B. C. 495 rose in open rebellion, and in
the following year seceded in arms to a hill a few miles distant from
Rome, where they encamped, fully resolved not to return until they
should obtain redress of their grievances. But Menenius Agrippa,
who was sent to them as deputy by the senate, prevailed upon them,
by the well-known fable of the Belly and the Members, to abandon
their useless scheme, and promised that the evils under which they
suffered should be remedied. A compact was then concluded
between the two estates, that all who had lost their freedom through
debt should be restored, and that five tribunes of the plebs should
be appointed, whose business it should be to protect the plebeians
against any abuse of the authority of a magistrate, and whose persons were to be sacred and inviolate. At the same time two
plebeian aediles were appointed, who had the superintendence of
public buildings, and exercised a control over usurers and merchants, to prevent unnecessary dearth of provisions. After the
conclusion of this solemn compact the plebeians quitted the hill,
which, from these transactions, was ever after called the Sacred
Mount.

5. The contest between the two orders had now commenced, and
some important advantages had been gained by the plebeians.
Throughout the noble struggles which succeeded, the patricians
acted more or less the part of an exclusive caste, while the plebeians represented what we may call the people. The stubbornness,
tenacity, and selfishness with which the former clung to their rights
and privileges, formed the strongest impediment to the steady and
progressive development of the institutions of the state. If they,
with their clients, had succeeded in maintaining their exclusive
rights of citizenship, Rome would have become a rigid oligarchy,
its place in the history of the world would not have risen above
that of many other petty republics, and in the end it would have
miserably perished from mere want of vitality. This latter principle rested with the plebeians, and in their struggles against aristocratic exclusiveness, it bore the noblest fruit, and made Rome the
mistress of the world.

6. Shortly after the secession of the plebs, during which the
cultivation of the fields had been almost entirely neglected, Rome
suffered from dearth and famine, and when at length ships laden
with corn arrived from Sicily, the insolent patrician C. Marcius
Coriolanus, proposed that none of it should be given to the plebeians unless they consented to renounce the advantages they had
gained by their secession to the Sacred Mount. At this the ple-

beians were so exasperated, that they outlawed him and obliged him, in B. C. 491, to take refuge among the Volscians, whom he persuaded to make an inroad into the Roman territory, promising that he would lead them as their commander. Under his guidance they advanced within five miles of the city, and nothing could induce him to abandon his hostile undertaking against his own country, until he was at length prevailed upon by the tears and entreaties of his mother and his wife to retreat. He is said to have died soon after, overwhelmed with grief and shame. The Volscians, however, retained possession of some of the Latin towns which they had conquered. In the year B. C. 486, the same Spurius Cassius, who had brought about the equal alliance with the Latin towns, concluded one on the same terms with the Hernicans. By this union of the Romans, Latins, and Hernicans, fresh strength was gained against the Æquians and Volscians. This same year, in which Cassius concluded the league with the Hernicans, is also remarkable as the one in which an agrarian law was first mentioned at Rome. The Roman state possessed very extensive domains of land conquered in war, which were not the property of any individual, but the use of which was given up to the patricians on condition of their paying to the treasury a small sum as an acknowledgment. This domain land (*ager publicus*), however, came gradually to be regarded by its occupants as their private property, which they had cultivated by their clients and slaves, and for which they did not always think it necessary to pay the rent to the state, for they themselves and they alone constituted the state. The plebeians from time to time demanded likewise to be permitted to occupy portions of the public land; but whenever such an agrarian bill (*lex agraria*) was brought forward, it was met by the most determined opposition on the part of the patricians. Sp. Cassius was the first Roman that is known to have proposed and carried an agrarian law, ordaining that a certain portion of the public land should be distributed among those plebeians who did not possess any landed property. The noble efforts of this man to prevent the growth of pauperism and to transform the poor into industrious husbandmen, who at all times constituted the mainstay of the Roman republic, were ill requited, for in the year after his consulship, B. C. 485, he was sentenced to death by the patricians, and beheaded. The house in which he had lived was levelled with the ground, and the spot itself was declared accursed. Although the law had been passed in due form, the patricians prevented its being carried into effect by every means in their power. Many years afterwards, B. C. 473, a tribune Genucius arraigned the consuls before the commonalty for not allowing the law to be put in operation, but on the morning of the day before the trial the tribune was found murdered in his own house. These acts of violence and injustice for a time intimidated the friends of the plebeians; but their perseverance did not abate, and ultimately compelled the pride of the patricians to succumb.

7. By these internal feuds and disputes, Rome was so much weakened that the Etruscans and Æquians were enabled to conquer one town after another; and when at length, in B. C. 477, the whole clan of the Fabii, amounting to three hundred and six men, marched out against them, they were all slain by the Etruscans on the banks of the river Cremera; one only had remained in Rome, and he became the ancestor of the Fabii, whom we meet with in later times. Not long before this event, the Fabii had been proud and haughty champions of their order against the plebeians, but afterwards siding with the oppressed, they brought upon themselves the hatred of the patricians. This seems to have called forth in them a desire to emigrate; they proposed to the senate to carry on a long protracted war against Veii at their own expense. The request was readily granted, and amid the good wishes of the people they marched against the enemy. They ravaged the country, and were successful in many an enterprise; but their success diminished their caution, and being drawn into an ambuscade by their desire to capture a herd of cattle which had been sent out on purpose, they were surrounded by the enemy, and cut to pieces to a man. This story of the Fabii is only a popular legend, though not without an historical foundation.

8. In the south and west the Æquians and Volscians continued their inroads into the Roman territory. The former, so the story runs, had concluded peace with Rome, but their commander Gracchus Cloelius nevertheless led his troops to mount Algidus, and thence they renewed their inroads every year. A Roman embassy appearing in his camp was scornfully received, and the Roman consul L. Minucius was defeated by the Æquians and besieged in his own camp. Five horsemen, who had escaped before the lines were closed around the camp, brought the disastrous news to Rome, and the senate appointed L. Quinctius Cincinnatus dictator, B. C. 458. The news of his elevation was brought to him on his farm, which consisted of four jugera or acres, and which he cultivated with his own hands. The next day at dawn the dictator appeared in the Forum, and nominated L. Tarquitius his master of the horse. All men capable of bearing arms were called upon to enlist, and in three days he marched with his army to mount Algidus. He surrounded the Æquians, and the Romans in the camp having received a signal that succour had arrived, broke through the surrounding enemy. A desperate fight then commenced; it lasted a long time, and when in the end the Æquians found that they were surrounded, they implored the dictator to spare them. Gracchus Cloelius and the other commanders were put in chains, and the rest were obliged

to lay down their arms and pass under the yoke. The town of
Corbio and the Æquian camp fell into the hands of the victors.
Cincinnatus then returned to Rome in triumph, and was rewarded
with a golden crown. After having been invested with the dictatorship for no more than sixteen days, he laid down his office and
returned to his farm. This is said to have happened in B. C. 458,
but the whole story, as related by Livy, seems to be only a beautiful poetical legend about the historical fact that Minucius was
rescued by succour sent to him from Rome. The Æquians were
indeed defeated, but the war against them was continued with
varying success, until B. C. 446, when in the battle of Corbio they
were so much weakened that for a time they were unable again to
take up arms against Rome.

9. There existed in ancient Rome no code of written laws; the
administration of justice, based upon hereditary usage, was altogether
in the hands of the patricians, who were often guilty of acts of the
most flagrant injustice. With the view to prevent their arbitrary
proceedings, and to acquire a knowledge of the law and its forms,
the plebeians began to demand that a code of laws should be drawn
up. The patricians, regarding this as an encroachment upon their
prerogatives, offered a long and violent opposition to the demand.
During these disputes, party animosity reached the highest pitch.
In B. C. 471, the tribune Publilius Volero, amid the most fearful
opposition, carried several laws, which enacted that the plebeian
magistrates (tribunes and aediles) should be elected by the plebeian
comitia of the tribes, and that these same comitia should have the
power of passing resolutions (*plebiscita*) on matters affecting the
interest of the whole state. The excitement produced by these
measures divided Rome into two hostile camps, and this feeling,
together with a terrible epidemic which carried off large numbers
of all ranks, weakened Rome so much, that the Æquians and Volscians dared to advance on their predatory excursions, which have
already been noticed, as far as the very gates of Rome ; and Her-
donius, a Sabine adventurer, with a band of runaway slaves and
exiles, who had actually taken possession of the Capitol, was expelled only with great difficulty. The first formal demand for a
written code of laws was made in B. C. 462 by the tribune C. Ter-
entillus Arsa, and although it was violently opposed, the idea could
not be crushed ; similar demands were afterwards repeated, and the
plebeians were determined to carry their point. In B. C. 457, the
number of tribunes was increased from five to ten, it having
probably been found that the previous number was insufficient to
afford protection in all cases. Three years later, the bill of Teren-
tillus Arsa was taken up again, and it was at last agreed that the
laws should be revised ; it was further resolved as a preliminary
step, that three senators should be sent to Athens to study the laws

and constitution of that republic and of other Greek states, and to bring back a report of such laws and institutions as it might seem desirable to adopt at Rome.

~~~~~~~~~~~~~~~~~~~~~~~~~~~~~~

CHAPTER IV.

FROM THE DECEMVIRAL LEGISLATION DOWN TO THE FINAL SUBJUGATION OF LATIUM.

1. AFTER the return of the ambassadors from Greece, both orders agreed that a commission of ten patricians should be appointed to draw up a code of laws, that they should have full power to act as they thought fit, and that for the time all other magistrates, perhaps with the exception of the tribunes, should have their powers suspended. The decemvirs who entered upon their office in B. C. 451, performed the duty intrusted to them honestly and satisfactorily; but as at the end of the year their task was not completed, they were unhesitatingly permitted to continue their office and their labours for another year. The expectations of the people, however, were now fearfully disappointed, and every kind of cruelty was resorted to in punishing those plebeians who ventured to express an opinion upon the proceedings of the Ten; nay, an aged and brave plebeian whose opposition they feared most, and who was serving against the enemies of Rome, was drawn into an ambuscade and assassinated by his own countrymen. At the close of the second year, when the legislation was completed and the laws were engraven upon twelve tables, the decemvirs still persisted in retaining their office, and would perhaps have succeeded in their usurpation, had not the haughty Appius Claudius, the most influential among them, by his brutal lust and injustice called forth a fearful outbreak of the smothered discontent. He had conceived a desire to possess Virginia, the beautiful daughter of the plebeian Virginius, who was already betrothed to another. In order to gain this object, he prevailed upon one of his clients to declare the maiden to be a runaway slave of his own, and to claim her as his property before the tribunal of the decemvir. A large concourse of people assembled in the Forum to witness the trial. Claudius assigned the maiden to his client; but her father having obtained permission to take leave of her, plunged a knife into her heart to save his child from dishonour.

2. The excitement in the city was immense; the authority of the decemvirs was set at defiance by the people, and the army,
~~~~~~~~~~~~~~~~~~~~~~~~~~~~~~

which was engaged against the Sabines, on learning what had happened, quitted the camp and took possession of the Aventine, resolved to leave Rome and seek a new home elsewhere. The plebeians with their families then proceeded to the Sacred Mount. Valerius and Horatius, two of the most popular among the patricians, were despatched to the plebeians to treat with them on any terms they might think fit. The plebeians demanded the right of appeal against any magistrate, an amnesty for themselves, and that the decemvirs should be deposed. All was granted and sanctioned by the senate, and the plebeians returned to Rome. Appius Claudius was thrown into prison and died by his own hand; one of his colleagues perished in the same manner, and the remaining eight went into exile. The laws of the Twelve Tables, however, remained in force, and ever after formed the basis of the Roman law. The only constitutional change which they seem to have introduced was that the patricians became members of the local tribes which had previously consisted of the plebeians alone. But this was for the present no great advantage, for the assembly of the tribes did not as yet possess any legislative power; the plebeians were still excluded from the highest magistracy and from a share in the public land, and marriages could not be legally contracted between patricians and plebeians. The mere fact, however, of the laws being now fixed was a great gain, inasmuch as the plebeians were no longer exposed to the arbitrary proceedings of the patricians.

3. After the recent reconciliation, the patricians still continued to annoy the plebeians in a variety of ways, and the hotter spirits among the latter were inclined to retaliate, but as a body the plebeians were moderate, though firm, and it was evident that they were aiming at nothing short of a perfect equality of rights with the patricians. In B. C. 445 the tribune Canuleius brought forward a bill demanding for the plebeians the right of contracting legal marriages with patricians (*connubium*), and the bill was passed amid the fiercest opposition. Another bill proposed that one of the consuls should always be a plebeian; but after long and violent discussions of this question, it was agreed that, instead of consuls, military tribunes with consular power should sometimes be elected, who should be taken indiscriminately from the plebeians, as well as from the patricians. The senate, however, retained the power of determining in each year whether consuls or consular tribunes should be elected. The ancient and venerable dignity of the consulship was thus saved for the patricians, who in most cases also contrived to keep the military tribuneship in their own hands; and in order that the plebeians might never enjoy the full powers of the consulship, two censors were appointed in B. C. 443, whose functions had previously belonged to the consuls. This new office was accessible to patricians only, and was filled anew every five

26

years, which period was called a *lustrum*, though the censors had
to perform their duties within the term of eighteen months. They
had to make up and keep lists of all the Romans, in which senators, equites, and the rest of the citizens, were classed according to
their rank and property; they collected the rent for the domain
land, superintended the building of temples, and the making of
roads and bridges, and exercised a severe control over the moral
conduct of citizens, offences against which they were empowered to
punish by depriving a person of his civil rights or of his rank and
station in society.

4. The establishment of the *connubium*, or right of contracting
legal marriages between the two orders, seems to have somewhat
softened their animosity; but patrician malice and intrigue nevertheless did not easily allow an opportunity to pass, where the plebeians could be humbled. In B. C. 440 Rome was visited by a
famine, and all endeavours of the government to mitigate the evil
were of no avail. A wealthy plebeian, Spurius Maelius, generously
purchased large quantities of grain, and sold it at a moderate price
to the famishing people. The popularity he thus acquired alarmed
the patricians; they feared treacherous plots and conspiracies, and
charged him with aiming at regal power. The aged Quinctius Cincinnatus, who was appointed dictator in B. C. 439, summoned Maelius before his tribunal; and as Maelius prepared to defend himself,
Servilius Ahala, the dictator's master of the horse, slew him in
broad daylight in the midst of the Forum.

5. During these internal struggles, the Roman armies, in which
the plebeians manfully and bravely defended their country, fought
many successful battles against foreign enemies. Allied with and
strengthened by the Latins and Hernicans, they repeatedly defeated
the Volscians and Æquians, and reduced their territories. The
town of Fidenae, which had been colonised by the Romans at an
early period, but had committed many outrages, was destroyed in
B. C. 426, notwithstanding the assistance it obtained from the
Etruscan city of Veii. This led to a desperate war with Veii,
against which Rome directed all her forces, and which was taken,
in B. C. 396, by Camillus, after a siege of ten years. The account
of the manner in which Veii was captured is nothing but a beautiful lay, in which that city acts a similar part to that of Troy in the
Trojan legends; but there can be no doubt that its inhabitants were
partly slain, and partly sold as slaves. During the protracted war
against Veii, the senate of its own accord decreed that in future
pay should be given to the soldiers from the public treasury, for
until then they had had to equip and maintain themselves. This
measure enabled the government to keep its armies longer in uninterrupted service than would otherwise have been possible, and the
men became no doubt more willing to serve than they had been

before. Camillus, the proud conqueror of Veii, celebrated a magnificent triumph, but as his soldiers considered themselves robbed by him of their legitimate share in the booty, and as he opposed the proposal to distribute the territory of Veii among the plebeians, he drew upon himself the hatred of the people. In B. C. 391, he was charged with having secreted a portion of the spoil taken at Veii; and in order to escape condemnation, he went into exile, at a time when Rome needed her great commander more than ever.

6. She was now on the eve of a conflict with a branch of one of the most widely spread nations of Europe, the Celts or Gauls, who are said to have crossed the Alps as early as the reign of Tarquinius Priscus. Soon after their arrival in Italy they drove the Etruscans from the plains in the north and east of the Appenines, and for a time those mountains seem to have formed the barrier between them and the Etruscans; but in B. C. 391, swarms of them crossed the Appenines, and under the command of their chief, Brennus, laid siege to the Etruscan town of Clusium. The Clusines solicited the assistance of the Romans, the most powerful neighbours of the Etruscans, and the Romans at first sent only ambassadors to the Gauls to induce them not to molest the Etruscans; but as their envoys did not succeed, a battle ensued between the Gauls and Etruscans, in which the Roman ambassadors took part and slew one of the Gallic chiefs. This violation of the law of nations enraged the barbarians, and as the Romans haughtily refused to surrender the offenders, the Gauls at once abandoned Clusium, and set out against Rome. On the banks of the little river Allia, about eleven miles from the city, they met the Roman army, and defeated it so completely that only a few escaped by flight to Veii and Rome, B. C. 390; Rome itself, from which the women and children had withdrawn, was in a defenceless state, and fell into the hands of the barbarians. The city became a prey to the flames, and eighty old men of high rank, who had sat down in the Forum to devote themselves as a propitiatory sacrifice to the gods, were massacred. The Capitol alone, to which many of the most valuable treasures had been carried, was occupied and defended by the Romans. Its garrison, commanded by the brave Manlius Capitolinus, offered a gallant resistance, while the Gauls like true barbarians, intoxicated with their recent victory, abandoned themselves to every kind of excess, in consequence of which their ranks were considerably thinned during the siege, which lasted seven months. This is said to have induced Brennus at length to accept one thousand pounds of gold, and to quit the territory of Rome; but the haughty Gaul increased the gold by throwing his sword into the scale. At this moment Camillus, who had been recalled from his exile by the army assembled at Veii, arrived at the gates of Rome, and defeated the Gauls in a battle in which all of them were slain, and all the booty carried off

was recovered. This is the famous story of the sacking of Rome by the Gauls, in B. C. 390, the latter part of which is fictitious, for we know that the Gauls left Rome unmolested, because their own country in the north was invaded by another enemy.

7. After the departure of the Gauls, the Roman people were so much disheartened, that they were unwilling to rebuild their ruined houses, and proposed to migrate to Veii and establish themselves in that deserted city. The patricians, however, feeling a stronger attachment to the place with which all their ancient associations were connected, by great exertion prevailed upon the people to give up this scheme; and in order that such a thought might never be conceived again, the people were allowed to demolish the houses still standing at Veii, and use the materials in rebuilding their own homes at Rome. Scarcely had Rome been hastily rebuilt, with crooked and narrow streets and small houses, when the patricians again began to enforce their ancient privileges, and above all, to carry into execution, with the utmost rigour upon the impoverished people, the severe laws of debt, which had been retained in the Twelve Tables. The plebeians having already suffered severely during the Gallic invasion and the rebuilding of their houses, excited the sympathy of Manlius Capitolinus, the gallant defender of the Capitol, who now came forward as their champion, proposing a reduction of the debts, and distribution of public land. This so much incensed his brother patricians against him, that, under the futile pretext of his aiming at kingly power, they procured his condemnation. The saviour of the Capitol was hurled down from the Tarpeian rock, his house was razed to the ground, and his name was treated as that of an accursed person. This disgraceful deed was perpetrated in B. C. 384.

8. During the humiliation of Rome, the Hernicans and many of the Latin towns renounced their alliance with her, and the Volscians, Æquians, and Etruscans also took arms again. The last three nations were successively humbled by Camillus, who was the soul of all Roman undertakings during this period, and the towns of Sutrium and Nepete in Etruria received Roman colonists. Some of the Latin towns also were subdued, and it may be said on the whole, that Rome was rapidly recovering from the wounds of the Gallic conquest, and the evils that followed in its train. But the distress of the poor was ever on the increase, although in B. C. 383 the senate had assigned to the plebeians the Pomptine district. The murder of Manlius also contributed once more to rouse the plebeians to action against their insolent oppressors. In B. C. 376, C. Licinius Stolo and Lucius Sextius, two bold and energetic tribunes, took upon themselves the task of stopping the state in its downward career. They brought forward three rogations or bills—1st. That consuls should again be elected as of old, but that one

of them should always be a plebeian; 2d. That no man should be allowed to occupy of the public land more than five hundred jugera, and that after a due measurement, the surplus should be taken from the former occupants, and assigned to the plebeians as their full property; and, 3d. That the interest already paid upon debts should be deducted from the principal, and that the remainder should be paid off in three annual instalments. The patricians, for a period of nearly ten years, contrived to thwart these proposals, and left no means untried to render them abortive; but all their efforts, and even the elevation of Camillus to the dictatorship, were of no avail against the firmness and perseverance of the tribunes, who continued to prevent both the election of magistrates and the levies for the armies; for it must be understood that the tribuneship—chiefly through the power of the *Veto*, that is, of prohibiting public acts—had become a much more influential office than at its first institution. At length, in B. C. 367, after a long period of strife and anarchy, the patricians were obliged to yield; the proposals of the tribunes became law, and in B. C. 366, L. Sextius was the first plebeian consul. But in order to reserve for themselves as much as possible, the patricians contrived to strip the consulship of the power of jurisdiction in civil cases, which was now assigned to the praetor, an officer who was to be taken from the patricians exclusively. These precautions, however, were of no avail, for the year B. C. 356 saw the first plebeian dictator, 351 the first plebeian censor, 337 the first plebeian praetor; and in B. C. 300, the priestly offices of pontiff and augur were opened to the plebeians. By these successive measures, the equalization of the two orders was gradually accomplished, and Rome, internally united and strong, was in a condition to enter upon the great career marked out for her by Providence.

9. The reconciliation of the two orders, after the passing of the Licinian laws, was celebrated by the dedication of a temple to Concord by the aged Camillus, who soon after died of the plague which raged at Rome for several years. The good results of the unity and harmony thus restored soon became manifest in the contests of the republic with her foreign enemies, especially in the conflicts with the hordes of Gauls who wandered through Italy, laying waste the country, and supporting the enemies of Rome. It was in the course of these Gallic wars that the first plebeian dictator was appointed, B. C. 356, and that Manlius Torquatus and Valerius Corvus gained their immortal fame by deeds of heroism which were celebrated in Roman song.

In B. C. 358, when the Gauls had pitched their camp on the banks of the river Allia, a Gaul of gigantic stature stepped upon the bridge which separated the two armies, and challenged any Roman to fight with him. Titus Manlius, a noble young Roman,

26 *

after having obtained the consul's permission, accepted the challenge. Lightly armed, he advanced against the boastful Gaul, and approached so closely, that the barbarian was unable to make use of his arms; he then pierced him through the side and belly, and when the enemy thus lay prostrate, stripped him of his gold chain (*torques*), and put it round his own neck. From this circumstance he was ever after called T. Manlius Torquatus. Eight years later, B. C. 350, when another host of Gauls had advanced to the very neighbourhood of Rome, a powerful Gaul, according to the usual practice of his nation, challenged the bravest of the Romans to single combat. M. Valerius, a young tribune of the soldiers, accepted the challenge. When the combat began, a raven, which had settled upon the helmet of the Roman, flew at each onset into the face of the Gaul, who, being unable to see, was slain by Valerius; the young Roman received from this miraculous ally the surname of Corvus. The successes gained by the Romans in these wars with the Gauls were in a great measure owing to the improvements in their armour and tactics which had been introduced by Camillus; and the same progress in the military art, together with the renewed alliance with Latium, enabled the Romans to engage in a contest with the Samnites, a powerful nation, not inferior to them either in valour or love of liberty.

10. The Samnites, the principal nation of the Sabellian race, occupied a country far more extensive than that of the Romans and Latins put together; they were more powerful than the Romans and Latins, together with whom they formed the great stock of nations which we have called specially Italian. In the earlier times they had colonized Capua and the plains of Campania and Lucania, but in the course of time these colonies had become estranged from the mother country. What the Samnites needed to make them successful against their foreign enemies, was union among themselves, for they consisted of four cantons, which were but loosely connected. At the time when they came into conflict with Rome, they had been in alliance with her for ten years, and the cause of the hostility between them is related as follows: The Samnites were involved in a war against the Sidicines, who, being too weak, applied for assistance to Capua. The Campanians, one of the most effeminate and luxurious peoples of Italy, willingly granted the request, but were defeated by the Samnites in two battles. The Campanians then applied to Rome for assistance; but as the Romans scrupled to support strangers against their own allies, the Campanians, it is said, offered to acknowledge the supremacy of Rome, if she would but comply with their request. The scruple being thus removed, Rome at once resolved to succour them. From this account we might expect hereafter to find the Campanians in the relation of subjects to Rome, but such is not the case; the fact

is, that Rome, in supporting them, evidently violated the treaty with Samnium ; and the above-mentioned story was devised only to disguise her unjust conduct. In this light it was viewed by the Samnites, and the war between the two nations broke out in B. C. 343, and lasted until 341. The series of wars, of which this was only the first, was destined to decide which of the two nations was to have the supremacy in Italy, and through it that of the whole of the ancient world. In the first campaign, the Romans, under M. Valerius Corvus, gained a great victory on mount Gaurus. The second consular army which was destined to invade Samnium, came, through the carelessness of the consul, into a position among the mountains, where it certainly would have been destroyed but for the boldness and skill of Decius Mus, who contrived to get possession of an eminence overhanging the enemy, and thus enabled his countrymen to pass safely through the defile. During the second year of the war, nothing of any importance was achieved, partly in consequence of disturbances at Rome arising from the severity of the law of debt, and partly on account of the disaffection of the Latins. The Romans, therefore, thought it prudent to conclude a peace with the Samnites, in which the old alliance with them was renewed, and fair terms were granted.

11. The Campanians, now forsaken by the Romans, saw no other means of safety except in an alliance with Latium, in consequence of which Rome, in B. C. 340, at once began hostile operations against the Latins. The Latins, however, would have liked to avoid active hostilities, and to come to an amicable understanding with Rome, which, though allied with them on equal terms, had always con rived to domineer over its confederates. The Latins, therefore, now demanded that Rome and Latium should be really united as one state, that one of the consuls should be taken from the Latins, and that one-half of the senators should always be Latins. This demand, reasonable as it was, exasperated all classes of the Romans to such a degree that war was declared at once. During the first campaign the Latins transferred the war to Campania, and at the foot of Mount Vesuvius a great battle was fought, in which one of the consuls, P. Decius, for the purpose of securing the victory to his own countrymen, caused himself to be devoted to death by a priest, and then rushed among the Latins like a spirit of destruction, until he himself was slain. During the same campaign, Manlius Torquatus, the other consul, exhibited an example of Roman severity which was revolting even to his own countrymen. Orders had been given that no man should engage in fighting out of his own line. The consul's son Manlius, on being taunted and provoked by a haughty Latin from Tusculum, was unable to control his anger, and slew the Tusculan. Delighted with his victory, he brought the spoils of his enemy before his father, but the latter

ordered the lictor to carry his threat into effect, by putting his son to death. The comrades of young Manlius honoured him with splendid funeral ceremonies, and the unnatural father was ever after shunned and scorned on account of this act.

12. After the first defeat, the Latins were deserted by the Campanians, who obtained favourable terms from the Romans. The Latins, however, continued the war two years longer, and at first made the most desperate efforts to maintain their independence. But another defeat in the second campaign led to the dissolution of the Latin confederacy, after which most of the towns surrendered one after another. Their example was followed by their allies the Volscians, so that, in B. C. 338, the subjugation of the country of the Latins and Volscians was completed. The conquered people, however, were treated with moderation; some obtained the full Roman franchise, such as the towns of Aricia, Lanuvium, Nomentum, and Pedum, while others received the franchise without the suffrage; others again became Roman municipia, that is, had an internal administration independent of Rome. Some of the more important towns, however, were humbled and weakened by their noble families being sent into exile, or by being deprived of portions of their territory. Each Latin town, moreover, was isolated as much as possible from the others, that is to say, the *commercium* and *connubium* among the several towns were abolished. The question as to whether Rome should be only one in the confederacy of the Latin towns, or rule over them as their mistress, was now decided for ever, and she secured her power in the newly-conquered countries by the means already mentioned, and still more by the establishment of Roman and Latin colonies, which were in reality military garrisons stationed in the conquered places, and generally received one-third of the landed property of the original inhabitants.

13. During the period of the wars against the Samnites and Latins, several important measures were adopted at Rome, partly to prevent the law of debt from weighing too heavily upon the plebeians, and partly to check abuses of the powers of the magistrates. In the year B. C. 339, the dictator Q. Publilius Philo enacted three important laws, the first of which abolished the veto of the patrician curiae on legal enactments passed by the comitia centuriata; the second gave to plebiscita the full power of laws binding on the whole nation; and the third ordained that one of the censors should always be a plebeian. The last vestiges of the patricians, as a privileged order, thus gradually disappeared one after another, without any great effort being made on the part of the patricians to maintain their once exclusive rights. The Roman republic now consisted of the Roman citizens, both patrician and plebeian, the Latins, and the allies as they were termed, though in reality they were the subjects of Rome, who provided the greater part of her armies in the wars against her more distant enemies.

CHAPTER V.

FROM THE SUBJUGATION OF LATIUM TO THAT OF ALL ITALY.

1. THE success of the Romans seems to have awakened the jealousy of the Samnites, and the Romans observing this feeling endeavoured to strengthen themselves partly by concluding treaties of alliance, but more especially by establishing colonies, that is, military garrisons, on or near the frontiers of Samnium. Such a colony was founded in B. C. 328, at Fregellae, a Volscian town, which had been conquered and destroyed by the Samnites, to whom, accordingly, the territory belonged. This led to disputes and even threats on the part of the Samnites; but war was not declared until B. C. 326, when the Samnites had sent reinforcements to Neapolis in Campania, which was then at war with Rome. Neapolis soon after concluded peace, but the Samnites were indemnified for the loss of this ally by Lucania renouncing its alliance with Rome. The Tarentines also supported Samnium. In the first campaign a Roman army marched into Apulia, part of which was allied with the Samnites, and where with great difficulty the Romans made themselves masters of some towns, but afterwards gained a great victory. The Samnites then obtained a truce for one year, after the expiration of which a body of them entered Latium and gained over some of the Latin towns, while the Roman army was in great danger in Apulia. Rome, however, was saved by the Latin towns returning to their duty, and thus enabling her to drive the enemy from Latium. Meanwhile, in B. C. 322, her arms in Apulia also were successful; Luceria and many smaller towns both in Apulia and in Samnium were conquered, and Fregellae was evacuated by the Samnites. The latter now offered to treat for peace, but the demands made by the Romans were of such a nature that the Samnites could not accept them.

2. After this unsuccessful attempt at negotiation, the Samnites made every effort to maintain their independence. Luceria was closely besieged by them, and in B. C. 321, the Romans, by the imprudent conduct of their consuls, Veturius and Postumius, lost nearly all the advantages they had gained in their previous campaigns; for the army being surrounded on all sides in the mountain pass of Caudium, and defeated in a fearful battle, was obliged to surrender. The survivors had to give up their arms and pass under the yoke, a symbolical act by which an army acknowledged itself to be vanquished. Pontius, the noble and modest commander of the Samnites, again offered fair terms of peace; these were accepted by the Roman commanders, and the army was then allowed to return home.

But the senate not only refused to ratify the peace, but decreed that those who had concluded it should be given up in chains to the enemy, as persons that had deceived them. Pontius refused to accept them, and the war was continued by the Romans with redoubled vigour, to wipe off the disgrace of Caudium. Great victories are henceforth ascribed to the Romans to make up for the great defeat. The first important advantages were gained in Apulia, where Papirius Cursor distinguished himself; but Fabius Maximus was defeated in a great battle at Lautulae, in consequence of which many towns revolted from Rome. The sufferings of the Samnites, however, were great, and their strength gradually sank. In B. C. 314 they were defeated in several engagements; in the following year Fregellae was recovered, together with several other towns, and the submission of Campania and Apulia was secured by various means. Rome had in fact the fairest prospects of speedily and thoroughly humbling her enemies, had not other events in different quarters prevented this consummation for a time.

3. The Etruscans, who had long been apprehensive of Rome's growing power, took up arms against her in B. C. 311, and thus obliged her to divide her forces. The Romans accordingly not being able to direct all their strength against the Samnites, suffered a great defeat near Allifae, and the legions in Samnium were in great distress. Under these circumstances Papirius Cursor, being appointed dictator, in B. C. 309, hastened to their assistance, and so completely defeated the Samnites, that they took to flight, leaving their camp in the hands of the enemy. But the Samnites were then joined by the Marsians, Pelignians, and Umbrians. The last of these were indeed soon brought to submission by Fabius Maximus; but a great coalition was forming against Rome, in which the Hernicans and Æquians also took part, and which gave the Samnites fresh hopes. Notwithstanding all this, however, Rome's power was irresistible; the war against Etruria was near its end, the Hernicans were easily overpowered, and the consuls Q. Marcius and P. Cornelius, directing their united forces against the Samnites, put them to flight in all directions, B. C. 306. The coalition on which they had relied being broken up, and their armies being defeated, they concluded a short truce in the hope of obtaining peace on tolerable terms. When hostilities were recommenced, the Romans ravaged Samnium far and wide, until the Samnites, after another defeat at Bovianum in B. C. 305, were completely crushed. Negotiations for peace accordingly were commenced, and the Samnites were obliged to accept the terms dictated by Rome, to give up their supremacy over Lucinia, as well as their alliance with the Marsians, Pelignians, Marrucinians, and Frentanians, while Rome reserved to herself the right to interfere in all the external relations of Samnium. This peace, hard as it was, was acquiesced in because

the Samnites were so much reduced that they could not continue the war. Thus ended the second Samnite war, which had lasted from B. C. 326 to 304.

4. The fate of the Hernicans after their reduction in B. C. 306, was on the whole the same as that of the Latins. The Æquians, who all along had supported the Samnites, rose in a body at the time when the Samnites had already concluded peace with Rome. The consequence of this thoughtless insurrection was that their towns in a short period were conquered one after another, and most of them were destroyed. About this same time the Romans concluded a treaty with Tarentum, in which it was stipulated that no Roman ships should sail beyond cape Lacinium. The Etruscan war above referred to broke out in B. C. 311, when the Etruscans, encouraged by the defeat of the Romans at Lautulae, hoped to be able to recover their ancient independence. Their country was no longer harassed by the wandering Celts, who had quietly settled down in the plains on the north and east of the Appenines. But the Etruscans began the war against Rome too late, and after it had lasted for some years, their cities began, in B. C. 308, to conclude peace with Rome each for itself for a fixed number of years. The interval between the second and third Samnite wars is marked only by the revolt of the Æquians already mentioned, and by the invasion of the Roman territory by a host of Celts who had just come across the Alps. But the barbarians did not stay long, and having collected vast quantities of booty returned to the north.

5. The peace concluded with the Samnites lasted only six years, of which period the Romans availed themselves for firmly establishing their power in the countries they had recently conquered. The Samnites were only waiting for a favourable opportunity to recommence hostilities, and being led to think that the Romans were afraid of entering upon a fresh war, they resolved to try to recover the supremacy of Lucania, which was torn to pieces by factions. The Lucanian nobles, however, placed themselves under the protection of Rome, whereupon the Romans demanded of the Samnites to evacuate Lucania. This demand irritated them so much that war was declared at once, B. C. 298. At the same time the Etruscans again rose in arms, allied themselves with the Umbrians, and even called in the aid of Gallic mercenaries. In the first two years of the third Samnite war, the Samnites were defeated in Lucania, at Bovianum, and at Maleventum in Samnium itself, which was fearfully ravaged. In the third year all Lucania was recovered by the Romans. The Etruscans were not more fortunate than the Samnites, and the latter sent out an army to their assistance; but all was to no purpose; the Roman arms were victorious everywhere, and a defeat of the Samnites in Campania delivered Rome from the fear of a revolt among her allies. But what

alarmed her, nevertheless, was a report that the Gauls were marching southward, and were allied with and supported by the Etruscans and Umbrians.   In B. C. 295, under the consuls Q. Fabius and P. Decius, the Romans made incredible efforts to meet the threatening storm.   In Etruria they had suffered some severe reverses, but Fabius' arrival soon produced a favourable change, and in the great battle of Sentinum in Umbria, which was nearly lost, the self-sacrifice of Decius, who caused himself and the hostile army to be devoted to the infernal gods, gained for the Romans a signal victory.   The Samnite army which had been sent into Etruria was cut to pieces, and twenty-five thousand Gauls and Samnites covered the field of battle, while eight thousand were made prisoners. From Umbria Fabius returned to Etruria, where he gained a victory over the Etruscans near Perusia.

6. While these things were going on in the north, where the enemies of Rome had endeavoured to unite their forces, another Samnite army had been engaged in fearfully ravaging part of Campania, but there too they are said to have been beaten with great loss by the Roman army returning from Sentinum.   In the two following years, the Romans continued to be successful both in Etruria, where most of the town thought it advisable to conclude peace with Rome, and in Samnium.   The people of the latter country now exerted all their strength, and having enlisted all their men capable of bearing arms, invaded Campania.   But an invasion of Samnium by the Romans obliged them to return, and the Romans having gained a great and decisive victory, carried off an immense quantity of booty.   No sooner, however, had they withdrawn from Samnium than the Samnites, under the command of the noble-minded Pontius, again invaded Campania.   At first, the Romans who met the enemy were defeated, and had it not been for the excessive caution of the Samnites, the Roman army would have been completely annihilated.   But soon after this, in B. C. 292, the aged Q. Fabius Maximus undertaking the command, a fierce battle was fought, which decided the contest between Rome and Samnium.   Twenty thousand Samnites were killed, and four thousand made prisoners, among whom was the brave Pontius.   The issue of the war was now decided, although the submission of Samnium was delayed for two years longer.   Pontius was led to Rome in chains, and then beheaded—a savage treatment of a man to whose generous forbearance it had been owing that the whole Roman army was not destroyed after the defeat of Caudium.   The Samnites do not appear after this to have ventured again to meet their enemies in the field; and in B. C. 290 they sued for peace, which was granted on condition that Samnium should acknowledge the supremacy of Rome.   The same soon afterwards became the fate of the Umbrians, Etruscans, and the Celtic tribes of the Senones

and Boians. Numerous colonies were established to secure the submission of these countries, and Rome, having now acquired the dominion of all central Italy, enjoyed a few years of peace.

7. Notwithstanding a few occasional attempts of the patricians to deprive the plebeians of the rights guaranteed to them by solemn laws, the two orders were placed upon a complete footing of equality during the period of the first and second Samnite wars. In B. c. 312, the censor Appius Claudius made the famous Appian road from Rome to Capua (which was afterwards continued to Brundisium), and the first aqueduct which supplied the city of Rome with water. In the same year a calendar was set up in public for the convenience of the people, that they might know on what days it was lawful to meet in the assembly and administer justice. A constitutional change appears to have been made about the same time, in consequence of which the comitia centuriata were engrafted upon the comitia tributa, though the latter still continued to be convened separately as before. The last great change, by which the equalisation of the two orders was completed, was effected by the Ogulnian law, B. c. 300, by which the number of pontiffs and augurs was increased, and at the same time it was enacted that one-half of these priestly colleges should be filled with plebeians. All public offices with which political power was connected, were now equally divided between patricians and plebeians, and the differences between the two estates were soon so far forgotten, that the question as to whether a man was a patrician or a plebeian was entirely lost sight of. The Licinian agrarian law, however, appears to have been constantly violated with impunity. The distribution of the public land among the poor citizens, though not absolutely refused, was but rarely resorted to; and the long wars carried on at a great distance from home continued to reduce to poverty many who shed their blood for their country. But notwithstanding these drawbacks, Rome was now enjoying, in some measure, the blessings of the legislation of Licinius, and the period of the Samnite wars may be regarded as the beginning of the golden age of Roman history.

8. The peace which Rome enjoyed after the termination of the third Samnite war was interrupted only by fresh attacks of the Gauls and Etruscans, who are said to have been stirred up by the Tarentines. This war, beginning in B. c. 285, ended in the total subjugation of the Senones and Boii in B. c. 282; but that against the Etruscans lasted for two years longer, when the Romans, on account of a defeat they sustained in southern Italy, granted them a most favourable peace. After this, the Etruscans made no further attempts to recover their independence, and seemed to have enjoyed a high degree of prosperity under the supremacy of Rome.

9. Tarentum, a colony of Sparta, which had been founded in B. c. 708, and had attained a very considerable degree of prosperity as a

commercial and manufacturing city, was looking with alarm upon
the spread of the power of the Romans in southern Italy; but being
unwilling itself to engage in a contest with Rome, it stirred up the
other nations of southern Italy to combine against their common
enemy.   This scheme succeeded so far as to induce even the Samnites to join the coalition in the hope of recovering their former
independence.   The first act of hostility consisted in the Lucanians
besieging Thurii, but C. Fabricius, after great difficulties, succeeded, B. C. 282, in relieving the place and gaining several victories
over the allies.   The necessity of communicating with Thurii by
sea led the Romans to violate the treaty subsisting between them
and the Tarentines, and ten Roman ships steered towards the harbour of Tarentum.   The Tarentines immediately sailed out to attack
them; and only five Roman ships escaped.   Thurii being then
attacked by the Tarentines was obliged to throw open its gates to
them.   Upon these proceedings the Roman senate sent an embassy
to Tarentum to demand reparation; but the Tarentines not only
refused to do this, but insulted the ambassadors in a most indecent
manner.   War was thus unavoidable.   The Tarentines had, in the
meantime, been joined by the Messapians; but as their hopes of a
general coalition of the nations of Italy against Rome were disappointed, they invited Pyrrhus of Epirus to come to their assistance.

10. Pyrrhus, the adventurous and chivalrous king of Epirus,
with whom we have already become acquainted,[1] gladly seized the
opportunity, in the hope of being able to establish for himself a
great kingdom, consisting of Epirus, Magna Graecia, and Sicily.
He arrival in Italy in B. C. 281, and immediately took possession
of Tarentum, whose inhabitants had to submit to severe military
discipline.   In the year following, the Romans, after concluding
peace with Etruria, sent out armies against the Samnites and Tarentines.   On the banks of the Siris, near Heracleia, the hostile armies
met, and Pyrrhus, partly by means of his Macedonian phalanx, and
partly by the terror of his elephants, with which the Romans were
unacquainted, gained a decisive victory over the Romans, though
they fought with the most admirable valour.   In consequence of
this victory many Italians, such as the Apulians, Locrians, and
many separate towns, openly joined Pyrrhus.   But as he himself
had sustained great losses in the battle, he sent his friend Cineas to
Rome to offer peace.   The senate, however, refused to listen to any
proposals until the king should consent to quit Italy.   Pyrrhus then
advanced to the very neighbourhood of Rome, but finding that
peace had been concluded with Etruria, he returned to Tarentum.
In the year B. C. 279, the Roman consuls met the enemy again in
the neighbourhood of Asculum, where Pyrrhus gained another
hand-won victory.   Notwithstanding this, however, he seems to

<hr>

[1] P. 258, &c.

have despaired of success, and in speaking of the Romans is reported to have said, "with such soldiers the world would be mine," while he described his own victory by saying, "one more such victory, and I shall be ruined."

11. After these disasters the Roman senate felt inclined to come to some understanding with Pyrrhus; but Appius Claudius the Blind strenuously opposed the scheme so long as Pyrrhus refused to quit Italy. Pyrrhus had lost his confidence in his Italian allies, while the Romans filled his soul with admiration and respect; and well it might be so when he compared their conduct with that of the degenerate Greeks, with whom alone he had hitherto had dealings. Under these circumstances, he gladly availed himself of an invitation sent to him by the Sicilian Greeks, who hoped with his assistance to drive the Carthaginians out of the island. A truce seems to have been concluded with Rome in b. c. 278, and Pyrrhus sailed over into Sicily. But he found his Sicilian allies even worse than those in Italy; their faithless and treacherous disposition thwarted nearly all his undertakings, though, if they had followed and obeyed him, he would, no doubt, have rescued Sicily from the hands of the Carthaginians. After a stay of three years in the island, he returned to Italy at the urgent request of his Italian allies, who were hard pressed by the Romans. During his absence the latter had punished their revolted allies or subjects, and victories had been gained over the Lucanians, Bruttians, Tarentines, and Samnites. Upon his arrival in Italy, Pyrrhus recovered some of the towns which had fallen into the hands of the Romans. The consul M.'Curius Dentatus was encamped near Beneventum, and thither Pyrrhus repaired to offer battle. But his army, now mainly composed of effeminate and fickle Greeks, was no longer what it had been in his former campaigns. He was so completely defeated, b. c. 275, that he escaped with only a few horsemen to Tarentum. Finding that his Italian allies in other quarters were not more successful, and that he could not expect any reinforcements from the kings of Macedonia and Syria, he at once resolved to quit Italy, leaving small garrisons at Tarentum and Rhegium. Two years after his return to Epirus, he was killed at Argos in a battle against Antigonus Gonatas.

12. After the departure of Pyrrhus, the Tarentines concluded peace with the Romans, who now resolved to crush the inhabitants of southern Italy for ever; and this was accomplished in b. c. 272, when the Samnites, Lucanians, and Bruttians did homage to the majesty of the great republic; but Rhegium was not recovered till the year after. Rome now was the virtual mistress of all Italy, from the northern frontier of Etruria to the straits of Sicily. There was, however, one nation, which, though often conquered and humbled, could not resign itself to its fate. This was the Samnites,

and in B. C. 268 the fourth and last Samnite war broke out; but it was brought to a close in the very first campaign. The conquered nations of Italy were treated differently, according to the degree of hostility they had shown during the war, and according to the manner in which they had succumbed to the Romans. All, however, had to recognise the supremacy of Rome, which as usual secured its dominion in the newly-conquered districts by the establishment of colonies or military garrisons. The vanquished nations lost the right of carrying on war on their own account, and of concluding treaties with foreign nations. The ships of the maritime cities enabled the Romans, in case of need, to form a fleet against any transmarine enemy with whom they might come in contact. At this time the fame of Rome's conquests had reached the ears of the princes in the distant East, and Ptolemy Philadelphus of Egypt, in B. C. 273, sent an embassy to conclude a treaty of friendship, which was willingly granted. Rome had now become one of the states of the first rank in ancient history, and well would it have been for her, had circumstances allowed her to limit herself to Italy, and develop a system of free institutions over the peninsula, so as to unite the whole in one compact state.

CHAPTER VI.

CARTHAGE AND SICILY.

1. CARTHAGE, a colony of Tyre, on the north coast of Africa, is said to have been founded by Dido, a Tyrian princess, about the year B. C. 814. Its inhabitants therefore belonged to the Phoenicians, a branch of the Semitic race. Carthage was not the only Phoenician colony on that coast, nor even the most ancient, for Utica and Tunis boasted a much higher antiquity; but Carthage soon rose to great power and prosperity, in consequence partly of its favourable situation, and partly of the decline of the commercial greatness of the mother city. From these and other circumstances, it exercised a sort of supremacy over the other Phoenician settlements on the same coast, though formally their independence was always recognised, and Utica in particular remained an independent political community down to the latest times. For a long period, down to the reign of Darius Hystaspis, the Carthaginians had to pay a tribute to the Libyans, that is, the natives among whom they had established themselves. But in the course of time they not only ceased to pay this tribute, but reduced the Libyans to com-

plete subjection. These were then treated by their new masters with cruel avarice; they had to till the land for them, and furnish them with armies, for the Carthaginian soldiers mentioned in history are always either Libyans or mercenaries, the purse-proud merchants of Carthage disdaining to serve their country in person. In the country round Carthage, the mixture of the Phoenician settlers with the native Libyans produced a race called the Libyphoenicians, who seem to have occupied and cultivated the rich lands about Carthage and the valley of the river Bagradas. The territory which the Carthaginian state acquired probably never reached further south than lake Triton, or further west than Hippo Regius. Its influence, however, was extended both in the west and in the east by a large number of colonies or factories, for they were all established for commercial purposes. Hence Carthage exercised her authority over the north coast of Africa, more or less, from the pillars of Hercules to the head of the great Syrtis.

2. The character of the Carthaginians as a commercial nation obliged them to make themselves masters of the islands nearest to Africa. About the middle of the sixth century B. C., Malchus, a Carthaginian general who had distinguished himself in the wars in Africa, is said to have undertaken a successful expedition against Sicily; but an attempt upon Sardinia failed, in consequence of which he was punished with exile. Instead of submitting to his fate, he proceeded with his army against Carthage, and made himself master of it. In the end, however, he was put to death, because he was accused of aiming at regal power. The work of conquest begun by him was continued by Mago, who also gave a better organisation to the military resources of his country. Shortly after this, the refusal to pay the customary tribute to the Libyans led to a war with them, in which Carthage was defeated, and had to purchase peace. The conquests in Sardinia and Sicily, however, were continued, and Sardinia became the first foreign province of Carthage, a condition in which that island appears as early as the first year of the Roman republic. Corsica was likewise occupied by them at an early period, though its possession was disputed for a long time by the Tyrrhenians.

3. Sicily, to which the attention of the Carthaginians was directed from the very first, was never entirely conquered by them. The island was inhabited by two peoples, the Sicani and Siceli, and its southern and eastern coasts were occupied by Greek colonists, called Siceliotae, whose steady advance displaced several of the Phoenician settlements, which had existed there from early times, until the Phoenicians retained their footing only on the western coast. These Phoenician colonies were first taken possession of by the Carthaginians, who with this firm footing in the island, endeavoured to extend their empire there by fomenting dissensions among the

27 *

Greeks until they were prepared to strike a great blow. Even before the invasion of Greece by the Persians, they had been involved in war with Gelo, the tyrant of Syracuse; and when they found that the Greeks of the mother country were fully engaged against the Persians, who may even have urged on the Carthaginians, they resolved to make a great effort against the Sicilian Greeks. An opportunity easily presented itself, and the Carthaginians, to support their friend Terillus, the exiled tyrant of Himera, invaded the island in B. C. 480 with a fleet of three thousand ships, and an army of three hundred thousand men, which was commanded by Hamilcar. But this grand armament was utterly defeated and its commander slain, it is said, on the very day on which the Greeks of the mother country fought the glorious battle of Salamis. The loss of this battle at once decided the fate of the Carthaginians in Sicily; they were driven back to their ancient positions in the west of the island, and, for a time at least, seem to have given up all thoughts of extending their dominion in Sicily, for no fresh attempts were made until the year B. C. 410, from which time they continued their wars with the Sicilian Greeks, until the Romans interfered in the contest.

4. Among the other foreign possessions of Carthage, we may notice the Balearic islands, and parts of the south and west coast of Spain. The first time that Carthage had any dealings with Rome was the year after the expulsion of the Tarquins, B. C. 509, when the two republics concluded a commercial treaty, which is preserved in Polybius, and is of extreme importance in determining the relations then subsisting between Rome and Carthage. In a second treaty of a similar nature, concluded in B. C. 348, the Roman merchants were excluded from Corsica and Libya. During this period, the relations between Rome and Carthage were of an amicable nature, as is attested by several occurrences, and also by the fact, that in B. C. 306 the ancient treaty was renewed. But the progress made by the Romans in southern Italy aroused jealousy and alarm in the minds of the Carthaginians; during the war against Pyrrhus, however, in B. C. 279, Carthage and Rome, being drawn together by the same interests, concluded a defensive alliance, which was directed against Pyrrhus, their common enemy. In consequence of this, a Carthaginian fleet of one hundred sail appeared at Ostia to assist the Romans, but it was dismissed with thanks, without being used. The fears entertained by Carthage in regard to Pyrrhus were realised by his crossing over into Sicily with the avowed purpose of driving the Carthaginians from it. But owing to the miserable conduct of his Greek allies, he was obliged to give up his enterprise. Throughout the war against Pyrrhus, both in Italy and Sicily, each of the two republics fought without being assisted by the other, which probably arose from mistrust which

they had conceived of each other after the conclusion of the last treaty, and the march of events soon brought them into violent collision.

5. The political constitution of Carthage was strictly oligarchical, and a few wealthy, ancient, and powerful families divided among themselves all the power and all the great offices of the state. The executive was in the hands of two chief magistrates called suffetes or judges, who appear to have been elected annually. We also hear of a senate of three hundred members, forming a sort of great council, out of which several smaller bodies or committees were chosen. The assembled people were sometimes consulted in cases where the suffetes and the council could not agree; but this popular assembly appears otherwise to have had little power, the wealthy families generally having everything their own way, for money seems to have been all-powerful at Carthage. The arts and sciences were cultivated only so far as they contributed to the comforts of life, or afforded the means of acquiring wealth. The religion of the Carthaginians was the same as that of the Phoenicians, and was occasionally stained by the offering of human sacrifices to their gods.

6. The most powerful among the Greek colonies in Sicily was Syracuse, and it was chiefly this city that had from the first disputed the sovereignty of the island with Carthage. Civil dissensions induced and enabled enterprising men at an early period to set themselves up as tyrants of Syracuse. After the great victory of Gelo over the Carthaginians at Himera, in B. c. 480, Sicily for a time was not again invaded by the Carthaginians, but about a century later the elder Dionysius, who was tyrant of Syracuse from B. c. 405 to 368, had to purchase peace from Carthage by giving up Agrigentum and other Greek towns. The Corinthian hero Timoleon afterwards, having delivered Syracuse from the tyranny of the younger Dionysius (who ruled from B. c 368 to 345), for a time checked the encroachments of the Carthaginians; but under Agathocles, who had raised himself from the lowest rank to that of tyrant of Syracuse, B. c. 317, the hostilities recommenced, and continued with such varying success, that at one and the same time, B. c. 310, Carthage was besieged by the army of Agathocles, and Syracuse by that of the Carthaginians; for as the Carthaginians who had been invited by the enemies of Agathocles were carrying on their siege operations somewhat carelessly, he seized a favourable moment, and sailed through the midst of the enemy's fleet to Carthage. After having landed on the coast, he ordered his fleet to be burnt, that his soldiers might have no choice between victory or death, and in a short time made himself, by his desperate courage, master of the whole territory of Carthage. The Carthaginian general Hamilcar in the meantime was defeated at Syracuse, and

died in captivity. Agathocles then, with brilliant promises, invited Ophellas, the governor of Cyrene, to come to his assistance, B. C. 308. But when he arrived with an army of twenty thousand men, the cunning Syracusan, alleging that the Cyrenean was meditating treason, unexpectedly attacked and slew him, and then compelled his men to enter into his own service. In the height of his pride he fancied himself already master of the whole of northern Africa, and assumed the title of king. But matters soon assumed a different aspect, for being defeated in a battle by the Carthaginians, he secretly made his escape to Sicily to secure his position at Syracuse, leaving his army to perish in a foreign land. The soldiers, enraged at such conduct, murdered the son of the tyrant, who had been left behind, and then entered the service of Carthage. By murders and acts of the most wanton cruelty, Agathocles now endeavoured to establish himself securely at Syracuse, and extended his dominion over the greater part of the island; but in the end a slow poison was administered to him, which induced him to order himself to be burned. He had been tyrant of Syracuse from B. C. 317 to 289.

7. After the death of this bold but unscrupulous adventurer, the whole island fell into a state of the wildest anarchy. His Campanian mercenaries, called Mamertines, on their return home took forcible possession of the town of Messene or Messana, B. C. 281; they murdered or expelled the male population, and then distributed their property as well as their wives and children among themselves. From Messana, they made predatory excursions in all directions, and thereby produced in the island a feeling of uneasiness and insecurity, which the Carthaginians were not slow to turn to their own advantage. Pyrrhus was invited from Italy to assist the Sicilian Greeks against both the Carthaginians and Mamertines. He went across, as we have seen,[1] but the Sicilian Greeks, who probably knew that he was really aiming at making himself master of the island, behaved towatds him in such a manner, that after a stay of three years he was glad to return to Italy. The island now fell again into its former state of anarchy, and the Mamertines, like a horde of robbers, ransacked the country, and secured their plunder behind the strong walls of Messana. At this time, B. C. 275, the Syracusans elected Hiero, a descendant of Gelo, as their general, and five years later he obtained the title of king. With a strong army he marched against Messana, defeated the Mamertines, and by besieging the town reduced them to such straits, that they were obliged to look about for foreign assistance. Some were of opinion that they should throw themselves into the arms of the Carthaginians, who, from hatred of Hiero and the Syracusans, had already offered their assistance, and soon after took possession of the acropolis of Messana; but the majority resolved to invoke the aid of the Romans.

[1] P. 314.

CHAPTER VII.

THE FIRST PUNIC WAR, DOWN TO THE OUTBREAK OF THE SECOND.

1. At the time when the Mamertines solicited the assistance of Rome, scarcely six years had elapsed since the Romans had inflicted the severest punishment upon a body of Campanians who had acted at Rhegium in the same manner as the Mamertines had done at Messana. The Roman senate, or at least the better part of it, felt that common decency forbade their entertaining the proposal; and accordingly referred it to the assembly of the people, with whom the love of war and conquest seems, at that time at least, to have stifled every other feeling. An alliance with the Mamertines was concluded in B. C. 264. As the Carthaginians were in possession of the citadel, Hiero, finding that he could effect nothing against the town, concluded peace with the Mamertines. This cut off at once every pretext for Roman interference; but the opportunity of commencing war against the Carthaginians was too tempting, and a fleet, furnished by the Greek maritime towns, and an army, at once assembled at Rhegium. A proclamation was sent to Messana, to announce to the Mamertines that the Romans were ready to deliver them from the yoke of the Carthaginians. The fleet then sailed across, and the Carthaginian general was treacherously induced to surrender the citadel of Messana to the Romans. The Carthaginians demanded of the Romans to quit Sicily, and as this was disregarded, a fresh army, in conjunction with king Hiero, laid siege to Messana. The consul Appius Claudius, who had in the meantime come across with his legions, defeated Hiero before his allies could come to his assistance. Hiero retreated to Syracuse, and the Carthaginians, being likewise defeated, dispersed among their subject towns in the island. In the year after, B. C. 263, Hiero and his Syracusans, tired of the war, concluded peace with Rome, and remained her most faithful allies for many years.

2 In the meantime, other Roman armies had landed in Sicily, and sixty-seven towns are said to have surrendered to them. The Carthaginians did not make their appearance in the field, and the conquest of the island at that time seemed a matter of no great difficulty. In B. C. 262, the Romans besieged Agrigentum, which was held by a numerous garrison of the Carthaginians. After a siege of seven months, the city was compelled to surrender; the garrison escaped, but the place experienced all the horrors of a town conquered by the sword. As Carthage was mistress of the sea, the Roman senate ordered a fleet to be built in all haste,

after the model of a Carthaginian quinquereme which had been thrown on the coast of Bruttium. In B. c. 260, C. Duilius undertook the command of the fleet, and in the ensuing engagement with the Carthaginians off Mylae, he changed, by means of boarding bridges, the naval battle into a land fight. This was the first battle fought by the Romans at sea, and their victory was so complete, that the enemy, after a loss of about ten thousand in killed and wounded, took to flight. The grateful Romans honoured their admiral with a column, adorned with the beaks of the captured ships (*columna rostrata*), and with an inscription recording the details of his victory. After this success, the Romans were so emboldened that they resolved to drive the Carthaginians from all their insular possessions, and expeditions were undertaken at the same time against Sardinia and Corsica. The operations in Sicily were in the meantime carried on with less vigour, and the Carthaginians gained some advantages; but the ascendancy of the Romans was restored in B. c. 258 by the consul Atilius Calatinus. Myttistratum, which had been besieged by the Romans for some time, was abandoned by the Carthaginian garrison, and fell into the hands of the Romans. Camarina and many other towns were either taken or surrendered.

3. But notwithstanding these and other successful enterprises, one half of Sicily was still in the hands of the Carthaginians, and the Romans had only recovered what they had previously lost. In B. c. 256, however, the Romans made immense exertions, and a large fleet of three hundred and thirty sail was got ready, intended to cross over into Africa under the command of the consuls L. Manlius and M. Atilius Regulus. But the fleet was met by a larger one of the Carthaginians near Ecnomus, and a decisive and destructive battle ensued, in which the Carthaginians were completely defeated. Offers of peace on the part of the Carthaginians were rejected, and the Roman fleet sailed to Africa. It landed near Clupea, and as the place was found deserted by its inhabitants, the Romans made it their head quarters, and in all directions ravaged the country, which was cultivated like a garden and studded with factories and country houses of the wealthy. At the close of the year Manlius returned to Italy with a portion of the forces and a vast number of prisoners. Regulus, remaining behind with his diminished forces, began the campaign of B. c. 255 by laying siege to the town of Adis. But owing to the inexperience of the enemy, Regulus, it is said, had the satisfaction of seeing a large number of towns submitting to him. The Carthaginians were so much reduced as to be obliged to seek shelter behind the walls of their own city. In this distress they sent to Regulus to sue for peace; but he, who might now have concluded the war in an honourable manner, proposed such humiliating terms, that the Cartha-

ginians could not accept them, and resolved to perish sword in hand rather than submit to the insolence of their enemy.

4. This would probably have been the result in a short time, had the Carthaginians not availed themselves of the services of the able Spartan Xanthippus, to whom they entrusted the supreme command of their forces. He increased the army, and by an improved discipline revived the spirit and confidence of the soldiers. When the army was sufficiently trained, he marched out to meet Regulus, and in the battle that ensued the whole Roman army was routed and dispersed. Regulus himself was taken prisoner with five hundred men, and only two thousand escaped to Clupea. The Roman consuls immediately sailed to Africa with a large fleet to rescue the men at Clupea, who defended themselves bravely; near cape Hermaeum it was attacked by the Carthaginians, but gained a brilliant victory over them, and continued its course to Clupea, where the Carthaginians were again defeated, and the two thousand Romans taken on board. But on its return to Sicily, the fleet was overtaken by a storm, during which most of the ships perished, all the coast from Camarina to Pachynus being covered with wrecks and corpses. The Carthaginians emboldened by their own success and the reverses of their enemies, re-commenced their operations in Sicily and made new conquests. The news of the destruction of the fleet, however, acted upon the Romans only as an incentive to greater exertions, and in B. C. 254, a new armada of two hundred and twenty ships sailed to Sicily, and took Panormus. This conquest was followed by the surrender of several towns which until then had been faithful to Carthage. As the progress of the Romans was slow, the fleet in B. C. 252 once more sailed to Africa, and laid waste its coast districts. But the dangers of the Syrtes induced the Romans to return, and when the fleet came within sight of cape Palinurus, a storm burst forth in which one hundred and fifty ships were wrecked. This second great disaster at sea discouraged the Romans, and it was resolved not to restore the fleet beyond what was necessary to protect Italy and convey troops to Sicily.

5. During the following years the Romans nevertheless continued to make progress; they confined the Carthaginians to the western corner of the island, and in B. C. 250 the consul Caecilius defeated them in a great battle in the neighborhood of Panormus. This was the third great battle fought during the whole period of the war, and it was at the same time the last. The Carthaginians had now lost all the towns in Sicily with the exception of the fortresses of Lilybaeum and Drepana, and anxious to obtain peace or at least an exchange of prisoners, they are said to have sent Regulus, who was still in captivity, to Rome, to prevail on his countrymen to grant either one or the other. But Regulus persuaded the Roman senate to enter into no negotiations and to continue the war. A

new fleet of two hundred sail was built, and the Romans began to besiege Lilybaeum, which was very strongly fortified. The siege lasted for a long time, until at length the Romans confined themselves to blockading the place. In B. C. 249 the fool-hardy and haughty Appius Claudius, who had gone to Sicily with a supplementary army, was defeated near Drepana both by land and by sea. This disaster of their enemy gave fresh courage to the Carthaginians, who followed up their victory with great vigour. But still more serious misfortunes befel the Romans, for a vast number of transports were destroyed during a storm, and their remaining ships of war were captured or sunk by the enemy. These things led them a second time to renounce the sea, of which the Carthaginians were now the undisputed masters. But their resources were exhausted, and their attempt to raise money by a loan was unsuccessful. In these circumstances, the great Hamilcar, the father of Hannibal, undertook the command of the forces in Sicily, B. C. 247. He first made some predatory descents upon the coasts of Italy, and on his return took up a strong position on mount Hercte, where for a period of three years he watched the proceedings of the Romans, and did them incalculable injury by his sallies. Afterwards he took up a similar position on mount Eryx, where he was besieged by the Romans, but continued to harass them as before, although he was surrounded by great difficulties and had only mercenaries for his soldiers.

6. In this manner the war was protracted without anything decisive being effected by either party. The Romans at length, seeing that it could not be brought to a close without some great effort, resolved, in B C. 242, to build another fleet. The funds were contributed by wealthy and patriotic citizens, and an armament of two hundred ships commanded by C. Lutatius Catulus, was soon under sail. He first made an attack upon Drepana, but being unsuccessful, resolved at once to offer battle to the Carthaginian fleet, which contained a large number of transports. The victory of the Romans was easy and complete; sixty-three of the enemy's ships were taken, one hundred and twenty were sunk, and the number of the slain and prisoners was immense. This great victory was gained in B. C. 241 off the Ægatian islands, and Eryx soon after fell into the hands of the Romans. The Carthaginians now sued for peace, which was granted on condition of their evacuating Sicily and the islands between it and Carthage, abstaining from war against Hiero and his allies, restoring the Roman prisoners without ransom, and paying two thousand three hundred talents in ten yearly instalments.

7. The first Punic war, which had lasted twenty-three years, and had been carried on with incredible efforts and losses on both sides, was now terminated, and in Sicily Rome made her first foreign

conquest. Sicily, as a country out of Italy, on coming into the hands of the Romans received a constitution different from that of the conquered countries of Italy—it became a province, that is, a country governed by a Roman praetor or proconsul, who was sent out every year with supreme civil and military power, and was assisted by a quaestor or treasurer. The revenues derived from a province by the Roman republic were of various kinds, such as taxes consisting of a tithe of all the produce of the soil, and the rent of the public or domain land. These revenues (*vectigalia*) were not levied by officers of the government, but were farmed by wealthy individuals (*publicani*) or companies of them. All the towns of a province, moreover, were not in the same relation to Rome, their condition generally depending on the manner in which they had behaved during the war preceding the conquest. In Sicily, for example, the little kingdom of Hiero and several other places remained perfectly free and independent. It was a maxim with the Romans that provincials should serve Rome only with money, and not with soldiers, whence they were not allowed to enlist in the Roman armies. It is a remarkable fact, that during the long period of the first war with Carthage, the Italian nations remained quiet, and did not attempt to shake off the yoke of Rome —a proof of the moderation with which she treated them.

8. When the Carthaginians evacuated Sicily and their mercenaries returned to Africa, the government was unable to give them the pay that was due to them. They accordingly rose in arms against their employers, B. C. 241, and were urged on by Italian deserters who were afraid of being delivered up to the Romans. This war between Carthage and her mercenaries was carried on with the utmost cruelty by both parties, and Carthage itself was brought to the brink of destruction, the whole of the surrounding country being at times in the hands of its enemies, for the insurgents were joined by the Libyans and even by other Phoenician colonies on the coast. The great Hamilcar at length, after the war had raged upwards of three years, succeeded in putting an end to it, B. C. 238. The fact that Carthage was enabled to crush the rebellious mercenaries, was partly owing to the generous conduct of the Romans, who not only refused to aid the rebels, but, protected the transports destined for Carthage. During this African war, the mercenaries in Sardinia likewise revolted; but the natives drove them from the island. The mercenaries then threw themselves into the arms of the Romans, who gladly availed themselves of the opportunity of seizing the island, in B. C. 238. When Carthage remonstrated with them for this act of aggression, the Romans treated them as if they were the offenders, and not only took possession of Sardinia and Corsica, but demanded of Carthage the additional sum of twelve hundred talents. The African republic

28

being in too exhausted a condition to offer any resistance, was obliged to yield; but its indignation and revenge were treasured up for a more convenient time; and Carthage, under the guidance of Hamilcar, at once began to make preparations to indemnify herself in another quarter for what she had lost.

9. The Romans had indeed gained possession of the islands of Sardinia and Corsica, but they had to carry on a long and tedious war with the natives, who were less patient of the Roman yoke than they had been of the Carthaginian. About the same time, the Romans were involved in an equally tedious war with the Ligurians and Boians, and while these wars were still going on, another struggle was commenced in B. C. 229, against the semi-barbarous pirates of Illyricum, who were then governed by a queen Teuta, and did great injury to the maritime cities of Greece. The barbarians were easily conquered, and the Greek towns which had formerly been plundered by the Illyrians, such as Corcyra, Epidamnus (Dyrrhachium), Apollonia, placed themselves under the protection of Rome. In this manner the Romans gained a footing on the eastern coast of the Adriatic, and a certain influence upon the affairs of Greece; that influence, however, was beneficial, for the Illyrians were humbled and obliged to give up their piracy. At the same time Corinth and Athens conferred certain marks of honourable distinction upon the Romans.

10. But all these were trifling compared with that which now burst upon the Romans. In B. C. 229, C. Flaminius, by an agrarian law, had distributed the lands on the north-east of the Appenines, which had been taken from the Gauls. For some years the Boians had been strengthening themselves by alliances with other Celtic tribes in the north of Italy, and even beyond the Alps. In B. C. 226, swarms of Celts came across the Alps, and as their formidable hosts moved southward, the Romans were seized with the greatest alarm. The Gauls, devastating everything by fire and sword, advanced as far as Clusium in Etruria. There the Roman army met them, determined to rescue Italy from their devastations. At first the Romans were nearly surrounded and annihilated, but in the neighbourhood of Telamon, on the coast of Etruria, they gained a decisive victory, the Gauls losing forty thousand in killed and ten thousand in prisoners. This memorable battle was fought in B. C. 225, and the year after the Romans compelled the Boians to submit, and for the first time crossed the river Po, where, in B. C. 223, the consul C. Flaminius gained a great victory over the Insubrians. In the year following, the war against the Gauls was brought to a close by M. Claudius Marcellus in the battle of Clastidium, where he slew the Gallic chief Viridomarus with his own hand. In the peace which was then concluded, the Gauls recognised the supremacy of Rome, which thus became the mistress of the wide plains of Lombardy,

known by the ancient name of Gallia Cisalpina; and she secured these conquests by the establishment of the colonies of Cremona and Placentia.

11. In the meantime, the Illyrians, and especially the Illyrian prince, Demetrius of Pharos, had renewed their piratical practices; but they were effectually put an end to, in B. C. 219, by the consul L. Æmilius Paulus, who subdued the whole of Illyricum; but Demetrius escaped to the court of Philip of Macedonia, whose attention had no doubt already been attracted by the progress made by the Romans on the east of the Adriatic.

12. After the loss of Sicily, Sardinia, and Corsica, the Carthaginians, guided by the wise counsels of Hamilcar, had endeavoured to indemnify themselves by making conquests and establishing a new empire in Spain. That country was inhabited by Iberians and Celts, who lived partly in separate districts, and partly mixed together under the name of Celtiberians. In some of the coast districts the Phoenicians and Greeks had already formed settlements. By a wise moderation and kind treatment, Hamilcar succeeded in attaching the natives to himself, though he neglected no precaution to insure their permanent fidelity. In B. C. 229, he fell in a bloody battle against the natives, leaving the command to his son-in-law Hasdrubal, who successfully pursued the same policy as his predecessor, and founded the town of New Carthage (Carthagena). The Romans, somewhat alarmed at the progress made by the Carthaginians in Spain, concluded a treaty with Hasdrubal, in which it was stipulated that they should not carry their conquests beyond the river Iberus. In B. C. 221, Hasdrubal was assassinated and succeeded by the great Hannibal, the son of Hamilcar, who had accompanied his father to Spain at the age of nine years, and had grown up in the camp under the eyes of his illustrious father, and in the midst of the greatest hardships.

13. Hannibal is one of the greatest generals of all ages and countries, and ought not to be judged of by the partial and prejudiced account which Livy gives of him. Immediately after his accession, he engaged in war with some tribes, and succeeded in conquering Spain as far as the Iberus, except the town of Saguntum, which is said to have been allied with the Romans. Availing himself of some dispute between it and a neighbouring tribe, he at once proceeded in B. C. 219, to lay siege to the town. Roman ambassadors in vain called on him to abstain from hostilities; he referred them to the senate at Carthage. Q. Fabius, the spokesman of the embassy, met with no better success at Carthage, for although the aristocratic party, headed by Hanno, was thoroughly opposed · to a war with Rome, the friends of Hannibal and the popular party refused to take their victorious general to account, or to recall him. Fabius, at length, making a fold of his toga, said, " Here I bring

you peace and war; take whichever you please." When the answer was, "Give us whichever you please," he, unfolding his toga, replied, " Well, then, I offer you war." War was thus declared. The inhabitants of Saguntum maintained themselves with the greatest fortitude against the besiegers, but after eight months of a most heroic defence, the town was taken and reduced to a heap of ruins. The inhabitants were partly buried under the ruins of their houses, and partly killed themselves by rushing into the fire which they had kindled in the market-place to destroy their remaining property; the survivors were put to the sword.

<center>~~~~~~~~~~~~~~~~~~~~~~~~~~~~~~~~~~~~~~~</center>

CHAPTER VIII.

THE SECOND PUNIC WAR, THE FIRST AND SECOND MACEDONIAN WARS, AND THE WAR AGAINST ANTIOCHUS.

1. AT the time when war was declared against Carthage, the Romans were still engaged in Illyricum, and the war against the Gauls had only just been brought to a close, whence we cannot be much surprised at finding that they did not at once act with the energy and quickness which they usually manifested on such occasions. Hannibal, on the other hand, assembling his troops at New Carthage, intrusted the supreme command in Spain to his brother Hasdrubal, while he himself, in the beginning of the summer of B. C. 218, crossed the Iberus with an army of ninety thousand foot, twelve thousand horse, and thirty-seven elephants; but before crossing the Pyrenees, he allowed all those who were unwilling to accompany him on his gigantic expedition, to return. By this means his forces were reduced to fifty thousand foot, and nine thousand horse. On his passage through Gaul he met with no opposition until he reached the river Rhone, the passage of which he had to force against hosts of Gauls drawn up against him on the eastern bank. He then began his ever memorable march across the Alps, by the Little St. Bernard, during which he and his army had to struggle with indescribable difficulties. When at length he arrived on the southern side of the Alps in the valley of Aosta, his forces were reduced to twenty thousand foot and six thousand horse; but though worn out, they were all soldiers on whom the great general could place full reliance. The passage of the Alps had been effected in fifteen days, and his arrival in Italy was hailed by the Gauls, who implored his protection against Rome.

2. When the Romans received intelligence of Hannibal's design

to cross the Alps, they sent the consul P. Cornelius Scipio with an army and fleet to Gaul, and his colleague Sempronius Longus with another army to Sicily. Scipio arrived in Gaul when Hannibal had already crossed the Rhone. Without, therefore, effecting anything of consequence, he slowly returned to Italy, and did not arrive on the banks of the Po until Hannibal had already descended from the Alps. The hostile armies met first on the banks of the Ticinus, and afterwards on those of the Trebia, and in each of these engagements the Romans were defeated, and Scipio himself received a severe wound in that on the Ticinus. Hannibal spent the winter in Lombardy, and in the beginning of B. C. 217 he with incredible difficulty crossed the Appenines into Etruria. On the banks of lake Trasimenus, the consul C. Flaminius, anxious to defend the road to Rome, met the Carthaginian army, and on a foggy morning a fearful battle was fought, in which no less than fifteen thousand Romans perished. Flaminius himself was among the slain, and the rest escaped to an Etruscan village. Another detachment which had been sent to assist the consul was likewise cut to pieces or taken prisoners. Hannibal's policy from the first was by kind treatment of the Italians to win their attachment, and induce them to throw off the yoke of Rome; but, as we shall see, hereafter, he had miscalculated: the Italian allies, and more especially the Roman and Latin colonies throughout Italy, remained faithful. This he experienced immediately after the battle of lake Trasimenus, for when he attacked Spoletium, the town offered a brave defence, and Hannibal, abandoning the place, marched along the eastern coast of Italy, through the countries inhabited by Sabellian tribes, towards Apulia, in the hope of arousing the nations of southern Italy against their rulers.

3. The news of the battle of Lake Trasimenus had thrown Rome into the greatest consternation. Q. Fabius Maximus, honourably surnamed the Slack (Cunctator), was immediately appointed dictator, for it was expected that Hannibal would march straightway against Rome. But finding that he had taken a different road, Fabius followed him at every step, but cautiously avoided giving battle, though he endeavoured to gain every possible advantage when opportunity offered. Near Casilinum, the prudence of Fabius, and a mistake on the part of Hannibal's guide, placed the latter in so difficult a position, that he extricated himself only by a stratagem, causing bundles of wood to be fastened to the horns of two thousand oxen, which were then driven in the night with the faggots blazing towards the Romans. The latter, terrified by the sight, quitted their favourable position, and thereby enabled the enemy to escape. Hannibal spent the winter in Apulia, and was greatly disappointed at finding that he was not yet joined by any of the Italian nations. The Romans began to be dissatisfied with the excessive

28 *

caution of Fabius, and for the year B. c. 216, appointed C. Terentius Varro, a man of a directly opposite character, to the consulship, along with L. Æmilius Paulus. They were expected to put an end to the war at one blow; they entered Apulia with an army of eighty thousand foot and six thousand horse, and pitched their camp near the little town of Cannae. The terrible defeat which the Romans sustained there at once showed them how wise had been the policy of Fabius. Forty-seven thousand Romans covered the field of battle; the consul Æmilius Paulus and eighty senators were among the slain. Varro escaped with only a few horsemen to Venusia. This day of Cannae was marked in the Roman calendar as a day equally disastrous with that on which they had been defeated by the Gauls on the Allia.

4. But although Rome was humbled, her spirit was not broken; and proposals for ransoming the prisoners, or concluding a peace, were indignantly rejected. Hannibal, after his victory, moved towards Capua, and at once reaped the fruits of his success in being joined by a number of Italians. Capua, next to Rome the greatest and wealthiest city of Italy, likewise openly declared for him, though its relation to Rome had been extremely favourable. He took up his winter quarters among his new allies at Capua, and his stay there forms the turning point in his career, which had hitherto been so glorious, and that too notwithstanding the numerous allies he had gained, and the reinforcements he had received from Carthage. The Romans made incredible efforts, and even enlisted a body of eight thousand slaves. In B. c. 215, Hannibal sustained considerable loss in an attack upon the fortified camp of M. Claudius Marcellus at Nola, and another great advantage was gained by Tib. Sempronius Gracchus near Beneventum. The confidence of the Romans was revived by these successes, and they now laid siege to Capua, which was forsaken by Hannibal, who lingered in Apulia and Lucania. At length, however, he advanced to the relief of Capua, but as the Romans declined a battle, he proceeded towards Rome, and pitched his camp near its very gates. A detachment from the besieging army at Capua was recalled, and battle was offered to Hannibal, but he, satisfied with having ravaged the country, returned to Capua which was still blockaded, and thence to Rhegium.

5. In the year of the battle of Cannae, Hiero, the faithful ally of the Romans, had died; and his successor Hieronymus, ceasing to fear Rome after her defeat, negotiated with Hannibal, who gladly accepted the proposal of an alliance. But Hieronymus was murdered by his own subjects, and two usurpers, who assumed the supreme power, treated Rome in the same way as their predecessor. The consequence was, that in B. c. 214, an army under M. Claudius Marcellus sailed across to Sicily, and laid siege to Syracuse, which

siege continued until B. C. 212, when the Romans became masters
of the place by treachery. The Syracusans, assisted by the mathematical and mechanical skill of Archimedes, defended themselves
bravely, and for this they had to pay dearly in the cruel treatment
they experienced at the hands of their conquerors. The greatness
and splendour of Syracuse were destroyed for ever, and the great
mathematician was murdered while pursuing his scientific studies.
All Sicily now again fell into the hands of the Romans. Hannibal
tried to make up for this loss by the conquest of Tarentum and
some other places in southern Italy. But it was all of no avail;
the genius of Rome was in the ascendant, and in the year after,
B. C. 211, Capua was taken. Its inhabitants were treated with true
Roman cruelty, and twenty-seven senators made away with themselves, while others killed their wives and children to save them
from inhuman treatment by the Romans. Two years after this,
B. C. 209, Tarentum was recovered by Fabius Maximus. This and
the cruel treatment inflicted on Syracuse and Capua intimidated
most of the Greek towns in Italy so much, that they abandoned the
cause of Hannibal. The Carthaginian now set his only hope on the
succours which he expected from his brother Hasdrubal in Spain.

6. At the very beginning of the war in B. C. 218, Cn. Cornelius
Scipio had been sent to Spain to oppose Hasdrubal, and had soon
after been joined by his brother Publius. The two Scipios remained in Spain for a number of years, ever harassing and checking
the Carthaginians. They not only prevented Hasdrubal from sending reinforcements to Hannibal, but even defeated him in several
battles. At the same time they formed connections with an African
chief Syphax, who then attacked Carthage. But in the year B. C.
212, the two Scipios were slain in battle within thirty days of each
other, and their armies were nearly annihilated. The Romans lost
all their possessions in Spain on the south-east of the Iberus, and
Hasdrubal made preparations to join his brother in Italy. At
Rome, no one was bold enough to undertake the command of a new
army in Spain, till young P. Cornelius Scipio, the son of P. Cornelius Scipio who had lately been slain in Spain, offered to do so,
though he was only twenty-four years old. This young man, in
every respect a most remarkable person, was scarcely inferior as a
general to Hannibal himself, and afterwards gained the imperish-
able glory of putting an end to the war. Immediately on his arrival
in Spain, B. C. 211, things took a different turn, and in his second
campaign, he took New Carthage, the most important possession
of the Carthaginians. By mildness and kindness he secured the
attachment of many of the Spanish chiefs, and his authority and
influence became so great that he quite eclipsed Hasdrubal, who
was defeated by him in B. C. 209, in a great battle near Baecula.
But notwithstanding this discomfiture. Hasdrubal ventured at length

to carry out his scheme of joining Hannibal in Italy. In B. C. 207, he arrived on the southern side of the Alps, and after some delay in Lombardy, marched through eastern Italy to join his brother in Apulia, but he was opposed by the consul C. Claudius Nero. Hasdrubal, while attempting to cross the river Metaurus in Umbria, was attacked by the Romans by night. He himself was killed, and his army, unacquainted with the locality, was entirely cut to pieces before Hannibal even knew of his arrival, for all letters had been intercepted. A Roman cut off the head of Hasdrubal, and on the return of the army to Apulia, flung it into the camp of Hannibal. This was the first intelligence which Hannibal received of his brother's misfortune, and in it he read his own fate.

7. After these occurrences, Hannibal confined himself to a defensive attitude in the country of the Bruttians, who still remained faithful to him. In this isolated and deserted condition, without assistance from home, and without allies in Italy, he displayed the greatest heroism; he maintained himself for several years, and whoever attacked him had to pay dearly for it. After the departure of Hasdrubal from Spain, the Carthaginians still had two armies there; but their commanders were not able to cope with Scipio, who gradually drove them out of Spain, and made himself master of the whole of the southern part of the peninsula. Scipio remained in Spain for several years, partly engaged in chastising the rebellious tribes, and partly in organising the administration of the conquered country. He also renewed the connection with Syphax, and concluded a treaty with him. After this, he went to Rome, where, notwithstanding his youth, he was elected consul for the year B C. 205. He had, however, many powerful enemies, and the cautious senate did not approve of his proposal to make a descent upon Africa. Sicily was assigned to him as his province, and he obtained permission to sail to Africa, if he thought it advantageous for the republic. The means placed at his disposal were very scanty, but the enthusiasm of the people in all Italy was so great, that he was plentifully provided with everything by their voluntary contributions. He established himself at Syracuse, and took Locri in southern Italy.

8. When all preparations had been made, Scipio in B. C. 204 crossed over into Africa. Syphax, from jealousy of the Numidian king Masinissa, had joined the Carthaginians, while Masinissa went over to the Romans. With his assistance Scipio, not far from Utica, set fire to the camp of Syphax and the Carthaginians, which consisted of tents made of straw and dry branches; and great havoc was made among the enemies. Syphax fled to his own kingdom, but was pursued and taken prisoner. His wife Sophonisbe, who had caused the jealousy between him and Masinissa, was now given to the latter; but afterwards when Scipio, who did not trust her,

demanded her surrender, Masinissa poisoned her. The last hope of Carthage now rested upon Hannibal, and a message was forthwith sent to summon him to return to Carthage. He obeyed the call without hesitation, but with a heavy heart, B. c 202. Soon after his arrival he had an interview with Scipio, and both commanders were willing to come to terms ; but the Carthaginian people, elated by the mere presence of their great general, resolved once more to try the fortune of arms. The battle of Zama, in B. c. 202, decided between the two nations. The Carthaginians fought with the courage of despair ; but the day was lost, and the greater part of their army cut to pieces. Hannibal himself escaped with only a few companions, and advised his countrymen to submit to necessity and accept the terms of peace offered by Scipio. Carthage was obliged to surrender all Roman deserters and prisoners without ransom, to give up its whole fleet with the exception of ten ships; to promise to abstain from war with foreign states without the sanction of Rome, to indemnify Masinissa for his losses, and to pay the enormous sum of ten thousand talents by fifty yearly instalments. This peace was ratified at Rome in B. c. 201; Scipio then returned to Rome in triumph, and was henceforth distinguished by the honourable surname of Africanus.

9. After the peace Hannibal shewed that he was not less great as a statesman and politician than as a general ; for he did all he could to heal up the wounds of his country by wise reforms in the administration. But not only did the Romans exert their influence to undermine his authority, but his own countrymen began to distrust him, so that the greatest man of his age was at last obliged to quit his country as an exile, B. c. 196, and seek protection at the court of an eastern despot, Antiochus the Great, king of Syria. His hatred of the Romans, however, remained as unquenchable as his love of his own country. The Roman republic, notwithstanding the fearful losses it had sustained, and notwithstanding the enormous devastations which Italy had experienced during the long war, came forth from the struggle more powerful than ever. She had conquered Spain, and Carthage and Numidia were virtually in a state of dependence on her. Their non-Italian possessions now obliged the Romans to keep a fleet; their name was known far and wide, and foreign states and princes eagerly sought their friendship and alliance.

10. During the time of the second Punic war, Macedonia was governed by the young and talented, but faithless and licentious king Philip. His fears of the Romans had been already excited by the influence they had acquired in the east of the Adriatic after the Illyrian wars, and these feelings were fostered by Demetrius of Pharos. After the battle of Cannae, when the power of Rome seemed to be broken, he concluded a treaty with Hannibal, in

which all the countries on the east of the Adriatic were secured to Philip, while Carthage was to rule over the west. But the document containing the treaty fell into the hands of the Romans, who at once adopted energetic measures to prevent the Macedonian king from sending succour to Hannibal. Philip, on the other hand, instead of trying to support his great ally, spent his time in useless struggles with the friends of the Romans in Asia Minor and Greece. A petty war was thus carried on for a period of ten years, from B. C. 215 to 205, during which neither party gained any great advantage. A peace was then concluded, in which neither the Romans nor the Macedonians had any honest intentions, for Rome having to make every effort against the Carthaginians could not afford at the same time to continue the war against Macedonia with vigour, and wished to postpone more active measures until the close of the Hannibalian war. The second war against Macedonia broke out in B. C. 200, because Philip had ravaged Attica, which was allied with Rome. This war was first carried on with little energy on the part of the Romans, and Philip, supported by the Achaean league and other Greek states, was successful for a time, but when T. Quinctius Flamininus in B. C. 198 undertook the command, and with extraordinary boldness attacked the enemy in his own country, things assumed a different aspect. In the battle of Cynoscephalae the Romans gained a complete victory over Philip, who was now obliged to conclude a peace, in which he recognised the independence of Greece, gave up a great part of his fleet, paid a large sum of money, and gave hostages as security for his future conduct. This peace was concluded in B. C. 197, and the year after Flamininus solemnly proclaimed the liberty and independence of Greece at the Isthmian games.

11. The rejoicing of the Greeks knew no bounds, but it soon became evident that they had only made a change of masters, the Romans having stepped into the place of the Macedonians. The enthusiasm for their liberators gradually subsided, and the rude Ætolians, being hostile to the Romans, partly because they did not consider themselves sufficiently rewarded for their services, and partly because they hated Nabis, the tyrant of Sparta, who had been too gently treated by the Romans, stirred up Antiochus the Great to a war against Rome. In this attempt they were supported by Hannibal, who was then staying at the king's court. The king himself, moreover, had been offended by the Romans, who demanded that he should restore the Greek states in Asia Minor to independence, and renounce his possessions in Thrace. Accordingly, in B. C. 192, on the invitation of the Ætolians, Antiochus crossed over into Europe; but instead of following the advice of Hannibal, to ally himself with Philip of Macedonia and attack the Romans in Italy, he wasted his time in festivities and amusements in Euboea, and

offended Philip, while the Romans rapidly advanc'd into Thessaly. In B. C. 191 Antiochus and the Ætolians were met at Thermopylae by the Romans under M. 'Acilius Glabrio, and were put to flight without any great struggle. The Ætolians now sued for and obtained pe;ce, for the Romans were desirous to continue the war against Antiochus in Asia, whither he had fled after his defeat.

12. In B. C. 190, a Roman army, under the command of C. Laelius and L. Cornelius Scipio (who was accompanied by his brother P. Scipio Africanus), crossed over into Asia with an army of twenty thousand men. As the haughty king still refused to accept the terms offered by the Romans, a great battle was fought near Magnesia, at the foot of mount Sipylus, in which the hosts of the Syrians were unable to resist the Roman legions. After the loss of this battle Antiochus fled to Syria and sued for peace, which was granted to him on condition that he should renounce all his possessions in Asia west of mount Taurus, give up all his ships of war, and pay a large sum of money. He was, moreover, required not to interfere in the affairs of the allies of Rome, and to deliver up Hannibal. This peace was not ratified at Rome until B. C. 188. The countries in Asia ceded by the Syrian king (including Galatia, which was conquered soon after), were, for the present, distributed among the allies of Rome, such as the Rhodians and Eumenes of Pergamus, for the time had not yet come when it was thought desirable to constitute them as a Roman province. Hannibal finding that his life was not safe in Syria, sought and found protection with Prusias, king of Bithynia; but when this prince also was unable to protect him against the restless persecution of the Romans, the unhappy Carthaginian poisoned himself B. C. 183. His conqueror Scipio Africanus died about the same time; he too spent the last years of his life in a kind of exile, into which he had been driven by the envy and jealousy of his enemies, though he had in some measure to blame his own overbearing haughtiness.

13. While the Romans were thus engaged in making vast conquests in the East, the peace had been disturbed in the north of Italy by the Ligurians, Insubrians, and Boians, who commenced hostilities in B. C. 200, and continued them until B. C. 181. In the course of this war, during which many a bloody battle was fought, these nations were compelled to submit to Rome, and the Boians seem to have been completely extirpated. In Spain, too, the Romans were obliged to maintain their dominion sword in hand, for, after the departure of Scipio, the cruelty and faithlessness of the Romans often drove the Spaniards into rebellion and insurrection. A great war broke out there in B. C. 181, and continued to rage until B. C. 179, when Tib. Sempronius Gracchus, the father of the two celebrated tribunes, concluded a fair and honourable peace, which was long and gratefully remembered by the Spaniards.

CHAPTER IX.

FROM THE THIRD WAR AGAINST MACEDONIA DOWN TO THE TIME OF THE GRACCHI.

1. THOUGH Philip of Macedonia had assisted the Romans in the war against Antiochus, still he cherished an implacable hatred of them, and when in B. C. 179 he died, he bequeathed the same feelings to his successor Perseus, who, being an illegitimate son, had by intrigues and calumnies induced his father to put to death his lawful son Demetrius. No sooner had Perseus ascended the throne than he began to form new alliances, and make preparations for a conflict with Rome, for which his father had left him ample means. But the unwillingness he felt to part with his treasures, and his ill-judged measures, after some momentary advantages, brought about his downfall. When defeated by Æmilius Paulus at Pydna in B. C. 168, he fell into the hands of the Romans, and, together with his children, treasures, and friends, was led in triumph through the streets of Rome. Macedonia was now divided into four independent districts, with republican institutions, and made tributary to Rome.[1] By this dismemberment, the unity, and with it the strength of the country, was broken.

2. Greece, too, distracted as it was by treachery, intrigues, and party feuds, was hastening towards its final dissolution. Shortly after the battle of Pydna, one thousand of the most illustrious Achaeans, charged with having secretly supported Perseus, were sent to Italy to be tried. Among them was the great historian Polybius. But instead of being allowed to account for their conduct, they were kept as hostages and prisoners. After seventeen years, B. C. 151, when death had reduced their number to three hundred, they were permitted to return to their country. A similar charge was brought against the wealthy and powerful island of Rhodes, which, in consequence, lost its Asiatic possessions, and was obliged to recognize the supremacy of Rome. About nineteen years after the battle of Pydna, B. C. 149, Andriscus, a runaway slave, came forward, and, pretending to be a son of the late king Perseus, claimed the throne of Macedonia. Many Macedonians flocked around his standard, being encouraged by the outbreak of a third war against Carthage, in which it was hoped that Rome would be defeated. But the praetor Q. Caecilius Metellus crushed the pretender and his followers, in B. C. 148, in a battle near Pydna. Some years after this, Macedonia was constituted as a Roman province.

[1] Compare p. 268, foll.

8. Metellus was still engaged in Macedonia when the Romans called upon the Achaeans to dismiss Lacedaemon and several other cities from their confederacy; the Achaeans assembled at Corinth treated the Roman ambassadors, who communicated this demand, with insult and violence. This act led to a war,[1] and in B. C. 147, Metellus, after settling the affairs of Macedonia, advanced southward, and defeated the Achaeans in two battles, at Thermopylae, and at Scarpheia in Locris. But he was obliged to leave the honour of bringing the war to a close to the rude L. Mummius, who, after a victory at Leucopetra on the Isthmus, took and destroyed the wealthy city of Corinth B. C. 146, and then traversed Greece, but especially Peloponnesus, spreading desolation wherever he appeared. The inhabitants of Corinth and other places were partly put to the sword, and partly sold as slaves; the treasures of art were ruthlessly destroyed, or carried away to Rome, to adorn the palaces and villas of the nobles. Greece, however, does not appear to have been made a Roman province, under the name of Achaia, till many years later. Under the oppressive administration of the Romans, the prosperity of the once flourishing little states gradually died away, and scarcely a trace was left of the ancient patriotism and love of liberty. The Spartans continued to indulge their warlike propensities by serving as mercenaries in the armies of foreign powers, while the Athenians continued to be valued by the Romans as scholars, artists, poets, actors, and dancers, who contributed to the entertainment and amusement of their haughty conquerors, though they rarely succeeded in gaining their esteem and respect. As a seat of learning, however, Athens continued to maintain its rank as one of the principal places in the ancient world, to which men, fond of ease and letters, flocked from all parts, as to a great university.

4. The peace which Carthage had concluded with Rome in B. C. 201, lasted for more than half a century, during which period the Carthaginians, by industry, commerce, and agriculture, to some extent recovered their former prosperity. But this prosperity only gave fresh fuel to the national hatred of the Romans, and excited their jealousy and fear. Masinissa, the neighbour of Carthage, who enjoyed the favour of the Romans, and seems even to have been instigated by them, neglected no opportunity of harassing and annoying the reviving state. The Roman Cato, who was infatuated by a blind hatred of Carthage, partly perhaps because the Carthaginians had rejected his proffered mediation between them and Masinissa, and partly from a real, though unfounded fear of the growing power of Carthage, urged in every speech he made in the senate the necessity of crushing the African republic. Masinissa, who well knew the feelings of the party at Rome hostile to Carthage, and was sure not only of impunity, but of support and pro-

[1] Compare p. 270, foll.

tection, increased his own dominion at the expense of Carthage, and by constant disputes and vexations drove the Carthaginians to the necessity of defending their rights by force of arms, because Rome, when appealed to, either delayed pronouncing sentence, or decided in favour of the aggressor. The Romans, gladly seizing the opportunity, charged the Carthaginians with having broken the peace. The people of Carthage implored their mercy; and to assure them that they had no hostile intentions, they not only sent three hundred of their noblest citizens as hostages to Rome, but delivered up all their ships and arms. This happened in B. C. 149; and when all this was done, the Romans further demanded that Carthage should be razed to the ground, and that the inhabitants should build a new town for themselves at a distance of many miles from the sea. The treacherous and insolent nature of this demand drove the people to despair and madness; they resolved to perish under the ruins of their own houses rather than yield to such insolence. A bold, patriotic spirit seized all ranks and all ages, and the women cheerfully sacrificed all their finery upon the altar of their country. The whole city was at once changed into a military camp, temples were transformed into manufactories of arms, and nothing was spared that could serve to deliver the country from its impending doom. Such a spirit was too much even for the Roman legions, accustomed as they were to conquest and victory. Several times they were repulsed, and thrown into such a perilous condition, that at last the Romans found it necessary to appoint P. Cornelius Scipio Æmilianus, the son of Æmilius Paulus, who had been adopted into the family of the Scipios, to the consulship for B. C. 147. He had not yet attained the age to qualify him for the consulship, but he had already given proofs of the highest military talent. Even he, however, was not able to take the city, which offered a most desperate resistance, until the inhabitants were reduced by the most fearful famine, and even then he had to conquer every inch of ground, during a murderous fight in the streets of Carthage, which lasted for six days, B. C. 146. The fury of the enraged soldiers, and a conflagration which continued without interruption for seventeen days, changed the once proud mistress of the Mediterranean into a heap of ruins. A small number of determined Carthaginians, who had manfully defended the temple of Æsculapius, the highest point in the city, when they saw that all was hopeless, set fire to the temple, and found their death in the flames. Fifty thousand inhabitants, who escaped from the carnage, are said to have been sold into slavery by Scipio, who, from this conquest, like his great namesake, obtained the surname Africanus. The territory of Carthage was changed into the Roman province of Africa, and a curse was pronounced upon the site of the ancient city, that it might never be rebuilt.

5. Rome had now become virtually the mistress of all the countries round the basin of the Mediterranean, for the few states, such as Numidia, Egypt, and Pergamus, which still enjoyed a nominal independence, were destined at no distant period to lose even this appearance of freedom, for Rome had become conscious that she must rule the world. This destiny of Rome, however, was not the effect of any settled plan of her rulers or statesmen; it was rather the result of circumstances, and she was forced, often very reluctantly, for the sake of her own peace and safety, to con tinue her conquests at an inconvenient distance. We have seen that newly conquered countries were sometimes not even retained, but given to those who had assisted Rome in conquering them. But great as was the prosperity abroad, at home the cancer of poverty was eating deeply into the vital parts of the state, while the upper classes indulged in every kind of foreign luxury. The political constitution had been finally fixed long ago, and the difference between patricians and plebeians was no longer thought of. But although not recognised by law, a new aristocracy (*nobiles, optimates*) had arisen which based its claims upon wealth, and more especially upon family honours; that is, those who could boast of a long list of ancestors who had been invested with the great offices of the republic looked upon themselves as being entitled to the same honours, whereas those who had no such ancestors to refer to were virtually almost excluded, and stigmatised by the name of obscure persons (*obscuri*); and if any such person succeeded in raising himself to the highest dignity, he was styled an upstart (*novus homo*). Henceforth, therefore, the struggle in the republic was between the rich and the poor, between those who were in possession of all the material and political powers, and those who possessed neither, but were anxious to secure, at least, the means of living.

6. Ever since the Romans had formed connections with the Greeks in southern Italy, and still more after the Illyrian and Macedonian wars, the intellectual superiority of the Greeks had manifested its influence in all the departments of public and private life. Greek gods and Greek forms of worship were adopted at a very early period, and threw many parts of the ancient national or Italian religion so much into the shade, that they became mere matters of antiquarian curiosity, whose meaning and import were forgotten. Greek education and an acquaintance with Greek arts and literature were regarded as necessary by the best among the Roman families, and no one can say to what this hellenizing spirit might have led, had it not been checked by a party which still clung tenaciously to the ancient and simple ways of their ancestors. This party was headed by M. Porcius Cato, who in his censorship manfully struggled against the prevailing fashion, and made his name proverbial as *Cato censorius*. The foreign influence which he combated showed itself not only in education and in literature, which was at first little more than translation and adaptation from the Greek, but extended over the whole life of the Romans, and was seen in the luxuries of dress and of the table, in the affectation of polished manners, and in sensual enjoyments; for along with the riches of the East the conquerors also imported its follies and vices. In B. C. 155 Cato carried a decree ordering the three Greek philosophers, Carneades, Diogenes, and Critolaus, who had been sent to Rome as ambassadors from Athens, and attracted crowds of young men to their lectures, to quit the city. Long before this time it had been found necessary to prohibit the celebration of the Bacchic festivals (*Bacchanalia*), which had been introduced from southern Italy and formed a focus for every vice and licentiousness. Cato endeavoured to counteract the evil tendency not only by legal enactments, but by literary productions, such as his works on agriculture, the foundation of Rome's greatness, and on the Italian nations, whose history formed as strong a contrast to that of Rome in his time, as his own frugal and simple mode of life, and his old-fashioned cheerfulness in his social circles, did to the lavish extravagance and fashionable refinement of his opponents. But still the very example of Cato, who himself commenced the study of Greek in his old age, shows that obstinate partiality for what is old and established must ultimately give way to the onward movement which nothing can completely stop.

7. The wealth carried to Italy after the Punic, Macedonian, and Syrian wars was immense, and exercised the greatest influence upon the manners and morality of the Romans. The families from whom the highest magistrates and generals were taken, accumulated such enormous riches, as to be able to live more like princes than plain citizens of the republic. Their humble dwellings were exchanged for stately villas surrounded by parks and filled with the most costly furniture and the most precious works of art, of which they had stripped the conquered countries and cities. In the acquisition of these treasures they were not very scrupulous as to the means employed, whence the constant complaints about bribery, avarice, and oppression in the provinces. The ladies especially, who possessed much more influence at Rome than in Greece, indulged in extravagant luxuries and dress, against which the laws proved powerless. The immorality and degeneracy of the wealthy were but too soon communicated to the great body of the people. The ancient and frugal mode of life, as well as the laborious pursuit of agriculture, was more and more abandoned. The young men preferred military service abroad where their toil was rewarded with wealth and enjoyment, to the peaceful employments at home; the soldiers always liked best to serve under a commander who was willing to allow them the greatest licence, and as his elevation depended upon their

votes in the assembly, the men aspiring to high offices neglected no means of gaining popularity, however immoral or illegal they might be. This hunting after popularity was, and remained, one of the most fatal disorders of the Roman republic. The wealthy vied with one another to win the favour of the multitude by splendid games and exhibitions, of which the Romans were always passionately fond; and by this means the people were demoralised and corrupted. Their sense of honour was stifled, and with it the source of virtue dried up. The public games exhibited at Rome for the amusement of the multitude show that the influence of Greek culture had affected only the surface of the great body of the Romans; for while in Greece the national games were a stimulus to great and noble efforts in war and in peace, the gladiatorial and animal fights of the Roman circus produced and could produce no other effect than that of fostering a delight in cruelty and bloodshed, and of familiarising the people with scenes that ought to have filled them with disgust and horror.

8. Reckless extravagance was indulged in not only by the wealthy but also by the poorer classes, so that Rome has not unfitly been called "an abyss which no treasures were able to fill up." The natural consequence was poverty and distress, with all the evils that generally accompany them. Usurers filled their coffers from the misery of thousands, who, notwithstanding their wretched condition, looked upon themselves as the lords of the earth, and treated with contempt those unfortunate foreigners whom war had reduced to slavery. A most lucrative trade was at this time carried on in slaves, and some of the best among the Romans did not disdain to enrich themselves by the odious traffic. The rude and half-savage natives of Sardinia and Corsica (probably Ligurians mixed with Iberians), who were employed for coarse labour, were sold at a very low price, while the more educated and refined Greeks and Asiatics, who served as secretaries, readers, teachers, tutors, and domestic servants, often fetched very high prices in the market. But notwithstanding all these symptoms of internal decay, Rome's outward prosperity was ever increasing, and the great public works, highroads, canals, and aqueducts, are sufficient attestations of the lofty spirit and persevering energy of this wonderful people.

9. The optimates, amassing their wealth chiefly in the provinces, were ever eager for fresh wars and conquests. When appointed governors of foreign provinces under the title of proconsul or praetor, they generally looked more to their own interests than to the welfare of the provincials. As the Roman government did not itself levy the taxes in the provinces, but left this duty to wealthy capitals (*publicani*), who paid to the state a stipulated sum, and then obtained the right either themselves or through their agents to collect the taxes and duties, a wide field for extortion and cruel

29 *

oppression was left open, and the most enormous sums were carried to Italy from the provinces. What was left by the publicani was speedily absorbed by hungry usurers and money-lenders, who usually inundated a country as soon as it became a Roman province; hence a few years were often sufficient to ruin the prosperity of a whole country. There existed, it is true, laws against extortion (*de repetundis*) in the provinces, and provincials might seek redress from the Roman senate; but as the judges were taken from the senators, who either had been guilty of the same crime, or were looking forward to similar opportunities of enriching themselves, the accused generally escaped unpunished, or were sentenced, for the sake of appearance, to pay a small fine.

10. Sometimes the misrule of the governors and the extortion of the publicani drove the provincials into despair and rebellion. The first instances of this kind occurred in Lusitania in Spain, where Ser. Sulpicius Galba, after having suffered a severe defeat, by his avarice and cruelty called forth a general insurrection. Galba treacherously causing the people to appear before him without arms, ordered them all to be massacred. Viriathus, a common Lusitanian, but a brave and patriotic soldier, who escaped on that fearful day, rallied round him as many of his countrymen as he could, and for a period of eight years, from B. C. 148 to 140, carried on a war which was most disastrous to the Romans. In B. C. 141 a peace was concluded with him, in which the Romans were obliged to recognise him as their friend and ally; but regarding this as an intolerable humiliation, they renewed the war in the year following, and got rid of their enemy only by hiring assassins, who murdered him in his own tent. The Lusitanians continued the war for a few years longer, but were in the end obliged to submit, B. C. 137.

11. Even before this war was brought to a close, another had broken out with the Celtiberians in B. C. 143. Their capital was Numantia, a city renowned in the history of Spain for the brave and noble resistance it offered to the valour of the Roman legions. It was situated on a lofty eminence on the upper Durius, and held out against the besieging and blockading armies for a period of five years. In B. C. 137 the Numantines put the consul C. Hostilius Mancinus in a situation so perilous, that he was obliged to conclude a peace with them, in which their independence was recognised But the senate again resorted to the miserable expedient which had been adopted after the defeat of Claudium: Mancinus was to be delivered up to the Numantines, and the war to be resumed with renewed vigour. The brave mountaineers remained undismayed, and for P. Cornelius Scipio, the destroyer of Carthage, was reserved the unenviable task of torturing to death the heroic citizens of Numantia. When he received the command of the Roman army, he

conduced the siege with the utmost vigour. The besieged suffered
from the most frightful famine, and for some time fed upon the
corpses of their fellow-citizens. At last, in B C. 133, they were
obliged to surrender, and having first killed their wives and children, they threw open the gates. Their number was very small,
and in consequence of their long sufferings, their features hardly
resembled those of human beings. Scipio then destroyed the
mountain fortress, the ruins of which, not far from Soria, are still
a monument of the noble struggle for freedom and independence.
Spain now became a Roman province, and being exhausted, remained quiet for more than thirty years, but fresh acts of oppression afterwards gave rise to new wars.

12. In the same year in which Numantia fell, Attalus, king of
Pergamus, died, and in his will bequeathed his kingdom to the
Roman people, probably in compliance with an express demand of
the senate. Soon afterwards, B. C. 131, Aristonicus, a relation of
the late king, came forward to claim the kingdom as his lawful
inheritance. Finding many supporters, he placed himself at the
head of a general insurrection of the Lydians and Ionians. The
war, in which the Romans sustained serious losses, was continued
into the year B. C. 130, when M. Perperna brought it to a close.
Aristonicus was taken prisoner and carried to Rome in triumph.
The kingdom of Pergamus, with the exception of Phrygia, which
was given to Mithridates V., king of Pontus, as a reward for his
assistance, was now constituted as a Roman province under the
name of Asia.

CHAPTER X.

FROM THE TIME OF THE GRACCHI DOWN TO THE FIRST WAR
AGAINST MITHRIDATES.

1. THE new aristocracy of the optimates, which had gradually
been formed after the two ancient estates of the patricians and plebeians had been placed upon a footing of political equality not only
endeavoured to exclude all *novi homines* from the great offices of
the republic, but also maintained themselves, like the patricians of
old, in the exclusive possession of the *ager publicus*, which in fact
they regarded as their private property, neither heeding the limita-
tion fixed by the Licinian law, nor particularly scrupulous about
paying the rent to the treasury. The number of these optimates
was comparatively small, but they held in their hands the adminis
tration of the republic and the provinces, and they alone earned

glory, wealth, and triumphs by foreign wars, while the great body of the people were oppressed by the constant necessity of serving in the armies, and were suffering from want, for the booty taken in war generally passed into the hands of the generals and other optimates. Nay, it would appear that in some instances the wealthy landed proprietor by fraud or violence deprived his weaker neighbour of his small patrimony, and reduced him and his family to beggary. In this manner the optimates amassed enormous riches, while multitudes were pining in abject poverty. The class of small landed proprietors, who once had constituted the strength of the republic, had almost entirely disappeared, and instead of them there had arisen a body of citizens without property, spending their life in idleness, and ready to sell their political birthright for miserable bribes. Their number had, moreover, been increased by the admission of strangers and freedom to the franchise. So long as the wealthy landed proprietors had cultivated their princely estates (*latifundia*) by free peasants or clients, no alarming symptoms showed themselves, because the impoverished husbandman might support himself and his family at least by working as an agricultural labourer; but when the avarice of the nobles led them to employ hordes of slaves on their estates instead of free labourers, who were now abandoned as homeless wanderers in their own country, a few of the nobler natures among the Romans began to feel uneasy, and were prompted by a feeling of humanity to devise a remedy for the ever increasing evil.

2. Formerly the people in the comitia had voted openly, but in B. C. 139 the Gabinian law introduced the vote by ballot in the election of magistrates, and two years later the same practice was extended by the Cassian law to the popular courts of law. By these measures the influence of the optimates over the poor became only more pernicious; the multitude became more venal, and the nobles had the best opportunities, by bribing or purchasing votes, and by manumitting their slaves, to carry the elections according to their own wishes and interests. These evils might have been remedied by creating an independent middle class, either by distributing the public land, of which the state possessed a vast amount, among the poor, or by conferring the full franchise upon the Latins. The latter of these remedies was unpalatable to the pride and ambition of the ruling people, and the former to the avarice and selfishness of the Roman nobility. The fears of the humane and truly patriotic citizens must have been increased by what was just happening in Sicily, where a war of the slaves, commanded by Eunus, one of their number, broke out in B. C. 134 against the free population, and was carried on with the horrors common in wars of slaves who break their chains. It raged for more than two years, and upwards of twenty thousand slaves are said to have been killed.

3. Occurrences like these, which showed to what disastrous consequences the present system, if persevered in, might ultimately
lead, emboldened the noble and patriotic tribune, Tib. Sempronius
Gracchus, a son of Cornelia, the daughter of the elder Scipio Africanus, in B. C. 133, to come forward as the friend and champion of
the poor. He proposed the re-enactment of the Licinian law, which
had, in fact, never been repealed, but had in the course of time
become a dead letter. No one, accordingly, was to be allowed to
possess more than five hundred jugera of public land; the surplus
was to be taken from the actual possessors, and distributed in small
lots as full property among poor citizens. A commission of three
men was to be appointed to superintend the measurement and distribution; and at the same time it was proposed that the property
which had just been bequeathed to the Roman people by king
Attalus of Pergamus, should be distributed among the poor to
enable them to purchase stock and the necessary agricultural implements. The optimates, headed by the violent and stubborn Scipio
Nasica, opposed the bill with all their might, and by intrigues induced another tribune, Octavius, to put his veto on the proposal of
his colleague, in which scheme they succeeded the more easily,
because Octavius, too, possessed more of the public land than the
law allowed. Gracchus left no means untried to induce his colleague to give up his opposition; but all was in vain; avarice and
the instigations of the optimates prevailed. Gracchus thus found
himself under the necessity of either giving up his noble and
patriotic scheme, or depriving his colleague of his powers. He
adopted the latter course, and in the assembly of the people, which
was numerously attended by men from the country, he proposed
the deposition of Octavius. This plan succeeded; Octavius was
stripped of his office, and a new tribune being elected in his stead,
the bill of Gracchus was passed. This procedure, which was contrary to established usage, gave his opponents a handle against him,
and they now endeavoured to persuade the people that Gracchus
aimed at subverting the constitution, and even spread the malicious
report that his object was to make himself king of Rome. The
people in their ignorance allowed themselves to be misguided, and
notwithstanding the purity of his intentions, Gracchus found that
his popularity was decreasing. When at the approaching election
of the tribunes for the next year he again presented himself as a
candidate, the optimates and their followers created a tumult, in
which the illustrious tribune was slain, together with three hundred of his friends and followers. These scenes of bloodshed were
followed by every kind of persecution, in which the nobles took
bloody revenge for the fears they had endured of being deprived of
their illegal possessions. During the night after the murder, Caius,
the brother of Tiberius Gracchus, wished to have the body of his

brother removed and decently buried, but was prevented; and before daybreak, it was thrown into the Tiber, together with those of all the others who had fallen during the tumult.

4. The aristocracy had gained a complete triumph, and made bloody use of it; but the tribunes also had become aware of their power, and the years which now follow are marked by several popular enactments. The triumvirs were to superintend the carrying into effect of the agrarian law, but the optimates continued to obstruct their working in every possible way, and contrived, by appointments abroad, to remove from the city those men whose spirit and energy they had most reason to dread. But all their machinations did not prevent C. Sempronius Gracchus, the younger and more talented brother of Tiberius Gracchus, after a lapse of ten years, from offering himself for the tribuneship. He was elected to the office for the year B. C. 123, in the course of which he carried a great many laws, all intended to improve the condition of the poor and to weaken the power of the senate and the nobles. One of them was a re-enactment of his brother's agrarian law. The popularity he thus acquired secured his re-election for the next year. He commenced his operations of the second year by an enactment, transferring the trial of political offences from the courts composed of senators to courts consisting of equites or wealthy capitalists. By this means, the offenders, generally senators, ceased to be tried by their peers, but became subject to courts composed of quite a different class of men, who seemed less likely to screen offenders or make justice a purchaseable article. This law remained in force until the time of Sulla. Gracchus' great eloquence and noble nature created for him a numerous and powerful party of supporters among the poorer classes, whose momentary wants he endeavoured to relieve by employing them in making public roads and constructing public buildings. His labours proceeded as satisfactorily as could be expected; but when, urged on by his somewhat vehement friend, Fulvius Flaccus, he proposed that the Roman franchise should be conferred upon the Italian allies, or at least, upon the Latins and Latin colonies, the optimates were seized with the greatest alarm, and resorted to an expedient which had been tried and found useful before. M. Livius Drusus, one of the tribunes, was gained over by the aristocrats and prevailed upon to outbid Gracchus in popular measures. He accordingly promised the people other and greater advantages, and by this means undermined the popularity of Gracchus; the aristocracy succeeded in preventing his re-election to the tribuneship for the third year, and even made preparations for a proposal to abolish all his enactments. As Gracchus was now divested of the sacred character of tribune, his opponents were less scrupulous. During the disturbances which arose, the consul L. Opimius, a personal enemy of Gracchus, was

invested with dictatorial power, to save the republic, as the cry was, from impending ruin. A battle was fought in the streets of Rome, and Gracchus and Fulvius Flaccus with their followers were over-powered. Flaccus and three thousand of his party were slain, and their bodies thrown into the Tiber. Gracchus escaped across the river into the grove of the Furies, where, at his own request, he was killed by a faithful slave. Exile, execution, and imprisonment then completed the work which had been left undone by the sword, and the aristocratic party, when satiated with blood, erected a temple to Concord! But peace was not restored, and the triumph achieved by the optimates was not of long duration: the measure of their misdeeds was not yet full.

5. The exertions and sacrifices made by the noble brothers were productive of no permanent good to the republic, and things went on much in the same way as they had done before. The optimates disgraced the victory they had won by insatiable avarice, acts of injustice, and the most barefaced bribery. But events were taking place destined soon to bring the evil to a head. The audacious and crafty Jugurtha, the adopted son of Masinissa, king of Numidia, knew the venal character of the Romans, and relying on their moral depravity, and feeling sure of impunity, murdered the two sons of Masinissa and took possession of their dominions. The Romans during these proceedings acted the part of mere lookers on, or allowed themselves by large bribes to be induced to connive at the crimes of Jugurtha. At length, however, the tribune C. Memmius gave vent to his indignation at the conduct of the nobles, and by exposing their conduct induced the senate in B. C. 111 to declare war against the Numidian usurper. An army was accordingly sent to Africa, but the commanders soon found out that they could derive greater personal advantages from negotiation and treating with Jugurtha, than from vigorously carrying out the decree of the senate. When these things became known at Rome, the honest and talented Memmius again came forward, and fearlessly exposed the shameless conduct of the Roman commanders in Africa. Jugurtha was summoned to Rome, but even now he might have escaped with impunity, had he not had the audacity to murder young Massiva, a grandson of Masinissa. The war was indeed continued, but it was conducted in a careless and slovenly manner, until at length, in B. C. 109, the senate endeavoured to allay the threatening storm, by giving the command against Jugurtha to the honest and brave, but proud Q. Caecilius Metellus. He managed the war for a period of two years in a highly creditable manner, and restored the honour of the Roman arms. But the people of Rome had lost confidence in their noble commanders.

6. When Metellus went to Africa, he took with him C. Marius as one of his lieutenants. This man was of humble parentage.

but of unbounded ambition, and full of hatred of the aristocracy, as well as of their polished manners and learning, of which it was his boast to be profoundly ignorant. Even before he went to Africa, he had attracted public attention by the vigorous manner in which he tried to secure the rights of the poorer classes against the encroachments of the optimates. His personal valour, and his talent as a military commander, were also generally known and acknowledged, and it was to him that the people of Rome seem to have been looking as the man who alone could and would bring the war against Jugurtha to a close. In B. c. 108 he formed the design of offering himself as a candidate for the consulship, and the insolent manner in which the proud Metellus received the announcement only fired his ambition; he therefore proceeded to Rome, where the popular party received him with the greatest enthusiasm. He obtained the consulship for B. c. 107, and the commission to proceed to Africa, as the successor of Metellus, and bring the war against Jugurtha to a termination. Marius, in forming his army, enlisted large numbers of the poorer classes and even freedmen, and having trained them well, his skill, bravery, and straightforwardness, were more than a match for the crafty Numidian. He was eminently successful, and reduced the enemy to such straits, that he was obliged to apply to Bocchus, his father-in-law, king of Mauritania, in the hope of stirring him up to a war against Rome. But L. Cornelius Sulla, a young noble, who was serving in the army of Marius as quaestor, induced Bocchus treacherously to deliver up his own son-in-law. Jugurtha was accordingly surrendered to Sulla, who forthwith delivered him up to the consul Marius. The war was thus terminated in B. c. 106, and Jugurtha, after adorning the triumph of Marius, died of starvation in a Roman dungeon.

7. Nothing could have been more fortunate for Rome, than this timely conclusion of the Numidian war, for Italy was threatened with an invasion of barbarians more terrible than any it had yet experienced. The Cimbri, a Celtic host, who had been pressed forward towards the west by commotions among the Sarmatians in the east, appeared in Noricum on the banks of the Danube, where they were joined by an equally numerous host of Teutones or Germans. This had happened in B. c. 113. The Cimbri, wandering about with their women and children, sought a new home in the western part of Europe, and promised to commit no act of hostility against either the Romans or their friends. They kept their promise; but being nevertheless treacherously attacked in the neighbourhood of Noreia, they completely defeated the Roman army, B. c. 113. After this, instead of invading Italy, they threw themselves into Gaul, being joined in Helvetia by other tribes. Gaul was fearfully ravaged, and scarcely any part of the country

was able to resist the invaders. In the course of four years, five consular armies were defeated by the barbarians on the Rhone and on the banks of the lake of Geneva. All Italy trembled as in the days of Hannibal; no one was anxious to obtain the consulship, and Marius was the only man to whom all looked with confidence. He had not yet returned from Numidia, but in his absence he was elected consul for the year B. C. 104, and the same dignity was conferred upon him in the four following years. Fortunately the Cimbri, after their victories over the Romans, invaded Spain, which they ravaged in the same manner as Gaul, but in B. C. 102 they returned to Gaul, where in the meantime the Teutones also had arrived.

8. Ever since his second consulship, Marius had exerted himself to train and discipline his army for the coming struggle, by accustoming the men to every kind of hardship. When the Cimbri arrived, Marius was with his army in Gaul, and fought a decisive battle in B. C. 102, near Aquae Sextiae (Aix), against the Teutones. After this defeat, the barbarians retreated to their waggons, but being unable to maintain themselves, the whole body was annihilated. Half the danger was now overcome; but the Cimbri were at the same time descending from the Raetian Alps into Italy, and the Roman army which was to oppose them under Q. Lutatius Catullus, was obliged to retreat before the invaders to the southern bank of the river Po. Marius, on being informed of this, hastened to the relief of his colleague, and in a place called the Campi Raudii, near Vercellae, he defeated in B. C. 101, the Cimbri as completely as he had the year before defeated the Teutones. Only a very small band escaped, who seem to have settled on the banks of the Meuse, where they were afterwards found by Julius Caesar. Marius was the deliverer of Italy, and the pride of the popular party; his sixth consulship, in B. C. 100, was the reward of his glorious victories, and under his auspices the democratic or popular party gained the upper hand.

9. The optimates, apprehensive of the growing power of their opponents, and of losing what they considered their rights, united under the leadership of Sulla, who was as ambitious as Marius, but combined in his person all the good and all the bad qualities of the Roman aristocracy. His connection with Marius in the Numidian war, and his success, had only increased the hatred of the popular leader against him. Marius, who had become giddy by his victories, acted in many respects as if he were the master of the republic. The lawless conduct of the infamous tribune, L. Appuleius Saturninus, who was supported by Marius, lorded it over the popular assembly by a band of followers, and endeavoured to increase the number of his own friends and party by a series of legislative enactments which were carried by force and violence. One of these

enactments ordained that the lands conquered by Marius in Gaul and Africa should be distributed among his veterans. The high-minded Q. Caecilius Metellus, who refused to be a party to the revolutionary schemes of Saturninus, was sent into exile; and Saturninus succeeded in raising himself twice to the tribuneship by causing his competitors to be murdered in broad daylight. At length, wishing to gain the consulship for Servilius Glaucia, one of his associates, he caused his competitor, the noble C. Memmius, to be murdered, B. C. 100. This and many other atrocious acts at length induced Marius to renounce his connection with Saturninus. Even his own party began to detest the monster, and when Marius called upon his fellow-citizens, they readily took up arms in the defence of the republic. Saturninus, Glaucia, and their followers, withdrew to the Capitol, where they were besieged; but want of water soon compelled them to surrender, and nearly all of them were put to death by command of Marius. After these horrible scenes, Marius himself for a time withdrew from public life, and the party strife seemed to subside. But the causes of discontent and disease were not removed, and every one capable of discerning the signs of the times must have looked forward with terror to the explosion which could not be far distant.

10. Sulla neglected no opportunity of wounding the already exasperated feelings of Marius. He was anxious to show that the honour of having brought the Numidian war to a close belonged to him alone, and that Marius had no share in it. But this and similar things were of minor importance. Far weightier matters were agitating the minds of thinking men. The reform introduced by Gracchus in the composition of the courts of justice had proved a complete failure, as the equites were found to be as accessible to bribes as the senators had been; the number of the poor and help-less was increasing every year in a most alarming ratio, which enabled the wealthy, by their money, to rule the state; and, lastly, the Latins and Italian allies of Rome had for some time been demanding the full franchise. It required a man of unusual bold-ness to grapple with these questions, but it was impossible to devise means satisfactory to all parties. At length, in B. C. 91, the elo-quent and talented tribune, M. Livius Drusus, undertook the task. He first endeavoured to remedy the scandalous mal-administration of justice by law in which the judicial power was divided between the senators and equites. He contemplated checking the growth of pauperism by agrarian laws, the establishment of colonies, and regular distribution of corn among the poorer classes. His third measure demanded the franchise for all the Italians, but before this could be carried, Drusus was murdered in his own house, and the Italians, seeing from this occurrence that it was hopeless to endea-vour to gain their rights in a constitutional and peaceful way, took

up arms to conquer by force what had been so obstinately refused to their petitions and demands. This was the beginning of the Social or Marsic war, which broke out in B. c. 90, and blazed forth at once in all parts of Italy.

11. In the earliest times, Rome had from time to time conferred the franchise upon the neighbouring districts, as they were successively incorporated with the state. The number of such districts, or tribes as they were called, had been increased to thirty-five about the end of the first Punic war, the city of Rome forming four tribes, and the surrounding country thirty-one; but after that time the franchise was not extended. The rights enjoyed by the Latins and Latin colonies approached nearest the Roman franchise, and it was evident that in any political reform they must be the first to obtain it. The Italian allies had for a long time demanded to be emancipated and placed on a footing of equality with the Romans; but whenever the question had been mooted, they were treated with haughtiness and contempt. They had set their last hope upon the efforts of Livius Drusus, and this time they were prepared to gain their point either by persuasion or by force. All the Sabellian nations, with the Marsians and Samnites at their head, had formed themselves into a confederacy, and, after the murder of Drusus, renounced their obedience to Rome. Their object was to establish an Italian republic governed by two consuls, and with the town of Corfinium, henceforth to be called Italica, as its capital. Armies well trained in arms, and a well supplied common fund, seemed to promise the best results. Fortunately for Rome, the Latins all over Italy, with the Etruscans and Umbrians, had not joined the insurgents, and the Romans, in order to prevent such a contingency, at once conferred the franchise upon the Latins by a law proposed by the consul L. Julius Caesar, B. c. 90. The war was carried on simultaneously in several parts of Italy, and many a bloody battle was fought. In B. c. 88, when the Etruscans and Umbrians were on the point of joining the Italians, Rome wisely propitiated them also by granting them the franchise. By these concessions the strength and still more the hopes of the allies were broken, and as Rome was threatened by a war with Mithridates in Asia, and was anxious to restore the peace in Italy, she promised the franchise to all those Italians who should lay down their arms. This measure produced the desired effect, and the Social War, in which Italy had lost three hundred thousand of her sons, terminated in B. c. 88. But the Samnites still held out with the same vigour and determination which they had displayed in their former conflicts with Rome, and afterwards, during the civil war between Marius and Sulla, they joined the former. The new citizens thus admitted to the franchise, however, were not put on a complete footing of equality with the old ones, and this arrangement contained of course the seeds of future discord and disturbances.

CHAPTER XI.

FROM THE FIRST WAR AGAINST MITHRIDATES, DOWN TO THE DEATH OF SULLA.

1. THE kingdom of Pontus, in the north-east of Asia Minor, had originally been a province subject to Persia, but in B. C. 363 Ariobarzanes, satrap of Phrygia, made himself independent, and constituted Pontus as a separate kingdom. Under his successor, Mithridates, who reigned from B. C. 337 to 302, the kingdom became consolidated and powerful.' Mithridates V. (B. C. 156–120) assisted the Romans in their war against Aristonicus, for which they rewarded him by adding Phrygia to his kingdom. But after his death, when his son and successor Mithridates VI. was still very young, they took Phrygia from him. The young king was at the time unable to resent this aggression, but strengthened himself and extended his kingdom as far as he could without coming into contact with the Romans. Mithridates was a man of great courage and enterprise, and possessed of all the advantages that Greek culture and civilisation could afford. When he was sufficiently prepared, he did not hesitate to interfere in the affairs of Cappadocia and Bithynia, and when opposed by the Romans, his well-disciplined troops had no difficulty in defeating them. He then advanced westward, and his arrival was hailed by the lightheaded Greeks, who looked upon him as their deliverer from the Roman yoke. In B. C. 88, no less than eighty thousand Romans residing in various parts of Asia Minor are said to have been put to death by his orders. Having made himself master of the whole of Asia Minor, he sent his general Archelaus with a large army into Greece, where the principal cities, and among them Athens and Thebes, threw their gates open to him as their deliverer.

2. The outrage committed by Mithridates, and his invasion of Greece, by which the safety of Italy itself was endangered, called for immediate and energetic measures, and the Roman senate conferred the supreme command in the war upon Sulla, who had greatly distinguished himself during the Social War, and was honoured with the consulship for the year B. C. 88. He still was the leader of the aristocratic party, and was at the time stationed with an army at Nola, conducting the war against the Samnites. Marius felt greatly hurt at finding himself in his old age superseded by his rival, who was now appointed to the command in a war, in which glory and wealth were sure to be the reward of success. Smarting under the feeling of jealousy, and wounded at being passed over on such an occasion, he formed a connection with the

bold tribune P. Sulpicius, who, partly by a cunning distribution of the new citizens among the ancient thirty-five tribes, which secured to them the full and unlimited franchise, and partly by violence, carried a law depriving Sulla of the command against Mithridates, and conferring it upon Marius. When this intelligence was brought to Sulla at Nola, he forthwith marched with his army against Rome, which, being taken by surprise, was easily forced to admit him and his soldiers. Notwithstanding the furious resistance offered to him in the streets of Rome, Sulla succeeded in putting his enemies to flight; he used his victory with moderation, and outlawed only Marius himself, and eleven of the most conspicuous ringleaders. Marius with great difficulty escaped to Minturnae, and thence crossed over to Africa, where he watched the course of events.

3. Sulla after his victory remained at Rome for a short time, to make such arrangements as might insure the peace and tranquillity of the city during his absence in the East. He restored the power of the senate, and limited the rights of the new citizens; his apparent moderation went so far that he even allowed L. Cornelius Cinna, a leader of the democratic party, to be elected to the consulship for B. C. 87, together with his aristocratic friend Cn. Octavius. Soon after these new consuls had entered upon their office, Sulla went with his army to Greece, leaving Pompeius Rufus to continue the war against the Samnites. On his arrival in Greece, Boeotia and Thebes submitted to him at once; but Athens had to do fearful penance for its revolt. The Pontian general Archelaus, after two bloody battles at Chaeroneia and Orchomenos, was obliged to take to flight, and Athens was taken and plundered in B. C. 86, after a long siege, during which the people had suffered from the most terrible famine. Sulla's conduct at Athens, notwithstanding his Greek culture, was marked by such barbarity as to make his name the terror and dread of all the Greeks. The fortifications, and even the ancient temples, were destroyed or pillaged, and a vast number of the treasures of art were carried away; among them was the library of Apellico, which is said to have contained the only complete copy of the works of Aristotle. When Archelaus, notwithstanding the reinforcements he had received, was obliged to quit Europe, Mithridates, being himself hard pressed in Asia by Fimbria, ordered Archelaus to commence negotiations for peace. While these transactions were going on, Sulla proceeded to the north, chastising those Greeks who had allied themselves with the Pontian king. Peace was not finally concluded until B. C. 84, when Sulla had a personal interview with the king in Asia. Mithridates had to surrender his whole fleet, pay all the expenses of the war, and give up all his conquests, so that his empire was limited to the original kingdom of Pontus. The revolted cities and provinces of Asia had to pay enormous sums to the conquerors; and the inhabitants, being

30 *

reduced by these extortions to poverty, became an easy prey to th Roman usurers, who like vultures flocked into the unhappy provinces. Fimbria, who belonged to the party of Marius, was, notwithstanding his victories over Mithridates, treated as an enemy by Sulla, and being deserted by his own soldiers, committed suicide.

4. While Sulla was engaged in Greece and Asia, Rome was again the scene of civil bloodshed, for no sooner had Sulla left, than Cinna attempted to abolish his regulations, to recall those who had been outlawed, and to distribute the new citizens among the thirty-five tribes. But the aristocratic party, in a fierce struggle, drove him out of the city and deprived him of the consulship. He then proceeded to the army at Nola, and rallying around him as many malcontents from all parts of Italy as he could, invited his friend Marius to return from Africa. The latter unhesitatingly obeyed the call, and landing in Etruria, collected an army consisting of hardened peasants, daring robbers, freedmen, and new citizens, and in conjunction with Cinna attacked and blockaded the city of Rome, which was compelled by hunger and internal discord to surrender. Marius now abandoned himself without restraint to taking vengeance upon his political opponents. Bands of savage soldiers, murdering and robbing, marched through the streets of the city, and the leading men of the aristocratic party, consulars and senators, such as Catulus, the consul Cn. Octavius, the orator M. Antonius, and many others, were killed, their houses plundered and devastated, their property confiscated, and their bodies left in the streets. For five days and five nights Rome experienced all the horrors of a city taken by the sword.

5. After these sanguinary proceedings, Marius caused himself to be elected to his seventh consulship for the year B. C. 86; but the terrible excitement of the time, and the debaucheries in which he indulged, during the short period of his power, together with the fear of Sulla's return and revenge, caused his death about the middle of January. In the meantime peace had been concluded with the Samnites, and the franchise had been conferred upon them. All Italy was now in the hands of Cinna, and the aristocracy repeatedly urged Sulla to return from the East, to save his friends and his party; but he refused to do so, until he should have discharged his duty to the republic. At the beginning of B. C. 83, he at length landed in Italy, and proceeded to Campania. Cinna, who had been invested with the consulship for four successive years, was murdered by his own soldiers. By this act the Marian party was deprived of the last able man among them; for Carbo, Marius the younger, and Norbanus, who were now at their head, did not possess the talent and energy required by their situation. Sulla in several battles defeated the armies opposed to him, and induced the soldiers belonging to them to serve under his own standard. In B. C. 82 he drove

young Marius to Praeneste, where he was closely besieged, and in despair killed himself. Sulla then entered Rome, where the democrats had perpetrated the greatest horrors against those who were suspected of favouring their opponents. At this moment an army commanded by the Samnite, Pontius Telesinus, marched against Rome, which he hoped to take by surprise; but Sulla met the enemy at the Colline gate, and a bloody and murderous battle was fought, in which the democratic party was so completely defeated, that in his despair, Pontius Telesinus made away with himself.

6. This battle was the death-blow of the Marian party, and Sulla was now undisputed master of Italy, from which all his enemies fled. A few days after the battle, eight thousand prisoners were butchered in the Circus, while Sulla had assembled the senate in the adjoining temple of Bellona, where the cries and shrieks of the unfortunate victims could be distinctly heard. The senators, terrified by these scenes, readily obeyed the commands of the conqueror. More than one hundred thousand lives had already been sacrificed during the civil war; but Sulla, not yet satisfied, devised a new and unprecedented measure for punishing those whom he suspected. He set on foot a proscription, that is, he drew up a list of all those whom he chose to regard as his enemies, and set it up in public. Any one might kill a person whose name was there registered, and rewards were given for the heads of the slain. Their estates were confiscated, and their descendants for ever deprived of the franchise. This measure, one of the most fearful on record, tore asunder every tie of blood, friendship, and hospitality; sons were armed against their fathers, and slaves against their masters; for those who concealed or protected a proscribed person, were punished in the same way as the proscribed themselves. No less than one thousand six hundred equites were thus murdered, and among the monsters who distinguished themselves during those days of terror, we find Catiline, who some years later planned the destruction of the city of Rome.

7. After having thus cleared Rome and Italy of all opponents, Sulla caused himself to be appointed dictator for an indefinite period, to enable him to reform the constitution and the law. He entered upon this office towards the end of B. C. 82. The first thing he did was to reward those soldiers through whose services he had gained his present position. Twenty-three legions had colonies assigned to them, consisting mainly of the towns which had supported his enemies. In these military colonies, the soldiers constituted the ruling body, and being scattered over all Italy, they afforded him the means of keeping the country in submission; ten thousand slaves were manumitted and formed his body-guard under the name of the Cornelii; the number of senators was increased by persons ready to do anything for the dictator, however low or vulgar their

origin might be. After these preliminary measures, by which he secured his power, he proceeded to reform the constitution. His object being to restore the ancient constitution of Rome, he first reduced the powers of the tribunes to what they had been originally, and by the same act he deprived the comitia tributa of all their legislative functions. His second measure consisted in restoring the courts for trying offences against the republic to the senators, to whom they had belonged before the time of the Gracchi. Lastly, Sulla increased the number of public officers, that of the praetors to eight, that of the quaestors to twenty, and the members of the colleges of pontiffs and augurs to fifteen. These and some regulations relating to the administration of the provinces were his chief political reforms, and they show that he was one of those shortsighted men who fancy that by restoring ancient forms they can restore the spirit of bygone times. The creation of Sulla was a mere body without a soul, and could not last. He was more successful in his reforms of the criminal law, which he was the first to place on a permanent basis. After having made these arrangements, Sulla, to the surprise of every one, in B. C. 79, laid down his dictatorship, and withdrew to Puteoli, where he lived as a private person, until, in B. C. 78, he died of a most disgusting disease which had probably been brought on by his voluptuousness and debauchery. Vice seems to have been his delight, and mimes, buffoons, and prostitutes were his favourite companions in his leisure hours, and during his luxurious meals. At the time of his death he was engaged in writing his memoirs in Greek; but the part he had finished has not come down to us.

8 During the time of Sulla's dictatorship, the few remnants of the Marian party were dispersed in Sicily, Africa, and Spain, where they maintained themselves and increased their numbers by malcontents from Italy. Cn. Pompey, who had gained his first laurels during the Social War, was sent by Sulla to Sicily and Africa, and annihilated the Marians in those countries, by causing Carbo to be assassinated in Sicily, and by defeating in Africa Domitius Ahenobarbus and his Numidian supporter, Hiarbas. On his return Pompey was honoured by Sulla with the surname of the Great, and obtained a triumph, although he was only an eques and no more than twenty-four years old. During the same period the Romans were engaged in a second war against Mithridates, from B. C. 83 till 81. Soon after Sulla's departure from Asia, the king repented of the terms of peace, and as it had not received the sanction of the Roman senate, he refused to give up Cappadocia to Ariobarzanes, as he had promised to do. Archelaus then deserted to the Romans, and persuaded L. Murena, the commander of the Roman forces in Asia, to attack the king at once, and not to wait until he should commence hostilities. This advice was adopted. Murena proceeded into Cap-

padocia and plundered the wealthy temple at Comana; in consequence of this aggression Mithridates attacked Murena in the vicinity of Sinope, and defeated him. Peace, however, was concluded in B. C. 81, and Mithridates remained in possession of a part of Cappadocia.

CHAPTER XII.

FROM THE DEATH OF SULLA TO THE OUTBREAK OF THE CIVIL WAR BETWEEN CAESAR AND POMPEY.

1. IN the very year of Sulla's death an attempt was made by M. Æmilius Lepidus to abolish his ill-judged constitution, but he was defeated by the party of Sulla. The attempt, however, did not remain without its effects, for the tribunes and others henceforth, year after year, endeavoured to demolish one part after another of the edifice reared by Sulla, until at length, in B. c. 70, Cn. Pompey, in his consulship, carried a law by which the power of the tribunes was restored to what it had been before the reforms of Sulla; and the praetor L. Aurelius Cotta enacted a law by which the courts of justice remodelled by Sulla were henceforth to be composed of senators, equites, and tribuni aerarii. Pompey, though a partizan of Sulla, carried or supported these measures, because he was anxious to obtain popularity at any cost. He gained his end most completely, for although there were among his contemporaries men of far greater abilities, yet, partly by his singular good fortune, partly by his kindly and sometimes chivalrous conduct, he succeeded in winning the confidence and admiration of the citizens as well as of the soldiers, and at this time no Roman enjoyed greater popularity than he.

2. In B. C. 82 when Sulla entered Rome, Q. Sertorius, the noblest and ablest among the democratic leaders, having become disgusted with the proceedings of his party, went with an army to Spain, in the hope of being able there to maintain the interests of the popular cause. Here he was joined by the exiled and persecuted remnants of the Marian party, and by his prudence and kindness, as well as by his honesty and military ability, he succeeded in winning the confidence of the Spaniards, and founded an independent republic of Spain, consisting of Romans and Spaniards, and defended by an excellently trained army. The new republic was to be governed by a senate of three hundred, and two consuls, the Spaniards being eligible to the great offices as well as the Romans. In the town of Osca he established a great school, in which the

sons of the Spanish nobles were to receive a Roman education. His plans succeeded admirably, and Sertorius was the darling of the Spaniards and the Romans. War was commenced against him in B. C. 79, but neither Q. Metellus nor Pompey was able to gain any advantages over him. In B. C. 74 Sertorius formed an alliance with Mithridates of Pontus, hoping thereby to place Rome between two fires; but disunion among the Spaniards brought about a change which saved Rome from this dangerous enemy. In B. C 72, Perperna, whose ambition had been thwarted by the great captain, formed a conspiracy against him, and murdered him during a banquet at Osca. Perperna then placed himself at the head of the army, but in his first encounter with Pompey his whole army was cut to pieces, and he himself fell into the hands of his enemy, and was put to death. The Spanish republic was overturned, and the last remnant of the Marian party was now annihilated.

3. The number of slaves that had been carried into Italy from all the countries round the Mediterranean, and the cruel manner in which they were occasionally treated, could not fail to give rise to insurrections. In Sicily a second servile war had been carried on from B. C 102 to 99, in which thousands were killed on both sides. A similar insurrection broke out in B. C. 73 at Capua in Campania, where about seventy slaves trained as gladiators, headed by the Thracian Spartacus, broke loose. Opening by force the prisons of other slaves in southern Italy, and calling on them to assert their freedom, they soon increased their number to ten thousand, all of whom were provided with arms. Spartacus seems at first to have intended only to restore the liberated slaves to their respective homes, or to find a country where they might be free; but having defeated several consular armies which attempted to prevent the escape of the slaves, he formed the plan of destroying the power of Rome, and of taking revenge on the oppressors of mankind. The free population of southern Italy had already been very much thinned during the Social War, and the sad effects of this now became visible during the conflict with the slaves, who murdered without mercy and destroyed everything that came in their way. What saved Rome and Italy was the want of military discipline among the slaves and their irregular movements through the country. It was these circumstances that enabled the praetor M. Licinius Crassus, who, in B. C. 71, overtook the army of slaves in Lucania on the river Silarus, to gain a complete victory over them. Spartacus himself was killed, and this loss deprived the slaves of all hopes. Thousands were slain, and their bodies were partly impaled along the high roads, and partly left unburied, to strike terror into their fellows. A body of about five thousand made their escape to the north of Italy, endeavouring to seek safety in Gaul; but they fell in with Pompey, who was just returning from Spain, and were completely cut to pieces.

4. On his return to Rome, Pompey was rewarded for his victories by the consulship for the year B. C. 70, during which, for the sake of increasing his popularity, he displayed the greatest liberality towards the people, and assisted in abolishing the reforms of Sulla. After the expiration of his consulship he lived for a few years in retirement, enjoying his reputation and his wealth, until a new opportunity offered itself. For several years past all parts of the Mediterranean had been so much infested by pirates that it was scarcely safe for merchant vessels to sail from port to port. The pirates plundered the maritime towns, and even ventured to land in the very vicinity of Rome and destroy ships in the port of Ostia. They consisted chiefly of people that had become homeless in consequence of the Roman conquests in the East, and were driven to piracy by sheer misery and poverty; they had their strongholds and warehouses to deposit their plunder principally in Cilicia, on the south coast of Asia Minor. The Romans had been warring against them ever since the year B. C. 78, but no impression had been made on them; and Rome itself was in constant danger of famine, as the necessary supplies could not be imported with safety. Under these circumstances the tribune Aulus Gabinius, in B. C. 67, proposed that Pompey should be invested for three years with the command of all the coasts of the Mediterranean to a considerable distance from the sea, and that he should be liberally provided with everything necessary to put an end to the war against the pirates. This measure was a dangerous one, and met with strong opposition, but the people readily consented to invest their favourite with all the powers and means demanded for him. His success more than justified their confidence, and the war which he now commenced, and which he gloriously terminated in about three months, is the most brilliant exploit of Pompey's whole life. He completely swept the Mediterranean from west to east, and drove the pirates into the Cilician sea, where he defeated them in a great battle; many of them were killed or taken prisoners, and the rest surrendered. He then took and destroyed their fortified places in Cilicia, and assigned settlements to the survivors, that they might be able to earn their livelihood without falling back upon their dangerous practices.

5. After the termination of this war, Pompey did not return to Italy, but remained in Asia Minor, probably in the hope of being appointed, in his absence, commander in the third war against Mithridates of Pontus, in which Rome had already been engaged for some years; for he well knew that his friends at Rome would do anything to gratify him. In B. C. 74, Mithridates had been tempted by Sertorius to commence fresh hostilities against Rome. King Nicomedes of Bithynia had just died, and bequeathed his kingdom to the Romans. Mithridates refused to recognise this

bequest, and at once invaded Bithynia, while his fleet sailed out against that of the Romans. Having gained a victory at sea, the king laid siege to the wealthy and populous town of Cyzicus, which was in alliance with Rome. While this siege was going on, L. Lucullus arrived with an army in Asia, and succeeded in cutting off the king from all supplies of provisions, B. C. 73. This and some other losses which he sustained for the moment deprived Mithridates of all hope, and in his despair he fled to his son-in-law Tigranes, king of Armenia, while Lucullus entered the kingdom of Pontus and compelled the towns to surrender one after another. After the conquest of Pontus, Lucullus spent some time in Asia to regulate the affairs of the conquered countries, which were inundated by greedy usurers and Roman officials. When at length Tigranes refused to surrender Mithridates, Lucullus, in B. C. 69, advanced against Tigranocerta, the capital of the Armenian king, near which he overpowered a vast army of Asiatics. Both kings took to flight, but Tigranes, who made an attempt to defend himself, was defeated a second time near Artaxata. Lucullus now made preparations to subdue the whole of Armenia, when a mutiny broke out in his army, which was headed by the notorious P. Clodius. Lucullus succeeded, indeed, in quelling the revolt, but Mithridates, availing himself of the favourable opportunity, effected his return to his own kingdom. Lucullus pursued him, but owing to the mutinous spirit of his soldiers, he was scarcely able to finish the campaign in which he was engaged. Just at this time, B. C. 67, M. Acilius Glabrio was sent from Rome as successor to Lucullus, who was obliged to give up the command to him. This man did absolutely nothing, but allowed all the advantages gained by Lucullus to slip out of his hands, while Mithridates re-established himself in Pontus and Cappadocia. Lucullus, who was possessed of enormous wealth, returned to Italy, where his numerous palaces, villas, and parks formed rallying points for men of refined taste in art and literature. He is said to have introduced into Italy the cherry-tree from Cerasus, a town of Colchis.

6. The inactivity of the Roman commander and the increasing power of Mithridates, afforded a welcome opportunity to the friends of Pompey who was still in Asia, of getting the command transferred to him. Accordingly, in B. C. 66, the tribune Manilius brought forward a bill to this effect. It was supported by Julius Caesar and Cicero, and Pompey was intrusted with additional powers in Asia Minor to enable him to bring the Mithridatic war to a close. Pompey, having received large reinforcements and concluded an alliance with the Parthians, fought a battle by night against Mithridates on the banks of the Euphrates, in which the king was defeated and put to flight. Tigranes became a vassal of the Roman republic, and Mithridates escaped into Colchis. After

having founded the town of Nicopolis, Pompey, in B. C. 65, pursued the king, and victoriously traversed Albania and Iberia, about mount Caucasus; but owing to the difficulties he had to contend with in those wild and remote countries, he gave up the pursuit of the enemy. The latter, still undismayed, formed the gigantic scheme of entering into alliances with the Scythians and invading Italy from the north-east. But his own son Pharnaces headed an insurrection of the soldiers against his father at Panticapaeum in the Crimea. Mithridates, to avoid falling into the hands of his enemies, took poison which for some time he had been carrying about with him, B. C. 63. Pompey, to whom the body was sent, ordered it to be buried with regal magnificence, but gave to the unnatural son of his great enemy, the sovereignty over the countries about the Cimmerian Bosporus.

7. After having concluded peace with the Albanians and Iberians, Pompey went to Syria, where he unceremoniously deposed king Antiochus XIII., and put an end to that effete kingdom, changing it, with Phoenicia, into the Roman province of Syria. In Asia Minor, Bithynia, with a part of Pontus, was likewise constituted as a province; but Armenia Magna, the northern part of Pontus, Paphlagonia, Galatia, and other countries, were given to tributary kings, who recognised the supremacy of Rome. The same was done in Judaea, where, after taking the temple of Jerusalem, he appointed Hyrcanus tetrarch, taking his brother Aristobulus, who had bravely defended himself, with his children, to Rome. Many Jews in their despair made away with themselves, throwing themselves down from the walls, or setting fire to their houses. The real ruler of Judaea, however, was the Idumaean Antipater, the father of Herod, and a cunning supporter of the Roman interest. When all these arrangements were made, Pompey, in B. C. 62, quitted Asia, and returned to Italy, but did not arrive at Rome until the beginning of B. C. 61. He celebrated a most splendid triumph, and the sums which he handed over to the treasury were enormous. His popularity was immense, and he took the greatest care to impress the people with the notion that he was happy in the condition of a simple Roman citizen. His great ambition was to induce the senate to sanction the arrangements he had made in Asia; and his vanity, therefore, was not a little wounded, when he found this desire opposed by men of the greatest influence. He felt so mortified that he resolved to abandon the optimates, and join the popular party, a step which ultimately led to his own ruin.

8. Some time before Pompey's return to Italy, M. Tullius Cicero had been honoured by his fellow-citizens with the name of father of his country. Cicero, born at Arpinum in B. C. 106, was the son of very respectable parents, and by his talent, industry, and irreproachable conduct, had so much distinguished himself, that although a

novus homo, he obtained in due time most of the great offices of the republic, and was in the end even raised to the consulship. He had studied at Athens and Rhodes, and had devoted himself with such zeal to his pursuits, especially those of oratory and philosophy, that as an orator he was surpassed by none, and was the first who successfully endeavoured to popularise the philosophical speculations of the Greeks among his countrymen. As a statesman he was less great, because his friendship for Pompey and Caesar led him often to act the part of a mediator between them, which led him into inconsistencies and contradictions. But his patriotism, his strong sense of justice, and his general virtues as a citizen, are acknowledged by all, and ought to make us judge leniently of his vanity and other foibles. In his consulship, B. c. 63, Catiline, a partizan of Sulla, and a man of patrician origin, but of most profligate character, and, like many others of his class, overwhelmed with debts, formed a conspiracy, which was joined by some reckless nobles of the highest rank, whose circumstances were so desperate that they saw no hope for themselves except in a revolution. Catiline had attempted similar things before, but had been thwarted by the vigilance of patriotic men, and by his own impatience. He and his associates now determined to murder Cicero, to set Rome on fire, to overthrow the constitution, and in the midst of the confusion to usurp the reins of government, and, probably, to establish a military despotism. But the watchfulness of Cicero, whose four speeches against Catiline, distinguished alike for manly courage and spirited eloquence, we still possess, prevented the infamous scheme. Catiline, in spite of his cunning and power of dissimulation, was unmasked by the consul, and obliged to quit the city. The senate, on the proposal of Cicero and Cato, condemned Catiline and some of his associates who had remained at Rome. His accomplices were strangled in the Capitoline prison; but Catiline himself, who with the rest of his followers had escaped to the north of Etruria, was killed in the battle of Pistoria, where he and all his friends fought with a bravery and courage worthy of a better cause. Cicero's joy at having saved his country and his fellow-citizens from dire destruction did not last long, for many of the secret friends and supporters of Catiline remained at Rome longing for an opportunity of taking vengeance upon the man who had so nobly defended his country's cause.

9. Ever since the time of Marius and Sulla, the leading men at Rome made all possible efforts and sacrifices to gain popularity; this popularity, however, was not sought after for the purpose of enabling them to serve the interests of their country, but to satisfy their own avarice and ambition, whence the history of that period down to the establishment of the empire is scarcely more than the personal history of the men who endeavoured to eclipse one another. By far

the most eminent and the most gifted among the men of this time,
was C. Julius Caesar, born in B. C. 100; he was fast rising in popular favour, while Pompey was reposing on his laurels, and enjoying the fruits of his previous victories. Caesar, though unscrupulous in the application of the means to gain his ends, had a thoroughly cultivated mind, and was indefatigable in his activity; he
was no less great as an orator and an author than as a general and
statesman. Julia, an aunt of his, had been married to C. Marius,
for whom he always entertained great affection, whence in the time
of Sulla his very life was threatened. In B. C. 65, he came forward
as the avowed leader of the remnants of the Marian or popular party.
His liberality was unbounded, and he became overwhelmed with
debts, but a campaign against the revolted Lusitanians in Spain, in
B. C. 61, enabled him to satisfy his creditors as well as his own extravagant wants. He obtained the consulship for B. C. 59, and in
that year strengthened himself by a close alliance with Pompey,
who had then renounced the party of the optimates, and by effecting a reconciliation between Pompey and Crassus. These three
men, forming what is commonly called the first triumvirate, agreed
that no political measures should be adopted which were displeasing
to any one of them. Being at the head of the democratic party,
they held the fate of the republic in their own hands. A number
of popular measures were passed, such as an agrarian law, by which
twenty thousand citizens received assignments of land. Caesar also
prevailed upon the senate to sanction the arrangements made by
Pompey in Asia. Having thus formed a powerful party for himself, he caused the provinces of Cisalpine and Transalpine Gaul with
Illyricum to be assigned to himself.

10. After the expiration of his consulship, however, he did not
proceed to his province at once, but remained in the neighbourhood
of Rome with his army to support the unprincipled P. Clodius in
his machinations against Cicero, who had offended Caesar. In B. C.
61, Clodius had committed some sacreligious act for which he was
brought to trial. Cicero then spoke against him, and provoked
him on several other occasions. Clodius vowed vengeance, and
after having caused himself to be adopted into a plebeian family, obtained, by the aid of Caesar, the tribuneship for B. C. 58. He first
secured the favour of the multitude by several popular measures,
and then carried a law that every one who had put to death a
Roman citizen without a formal trial should be outlawed. This law
was aimed at Cicero, who, on the authority of a mere decree of the
senate, had caused some of the associates of Catiline to be strangled
in prison. Cicero was abandoned by the triumvirs, who alone had
it in their power to save him, and in order to escape condemnation
went into exile. After this he was formally declared an outlaw, his
house was burned down, and two of his villas were destroyed This

measure was followed by others of an equally atrocious character. In order to get rid of a troublesome critic at Rome, Clodius sent Cato to Cyprus with orders to expel the king of the island, who was a brother of the king of Egypt, and to make Cyprus a Roman province. But no sooner had Clodius' tribuneship expired, than a reaction took place in the public mind, in consequence of which Cicero was recalled from exile, B. c. 57. Caesar had not departed for Gaul until the end of April, B. c. 58, when Clodius had gained his end.

11. While Caesar was engaged in Gaul, which had been assigned to him for five years, things at Rome became worse and worse. In B. c. 55 Pompey and Crassus obtained the consulship, and a law was carried by which Caesar's governorship of Gaul was prolonged for other five years, while Pompey obtained Spain, and Crassus Syria. Pompey did not go to his province, but allowed it to be governed by his legates, while he himself remained at Rome, where he exercised a sort of dictatorial power; but Crassus, though advanced in years, could not resist the temptation to go to Syria himself, where he hoped to be able to satisfy his insatiable avarice. He robbed and plundered wherever he appeared, and in B. c. 54 undertook an expedition against the Parthians, who had formed a powerful empire on the east of the Euphrates, and regarded themselves as the successors of the ancient Persians. They were governed by the dynasty of the Arsacidae, and their king at this time was Orodes or Arsaces XIV., who had assembled a powerful army in Mesopotamia to oppose the Romans. Crassus, guided by a treacherous Arab, boldly crossed the Euphrates, but in a sandy desert near Carrhae he was defeated, taken prisoner, and killed, after his son had been put to death before his own eyes. The Roman army was nearly annihilated, and the whole camp and all the standards fell into the hands of the conquerors. The war against the Parthians, however, was continued for several years, after the remnants of the army of Crassus had been led back to Syria by the brave legate C. Cassius.

12. At the time when Caesar undertook the conquest of Gaul, the whole country between the Rhine and the Atlantic was inhabited by a number of Celtic tribes, the south-western part, called Aquitania, alone being occupied by Iberians. On the eastern frontier the Germans had already commenced making encroachments. The southern part of Gaul, that is, the country about the mouth of the Rhone, had been conquered by the Romans as early as B. C. 126, and a few years later the towns of Aquae Sextiae (Aix) and Narbo Marcius (Narbonne) were founded. This part of Gaul was constituted a Roman province (whence its modern name Provence), and the Greek colony of Massilia was the means of spreading civilisation not only over the coast districts, but over the whole of Gaul.

Among the numerous Celtic tribes, one, such as the Arverni, Sequani, and Ædui, appears always to have exercised a kind of supremacy over the rest, though this did not produce any political union among them. Their common characteristics, however, were, that they were governed by a chivalrous kind of nobility, and by a powerful priesthood called Druids, while the great body of the nation were little better than serfs. The people were skilled in several of the arts of civilised life, and in many parts lived together in towns; but they were fierce and warlike, and, urged on by their priests and bards, rushed into battle with great vehemence, though they were wanting in perseverance. Caesar undertook the conquest of the whole country, for which its invasion by the Germans, and a migration of the Helvetii, likewise a Celtic people, afforded a welcome pretext.

13. The Helvetii had just at that time been tempted to quit their own poor and unproductive country, and seek new homes in the south-western parts of Gaul. Caesar, apprehending great danger to the Roman province from this migration, attacked and defeated first one numerous clan of the nation, and soon after the remainder in a great battle near Bibracte. These disasters obliged the Helvetii to return to their own devastated country, on quitting which they had burned and destroyed everything. About fourteen years before this time the Germans under Ariovistus had crossed the Rhine, having been invited by the Sequani to assist them against the Ædui. Ariovistus had repeatedly defeated the Ædui, and had compelled even the Sequani to give up to him one-third of their country; in consequence of which large numbers of Germans had taken up their abode in Gaul. At the request of the Ædui, Caesar now attacked the Germans, and having completely defeated them in a pitched battle near Vesontio, he compelled Ariovistus with the remainder of his army to retrace his steps across the Rhine. In B. C. 57, Caesar was successful against the Belgæ in the north of Gaul, who had formed themselves into a confederacy, and now took up arms against the Roman invaders. He managed to prevent their union, and defeated the several tribes one after another. In the following year he subdued the people in the north-west of Gaul.

14. By these repeated losses, the strength of Gaul was nearly broken, and Caesar now turned against two German tribes, the Usipetes and Tenchteri, who had crossed the Rhine, near its mouth, with the intention of settling in Gaul. The unfortunate barbarians, trusting to the honesty of the Roman proconsul, were treacherously attacked and butchered, while the negotiations for peace were going on. After this Caesar returned southward, and crossed the Rhine, by a wooden bridge of his own construction, in the neighbourhood of Neuwied; his object was probably to strike terror into the Germans; for after having ravaged their country, which was thickly covered

31*

with forests, he returned to Gaul, and broke down the bridge. In the same summer, B. C. 55, he also made an expedition into Britain, which, like Gaul, was inhabited by Celts. He landed, after a vigorous resistance, on the coast of Kent, and some of the British tribes offered to submit to him, but on being informed of his fleet having sustained a great loss at sea, they took up arms to repel the invader. Being defeated, however, they were obliged to submit to Caesar, who, immediately after his victory, was compelled by the late season of the year, to return to Gaul. In B. C. 54, he invaded Britain a second time ; the natives, under their chief Cassivelaunus, fought bravely, but were defeated several times, and Caesar conquered the greater part of Essex and Middlesex. Peace was then concluded, and the Britons having promised to pay a fixed annual tribute, and given hostages, Caesar returned to Gaul. But as he could not afford to leave any troops behind in the island, these promises were soon forgotten and neglected.

15. In B. C. 53, several of the Gallic tribes formed a confederacy to recover their independence, and were supported by some Germans who had come across the Rhine. But the insurgents were subdued, and Caesar pursued the Germans across the Rhine, where they found shelter in their forests and marshes, into which Caesar could not follow them with safety. The cruelty with which Caesar treated the leaders of the Gallic tribes which had risen in arms, at length set the whole of Gaul in a blaze. Even the Ædui, who had hitherto been the steady friends of the Romans, joined the insurrection, and the Arvernian Vercingetorix was the soul of the whole undertaking. The war in Gaul now assumed a more formidable aspect than ever. After various enterprises, Vercingetorix retreated to Alesia in Burgundy. Caesar laid siege to the town, which was believed to be impregnable ; he himself was surrounded by swarms of Gauls, and his position was perilous in the highest degree, but his genius overcame every obstacle, and, in B. C. 52, Alesia was compelled by famine to surrender. The fall of this town virtually decided the fate of Gaul, though some tribes still continued in arms. They were reduced, however, in the course of B. C. 51, when the Belgae also began to stir ; but it was now too late. Caesar, having subdued the Belgae, all Gaul, and the Helvetii, returned in B. C. 50 to Cisalpine Gaul, leaving his army in the country beyond the Alps. His men were attached to him in the highest degree, and his extraordinary exploits in Gaul had excited universal admiration of his genius and skill.

16. While Caesar was engaged in Gaul, Pompey had endeavoured, by every means, to increase his popularity ; his marriage with Caesar's daughter Julia for a time served as a bond of union between the two ambitious men ; but her death, in B. C. 54, rent asunder the tie, and the fall of Crassus in Mesopotamia in B. C. 53

left the Roman empire the bone of contention between Caesar and
Pompey. Caesar had kept up an active correspondence with his
friends at Rome, and considerable apprehensions prevailed in the city
in consequence of the turbulent and riotous proceedings of his partizans, such as Clodius, C. Curio, and others, who received enormous
bribes from Gaul. In B. c. 52, Pompey was for a time sole consul,
until he chose Metellus Scipio, his father-in-law, for his colleague.
The aristocracy again began to look upon Pompey as their only safe-
guard against the machinations of Caesar. In B. c. 51, Claudius
Marcellus, one of the leading optimates, proposed that Caesar
should be recalled from Gaul, and a successor appointed; no opportunity was, in fact, overlooked for hurting or insulting him. In
B. c. 50 the consulship was in the hands of two aristocrats; but
Caesar by his bribes succeeded in gaining over some of the leading
men. The time had now come when the optimates thought it right
to resort to energetic measures, and although the proconsulship of
Caesar had not yet expired, the senate, on the proposal of Metellus
Scipio, passed a decree peremptorily demanding of him to disband
his army by a certain day, and declaring him a public enemy, in
case he should refuse compliance. Two tribunes, M. Antonius and
Q. Cassius, who had in vain opposed the decree, and demanded that
Pompey should likewise resign his power and disband his armies,
fled to Caesar, who was stationed at Ravenna in Cisalpine Gaul
with only a small part of his forces; they called upon him to come
to Rome as the avenger of the tribunician power, which had been
trodden under foot by his adversaries. Pompey was full of confi-
fidence that he would be successful in the ensuing struggle, and
the optimates entertained the same feelings, so that even the most
necessary precautions were neglected. But recklessness and foolish
conceit found out too soon that they had miscalculated.

CHAPTER XIII.

THE CIVIL WAR BETWEEN POMPEY AND CAESAR, AND THE SUB-
SEQUENT EVENTS DOWN TO THE BATTLE OF ACTIUM.

1. THE arrival of the tribunes before Caesar at Ravenna, in B. c.
49, was a decisive moment, and after a short hesitation, as to whether he should cross the little stream Rubicon, which separated
Cisalpine Gaul from Italy, he called out, " The die is cast!" and
crossed the river with a small force, having sent orders to Gaul for
the other legions to follow him. Accompanied by his faithful vete-

rans, he hastened rapidly through Umbria and the Sabellian districts, to prevent his adversaries completing their preparations before
his arrival. His renown went before him, his kindness and affability won the hearts of all, and the gates of the towns on his route
were thrown open to him. Pompey, who had been roused too late
from his feeling of security, did not venture to await the enemy's
arrival at Rome, but with newly enlisted and untrained recruits, a
few trustworthy soldiers, and a large number of senators and optimates, fled to Brundusium; and when Caesar approached that port,
Pompey and his retinue sailed across to Epirus. His vaunting
boast, that he need only stamp upon the ground with his foot to
call forth legions, had all its emptiness now fully proved. After his
departure, all Italy joined Caesar, who now returned to Rome, where
he acted with great mildness, though showing in every thing that
he regarded himself as the real sovereign of the state. He took
possession of the treasury, and, leaving Pompey for the present to
his fate, immediately set out for Spain against Pompey's lieutenants
and armies. By his surpassing talent as a commander, and the
astonishing rapidity of his movements, he drove them into such
straits that, after most of their troops had deserted, they were compelled to surrender. Afranius and Petreius, the legates, were dismissed unhurt, and the remnant of the army was disbanded. On
his return from Spain, Caesar had to compel Massilia, which desired
to remain neutral, to side with him; the city was taken, but treated
with great mildness. In the meantime, C. Curio had taken possession of Sicily, the Pompeian party having evacuated it, but in an
attempt to conquer Africa also, he was killed.

2. While yet engaged at Massilia, Caesar was made dictator; as
such he returned to Rome, but in order not to alarm the republicans
too much, he caused himself to be elected consul for B. C. 48, and
laid down the dictatorship. He then passed several measures to
restore order and tranquillity to the city; he extended the franchise
to Cisalpine Gaul, reduced debts, and restored exiles and the children of those who had been proscribed by Sulla. His stay at Rome
was very brief; and as soon as the necessary preparations were
made, he crossed the Adriatic from Brundusium in pursuit of
Pompey, B. C. 48. Pompey had not been inactive, but had collected troops, ships, and supplies from all parts of the East, so that
in point of numbers he had the advantage over Caesar. The latter
besieged his enemy at Dyrrhachium, but with so little success that
he almost despaired; instead, however, of giving way to this feeling, he boldly marched from the coast towards Thessaly, where
every inch of ground had to be conquered. Pompey's former confidence now returned, and imagining that his enemy had taken to
flight, he followed him with all speed, hoping to annihilate him at
one blow. Caesar pitched his camp near Pharsalus, and Pompey,

being urged on by the inexperienced nobles, fought the decisive battle of Pharsalus on the 9th of August, b. c. 48. His army was completely defeated, though it was twice as numerous as that of his opponent, and the camp, filled with treasures and luxuries of every kind, fell into the hands of the conquerors. Pompey, having now lost all hope, fled to Le-bos, and thence to Egypt, where he had reason to expect a hospitable reception; but young Ptolemy Dionysius, the king of Egypt, in the hope of securing the favour of Caesar, ordered him to be murdered even before he reached the shore, and his body was left unburied on the beach.

3. A few days after this tragic end of Pompey, Caesar arrived with a small force in Egypt, and the sad fate of his rival is said to have brought tears into his eyes. The author of the murder did not receive the expected reward, and being called upon to act as mediator between the young king and his sister Cleopatra, who by their father's request ought to have reigned in common, Caesar decided in favour of the beautiful and fascinating Cleopatra This decision involved him in a war with the young king and the people of ₋Alexandria; for a time he was exposed to very great danger, as he had only few troops with him. With wonderful skill and adroitness he defended himself in the royal palace against the infuriated and demoralised populace, and when the palace was set on fire, he escaped by swimming to a ship lying at anchor. But when his reinforcements arrived he compelled Alexandria to surrender, and as the young king had been drowned in the Nile during the disturbances, he restored Cleopatra to the throne, and spent nine months with her, during which time he appears to have forgotten everything in the luxuries of the Alexandrian court. At length he received information that Pharnaces, the son of Mithridates, had availed himself of the civil war among the Romans for the purpose of extending his kingdom, and that one of the Roman legates had been defeated by him. Accordingly, in the spring of b. c. 47, he marched through Syria into Pontus, and defeated the Asiatics in a decisive battle near Zela. This victory is celebrated on account of the laconic despatch which Caesar sent to Rome regarding it, "I came, saw, conquered" (*veni, vidi, vici*). Pharnaces lost all his conquests, and was soon afterwards murdered by one of his own subjects.

4. Soon after this he was informed of disturbances at Rome, in consequence of which he hastened back. He arrived in the city in the autumn of b. c. 47. After the battle of Pharsalus, the enthusiasm of the senate and people at Rome was so great that the most extraordinary honours and powers were conferred upon him, which in reality made him the sole ruler of the republic. This was in some measure the result of his unexpected mildness towards his conquered enemies. During his absence in the East, the partizans of Pompey

had been active in collecting their scattered forces in Africa, where they were supported by Juba, king of Numidia. In Rome quarrels had broken out between his own friends M. Antony and Dolabella, a profligate young man, and bloody riots had taken place in consequence. Caesar being anxious to bring the war against the Pompeians to a close, confined himself at Rome to conciliatory measures, rewarding his friends by increasing the number of praetors, quaestors, aediles, and of the members of the priestly colleges, by making liberal promises to the soldiers, and stirring up their military ambition. When all these matters were settled, he set out at the end of B. C. 47 for Africa, and very soon afterwards the bloody battle of Thapsus, in B. C. 46, decided the fate of the Pompeian party for a time; fifty thousand dead covered the field of battle, and many of the survivors made away with themselves; among these latter were Pompey's own father-in-law Metellus Scipio, the Numidian king Juba, whose kingdom became a Roman province, the warlike Petreius, and the stern Cato, who with stoic calmness put an end to his own life at Utica. But the two sons of Pompey, Cneius and Sextus, escaped to Spain, where somewhat later they stirred up a fresh war.

5. Caesar was now the sole master of the Roman world, and on his return to Rome silenced all fears and apprehensions by proclaiming a general amnesty, and assuring the senate and people that his great object was the restoration of peace and order. He celebrated at once four triumphs, carefully avoiding hurting any one's feelings, and amused both soldiers and citizens with every kind of public amusements. During his stay at Rome, B. C. 46, Caesar, in his capacity of pontifex maximus, introduced his celebrated reform of the calendar, which, owing to the ignorance or caprice of the pontiffs, had fallen into such disorder, that it was three months in advance of the real time. Caesar remedied the actual evil, and made regulations to prevent its recurrence, which were observed until, in A. D. 1582, Pope Gregory XIII. introduced another reform. While Caesar was thus peacefully and usefully employed at Rome, he was informed that the sons of Pompey had collected a fresh army in Spain, and that the whole of the southern part of that country was in a state of insurrection. Towards the end of B. C. 46, he set out for Spain, to face his enemies in their last and desperate struggle. His difficulties were very great, and it was only his undaunted courage and perseverance that enabled him to overcome them. The fearful battle of Munda, in the spring of B. C. 45, decided the fate of the Pompeian party for ever. Cneius, one of the two brothers, was killed after the fight while attempting to make his escape; but Sextus fled from the field, and for some years after this led the life of a robber and pirate chief.

6. On his return to Rome Caesar celebrated a triumph over the

Pompeians, and was received by the senate with the most abject flattery and servility. Distinctions of every kind were literally showered upon him; he was called "father of his country;" the month of Quintilis, in which he was born, was called after him Julius (July); the powers which he had gradually received were conferred on him for life; he received the permanent title of impe- ¬ator, the consulship for the next ten years, and the offices of lictator and praefectus morum for life. These and many other powers and distinctions virtually made Caesar the acknowledged ruler of the Roman world, and nothing but the outward signs of absolute sovereignty were wanting. But however much he endea- voured, by observing the ancient forms, to allay the fears of the republicans, and however much he tried to pacify the wealthy and noble by increasing the number of senators, and to satisfy the sol- diers by the distribution of lands—however much he did to improve the laws and their administration, to raise commerce and agricul- ture, to embellish the city with temples and theatres, and to benefit Italy by making roads, canals, and harbours, he could not make the people forget that they had been free; it was evident to them that he was not satisfied with the substance of sovereign power, but also aimed at the outward marks and distinctions of a monarch. There still existed many deluded enthusiasts who imagined that it was possible to maintain the republic, and that, by preserving the ancient forms, the spirit of freedom might be revived. Besides these there were many, also, who, although they had received from Caesar posts of honour and distinction, yet thought them- selves slighted and neglected, and secretly plotted against him. The increasing pride of the dictator, and his too obvious desire to obtain the title of king, at length induced the republicans to make common cause with his personal enemies. A conspiracy was formed against his life in the beginning of B. C. 44; it was headed by M. Junius Brutus, a genuine though deluded republican, and C. Cassius, who bore a personal grudge against Caesar. Both had been partizans of Pompey, but had nevertheless been raised by Caesar to the praetorship, and had been treated by him with kind ness and confidence; but all considerations of a private nature were set aside under the specious pretext that the liberty of their country had higher claims upon them. The plan for the murder of Caesar was formed with the greatest caution and secrecy. On the ides (the 15th) of March B. C. 44, Caesar convened a meeting of the senate in the curia of Pompey, for the purpose of receiving the title of king out of Italy, to enable him, under this designation, to under- take a war against the Parthians. That day was fixed upon by the conspirators for carrying out their design. He was attacked at the meeting of the senate, and sank overwhelmed by the daggers of his assailants. At first he made an attempt to defend himself, but perceiving Brutus among his murderers, he exclaimed, " You, too, Brutus?" wrapped himself up in his toga, and sank at the base of Pompey's statue. Thus fell the only man that was then both able and willing to save Rome from internal war and bloodshed, and whose reign might have become the beginning of a happy and prosperous era in Roman history. But the cup of suffering for Rome was not yet full.

7. The conspirators soon found to their own cost, that it is more easy to destroy than to build up; of the latter, they had in fact scarcely thought, and were not a little alarmed by the discovery, that the slight enthusiasm produced by the murder gave way to hatred and detestation, when the crafty M. Antony in his funeral oration over the body of Caesar, set forth his great merits and his many excellent qualities, and mentioned the liberal bequests and donations which he had made in his will to the people. The multitude became infuriated, and the murderers were obliged to take to flight. Decimus Brutus went to his province of Cisalpine Gaul, and M. Brutus and Cassius proceeded to the East, where provinces had previously been assigned to them. After they had gone, Antony caused Cisalpine Gaul to be transferred to himself, and proceeded at once with an army to Mutina to expel D. Brutus, who had taken up his position in that city. The senate, being in the meantime stirred up by Cicero, invested C. Julius Caesar Octavianus, the adopted son and heir of Caesar, who was only nineteen years old, and had come over from Apollonia, with the powers of a praetor; and as many of the veterans of Antony joined the young avenger of Caesar, Octavianus was sent along with the consuls of B. C. 43, A. Hirtius and Vibius Pansa, to the north of Italy, to prevent Antony, who had in the meantime been declared a public enemy, from gaining his object. Antony, being defeated in this war by the armies of his opponents, fled across the Alps into Gaul, where he was favourably received by the governor Lepidus. As the two consuls had been killed in the war, and the senate conferred the command of its armies on D. Brutus, Octavianus, exasperated at the slight, compelled the senate to allow him to be elected to the consulship in spite of his youth. A law was passed, declaring all the murderers of Caesar outlaws, and Octavianus then marched with his army to the north. D. Brutus took to flight, and was murdered at Aquileia, while Lepidus and Antony, against whom the decree of outlawry was repealed, returned to Italy.

8. A conference then took place between Octavianus, Antony, and Lepidus, in the neighbourhood of Bononia, at which the three assumed the title of triumvirs for regulating the affairs of the republic (*triumviri rei publicae constituendae*), and distributed the provinces among themselves. Octavianus received Africa, Sicily,

and Sardinia, Antony Gaul, and Lepidus Spain, and Antony and Lepidus undertook to carry on the war against Brutus and Cassius in the East. The triumvirs then, to rid themselves of all their enemies and opponents, adopted the plan of Sulla, and drew up a proscription list, in which each entered the names of those specially obnoxious to himself. This proscription, ostensibly directed against their political opponents, was, in point of fact, a legalised wholesale murder of wealthy persons, whose property was in many instances the sole reason why their names appeared among the proscribed. The triumvirs entered Rome at the head of their armies, compelled the people to sanction their arrangements, and then let loose the soldiery upon the devoted victims. The most illustrious and patriotic men fell under the strokes of the rapacious and reckless soldiers; all the ties of blood and of friendship were rent asunder, nothing was sacred, and murder was the order of the day. Two thousand equites and three hundred senators were massacred, and those who could make their escape fled to Brutus and Cassius, or to Sextus Pompeius, who had returned from Spain and made himself master of Sicily. The great orator Cicero, who had looked upon Octavianus as the champion of the republic and supported him on all occasions, was one of the many victims who fell during this time: he was murdered on the 7th of December B. C. 43, and Antony's wife Fulvia feasted her eyes on the dead features when his head was brought to her.

9. When the triumvirs had sufficiently punished Italy by murder, confiscation, and extortion, Octavianus and Antony sailed over to Greece to make war against Brutus and Cassius. Shortly after quitting Italy, Brutus had gone to his province of Macedonia, where he was recognised as the rightful governor, and where in a short time he was amply provided with everything necessary to carry on a war against his enemies. Cassius had in the meantime displayed great vigour in Syria and Asia Minor; the two republican chiefs were in point of fact masters of all the countries to the east of the Adriatic, and at a meeting in Sardes they agreed to operate together against their common enemies. But while they were preparing themselves, Octavianus and Antony had already made themselves masters of Greece, and taken up their quarters at Amphipolis. The republicans pitched their camp in the neighbourhood of Philippi, and in the first battle Cassius was obliged to retreat before Antony, while Brutus succeeded in repelling the legions of Octavianus, who is said to have been ill on the occasion. Soon after, Cassius, deceived by erroneous information, threw himself on his own sword, and when, twenty days after the first battle, the triumvirs renewed the contest with fresh vigour, Brutus was also defeated, and made away with himself. Many other republicans followed his example; but most of the soldiers sur-

rendered to the triumvirs, while others fled to Sext. Pompeius in Sicily. The battles of Philippi, which were fought in the autumn of B. C. 42, were the death-blow of the republic, and Brutus and Cassius have often been called "the last of the Romans."

10. The conquerors now again divided the empire among themselves; Lepidus obtained Africa, and Antony the eastern provinces, while Octavianus returned to Italy to satisfy his greedy and rapacious soldiers by the distribution of lands and the establishment of military colonies. Antony, intoxicated by the incense of the Greeks and the luxuries of Asia, began a senseless and voluptuous career in the East. The sums he extorted in Asia were lavished upon the coquettish and dissolute Cleopatra, queen of Egypt. His wife Fulvia, who loved him with all the passion of her passionate nature, scrupled at nothing which seemed to her likely to effect his return and secure to him the possession of the western world. The misery and wretchedness into which thousands of Italians were thrown in consequence of the establishment of military colonies, afforded a fair pretext for Fulvia and L. Antonius, her husband's brother, to come forward as the protectors of the suffering and oppressed. L. Antonius was consul in B. C. 41, and proclaiming himself the friend of the poor and distressed, he, with Fulvia and others, established themselves at Perusia in Etruria, where large numbers of malcontents gathered around them. Towards the end of B. C. 41, Octavianus proceeded to blockade the rebels with three armies; and when at length the besieged began to suffer from famine and found it impossible to escape, L. Antonius capitulated, and Fulvia was set free on condition of her quitting Italy; but all the senators of Perusia were put to death, and upwards of three hundred of its most illustrious citizens were sacrificed on the 15th of March B. C. 40 at the altar of Julius Caesar. The ancient town of Perusia itself was reduced to a heap of ashes. Fulvia went to Greece, where she met Antony, but soon after died at Sicyon.

11. The war of Perusia nearly produced a struggle between Antony and Octavianus, for the former actually advanced with his fleet to Brundusium, and prevailed on Sext. Pompeius to co-operate with him; but a reconciliation was brought about, and Sext. Pompeius, betrayed by Antony, was declared the common enemy of the triumvirs. Pompeius now continued his former piratical practices, infesting the coasts of Italy and preventing supplies of grain from being imported from abroad, in consequence of which Rome was often suffering from scarcity of provisions. The people therefore complained loudly, demanding of the triumvirs to come to some understanding with him. A peace accordingly was concluded at Misenum in B. C. 39, in which Pompeius obtained proconsular power over Sicily and several other provinces. Antony, who ever since

the treaty of Brundusium had been at Rome, now married the noble Octavia, sister of Octavianus, and then went to Greece, where for a time he lived as a private person. Pompeius, who felt himself wronged by Antony, did not altogether abstain from piracy, and this afforded Octavianus a welcome pretext for undertaking a war against him. It was commenced in B. c 38, and at first the triumvir was not very successful; but in B. c. 36, he appointed his friend Agrippa commander-in-chief of the whole fleet. The island was then surrounded, but although Agrippa was supported by the fleets of Antony and Lepidus, no decisive impression was made until the great battle of Mylae, in which Pompeius was completely defeated. His land army surrendered, and he himself escaped with a few ships to Asia, where soon after he was murdered. Lepidus now claimed Sicily for himself, but as he was not a man of much influence or spirit, Octavianus unceremoniously commanded his soldiers to join him, and Lepidus was sent to Rome, where he enjoyed the empty honour of chief pontiff until his death in B. c. 12.

12. Even before the treaty of Brundusium, in B. c. 40, a war had broken out with the Parthians, who had made inroads into Syria. At first the war against them was conducted successfully by Antony's lieutenants; in B. c. 37, Octavia returned to Italy, and Antony hastened to Syria to undertake the command against the Parthians in person. He had a large army, and was allied with Artavasdes, king of Armenia. But his plans were ill laid, and the Parthian king Phraates, attacking him in Media, nearly annihilated his legions, and obtained possession of all his ammunition and provisions. Antony himself narrowly escaped the fate of Crassus. After having brought this disgrace upon himself and the Roman arms, he returned to Alexandria, where he forgot himself and everything else in the sensual pleasures of the court. He gave to Cleopatra Coelo-Syria, Judaea and Cyprus, to which in B. c. 34 he added Armenia, whose king was taken prisoner. He even forgot himself so far as to celebrate a triumph at Alexandria, and soon after divorced the noble Octavia, who had acted with the greatest forbearance towards him, and had often prevented a rupture between her brother and her husband. Octavianus and his sister were now in the position of the injured party, and all became ashamed of Antony's conduct in the East. At last, in B. c. 32, war was declared against the queen of Egypt, and in the spring of the following year, the fleet of Octavianus, under the able command of Agrippa, spread over the whole of the Adriatic, while Octavianus himself with his legions landed in Epirus.

13. Antony, accompanied by Cleopatra, sailed leisurely to Corcyra, where his forces were assembled. On the 2d of September, B. c. 31, the memorable sea-fight off the promontory of Actium in Acarnania took place : its issue was at first doubtful, but Cleopatra

soon losing courage took to flight; Antony followed her, and both together returned to Alexandria, leaving their fleet and army to their fate.   The fleet was soon destroyed by Agrippa, and when the land forces found that their commander had abandoned them, they surrendered to Octavianus.   The town of Nicopolis opposite Actium was afterwards built to commemorate this victory, and the moderation displayed by Octavianus towards the vanquished excited general admiration.   Soon after his victory, Octavianus followed his conquered enemies to Alexandria.   Cleopatra made an attempt to see whether she could not charm her conqueror as she had charmed Caesar and Antony; but it was all in vain.   Antony being prematurely informed of the death of his mistress, threw himself upon his sword, B. C. 30, and Cleopatra soon after made away with herself, by putting a viper to her breast, that she might not be compelled to adorn as a captive the triumph of her conqueror.   Egypt, where the race of the Ptolemies was now extinct, was made a Roman province.   In the spring of B. C. 29, Octavianus returned to Rome, where the temple of Janus was closed, as a sign that peace was restored throughout the empire, of which Octavianus was now the sole master.

<center>~~~~~~~~~~~~~~~~~~~~~~~~~~~~~~</center>

CHAPTER XIV.

THE REIGN OF AUGUSTUS.

1. IF we consider the state of political and social morality of the Romans at the time, and the fearful convulsions through which they had passed ever since the days of Sulla, it must be owned that it was a real blessing for the empire to have fallen at length under the sway of one who, though neither so great nor so noble-minded as Caesar, yet had the desire to restore order, peace, and prosperity to his country.   On the whole it seems that the greater part of the Romans, and many even of those who had fought under the banner of the republic, had arrived at the conviction that the republic was irrecoverably gone, and that its restoration was not even desirable. Octavianus, however, was very careful in preserving the ancient republican forms, such as the meetings of the comitia and of the senate, while, on the other hand, he avoided with equal care such titles as "king," which had always been detested by the Romans, and "dictator," which had been abolished for ever after the murder of Caesar.   As far as outward appearance was concerned, Octavianus, notwithstanding the extraordinary powers conferred upon him,

was no more than a republican magistrate. The Roman populace had come to regard republican freedom with indifference, and were satisfied if plentifully provided with bread and amusements (*panis et circenses.*)

2. On the return of Octavianus from the East, B. c. 29, he was overwhelmed by the adulation and servility of both the senate and people. Two years later he received the novel title of "Augustus," that is, "the Venerable," which was afterwards assumed by all the Roman emperors. To it was added the title of "Imperator," or emperor, for ten years, by virtue of which he had the supreme command over all the armies, and which was subsequently renewed from time to time. In B. c. 23, he was invested with the tribunician power for life, whereby his person became sacred and inviolable; at the same time he obtained the tribunician veto, as well as the right to convene the senate whenever he pleased. In like manner he acquired the office of censor, and proconsular power in all the provinces. In the course of a few years he thus concentrated in his own person all the powers which had formerly belonged to the several republican magistrates; but the consulship and the other magistracies were nominally left to others, and continued to be looked upon as high honours down to the overthrow of the empire. In his capacity of censor, Augustus directed his attention first to the purification of the senate by excluding unworthy members, and reducing its number to six hundred. The senate gradually became a sort of state council and supreme court of justice for all cases in which the majesty of the emperor was violated. Augustus had no ministers of state in our sense of the term, but he was assisted and supported by a number of able friends, such as Agrippa, Mæcenas, Valerius Messalla, and Asinius Pollio.

3. In regard to the internal administration, Augustus bestowed particular care upon the safety of life and property in the city of Rome, which had before been little better than a den of robbers. With this view he divided the city and its suburbs into fourteen regions, and the whole of Italy into a number of districts or provinces. For himself he established a numerous body-guard of ten praetorian cohorts; three of which were stationed in the city, and the rest in different parts of Italy, until, in the reign of Tiberius, they were all collected in a fortified camp near Rome, called the *castra praetoria*. Augustus also made several useful and necessary regulations concerning the administration of the provinces, the number of which then amounted to twenty-five. In B. c. 27, they were divided between himself and the senate, that is, into *provinciae senatoriae* or *populi*, and *provinciae Caesareae*—the emperor reserving for himself those which were not completely subdued, and required the presence of a military force, and for these the emperor himself appointed the governors. Under the control of Augustus

32 *

the administration of the provinces was conducted much more fairly and honourably than had been the case during the last century of the republic. The two classes of the provinces also rendered necessary a division of the revenues derived from them; the revenues of the senatorial provinces went into the *aerarium* or state treasury, while those obtained from the imperial provinces went into the treasury of the emperor, called the *fiscus.*

4. Augustus also bestowed great attention upon the moral and social improvement of his people, by encouraging marriage and punishing adultery, and nothing was neglected which tended to increase the material prosperity of his subjects. He hoped much, also, from a revival of the ancient piety and religious worship of the Romans; but these and many other things are of such a nature that laws, however well meant, must remain inefficient so long as the spirit of the people is not improved; and this can be the work only of time and long perseverance. Notwithstanding the mildness with which Augustus ruled, and the anxiety he displayed to conceal the fact that he was the real sovereign, conspiracies against his life broke out from time to time; and these evidences of secret enemies intimidated him so much, that during the latter part of his reign he always took precaution against any sudden attack.

5. Augustus, throughout his long reign, was more concerned about securing the frontiers of his vast empire than about making additional conquests. In B. C. 27, he himself went through Gaul to the north of Spain, for the purpose of subduing the Astures and Cantabri, and making the Atlantic the boundary of the empire in the west. For three years he carried on war against them, and when at length, in B. C. 24, those brave tribes submitted, and gave hostages, he returned to Rome; but soon after the Cantabri again revolted, and were finally subdued by Agrippa, in B. C. 19. About the same time Ælius Gallus, the first governor of Egypt, made an unsuccessful expedition into Arabia; but in Africa the frontier was secured by victories over the Ethiopians and Garamantes. In B. C. 20 the Parthians who had until then been the most formidable enemies of Rome in the East, thought it advisable to return to Augustus the standards which had fallen into their hands during the wars of Crassus and Antony. This event filled every Roman with joy. The existence of numerous independent tribes in the Raetian and Graian Alps, and in Vindelicia and Noricum, was thought to be incompatible with the safety and peace of Italy; war accordingly was waged against them in B. C. 25, and was continued for many years, until the Alpine tribes were completely subdued in B C. 13. But the war against them stirred up commotions in Gaul and in the south of Germany. Some German tribes even crossed the Rhine and invaded Gaul, an event which created so much alarm at Rome, that Augustus himself, in B. C. 16, went to Gaul for the purpose of

securing its eastern frontier. But after an absence of three years, he returned, leaving the command of the troops on the Rhine to his step-son Drusus, who with his brother Tiberius had till then been conducting the war against the Alpine tribes.

6. The appointment of Drusus marks the commencement of a series of dangerous wars with the Germans on the east of the Rhine, the object of which was not so much to gain a permanent footing in Germany as to crush that nation, which was thought to be a most dangerous neighbour of Gaul. Germany itself was for the most part a wild and uncultivated country, covered with immense forests and marshes, and holding out little or no temptation to a conqueror. The southern parts about the Danube, perhaps as far as the Maine, were inhabited by Celtic nations; the rest, with the exception of some portions in the north-east, was inhabited by a vast number of German tribes, which led a free and roving life, and were unable to bear the yoke of foreign rulers. But their great misfortune then, as ever after, was their incessant quarrels and wars with one another, which greatly facilitated the work of conquest. Drusus, when he undertook the command in B. C. 12, at once resolved to conquer the part of Germany between the Rhine and the Elbe. From Mayence he made several successful expeditions against the Sigambri, Usipetes, Bructeri, Chatti, and others, and by the establishment of the fortress of Aliso near the sources of the Lippe, he endeavoured to secure his conquests. In B. C. 9 he advanced as far as the Elbe; but want of provisions obliged him to return; on his journey he fell from his horse, and died thirty days later in consequence of the injury he received.

7. His brother Tiberius, who until then had been conducting a war in Dalmatia and Pannonia, succeeded to the command of his forces, and in B. C. 8 crossed the Rhine to complete what his brother had commenced. For two years he continued the war with great skill and valour, though not always with that honesty which becomes a great general; but he was unable completely to subdue the west of Germany. In B. C. 6 he returned to Rome, and was succeeded by Domitius Ahenobarbus, a bold but at the same time a prudent man, who endeavoured to push his conquests even beyond the Elbe. After various undertakings, none of which was crowned with permanent success, Tiberius, in A. D. 4, resumed the command of the legions on the Rhine, and by victories on the field of battle, as well as by prudent negotiations, succeeded in subduing the country between the Rhine and the Weser, which in A. D. 5 was constituted as a Roman province. Peace being thus restored in that part of Germany, he meditated a war against Maroboduus, a powerful king of the Marcomanni, in the south-east of Germany; but the tidings of a great insurrection which had broken out in Pannonia and Dalmatia, obliged him to conclude peace with the king and direct his

forces against the rebels. This war lasted for two years, and obliged the Romans, who were at first unsuccessful, to make the greatest efforts. At length in A. D. 9 the fall of the fortress of Anderion decided the fate of the insurgents, who now again submitted to Rome; but their country, between the Danube and the Adriatic, had been fearfully ravaged during the war.

8. In the meantime the work of Romanising western Germany was commencing: many Germans served in the Roman armies, and young nobles delighted in the distinctions with which they were honoured by their conquerors; but the avarice and rapacity of the Roman governor Quintilius Varus, combined with his haughty and insolent manners, roused the aversion and hatred of the barbarians. A conspiracy accordingly was formed against him by Arminius, a young Cheruscan chief, who had served among the Romans, and was well acquainted with their mode of warfare. The Cheruscans were joined by several other tribes. Segestes, the father-in-law of Arminius, who bore him a grudge, informed Varus of the dangerous plot; but in vain: in A. D. 9, the Roman governor set out against some rebels whose only object was to draw him into a snare. He marched heedlessly with three legions, many auxiliaries, and a quantity of baggage, through the forest of Teutoburg, and in a battle during three very stormy days, he suffered so complete a defeat that the ground far and wide was covered with the dead bodies of the Romans; all those who fell into the hands of the conquerors were made slaves; the Roman standards were lost, and Varus, in despair, put an end to his own life. The Germans had been commanded by Arminius, who was looked upon in after times as the great deliverer of his country from the yoke of the Romans. Augustus, on receiving intelligence of this disaster, is said to have been seized with rage and despair. As the fortress of Aliso had been taken and destroyed by the barbarians, the Romans found it impossible to maintain themselves on the eastern bank of the Rhine, and henceforth confined themselves to protecting the left bank and compelling the Germans to keep to their own side of the river.

9. In this manner the reign of Augustus came to its close. The most eventful occurrence which marks it is the birth of our Lord Jesus Christ at Bethlehem in Judaea. His birth is the beginning of the Christian era, and the date of the present year marks the number supposed to have elapsed since his birth; but more accurate chronological calculations have shown that the birth of Christ must be dated four or five years before the commencement of the vulgar era. The age of Augustus, or, more correctly, the period from the death of Sulla to that of Augustus, must be regarded as the golden age of Roman literature. The Latin language had then reached its highest development, and the greatest poets, orators, and historians

that Rome produced belong to that memorable period, the study of which is of the highest interest also, because in it was first formed and consolidated that system of government and administration which has in a great measure determined the character of our modern civilisation.

10. The happiness of Augustus was greatly disturbed during his later years by domestic misfortunes and afflictions. His promising grandsons, Caius and Lucius Caesar, the sons of his daughter Julia by his friend Agrippa, died prematurely in their youth, not without a suspicion of their having been poisoned by his ambitious wife Livia, who was anxious to secure the succession to Tiberius, her own son by her former husband Augustus' daughter Julia, herself, a talented but licentious woman, caused her father so much grief by her dissolute life, that in the end he found it necessary to banish her. A posthumous son of Agrippa by the same Julia, Agrippa Postumus, died by the hand of a hired assassin in a distant island, to which he had been banished in order that he might not put forward any claims against Tiberius. This murder was perpetrated immediately after the death of Augustus, which took place on the 19th of August A. D. 14, at Nola in Campania, whither he had gone to restore his enfeebled health. He was succeeded without any difficulty by Tiberius, his step-son, who owed his elevation to the cunning contrivances of his mother Livia. The imperial dignity remained in the same family until Nero, who was the last of the line, for after his time the imperial throne was generally filled by the choice of the soldiery.

CHAPTER XV.

THE SUCCESSORS OF AUGUSTUS DOWN TO THE DEATH OF NERO.

1. In his earlier days Tiberius had acquired great renown for the ability with which he had conducted the various wars in the East, in Pannonia and on the Rhine; but his temper had been soured, and after his accession he seemed to have become quite a different man. He was a great proficient in dissimulation, and at first succeeded for a time in concealing the viciousness of his character and disposition; but after the year A. D. 20, when his friend Ælius Seianus gained paramount influence over him, the despot committed a series of most revolting atrocities. It was on the advice of Seianus that in A. D. 23 the praetorian cohorts received their stationary camp near Rome, whereby the government was at

once changed into a military despotism, for those praetorians became
the ever ready tools of tyranny, and in the course of time usurped
the power of electing and deposing emperors at their pleasure.
Augustus had allowed the people to assemble in their comitia, and
even to pass laws in the ancient form, but Tiberius abolished this
last shadow of republican freedom, and transferred the functions
of the assembled people to the senate, which degraded itself by its
servile flattery, and readiness to do or sanction deeds which the
despot himself shrunk from attempting. The trial of cases of high
treason against the person of the emperor became one of the duties
of the senate, which was thus obliged to inflict punishment on persons whom Tiberius himself could scarcely have ventured to con-
demn. Every one was declared guilty of high treason who either
by speech, deed, or writing, should offend the emperor. This
measure called into existence a host of well-paid crafty spies and
informers, who crushed and stifled every honest expression of
opinion, and extinguished the last spark of freedom and independence, while, on the other hand, they increased the tyrant's
fears and cruelty. Seianus, whose character very much resembled
that of his master, had the executive in his own hands, while Tiberius abandoned himself to the basest sensual lusts; and in order to
be able to indulge them more freely and unrestrainedly, he withdrew in A. D. 26 from Rome, and finally took up his abode in the
island of Capreae, in the bay of Naples. There he gave himself up
to the grossest sensuality, and took a delight in torturing the unfortunate victims of his lust. This period of his absence from Rome
was the most frightful of his frightful reign, for Seianus now ruled
without restraint, endeavouring to exterminate the family of his
sovereign, and thus to secure the succession to himself. He had
already despatched by poison Drusus, the only son of Tiberius.
This had happened in A. D. 23; six years later several other members of the imperial family, and among them Agrippina and her
three sons, were got rid of by being sent into exile, and were afterwards killed by starvation or otherwise; Caius (afterwards the
emperor Caligula), the youngest of the sons of Agrippina and
Germanicus, was the only one that escaped. At length, when all
obstacles were removed, Seianus sued for the hand of the widow
of Drusus, whom he himself had poisoned. When, notwithstanding his great precaution, this was reported to Tiberius, the emperor
addressed a letter to the senate, in which he accused his minister
of high treason, and demanded his execution. The order was
immediately and joyfully obeyed, A. D. 31, and Tiberius now took
vengeance on all the friends and relations of Seianus. Macro, the
successor of Seianus, was scarcely better than his predecessor; and
Tiberius, by his experience of the past, became still more distrust-
ful and cruel than before. His debauches had destroyed his health,

and he appears to have felt his end approaching. But carefully concealing his condition, he resolved to return to Rome. In the meantime Macro, in conjunction with Caius (Caligula), had formed the design of getting rid of the aged tyrant. At a villa near Misenum, Tiberius fell into a deathlike state of lethargy, which induced some persons of his suite to proclaim Caligula, who happened to be with his uncle, as his successor. But Tiberius recovered, and as both Macro and Caligula had reason to fear his vengeance, they caused him to be suffocated between beds and pillows, A. D. 37, when he had attained his seventy-eighth year.

2. The most remarkable event in the external history of the reign of Tiberius is the crucifixion of Jesus Christ, according to the common chronology, in A. D. 33. We may also mention a fearful earthquake, by which many flourishing cities in Asia were reduced to heaps of ruins; and the great catastrophe at Fidenae, where a temporary wooden amphitheatre fell during a show of gladiators, which had drawn together vast multitudes from Rome and other neighbouring towns; no less than fifty thousand persons were killed or seriously hurt on that occasion. The last great event we shall here notice, the war against the Germans, was in point of time the first, for in the very year in which Tiberius obtained the imperial dignity, A. D. 14, a great insurrection broke out among the legions on the Rhine and in Pannonia. Germanicus, the noble son of Drusus, commanding on the Rhine, was generous enough to quiet the soldiers, who demanded that he should assume the imperial dignity instead of Tiberius. The revolt in Pannonia was quelled by prudent concessions on the part of Tiberius. Germanicus, after appeasing his troops, crossed the Rhine to wipe off the stain cast on the Roman name under the bad management of Varus; he penetrated into, and ravaged, the country of the Chatti, buried the remains of the Romans he found in the Teutoburg forest, and made Thusnelda, Arminius' wife, his captive, she having been betrayed into his hands by her own father Segestes, who had always been well disposed towards the Romans. In consequence of this, Arminius exerted all his energy to rouse the Cheruscans and· the neighbouring tribes to a vigorous resistance against the common enemy. A. Caecina, the legate of Germanicus, was brought into imminent danger; but owing to the superior tactics of the Romans and the prudence of Germanicus, the Germans were defeated in two battles. Nevertheless, however, the dominion of Rome could not be firmly and permanently re-established on the eastern bank of the Rhine. For when, in A. D. 16, Germanicus was recalled by Tiberius, who looked with jealousy upon his success and popularity, the Germans were for a time left without any further molestation. Germanicus was sent to the East, and died at Antioch in A. D. 19, having probably been poisoned by Piso, the governor of Syria. About this time

Tiberius, or rather his son Drusus, undertook an expedition against Maroboduus, king of the Marcomanni. But to facilitate the undertaking, another German tribe was induced to attack Maroboduus in another quarter. As the king's capital was taken by the enemy, he sought the assistance of the Romans, whom he did not suspect of hostile intentions; but Tiberius ordered him to renounce his kingdom, and spend the remainder of his life at Ravenna. Catualda, the conqueror of Maroboduus, soon after experienced the same fate, for being driven from his kingdom, he sought refuge with the Romans, and was ordered to take up his residence at Forum Julium, in the south of Gaul. Arminius, the deliverer of Germany, was afterwards murdered by his own ungrateful countrymen. These occurrences and insurrections in Gaul and Africa, which were quelled without much difficulty, are the only important events in the Roman empire during the reign of Tiberius.

3. Tiberius, as we have already noticed, was succeeded by Caius, commonly called Caligula, who reigned from A. D. 37 till 41. He was the son of the noble-minded Germanicus, by Agrippina, and as he resembled his father in appearance, every one hoped that he had also inherited his father's virtues. During the first eight months, these hopes seemed to be realised, when he was suddenly taken ill. He did indeed recover his bodily health, but in his conduct he was completely altered. The vicious disposition, which until then had been carefully concealed, now burst forth without scruple or restraint, and there can be little doubt that he was labouring under insanity. Without entering into the disgusting details of his reign, we shall briefly sum up the most prominent features of his character. He was a blood-thirsty tyrant, who took a delight in signing death-warrants and witnessing the agonies of his victims; a senseless squanderer of the public treasures, which he spent upon the gratification of his lusts and the erection of absurd buildings; a vain boaster, who celebrated triumphs over the Germans and Britons, whom he had never encountered on the field of battle, and ordered himself to be worshipped as a god; a glutton, who by his excesses drained the provinces as well as the treasury; and a low and vulgar sensualist, whose favourite companions were actors, gladiators, and prostitutes. A conspiracy was formed against this monster as early as B. C. 39, but it was discovered and its authors were put to death: soon after another was formed by some officers of the praetorian guards, and in A. D. 41 he was murdered in his own palace while attending the rehearsal of some actors. His wife and daughters were likewise put to death. During the tumult the murderers dragged forth Tiberius Claudius, who from fear had concealed himself, and proclaimed him emperor.

4. Cladius was a brother of Germanicus, and a son of Drusus and Antonia. His life had been spared during the reigns of Tiberius

and Caligula, merely because he was despised and looked upon as an idiot, who was not likely ever to claim the succession. When he ascended the throne, he had reached the age of fifty-one years. The manner in which he had been treated by his own family had intimidated him and made him cowardly. His favourite pursuits had been history and antiquities, and he himself wrote a history of his own times, memoirs of his own life, and, in the Greek language, histories of Carthage and Etruria. While he occupied himself with these pursuits, his freedmen and favourites, Narcissus, Pallas, Callistus, and others governed the empire, exercising unlimited influence over him, and his dissolute wife Messalina scorned every law of decency and morality. At the suggestion of these unworthy advisers, Claudius put to death the noblest men of the time, and the licentiousness of the court destroyed the last vestiges of virtue among the higher classes, especially among females. Messalina went so far in her shamelessness, as publicly to solemnise her marriage with a handsome young Roman, although she was lawfully married to Claudius. This step at length opened the eyes of the infatuated emperor, and, terrified by the prospect of greater dangers, he ordered Messalina to be put to death, and married his niece, the beautiful and talented, but licentious and ambitious Agrippina. She was anxious to get rid of his children by his former wife, and to secure the succession to Nero her own son, by her former husband, Domitius Ahenobarbus. When her schemes were discovered, and the voluptuous emperor was on the point of thwarting her, she anticipated him by causing him to be poisoned, in the month of October, A. D. 54. The reign of Claudius, so far as he was not under the influence of women and freedmen, was mild and popular. He was very fond of building, and undertook and completed some very important works: he deepened and fortified the port of Ostia, and drained the Fucine lake by constructing an immense tunnel, at which thirty thousand men are said to have been at work for eleven years, and which led the waters of the lake into the river Liris. In spite of the moral degeneracy of the times, the Roman arms were victorious abroad under Claudius and his successors. In A. D. 50, a successful war was commenced against the Parthians, who attempted to conquer Armenia. In Germany, quarrels arose after the death of Arminius, which led to Claudius appointing Italicus, a nephew of Arminius, king of the Cheruscans, and considerably weakened the German tribes, so that the whole of western Germany might again have become a Roman province, had not Claudius recalled his victorious general Corbulo, and ordered him to confine himself to defending the western banks of the Rhine. The reign of Claudius is also remarkable as the period in which the Romans first made permanent conquests in Britain. On the invitation of an exiled British chief, a Roman army, in A. D. 43. invaded the island.   Claudius himself visited it for a short time, but left the management of the war to his lieutenants, who continued it for nine years.   Vespasian and his son Titus acquired their first military laurels in this war, and the south-eastern part of Britain, which was finally conquered in A. D. 51, was constituted a Roman province.

5. Agrippina succeeded in her plan of securing the succession to her son Nero, and soon after the murder of Claudius, the young man, only seventeen years old, was proclaimed emperor.   He had been educated by the philosopher Seneca and Burrus, an officer of the praetorian guards, and was possessed of considerable talent, but the influence of the corrupt and licentious court, the obsequiousness of the senate, and the servility of the people, could not but ultimately produce their effects.   During the first five years of his reign, however, Seneca, and Burrus so far succeeded in controlling his vicious propensities, that this period, compared with that which followed, appeared to the Romans as a most happy time. Things assumed a different aspect, when Nero began to quarrel with his ambitious mother, who interfered in the government, and even threatened to raise Brittanicus, the son of Claudius, to the throne.   He now in rapid succession murdered Brittanicus and his mother, whom he intended to drown by means of a boat constructed in such a manner that it went to pieces when on the waters; but as she saved herself by swimming, he ordered her to be assassinated, and this deed was not disapproved of by Seneca and Burrus.   His mistresses Acte and Poppaea Sabina led him from one crime to another, and when Burrus was removed from the court, B. C. 62, Nero threw off all restraint: he banished his wife Octavia to the island of Pandataria, where she was soon afterwards murdered, and then married the adulterous Poppaea Sabina.   Two years later, a fearful conflagration broke out at Rome, which lasted for six days, and during which the greater part of the city was reduced to ashes. It is said that this fire was the work of Nero, who was anxious to have a vivid representation of the burning of Troy.   The emperor, however, charged the Christians, who as yet formed an obscure sect, with having caused the conflagration, and instituted a cruel persecution against them, in which the apostles Peter and Paul are said to have perished.   The magnificent restoration of the city, and the building of Nero's golden house on the Palatine hill, increased the oppressive character of his rule, though the populace was kept in good humour by being fed and amused with the plunder of the provinces.

5. In B. C. 65, a formidable conspiracy was formed by Calpurnius Piso, but it was discovered, and Piso himself, the poet Lucan, and a great many others, had to pay for the attempt with their lives.   Seneca, who was also suspected of having been an

accomplice, died by opening his own veins. His next victims were his wife Poppaea Sabina, whom he killed in a brutal fit of passion, and Antonia, a daughter of Claudius, whom he murdered because she refused to marry him. Virtue, in whatever form it appeared, now became an object of the tyrant's fear and hatred. In A. D. 67, Nero went to Greece to take part as a player on the lyre in the great games at Olympia and on the Isthmus, and signalised himself by the grossest follies and cruelties. In the following year, soon after his return, an insurrection, headed by Julius Vindex, broke out in Gaul, on account of the fearful oppression to which that country had been subjected. Vindex offered the sovereignty to Servius Galba, governor of Spain, who was at once proclaimed emperor by his soldiers. But Rufus, the governor of southern Germany, marched into Gaul against Vindex, and although the two appear to have come to an amicable arrangement, Vindex by some mistake was murdered. The praetorians at Rome were soon induced likewise to proclaim Servius Galba, whereupon Nero, abandoned by every one, took to flight, and on being discovered, inflicted a wound on himself, in consequence of which he died, in June A. D. 68. With him the house of the Claudii or of Augustus became extinct, and henceforth the praetorian guards, and sometimes the legions in the provinces, assumed the right of electing the emperor, who generally obtained the sanction of the senate, which, however, was a mere matter of form.

7. In the meantime the Parthians in the East had succeeded in making themselves masters of Armenia. In A. D. 54, Domitius Corbulo, one of the ablest generals of the time, was sent against them, and in a long protracted war recovered the whole of Armenia; his successor, however, was unable to maintain his ground, and Tiridates, a brother of the Parthian king, in A. D. 66 again ascended the throne of Armenia. Germany was tolerably quiet during the reign of Nero, but in Britain an alarming insurrection broke out in A. D. 61, in consequence of the fearful rapacity of the Roman governor. During his absence on an expedition against the island of Mona, the Britons under their queen Boadicea took up arms, and succeeded in destroying a whole Roman legion and several colonies. But the governor Paulinus speedily returned, and defeated them in a great battle, in which eighty thousand of them are said to have been slain. Boadicea put an end to her own life, and peace was concluded with the Britons. During Nero's stay in Greece, the Jews also rose in open rebellion against their oppressors, and after the first defeat of the Roman army by them, the emperor gave the command to Vespasian, who had already greatly distinguished himself by extending the Roman dominion in Britain.

CHAPTER XVI.

FROM THE DEATH OF NERO TO THAT OF DOMITIAN.

1. ON learning that he had been proclaimed by the praetorians, and that the choice was sanctioned by the senate, Servius Galba hastened to Rome, accompanied by Salvius Otho, the governor of Lusitania.   He was the first emperor that was raised to the throne by the soldiery, and they expected that he would be particularly liberal towards them.   In this hope they were disappointed, and as, moreover, he attempted to restore discipline among them, and was also guilty of some arbitrary proceedings, to which he was led by his freedmen, who had entire control over him, Salvius Otho formed a conspiracy against him, and Galba was murdered while crossing the Forum, in January, A. D. 69, at the advanced age of seventy-three, and after a reign of scarcely eight months.   His adopted son, Piso Licinianus, who was to have been his successor, and whose adoption had offended Otho, was likewise murdered.

2. The praetorians now proclaimed Otho emperor, and the servile senate sanctioned their choice.   Otho had been the contemptible husband of Poppaea Sabina before her marriage with Nero; but he commenced his reign by taking to account some of the persons who had been most conspicuous under Nero.   He had, however, scarcely entered on his duties, when he received tidings that the legions stationed on the Rhine had proclaimed Vitellius, their own commander, emperor.   The latter immediately sent an army across the Alps, and in a great battle near Bedriacum, gained a decisive victory over Otho, who a few days later made away with himself in despair, in April, A. D. 69.   Otho's army surrendered to Vitellius, who was now the undisputed sovereign of the empire.   He was a vulgar glutton, who had spent all his life in coarse sensual pleasures. He took no interest in the duties of his station, allowed the praetorians to act as they pleased with impunity, and distinguished himself only by extorting money to satisfy his low appetites.   This conduct aroused general indignation against him, and the legions in Syria, Moesia, and Pannonia, renounced their allegiance; during these insurrections, Flavius Vespasianus, who was successfully carrying on the war against the Jews, was proclaimed emperor.   Being supported by the governors of several other provinces, and leaving the continuation of the siege of Jerusalem to his son Titus, he at once prepared for war against Vitellius.   The hostile armies met in the north of Italy, and Antonius Primus, a staunch supporter of Vespasian, who had come with an army across the Alps, defeated Vitellius near Bedriacum, and the town of Cremona was completely

ravage l for its attachment to him.   Vitellius was now forsaken by
all parties except the praetorians and the Roman populace.   When
the hostile army arrived at Rome, a frightful massacre took place
in the streets of the city.   Sabinus, a brother of Vespasian, who
had thrown himself into the Capitol, was taken and murdered by
the partizans of Vitellius, and the magnificent Capitoline temple
was destroyed by fire.   At length the praetorian camp in which
Vitellius had taken refuge fell into the hands of the enemy, and the
emperor being dragged forth was cruelly murdered, in December,
A. D. 69, after a reign of scarcely eight months.

3. While these things were going on in Italy, Vespasian was
still at Alexandria, in Egypt, and the affairs at Rome were managed
by his son Domitian, and Mucianus, the late governor of Syria.
The new emperor himself did not arrive in Rome until A. D. 70,
when he found the praetorians completely subdued.   All the successors of Augustus had been cruel tyrants or contemptible imbe-
ciles.   Vespasian was a man of quite a different character, and the
very ruler whom Rome required at the time; he may be called the
true renovator of the state.   Immediately after his arrival at Rome
he set about restoring discipline among the troops and the praetorians, excluded unworthy men from the senate, watched over the
administration of justice, suppressed the detestable class of informers, stopped the trials for high treason against the person of the emperor, and economised the finances of the empire by a wise regulation of the taxes and tolls, though he was not niggardly when the
public good or the embellishment of the city required it.   He spent
enormous sums upon the rebuilding of the Capitoline temple, upon
the construction of the great amphitheatre called the Colosseum,
which even in its present dilapidated state excites the wonder and
admiration of all travellers, and upon the building of the temple of
Peace.   By his own example he endeavoured to put an end to the
profligacy of the higher orders, and gave to the empire a greater
degree of unity and compactness than it had hitherto possessed, by
raising the most illustrious men from the provinces to the places
which became vacant in the senate, so that Italy virtually ceased to
be the exclusive mistress of the world.   Vespasian was what we
may call a plain, practical man; he had a great aversion not only to
every kind of luxury, but also to the numerous philosophers and
astrologers who then resided at Rome, and whom in A. D. 74, he
expelled from the city.   He hated the Christians and republicans;
the former he confounded with the Jews, and the latter, who were
found principally among the Stoic philosophers, he regarded as foolish and audacious speculators.   Hence the noble Helvidius Priscus,
who, like his father-in-law Paetus Thrasea, was a great Stoic and
republican, and had often been troublesome to the emperor by his
opposition in the senate, was first exiled and then put to death.

33 *

4. Among the most remarkable occurrences in the history of the empire during Vespasian's reign is the capture of Jerusalem by his son Titus, in A. D. 70. Judaea had for many years been governed by Roman *procuratores*, who not only oppressed the people, but by their insolence and scorn wounded their deepest feelings. Gessius Florus, who had been appointed procurator by Nero, combining cruelty with the ordinary qualities of a Roman governor, drove the Jews, who were also urged on by a strong national party, into open rebellion, and the Romans were compelled to evacuate Jerusalem. But the victorious party now established a reign of terror in the city, during which many of the moderate party and the Roman prisoners were murdered. Vespasian then, A. D. 67, undertook the war against the Jews with a powerful army. Being misguided by their own leaders, distracted by internal dissensions, and mortally hated by the Romans, they fought with the courage of despair against the legions. After the fall of the strong fortress of Jotapata, and a fearful defeat in which forty thousand Jews are said to have been killed, they were obliged to confine themselves to the defence of their city of Jerusalem, which, after Vespasian's elevation to the sovereignty of the empire, was besieged by his son Titus. The city being overcrowded with men from all parts, suffered severely from famine, and the distress was increased by epidemic diseases and furious party feuds. It was in vain that Titus offered to spare the Jews, if they would lay down their arms; rage against their enemies and a blind confidence in the speedy help of Jehovah, goaded them on to the last extremity. When at length the city was taken, the Jews defended themselves in the Temple, until that magnificent and venerable building, too, became a prey to the flames on the 2d of September, A. D. 70. The city was then destroyed, and upwards of a million of Jews are said to have perished. They lost their independence for ever, and being forbidden to rebuild their city, scattered over the whole of the Roman empire, where they were subject to the payment of an annual tax. The triumphal arch, afterwards erected by Titus at Rome, still bears witness to that memorable event.

5. Even before Vespasian's arrival at Rome, a great insurrection, headed by Claudius Civilis, had broken out among the Batavi, whose example was speedily followed by the Frisians and some Gallic tribes; but owing to the energy of Petilius Cerealis, they were defeated one after another, and compelled to sue for peace, A. D. 70. In the following year Cerealis obtained the administration of Britain, and was accompanied thither by Agricola, the father-in-law of the great historian Tacitus, by whom we have a life of him. In A. D. 77, Agricola was himself appointed governor of Britain, a post which he filled until A. D. 85, to his own honour and that of his countrymen. During this period he conquered not only all England but the south of Scotland

as far as the Firths of Clyde and Forth.   He carried his victories even to the Highlands, and explored the coasts of the country, though he was unable tó establish the Roman dominion beyond the Forth.

6. The reign of Vespasian was extremely beneficial to the empire, although he did things which cannot be called otherwise than cruel. Towards the end of his life a conspiracy was formed against him ; but it was discovered and its authors were put to death.   Soon afterwards he was taken ill, and having died on the 23d of June, A. D. 79, at the age of seventy, he was succeeded by his son Titus, who had latterly governed the empire in conjunction with his father. His short reign lasted only till the middle of September A. D. 81, and at first considerable apprehension prevailed at Rome, as he had been previously guilty of several acts of cruelty.   But after his accession he showed himself so kind and benevolent as to obtain and deserve the title of "the love and delight of mankind."   The calamities which visited several parts of the empire during his brief reign afforded him excellent opportunities for displaying his kindly benevolence.   In the month of August A. D. 79, a fearful eruption of mount Vesuvius, the first recorded in history, destroyed and buried under burning lava and ashes the towns of Herculaneum, Pompeii, and Stabiae.   Pliny the elder, who ventured too near to satisfy his curiosity, lost his life; the whole eruption has been minutely described by his nephew, the younger Pliny, in two letters addressed to Tacitus the historian.   Portions of these buried towns which have been laid open in modern times, furnish the most inte- resting information on antiquities and ancient art.   It is said that the emperor Titus spent nearly his whole property in relieving the sufferers who survived the terrible catastrophe.   In A. D. 80 a fire broke out at Rome, which raged for three days, destroying the finest parts of the city; and no sooner had this misfortune passed away, than a fearful pestilence came, which carried off thousands of people in all parts of Italy.   The last year of Titus' reign is marked by the inauguration of the Colosseum, which had been commenced by his father, and by the building of the Thermae, which bear his name.   He died in the same villa in which Vespasian had breathed his last, in the country of the Sabines ; and all the Romans mourned over his death as over that of a father.   During his reign the frontiers of the empire were not disturbed by any aggressions, and Agricola was engaged in the conquest of Britain, which he secured by forti- fications between the Clyde and Forth.

7. Titus was succeeded by his brother Domitian, a man who had already given numerous proofs of his cruel and tyrannical disposi- tion, and was even believed to have made attempts upon the lives of his father and brother.   At first, however, his conduct led his subjects to believe that he was better than his reputation, but after- wards he displayed his real character, and became one of the darkest

and most detestable tyrants that ever disgraced a throne.   Hosts
of informers again arose as in the worst days of his predecessors.
He increased the pay of the soldiers to make himself popular with
them, and in order to obtain the means necessary for this and other
extravagances, he had recourse to confiscations, and wealthy persons
were treated as criminals merely to enable the despot to gain possession of their property.   His only delights were the gladiatorial
exhibitions, and the torturing of his victims.   He was by no means
devoid of talent, but his occupation with poetry and literature did
not improve his savage nature.   In A. D. 83 he undertook an expedition against the Chatti, and built a frontier wall between the free
Germans and those who were subject to the empire.   In the year
following Agricola gained a great victory over the Caledonians, who
were commanded by their chief Galgacus, at the foot of the Gram-
pians; but as Domitian was jealous of the success of his general, he
recalled him to Rome.   Two years later, A. D. 86, the warlike nation
of the Dacians crossed the Danube and defeated the Roman army
in Moesia.   Domitian himself took the field, but was unable to
repel them.   The Marcomanni and other tribes which were allied
with Rome, refused to support the emperor, and thus obliged him
to purchase a disgraceful peace from the Dacian king Decebalus,
A. D. 90.   Notwithstanding this ignominy, Domitian did not blush
to celebrate a triumph over the Dacians, and assume the name of
Dacicus; but as he nevertheless felt his humiliation keenly, he
became still more ferocious, and went so far in his madness as to
order himself to be worshipped as "Lord and God."   The noblest
men were put to death for opinions they ventured to express;
the philosophers, one of whom was the great Epictetus, were
expelled, and the Christians, whose number had been steadily
increasing at Rome, were murdered and persecuted without mercy.
In the end, however, his own wife Domitia, whom he intended to
put to death, formed a conspiracy against him, and the tyrant was
stabbed in his bed-room by one of her freedmen, on the 18th of
September A. D. 96.

<hr>

CHAPTER XVII.

FROM THE ACCESSION OF NERVA, TO THE DEATH OF M. AURELIUS.

1. HITHERTO all the Roman emperors had been natives of Italy;
but henceforth we frequently find provincials raised to the imperial
dignity, and it was fortunate for the empire that it was so, for the

moral corruption and degradation of Rome and Italy had not yet spread over all the provinces, and the five emperors who followed after Domitian form so noble a contrast with their unworthy predecessors (always excepting Vespasian and Titus), that the period of their reign from A. D. 96 to A. D. 180, is regarded as the happiest in the whole history of the Roman emperors. Immediately after the murder of Domitian, the people and soldiers proclaimed Nerva, a venerable senator of mild disposition. He was, however, not the man whom the praetorians wished to see at the head of affairs, and was therefore obliged to be cautious, both in punishing offenders and in restoring those who had been exiled by Domitian. But the insolence of the praetorians knew no bounds, and in order to strengthen himself, he adopted Ulpius Trajan, a man of unblemished character, who at the time had the command of the legions in Germany. But three months after he had taken this step he died of a fever on the 27th of January A. D. 98. If he had lived longer, he would unquestionably have wrought a great moral change among his subjects.

2. Trajan was a native of Italica in Spain, and arrived at Rome in the year A. D. 99. His administration of the internal affairs of the empire gained for him the surname of "the Best," while his military undertakings showed him to be a man of great military talent. He first of all got rid of the infamous class of informers, many of whom were exiled, and punished the most turbulent among the praetorians. He restored to the senate its power, and founded an institution for the education of poor children of both sexes; he facilitated trade and commerce by making new roads, canals, bridges, and by extending the port of Civita Vecchia; he adorned Rome, Italy, and the provinces with triumphal arches, porticoes, temples, and Rome in particular with the institution of a public library, and the building of a new Forum, in the centre of which rose the celebrated column of Trajan with its bas-relief sculptures representing his own exploits against the Dacians. He honoured men of intellectual culture, and loved their society, as we see from the relation subsisting between him and the historian Tacitus and the younger Pliny. Trajan's own mode of life was simple and without any pomp or ostentation. His wife Plotina and his sister Marciana are among the most estimable female characters in Roman history, and contributed by their example not a little towards the improvement in the conduct of Roman ladies, which henceforth is not disgraced by that licentiousness which forms so deplorable a feature in their character during the first century of the empire.

3. Trajan deeply felt the humiliation of paying to the Dacians the tribute with which Domitian had purchased peace, and in A. D. 100, he set out with a large army against Dacia, which was still governed by king Decebalus. Trajan took his capital Zarmizege-

thusa, defeated him in several battles, and compelled him, in A. D. 103, to sue for peace, which was granted to him on condition of his ceding a portion of his dominions to the empire. This peace, however, did not last long, for in A. D. 104 the Dacians rose again. Trajan then caused a stone bridge to be built over the Danube to facilitate his operations, and marching into Dacia, pressed the enemy so hard, that Decebalus in despair made away with himself, A. D. 106. Dacia (*i. e.* Moldavia, Wallachia, and Transylvania) then became a Roman province, and received numerous colonies, which in a short time firmly established Roman culture and civilisation among the Dacians. Trajan, on his return to Rome, erected the above-mentioned column, which is still one of the most interesting remains of ancient Rome. In A. D. 114, the Parthians again menaced the eastern frontiers of the empire, for their king, deposing the king of Armenia, raised his own brother to the throne. Trajan immediately took the field against them. The Armenians received him with open arms, and their country was made a Roman province, A. D. 115; Nisibis then fell into his hands, and with it the whole of Mesopotamia. The emperor even crossed the Tigris, subdued Assyria, and took the towns of Seleucia and Ctesiphon, the capital of the Parthians, who were obliged to accept Parthamaspates as their king. When the affairs of the Parthians were thus settled, Trajan entered Arabia, where some of his lieutenants had made conquests before, but being taken ill, he left his legate Hadrian in the command of his forces, and hastened to return to Rome; death, however, overtook him at Selinus in Cilicia, on the 9th of August, A. D. 117. His remains were carried to Rome and deposited under the column which he had erected in his Forum.

4. After the death of Trajan, his wife Plotina spread a report that during his illness he had adopted Hadrian, who accordingly undertook the sovereignty at Antioch, where he was then staying, and where he was proclaimed. Hadrian was a native of Picenum, and his father had been married to a relation of Trajan. His disposition was less warlike than that of his predecessor, and seeing that the maintenance of the conquests made by him would involve the empire in perpetual wars, he made the Euphrates the boundary in the East, restoring Assyria and Mesopotamia to the Parthians, and Armenia to the rank of an independent kingdom. Having thus settled the affairs in the East, he returned to Rome, A. D. 118, and then marched into Moesia, which had been invaded by Sarmatian tribes. As he did not wish to make conquests, but only to protect the frontiers of the empire, he concluded peace with the Roxolani. In the meantime, a plot was formed against him by a number of his personal enemies; but the scheme was discovered, and as his severity in punishing the leaders created ill feeling both in the army and at Rome, Hadrian, fearing serious consequences,

returned to Rome, where he did everything in his power to conciliate the senate and the people, while the war against the Sarmatians was continued by his legates.

5. When the frontiers of the empire had been secured, Hadrian, in A. D. 120, undertook a journey through all the provinces of the empire, a great part of which he made on foot, accompanied by only a small retinue. He visited Gaul, Germany, Britain, the northern part of which he secured against the invasions of the Scots by the famous wall extending from the mouth of the Tyne to the Solway; Greece, Asia, and Egypt, where his favourite Antinoüs was drowned in the Nile. These journeys were undertaken, partly on account of a certain restlessness in his disposition, partly to satisfy his curiosity, and partly to make himself personally acquainted with the wants of the provinces, and discover the means for improving their condition. Everywhere he left memorials of his visits, which were designed either to defend and strengthen towns and provinces, or to embellish them, for he was a man of high intellectual culture, and capable of noble feelings, though vanity and conceit rendered him easily accessible to flattery, and towards the end of his life, mistrust and weariness of life often led him to harshness and cruelty. Athens, where he loved to dwell, was embellished by him with extraordinary splendour. His taste for the arts, not to mention the aqueducts, bridges, and temples, with which he adorned Rome, Athens, Nemausus, and other places, was displayed especially in his villa below Tibur, which is still a real mine of valuable antiquities, and his magnificent mausoleum at Rome (Castle St. Angelo). Hadrian was also a liberal patron of literature and science, though in this respect, as well as in his cultivation of the arts, he was very capricious, and much given to astrology and other superstitious pursuits. The philosophers and rhetoricians who were his friends, and lived at his court, such as Plutarch, Herodes Atticus, and Fronto, were men skilled in the use of courtly and tinkling phrases, but deficient in manly spirit and independence.

6. Shortly after Hadrian's return from his travels, A. D. 131, a fearful insurrection broke out among the Jews. Jerusalem had been made a Roman colony under the name of Ælia Capitolina, pagan worship had been introduced, and the religious rites of the Jews rudely interfered with. In consequence of these things they now rose in arms, and carried on a desperate war for many years, but in the end they were crushed by Julius Severus, who was summoned from Britain to conduct the war against them. The Jews henceforth were forbidden to live at Jerusalem, or in its immediate vicinity, and thousands were sold into slavery. Hadrian, in the meantime, lived in retirement; the fatigues he had undergone had impaired his health, and he was so tired of life that he made several attempts at suicide; but he died at Baiae on the 10th of July,

A. D. 138.   As he had no children, he adopted during his illness Arrius Antoninus (Antoninus Pius), whom he obliged to adopt Annius Verus (M. Aurelius).   During the last three years of his life, Hadrian, in consequence of the state of his health, had committed many acts which rendered him unpopular; but Antoninus, with true filial affection for him, did all he could to prevent an outbreak of popular indignation, and hence deserved his surname of Pius.

7. Antoninus Pius, who was descended from a family belonging to Nemausus in Gaul, owed his adoption by Hadrian solely to his virtues.   He had already distinguished himself by his wisdom and mildness in various high offices with which he had been invested. His reign, from A. D. 138 to A. D. 161, forms the happiest period of the Roman empire.   He strictly adhered to the principles of his predecessor, and used to say, that he would rather save the life of one citizen than slay a thousand enemies.   He was a real ornament of the imperial throne, and was beloved throughout the empire perhaps more than any sovereign has ever been beloved either before or since.   His whole care was devoted to the advancement of the arts of peace and the happiness of his people.   These objects he endeavoured to attain by the proper administration of justice, and by educational and charitable institutions for the poor and for orphan children.   The peace which prevailed during his reign, and his own fervent piety, gained for him the name of a second Numa.   The Christians, who then existed in large numbers both at Rome and in the provinces, were not disturbed in their religious observances. He died on the 7th of March, A. D. 161, in one of his villas where he loved to reside in rural retirement.   The Roman empire was so situated that it could not be safe for any length of time without war, and as the troops had been inactive throughout his reign, they had become idle and unwarlike, and when dangers burst in upon the empire under his successor, it was found that the armies were no longer what they had been.

8. As the two sons of Antoninus had died before their father, he was succeeded, according to the established custom, by his adopted son M. Aurelius, surnamed the Philosopher, a native of Rome.   He had been educated with the greatest care, and had from his earliest days shown an extreme love of truth and thirst for knowledge. The doctrines of the Stoic philosophy had a peculiar charm for him, and he continued his favourite pursuit even after he had ascended the throne, though he did not neglect his duties as a ruler when the empire was in danger.   As, however, he was of a weakly constitution, he admitted his adopted brother, L. Verus, a young and active man, to a full participation of the sovereign power; Verus, however, was addicted to debauchery and voluptuousness, which dispositions he had until then carefully concealed from M. Aurelius; but he indulged in them without restraint as soon as he found him-

self abroad at the head of the armies. The Parthians, who had been restrained by the remonstrances of Antoninus, now began making inroads into the Roman provinces, and L. Verus set out against them in A. D. 162. On arriving in Syria, he at once abandoned himself to his voluptuous propensities, leaving the command of the forces to his lieutenants, one of whom invaded Mesopotamia and destroyed Seleucia and Ctesiphon, while another made himself master of Armenia. Peace was at last concluded with the Parthian king, in which he was obliged to cede Mesopotamia to the Romans, A. D. 166.

9. But still more serious dangers were threatening the empire in the north-east, for a number of German and Sarmatian tribes, such as the Marcomanni and Quadi, were on the point of invading Italy, and had already advanced as far as Aquileia. Soon after Verus' return from Syria, the two emperors marched out together against the barbarians, and displayed such overwhelming power that the enemies retreated before them. In A. D. 169 L. Verus died of a fit of apoplexy, and M. Aurelius, now sole emperor, continued the war with great vigour. On one occasion a great battle was fought on the frozen Danube. In A. D. 174, the whole of the Roman army was surrounded, and was saved from destruction only by a violent storm. This sudden and unexpected success of the Romans struck the barbarians with awe, and they sought and obtained peace, on condition of their withdrawing beyond the Danube, A. D. 175. After the pacification of the Danubian frontier, M. Aurelius was called to the East by an insurrection of Avidius Cassius, who had been instigated by the emperor's own wife, Faustina, the unworthy daughter of Antoninus Pius. While he was engaged in quelling the insurrection with a moderation and mildness to which history scarcely presents a parallel, the Marcomanni and their allies renewed the war. In A. D. 178 he therefore once more set out against the Germans and Sarmatians, and fought several successful battles; but before the war was brought to a close he died at Sirmium, on the 17th of March, A. D. 180. His son Commodus, who had accompanied him, now made haste to purchase peace of the barbarians, and thereby revealed to them the weakness of the empire, or rather his own. M. Aurelius had been a philosopher on the throne, in the noblest sense of the term. Notwithstanding the almost uninterrupted wars of his reign, he found leisure to compose his celebrated "Meditations," in which he has portrayed himself with all his amiable, affectionate, and benevolent sentiments. His reign closes the series of really good emperors. His son Commodus, who succeeded him, was one of the most contemptible and insane tyrants known in history.

34

CHAPTER XVIII.

FROM THE ACCESSION OF COMMODUS TO THAT OF DIOCLETIAN.

1. THE accession of Commodus forms the beginning of the decline of the empire, both internally and externally. The best age of Roman literature and the arts had come to a close even before the death of Augustus; the subsequent period, though much inferior in many respects, yet produced a Tacitus and a Juvenal; the arts also revived under Hadrian; but all is now over, and everything tends downwards. The praetorian guards henceforth exercised a most frightful military despotism; and as the troops stationed in the provinces did not always acquiesce in the choice of the praetorians, sometimes two or even more emperors were proclaimed at once in different parts of the empire. From the time of Commodus there is an irregular succession of emperors, who, with very few exceptions, are distinguished only for tyranny and baseness, or impotence and weakness.

2. After having purchased peace of the Marcomanni, Commodus, not yet twenty years old, hastened to Italy, to indulge in all the pleasures and licentiousness of the capital; for the excellent education he had received, and the noble example of his father, were lost upon him. During the first two years of his reign there was not much to complain of, and the best hopes were entertained of him; but a conspiracy formed against him in A. D. 183, by his own sister, changed everything, and the whole remaining period of his life was an uninterrupted series of sanguinary and disgusting excesses. The friends and advisers of his father were put to death, and the business of the state was left to the lowest creatures, while Commodus abandoned himself publicly and without shame, to the grossest vices and most brutal debaucheries. His greatest ambition was to shine as a gladiator in the circus, both against wild beasts and human beings, and his athletic strength led him to regard himself as a second Hercules. In A. D. 185, he was forced by his troops in Britain to recall their commander Perennis, whose tyranny was unbearable to the men; but at the same time he appointed his favourite freedman, Cleander, prefect of the praetorian guards. The exasperation against the unworthy favourite soon rose to such a pitch that he was literally torn to pieces by the populace. At the same time Italy was suffering from plague and famine, while the emperor amused himself with his concubines, and with butchering the noblest among the senators. At length he formed the design of entering the senate-house on the 1st of January, A. D. 193, with a band of gladiators, and of murdering the consuls and many other

persons of eminence. The list of the victims fell into the hands of his mistress, Marcia, and finding her own name among them, she, in conjunction with others, caused the tyrant to be strangled in his bed, on the 31st of December, A. D. 192. During his whole reign he had never troubled himself about the safety of the empire, but its integrity was nevertheless maintained by the valour of his generals. Britain was disturbed by invasions of the Caledonians, who defeated the Roman legions, and spread devastation far and wide; but Ulpius Marcellus drove them back into their own country, and terminated the war against them in A D. 184.

3. The death of Commodus spread joy throughout Rome, and the senate cursed his memory; the praetorians alone were dissatisfied, for upon them he had most lavishly squandered the treasures of the empire. His murderers proclaimed Pertinax, the prefect of the city, emperor, and he accepted the proffered dignity not without great reluctance. In order to replenish the empty treasury, he sold all the costly and luxurious furniture, the mistresses and favourite boys of Commodus, and commenced a series of useful reforms. But the praetorians, vexed at the attempts to curb their licentiousness, which had been connived at by Commodus, rose in open rebellion, and Pertinax was murdered before the end of March, after a reign of scarcely three months. This murder was the commencement of a state of perfect anarchy. The praetorians, who now amounted to sixteen thousand men, ascended the walls of their fortified barracks, and offered the sovereignty to the man who would give them the largest donative. All competitors were outbidden by the wealthy glutton Didius Julianus, who promised to give to every praetorian about one hundred and eighty pounds, and was accordingly proclaimed emperor. The senate, however, detested him, and the people refusing to recognise him, took up arms. The praetorians also grew lukewarm in his defence, as he did not at once give them the promised sum of money. At the same time the army in Syria proclaimed Pescennius Niger, and the legions of Illyricum raised Septimius Severus to the imperial dignity. The latter, wiser than his competitor, advanced with his army into Italy; Didius Julianus, who in vain offered to share the government with him, was put to death by order of the senate on the 1st of July, and Severus was recognised as emperor.

4. Septimius Severus, after being raised to the throne, determined to maintain himself by inexorable severity. Disbanding the praetorian guards, he selected others four times more numerous, and instituted a complete military despotism. He then marched to the East against Pescennius Niger; three battles were fought, and it was only in the third, in the neighbourhood of Issus, A. D. 194, that Niger was completely defeated; he was

afterwards killed while endeavouring to escape by flight. The city of Byzantium, which was in the hands of the partizans of Niger, was defended for two years by the valour of its garrison and its strong fortifications; but when in the end it was compelled by famine to surrender, Severus took fearful vengeance, and ordered its fortifications to be demolished, whereby he unwisely deprived the empire of one of its strong frontier fortresses. Clodius Albinus, the governor of Britain, who had openly declared himself against Didius Julianus and Niger, was rewarded by Severus with the title of Caesar, which conferred upon him the right of succession; but afterwards discovering that Severus had formed a plan for procuring his assassination, he took up arms against him, and found many followers among those who were displeased with the emperor's severity. The latter accordingly was obliged to hasten from the East to Gaul, where a schoolmaster had already collected an army for him. Clodius Albinus was defeated in A. D. 197 near Lyons in Gaul: he himself perished, and all his friends and relations were put to death with cruel tortures. On his return to Rome the emperor behaved with equal sternness. In A. D. 198 he made a successful expedition against the Parthians, whom he deprived of the province of Mesopotamia together with the towns of Dara and Nisibis; but Atra in Arabia was besieged in vain. He also paid a visit to Egypt, where some new regulations were made. When at length he had got rid of all his competitors and felt himself safe in the possession of the sovereignty, he endeavoured to improve the laws, and through them public morality; in these endeavours he was assisted by the great jurists Papinian and Ulpian, who may be termed his ministers of justice. At the same time he took upon himself the whole administration of the empire,—its finances, and its stores, thereby depriving the senate of nearly all its powers. In A. D. 208 the Caledonians repeated their invasion of the north of England, in consequence of which he proceeded to Britain, taking with him his two sons Antoninus Caracalla and Septimius Geta. He penetrated indeed far into the northern part of Britain, but sustained severe losses, until in A D. 210 he succeeded in compelling the Caledonians to submit, and completed the fortification which had been erected between the Solway and Tyne. While engaged in this manner he was taken ill; grief at the faithless conduct of his son Caracalla aggravated his illness, and he died at York on the 4th of February A. D. 211.

5. The two brothers Caracalla and Geta, who had both been destined by their father to succeed him, concluded a treaty with the Caledonians, who had again revolted, and then returned to Rome. The hatred which they had cherished against each other from their boyhood now burst forth with greater animosity, and it was in vain that their mother Julia Domna attempted to bring

about a reconciliation: Caracalla, the more cruel of the two, caused his brother to be murdered in the very arms of his mother, and then declared him to be a god, A. D. 212. No one, however, was allowed to mention the name of Geta, and all his friends were put to death. Among these victims was Caracalla's own instructor, the great jurist Papinian, who refused to justify the fratricide. Besides these, thousands of others were murdered in order that the tyrant might gain possession of their property. When these means no longer sufficed to provide him with what he wanted to gratify his lusts, he deteriorated the coinage, and in order to be able to increase the taxes, conferred the Roman franchise upon all free-born subjects of the empire. But all these things made his name so odious at Rome that he felt uneasy, and resolved to travel through the various countries of the empire, all of which were now equally robbed and plundered, and deprived of their best inhabitants. Thus he devastated Gaul in A. D. 213, and in the year following, he was obliged to purchase peace of the Germans, notwithstanding which he assumed the title Germanicus. After this he traversed Macedonia, aping Alexander the Great in his dress, gestures, and the inclination of the head; thence he proceeded to Asia Minor, where he imitated Achilles. Osrhoëne was made by him a Roman province, but an attempt upon Armenia failed At last he arrived in Alexandria, where some pasquinades upon him had been circulated. For this offence he now punished the city, in A. D. 215, by ordering the greater part of its inhabitants to be butchered by his soldiers. The place is said to have been literally deluged with blood. After this atrocity he proceeded to Antioch, being desirous to obtain the surname Parthicus. He gained his object, without fighting a battle, by treacherously causing Artabanes, the king of the Parthians, to be put to death. But on his return he himself was murdered, on the 8th of April, A. D. 217, near Edessa by his own soldiers, headed by Macrinus, the prefect of the praetorians. His memory was cursed and his name effaced from all public monuments.

6. Macrinus, the murderer, was then proclaimed emperor by the soldiers, and continued the war against the Parthians, but without success, and was obliged to purchase peace of them with an enormous sum of money. The Roman senate disliked Macrinus, because, being himself a Mauritanian of low origin, he raised vulgar persons to rank and station, and with the soldiers he was unpopular, on account of his harshness. Maesa, a sister of Julia Domna, the wife of Septimius Severus, accordingly had no difficulty in exciting the soldiers against him, and persuading them to confer the imperial dignity upon her own grandson Elagabalus, a priest of the Sun at Emesa. This happened on the 8th of June A. D. 218. In the ensuing struggle between the two emperors, Macrinus and his son
34 *

Diadumenianus were murdered at Chalcedon.   The mad and brutal lusts, and the fearful extravagance of Elagabalus, however, soon created universal disgust.   It would almost seem that at times he was actually labouring under insanity; he raised his grandmother to the rank of a senator, and instituted a senate of ladies, to honour his mother, and to determine the fashions and ceremonies.   He also introduced at Rome the Syrian worship of the Sun, by which he destroyed the last traces of the ancient Roman discipline and morality.   As Maesa perceived that the Romans would not tolerate the young and cruel voluptuary much longer, she persuaded him to raise Alexander Severus, another grandson of hers, to the rank of Caesar; Elagabalus complied with the request, but finding that the Caesar daily rose in popularity, he attempted to murder him; at length the praetorians, utterly disgusted with him, put him and his mother to death on the 11th of March A. D. 222.

7. Alexander Severus was only in his seventeenth year when he ascended the throne; he was a simple-hearted man of good moral principles, who made many useful regulations, and followed the advice of his intelligent mother Mammaea, who was well disposed towards the Christians; but he did not possess the strength of character required by the exigencies of the times.   Assisted in the government by his mother and a council of sixteen senators, he endeavoured to restrain within proper bounds the lascivious manners of his subjects, exiled useless servants and faithless governors of provinces, promoted commerce, and reduced oppressive taxes. Notwithstanding all this, attempts were made to dethrone him, and the praetorians, exasperated at the severity of the great jurist Ulpian, murdered him with impunity before the emperor's own eyes, A. D. 228.   Alexander Severus had not only to contend with enemies at home, but the frontiers of the empire were threatened by foreign foes.   In A. D. 226, the Persians under Artaxerxes (Ardishir) over-turned the kingdom of the Parthians, and founded the dynasty of the Sassanidae, so called from Artaxerxes being a son of Sassan. The object of the new rulers was to restore the ancient Persian empire in its whole extent, and accordingly they invaded Mesopo-tamia and Syria.   The feeble garrisons were unable to offer any effective resistance, and some even went over to the enemy.   In A. D. 231 Alexander Severus himself proceeded to the East, and, having restored discipline among the troops, commenced a war against Artaxerxes, in which, according to some authorities, he was very successful against the proud Persian.   At all events, the Per-sians for some time after this remained quiet or made conquests in other quarters.   Severus returned to Rome in triumph A. D. 233, and soon after, being informed that German tribes were harassing Gaul, he hastened to the aid of the threatened province.   But before he had an opportunity of fighting a battle, he and his mother were

murdered in the camp near Mayence on the 10th of February
A. D. 235, by his soldiers, who wanted a more valiant and liberal
ruler.

8. Maximinus, a rude Thracian, but a man of great bodily strength
and experience in war, was then proclaimed emperor by the soldiers.
He was an enemy to the Christian religion, and immediately on his
accession, he showed the rudeness of his character, by causing many
of his own benefactors to be put to death, and dispatching all those
who showed the slightest symptoms of attachment to others.   He
was, however, successful against the Germans, whose country he
devastated far and wide.   His elevation, which was not approved
of by the Roman senate, threw the empire into such confusion, that
within twenty years no less than twelve emperors were set up and
deposed.   In A. D. 238, the legions stationed in Africa, with the
consent of the senate, proclaimed Gordian emperor, who being
already at the advanced age of eighty, assumed his son as his colleague.   This happened in the month of February, but in March
of the same year, Capelianus, Maximinus' prefect of Mauritania,
defeated and slew the younger Gordian in a battle, and drove the
aged father to kill himself in despair.   Terrified by this news, the
senate raised two eminent senators, Maximus and Balbinus, to the
imperial dignity, and by the demand of the people, Gordian, a boy
of thirteen years, and a grandson of the elder Gordian, was raised
to the rank of Caesar.   In A. D. 238 Maximinus advanced with his
army from Germany into Italy.   Terror preceded him everywhere,
and the citizens leaving their unprotected homes took refuge in the
fortresses, which the invader did not find it easy to take.   While
besieging Aquileia, the soldiers suffering from want, and seeing
that the whole empire was opposed to Maximinus, put him and his
son to death in the month of April, and joined the army of Maximus, who was encamped in the neighbourhood of Ravenna.

9. In the meantime the praetorian guards at Rome being dissatisfied with the emperors Maximus and Balbinus, who had been
appointed by the senate, murdered them in the month of July
during the Capitoline games, and proclaimed young Gordian emperor.
This boy, who was thus raised to the throne, was at first misled and
deceived by dishonest advisers; but from A. D. 241, in which he
married a daughter of Misitheus, he allowed himself to be guided
by the prudent and disinterested advice of his father-in-law.   In
the same year the Persians renewed the war with greater vehemence
than ever under their king Sapor I.; and Gordian, accompanied by
Misitheus, set out for the East, and drove the enemy from Syria
and Mesopotamia, which had been ravaged by them.   Unfortunately
Misitheus died two years later, and Philippus, an Arab by birth,
who was appointed his successor as prefect of the praetorians, stirred
up a mutinous spirit among the soldiers.   By this means he com-

pelled Gordian to make him his colleague in the empire, and afterwards, in the month of April A. D. 244, caused the young prince to be murdered near Circesium on the confines of Assyria. Philippus then concluded peace with the Persians and returned to Rome, where he favoured the Christians, and carried on the government not without wisdom and moderation; but these very circumstances combined with his eastern origin made him unpopular, and it was in vain that, in A. D. 247, he entertained the people with magnificent *ludi saeculares* to commemorate the thousand years' existence of Rome. In A. D. 249 the legions stationed in Moesia compelled Decius against his will to assume the imperial dignity. He informed Philippus by letter that he would resign his power as soon as he arrived at Rome, but Philippus, distrusting him, marched with an army to the north of Italy, where he was defeated and killed in a battle near Verona.

10. Decius ascended the throne about the middle of A. D. 249, and after quelling some disturbances in Gaul, returned to Rome, where he commenced a fearful persecution of the Christians throughout the empire, and endeavoured by the revival of ancient institutions to check the downward course of the empire. But it was in vain, and the more the state suffered from internal decay and dissolution, the more did the barbarians on the frontiers, especially the Germans, become emboldened. The Goths, a numerous German tribe, who first appear in history as inhabitants of the banks of the Vistula, had advanced southward to the frontiers of Dacia as early as the time of Caracalla. In alliance with many other German tribes, and commanded by their own kings, they first attacked the provinces about the Danube. In A. D. 250, the Goth Cniva, with an army of seventy thousand men, crossed the Danube, and advanced as far as Philippopolis in Thrace; Decius marched into Thrace, and succeeded in driving the barbarians back across the Danube, but owing to the treachery of his own general Gallus Trebonianus, he was killed with his son during an engagement in a marshy district of Moesia, A. D. 251. Gallus, who was then proclaimed emperor by the legions, made Hostilianus, a son of the brave Decius, his colleague in the empire, and his own son Volusianus was raised to the rank of Caesar. A pestilence was then beginning to rage in all parts of the empire, and continuing for the long period of fifteen years, carried off a vast multitude of men. Hostilianus was one of its victims in A. D. 252. Throughout this time, Gallus remained inactive at Rome, while the Goths and other tribes again invaded Moesia and Pannonia. But his brave general Æmilius Æmilianus repelled the enemy, and, proud of his victory, accepted the purple offered to him by his soldiers. The new emperor forthwith proceeded with his army to Italy; Gallus met the usurper in Umbria, but both he and his son Volusianus were put to death by their mutinous soldiers, in May A. D. 253. Æmilia-

nus now took possession of the throne, but scarcely four months later he too was killed by his faithless soldiers in the neighbourhood of Spoleto.

11. Just at this time, Valerian, a most distinguished man, and a friend of Gallus, was approaching Italy with Gallic and German legions to avenge the murder of his friend. His army at once saluted him as emperor; in Rome, too, his arrival was welcomed, and he appointed his own son Gallienus his colleague in the administration of the empire. He did all he could to restore the internal tranquillity of the empire, carefully watched over the execution of justice, and reduced obnoxious taxes; but unfortunately he had not much leisure to devote to these internal reforms, for the empire was at the time threatened on all sides; the Franks and Alemanni were crossing the Rhine, the Goths invaded Moesia, and the Persians in the East, under their powerful king Sapor, crossed the Euphrates and even made themselves masters of Antioch. Gallienus, or rather his brave legato Postumus, in A. D. 256 fought successfully against the Franks, a confederation of German tribes dwelling between the Rhine and the Weser, such as the Bructeri, Sigambri, and Chatti. Valerian himself, in A. D. 258, marched against the Persians, recovered Antioch, and penetrated into Mesopotamia; but two years later, he was defeated and taken prisoner by the Persians, in the neighbourhood of Edessa. Valerian never recovered his freedom, but remained in captivity until his death, enduring the most insolent treatment at the hands of his enemies, who now recovered Antioch and even made conquests in Asia Minor, until the Roman general Balista forced them to return across the Euphrates.

12. From A. D. 260, Gallienus was sole emperor until A. D. 268, and, on the whole, did his best to promote the prosperity of the empire. But things had come to a pass when it required more than human strength to keep the tottering edifice together. In the reign of Gallienus, insurrections broke out in nearly all the provinces of the empire, each of which proclaimed its own sovereign. This period is foolishly called the period of the Thirty Tyrants, from the thirty who governed Athens after the close of the Peloponnesian war; for the number of pretenders to the imperial throne did not amount to more than nineteen or twenty. While the empire thus seemed to fall to pieces, the barbarians invaded it on all sides; the Franks and Alemannians advanced as far as Italy, the Quadi even entered Spain, and the Goths Asia Minor. The Isauri in Asia revolted and became for ever separated from the empire. In Palmyra, Odenathus made himself independent, after having defeated the Persians, and his independence was recognised by Gallienus in A. D. 264. The ancient city of Palmyra, situated in an oasis in the Syrian desert, and said to have been built by Solomon, had become wealthy and powerful through commerce; and in

the time of Hadrian and the Antonines, it was a great centre of
Greek art and culture.   The splendid ruins of Palmyra, which were
discovered about the end of the seventeenth century, still attest its
ancient magnificence.   Postumus, who had defeated the Franks, set
himself up as emperor in Gaul, A. D. 258, and maintained himself
for nearly seven years, after which he was murdered by his soldiers,
because he would not allow them to plunder the rebellious city of
Mayence.   Macrianus, the commander in Syria, by whose treachery
Valerian had fallen into the hands of the Persians, assumed the
imperial purple in A. D. 261, and appointed his two sons his colleagues; but he was conquered by Odenathus, who, in A. D. 264,
was made the colleague of Gallienus.   Three years later Odenathus
was killed by a relative, and his wife Zenobia, who undertook the
government of her kingdom, became the real founder of the empire
of Palmyra in Syria.   Egypt was in the meantime ravaged by
plague and civil wars.   The other usurpers, such as Valens, Piso,
Tetricus, and others, did not maintain their power for any length
of time.   The last of them was Aureolus, who assumed the purple
in Ractia, A. D. 262.   Gallienus, assembling all his forces, besieged
him at Milan; but, in the beginning of A. D. 268, a conspiracy was
formed against Gallienus, who was assassinated in his camp before
Milan.   Aureolus, however, was unable to maintain himself, and
was killed in the same year, whereupon Claudius, surnamed Gothi-
cus, was proclaimed emperor by the soldiers.

13. Claudius had already distinguished himself as a brave warrior, and a lover of strict justice, and now commenced the restoration of the empire by successful campaigns against the barbarians.
The Alemanni, who had invaded Italy, were defeated near Lake
Benacus, and in A. D. 269 he set out against the Goths, who had
penetrated into Macedonia, and were besieging the towns of Cassan-
dreia and Thessalonica.   In a decisive battle near Naissus in Serbia, the Goths were overpowered and compelled to retrace their
steps.   But not long afterwards, in the month of April, A. D. 270,
the emperor died at Sirmium, of a disease which carried off thousands both of Romans and Goths.   At the time of his death, Claudius was preparing for an expedition against Zenobia, who had subdued Syria and Egypt.   After his death the legions at Aquileia
proclaimed his brother Quintullus, who, on hearing that the legions
on the Danube had offered the purple to Aurelian, ordered his veins
to be opened, and died on the seventeenth day after his accession.

14. Aurelian, a native of Pannonia, completed the work so
nobly commenced by Claudius, and became the real restorer of the
Roman empire.   After a brief visit to Rome he marched against
the Goths and their allies, and a battle having been fought on the
banks of the Danube, in which neither party could claim a decisive
victory, he concluded a peace, in which the province of Dacia was

given up to the Goths. Tranquillity being thus restored in that quarter, he proceeded, in A. D. 272, to the East against Zenobia, and, after several victories over the queen recovered Syria, while his legate Probus was equally successful in Egypt. In the following year he besieged Zenobia in her own capital of Palmyra, and, on the surrender of the city, made her his prisoner; but as the city soon after revolted, Aurelian ordered it to be destroyed. Having thus reunited Syria, Mesopotamia, and Egypt with the empire, he returned to Europe, and forthwith made war against Tetricus, who still maintained himself in Gaul. In a battle near Chalons, in A. D. 274, Tetricus, who did not feel safe among his own troops, went over to Aurelian, by whom he was kindly treated. The emperor returned to Rome, and celebrated a triumph, adorned by the presence of Zenobia, such as the city had not seen for a long time. He now endeavoured, by internal reforms, to ameliorate the condition of his subjects, and restore ancient morality and simplicity; but his wise measures were not always well received by the demoralised people. It also gave offence that he assumed the diadem, which no emperor had done before him. In order to give occupation to his restless legions, he undertook an expedition against the Persians, who still defied the majesty of Rome; but in March A. D. 275 he was murdered, on his road between Heracleia and Byzantium, by his own servants, who had reason to fear his severity.

15. The soldiers not having a general of sufficient popularity among them, reduested the senate to appoint a successor; but as emperors nominated by the senate had generally been rejected by the soldiers, the senate at first declined, and several months elapsed in correspondence, until in September the senate offered the imperial dignity to Claudius Tacitus, a venerable senator of the age of seventy-five. After his elevation he immediately proceeded to the East, where he was welcomed by the army. He repelled the Alani, who had invaded Cappadocia, and advanced as far as mount Caucasus to carry on the war against the Persians, but in consequence of his exertions he was seized with an illness, of which he died on the 12th of April A. D. 276. His brother Annius Florianus assumed the imperial dignity, but scarcely three months later he was murdered by his own soldiers at Tarsus, as it became known that Tacitus had recommended Probus, the commander of the eastern forces, who was very popular among the soldiers. Probus' antecedents were very promising, and after his accession to the empire, he displayed qualities both of a great general and an able ruler. After having paid a visit to Rome, he marched with a strong army into Gaul, a great part of which was occupied by the German tribes of the Franks, Lygians, Burgundians, and Vandals. He rescued sixty large towns from them, pursued them across the

Rhine, and in Germany itself established Roman garrisons as colonies, securing the conquered country by a strong wall extending from Ratisbon to the banks of the Neckar and the Rhine. Having extended and secured the frontiers in that quarter and subdued some rebels in Gaul, he marched to Illyricum and Thrace, where he conquered the Sarmatians and the tribes of the Getae; then crossing over into Asia Minor and restoring peace in some of its provinces, he advanced into Syria and Egypt. In the latter country he expelled the Blemmyae, a Nubian tribe, which had made itself master of several towns, A. D. 279. The Persian king Narses, alarmed by the emperor's success, concluded peace with him. From Egypt Probus returned to Thrace, and transplanted one hundred thousand Bastarnae and other tribes from the left bank of the Danube into Thrace. He then celebrated a great triumph at Rome over the Germans and Blemmyae. As peace was now restored in all parts of the empire, he began employing his armies in various useful works, such as the rebuilding of ruined towns, draining of marshes, and the like; but the severity with which he exacted these services called forth a formidable insurrection, during which, in the month of September A. D. 282, the infuriated soldiers slew their excellent emperor, whose death they soon after deplored. He is said to have been the first to introduce the cultivation of the vine into Hungary and the countries on the Rhine.

16. The legions now proclaimed Carus emperor. He was an able general, but too indulgent towards his two sons Carinus and Numerianus, on whom he conferred the dignity of Caesar. On receiving the news of the death of Probus, the Sarmatians invaded Thrace and Illyricum. Numerianus obtained the command against them and defeated them, while his brother was intrusted with the administration of the western provinces. In A. D. 283, Carus with Numerianus set out against the Persians, who were likewise preparing for war. The Romans were very successful: they ravaged Mesopotamia, took Seleucia and Ctesiphon, and even advanced beyond the Tigris, when suddenly Carus was killed by a flash of lightning, on the 25th of December A. D. 283. His sons were immediately recognised as emperors. Numerianus, who deserved to have lived in happier days, gave up the war with the Persians, and was murdered on his return, during a review of the troops, by his own father-in-law, in September A. D. 284. The army at once proclaimed Diocletian, a Dalmatian, who was then prefect of the praetorians, emperor. Carinus, the profligate son of Carus, endeavoured to assert his claims, and set out against his rival, but near Margus in Serbia, he was killed by a man whose wife he had ill-used, in May A. D. 285, and the civil war was thus brought to a speedy termination.

CHAPTER XIX.

1. DIOCLETIAN, a man of humble origin, had worked his way
up to the highest military stations by his prudence, talent, and
ambition. His reign is particularly remarkable for the great
changes he introduced in the administration of the empire. The
despotism of the soldiers, who had until then appointed and deposed emperors, was put an end to, every trace of republican Rome
which yet remained was done away with, and the spirit of the
government and the character of the sovereign henceforth display
much of what is commonly observed in Eastern despotisms.
From this time the seat of the government was no longer exclusively at Rome, but Nicomedeia became the capital for the
eastern provinces, Milan tor Italy and the countries south of it,
Treves for Gaul, Britain, and Spain, and Sirmium for Pannonia and
Illyricum. The religion of the ancient world also was fast hastening towards its final extinction, for Christianity had already extended far and wide. Diocletian was quite conscious of the
duties he had to perform; but he also knew the dangers and difficulties he had to contend with, and in order to strengthen himself,
assumed Maximian as his colleague in the imperial dignity. This
man was a rude, but able soldier, and Diocletian, assigning to him
the western parts of the empire, at once entrusted to him the war
against the Gauls and Germans. In Gaul the Bagaudae, that is,
the peasants, provoked by the oppression of their governors, had
risen in arms against them; but Maximian defeated them in A. D.
286. The Alemanni, who had invaded Raetia and the Gallic side
of the Rhine, were driven back into their own country, which was
ravaged by Maximian. It is about this time that we first hear of
the Saxons, who infested the coasts of Britain and Gaul with their
piratical fleets, and in conjunction with the Franks traversed and
plundered the north of Gaul. Carausius, an experienced Belgian
chief, was commissioned by Maximian to protect the coasts against
those German pirates, but as after a while he drew upon himself
the suspicion of favouring the barbarians, Maximian ordered him
to be put to death. But Carausius escaped into Britain, where he
assumed in A. D. 287 the imperial dignity, allied himself with the
piratical Franks and Saxons, and maintained himself until A. D.
293, when he fell by the hand of another usurper, Alectus, who
ruled over Britain for a period of three years.

2. While Maximian was thus engaged in Gaul and Germany,

Diocletian carried on a successful war against the invaders in Raetia, and then proceeded to Nicomedcia, in Asia Minor, which he had chosen for his residence. Thinking that the two emperors were not sufficient to protect the empire against both domestic and foreign enemies, Diocletian, in A. D. 292, nominated at Nicomedcia two Caesars, Constantius Chlorus and Galerius, both Illyrians, who by marriages connected themselves with the imperial families. The empire was then divided among the four rulers: Diocletian retained for himself the eastern provinces, Galerius obtained Thrace and the Danubian countries, Maximian Italy, Africa, and the western islands, while Constantius received Gaul, Spain, Britain, and Mauritania. The unity of the empire, however, was not affected by this division, for Diocletian was at the head of the whole, and in the internal administration none of his colleagues could undertake anything without his consent. The power of the praetorian guards was reduced, and Diocletian surrounded himself at Nicomedcia with all the pomp and ceremonial of an eastern despot. In the very year in which he divided his dominions, fresh enemies arose both within and without the empire; the Persians threatened to invade Syria, some African tribes in Mauritania revolted, and soon after, Julian came forward as a usurper in Italy, and Achilles in Egypt. But the usurpers were easily overcome by Maximian and Diocletian, and the former also subdued the Mauritanians. In A. D. 295, Galerius conquered the Carpi, in the neighbourhood of the Carpathian mountains, and other tribes in the countries about the Danube, and then proceeded against the Persians. He was at first not very successful, but in the following year, the Persians were compelled in a pitched battle to sue for peace, in which they gave up all Mesopotamia, and even certain provinces beyond the Tigris, A. D. 298. In the meantime Constantius expelled the Franks from Gaul and the country of the Batavi, crossed over into Britain, and defeating the usurper Alectus, reunited, in A. D. 296, Britain with the empire, from which it had been separated for ten years. Constantius then returned to Gaul, and in A. D. 301, defeated the Alemanni near Lingonae. In A. D. 303, the four sovereigns met at Rome, where they celebrated a splendid triumph, and consulted for a long time about the means to be adopted to prevent the spreading of Christianity. An edict was issued ordering all the Christian churches to be destroyed, the sacred books to be burned, the priests to be thrown into prison, and to use every means to extirpate the new religion. This decree, however, was not executed everywhere with the same rigour, especially in those parts where the mild and tolerant Constantius commanded. Shortly after this, Diocletian was taken ill, and returned to Nicomedcia, where, on the first of May, A. D. 305, he resigned his imperial dignity, and retired as a private person to his magnificent villa near Salouae, on the coast of Dalmatia. Maximian was obliged against his own inclination, to take the same step at Milan on the same day. Diocletian died in A. D. 313.

3. Immediately after the abdication of the two emperors, the two Caesars, Galerius and Constantius, were raised to the imperial dignity, and at once nominated two Caesars, Valerius Severus and Maximinus Daza, Italy and Africa being assigned to the former, and Egypt and Syria to the latter. Constantine and Maxentius, the sons of Constantius and Maximian, were passed over in this arrangement. But when Constantine heard that his father was ill at York, he hastened thither from Rome, and on the death of Constantius, on the 25th of July, A. D. 306, at once undertook the administration of the provinces of his father, and assumed the title of Caesar. Galerius, though reluctantly, recognised him in his assumed dignity, as he was very popular with the army. Galerius himself was so much detested at Rome, on account of his harshness and cruelty, that the practorians, once more availing themselves of their ancient prerogative, proclaimed Maxentius, the son of Maximian, emperor, and as Maximian himself also resumed the purple, the empire all at once had six rulers, and civil wars were unavoidable. In A. D. 307, Severus marched into Italy against Maxentius, but being deserted by his soldiers, he was put to death at Ravenna by Maximian. Galerius, then greatly enraged, marched with an army into Italy, and conferred the title of Augustus or emperor on his friend Licinius. Maximinus, who governed Egypt and Syria, also assumed the title of Augustus. The old and ambitious Maximian, unable to maintain himself in Italy, fled to Constantine at Treves. But as he was planning his destruction, he was betrayed and fled to the south of Gaul; here he was obliged to surrender at Marseilles, A. D. 310, and hanged himself. In the following year, Galerius died in consequence of his excesses; Maxentius through his legates recovered Africa, where a usurper of the name of Alexander had started up, and then prepared for war against Constantine; but the latter, anticipating him, invaded northern Italy, and defeated him in a great battle, A. D. 312, near a place called Saxa Rubra. Maxentius took to flight, and as he was riding across the Milvian bridge, his horse took fright and threw him into the Tiber, where he was drowned. Having secured the possession of Italy and Rome, Constantine hastened back to the Rhine, repelled the Franks, crossed the river, and caused a stone bridge to be built over it at Cologne.

4. While Constantine was thus successfully engaged against the Germans, a war broke out in the East between Licinius, who had married a sister of Constantine, and Maximinus, the ally of Maxentius. Maximinus suffered a severe defeat at Adrianople, and was poisoned A. D. 313, at Tarsus, in Cilicia. Two sovereigns were now left, Constantine and Licinius, the former governing the West, and the latter the East. Peace might therefore have continued for some

time, but the two emperors were equally ambitious, and equally faithless and crafty, and each was anxious to get rid of the other. Licinius took part in a conspiracy against Constantine, who, on being informed of it, began a war, A. D. 314, and defeated the troops of his rival in two battles, at Cibalae in Pannonia, and at Adrianople. A peace was then concluded, in which Licinius gave up to Constantine all Illyricum, with Macedonia and Greece. There now followed a period of tranquillity, which lasted for seven years, and during which Constantine regulated the administration of the empire, defeated the Goths, and received from them a corps of forty thousand men into his service. After this Constantine again directed his arms against Licinius, who cruelly persecuted the Christians; the two armies met at Adrianople, and on the 3d of July, A. D. 323, Licinius was completely defeated. He fled to Byzantium, whence he crossed over to Chalcedon, and being there beaten a second time, on the 18th of September, he surrendered to the conqueror, who stripped him of his purple, and promised to allow him to live in honourable retirement; but soon afterwards caused him to be strangled at Thessalonica.

5. After these severe struggles, which had lasted many years, Constantine, surnamed the Great, was the sole ruler of the empire. His faithlessness, his boundless ambition, and the heartless cruelty he displayed towards his friends and nearest relations, render it impossible to rank him among the good rulers. Even the good he did in protecting the Christian religion did not proceed from pure motives, but from a desire to promote his own interests, for Christianity exercised no influence on his character and conduct. But he nevertheless exercised an important influence upon Europe, by raising Christianity to the rank of the state religion, and by transferring the seat of empire from Rome to Byzantium, which from him received its present name of Constantinople. He was at the same time the founder of the Court despotism, which he substituted for the military despotism, and of hierarchy in the Christian church.

6 Even while yet only Caesar in Gaul, Constantine, imitating the example of his father, had protected the Christians in that province and in Britain; during his war against Maxentius, he was induced, it is said, by the appearance of a cross in the sun, to adopt Christianity himself. In A. D. 313, he issued at Milan the memorable edict of toleration, which granted perfect religious liberty to all his subjects. The Christians thereby recovered their lost property, obtained access to the great offices of state, and permission to build churches. Christianity, which had even before been adopted by millions, now spread over all parts of the empire. Constantine himself was not drawn towards it by any inward desire, or by a conviction of its truth, but because he hoped by the help of the Christians to crush his opponents who were hostile to Christianity.

The disputes between the Arians and followers of Athanasius about the nature of the Redeemer, offered Constantine an opportunity at the general council of Nicaea, A. D. 325, to interfere in matters of ecclesiastical law. It was at this council that what is called orthodoxy was first clearly defined. The pure and simple doctrines of Christ were more and more disfigured by decrees of councils; the clergy became more and more distinct from the laity; the church acquired great privileges, jurisdiction, large domains, well-paid priests, a splendid outward ceremonial, until in the end the Christian religion sank down to a worship of images and relics. The bishop of Rome naturally claimed a higher power than his colleagues, and his pretensions were strengthened by the fact, that the barbarous nations in the north-western provinces readily submitted to the orders of the bishop of the great western capital. In this manner, and supported by the secular power of the emperors, the bishop of Rome was enabled gradually to develop the vast hierarchical system under which afterwards Europe groaned until the time of the Reformation.

7. Rome, with all its ancient pagan and republican associations, was not a fit place for establishing the despotism of a Christian emperor, with his servile court ceremonial. Constantine accordingly selected Byzantium for the capital of the empire, which nature herself seems to have destined to be the seat of a great empire. The building and extension of the city occupied nearly ten years, from A. D. 325 till A. D. 334, and cost enormous sums of money. But more important still, was the entire change of the government and administration, which was introduced by Constantine. The changes were entirely of an oriental character; his object was to give unity and compactness to the empire, and to secure to the throne as its centre the supreme power in every respect. He accordingly divided the empire into four prefectures, fourteen dioceses, and one hundred and sixteen provinces. The first prefecture, that of the East, contained five dioceses, viz., the East, Egypt, Pontus, Asia, and Thrace, all of which formed forty-eight provinces. The second prefecture, or Illyricum, contained the dioceses of Macedonia and Dacia, forming together eleven provinces, including Greece and Crete; the prefecture of Italy had three dioceses, Italy, the western part of Illyricum, with the countries south of the Danube, and Africa with the western islands of the Mediterranean, forming altogether twenty-nine provinces; the fourth prefecture, that of Gaul, forming three dioceses, Gaul, Spain, and Britain, contained twenty-eight provinces. Rome and Constantinople belonged to no prefecture, but had their own administration under prefects of the city. Each prefecture was governed by a *praefectus praetorio*, who had no military power; the highest magistrate in a diocese was called *vicarius*, while the governor of a province bore the title of proconsul, consular, cor-

rector, or praeses. The civil and military powers were completely separated, and it was therefore necessary to create a number of new military dignitaries, all of whom stood under a commander-in-chief, called *magister utriusque militiae*. The emperor's court was constituted upon the model of that of Persia, and a vast number of court officials and dignitaries were appointed with a scrupulously distinguished gradation of rank. Consuls were still annually appointed both at Rome and at Constantinople, though the honour of the consulship was nothing but an expensive luxury.

8. The new and expensive system of administration, with its numerous officials, rendered it necessary to increase the taxes. The severity with which they were exacted, and the unfairness with which they were distributed, were in many instances the source of much unhappiness and discontent in the various provinces of the empire. Another circumstance which rendered an increase of the public revenue unavoidable, was the system of engaging mercenaries from among the barbarians, for at this time they formed the greater part of the Roman armies. The empire had been in a state of recovery ever since the time of Diocletian, and things were still improving during the reign of Constantine, notwithstanding the extremely heavy taxes. For after the defeat of Licinius, the empire enjoyed peace until A. D. 332, when the Goths, under their king Alaric, again crossed the Danube, and ravaged the country; but they were driven back by Constantine; and the Sarmatae, who had to suffer much from the Goths, were protected by the emperor, who in A. D. 334 assigned habitations to three hundred thousand of them within the Roman empire, in Pannonia, Thrace, and Macedonia. During the last years of his life, Constantine favoured the Arians, whom he had formerly condemned as heretics; this change in his mind had been brought about by the Arian bishop Eusebius of Nicomedeia, at whose hands he also received baptism when he felt the end of his life approaching, for he believed that baptism would wipe away at once all the sins of his life. He died on the 22d of May A. D. 337 in his palace near Nicomedeia, while he was occupied with preparations against the Persians, who appear to have resolved to recover their lost provinces.

9. Before his death, Constantine had divided the empire among his three sons, assigning Gaul to Constantine II., the East to Constantius, and Italy to Constans, while his two nephews, Dalmatius and Hannibalianus, who were raised to the rank of Caesars, received Illyricum and the kingdoms of Armenia and Pontus. Constantius, after his father's death, hastened to Constantinople, and caused or allowed all his relations to be put to death; no one was spared except Gallus, who was ill, and Julianus, who was a mere boy. The three brother emperors then met and made a new division of the empire, in which all Illyricum was added to the portion of

Constans, and Africa was divided between him and Constantine. After this Constantius undertook with great vigour the war against Persia, for which his father had already made preparations, and which detained him nearly all the remainder of his life in Syria. Constantine II., who resided at Treves, not being satisfied with the empire assigned to him, and wishing to rob his brother Constans of Italy, marched southward with his army, but in A. D. 340 he was defeated and killed near Aquileia, and his portion of the empire was taken possession of by Constans. Ten years later, Magnentius, a Frank, who had received a Roman education, was raised to the rank of Augustus at Autun (Augustodunum) in Gaul, and found numerous adherents. Leaving Gaul to his brother Decentius, he marched into Italy; and Constans, whose vicious conduct had made him unpopular, both with the provincials and soldiers, was killed during his flight in a place at the foot of the Pyrenees. Magnentius thus became master of Italy. Simultaneously, Vetranio, a brave general, was raised by the army in Illyricum to the rank of Augustus; but a few months later he abdicated, having received orders to do so from Constantius, who, leaving the management of the Persian war to Gallus, proceeded against the usurper Magnentius. In the neighbourhood of Mursa in Pannonia, he gained a victory, A. D. 351, whereupon Magnentius withdrew to Italy. But being unable to maintain himself, he put an end to his life, A. D. 353.

10. Constantius was now the sole ruler of the empire; he was timid and suspicious, and completely under the control of women, eunuchs, and flatterers. He zealously engaged in the religious disputes of the time, though he did not adopt any fixed principles himself. While staying at Milan, he concluded a treaty with the Alemanni; and as Gallus, who had been raised to the rank of Caesar, displayed too much ambition in the East, Constantius summoned him to come to Italy, and ordered him to be killed on his journey at Pola in Istria, A. D. 354. A similar fate was hanging over Julian, but the empress Eusebia averted it by her entreaties; and Julian was banished to Athens, where he occupied himself with the study of philosophy. Shortly after this, the valiant general Sylvanus, who had acquired great fame in his war against the Germans, entered into connection with the Franks, and fearing the consequences of this step, assumed the title of Augustus at Cologne, in A. D. 355. But Ursicinus, a general of Constantius, and the historian Ammianus Marcellinus, speedily put an end to his usurpation: he was dragged forth from a chapel and cut down by the soldiers. Constantius now recalled Julian, gave him his sister Helena to wife, and entrusted to him the administration of Gaul, which was ravaged by the Germans, for the Franks had taken Cologne, and the Alemanni had destroyed Strasburg and Mayence.

Julian, though he had not been brought up as a soldier, first
defeated the Alemanni, and then advancing to the lower Rhine
recovered Cologne : in A. D. 357 he gained a great battle near
Strasburg, in consequence of which the whole line from Basle to
Cologne was freed from the enemies, who had to purchase peace.
This success roused the jealousy of Constantius, who had in the
meantime been engaged against the Germans on the Danube, and
was now preparing to take the command against the Persians,
because his lieutenants were unsuccessful in the East.   But when
he demanded from Julian a portion of his forces, the soldiers, with
whom Julian was very popular, proclaimed him emperor, A. D. 360,
at Paris, where he had his winter quarters.   This honour he had
well deserved by his moderation and justice during the administration of Gaul.   Constantius rejected all offers to come to terms, and
prepared for war.   Julian therefore quickly set out and arrived in
Illyricum, when unexpectedly Constantius died in Cilicia, on the
3d of November A. D. 361.

11. Julian, surnamed the Apostate, was now sole Augustus.
He owes his surname to the fact that, although brought up as a
Christian, he renounced Christianity ten years before his accession,
and being disgusted with the unprofitable disputes of the Christians,
their monastic tendencies, and other abuses, exerted himself to
restore the ancient pagan religion of the Romans, though he was
not averse to borrowing some things from the Christians by which
he thought Paganism might be improved; nor did he close the
Christian churches, and in A. D. 363 he even allowed the Jews to
rebuild their temple at Jerusalem.   But fires bursting from the
ground, and earthquakes, are said to have prevented the undertaking.   Julian professed to imitate the example of Antoninus the philosopher, and set the example of abstinence and severity towards
himself, in order to be able to demand the exercise of similar virtues from his subjects.   He was thoroughly imbued with the spirit
of the classical literature of Greece, and even during his most important engagements he never neglected the cultivation of his own
mind, as we still see from his writings.   But his opposition to
Christianity was an attempt to turn the current of a mighty river;
paganism could not for any length of time maintain itself against
the Christian religion, which offered to oppressed humanity conso-
lation for present sufferings, and a prospect of a better life to come.
After a stay of about eight months at Constantinople, Julian set out
against the Persians.   He entered Mesopotamia with a large army,
and gained a great victory near Ctesiphon.   He and his soldiers suffered much from want of provisions, the Persians having laid waste
the country during their retreat; but he pursued his objects with
undaunted spirit, until, on the 26th of June, A. D. 363, he died
of a wound, inflicted either by an enemy or by some incensed
Christian.

12. The army suffering severely from want in the desert steppes, and being hard pressed by the enemy, saluted Jovian as emperor. He was an intelligent and sincere professor of Christianity, though greatly addicted to sensual pleasures. The distressing circumstances in which the army was placed, rendered the conclusion of peace with the enemy unavoidable, however humiliating the terms were. The Persians thus recovered their five provinces beyond the Tigris, the great fortress of Nisibis, and other Mesopotamian towns On his return to Constantinople, Jovian died at Dadastana, in Galatia, on the 16th of February A. D. 364. In his short reign the Christians recovered their former rights and privileges, though the pagans also enjoyed toleration.

13. Ten days after the death of Jovian, the troops at Nicaea conferred the imperial dignity upon Valentinian, a Pannonian, who soon afterwards assumed his brother Valens as his colleague, and assigned to him the administration of the East, with Constantinople for his capital, while he himself undertook the government of the West. Valentinian was a wise and moderate ruler, permitting in religious matters every one to follow the dictates of his own conscience, but at the same time he was of an irascible temper. In A. D. 366, the Alemanni, who had again invaded Gaul, were repulsed by one of his generals, and in the following year the emperor, having recovered from a serious illness, raised his son Gratian to the rank of Augustus. At the same time the north of Roman Britain was much harassed by invasions of the Picts and Scots, against whom the ancient fortification of Antoninus was renewed In A. D. 368, the Alemanni, under their chief Rando, sacked and plundered the city of Mayence, which induced Valentinian, who was then residing at Paris, to wage war against them. He drove them across the Rhine, and defeated them in their own country. The next years were mainly spent in fortifying the banks of the Rhine against similar incursions. In A. D. 371, Saxon pirates infested the coasts of Gaul, and being surrounded by the Romans, were all treacherously cut to pieces, and at Treves, Valentinian and his son Gratian, who had been carefully educated by the poet Ausonius, celebrated splendid triumphs over the barbarians, on which occasion the orator Symmachus proclaimed their exploits to the world. As the Quadi and Sarmatians had invaded Pannonia, Valentinian marched against them, and crossing the Danube, fearfully ravaged their country, and butchered them without mercy. While in his winter quarters at Bregetio, some ambassadors of the Quadi appeared before him, and in his reply to them, he was seized with such a fit of anger, that he burst a blood-vessel, and died on the 17th of November A. D. 375.

14. Meanwhile his brother Valens, a passionate, cruel, and intolerant prince, who persecuted all those who did not adopt the Arian

creed, had in the very first year of his reign to contend with Procopius, who, while Valens was in Asia, had usurped the purple at Constantinople, and had gained over the Goths to his interest. But his successful career was cut short in A. D. 366, in a defeat which he sustained in Phrygia. In order to chastise the Goths for having supported the usurper, Valens crossed the Danube and laid waste their country, until, in A. D. 370, the Visigoth, Athanaric, being completely exhausted, sought and obtained peace. Scarcely was tranquillity restored in that quarter, when the Persians interfered in the affairs of Armenia, which Valens took under his protection, though he did not venture to declare war. Being a zealous Arian, he caused the Arian doctrines to be preached to the Goths by their bishop Ulphilas, who is celebrated in history for having translated the Scriptures into the Moeso-Gothic language, for which purpose he contrived a Gothic alphabet based upon that of the Greeks. But the unfortunate Goths were not able to enjoy the blessings of Christianity in peace, for a terrible hurricane which swept over their country from the East, drove them from their homes on the Danube and the Black Sea.

15. The commotions which were then going on in the interior of Asia, form the beginning of what is generally called the migration of nations. The most formidable among these were the Huns, a Kalmuck or Mongol tribe, of ugly appearance (they are compared to walking lumps of flesh), which had from time immemorial traversed the steppes of Asia as nomadic hordes, and had made conquests as far as China. After long wanderings, a portion of this race, in A. D. 375, crossed the Volga, the Don, the sea of Azof, and threw themselves upon the Alani, a part of the Goths. Unable to resist the invaders, the Alani partly submitted to them, and partly escaped to Mount Caucasus, where their descendants are said still to exist. The eastern Goths, or Ostrogoths, also called Guthrungi, dwelt between the lower Danube and the Dniester along the Euxine, while the western or Visigoths occupied the banks of the Danube. The shock of the Huns first fell upon the Ostrogoths, whose king, being too weak to offer resistance, threw himself upon his own sword, leaving his kingdom a prey to the Huns. His successor Withimer, however, trying to oppose them, fell in battle, and his people withdrew to the Visigoths, whose king Athanaric determined to oppose the Huns; but he too was defeated, and escaped into the inhospitable Carpathian mountains. The Thervingi, a portion of the Visigoths, in A. D. 376, implored the emperor Valens to assign to them within his empire the deserted districts of Moesia and Thrace. Valens granted their request on condition that, before crossing the Danube, they should give up their arms. A host of two hundred thousand men, with their wives and children, accordingly crossed the Danube. The sufferings of the Goths

in the marshes and deserts of Moesia were immense, and their distress was aggravated by the avarice of the Roman governors. Their prince Fritigern, irritated by the brutality of the Romans, called his people to arms, for they had evaded the demand to surrender them. The Goths then, accompanied by some Huns and Alani, fell upon the extensive plains of Thrace, devastating with fire and sword everything that came in their way between the Danube and the Hellespont. At length Valens marched with an army against them, but in a great battle near Adrianople, A. D. 378, he suffered a severe defeat. He took refuge in a cottage, which was set on fire by the barbarians, and Valens perished in the flames. Scarcely the third part of his army escaped. The whole country south of the Danube, including Thessaly and Greece, fell into the hands of the conquerors, the fortresses alone maintaining themselves.

16. Gratian, the son of Valentinian, had in the meantime signalised himself in Gaul against the Alemanni, and after having defeated them in A. D. 378 near Argentari, and compelled them to conclude a peace, in which they promised to furnish a contingent to the Roman army, he was preparing to hasten to the assistance of his uncle Valens; but being informed of his death, he raised Theodosius, a brave Spaniard, to the rank of Augustus, on the 16th of January A. D. 379, and assigned to him the prefectures of the East and of Illyricum. Theodosius soon crushed the Goths in Thrace, and his quick and energetic measures so much increased the respect of the barbarians for him, that after the death of Fritigern, Athanaric concluded peace with the empire, and willingly furnished the Gothic auxiliary corps of forty thousand men, which had been instituted by Constantine the Great. The Visigoths now obtained permission to settle in Dacia and Moesia. In the meantime, Gratian in the West, guided by bishops and hated by his soldiers, gave himself up to pleasure, rather than to his duties. The legions in Britain A. D. 383, raised Maximus to the dignity of emperor, and having assembled a large army, crossed over into Gaul. Gratian being betrayed by his own troops, endeavoured to escape into Italy, but was overtaken and killed at Lyons on the 25th of August, A. D. 383. Maximus, although he obtained from Theodosius the title of Augustus, on condition of his not molesting young Valentinian II., who had been made Augustus in A. D. 375, when he was only four years old, nevertheless invaded Italy, where Valentinian was residing, and occupied the passes of the Alps, A. D. 387. Valentinian, with his mother Justina, fled to Theodosius at Thessalonica, who now married Galla, a sister of Valentinian, though he had two sons, Arcadius and Honorius, by his first wife, who had died. In A. D. 388 Theodosius set out against the faithless usurper Maximus, who was delivered up by

his own soldiers and put to death.   Theodosius then went to Rome
and appointed Arbogastes, a distinguished Frank, counsellor and
guide of young Valentinian.   Arbogastes after this was the real
sovereign of the West, but Valentinian being anxious to get rid of
his troublesome adviser, transferred his residence to Vienne on the
Rhone, where soon after, on the 15th of May A. D. 392, he was
murdered, probably at the instigation of Arbogastes.   The cunning
Frank, in order not to appear himself as a usurper, raised the
learned and eloquent Eugenius to the imperial dignity; but in
A. D. 394 Theodosius broke up from Constantinople on an expedition against Arbogastes and Eugenius, and both were defeated near
Aquileia : Eugenius was made prisoner and beheaded, and Arbogastes committed suicide.   Theodosius now was the sole ruler of
the empire, but four months later he died at Milan on the 17th of
January A. D. 395.

17. Although Theodosius had managed the affairs of the empire
with vigour and energy, yet the necessity of increasing the taxes
threw a heavy burden upon the provinces, which had become de-
populated and miserably devastated.   In addition to this, the
empire was shaken by the passionate zeal which Theodosius displayed against the Arians in the East, and against the pagans, who,
not daring to show their faces in the towns and cities, lived for the
most part in retired country places (*payi*), whence their name
pagani or pagans.   Bands of fanatic monks wandered about from
place to place, destroying with impunity the finest monuments of
ancient art, and contributing as much as they could towards bringing about what are called the dark ages.   The great emperor himself humbly submitted to the penance imposed on him by the stern
Ambrose, bishop of Milan.   When the usurper Maximus had left
Britain, that province, being no longer protected by Roman garrisons, was given up to the inroads of the Picts and Scots.   From
time to time small armies were indeed sent into the island, but they
were unable to afford it any efficient protection, and the native
Britons, who had become unwarlike under the Roman dominion,
now were an easy prey to other conquerors.

CHAPTER XX.

FROM THE DIVISION OF THE EMPIRE, TO THE OVERTHROW OF THE WESTERN EMPIRE.

1. BEFORE his death Theodosius had divided the empire between his two sons, Arcadius and Honorius. The former being a youth of only eighteen years, was placed under the guardianship of Rufinus, a Gaul, and was to govern the eastern part of the empire, with Constantinople for his residence. Honorius, who was only eleven years old, had received Flavius Stilicho, a Vandal, for his guardian, and was to govern the western parts of the empire, having his residence at Rome or Ravenna. The line of demarcation between the two divisions of the empire was formed by the Danube, so far as its course is from north to south, that is, from Waitzen to the mouth of the Drave; then by the river Drino Blanco, which flows from the mountains of Macedonia towards the Save; while further south the frontier was a line drawn through Scutari towards the head of the great Syrtis on the coast of Africa. Theodosius had not intended by this division to abolish the unity of the empire, but the internal condition of the two parts under existing circumstances could not but lead to a permanent separation of the two empires, and thus accelerate the downfall of the western half, which was more exposed to attacks from without, and internally more decayed than the other. The policy of the eastern court, moreover, was to avert the attacks of the barbarians by directing them to the provinces of the west. Constantinople, lastly, was safer by its position and its fortifications than Rome, and able to defend and maintain itself even when all the provinces around it were in the hands of enemies.

2. Honorius, who was of a sickly constitution and too young to take a part in public matters, remained in his palace at Ravenna enjoying and amusing himself, while the empire was threatened on the Rhine and Danube by invasions of barbarians. The administration and defence of the empire were left to Stilicho, the ablest man both at the court and in the camp. Perceiving the disadvantages of the separation of the empires at a time when unity was most needed, he attempted to reunite the two parts, but this involved him in an unfortunate quarrel with Rufinus. The Visigoths, then governed by their bold king Alaric, invaded Greece and devastated Thrace. Stilicho, indeed, offered his assistance to the eastern empire, but it was declined, because Rufinus suspected him. Stilicho, deeply mortified at this, caused Rufinus to be murdered by the Gothic troops stationed at Constantinople, on the 27th of

36

November A. D. 395. But his successor, the eunuch Eutropius, and Gainas, the commander of the Goths in the eastern capital, now openly declared against Stilicho. The Goths under Alaric in the meantime traversed Greece, laying desolate the whole country, with the exception of Athens, and advanced even as far as Sparta. In A. D. 397 Stilicho went across, and surrounded them in Arcadia, but owing to the carelessness of his officers, they escaped to Epirus. Arcadius, in order to propitiate the formidable Alaric, made him commander of Eastern Illyricum, and declared Stilicho an enemy of the empire. At the same time Eutropius induced Gildo, the commander in Africa, to revolt from Honorius, with the view to gain Africa for the Eastern empire. But the attempt failed, and in A. D. 398 the rebel was defeated and killed. Stilicho then went into Raetia and Gaul for the purpose of either maintaining or restoring friendly relations with the German tribes in the neighbourhood.

3. After these events, Italy suffered all the miseries that can be inflicted on a country invaded by hordes of rude and rapacious barbarians. Alaric the Visigoth was commissioned to carry into effect the sentence which had been pronounced against Stilicho, and in A. D. 402 he undertook his first expedition; but, probably induced by bribes, returned after his arrival before the strong fortress of Aquileia. In A. D. 403, however, he returned and plundered the country about the Po, the towns alone offering resistance. All Italy was in alarm; Honorius protected himself at Ravenna, and the Romans began putting their walls in a state of defence. But Stilicho quickly assembled an army in Raetia, and advanced against Alaric, whom he overtook near Pollentia. The success of the Romans was insignificant, although the poets Claudian and Prudentius composed poems in praise of Stilicho's victory. Alaric had so much frightened the Romans, that Honorius concluded a treaty with him, in which he gave up the western part of Illyricum and promised to pay him an annual tribute. Scarcely had Alaric quitted Italy, when a new and fearful invasion increased the sufferings of the Italians. In A. D. 406 the Gothic chief Radagaisus, accompanied by a host of two hundred thousand men, partly Goths and partly other Germans, being pressed onward by hordes from Asia, poured into Lombardy from the Alps. Stilicho surrounded and defeated them near Faesulae; the greater part of the barbarians were taken prisoners, and Radagaisus was killed during his flight. But as Stilicho had been obliged for the purpose of protecting Italy to withdraw all the garrisons from Gaul, the Rhine was crossed by the Vandals, Alani, Burgundians, and Alemannians: horde followed upon horde, the towns on the Rhine were destroyed, and in A. D. 407 nearly the whole of Gaul, where the invaders were joined by the unfortunate Bagaudae, was ravaged. At the same time

Constantine, a common soldier, usurped the imperial purple in Britain, and crossing over to the continent succeeded in subduing Gaul and Spain. Honorius being quite powerless, was obliged to recognise his usurped power.

4. As the tribute promised to Alaric was not paid, he appeared in A. D. 408 again on the frontiers of Italy demanding payment. The senate assembled to deliberate, and Stilicho advised the members to adhere to the promise made to the Goths, and pay the tribute. Some personal enemy suggested to the timid Honorius that Stilicho had probably entered into an understanding with Alaric in order to secure the succession to his son Eucherius. Upon this the credulous emperor ordered Stilicho, whose daughter was married to him, to be murdered on the 23d of August A. D. 408. All his relations and friends were likewise put to death, and with a senseless cruelty, the emperor ordered the wives and children of thirty thousand Germans who served in the Roman army to be murdered. These soldiers, infuriated with rage, at once went over to Alaric, who, not obtaining the money he demanded, and hearing of Stilicho's fate, vowed to avenge him and crossed the Po. He straightway proceeded to Rome, which he commenced besieging. Famine and disease at length obliged the Romans to capitulate. Alaric was induced by a vast quantity of gold, silver, silk, and pepper, to depart. Some other promises which had been made, not being fulfilled, Alaric, reinforced by the troops of Adolphus, his brother-in-law, returned in A. D. 409 against Rome; he occupied Ostia, and compelled the terrified Romans to proclaim Attalus, the city prefect, emperor. The Goths then entered Rome, and Alaric undertook the supreme command of the new emperor's forces, whereby he virtually possessed the sovereign power. Honorius still clinging to his post offered to share the imperial dignity with Attalus. When Alaric found that the emperor of his own choice proved an obstacle in his way, he stripped him of his purple in presence of the whole army, and attempted to come to an understanding with Honorius; but as his terms were not accepted, he gave vent to his rage and marched against Rome, which he took for the third time on the 24th of August A. D. 410. Although he wished to spare the city, the Goths plundered it and destroyed some parts by fire. Galla Placidia, the sister of Honorius, fell into Alaric's hands, and he carried her with him as a hostage; after three days he left the city and marched southward with the intention of sailing to Sicily and Africa. But on his march thither he died at Cosenza.

5. Alaric was succeeded by Adolphus, who led the troops back in the hope of making Rome the seat of his government. Placidia, who had been intrusted to his keeping, dissuaded him, and advised him to make peace with her brother. Two years thus passed away in negotiations, after which Adolphus, evacuating Italy, marched

with his Goths into Gaul, where some usurpers had started up.   The brave general Constantius easily put them down, and also made the emperor Constantine his prisoner, and put him to death, A. D. 411. Constans, a son of Constantine, still maintained himself at Vienne, but was soon after killed.   All Gaul was thus recovered for Honorius; but Jovinus, supported by the Burgundians, assumed the purple at Mayence.   Adolphus at first made common cause with him, but in the end he turned his arms against him, made him his prisoner, and sent him captive to a general of Honorius.   A definite peace was at length concluded between Adolphus and Honorius, and the former, marrying Placidia, took up his residence in Gaul. But notwithstanding the peace, Constantius, the conqueror of Constantine, in A. D. 414, took up arms against Adolphus, and expelled him from Gaul.   Adolphus then went to Barcelona in Spain, where in the following year he was murdered by one of his own servants. After an interval of a few days Wallia succeeded Adolphus, and became the founder of the empire of the Visigoths, of which Toulouse was the capital, and which continued to flourish, until in A. D. 711 it was destroyed by the Arabs.   It extended at first from the Garonne to the Ebro, but subsequently embraced the whole of Spain.   Placidia married Constantius, whom Honorius in A. D. 421 made his colleague in the empire.   Constantius, however, died soon after at Ravenna; after his withdrawal from Gaul, the Franks and Burgundians made themselves masters of the country without any opposition.   The Burgundians founded an empire extending over the fertile fields of the Rhone, about Mount Jura and the countries on the upper and middle Rhine.   The Franks, from whom the country derives its modern name, established themselves in the northern parts of Gaul.   Britain had been left almost entirely to itself ever since the usurpation of Constantine; but in A. D. 426 the last garrisons were withdrawn, and the country was left to the invasions of the Saxons, Picts, and Scots.   Thus one province of the empire was lost after another, while Honorius spent his time in indolence at Ravenna until his death in A. D. 423.

6. Placidia had incurred the displeasure of her brother; at his death she was still staying at Constantinople with her son Valentinian, and as Honorius had made no arrangements about a successor, his private secretary Joannes assumed the purple at Ravenna. Arcadius, the emperor of the East, had died in A. D. 408, and was succeeded by Theodosius II., a boy of seven years, in whose name Anthemius, the *praefectus praetorio*, managed the affairs of the state with great prudence and wisdom.   On the usurpation of Joannes, Theodosius II. raised Valentinian III., Placidia's son, then only six years old, to the imperial throne of the West, and sent an army against the usurper, who was defeated and put to death at Aquileia in A. D. 425.   For a period of twenty-five years

Placidia managed the affairs of the empire in the name of her son Valentinian, but she was neither able to preserve nor restore anything during the general confusion of the time. Weakness was combined with demoralisation, and in the midst of plague, famine, and the ravages of barbarians, the Romans recklessly plunged into enjoyments and pleasures. The best provinces of the empire were lost. We have already noticed that Britain was finally given up in A. D. 426, notwithstanding the entreaties of the inhabitants, who were hard pressed by the Picts and Scots, so that in the end they were obliged to call in the assistance of the Angles and Saxons, two German tribes occupying the banks of the Elbe. The assistance was granted, but the Saxons being followed by other tribes, and being unwilling to quit Britain, turned against the natives, and permanently established themselves in Britain, about A. D. 449.

7. In Africa, the governor Bonifacius, against whom the ambitious general Aëtius had roused the suspicion of Placidia, was recalled; but thinking that his life was endangered, he refused obedience, and, A. D. 429, invited Genseric, king of the Vandals, who had been established in Spain ever since A.D. 409, to come over with an army to assist him. Genseric, with a host of eighty thousand barbarians, men, women, and children, crossed over into Africa. When at length the innocence of Bonifacius became known, and he wished to induce the Vandals to return to Spain, he found it impossible. He himself was defeated by them in a battle, and besieged at Hippo, where his friend St. Augustin died during the siege, A. D. 430. The whole province of Africa fell into the hands of those formidable barbarians, whose ravages in Spain and Africa have made their name proverbial. The fortresses Hippo, Cirta, and Carthage, maintained themselves for a time against them; but Bonifacius, after repeated defeats, went to Placidia, who received him kindly. Aëtius his enemy was now obliged to quit the court, and went to the Huns, with whom he had already had some transactions during the short reign of the usurper Joannes. Supported by an army of Huns, he returned into Italy, and as Bonifacius died soon after, Placidia felt herself obliged to restore him, in A. D. 433, to the office of commander-in-chief. But as it was impossible to continue the war against Genseric, Placidia, in A. D. 435, concluded peace with him, in which she formally ceded to him a part of Africa. Carthage still continued to belong to Rome, but, in A. D. 439, Genseric took the city by surprise, and treated its inhabitants most cruelly. After this the war between the Romans and Vandals was still carried on for several years, and during that period the coasts of Sicily and Italy suffered severely, for the barbarians were excellent sailors, and kept up a powerful fleet. At length, in A. D. 442, the emperor Valentinian, finding himself disappointed in his hope of support from the East, again

36*

concluded a treaty with Genseric, in which Africa, with the exception of Mauritania and western Numidia, was given up to the Vandals. Thus commenced the great empire of the Vandals in Africa, which continued to flourish as a maritime power for more than a century. But notwithstanding the peace, the barbarians continued their piratical expeditions by sea in all directions.

8. At that time, the Huns, under their king Attila, dwelt in Hungary, on the Danube, and in the plains of the Theiss. Attila was the terror of many kings and nations. In A. D. 441, he broke up with his hordes, many German tribes being obliged to join him, crossed the Danube, ravaged Moesia, and destroyed many towns. A similar invasion was made in A. D. 447, and on that occasion he carried his devastations as far as Constantinople and Thessaly. The emperor Theodosius had to purchase peace at an enormous price of the rapacious Hun, who treated the emperor and his ambassadors with great insolence. Being determined to crush both empires, Attila, in A. D. 451, advanced towards the Rhine, which his forces crossed in several detachments. Many towns on the river, were reduced to ashes; the king of the Burgundians was defeated and Orleans besieged. The Romans, under the able command of Aëtius, had united with the Visigoths and other German inhabitants of Gaul, such as the Burgundians, the Alani, and the Franks in the north, when the Huns advanced towards the river Marne. A most bloody battle in the plains near Chalons decided the fate of Gaul and of Europe. The Huns were defeated chiefly through the valour of the Visigoth Theodoric, and after his fall, through that of his brave son Torismund. One hundred and sixty-two thousand dead are said to have covered the field of battle, and the surviving Huns returned to the regions whence they had come. But undismayed by this loss, Attila, in the following year, A. D. 452, invaded Italy from Pannonia, probably invited by the licentious Honoria, a sister of Valentinian, who is said to have offered Attila her hand. He accordingly demanded her for his wife and a part of Italy as her portion. Aquileia was razed to the ground, and its inhabitants who escaped the sword are said to have taken refuge in the lagunes, and there to have built the town of Venice. Many other flourishing cities of Lombardy fell into the hands of the barbarians. Valentinian had no army to defend Italy, and Rome was in the greatest terror. An embassy, headed by the Roman bishop Leo I., was despatched with rich presents to Attila, and at length induced him to depart. He did so, however, persisting in his demand that Honoria should be given up to him, and threatening to return if this were not complied with. On his way back he once more invaded Gaul, but Torismund and the Visigoths hastened to the assistance of the Alani, and defeated the Huns, whereupon they returned to the Danube. In the following

year, A. D. 453, Attila suddenly died, and as the terror of his name no longer kept the nations together which he had united under his terrible rule, they, but especially the Gepidae, Ostrogoths, Suevi, and Heruli, made themselves free. The Ostrogoths obtained habitations between Sirmium and Vindobona. Scarcely had Aëtius averted the great danger from the empire, when the voluptuous and superstitious Valentinian began to suspect him, and in A. D. 454 plunged his sword into the breast of the only general capable of saving his empire. Soon after a conspiracy was formed against Valentinian himself, in consequence of which he was murdered on the 16th of March A. D. 455.

In the East, Theolosius II. had died in A. D. 450, after a reign remarkable only for the formation of the *Codex Theodosianus,* which was drawn up by his command in A. D. 438, and contains all the constitutions of the emperors from the time of Constantine the Great. His daughter Pulcheria married Marcianus, who was declared emperor, and reigned till A. D. 457.

After the murder of Valentinian, nine emperors succeeded one another in rapid succession, and the tottering remnant of the empire was kept together only by barbarian mercenaries. The day after the murder of Valentinian, his murderer Maximus assumed the purple, and forced his widow Eudoxia to marry him. In order to avenge herself, she invited, it is said, Genseric to come to Italy to assist her. The Vandal landed with a large fleet at Porto, near the mouth of the Tiber, and marched towards Rome. All who could make their escape took to flight, and the emperor himself would have run away had not a formidable insurrection broken out, during which he was slain by a soldier. His body was torn to pieces and thrown into the Tiber. After this, about the beginning of June A. D. 455, the Vandals entered Rome, and for fourteen days plundered and sacked it. All the remaining treasures of the imperial palaces, the temples, and the houses of the nobles, and everything which was thought worth carrying away, were seized by the barbarians and conveyed to Africa. A whole shipload of bronze statues perished on their way to Carthage. The principal churches and buildings themselves, however, were spared, and a few houses only were destroyed by fire during those days of terror. Several thousand prisoners, and among them the empress Eudoxia and a number of senators, were carried to Africa. After the departure of the Vandals, who during their stay also plundered and ravaged Capua, Nola, and all Campania, the populace of Rome was diverted by games in the Circus, and forgot its wretchedness.

10. In the meantime, the north-western part of Gaul was seized upon by Franks from the country of the Batavi and the lower Rhine; but the Roman commander Ægidius still maintained himself with his army in the neighbourhood of Soissons, though he

was surrounded by Goths, Burgundians, Alemannians, and Franks. His son Syagrius also continued to reign as an independent Roman prince in the same district, until in A. D. 486 he was attacked by the great Frankish king Clovis, who in the battle of Soissons destroyed the last remnant of the Roman dominion in Gaul. At the time of the murder of Maximus, the imperial general Avitus was staying at Toulouse with Theodoric II., who on learning the fate of the emperor urged him to assume the purple and promised him his assistance. Avitus accordingly caused himself to be proclaimed emperor on the 10th of July A. D. 455. The Gallic legions at Arles at once recognised the new emperor; but when soon afterwards he entered Italy, he was arrested at Placentia, a conspiracy having been formed against him by the powerful general Ricimer. In consequence of this, Avitus was obliged to abdicate on the 16th of October A. D. 456. This Ricimer, who was descended from Wallia, the king of the Visigoths, and had defeated the fleet of Genseric, being the commander of the foreign mercenaries in the pay of the Romans, henceforth disposed at his pleasure of the imperial throne for a period of sixteen years, but at the same time endeavoured to protect the empire against the Vandals, Alani, Ostrogoths, and Franks.

11. After the abdication of Avitus, the throne of the western empire remained unoccupied for more than a twelvemonth, until at the end of A. D. 457, Majorian, a friend of Ricimer, was invested with the purple at the request of the senate and people of Rome. Majorian was a brave soldier, who fought against the Burgundians in Gaul, and the Vandals in Africa, and did his best to promote the good of the yet remaining provinces of the empire. He equipped a large fleet against Genseric, and in A. D. 460 proceeded to Spain, in order to cross over into Africa and attack the Vandals in their own country. But they contrived treacherously to intercept a large part of the transports, and thus frustrated the whole undertaking. On his return to Rome, Ricimer caused him to be deposed, A. D. 461, and soon afterwards ordered him to be put to death. Thereupon Ricimer, on the 19th of November A. D. 461, proclaimed Libius Severus, a man not distinguished for anything, emperor at Ravenna, but carried on the government himself in the name of the nominal emperor. While these things were going on in Italy, Ægidius in Gaul, and Marcellinus in Dalmatia, made themselves independent of the empire, and governed their respective provinces as kings. Severus died in A. D. 465, either from poison or by his own hand, and Ricimer, without assuming the title of emperor, ruled as sovereign, until, with the consent of the eastern emperor Leo, the Greek patrician Anthemius was declared emperor of the West, A. D. 467. In order to secure Ricimer, the new emperor gave him his daughter in marriage. As the Vandals still continued by their

piratical expeditions to cause fearful devastations, not only in Sicily
and Italy but in Greece, the emperor Leo of Constantinople resolved,
in conjunction with Anthemius, to strike a decisive blow at them.
Preparations were made upon a gigantic scale. The main army
had already landed in Africa, and gained some advantages over the
barbarians, when, through the folly or treachery of the general
Basiliscus, a truce of five days was granted to Genseric, who, availing himself of the respite, attacked the Greek fleet during the
night with a number of fireships, and having destroyed half of it,
compelled the rest to take to flight, A. D. 468. After the defeat
of this great undertaking Genseric was enabled with impunity to
continue his devastations of both the western and eastern empires.
Anthemius then fought, though unsuccessfully, in Gaul, against
Euric, the king of the Visigoths, who subdued the Roman cities in
Gaul and Spain, which still recognised the supremacy of Rome.

12. In A. D. 472 the ambition of Ricimer was the cause of a
civil war between him and Anthemius, in which the latter lost his
life on the 11th of July. Ricimer took Rome by assault, and on
the following day proclaimed Olybrius, a brother-in-law of Valentinian III., emperor. This civil war lasted only three months, but
Rome suffered most severely from famine, epidemics, conflagrations,
murders, and rapine. On the 20th of August of the same year,
Ricimer died, and as there was no one ambitious enough to seek to
be invested with the purple, Gundobald, king of the Burgundians,
caused Glycerius, a brave general, to be proclaimed emperor at
Ravenna, A. D. 473. The court of Constantinople, however, not
recognising him, conferred the dignity upon Julius Nepos, a prince
of Dalmatia, who, in the month of May A. D. 474, took his rival
prisoner, and made him bishop of Salona; but he in his turn was
dethroned, in A. D. 475, by Orestes, who revolted in Gaul, whither
he had been sent to settle a peace with the Visigoths. Nepos fled
into Dalmatia, and Orestes by the votes of the soldiers conferred
the imperial dignity upon his son Romulus, who on account of his
youth was surnamed Augustulus.

13. The numerous bodies of German mercenaries and allies in
Italy, among whom Heruli, Rugii, Scyrri, Turcilingi, and Goths
are mentioned, were commanded by Odoacer, a chief of the Scyrri,
and a man distinguished both for bodily strength and intelligence.
When Romulus Augustulus was proclaimed emperor, the soldiers
demanded as a reward for their services that a third of the land in
Italy should be assigned to them as their property. As Orestes,
who spoke in the name of his son, refused to grant their request, all
the German troops in Italy assembled under the banners of Odoacer;
they besieged Orestes in the strong fortress of Pavia, and having
made him their prisoner, put him to death, on the 28th of August,
A. D. 476, at Placentia. Ravenna also fell into the hands of the

conquerors, and the helpless Romulus Augustulus, whose life Odoacer spared on account of his youth, resigned his dignity of his own accord.   Hereupon Odoacer, accepting the title of king of Italy, offered to him by his soldiers, though he did not use it among the Romans, for whom it was not suited, sent an ambassador to the court of Constantinople, intimating that Rome no longer required an emperor, and demanding for himself the title of patrician and prefect of the diocese of Italy.

14. Thus ended the Roman empire of the West.   Augustulus received a handsome annuity and withdrew to an estate in Campania, where he spent the remainder of his life in quiet retirement. All Italy fell into the hands of the German soldiers, and Odoacer reigned for a period of fourteen years, during which the unfortunate country gradually recovered from its previous sufferings.   But in A. D. 489 the kingdom of Odoacer was conquered by Theodoric, king of the Ostrogoths, who in A. D. 500 was recognised by the emperor of the East and entered Rome in triumph.   The eastern empire, where Marcianus had been succeeded by Leo I. (A. D. 457-474) and Zeno (A. D. 474-491), continued its existence for nearly a thousand years longer, but its history is that of a corrupt and contemptible court, in which only a few noble characters shine forth among the crowd of imbecile voluptuaries and tyrants.

15. During the last hundred years the state of the west and south of Europe, if we except Greece, had gradually become quite different from what is generally understood by the name ancient, for paganism had given way to Christianity, and Rome had ceased to be mistress of the world.   We cannot describe the changes which had been wrought in that part of Europe better than by saying that it had been *Christianised* and *Germanised.*   The countries which Rome had ruled over during the previous five hundred years, and even Italy itself, had been invaded and conquered by barbarians of the Teutonic race, who established in Britain, Gaul, Spain, the south of Germany, Italy, and the north of Africa, new and independent kingdoms, and laid the foundation of an entirely new state of things. Those countries which had experienced all the blessings and all the curses of Roman civilisation, and had sunk with the empire into vice and wretchedness, were violently shaken and ravaged by the conquering barbarians, who in many instances destroyed almost every vestige of the ancient civilisation.   But they could not destroy everything, for it is a law of history that, wherever a barbarous nation conquers a civilised people and rules over it, the barbarians gradually adopt the civilisation of the conquered, and become absorbed by them.   Hence the Teutonic tribes in Gaul, Spain, and Italy soon became Romanised, adopting the language, customs, and laws of the conquered people; hence even at the present day these countries form the links which connect our modern civilisa-

tion with that of the Roman empire, and their languages still are living monuments of the dominion of Rome. But the infusion of Teutonic blood into the demoralised and effete populations of south-western Europe was the beginning of their regeneration. This process was a slow one during the first thousand years, and could not be otherwise, so long as the spiritual tyranny exercised by the papacy over all Christendom kept the human mind in bondage. But ever since that bondage was broken in the sixteenth century, the advance of civilisation has been prodigious, and has at the present day reached a point which in many respects is much superior to that of any country in the ancient world. We should, however, learn modesty from the reflection that, with the example of the ancients before it, so many centuries have been spent before modern Europe reached the point at which it could stand any comparison with the wonderful civilisation attained by many of the ancient nations more than two thousand years ago.

CHRONOLOGICAL TABLE.

THE ISRAELITES.

* B.C. 4004	Creation of Man.
* 2400	The Deluge.
2000	Abraham.
1921	Joseph in Egypt.
1491	The Exodus.
1451	Death of Moses.
1426	Death of Joshua.
1128-1096	Samuel, the last of the Judges.
1095	Saul, anointed king of Israel.
1055	Death of Saul, and accession of David.
1015	Solomon succeeds David.
1012	Commencement of the Temple.
976	Death of Solomon. Revolt of the Ten Tribes. Judah and Israel.

KINGDOM OF JUDAH.		KINGDOM OF ISRAEL.	
B.C. 976-959	Rehoboam.	B.C. 976-955	Jeroboam.
959-956	Abijah.	955-954	Nadab.
956-915	Asa.	954-931	Baasha.
915-891	Jehoshaphat.	931-930	Elah.
891-884	Jehoram.	930	Zimri.
884-883	Ahaziah.	930-919	Omri. Samaria built.
883-877	Athaliah.	919-897	Ahab.
877-837	Joash.	897-895	Ahaziah.
837-808	Amaziah.	895-883	Joram.
808-756	Uzziah.	883-855	Jehu.
756-741	Jotham.	855-839	Jehoahaz.
741-726	Ahaz.	839-823	Jehoash.
726-697	Hezekiah.	823-782	Jeroboam.
697-642	Manasseh.	782-771	Interreign.
642-640	Amon.	771	Zachariah.
640-609	Josiah.	770	Shallum.
609	Jeoahaz.	770-760	Menahem.
609-598	Jehoiakim.	760	Interreign.
598	Jehoiachin.	759-757	Pekaiah.
598-587	Zedekiah.	757-738	Pekah.
587	Jerusalem taken by Nebuchadnezzar. End of the kingdom of Judah, which remains subject to Assyria until B.C. 538.	738-729	Interreign.
		729-720	Hoshea.
		720	Israel conquered by the Assyrian Salmanassar. Samaria subject to the Assyrians until B.C. 538.

* These two dates have been adopted, because they are the most generally received by English writers. It must, however, be observed that, according to the Septuagint the Creation is referred to B.C. 5508, and the Deluge to B.C. 3246. The date of the Creation is, in fact, carried back by some as far as B.C. 6984, while others bring it down to B.C. 3616 See *Encyclop. Brit.*, article *Chronology*, p. 669.

B.C. 538	**Cyrus**, after conquering **Babylon**, allows the Jews to **return to their country.**
538-332	All Palestine subject to Persia.
520	Building of the second Temple.
332	Alexander the Great at Jerusalem, to whom Palestine is subject until his death in B.C. 323.
323-301	Palestine subject to Syria, and from 301 to 203 to the kings of Egypt.
277	Origin of the **Septuagint.**
170	Jerusalem taken, and its temple polluted by Antiochus Epiphanes.
166	**Judas Maccabaeus** frees Judaea from the Syrians.
162	Death of Judas Maccabaeus.
162-143	Jonathan.
143-136	Simon.
136-107	John Hyrcanus.
106	Aristobulus, son of Hyrcanus, assumes the title of king.
105-78	Alexander Jannacus.
78-69	Queen Alexandra.
69	Hyrcanus II.
69-63	Aristobulus II. Dispute between Aristobulus and Hyrcanus decided by Pompey in favour of the latter.
63-41	Hyrcanus II. restored.
41-3	**Herod the Great.**
5 or 4	**Birth of Jesus Christ.**
A.D. 26-37	Pontius Pilate, governor of Judaea.
33	Jesus Christ crucified.
70	Siege, capture, and destruction of Jerusalem.

CHINA.

B.C. 2207	**Han.** the first historical dynasty.
500	**Confucius** (Kong-fu-tse), Chinese philosopher and reformer.
250	Destruction of Chinese literature in the reign of Shi-hoang-ti.
200	Death of Shi-hoang-ti, and restoration of literature.

INDIA.

B.C. 1400	Beginning of the historical period. Origin of the most ancient parts of the **Vedas.**
525	Origin of **Buddhism.**
327	**Alexander the Great** in India.
250	King Acoca promotes Buddhism, which is introduced also into Ceylon. Tibet. China, and other parts.
A.D 1	King **Vikramaditya**, patron of literature. **Kalidasa**, the dramatio poet.

IRANIAN NATIONS.

a BACTRIA.

B.C. 1230	The Assyrian **Ninus** invades Bactria.
1000	**Zoroaster**, the founder of the religion of light.
540	**Cyrus** subdues Bactria.
329	Alexander the Great conquers Bactria.
256	Bactria, an independent kingdom under **Antiochus Theus**
181	King **Eucratidas** extends the Bactrian empire.
100	Overthrow of the Bactrian kingdom by the **Scythians.**
A.D. 226	Bactria becomes a province of the Persian empire of the **Sassanidae.**

b. MEDIA.

B.C. 1230	Media becomes subject to Assyria.
713	The Medes throw off the yoke of Assyria.
709-656	**Deioces,** king of Media, built Ecbatana, his capital.
656-634	**Phraortes** perishes in a war against Assyria.
634-594	**Cyaxares** greatly extends his empire.
605	**Cyaxares** destroys Nineveh.
594-559	**Astyages.** The Median empire overthrown by the Persians.

c. PERSIA.

B.C.	
559-531	**Cyrus,** founder of the Persian monarchy.
546	Croesus, king of Lydia, conquered by Cyrus.
538	Cyrus conquers Babylon.
531	Cyrus is killed in a war against the Massagetæ
530-522	**Cambyses** succeeds Cyrus.
526	Cambyses conquers Egypt.
522	Smerdis revolts, and maintains himself on the throne of Persia for seven months.
521-486	**Darius,** son of Hystaspes, is chosen king of Persia.
516	An insurrection of Babylon is quelled. Zopyrus.
507	Unsuccessful expedition against the Scythians in Europe.
500	Revolt of the Ionians.
493	The Persians are again masters of all Asia Minor.
492	Mardonius' invasion of Europe fails.
490	The Persians defeated at Marathon.
487	Insurrection of Egypt.
485-465	**Xerxes.**
484	The Egyptian insurrection quelled.
480	Xerxes invades Europe, but is defeated at Artemisium and Salamis.
479	His general Mardonius defeated at Platacae, and on the same day the Persians defeated at Mycale.
465	**Artabanus** reigns only seven months.
465-425	**Artaxerxes I.** (Longimanus).
460-455	Revolt of Egypt under Inarus.
450	Revolt of Egypt under Amyrtaeus.
425	**Xerxes II.** reigns only two months.
425	**Sogdianus** reigns seven months.
24-405	**Darius II.** (Nothus).
412	A treaty between Sparta and Persia concluded.
408	Cyrus the younger in Asia Minor supports Sparta.
405-359	**Artaxerxes II.** (Mnemon.
400	Insurrection and defeat of the king's brother Cyrus.
396-394	Agesilaus carries on the war against Persia in Asia.
359-338	**Ochus.** Bagoas, the all-powerful eunuch.
350	Phoenicia revolts.
350-347	Revolt of Egypt under Nectanebus.
338-336	**Arses.**
336-331	**Darius III.** (Codomannus).
334	The Persians defeated by Alexander on the Granicus.
333	Battle of Issus.
331	Battle of Gaugamela, and end of the Persian empire.

ASSYRIA.

B.C. 1230	**Ninus,** the founder of the Assyrian empire and of Nineveh, succeeded by Semiramis and Ninyas.
770	**Phul** makes conquests in western Asia.
740	**Tiglath-Pileser** continues the conquests.

B.C. 720	Salmanassar takes Samaria.
712	Sennacherib penetrates into Egypt, but is unsuccessful.
675-626	Assarhaddon. In his reign the Assyrian empire begins to decline.
605	Sardanapalus. Under him **Nineveh** is taken and destroyed by Cyaxares, and Assyria becomes a province of the Median empire.

BABYLONIA.

B.C. 1903	The earliest date to which native traditions ascend.
747	**Nabonassar** shakes off the yoke of Assyria, to which Babylonia had been subject for more than 500 years.
625	**Nabopolassar** assists Cyaxares against Assyria.
604-561	**Nebuchadnezzar**, son of Nabopolassar, a great conqueror, leads the Jews captive to Babylon. After him the empire decays.
538	Under its last king **Nabonedus**, Babylon is conquered by Cyrus.
516	Revolt of Babylon. Zopyrus.

PHOENICIA.

B.C. 730	Phoenicia subdued by the Assyrian Salmanassar.
1100	**Gades**, a colony of Tyre, founded in Spain.
814	**Carthage**, a colony of Tyre, founded in Africa.
595-582	Tyre besieged by Nebuchadnezzar.
540	Phoenicia submits to Persia.
332	Tyre taken and destroyed by Alexander the Great.

LYDIA.

B.C. 1200	**Agron**, first king of the Heracleid dynasty.
716	**Candaules**, the last king of that dynasty, murdered
716-678	**Gyges**, first king of the Mermnad dynasty, conquers Mysia, Colophon, and Magnesia.
678-629	**Ardys.** The Cimmerians and Treres overrun Asia Minor.
629-617	**Sadyattes.**
617-560	**Alyattes** expels the Cimmerians and Treres, and extends his kingdom to the river Halys.
560-546	**Croesus**, a mild and beneficent ruler.
546	Croesus conquered and taken prisoner by Cyrus.

EGYPT.

B.C. 3892	**Menes**, the mythical founder of the kingdom.
1655-1326	Period of the eighteenth dynasty, the first that can be regarded as historical. **Rameses** the Great. Egypt at the height of its power.
1326-1183	Period of the nineteenth dynasty. Egypt still prosperous, but afterwards declines.
712	**Sennacherib** invades Egypt.
700-670	Period of the **dodecarchy.**
670-617	**Psammetichus** overthrows the dodecarchy, and becomes sole king of Egypt.
617-601	**Necho.** Circumnavigation of Africa.
608	Necho conquers the Jews, and takes Jerusalem.
604	Necho defeated by Nebuchadnezzar at Circesium.
601-595	**Psammis.**
595-570	**Apries** conquers Phoenicia and Cyprus, but is defeated by the Cyreneans.
570-526	**Amasis.** Egypt is very prosperous.
526	**Psammenitus.** Egypt is conquered by Cambyses.
487	**First insurrection** against Persia.
484	Xerxes quells the insurrection.

B.C. 460-455	Second revolt of Egypt under **Inarus.**
450	Revolt under **Amyrtaeus.**
350-347	The last revolt, under Nectanebus,
332	Egypt is conquered by **Alexander the Great.**
323-285	**Ptolemy Soter,** the son of Lagus.
306	Ptolemy assumes the title of king. Under him Egypt a great military and maritime state. The Museum.
285-247	**Ptolemy Philadelphus** bestows all his care on the internal administration. Egypt very powerful. Manetho. The Septuagint.
283	Death of Ptolemy Soter.
247-222	**Ptolemy Eurgetes** makes great conquests in Asia, but they are not lasting.
222-205	**Ptolemy Philopator.** The Egyptian empire begins to decline.
205-181	**Ptolemy Epiphanes** succeeds at the age of five, and many of his possessions are snatched from him by Syria and Macedonia.
193	Ptolemy marries a Syrian princess, whereby the disputes are settled.
181-146	**Ptolemy Philometor** ascends the throne as an infant. He is guided by his mother Cleopatra until her death, B.C. 173. Egypt is almost wholly dependent on Rome.
146-117	Ptolemy Eurgetes or Physcon, is said to have been a pupil of Aristarchus; was a most cruel tyrant.
117-81	Ptolemy Soter or Lathyrus. Great confusion in Egypt. (Ptolemy Alexander, Cleopatra).
96	Cyrene becomes a Roman province.
81-80	Ptolemy Alexander.
80-51	Ptolemy Dionysus or Auletes, leaves behind four children, one of whom is the celebrated Cleopatra.
51-30	Cleopatra at first rules with her brother Ptolemy, and, after several vicissitudes, alone.
30	Egypt becomes a Roman province.

GREECE.

1400-1200	The heroic age of Greece.
1194-1184	The war against **Troy.**
1130	Establishment of the Æolian colonies in Asia.
1104	Conquest of Peloponnesus by the **Dorians.**
1068	Medon, first archon for life at Athens.
900-800	The age of **Homer** and **Hesiod.**
884	**Lycurgus,** the Spartan lawgiver.
776	Commencement of the era of the **Olympiads.**
752	Decennial archons at Athens.
746	Rheginm in Italy founded.
743-724	The first Messenian war.
735	Naxos in Sicily founded by Theocles.
734	Syracuse, a Corinthian colony, founded by Archias.
723	Sybaris in Italy founded.
708	Tarentum founded by Laconians under Phalanthus.
690	Gela in Sicily founded by Cretans and Rhodians.
685-668	The second Messenian war.
683	First annual archons at Athens.
658	Byzantium founded by Megarians.
637	Cyrene receives additional colonists from Greece, and changes its constitution.
629	Selinus in Sicily founded.
624	**Draco's** legislation at Athens.
623-612	War between Lydia and Miletus.
612	**Cylon's** conspiracy at Athens.
604	Solon recovers Salamis for Athens.

B.C. 600	Massilia founded by Phocaeans.
597	Megacles and his partizans banished from Athens.
594-585	**The Crissaean or first Sacred War.**
594	Solon, as archon, reforms the constitution of Athens.
582	Agrigentum founded.
572-562	Solon travels in various countries.
570	**Pythagoras, the philosopher.**
560	**Pisistratus** becomes tyrant of Athens.
559	Solon dies, and Pisistratus is expelled.
550	Pherecydes of Syros, first Greek prose writer.
542	Pisistratus finally established as tyrant.
536	Xenophanes emigrates from Colophon to Elea, and founds the Eleatic school of philosophy.
527	**Pisistratus dies.**
522	Polycrates, tyrant of Samos, murdered at Sardes.
514	Conspiracy of Harmodius and Aristogeiton against the Pisistratids.
510	**Expulsion of the Pisistratids.** Constitutional reforms by Cleisthenes.
510	Sybaris destroyed by the Crotoniats.
508	Cleisthenes returns to Athens. War between Athens and Sparta and her allies.
504	The Crotoniats rise against the aristocracy and the Pythagoraeans.
501	Aristagoras of Miletus fails in his undertaking against Naxos.
500	**Revolt of the Ionians in Asia Minor.**
499	Sardes burnt.
494	Miletus taken by the Persians.
493	**Complete subjugation of the Asiatic Greeks.**
492	The Persian **Mardonius** invades Europe.
490	Second invasion of Europe by the Persians, and battle of **Marathon.**
483	**Aristides** exiled by ostracism.
480	Xerxes invades Europe. **Battles of Thermopylae, Artemisium, and Salamis.**
480	The Greeks in Sicily gain a great victory over the Carthaginians.
479	Battles of **Plataeae** and **Mycale.**
478	Athens rebuilt, and its harbours fortified.
477	The Greek fleet conquers Cyprus and Byzantium.
477-404	**Period of the supremacy of Athens.**
476	Cimon conquers Eion and Scyros.
471	Conviction and death of Pausanias, and flight of Themistocles to Epirus, and afterwards to Persia.
468	Death of Aristides.
466	Naxos conquered by the Athenians.
465	**Cimon** defeats the Persians on the **Eurymedon.**
464	Revolt of Thasos. **Pericles** enters on public life.
464-455	**The third Messenian war,** in consequence of an earthquake.
463	Cimon subdues Thasos.
461	Cimon is exiled.
460-455	Revolt of Inarus in Egypt, who is supported by the Athenians, but fails.
457	War between Athens and the Corinthians with their allies. The Athenians defeated at Tanagra.
456	Myronides defeats the Thebans at Œnophyta.
455	The Athenians gain possession of Naupactus.
454	Murder of Ephialtes, the friend of Pericles.
453	Cimon recalled from exile.
450	A truce of five years concluded between Athens and Sparta.
449	Death of Cimon at Citium, in Cyprus.

B.C. 448	War between the Delphians and Phocians, the former being supported by Sparta, the latter by Athens.
447	Battle of Coroneia, in which Tolmides the Athenian is defeated.
445	Revolt of Euboea and Megara. **A truce for thirty years** concluded between Athens and Sparta.
445-432	**Administration of Pericles.**
443	The colony of Thurii founded in Italy by Athenians and other Greeks.
440	**Revolt of Samos.** Sophocles one of the generals. Samos is reduced and Byzantium conquered.
435	**War between Corinth and Corcyra about Epidamnus.**
434	The Corinthians defeated in a naval action.
433	**Alliance between Atheus and Corcyra.**
432	Battle of Sybota. Beginning of **the Peloponnesian war.**
431	The Thebans attack **Plataeae.** The Spartans invade Attica, and the Athenians retaliate.
430	Second invasion of Attica, which is visited by **the plague.** Surrender of the revolted Potidaea.
429	**Death of Pericles.** Siege of Plataeae.
428	Third invasion of Attica. Revolt of Lesbos.
427	Fourth invasion of Attica. Lesbos reduced by **Paches. Cleon** the demagogue.
426	The Athenians are successful in Boeotia, Locris, Ætolia, Sicily, and Italy.
425	Fifth invasion of Attica. **Pylos** taken and fortified by the Athenians. Cleon takes Sphacteria and the Spartans in the island.
424	Nicias takes Cythera. **General peace in Sicily. Brasidas** at Megara and in Thrace. The Athenians defeated at Delion.
423	Truce for one year.
422	**Death of Brasidas,** and Cleon at Amphipolis.
421	**Peace of Nicias** concluded for fifty years. Offensive and defensive alliance between Athens and Sparta. Argive confederacy.
420	Alliance between Argos and Athens. **Alcibiades.**
418	War between Sparta and Argos. Battle of Mantineia, in which the Spartans are victorious. Alliance between Sparta and Argos.
417	The alliance broken, and war renewed.
416	**Alcibiades at Argos.** Conquest of **Melos.** Egesta in Sicily solicits the aid of the Athenians.
415	**The great Sicilian expedition.** Mutilation of the Hermae. Alcibiades recalled.
414	**Siege of Syracuse,** which is relieved by Gylippus.
413	The Spartans establish themselves at **Decelea** in Attica. **Fearful defeat of the Athenians in Sicily.**
412	Alcibiades, with the Spartan fleet, on the coast of Asia.
411	**Oligarchy established at Athens,** but overthrown in the same year. Battles of Cynossema and Abydos.
410	**Alcibiades** defeats the Lacedaemonians in Asia.
409	The Athenians conquer Byzantium.
408	**Alcibiades returns to Athens.** Lysander commands the Spartan fleet. Cyrus the younger supports Sparta.
407	The Athenians defeated at Notion. Alcibiades withdraws to Chersonesus, and is succeeded by Conon.
406	**Battle of Arginusae.** Misfortune of the Athenian generals.
405	**Battle of Ægospotomi,** in which the Athenians are defeated by Lysander. Siege and surrender of Athens.
404	Lysander enters Athens. **The Thirty Tyrants.**
403	**Thrasybulus** delivers Athens from the tyranny of the Thirty. Restoration of the constitution.

b. c. **400**	**Cyrus the younger**, assisted by Greeks, revolts against Artaxerxes. Battle of Cunaxa.
399	Dercyllidas, the Spartan, carries on war in Asia against Persia.
399	**Socrates** condemned to death.
399 & 398	War between Sparta and Elis.
398	**Agesilaus** becomes king of Sparta.
398 & 397	Conspiracy of Cinadon at Sparta.
396	Agesilaus takes the command in Asia against the Persians.
395	Agesilaus defeats the Persians. A coalition formed in Greece against Sparta. Lysander killed at Haliartos.
395-387	The **Corinthian** or **Boeotian war.**
394	Agesilaus recalled from Asia. Defeats the Boeotian confederates at Coroncia.
393	Massacre at Corinth. **Rebuilding of the walls of Athens by Conon.**
392	Agesilaus repulsed by Iphicrates.
391	Antalcidas negotiates with Persia for a peace.
390	**Death of Thrasybulus.**
389	Iphicrates defeats the Spartans at Abydos.
388	The Spartans take Ægina and harass Attica.
387	**The peace of Antalcidas** concluded.
385	Mantineia destroyed by the Spartans.
383-379	**The Olynthian war.**
382	**Thebes seized by the Spartan Phoebidas.** Pelopidas escapes to Athens.
379	Olynthos is compelled to surrender to the Spartans. **Pelopidas liberates Thebes.**
378-362	**The Theban war.** The Spartans invade Boeotia.
377	The invasion of Boeotia repeated.
376	The Spartans compelled to retreat from Boeotia.
375	The Spartans defeated at Orchomenos.
374	Peace between Athens and Sparta, but not of long duration.
373	The Spartans are obliged to raise the siege of Corcyra.
371	**Battle of Leuctra,** in which the Spartans are totally defeated.
370	Jason of Pherae assassinated.
369	First invasion of Peloponnesus by **Epaminondas. Restoration of Messenia.**
368	Second invasion of Peloponnesus. Pelopidas taken prisoner by Alexander of Pherae.
367	The Arcadians defeated by the Spartans.
366	Third invasion of Peloponnesus.
365	War between Arcadia and Elis.
364	**Pelopidas is killed** in Thessaly, but Alexander of Pherae forms an alliance with Thebes.
362	Fourth invasion of Peloponnesus. **Battle of Mantineia.** Death of Epaminondas.
361	A general peace concluded. Death of Agesilaus.
360	Amphipolis falls into the hands of the Olynthians.
359	Accession of **Philip of Macedonia.**
357-355	Social war between Athens and her allies, at the close of which Athens loses most of her allies.
355-346	Sacred war against the Phocians.
353	Defeat of the Phocians at Neon. War of Sparta against Megalopolis. Olynthos allies itself with Athens.
352	The Phocians compel Philip to return to Macedonia. First Philippic of Demosthenes.
351	The Phocians carry on the war in Boeotia.
347	Olynthos and other Thracian towns are taken by Philip.
346	The Boeotians defeated by the Phocians at Coroneia. But the Phocians submit, and their towns are destroyed.
344-341	Philip continues his conquests.

B.c. 340	Athens resolves upon war against Philip.
339	Phocion obliges him to raise the siege of Perinthos and Byzantium.
338	War against Amphissa. **Battle of Chaeroneia.**
337	Congress of Greek states at Corinth, and Philip appointed commander-in-chief against Persia.
336	**Murder of Philip, and accession of Alexander.**
335	Rise of the Greeks against Macedonia. **Destruction of Thebes.**
334	**Alexander sets out for Asia.**
333	Agis, king of Sparta, forms a confederacy against Macedonia Memnon of Rhodes dies.
331	Agis defeated by Antipater near Megalopolis.
324	Alexander orders the exiles to be recalled in the various parts of Greece. **Harpalus in Greece.** Demosthenes exiled.
323	**Alexander dies** at Babylon. Fresh revolt of Athens.
322	Battle of Crannon. Surrender of Athens. Death of Demosthenes.
318	Polysperchon proclaims the independence of Greece.
318-307	Administration of Athens by Demetrius Phalereus.
317	Athens submits to Cassander. Death of Phocion.
315	Thebes rebuilt by command of Cassander.
314	Greece declared free by Antigonus and Ptolemy.
312	Ptolemy makes himself master of several parts of Greece.
311	**General peace;** the independence of Greece guaranteed.
307	Demetrius Poliorcetes becomes master of Athens.
304	Demetrius returns to Greece against Cassander, who had made attempts upon Athens.
301	Demetrius, after the battle of Ipsus, is refused admission into Athens.
296	Athens, besieged by Demetrius, surrenders to him.
287	Athens recovers her freedom during the brief reign of Pyrrhus. Demochares returns from exile, and undertakes the administration of Athens.
280	Beginnings of the **Achaean league.** Celts in Greece.
279	The Celts routed at Delphi.
275	Extension of the Achaean league.
269-262	Athens besieged, and obliged to surrender to Antigonus Gonatas.
251	Flourishing period of the Achaean league. **Aratus** strategus.
244-241	**Agis IV.,** king of Sparta, attempts reforms.
243	The Macedonian garrison driven from Acrocorinthus.
241	Agis IV. murdered.
236-220	**Cleomenes III.** and his reforms at Sparta.
229	Athens freed from the Macedonian garrison.
226	Aratus strategus for the eleventh time. Cleomenes at war with the Achaean league.
224	The Achaeans seek the aid of Macedonia against Sparta.
223	Antigonus Doson in Peloponnesus.
222	Cleomenes takes Megalopolis, and invades Argolis.
221	**Battle of Sellasia.** The Spartans utterly defeated, and Sparta taken. Cleomenes flees to Egypt.
220	Cleomenes kills himself. **Lycurgus** sole king of Sparta.
220-217	**Social war** between the Achaean and Ætolian leagues.
219	Philip V. invades Ætolia, and the Ætolians invade Achaia.
218	Philip defeats Lycurgus.
217	Philip's attention being drawn to Italy, he concludes peace with the Ætolians.
213	**Aratus** poisoned by order of Philip.
211	The Ætolians conclude a treaty with Rome. Death of Lycurgus. **Machanidas,** tyrant of Sparta.
208	The Ætolians defeated by Philip. **Philopoemen.**
207	Philopoemen defeats Machanidas at Mantineia.

B.C. 205	The Ætolians are obliged to make peace with Philip.
200	Attica invaded by Philip, which is the cause of the second Macedonian war with Rome.
197	**Battle of Cynoscephalae.**
196	**Flamininus proclaims the independence of Greece.**
195	Nabis, tyrant of Sparta, is compelled to submit to a peace dictated by Flamininus.
194	War between Nabis and the Achaeans.
192	Nabis defeated by Philopoemen, and killed by the Ætolians. The Achaean league embraces all Peloponnesus. The Ætolians invite Antiochus, king of Syria.
191	**The Ætolians and Antiochus defeated at Thermopylae.**
190	A truce of six months between the Ætolians and Romans.
189	War recommenced, and the **Ætolian confederacy broken up.**
188	War between Sparta and the Achaeans. Sparta conquered, and its ancient constitution abolished by Philopoemen.
183	Messenia revolts from the Achaean league. Philopoemen put to death.
181	Sparta recovered by the Achaean league.
168	**Battle of Pydna.** End of the kingdom of Macedonia.
167	One thousand Achaean hostages, including Polybius, sent to Italy.
155	Athenian ambassadors at Rome.
151	Return of the surviving Achaean hostages from Italy.
147	**The Achaeans declare war against Rome.** The strategus Critolaus perishes after two defeats.
146	**Battle of Leucopetra. Corinth destroyed by Mummius.** The Achaean confederacy broken up. Greece subject to Rome.
86	Athens besieged, taken, and plundered by Sulla.

MACEDONIA.

B.C. 750	Carcanus, the alleged founder of the Macedonian dynasty.
413-399	Archelaus, the first great king.
399-394	Orestes, a minor, under the guardianship of Aëropus, who usurps the throne, and is succeeded by his son.
394-393	Pausanias, assassinated by Amyntas.
393-369	Amyntas II. leaves behind him three sons, Alexander, Perdiccas, and Philip.
369-367	Alexander is murdered by a usurper, Ptolemy Alorites.
367-364	Ptolemy Alorites, the usurper, is assassinated by Perdiccas.
364-359	Perdiccas is killed in a war against the Illyrians.
359-336	Philip III., son of Amyntas II., and father of Alexander the Great.
358	Philip is successful against the Illyrians, and interferes with the Greek towns in Thrace.
356	**Birth of Alexander.** Philip interferes in the affairs of Thessaly.
352	Philip takes part in the Sacred War against the Phocians; but being repulsed at Thermopylae, returns to Macedonia.
349	Philip attacks Olynthos.
347	Olynthos and other Thracian towns are conquered.
346	Philip concludes peace with Athens.
344-341	Philip makes conquests in Illyricum and Thrace.
340	Philip besieges Perinthos and Byzantium.
339	Is obliged by Phocion to raise the siege.
338	War against Amphissa, in which Philip is made commander-in-chief by the Amphictions. **Battle of Chaeroneia.** Peace with Athens and Thebes.
336	Philip assassinated at Ægeae.
336-323	**Alexander the Great.**
335	Expeditions against the Triballi, Getae, and Illyrians. Revolt of Greek states. Destruction of Thebes.

B.C. 334	Alexander sets out for Asia. Battle on the Granicus.
333	Battle of Issus.
332	Alexander takes Tyre. Egypt submits to him, and he plans the building of Alexandria.
331	Battle of Gaugamela.
330	Alexander takes Ecbatana. Darius murdered.
329-328	Alexander marches across the Paropamisus, and the rivers Oxus and Jaxartes. He marries Roxana.
327	Alexander in India. Defeat of Porus.
326	Alexander returns through the Gedrosian desert. Nearchus, with the fleet, sails from the Indus to the Persian gulf.
325	Alexander in Persia assumes the customs of eastern despots.
324	Mutiny among Alexander's troops. Philotas put to death. Alexander at Babylon plans new conquests.
323	**Alexander dies at Babylon.** His empire divided.
323-322	**Lamian war,** in which the Greeks are compelled to submit to Antipater.
321	Perdiccas, regent of the empire, murdered, and the empire distributed anew.
318	**Death of Antipater:** is succeeded by **Polysperchon.**
316	Cassander, Antipater's son, causes Olympias to be put to death, she having murdered Arrhidaeus and Eurydice in B.C. 317.
316	Craterus, taken prisoner by Antigonus, dies in a dungeon.
315-311	War of Ptolemy, Seleucus, Lysimachus, and Cassander, against Antigonus.
315-296	**Cassander,** at first regent, then king of Macedonia.
312	Seleucus establishes himself in the East. Era of the Seleucidae.
311	Murder of Roxana and her son Alexander by Cassander. General peace among the successors of Alexander.
309	Murder of Barsine and her son Heracles.
308	Cassander comes to terms with Ptolemy.
306	Ptolemy defeated in Cyprus. Antigonus and his son Demetrius assume the title of king, and their example is followed by the others.
301	Battle of Ipsus. Macedonia, Thrace, Syria, and Egypt recognised as independent kingdoms.
296-295	**Philip IV.** Civil war in Macedonia.
294-287	**Demetrius Poliorcetes** usurps the throne.
287	Demetrius dethroned by **Pyrrhus,** who reigns over Macedonia for seven months.
286-281	**Lysimachus** expels Pyrrhus, and becomes king of Macedonia.
283	Demetrius Poliorcetes dies as a prisoner of Seleucus.
281	Lysimachus slain in battle against Seleucus.
281-280	**Ptolemy Ceraunus.**
280	Invasion of Macedonia by the Celts.
280-274	**Antigonus Gonatas.**
274-272	**Pyrrhus** again king of Macedonia.
272-239	**Antigonas Gonatas** again king of Macedonia.
269-262	War against Athens, which in the end surrenders, and receives a Macedonian garrison.
239-229	**Demetrius II.**
229-220	**Antigonus Doson** reigns as guardian of Philip, the son of Demetrius.
223	Antigonus Doson, called to the assistance of the Achaeans against Sparta, enters Peloponnesus.
221	Battle of Sellasia. Antigonus takes Sparta.
220	Death of Antigonus Doson.
220-179	**Philip V.**
220-217	Social war in Greece, in which Philip supports the Achaeans against the Aetolians.
216	Philip concludes a treaty with Hannibal against Rome.

B.C. 215-205	First war with Rome carelessly conducted
205	Peace between Philip and the Ætolians.
200-197	Second War with Rome.
197	Philip defeated by Flamininus in the battle of Cynoscephalae.
196	Peace between Rome and Macedonia ratified, and Greece declared free.
179-168	Perseus, last king of Macedonia.
171-168	Third War with Rome.
168	Battle of Pydna, in which Perseus is defeated by L. Æmiliu Paulus.
149	**Andriscus,** a pretender under the name of Philip, raises himself to the throne of Macedonia.
148	Andriscus defeated by Caecilius Metellus. Macedonia a Roman province.

SYRIA.

B.C. 312-280	Seleucus Nicator, founder of the Syrian empire, assassinated at Lysimachia.
280	State of Galatia formed.
280-261	Antiochus Soter, is killed in a battle against the Celts in Asia Minor.
261-246	Antiochue Theos. War against Egypt. Is murdered by his wife.
250	Foundation of the Parthian empire by Arsaces. Bactria also makes itself independent.
246-226	Seleucus Callinicus. A part of his kingdom conquered by Ptolemy Euergetes of Egypt. War against his brother Antiochus Hierax, who is defeated. Seleucus dies in consequence of a fall.
226-223	Seleucus Ceraunus, an imbecile ruler, murdered by his own officers.
223-187	**Antiochus III., the Great.**
217	Antiochus is defeated at Gaza, and Phoenicia and Palestine are ceded to Egypt.
214	The usurper Achaeus defeated.
212-205	War with Parthia and Bactria, the independence of which is finally recognised.
196	Antiochus crosses over into Europe, and conquers the Thracian Chersonesus.
195	Hannibal goes to Antiochus.
192	Antiochus invades Greece by the desire of the Ætolians.
191	Antiochus, defeated in the battle of Thermopylae, quits Europe.
190	Antiochus defeated by the Scipios in the battle of Magnesia. All Asia west of Mount Taurus is lost, and the power of Syria broken.
187-175	**Seleucus Philopator.** The decay of the empire continues.
175-164	Antiochus Epiphanes, is forced by the Romans to abandon Egypt.
164-162	Antiochus Eupator.
162-150	Demetrius Soter.
150-146	Alexander Bala.
146-137	Demetrius Nicator (Antiochus Trypho).
137-128	Antiochus Sidetes (Demetrius Nicator, again).
125	Seleucus V.
125-95	Antiochus Grypus (Antiochus Cyzicenus).
95-83	Seleucus VI. (Antiochus Eusebes, Philip, Demetrius Eucaerus, Antiochus Epiphanes, Antiochus Dionysius).
83-69	Tigranes, king of Armenia.
69-65	Antiochus Asiaticus.
65	Syria becomes a Roman province.

CARTHAGE AND SICILY.

B.C. 814	Foundation of Carthage.
734	Syracuse founded by the Corinthian Archias.
550	Malchus conquers part of Sicily, but is unsuccessful against Sardinia.
509	**Treaty of commerce between Carthage and Rome.** Sardinia a Carthaginian province.
480	The Carthaginians defeated at **Himera** by the Greeks.
410	Renewed attempts of the Carthaginians upon Sicily.
348	Renewal of the **commercial treaty between Rome and Carthage.**
306	Second renewal of the **ancient commercial treaty with Rome.**
279	Defensive alliance between Rome and Carthage.
405-368	**Dionysius the elder,** tyrant of Syracuse. The war with Carthage is renewed, and Carthage is in the end successful.
368-345	**Dionysius the younger** is hard pressed by the Carthaginians towards the end of his rule.
345-337	Timoleon checks the Carthaginians. After him Syracuse an oligarchy, until the time of Agathocles.
317-289	**Agathocles,** tyrant of Syracuse.
310	The Carthaginians besiege Syracuse, while Agathocles attacks Carthage.
308	Agathocles invites Ophellas of Cyrene to join him against Carthage.
281	The Mamertines take possession of Messene.
278	**Pyrrhus arrives in Sicily** to assist the Greeks against the Carthaginians and Mamertines.
275	Hiero elected general by the Syracusans.
270	**Hiero obtains the title of king.**
264	The Mamertines ally themselves with the Romans.
264-241	**First war of Carthage against Rome.**
264	Hiero concludes peace with Rome.
241	**Sicily, evacuated by the Carthaginians,** becomes the first Roman province.
241-238	War of Carthage against her revolted mercenaries.
238	Carthage loses Sardinia and Corsica.
229	Hamilcar dies in Spain.
221	Hasdrubal is assassinated in Spain, and succeeded by the great **Hannibal.**
219	Hannibal besieges and destroys Saguntum.
218-202	**Second war of Carthage against Rome.**
216	Death of Hiero, who is succeeded by Hieronymus.
215	Murder of Hieronymus, after which Hippocrates and Epicydes join the Carthaginians.
212	**Capture of Syracuse by M. Marcellus.** The eastern portion of Sicily also becomes part of the Roman province.
183	Death of Hannibal.
149-146	**Third and last war between Carthage and Rome.**
146	**Carthage taken and destroyed.** Its territory a Roman province.
134-132	First servile war in Sicily.
102-99	Second servile war in Sicily.

ROME.

B.C. 753	Foundation of Rome.
753-716	**Romulus.** Political institutions.
715-672	**Numa Pompilius.** Religious institutions.
672-640	**Tullus Hostilius.** War against Alba. The Horatii and Curiatii. Alba Longa destroyed. Beginnings of the **plebs.**

B.C. 64-616	Ancus Marcius. Formation of the plebeian order by the conquest of the Latins. Ostia built.
616-578	Tarquinius Priscus, attempts reforms, but is thwarted.
578-534	Servius Tullius. Organisation of the plebs, and reforms of the constitution.
534-510	Tarquinius Superbus.
509	Establishment of the republic. First consuls. Conspiracy at Rome. War with Porsenna.
505	War against the Sabines.
501	War with the Latins.
498	T. Larcius, first dictator.
496	Battle of Lake Regillus, in which the Latins are defeated.
495	Death of Tarquinius Superbus. Insurrection of the plebs.
494	Secession of the plebs to the *Mons Sacer*.
493	Appointment of the tribunes of the plebs. The Ædiles. League of Sp. Cassius with the Latins.
491	Coriolanus stirs up the Volscians against Rome.
486	League of Sp. Cassius with the Hernicans. First attempt at an agrarian law.
485	Sp. Cassius put to death, and his agrarian law is disregarded.
477	Defeat of the Fabii on the Cremera.
473	The tribune Genucius murdered.
471	The tribune Publilius Volero carries several laws to protect the plebs.
462	The tribune C. Terentillus Arsa demands a revision of the laws.
458	The dictator L. Quinctius Cincinnatus defeats the Æquians.
457	The number of tribunes of the plebs is increased to ten.
454	The bill of Terentillus Arsa is at length carried.
451	The first decemvirate.
450	The second decemvirate. Laws of the Twelve Tables.
449	Secession of the plebs to the *Mons Sacer*. Deposition of the decemvirs. Laws of Valerius and Horatius.
445	The tribune Canuleius carries a law establishing the *connubium* between patricians and plebeians.
443	Institution of the censorship.
440	Famine at Rome. Sp. Maelius assists the poor.
439	Sp. Maelius murdered by Servilius Ahala.
438	The first military tribunes instead of consuls.
426	Fidenae destroyed.
396	Capture of Veii by Camillus after a siege of ten years.
391	Camillus goes into exile. The Gauls besiege Clusium.
390	Battle of the Allia. Rome taken and destroyed by the Gauls.
384	M. Manlius Capitolinus condemned to death.
383	The Pomptine district assigned to the plebeians.
376	C. Licinius Stolo and L. Sextius bring forward their rogations.
367	The Licinian rogations are passed after a struggle of nearly ten years.
366	L. Sextius, the first plebeian consul. First appointment of a praetor.
358	T. Manlius Torquatus defeats a gigantic Gaul on the Allia.
356	The first plebeian dictator, C. Marcius Rutilus.
351	The first plebeian censor.
350	M. Valerius Corvus slays a Gallic chief by the aid of a raven.
343-341	First war against the Samnites.
340-338	War against the Latins. Self-sacrifice of P. Decius.
339	The laws of Q. Publilius Philo.
338	Final subjugation of Latium.
337	The first plebeian praetor.
328	Foundation of the colony of Fregellae.

B.C. 326-304	Second war against the Samnites.
322	Luceria in Apulia conquered by the Romans.
321	**Defeat of the Romans at Caudium.** Afterwards they gain several victories.
315	War declared against Rome by the Etruscans.
314	Great success of the Romans against Samnium.
312	The Appian road made.
311	War with the Etruscans breaks out.
309	The dictator L. Papirius Cursor defeats the Samnites.
308	The Etruscan towns conclude peace.
306	The Samnites defeated in all directions. Subjugation of the Hernicans.
305	The Samnites, defeated at Bovianum, sue for peace. The Æquians rise, but are completely crushed.
300	The colleges of augurs and pontiffs thrown open to the plebeians by the **Ogulnian law.**
298-290	**Third war against the Samnites.** The Etruscans and Umbrians also rise again.
295	The Romans recover all Lucania. Victory of the Romans at Sentium in Umbria. Decius Mus.
292	The Samnites totally defeated; their commander Pontius taken.
290	Samnium, and soon after Etruria and Umbria, recognise the supremacy of Rome.
285-282	**War against the Gauls.** Subjugation of the Senones and Boii.
282	The Romans relieve Thurii, which is besieged by the Lucanians.
281	**Pyrrhus,** king of Epirus, lands in Italy.
280	The Romans defeated by Pyrrhus near Heraclein.
279	The Romans again defeated by Pyrrhus at Asculum.
278	Truce between the Romans and Pyrrhus, who goes to Sicily.
276	Pyrrhus returns to Italy.
275	**Pyrrhus, defeated at Beneventum, abandons Italy.**
273	Embassy of Ptolemy Philadelphus to Rome.
272	All southern Italy submits to Rome.
271	Rhegium also is recovered by the Romans.
268	**Fourth and last war against the Samnites,** lasts only one year.
264	The Romans ally themselves with the Mamertines of Messene. Peace with Hiero.
264-241	**The first Punic war.**
261	Agrigentum besieged and taken by the Romans.
260	C. Duilius defeats the Carthaginians off Mylae.
258	Atilius Calatinus carries on the war in Sicily.
256	The Carthaginians defeated off Ecnomus by M. Atilius Regulus, who sails with his fleet to Africa.
255	Success of Regulus in Africa, but he is afterwards defeated by Xanthippus and taken prisoner. Wreck of the Roman fleet on the coast of Sicily.
254	A new fleet is equipped, and Panormus taken.
252	The Roman fleet sails to Africa, but is wrecked on its return.
250	The Carthaginians defeated near Panormus. Regulus sent as ambassador to Rome. Siege of Lilybaeum.
249	Defeat of Appius Claudius by land and sea.
247	**Hamilcar** undertakes the command of the Carthaginians.
242	The Romans build a new fleet.
241	C. Lutatius Catullus defeats the Carthaginians off the Ægates insulae. Peace with Carthage. **Sicily the first Roman province.**
238	Sardinia and Corsica are taken from Carthage.
229	War against the Illyrian pirates. Agrarian law of C. Flaminius. Death of Hamilcar in Spain; he is succeeded by Hasdrubal.

B.C. 228	Peace with the Illyrians.
226	The Gauls invade Etruria.
225	The Gauls defeated in the battle of Telamon.
224	Reduction of the Boii.
223	C. Flaminius conquers the Insubrians.
222	M. Claudius Marcellus, in the battle of Clastidium, brings the Gallic war to a close. Cremona and Placentia founded.
321	Assassination of Hasdrubal, who is succeeded by **Hannibal.**
219	Second war against the Illyrians, who are conquered by L. Æmilius Paulus. Capture of Saguntum.
218-202	**The second Punic or the Hannibalian war.**
218	The Romans defeated on the **Ticinus** and the **Trebia.** Cn. Cornelius Scipio goes to Spain.
217	Defeat of the Romans on **Lake Trasimenus.**
216	The Romans defeated at **Cannae.**
215	Losses of Hannibal at Nola and Beneventum. Syracuse revolts from Rome. Treaty of Hannibal with Philip of Macedonia.
215-205	**First war against Macedonia.**
214-212	**Siege and capture of Syracuse** by M. Claudius Marcellus.
212	The two Scipios slain in battle in Spain.
211	The Romans conquer Capua. P. Cornelius Scipio goes to Spain.
210	Scipio takes Carthago Nova in Spain.
209	Tarentum recovered by the Romans. Hasdrubal defeated at Baecula.
207	**Hasdrubal** goes to Italy, but is defeated and slain on the Metaurus.
205	P. Cornelius Scipio, consul, goes to Sicily.
204	Scipio crosses over into Africa.
203	Syphax taken prisoner.
202	Hannibal, recalled to Africa, is defeated in the **battle of Zama.**
201	Peace with Carthage ratified at Rome.
200-197	**Second war against Macedonia.**
200-181	War against the Ligurians, Insubrians, and Boians.
198	T. Quinctius Flamininus undertakes the war against Macedonia.
197	Philip defeated in the battle of Cynoscephalae. Peace between Macedonia and Rome.
196	Flamininus proclaims the independence of Greece.
192	Antiochus, invited by the Ætolians, crosses over into Europe.
191	Antiochus and the Ætolians defeated at Thermopylae.
190	L. Cornelius Scipio crosses over into Asia, and defeats Antiochus in the **battle of Magnesia.** Peace concluded.
188	Peace with Antiochus ratified at Rome.
183	**Death of Hannibal.**
181-179	War in Spain brought to a close by Tib. Sempronius Gracchus.
171-168	**Third and last Macedonian war.**
168	Battle of Pydna, in which Perseus is defeated. One thousand Achaeans sent to Italy.
155	Greek philosophers expelled from Rome.
151	The surviving Achaeans return to Greece.
149	Andriscus, a pretender to the throne of Macedonia.
149-146	**The third and last Punic war.**
148	Andriscus is defeated and slain by Q. Caecilius Metellus.
148-140	War in Spain. Viriathus.
147-146	War against the Achaeans.
146	**Destruction of Corinth,** and subjugation of Greece. **Capture and destruction of Carthage.**
143-133	War against the Celtiberians in Spain. Siege of **Numantia.**
141	Peace with Viriathus.
140	Viriathus murdered by hired assassins.
139	The Gabinian law, ordaining vote by ballot at the elections.

B.C. 137	Final subjugation of the Lusitanians. C. Hostilius Mancinus concludes peace with the Numantines. The Cassian law, ordaining vote by ballot in the courts of law.
134-132	**Servile war in Sicily.**
133	Numantia taken and destroyed. Attalus of Pergamus dies, bequeathing his kingdom to the Roman people. **Tribuneship of Tib. Sempronius Gracchus**: is murdered.
131-130	War against Aristonicus, who claimed the kingdom of Pergamus.
126	First conquests of the Romans in Gaul.
123	**Tribuneship of C. Sempronius Gracchus.**
122	Second tribuneship of C. Sempronius Gracchus.
121	Murder of C. Gracchus, and civil bloodshed at Rome.
113	The Cimbri and Teutones begin their migration westward.
111-106	**The Jugurthine war.**
109	Q. Caecilius Metellus undertakes the command against Jugurtha. **C. Marius.**
107	First consulship of C. Marius, who succeeds Metellus in Africa.
106	Jugurtha taken prisoner by **L. Cornelius Sulla.** Birth of Cicero.
104	Marius consul, and appointed to conduct the war against the Cimbri and Teutones.
102	The Cimbri return from Spain, and are joined in Gaul by the Teutones. **Battle of Aquae Sextiae**, in which the **Teutones** are defeated.
102-99	Second servile war in Sicily.
101	The **Cimbri** defeated in the **Campi Raudii.**
100	C. Marius consul for the sixth time. The seditious tribune, L. Apuleius Saturninus, and his party besieged in the Capitol, and afterwards put to death.
91	The tribune, M. Livius Drusus, attempts to confer the franchise upon the Italian allies, but is murdered.
90-88	**The Social or Marsic war.**
90	The Lex Julia confers the franchise on the Latins.
88	The Etruscans and Umbrians obtain the franchise. End of the Social War.
88-84	**First war against Mithridates.** Civil war between **Marius and Sulla.** Marius flees to Africa.
87	Marius returns to Rome. Scenes of horror at Rome.
86	Siege and capture of Athens by Sulla. Marius dies in his seventh consulship.
84	Peace concluded with Mithridates.
83	Sulla returns to Italy, and is successful against his opponents.
83-81	**Second war against Mithridates.**
82	Capture of Praeneste. Young Marius kills himself. Battle at the Colline gate. Q. Sertorius goes to Spain. Sulla enters Rome. First proscription. **Sulla dictator.** Political and legal reforms.
79	Sulla lays down his dictatorship, and withdraws to Puteoli.
79-72	**War against Sertorius.**
78	**Death of Sulla.** Commencement of the war against the pirates.
74-64	**Third war against Mithridates.**
74	Sertorius allies himself with Mithridates of Pontus.
73-71	Servile war in Italy. Spartacus.
73	Lucullus defeats Mithridates.
72	Murder of Sertorius at Osca.
71	The slaves defeated by M. Licinius Crassus.
70	**Cn. Pompey consul.** The political reforms of Sulla abolished
69	Lucullus defeats Tigranes and Mithridates at Tigranocerta.
67	**Cn. Pompey undertakes the war against the pirates.** Lucullus recalled.
66	Cn. Pompey obtains the command against Mithridates.

B.C. 65	Cn. Pompey pursues Mithridates into Albania and Iberia. J. Caesar is curule aedile, and puts himself at the head of the popular party.
63	Mithridates, being conspired against by his own son, takes poison. **Consulship of Cicero. Catilinarian conspiracy.**
62	Cn. Pompey returns to Italy.
61	Caesar as propraetor in Spain. **P. Clodius.**
59	**J. Caesar consul.**
58	P. Clodius tribune. Cicero goes into exile. Caesar proceeds to Gaul.
57	Cicero recalled.
55	Caesar receives the administration of Gaul for five years more. He crosses the Rhine, and **invades Britain.**
54	Caesar invades Britain a second time. Death of Julia, Caesar's daughter.
53	Caesar again crosses the Rhine. **Crassus defeated in Syria.**
·52	General insurrection in Gaul. Fall of Alesia. Pompey for a time sole consul.
51	Caesar returns to Cisalpine Gaul. Claudius Marcellus proposes measures against Caesar.
50	Caesar is called upon to disband his army.
49	**Caesar crosses the Rubicon.** Pompey and his party flee from Italy. Caesar in Spain. On his return he is made dictator.
48	Caesar consul. **Battle of Pharsalus.**
47	Caesar defeats Pharnaces of Pontus: crosses over into Africa.
46	**Battle of Thapsus,** in which the Pompeians in Africa are defeated. Caesar reforms the calendar, and goes to Spain against the sons of Pompey.
45	**Battle of Munda:** the Pompeians defeated.
44	**Caesar murdered.**
43	War of Mutina. The **triumvirate** between Octavanus, Antony, and Lepidus. Proscription. Death of Cicero.
42	**Battles of Philippi.**
41	**War of Perusia.**
40	Capture and destruction of Perusia. War with the Parthians begins.
39	Peace of Misenum with Sext. Pompeius.
38-36	**War against Sext. Pompeius.**
36	Sext. Pompeius defeated in the battle of Mylae. Lepidus deposed. Antony sustains great loss against the Parthians.
34	Antony conquers Armenia, and gives it to Cleopatra.
32	War declared against the queen of Egypt.
31	**Battle of Actium.**
30	Death of Antony and Cleopatra.
29	Octavianus returns to Rome.
27	Octavianus receives the title of **Augustus** and **Imperator.** Division of the provinces. Augustus goes to Spain.
25-13	War against the Alpine tribes.
24	Augustus returns from Spain.
23	Augustus obtains the tribunician power for life.
20	The Parthians send back the Roman standards.
19	The Cantabri finally subdued by Agrippa.
16-13	Augustus in Gaul, to protect its eastern frontiers.
12	Death of Lepidus and Agrippa.
12-9	Drusus has the command against the Germans.
8-6	Tiberius succeeds Drusus against the Germans.
6	Domitius Ahenobarbus takes the command against the Germans.
5 or 4	**Birth of Jesus Christ.**

A.D. 4	Tiberius resumes the war against the Germans.
5	Western Germany a Roman province.
6-9	War against the revolted Dalmatians and Pannonians.
9	Defeat of Varus.
14	**Death of Augustus.**
14-37	**Reign of Tiberius.**
14	Revolt of the legions in Germany and Pannonia.
16	Germanicus recalled from Germany.
19	Germanicus dies in Syria.
20	Ælius Seianus guides the counsels of Tiberius.
23	The *castra practoria* established near Rome. Drusus, son of Tiberius, poisoned.
26	Tiberius withdraws to Capreae.
31	Execution of Ælius Seianus.
33	Crucifixion of Jesus Christ.
37	Tiberius murdered by suffocation.
37-41	**Reign of Caligula.**
39	A conspiracy formed against Caligula.
41	Caligula murdered.
41-54	**Reign of Claudius.**
43	Commencement of permanent conquests in Britain.
50	Successful war against the Parthians.
51	The south-eastern part of Britain a Roman province.
54-68	**Reign of Nero.**
54	Corbulo drives the Parthians from Armenia.
61	Insurrection in Britain under Boadicea.
62	Nero banishes Octavia. Burrus put to death.
64	Great fire at Rome.
65	Seneca the philosopher and Lucan the poet put to death.
66	Tiridates recognised as king of Armenia.
67	Nero goes to Greece. Insurrection of the Jews. Vespasian conducts the war against them.
68-69	**Servius Galba is murdered.**
69	**Salvius Otho** defeated at Bedriacum, kills himself.
69	**Vitellius,** is murdered in the practorian camp.
69-79	**Vespasian.** The siege of Jerusalem is left to Titus.
70	Vespasian arrives at Rome. Capture and destruction of Jerusalem. Insurrection of Claudius Civilis and the Batavi.
71	Petilius Cerealis, governor of Britain, is accompanied by Agricola.
74	Philosophers expelled from Rome.
77-85	Agricola governor of Britain.
79-81	**Reign of Titus.**
79	First recorded eruption of Vesuvius, and destruction of Herculaneum, Pompeii, and Stabiae.
80	Great fire at Rome. Completion of the Colosseum.
81-96	**Reign of Domitian.**
83	Domitian undertakes an expedition against the Chatti.
84	Agricola defeats the Caledonians under Galgacus.
86	The Dacians make war against the Romans.
90	Domitian purchases peace of the Dacians.
96-98	**Reign of Nerva.**
98-117	**Reign of Trajan.**
100	Trajan sets out against the Dacians.
103	Peace with the Dacians.
104-106	Second Dacian war, at the end of which Dacia becomes a Roman province.
114	War against the Parthians.
115	Armenia a Roman province.
117-138	**Reign of Hadrian;** he makes the Euphrates the boundary in the East.

A.D. 118	Hadrian returns to Rome from the East. War against the Sarmatians. A conspiracy against him suppressed.
120-131	Hadrian travels through the provinces of the empire.
131-136	War against the Jews.
138-161	Reign of **Antonius Pius**. Peace throughout the empire.
161-180	Reign of **M. Aurelius**.
162	L. Verus goes to the East against the Parthians.
166	Peace concluded with the Parthians.
167	War against the Marcomanni and Quadi.
169	Death of L. Verus.
175	Peace with the Marcomanni concluded. Revolt of Avidius Cassius in the East.
178	Renewal of the war against the Marcomanni.
180-192	Reign of **Commodus**.
180	Commodus purchases peace of the Marcomanni.
183	Conspiracy against Commodus, headed by his sister Lucilla.
184	War against the Caledonians terminated.
185	Perennis recalled from Britain, and put to death.
193	Reign of **Pertinax** lasts only three months.
193	Reign of **Didius Julianus**. Purchases the imperial dignity, but reigns only two months.
193-211	Reign of **Septimius Severus**.
194	Pescennius Niger, who had been proclaimed in Syria, is defeated.
197	The rebel Clodius Albinus defeated in Gaul.
198	Severus carries on a successful war against the Parthians.
208	Severus goes to Britain, which had been invaded by the Caledonians.
210	The wall between the Tyne and Solway completed.
211-212	Reign of **Caracalla** and **Geta**.
212	Geta murdered by Caracalla.
212-217	**Caracalla** reigns alone.
213	Caracalla visits Gaul.
214	He invades Germany, but purchases peace.
215	Massacre at Alexandria in Egypt.
217-218	Reign of **Macrinus**. Purchases peace of the Parthians.
218-222	Reign of **Elagabalus**.
222-235	Reign of **Alexander Severus**.
226	Foundation of the new Persian empire of the Sassanidae on the ruins of that of Parthia.
228	Ulpian the jurist murdered by the soldiers.
231	Alexander Severus makes war upon the Persians.
233	He returns to Rome, and triumphs.
234	He proceeds to Gaul, to protect it against the Germans.
235-238	Reign of **Maximinus**: is successful against the Germans.
238	Gordian and his son proclaimed emperors by the senate.
238	**Maximus** and **Balbinus** made emperors by the senate. Young Gordian raised to the rank of Caesar.
238-244	Reign of **Gordian III**.
241	Gordian marries the daughter of Misitheus, and sets out against Sapor I., king of Persia.
244-249	Reign of **Philippus**. Makes peace with the Persians.
248	**Ludi Saeculares** at Rome.
249-251	Reign of **Decius**.
250	The Goths cross the Danube and invade Thrace.
251-253	Reign of **Gallus Trebonianus**.
252	Death of Hostilianus by the plague, which rages for fifteen years.
253	Æmilianus proclaimed emperor in Moesia, but is murdered after a reign of four months.
253-268	**Valerian** and **Gallienus** emperors. The barbarians invade the empire on all sides.

A.D 256	Successful war against the Franks.
258	Valerian sets out against the Persians. Postumus sets himself up as emperor in Gaul.
260	Valerian taken prisoner by the Persians.
260-268	**Gallienus** sole emperor. Period of the Thirty Tyrants.
261	Macrianus assumes the purple.
262	Aureolus proclaimed in Raetia.
264	Odenathus of Palmyra recognised as an independent sovereign.
267	Odenathus is slain, and succeeded by his wife Zenobia. Tetricu sets himself up as emperor in Gaul.
268-270	**Claudius II.**, surnamed Gothicus, emperor. Defeats the Alemanni.
269	Claudius sets out against the Goths, who are defeated.
270	Claudius dies at Sirmium.
270-275	Reign of **Aurelian**; he concludes peace with the Goths.
272	Aurelian proceeds to the East against Zenobia, who had invaded Egypt.
273	Zenobia besieged at Palmyra and taken prisoner.
274	Tetricus in Gaul submits to Aurelian.
275	Aurelian murdered. Interreign of six months.
275-276	**Claudius Tacitus** emperor, successful in the East.
276	**Annius Florianus** emperor for scarcely three months.
276-282	**Probus** defeats the barbarians in Gaul, and secures the German frontier.
279	Probus reduces the Isaurians and Blemmyae.
282	Probus murdered by his soldiers at Sirmium.
282-283	**Carus** emperor.
283	Carus with his son Numerianus sets out against the Persians, but dies at Ctesiphon. **Numerianus** and **Macrinus** recognised as emperors, but the former is murdered and the latter defeated by Diocletian.
284-305	Reign of **Diocletian**; he assumes **Maximian** as his colleague.
286	Maximian defeats the Bagaudae in Gaul, and drives the Alemanni across the Rhine. The Saxons.
287-293	Carausius assumes the imperial dignity in Britain.
292	Diocletian at Nicomedeia nominates Constantius, Chlorus, and Galerius Caesars. The empire divided among the four rulers.
293	Carausius slain by Alectus, who maintains himself for a period of three years.
295	Galerius defeats the Carpi.
296	Constantius defeats Alectus and recovers Britain.
298	Galerius compels the Persians to conclude peace.
301	Constantius defeats the Alemanni.
303	The four sovereigns meet at Rome to devise means against Christianity, which they attempt to suppress.
305	Diocletian abdicates and retires to Salonae. Maximian follows his example.
305	**Constantius and Galerius** succeed as emperors, but the former dies the year after.
306	Constantine assumes the rank of Caesar in Britain.
306-337	Reign of **Constantine**.
307	Severus, one of the Caesars, put to death at Ravenna. Licinius raised to the imperial dignity by Galerius.
310	Maximian commits suicide.
311	Death of Galerius.
312	War between Maxentius and Constantine. The former is defeated, flees, and perishes in the Tiber.
313	Maximinus defeated at Adrianople. Death of Diocletian. Constantine and Licinius the only surviving sovereigns. Edict in favour of the Christians.

A.D.	
314	War between Constantine and Licinius, in which the latter, on being defeated, make concessions to his conqueror.
323	War between Constantine and Ticinius, in which the latter is completely defeated, and Constantine remains sole emperor.
325	The Council of Nicaea. Orthodoxy defined.
325-331	Extension and fortification of Constantinople.
332	War against the Goths.
334	A large body of Sarmatians receive settlements in the empire.
337	**Death of Constantine** near Nicomedeia. **Constantine II.**, **Constantius**, and **Constans**, divide the empire.
338	Constantius commences war against Persia.
340	War between Constantine II. and Constans, in which the former is defeated and killed. Constans sole emperor of the West.
350	**Magnentius** assumes the purple at Autun in Gaul. Death of Constans.
351	War between Magnentius and Constantius, in which the former is defeated.
353	Magnentius kills himself. Constantius sole emperor.
354	Gallus is recalled from the East, and murdered at Pola.
355	Silvanus assumes the purple in Gaul, but is slain. Julian appointed to the command in Gaul.
356	Successful campaign of Julian against the Germans.
357	Julian clears the eastern frontier of Gaul from enemies.
360	Julian proclaimed emperor at Paris.
361	**Death of Constantius.**
361-363	Reign of **Julian** the Apostate.
363	Julian attempts to have the temple of Jerusalem rebuilt. Sets out from Antioch against the Persians. Gains a victory near Ctesiphon. Is slain.
363-364	**Jovian** emperor. Concludes peace with the Persians, who recover their lost provinces.
364-375	**Valentinian** emperor. Associates his brother **Valens** with himself in the empire.
365	War between Valens and the usurper Procopius.
366	The Alemanni repulsed in Gaul. Procopius defeated by Valens.
367	**Gratian**, son of Valentinian, declared Augustus.
368	The Alemanni again defeated.
370	Peace concluded with the Goths.
371	Saxon pirates cut to pieces.
375	Valentinian takes the field against the Quadi and Sarmatians. Death of Valentinian. The Huns cross the Volga, and throw themselves upon the Goths. Valentinian II. made Augustus, though only four years old.
376	A portion of the Goths are allowed by Valens to settle in Moesia and Thrace.
377	The Goths rise against the Romans.
378	The Goths defeat Valens with immense slaughter at Adrianople. Death of Valens. Gratian defeats the Alemanni.
379	Gratian raises **Theodosius I.** to the rank of Augustus, who defeats the Goths.
383	Revolt of **Maximus** in Britain. Death of Gratian.
387	Maximus expels Valentinian II. from Italy.
388	Theodosius sets out against Maximus, who is put to death. Arbogastes guardian of Valentinian.
392	Valentinian murdered in Gaul. Arbogastes proclaims **Eugenius** emperor.
394	Theodosius defeats both Arbogastes and Eugenius near Aquileia.
395	**Death of Theodosius** at Milan. He is succeeded by his sons **Arcadius** and **Honorius**, the former emperor of the East, and the latter of the West. **Stilicho**, guardian of Honorius, causes the murder of Rufinus, the guardian of Arcadius.

A.D. 397	Stilicho sets out against the Goths who are devastating Greece. Revolt of Gildo in Africa.
398	Gildo defeated and killed.
402	Alaric and his Goths invade Italy, but are induced to return.
403	Alaric plunders the north of Italy. Battle of Pollentia. Peace with Alaric.
406	The Goth Radagaisus with a numerous horde invades Italy; but is defeated and slain by Stilicho. The Vandals enter Gaul.
407	Ravages in Gaul continued. **Constantine in Britain usurps the** imperial title, and crosses over into Gaul.
408	Alaric again appears in Italy. **Stilicho murdered.** Alaric lays siege to Rome, which in the end capitulates. **Death of Arcadius.**
409	Alaric again appears before Rome. **Attalus** proclaimed emperor instead of Honorius. The Vandals establish themselves in Spain.
410	Alaric besieges and takes Rome the third time. Death of Alaric.
411	The usurper Constantine taken and killed.
412	Jovinus assumes the purple at Mayence.
414	Peace between Adolphus and Honorius.
415	Adolphus is murdered in Spain, and succeeded by Wallia, the founder of the empire of the Visigoths in Spain. The Burgundians and Franks become independent.
421	**Constantius** made Augustus by Honorius.
423	**Death of Honorius. Joannes** assumes the purple.
425	Joannes is defeated. **Valentinian III.** emperor.
426	The last Roman garrisons are withdrawn from Britain.
429	Bonifacius invites the Vandals under their king Genseric to come to Africa.
430	Bonifacius defeated by the Vandals at Hippo.
432	War between Bonifacius and Aëtius.
433	Restoration of Aëtius.
435	Peace with Genseric, to whom a part of Africa is ceded.
438	The **Codex Theodosianus** published.
439	Carthage taken by Genseric.
441	The **Huns** under **Attila** cross the Danube.
442	New peace with Genseric, in which further concessions are made to him.
447	Attila invades Thrace and Thessaly.
450	Death of Theodosius II., who is succeeded by Marcianus.
451	Attila crosses the Rhine and invades Gaul. **Battle of Chalons,** in which the Huns are defeated.
452	Attila invades Italy.
453	Death of Attila.
454	Aëtius murdered by Valentinian.
455	**Valentinian** slain by conspirators. **Maximus,** one of them, assumes the purple, but is killed by the soldiers. The Vandals enter Rome, which they plunder and sack. **Avitus** proclaimed emperor in Gaul.
456	Avitus is obliged to abdicate. Interregnum of more than a year. Ricimer has all the power in his hands.
457-461	**Majorian.**
460	Majorian goes to Spain, intending to cross over into Africa against the Vandals.
461	Majorian deposed, and put to death. **Severus** proclaimed, but Ricimer reigns in his name.
465	Death of Severus, after which Ricimer rules until 467.
467-472	**Anthemius** emperor.
468	A great undertaking against the Vandals fails through the misconduct of Basiliscus.

A.D. 472	Civil war between Anthemius and Ricimer. The former is killed, and Ricimer having captured Rome, proclaims **Olybrius** emperor. Death of Ricimer and Olybrius.
473	**Glycerius** proclaimed emperor.
474	**Julius Nepos** made emperor. Deposes Glycerius.
475	Nepos is dethroned by Orestes, who causes his son **Romulus Augustulus** to be proclaimed.
476	Orestes defeated and slain at Placentia by the German troops under Odoacer. Romulus resigns his dignity. **Odoacer,** king of Italy. End of the Western Empire.

THE END.

www.ingramcontent.com/pod-product-compliance
Lightning Source LLC
Chambersburg PA
CBHW020857130726
47900CB00014B/904